THE IRAQ WAR

Other Books by Anthony H. Cordesman

Saudi Arabia Enters the Twenty-first Century: The Military and National Security Dimensions (Westport, CT: Praeger/CSIS, 2003)

Saudi Arabia Enters the Twenty-first Century: The Political, Foreign Policy, Economic, and Energy Dimensions (Westport, CT: Praeger/CSIS, 2003)

The Lessons of Afghanistan: War Fighting, Intelligence, and Force Transformation (Washington, DC: CSIS, 2002)

Iraq's Military Capabilities in 2002: A Dynamic Net Assessment (Washington, DC: CSIS, 2002)

Strategic Threats and National Missile Defenses: Defending the U.S. Homeland (Westport, CT: Praeger, 2002)

A Tragedy of Arms: Military and Security Developments in the Maghreb (Westport, CT: Praeger, 2001)

Peace and War: The Arab-Israeli Military Balance Enters the 21st Century (Westport, CT: Praeger, 2001)

Terrorism, Asymmetric Warfare, and Weapons of Mass Destruction: Defending the U.S. Homeland (Westport, CT: Praeger, 2001)

Cyber-threats, Information Warfare, and Critical Infrastructure Protection: Defending the U.S. Homeland, with Justin G. Cordesman (Westport, CT: Praeger, 2001)

The Lessons and Non-Lessons of the Air and Missile Campaign in Kosovo (Westport, CT: Praeger, 2000)

Transnational Threats from the Middle East: Crying Wolf or Crying Havoc? (Carlyle, PA: Strategic Studies Institute, 1999)

Iraq and the War of Sanctions: Conventional Threats and Weapons of Mass Destruction (Westport, CT: Praeger, 1999)

Iran's Military Forces in Transition: Conventional Threats and Weapons of Mass Destruction (Westport, CT: Praeger, 2000)

U.S. Forces in the Middle East: Resources and Capabilities (Boulder, CO: Westview, 1997)

Perilous Prospects: The Peace Process and Arab-Israeli Military Balance (Boulder, CO: Westview, 1996)

The Lessons of Modern War, Volume IV: *The Gulf War,* with Abraham R. Wagner (Boulder, CO: Westview, 1995; paperback 1999).

US Defence Policy: Resources and Capabilities (London: RUSI Whitehall Series, 1993)

After the Storm: The Changing Military Balance in the Middle East (Boulder, CO: Westview, 1993)

Weapons of Mass Destruction in the Middle East (London: Brassey's, 1991)

The Lessons of Modern War, Volume III: *The Afghan and Falklands* Conflicts, with Abraham R. Wagner (Boulder, CO: Westview, 1990)

The Lessons of Modern War, Volume II: *The Iran-Iraq Conflict,* with Abraham R. Wagner (Boulder, CO: Westview, 1990)

The Lessons of Modern War, Volume I: *The Arab-Israeli Conflicts,* with Abraham R. Wagner (Boulder, CO: Westview, 1990)

The Gulf and the West: Strategic Relations and Military Realities (Boulder, CO: Westview, 1988)

NATO's Central Region Forces: Capabilities, Challenges, Concepts (London: RUSI/Jane's, 1987)

Western Strategic Interests in Saudi Arabia (London: Croom Helm, 1986)

The Gulf and the Search for Strategic Stability: Saudi Arabia, the Military Balance in the Gulf, and Trends in the Arab-Israeli Military Balance (Boulder, CO: Westview, 1984)

Jordanian Arms and the Middle East Balance (Washington, DC: Middle East Institute, 1983)

Imbalance of Power: An Analysis of Shifting U.S.-Soviet Military Strengths, with John M. Collins (Monterey, CA: Presidio, 1978)

THE IRAQ WAR

Strategy, Tactics, and Military Lessons

Anthony H. Cordesman

PUBLISHED IN COOPERATION WITH THE
CENTER FOR STRATEGIC AND INTERNATIONAL STUDIES,
WASHINGTON, D.C.

Westport, Connecticut
London

The author and publisher gratefully acknowledge permission to reprint the following materials:

Excerpts from James Kitfield, "Attack Always," *National Journal.* © 2003 by National Journal Group, Inc.

Excerpts from Joshua Davis, "If We Run Out of Batteries, This War Is Screwed," *Wired Magazine.* © 2003 Condé Nast Publications.

Excerpts from Carl Bildt, "Hard-earned Lessons on Nation Building: Seven Ways to Rebuild Iraq," *International Herald Tribune.* © 2003 International Herald Tribune.

Library of Congress Cataloging-in-Publication Data

Cordesman, Anthony H.
    The Iraq War : strategy, tactics, and military lessons / Anthony H. Cordesman.
        p. cm.
    Includes bibliographical references.
    ISBN 0-275-98227-0 (alk. paper)
    1. Iraq War, 2003. 2. Strategy. 3. Tactics. 4. National state. I. Title.
DS79.76.C67 2003b
956.7044′3—dc22   2003058922

British Library Cataloguing in Publication Data is available.

Library of Congress Catalog Card Number: 2003058922
ISBN: 0-275-98227-0

First published in 2003

Praeger Publishers, 88 Post Road West, Westport, CT 06881
An imprint of Greenwood Publishing Group, Inc.
www.praeger.com

Printed in the United States of America

The paper used in this book complies with the
Permanent Paper Standard issued by the National
Information Standards Organization (Z39.48-1984).

10 9 8 7 6 5 4 3 2 1

CONTENTS

LIST OF TABLES AND MAPS

ACKNOWLEDGMENTS

The author would like to thank Brian Hartman and Julia Powell of ABC for help in the research for this book, and Brian Hartman for many of the numbers on the size of the Coalition air effort, and Coalition Forces. Ryan Faith helped with the research for the chronology of events and both Ryan Faith and Jennifer Moravitz helped with the organization and editing during the drafting of the manuscript. Roberta Howard took on the task of editing the book manuscript during a period of nearly constant revisions and updates.

The reader should also be aware that this book makes extensive use of reporting on the war from a wide range of press sources, only some of which can be fully footnoted, interviews with serving and retired officers involved in various aspects of the planning and execution of the war, and the extensive work done by Australian, British, and U.S. officers in preparing daily briefings and official background materials on the conflict.

CHAPTER ONE
_____

INTRODUCTION

It is important to begin this analysis with an admission of ignorance. It is almost as arrogant to rush to judgment on the lessons of a war before all the data on military operations become available as it was to rush to judge the war plan before the success of coalition operations became apparent. History is filled with efforts to make instant judgments about the lessons of war that ultimately proved to be based on false information and assumptions.

Some important lessons of the war are clear. Secretary of Defense Donald Rumsfeld and General Tommy Franks, the commander of the U.S. Central Command (USCENTCOM) and the overall commander of the coalition forces, summarized these lessons in testimony to Congress on July 9, 2003. Secretary Rumsfeld summarized the key lessons as follows:[1]

> ...In less than a month, they [U.S. military planners] had developed and were executing a war plan for Afghanistan employing a range of capabilities—from the most advanced (such as laser-guided weapons), to the antique (40-year-old B-52s updated with modern electronics) to the rudimentary (a cavalry charge)—they and our Afghan and coalition allies drove the Taliban and al-Qaeda from power in a matter of months. The plan they developed for Operation Iraqi Freedom was even more innovative and transformational—employing an unprecedented combination of speed, precision, surprise, and flexibility.
>
> The Iraqi regime very likely expected the war to begin, as did the 1991 Gulf War, with a sustained bombing campaign. Instead, General Franks started the ground attack before the air campaign—sending a large force of Special Operators into Western Iraq, followed by thousands of coalition forces streaming across the Kuwaiti border. Instead of a long march through the South, with pitched battles for each city along the way, they drove through to reach the gates of Baghdad in a matter of weeks—liberating the Iraqi capital and toppling the regime in less than a month.

The plan was adaptable and flexible, allowing General Franks and his team to turn difficulties into opportunities. For example, the inability of coalition forces to enter Iraq from the north was disappointing. But instead of bringing the 4th Infantry Division out of the Mediterranean to the Gulf, General Franks kept them in the Mediterranean—creating the impression in Baghdad that the attack would not start until the coalition could open the northern front. This very likely contributed to the surprise of the Iraqi regime when the war began without those forces in the fight.

One of the most interesting aspects of the campaign was the fact that the "lessons learned" process began before the war began. General Franks installed a "lessons learned" team from Joint Forces Command with his command from the start. They did more than take notes to improve our performance for the next war—they provided immediate feedback, allowing CENTCOM leadership to apply "lessons learned" in real time and improve coalition performance in *this* war.

I'll leave it to General Franks to describe in detail the lessons he believes are most important. For my part, I'd say some key lessons so far include:

- the importance of *speed*, and the ability to get inside the enemy's decision cycle and strike before he is able to mount a coherent defense;
- the importance of *jointness*, and the ability of U.S. forces to fight, not as individual de-conflicted services, but as a truly joint force—maximizing the power and lethality they bring to bear;
- the importance of *intelligence*—and the ability to act on intelligence rapidly, in minutes, instead of days and even hours; and
- the importance of *precision*, and the ability to deliver devastating damage to enemy positions, while sparing civilian lives and the civilian infrastructure.

Another lesson is that in the twenty-first century "overmatching power" is more important than "overwhelming force." In the past, under the doctrine of overwhelming force, force tended to be measured in terms of mass—the number of troops that were committed to a particular conflict. In the twenty-first century, mass may no longer be the best measure of power in a conflict. After all, when Baghdad fell, there were just over 100,000 American forces on the ground. General Franks overwhelmed the enemy not with the typical three-to-one advantage in mass, but by overmatching the enemy with advanced capabilities, and using those capabilities in innovative and unexpected ways.

General Franks added the following points:[2]

Decisive combat in Iraq saw a maturing of joint force operations in many ways. Some capabilities reached new performance levels. From a joint integration perspective, our experience in Operations Southern and Northern Watch, and Enduring Freedom helped to develop a joint culture in our head-quarters and in our components. These operations helped to improve joint interoperability and improve our joint C4I [command, control, communications, computers, and intelligence] networks as joint force synergy was taken to new levels of sophistication.

Our forces were able to achieve their operational objectives by integrating ground maneuver, special operations, precision lethal fires, and non-lethal effects. We saw for the first time integration of forces rather than deconfliction of forces. This integration enabled conventional (air, ground, and sea) forces to leverage SOF [special operations forces] capabilities to deal effectively with asymmetric threats and enable precision targeting simultaneously in the same battle space.

Likewise, Special Operators were able to use conventional forces to enhance and enable special missions. Operational fires spearheaded our ground maneuver, as our forces sustained the momentum of the offense while defeating enemy formations in open, complex, and urban terrain.

We saw jointness, precision munitions, C2, equipment readiness, state of training of the troops, and Coalition support as clear "winners" during Operation Iraqi Freedom (OIF).

That said, we also identified a number of areas which require additional work. Fratricide prevention suffered from a lack of standardized combat identification. Units in theater arrived with seven different combat ID systems, and our commanders were forced to overcome these shortcomings "on the fly." Deployment planning and execution were cumbersome, and need to be improved to meet the operational demands of the twenty-first century. And, Coalition information sharing must be improved at all levels. Finally, human intelligence and communications bandwidth are also areas which will require continuing focus.

General Franks also noted that a number of important lessons learned during Operation Enduring Freedom (OEF) in Afghanistan carried over into Operation Iraqi Freedom (OIF):[3]

...we saw a number of functional areas and capabilities that reached new levels of performance. In some areas, improvements were made prior to Operation Iraqi Freedom. For example the DoD/CIA synergy which worked well during OEF was built upon the integration of liaison officers in each of our headquarters which facilitated teamwork and paid great dividends in Iraq.

Also, we continued to leverage coalition strengths as new Coalition members were added. "The mission determines the Coalition; the Coalition does not determine the mission." Advanced technologies employed during OEF were also critical. The command and control of air, ground, naval, and SOF from 7,000 miles away was a unique experience in warfare as our forces achieved unprecedented real-time situational awareness and C2 connectivity.

We learned that precision-guided munitions represent a force multiplier. Low collateral damage during both OEF and OIF was a fundamental factor in achieving our objectives. Early in OEF we saw the need for an unmanned sensor-to-shooter capability to support time-sensitive targeting (TST). The armed Predator demonstrates great potential and will be a high payoff system in the future. Blue Force Tracking and enhanced C4I systems increase lethality and decrease response time, and also represent transformational technologies. We will continue with development of Global Hawk as an unmanned, high-altitude, long loiter time, beyond line-of-sight multi-sensor UAV [unmanned aerial vehicle], and will work to incorporate laser designation and delivery of precision weaponry from that platform.

The integrated common operating picture (COP) was a very powerful tool. Tracking systems were previously Service unique. Workarounds were developed for OIF, but there is a need to develop one integrated, user-friendly, C4I architecture that captures blue and red air, ground, and maritime forces.

Strategic lift and tanker aircraft availability were stretched during OEF and OIF. These forces are critical to rapid future force projection and we must enhance this vital capability in the years ahead.

Combined and joint training of our forces was also a key factor during OEF and was carried over into OIF. Our military forces are the best-prepared forces in the world and I thank the members of Congress for providing assets and funding to train these wonderful fighting men and women to give them every possible advantage. Finally, our ability to take action in OEF was predicated on "Strategic Anchors," one of which was "Cooperative Security" relationships, which paid high dividends in basing, staging, and overflight rights during the present crisis.

No one can quarrel with these broad lessons. They have been validated in separate studies of the lessons of the war by the British Ministry of Defense and the U.S. military services; and they are validated in detail by the analysis in this book. At the same time, war is extraordinarily complex and uncertain. It is all too easy to oversimplify the lessons of training, tactics, technology, and strategy, and find dominant themes. Even when these themes are correct, however, the impact of complex mixes of less important factors is often cumulatively critical to a realistic understanding of what has actually occurred and its lessons for the future.

"Instant history" is an oxymoron. As the following chapter notes, much is still unknown about the Iraq War. The details of the diplomatic interactions between governments that shaped the prelude to the war are known in broad terms, but scarcely in detail. The debates that shaped U.S., British, Australian, and Iraqi war plans are largely unknown—except for some controversial press reports on U.S. plans.

Only limited information is available on the details of the buildup of U.S. and British forces before and during the Iraq War, except for nominal data on force deployments. Only limited information is available about the Iraqi preparations for war. One key issue that cannot yet be addressed is how much of the Iraqi defeat was the result of the war plan, technology, tactics, and readiness of coalition forces and how much was the result of the mistakes by the Iraqi leadership and the weaknesses of Iraqi forces. Both sets of factors are clearly involved, but far too little information is yet available on the Iraqi side of the war to make clear judgments.

Chapter 3 describes the history of the war using data based largely on official statements by the U.S. Department of Defense, the U.S. Central Command, the British Ministry of Defense, and the Australian Ministry of Defense. However, these data are drawn from wartime reports and not from the kind of meticulous historical research that war after war has shown is necessary to get an accurate picture of combat history.

Extensive information has become available in some areas, and this book draws upon a wide range of such sources. However, many of the key details of combat that could allow clear judgments to be made about given tactics, the interaction of combined and joint arms, and the impact of given weapons and technology are not yet available. Military history has shown again and again that any detailed lessons of war need extensive validation and that even the observations of the commanders and warriors most deeply involved can be wrong.

While it is possible to draw conclusions about many of the broader lessons of the war, there are other lessons that this book does not attempt to address. The road that led to the war must eventually involve a systematic reassessment of the way in which the Gulf War was terminated in 1991, the process of containment and confrontation that followed, and the public and private diplomacy that helped shape both the political struggles between 1991 and the Iraq War.

The problems that led Turkey to refuse to base U.S. and British forces and the success the United States and Britain had in dealing with friendly Gulf states like Bahrain, Kuwait, Oman, Qatar, and Saudi Arabia need detailed analysis. There is a need to better understand the attitudes of the Iraqi people toward Saddam Hussein's regime and toward coalition forces at the start of the war and as the war progressed.

As the final chapters of this book suggest, it is too soon to judge critical aspects of the grand strategic outcome of the war. It is clear that military victory is meaningful only to the extent that it is a prelude to successful nation building in Iraq, but it will be years before it is clear just how successful the coalition effort will be and what kind of Iraq will emerge from the ashes of Saddam Hussein's dictatorship. It is also unclear what the regional and global impact of the Iraq War will be. It seems unlikely that the war will really reshape the Middle East for either good or ill. It will certainly have a grand strategic impact, however, and that impact remains unclear.

Nevertheless, there are many "lessons" that are worth raising. Some are valuable because they provide new insights into the ongoing changes in warfighting that some call the "new way of war," and others because they provide detailed insights into changes in tactics, training, and technology. Still others are worth raising because they reiterate the importance of military fundamentals and of long-standing developments in U.S. and British forces. Even where full information is lacking, other points are worth raising to broaden the debate to come and to avoid a "sound bite" approach to analyzing the lessons of war.

Finally, a few words about sources and methods. This book relies heavily on interviews conducted under the ground rules that those interviewed could not be named. It also draws heavily on media reports as well as official reports; much of this reporting came via the Internet and is shown by source and date, but without page numbers. Where possible, serving officers and official reports have been quoted at length in an effort to avoid drawing lessons based solely on the author's background and judgments. There are many areas, however, where such sources are not available, at least at an unclassified level. Only a minimal effort has been made to standardize the spelling of Arabic names, in part because this book depends to some extent on a database where specific phrases and spellings allow rapid reference to the original source.

Notes

[1] Prepared testimony by U.S. Secretary of Defense Donald R. Rumsfeld, U.S. Senate Armed Services Committee, July 9, 2003.

[2] Statement of General Tommy R. Franks, former commander of U.S. Central Command, before the U.S. Senate Armed Services Committee, July 9, 2003.

[3] Ibid.

CHAPTER TWO

THE LIMITS OF ANALYSIS
WHAT WE DON'T YET KNOW

As the following chapters show, extensive official data, as well as many unofficial comments and reports, have become available on the war. The strengths and limits of this information are described in detail in the text and footnotes in these chapters. At the same time, it is important that the reader have a full understanding of the limits to what is and is not known as of this writing.

One of the more striking aspects of the Iraq War was that the U.S. and British commands issued far fewer "facts" about the conduct of the war and performance of weapons during the actual conflict than were issued in the Gulf War of 1990–1991. Few data were provided during the war on one of the most critical aspects of the war—the air and missile campaign. The U.S. Air Force has since provided significant data on the size of the forces, sortie numbers, and the numbers and types of munitions used. Almost no data have been made available, however, on the effectiveness of air and missile strikes, and few reliable data are available on the size and equipment of the land forces engaged and the effectiveness of their weapons.

The information the Iraqi government issued during the war was so decoupled from reality that the statements of the Iraqi Ministry of Information ranged between tragicomedy and an international practical joke. At the same time, U.S., British, and Australian forces encountered new mixes of Iraqi forces that involved irregular elements like Saddam's Fedayeen (Saddam's "Men of Sacrifice") as well as new asymmetric tactics. Little reliable data are available on these mixes of Iraqi Republican Guard, regular army, and irregular forces, or on how well they fought in given engagements, and on the successes and failures of these new force mixes and their tactics.

The basic course of the fighting is clear, and the history of the war in chapter 4 is drawn largely from briefings by the U.S. Central Command and materials developed by the British Ministry of Defense. There are no sweeping controversies about the outcome of individual battles or about many of the strengths and weaknesses in coalition and Iraqi forces.

Nevertheless, many patterns of events are not yet clear, and the devil often lies in the details. For example, the general merits of precision-guided weapons are clear. What is not clear is how reliable, accurate, and destructive given weapons have been, how good the targeting was, how well they were employed, and how they altered the nature of joint warfare and traditional balance between forces. The same uncertainties surround such key interactions as the changes made in the organization and technology used in the rapidly evolving command and control, communications, computer, intelligence, and strategic reconnaissance systems used in the war. The overall merits of these changes are clear. The details, however, are invisible.

At a broader level, it is all too easy to focus on the most dramatic changes in tactics and technology, but there is no clear way to weigh what is known about these changes against the impact of fundamentals like military professionalism, training, readiness, sustainability, and logistics. It seems likely that the coalition had an advantage in military professionalism that would have allowed it to win, albeit more slowly and with far more casualties, if U.S., British, and Australian forces had had to fight with the technologies they had in the Gulf War. It is far from clear that they could have won if the emphasis these forces placed on military professionalism had been lacking and if the coalition had relied primarily on advances in tactics and technology.

There are other key areas where insufficient data present major problems for analysis:

- There are few damage assessment data on the impact of firing some 800 Tomahawk and 100 conventional air-launched cruise missiles (CALCMs), and some 17,000 precision-guided munitions and 8,500 unguided weapons as of April 11. Such data may never be available in reliable form. Some senior officers involved in the conflict indicate the battle damage assessment process essentially broke down by the third day of the war, and question how much information can be reconstituted after the fact. (There are even some questions regarding the relative efforts using precision and unguided weapons. USCENTCOM reports some 65 percent of all strikes were precision strikes versus 7 percent for the first Gulf War. Reports of 90 percent versus 10 percent definitely do not fit the facts to date.)[1] Data on the use of new concepts of precision warfare, like the first uses of the Sensor Fused Weapon (SFW)—the first guided area weapon—are not available.[2]

- There are few data on the nature and flow of reinforcements between the start of the war on March 19 and April 9, aside from the movement of the 173rd Airborne Brigade into northern Iraq and rushing elements of the 2nd Armored Cavalry Regiment into the south to protect the logistic lines there. Some 62,000 men and women were moved by air, however, between the start of the war and April 6.

- The history of battles and clashes laid out in chapter 4 describes the dynamics of the fighting but not the scale of individual battles or the nature of the forces on each side. In many cases, intelligence analysis did not support initial estimates of the size of the Iraqi forces involved or their unit identification and mix of combat elements. Little or no data are available on the effectiveness of given elements of U.S. and British joint forces and their interactions.

- It is particularly difficult to trace the interaction between land and air forces, the extent to which land action forced Iraqi forces into exposed maneuvers, and the extent to which air strikes exhausted the Iraqi land forces before they could engage coalition forces. Anecdotal accounts to date indicate that maneuvering Iraqi forces often took so much damage from the air that they could not close cohesively on coalition ground forces. At the same time, reports from some U.S. Army and Marine units refer to major clashes with Iraqi land forces, problems with low-level mortar and rocket propelled grenade attacks, and, in one case, "body parts about knee deep, with hundreds of vehicles burning, including the occupants."

- It is clear from the history in chapter 4 that Special Forces and Ranger forces played a major role in the fighting throughout Iraq. The new interactions between special operations forces, precision airpower, and advanced intelligence, surveillance, and reconnaissance (IS&R) systems that were demonstrated during the Afghan conflict clearly continued to redefine the role of these forces. Special operations forces were able to secure Iraq's offshore oil loading terminals and help secure its oil fields, and in at least one case in the attack on Tikrit Special operations forces operated directly with heavy tanks. Still, many key details are not available.

- Less is known about the details of the fighting in the west and the north than about the fighting in southern and central Iraq, in part because much of this fighting involved elements of special operations forces, operations with elements of the Iraqi opposition, and operations by the 173rd Airborne Brigade—all of which required a high degree of wartime operational secrecy.

Map 1
Arabian Peninsula

Source: U.S. Government, CIA.

Map 2
Iraq

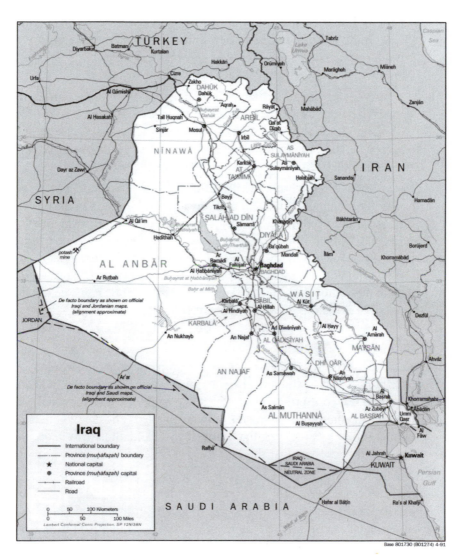

Source: U.S. Government, CIA.

- Much of the combat outside Baghdad and during the clashes on the way to Baghdad seems to have occurred in the form of air strikes against Iraqi ground forces that were trying to close on U.S. ground forces, and in the form of helicopter and artillery engagements against Iraqi ground forces rather than in the form of traditional ground force versus ground force engagements. There are few data on the nature of this "beyond-visual-range" combat.

- The role of "precision artillery" and helicopters is even harder to characterize than targeting and battle damage assessment (BDA) for fixed-wing aircraft. No reliable data are as yet available on attack helicopter sorties, the munitions fired, the forces and types of targets engaged, or the result. The same is true of artillery fire.

- Any effort to characterize the intentions, capabilities, and nature of the Iraqi leadership from night one onward, and the rate of decline in Iraqi command, control, communications, computers, and intelligence (C4I) capabilities during the war, must have a high degree of speculation. Far too many claims are being made about the degradation of Iraqi command, control, and communications (C3) capabilities that cannot be substantiated in detail, and it is generally impossible to distinguish the impact of Iraqi incompetence from Iraqi problems in communicating.

- The outcome of the war and the fact that Iraqi ground forces were decisively defeated are clear. So is the fact that most of Iraq's Republican Guard forces lost the bulk of their major weapons during the fighting and could not continue to fight. The fate of individual elements of the Republican Guard during the fighting is not clear. The detailed nature of operations by Iraqi regular army forces, and the impact of the strikes and battles against them, is even less clear.

- Only rough data are available on the role and mix of Iraqi Special Republican Guard, Republican Guard, regular army, Saddam's Fedayeen, Popular Army, and other forces in given battles and clashes. The same holds true on exactly what Iraqi forces were involved in the attacks conducted by Iraq's irregular and asymmetric forces. The Fedayeen are often credited for battles where other irregular Iraqi forces may have been involved.

- Few meaningful data are yet available on Iraq's capability and plans to use weapons of mass destruction (WMD)—if any—and only minimal data are available on its missile operations. It is possible that Iraq destroyed much of its weapons before the war in an effort to conceal them from the United Nations Monitoring, Verification, and In-spection Commission (UNMOVIC), and that it had adopted a strat-egy of focusing on development and creating dual-use facilities that could be used for production once UN sanctions were lifted. At this writing, such conclusions remain speculative.

- The full nature of Iraq's plans and tactics to use its ground-based air defenses is unclear, as are the scale of its use of surface-to-air missiles and anti-aircraft (AA) guns and the deployment of these forces.

- There is no way to confirm exactly why the Iraqi Air Force was com-pletely passive. The impact of the Gulf War, the inability to contest the "no-fly zones" over Iraq in the years that followed, and the mas-sive superiority of coalition airpower explain why Iraq's air force had few practical prospects and may have felt it could not engage or sur-vive successfully in combat, but this still does not explain its total lack of activity.

- It is clear that the United States dropped some 50 million leaflets be-tween October 2002 and April 11, 2003, but the full scale of psycho-logical warfare operations remains unclear, as does the nature of U.S. efforts to deny Iraqi capability to communicate.

- There are few data on Iraqi plans and capabilities to conduct acts of terrorism, try to bring Israel into the war, or use asymmetric warfare beyond its actions in the cities in the south and its use of the Fedayeen and other irregulars.

- It is still unclear why so many massive caches of conventional weap-ons were found in various cities, and whether Iraq had planned for a much larger role for its Popular Army and mass volunteers than was ever possible and/or whether it planned for "stay behinds" and con-flict after the fall of the regime. It seems most likely that the regime of Saddam Hussein planned on the massive mobilization of the Popular, or Al Quds, Army and that most Iraqis pressed into service in this force never showed up. The facts, however, remain uncertain.

- The Iraqi regime's overall defensive plan for Baghdad is unclear be-cause it failed so quickly that it is not possible to fully characterize Iraqi intentions.

- It is clear that many important aspects of the war actually began be-fore March 19. These include CIA and special operations forces ef-forts in the north and west, CIA efforts to suborn or bribe Iraqi commanders, deception efforts to tie down Iraqi forces in the north, and efforts to suppress Iraqi air defenses as part of the enforcement of the northern and southern no-fly zones.

Many of these data normally become available over time. Still, the truth is often complex, and validating military lessons takes and requires a great deal of objectivity. Far too often, "lessons" consist of arguments for a given strategy, force plan, tactic, weapon, or technology, with evidence selected to suit a given argument and alternative data ignored. Also note-worthy is the fact that key data often simply never become available. This study is in many ways a guide to issues that will take years to resolve.

As a final, and perhaps most important, caution, even a perfect under-standing of the lessons of the Iraq War does not mean that these lessons can easily be applied to the next. The United States and Britain may have developed a form of coalition and joint warfare more advanced than the capabilities of any other powers. As the next two chapters show, however, they faced a unique enemy in Iraq and one with many weaknesses. Prudent risks in fighting Iraq could prove to be remarkably imprudent in dealing with an enemy like North Korea, and other powers may prove to be far more effective in asymmetric warfare. Learning from history never means that it can be repeated.

Notes

[1] Sortie and munitions numbers shown here include CFACC strike and strike support missions; they do not include CFSOCC sorties or munitions or CFLCC and CFMCC helicopter and small fixed-wing sorties.

[2] Reporting by Stephen Trimble indicates that Air Force B-52s dropped six CBU-97 SFWs on a column of Iraqi vehicles moving south out of Baghdad on April 2. The Air Armament Center (AAC) has developed and fielded two versions of the weapon. The baseline SFW is anti-armor and identifies targets by sensing heat radiating from their engines. An upgraded variant—called the Pre-Planned Product Improvement (P3I) SFW—can identify "cool" man-made objects that are not emitting a heat signature. Both versions are designed with a dispenser that ejects four BLU-109 canisters, each containing a "smart" skeet warhead, for a total of 40 bomblets. Each variant uses a different skeet. The baseline SFW's skeet muni-tion is a solid warhead, but the P3I variant contains 16 tiny projectiles that create an effect similar to a shotgun blast. U.S. Air Force officials are discussing integrat-ing a single smart skeet on unmanned aerial vehicles. The concept is to employ the roughly eight-pound projectile on individual targets without the cluster effect that is dangerous in urban warfare settings. The U.S. Army also is testing skeet for use with the Guided Multiple Launch Rocket System. See Stephen Trimble, "Pentagon Eyes Larger Role for Battle Tested Sensor Fused Weapon," *Aerospace Daily*, April 22, 2003.

CHAPTER THREE

THE FORCES ENGAGED

The Iraq War was an asymmetric war in several senses of the term. Iraq made extensive use of irregular forces and unconventional warfare techniques, ranging from the use of its cities as sanctuaries for light armed paramilitary forces like Saddam's Fedayeen to the use of suicide bombers. It disguised some forces in civilian dress and may have attempted to make others look like they were wearing U.S. uniforms. The fundamental asymmetry, however, lay (1) in the radically different capabilities of the Iraqi forces and those of the coalition in technology, training, and readiness, and (2) in Iraq's lack of joint warfare capability against U.S. and British forces that had a degree of "jointness" that had never been approached in any previous war.[1]

THE CHANGING AND UNCERTAIN NATURE OF FORCE RATIOS

The Iraq War did not make force ratios meaningless. It did demonstrate, however, that traditional comparisons of force numbers can be virtually meaningless in shaping the outcome of modern joint warfare. Iraq was still a major military power by regional standards and had more than 400,000 conventional and paramilitary troops in its order of battle.

The total forces committed by the coalition actually outnumbered Iraq's forces, although many of these forces were support forces outside the combat zone and were not to be deployed in direct combat against Iraq. A U.S. Air Force (USAF) database shows that nearly 30 percent of all active duty U.S. military personnel, plus 40,397 reservists, were committed in some way to Operation Iraqi Freedom. The same database shows 42,987 active coalition personnel: 40,906 from Britain, 2,050 from Australia, and 31 from Canada.[2] The detailed breakout reported by the USAF is as follows:

Total U.S. Personnel Deployed	**466,985**	
USAF (10 Apr 03)	54,955	
USAF Reserve	2,084	
National Guard	7,207	
USMC (20 Apr 03)	74,405	
USMC Reserve	9,501	
USN (5 Apr 03)	61,296	(681 are USCG)
USN Reserve	2,056	
USA (17 Apr 03)	233,342	
USA Reserve	10,683	
National Guard	8,866	
Coalition	**42,987**	
British	40,906	
Australian	2,050	
Canadian	31	

These data undercount some allied forces and do not necessarily reflect the forces actually deployed forward into combat. However, press estimates indicate that Iraq's approximately 400,000 troops compared with a total of some 231,000 forward-deployed service men and women in U.S. forces, of which only 130,000 were in Kuwait. Another 8,500 were in Saudi Arabia, 8,300 in Qatar, 3,400 in Oman, 5,500 in Bahrain, 1,400 in the United Arab Emirates, 750+ in Diego Garcia, and 50,000 afloat. The British had 28,00 ground forces, including reservists.

The British had a total of approximately 45,000 troops in the theater plus 1,000 more in the National Contingent Headquarters. The Australians deployed approximately 2,000, and the Poles approximately 180. Some 20 countries provided or offered troops, and many others provided intelligence, logistics, and deployment support. President Bush stated on March 18 that a total of 40 countries were supporting the coalition.[3]

Iraq still had major holdings of armor and artillery, a significant air force, and extensive ground-based air defenses. If it had fought some combination of regional opponents, it would probably have been far more effective and might well have won any defensive battle. From a joint warfare perspective, however, Iraq had only limited capability. It had no meaningful navy and lacked an air force that could survive in the face of coalition airpower. It had poor combined armed capabilities, and much of its order of battle was designed more for regime security than for warfighting. Many Iraqi combat elements were better at watching each other, and at suppressing the Iraqi people, than at fighting a foreign opponent.

Iraq had some successes in using irregular forces and in asymmetric warfare, but it failed to make effective use of its strategic geography and organize its forces effectively despite more than a year of strategic warning. In retrospect, the surprise that limited numbers of loyalists like the Fedayeen Saddam achieved in controlling cities in the south and raiding U.S. forces and lines of communication disguised serious problems in Iraq's effort to organize for asymmetric warfare.

Iraq sought to create a massive Popular Army with the capability to draw on a mobilization base of some 7 million and the goal of actually arming up to 1 million men. Had this force become real, it might have enabled Saddam Hussein's regime to create massive popular defenses of Iraqi cities, create a "fortress" of defenses in depth around Baghdad, and conduct far more successful asymmetric fighting. Arms caches found throughout Baghdad and in many parts of the country indicate that the regime thought it could actually mobilize and arm such a force. There were also many revetments and defensive points around Baghdad, including oil-filled trenches that the regime lit early in the war.

In broad terms, however, the regime created a Popular Army that never showed up. As a result, Iraq's paramilitary forces were never strong enough to truly challenge coalition capabilities, although they achieved significant tactical surprises in some clashes in the south and did force the United States to devote forces to urban fighting and securing its lines of advance.

Iraq left virtually all of its regular forces deployed in their normal peacetime positions. The bulk of its armed forces were in the north and east at the start of the fighting. Moreover, they were deployed largely in forward areas against Iran and near the Kurdish security zone. It may be that Iraqi decisionmaking was heavily influenced by a debate in the United Nations that convinced it that the United States, Britain, and Australia could not go to war for political reasons.

It could also be that Iraq waited until the last moment to see if Turkey would permit the United States to deploy a second front that could attack Iraq through Mosul and create a major threat in the Kurdish security zone. In any case, all of the Iraqi forces in the north were left largely in their peacetime positions when the coalition attacked. Only one Republican Guard division executed major movements to strengthen the defense of Tikrit and Baghdad, and it was left in the north.

Iraq dispersed its air force in order to preserve it, with no apparent concept of using it in military operations. It seems to have calculated, as a result of the

Gulf War and more than a decade of encounters in the northern and southern "no-fly zones," that the air force simply could not survive in air combat. If Iraq had any concept of air operations like last-ditch or suicide raids, such strikes were never implemented. There is no way yet to determine the exact reason, but it seems likely that this was the result of years of defeat and weakness, a command decision, and the impact of coalition air strikes. The key unknown is whether the Iraqi Air Force ever intended to, or was ordered to, fight, and if so, what happened?

IRAQ'S MISUSE OF ITS FORCE STRENGTH DURING THE FIGHTING

Once the war began, Iraq could only maneuver in the face of massive assaults by coalition precision airpower. That airpower could locate all major armored movements using sensors like the E-8C JSTARS (Joint Surveillance Target Attack System), could strike during any time of day and in most forms of weather, and could either paralyze movement or exact a high price in terms of disruption and attrition. In broad terms, the regular army never moved, and the Republican Guard units in the north paid an extremely high price for moving south to try to defend the southern approaches to Baghdad.

Similar problems emerged in the south. When the war began, Iraq did have some regular army forces defending the approaches to Baghdad along the Euphrates and Tigris Rivers. A large number, however, were still in their peacetime positions and some forward-deployed elements forced, but most were still largely postured in their peacetime positions around Baghdad rather than dispersed and prepared for defense in depth.

No cohesive prewar effort was made to create an in-depth defense of Baghdad or to protect the lines of advance up the Euphrates. Although one division was moved south from the area around Mosul to the area around Tikrit, Iraq's Republican Guard did not begin to move to position themselves where they could oppose the United States' advance from the south until the war began and they were exposed to coalition airpower. The Republican Guard then moved largely in response to the coalition advance and had to fight mainly in scattered engagements rather than as part of a coherent, in-depth defense. In many cases, they intermingled their brigade elements with scattered elements of regular army forces and paramilitary units in ways that made well-organized defensive action difficult or impossible and compounded the impact of coalition strikes on Iraq's weak command and control capabilities.

There was no real effort to prepare the regular army in the south for defense in depth. The coalition seems to have successfully subverted the Iraqi 51st Mechanized Division in Basra to the point it disrupted the defense of Basra. It largely bypassed the Iraqi regular army corps defending the Iranian border, although elements of that corps did move to challenge the 1st Marine Division advance on Al Kut.

The remaining elements of the other regular army corps in the south attempted to maneuver to defend the lines of attack up the Euphrates, but never could keep up with the U.S. Army's V-Corps advance up the western side of the river, which was largely undefended except for paramilitary elements in the cities along the route—most of which could be bypassed.

There was heavy fighting for the key road junctions around Nasiriyah, and the 1 MEF had to fight through Iraqi regular army units on the way from Nasiriyah to Al Kut. In virtually every case, however, Iraqi forces had to maneuver and expose themselves to air attack to close on the advancing U.S. forces; they moved far too slowly to improvise a cohesive defense; and they fought at the small-unit element level and suffered massive attrition from coalition air attacks.

As the next chapter describes, Iraq never succeeded in exploiting its water barriers with any meaningful success. It left major gaps in its defenses of the Karbala Gap and southwestern approaches to Baghdad. It could not improvise an effective defense of the road from Al Kut to Baghdad in the east. And it continued to commit its Republican Guard piecemeal to the defenses of the approaches to Baghdad against both the 5th Corps and the 1st Marine Expeditionary Force in a manner that largely destroyed them and deprived the regime of the ability to create a cohesive defense of the city.

FAILURES IN IRAQI LEADERSHIP

It is impossible at this point to determine why the regime of Saddam Hussein failed to act decisively in so many ways, including why it never made effective use of any missiles and chemical and biological weapons it retained. The result, however, was that the coalition forces achieved a high degree of both strategic and tactical surprise. Moreover, much of what Iraq did greatly enhanced the advantages the coalition had in joint warfare and allowed the United States to exploit Iraq's own strategic geography in ways that denied Iraq the ability to develop a cohesive defense in depth.

The almost universal failures in Saddam Hussein's strategic leadership cannot be explained as the result of ignorance or "shock and awe." The Iraqi regime had already lost one war to a U.S. led-coalition and joint arms. It had seen what the United States and Britain could do in some 12 years of postwar clashes and in the fighting in Afghanistan. The broad details of the coalition buildup were fully revealed in the media during the months of debate within the UN, and so were many of the details of the coalition war plan.

If there are excuses for the failures of the Iraqi leadership, they could include the following:

- the belief that the UN debate would paralyze the ability of the coalition to take military action;
- belief that Turkey's decision not to base coalition land and air forces would delay or prevent military action (while Iraq's uncertainty regarding Turkey's ultimate intentions led it to leave its forces in the north);
- belief that a Popular Army that did not in reality exist could be mobilized;
- an inability to support and sustain most forces outside their peacetime barracks and bases that forced Iraq to wait to deploy them until the war began;
- an inability to translate a theoretical knowledge of coalition joint warfare capabilities into practical estimates of the lethality of the coalition's airpower, rates of maneuver, and capability to disrupt Iraqi movement and command and control capability once the war began;
- an unrealistic faith in unconventional and asymmetric warfare and the impact of delay, deception, and potential casualties on the willingness of the United States and Britain to sustain the war;
- a worldview that mixed the cult of the leader with an inability to realistically assess the strengths and weaknesses of Iraqi forces; and
- a series of actions to conceal and destroy Iraq's weapons of mass destruction in the face of UNMOVIC that continued virtually until the war began and meant that Iraq could never make effective use of any such weapons that remained.

All that said, it is difficult not to draw the conclusion that one of the major asymmetries in the military balance at the start of the war and during it was that the coalition had highly effective leadership and that Iraq was led by a military jackass.

THE IMPACT OF SEAPOWER

The coalition had a near monopoly of seapower. Iraq had a small 2,000-man navy with nine small, obsolete or obsolescent combat ships, an unknown number of mines, and Silkworm land-based anti-ship missiles.[4]

The United States had five carrier task forces, two amphibious task forces, and a total of 47 major surface ships, 12 submarines, and extensive additional support ships. These included roughly one-third of the total in the U.S. Navy. There were some 70,000 sailors and airmen deployed in the region. The U.S. Navy was able to sustain sorties from roughly 65 combat aircraft per carrier, and launch some 700 sea-based cruise missiles. At the same time, naval forces provided warning and air defense assets and radar support to the operation of the Patriot as a missile defense system.[5]

This was a massive commitment in terms of total U.S. naval forces, both in the theater and in terms of worldwide naval activity. According to the U.S. Congressional Research Service, the U.S. Navy put to sea 67 percent to 68 percent of its ships (54 percent or 55 percent in deployed status and another 13 percent in non-deployed operations). These forces included 7 or 8 of its 12 aircraft carriers, 7 of its 11 carrier air wings, 25 to 29 of its 38 amphibious ships, and 9 or 10 of the Navy's 12 "large-deck" amphibious assault ships.[6]

The British Royal Navy deployed Naval Task Group 2003. The task group was headed by the aircraft carrier HMS *Ark Royal*, accompanied by the helicopter carrier HMS *Ocean*, the destroyers HMS *Liverpool*, HMS *Edinburgh*, and HMS *York*, and a nuclear-powered submarine. The amphibious force deploying with the ships included the Headquarter 3rd Commando Brigade, the 40th Commando Royal Marines, the 42nd Commando Royal Marines (a total of some 4,000 men), and helicopter air groups aboard *Ark Royal* and *Ocean*.[7] The Royal Navy also deployed a Maritime Counter Measures Group to deal with the Iraqi mine threat, and an Afloat Support Group.

The Royal Australian Navy deployed the frigates HMAS *Anzac* and *Darwin* in the Persian Gulf and the sea transport ship HMAS *Kanimbla*, which carried about 350 sailors and soldiers, a Sea King helicopter, army landing craft, an army air defense detachment, and a specialist explosives ordnance team.[8]

The result was that the United States, Britain, and Australia not only had total domination of the sea, but also could operate carriers and cruise-missile launch ships from virtual sanctuary. Moreover, Iraq had been effectively "landlocked" since the summer of 1990, shortly after its invasion of Kuwait, by UN sanctions that denied it the ability to import arms, military supplies, and many dual-use items. Iraq's chief source of export income was under UN control, as were the items it imported. Although it did smuggle out oil through Turkey, Iranian waters, and Syria—and smuggled in some arms and military spare parts through Syria—Iraq had lost access not only to the sea but also to the land for most military purposes, and its overall military modernization and sustainability efforts had been crippled for more than a decade.

THE IMPACT OF AIRPOWER

In terms of sheer numbers, the coalition did not have the dominance in airpower that it had in seapower. Nevertheless, it had a nearly infinite force ratio in terms of military effectiveness. The Iraqi Air Force never flew a combat mission.

The Size and Nature of the Iraqi Air Force

As has been discussed earlier, the total passivity of the Iraqi Air Force is still difficult to fully explain. It dispersed, took shelter, and remained passive for the entire war, but this was scarcely inevitable. The Iraqi Air force had around 20,000 men when the war began. It still had between 316 and 325 combat aircraft, although only about 50 percent to 60 percent were serviceable. Senior pilots still flew 60 to 120 hours a year, depending on the aircraft, although most pilots flew as few as 20.[9]

There are no reliable estimates of Iraq's exact air strength. The IISS estimates that the Iraqi Air Force had 6 obsolete H-6D and Tu-22 bombers and 130 attack aircraft, including Mirage F-1EQs, Su-20s, 40 Su-22s, 2 Su-24s, and 2 Su-25s. Iraq still had extensive stocks of short-range air-to-ground missiles and cluster bombs. It also had 180 air defense fighters, including 12 MiG-25s, 50 Mirage F-1EQs, and 10 MiG-29s, plus 5 MiG-25 reconnaissance aircraft. Additionally, the air force had extensive stocks of MiG-21s, training aircraft, and drones, and had experimented with using them as unmanned aerial vehicles (UAVs) and unmanned combat aerial vehicles (UCAVs). It still had 2 IL-76 tankers and large numbers of transport aircraft.

Jane's Information Group provided a different estimate, with the following key combat types (the number estimated to be in service are shown in parentheses): 40 (0) F-7s, 30 (13) Mirage F-1EQs, 36 (15–25) MiG-21s, 35 (15–20) MiG-23s, 6 (3–6) MiG-25s, 17 (1) MiG-29s, 33 (15–18) Su-20/22s, 21 (6–11) Su-25s, 2 T-22s, and 3 Tu-16s.[10]

The Iraqi Air Force's key holdings seem to have included a total inventory of 255 fighters and fighter-bombers and some 80 trainers—some of which were combat capable.[11] Iraq's total holdings seem to have included a total of 130 J-6, MiG-23BN, MiG-27, Mirage F-1EQ5, Su-7, Su-20, and Su-25 attack fighters; 180 J-7, MiG-21, MiG-25, Mirage F-1EQ, and MiG-29 air defense fighters; MiG-21 and MiG-25 reconnaissance fighters; 15 old Hawker Hunters; a surviving Il-76 Adnan AEW (airborne early warning) aircraft (not operational); 2 Il-76 tankers; and large numbers of transports and helicopters. Estimates of its total surviving inventory by aircraft type vary by source, but Iraq probably retained about 30 Mirage F-1s, 15 MiG-29s, 50-60 MiG-23s, 15 MiG-25s, 150 MiG-21s, 25-30 Su-25s, and 60 Su-17s, Su-20s, and Su-22s.

Although it is unclear how many air munitions Iraq retained after the Gulf War, some estimates put this figure far below 50 percent of the pre-war total. Iraq retained significant numbers of modern air-to-air and air-to-ground munitions, however. These stocks included AA-6, AA-7, AA-8, AA-10, Matra 530, Matra 550, and Matra Super 530 air-to-air missiles, and AM-39 Exocet, AS-11, AS-12, AS-6, AS-14, AS-301, AS-37, C-601 Silk-worm air-to-surface missiles; laser-guided bombs; and cluster bombs.

Iraq deployed Matra Magic 2 "dogfight" air-to-air missiles on its Mirage F-1s after the Gulf War. This was virtually its only major improvement in air force equipment since 1990. It is not clear whether these missiles were delivered before the war, were stolen from Kuwait, or were smuggled in before the coalition attack. They are an advanced type of missile similar to the more advanced export versions of the U.S. AIM-9, with high energy of maneuver and a maximum range of three nautical miles.[12]

Iraq retained large numbers of combat-capable trainers, transport aircraft, and helicopters, and had some unmanned aerial vehicles. The trainers included some Mirage F-1BQs, 25 PC-7s, 30 PC-9s, 50 to 60 Tucanos (EMB-312s), 40 L-29s, and 40 L-39s. Transport assets included a mix of Soviet An-2, An-12, An-24, An-26, and Il-76 jets and propeller aircraft, and some Il-76s modified to act as tankers. The UAVs included some Iraqi-made designs, Italian designs, and Soviet designs. It is unclear how effectively Iraq used any of these UAV systems, but it did make limited use of them during the Gulf War.[13]

An air force, however, is not measured by its strength on the ground or by how many aircraft it can park. The Iraqi Air Force's air-to-air and air-to-ground training was limited and unrealistic. Its command and control was overcentralized, and its mission planning often set impossible goals. The two no-fly zones further limited air training and combat experience. It had no modern airborne sensor, command and control, or intelligence capabilities, other than its small number of UAVs. Its air control and warning was still heavily dependent on outdated ground-based intercept capabilities.

The Iraqi Air Force had, however, practiced penetration raids by single low-flying aircraft and had shown that it could conduct independent offensive operations at the small formation level. Iraq had repaired many of the bases and air facilities that were destroyed or damaged during the Gulf

War. It had 16 to 20 major air bases, with H-3, H-2, and Al Asad in the west; Mosul, Qayarah, and Kirkuk in the north; Al Jarah, Tallil, and Shaybah in the south; and 5 to 7 more bases within a 150-kilometer radius of Baghdad. Many of those bases had surface-to-air missile defenses. At the least, Iraq could have disrupted and delayed coalition air operations for a while, although at a terrible cost in pilots and aircraft.

THE SIZE AND NATURE OF THE COALITION AIR COMPONENT

The United States, in contrast, built up to more than 1,000 aircraft in theater before the war began and used 1,663 fixed-wing aircraft at the peak of the fighting, including virtually every type in the U.S. inventory.[14]

According to USCENTCOM, on March 17, 2003, the U.S. Air Force had 37,000 service members directly assigned to the Iraqi buildup, Operation Northern Watch, and Operation Southern Watch, with 300 fighter-bombers; 70 command and control (C2), surveillance and electronic warfare aircraft; 80 special operations and rescue aircraft; 160 tanker aircraft; and 120 airlift aircraft, for a total of 730. These did not include aircraft in Diego Garcia or the UK. The U.S. Navy added another 425 planes, with 250 "shooters" and 175 others, and the U.S. Marine Corps added 75 more aircraft.

According to the U.S. Air Force, the USAF had a peak total of 863 aircraft, the U.S. Navy had 408, the U.S. Marine Corps had 372, and the U.S. Army (less helicopters) had 20. The Royal Air Force (RAF) had 113 aircraft, the Royal Australian Air Force had 22, and the Canadian Air Force had 3. These numbers are shown below by major category:[15]

Aircraft Type	USAF	USMC	USN	U.S. Army	Canadian	Australian	British
Total	863	372	408	20	3	22	113
Fighters	293	130	232	—	—	14	66
Bombers	51	—	—	—	—	—	—
C2	22	—	20	—	—	—	4
IS&R	60	—	29	18	—	2	9
Sp Ops/Rescue	58	—	—	—	—	—	14
Special Forces	73	—	—	—	—	—	—
Tankers	182	22	52	—	—	—	12
Airlift	111	—	5	—	3	—	4
Other	13	220	70	2	—	3	—

The primary U.S. holdings of combat aircraft included 11 B-1B, 4 B-2, and 28 B-52 bombers. The main fighter and fighter attack aircraft included 60 A-10/OA-10s, 70 AV-8B Harriers, 56 F-14s, 42 F-15Cs, 48 F-15Es, 60 F-16s, 250 F/A-18s, and 12 F-117s. The special purpose combat aircraft included 8 AC-130 gunships and 71 Wild Weasel F-16Cjs equipped with HARM anti-radiation missiles. The United States had 1 RQ-1 Global Hawk and 4 RQ-4 Predators. The Iraq War was the first time the USAF ever flew four RQ-4s or 6 U-2s simultaneously.[16]

U.S. holdings also included 20 E-2, 19 E-3, 7 E-8C, 35 EA-6B, 8 EC-130, 3 EP-3, 1 R-1, 18 RC-12, 15 U-2, 8 HC-130, and 9 RC-135 electronic warfare and intelligence aircraft. There were 28 P-3, 1 PC-6, 40 S-3, and 2 PR-9 patrol aircraft.

The tanker forces included 4 KC-1s, 33 KC-10s, 22 KC-130s, and 149 KC-135s. Airlift aircraft included 10 C-2s, 5 C-9s, 7 C-17s, 3 C-20s, 7 C-21s, 1 C-32, 1 C-40, 1 CN-235, 1 DC-130, and 124 C-130s.

The database on helicopters is more uncertain because the USAF did not include U.S. army helicopters in its database. It shows a total of 58 AH-1s, 8 AH-6s, 67 CH-46s, 11 CH-47s, 54 CH-53s, 16 HH-60s, 7 MH-6s, 14 MH-47s, 31 MH-53s, 18 MH-60s, 30 UH-1s, 4 UH-3s, and 3 UH-60s.

There is no way to put together an exact count of U.S. air strength because the United States changed its number of aircraft and force mix during the war. In any case, the total numbers of aircraft were far less important than the fact that the United States had enough support and sustainability to use its air force, its navy, its marine corps, and its army to generate immense numbers of sorties. Moreover, virtually all of its combat aircraft not only could use precision-guided weapons; they could also acquire targets effectively, they could illuminate and/or track them, and they could fire at standoff ranges from Iraq's low-altitude air defenses.

The resulting combination of sortie generation numbers and sortie quality allowed the coalition to generate 41,404 sorties against an Iraqi Air Force that generated none. The United States alone generated 38,358 sorties, or more than 93 percent of the total. The coalition flew at least 20,753 fighter and bomber sorties, of which the United States alone flew all of the 505 bomber sorties and 18,190 of the fighter sorties for a total of 18,695 fighter/bomber sorties. The USAF estimate of these sortie numbers is as follows: [17]

Aircraft Type	USAF	USMC	USN	U.S. Army	British	Australian
Total	24,196	4,948	8,945	269	2,841	565
Fighters	8,828	3,794	5,568	-		302
Bombers	505	-	-	-	-	-
C2	432	75	442 (E2)	-	112 (E3D)	-
IS&R	452	305	357	269	273	-
Sp Ops/Rescue	191	-	-	-	-	-
Tankers	6,193	454	2,058	-	359	-
Airlift	7,413	-	-	-	-	263
Other	182	320	520	-	1	-

British reporting indicates that the Royal Air Force deployed 115 fixed-wing aircraft and 27 helicopters, and that the Royal Navy deployed an additional 43 helicopters. The British count shows a total of 2,519 sorties, with 1,353 offensive strike sorties, 169 air defense sorties, 87 airborne early warning sorties, 274 reconnaissance sorties, 355 air-to-air refueling sorties, 263 intertheater airlift sorties, and 18 aero-medical sorties.[18]

Even sortie numbers do not give a clear picture of the massive impact of coalition airpower. The coalition dropped a ratio of 19,948 precision-guided weapons, plus nearly 9,251 unguided weapons; the Iraqis dropped none.[19]

The U.S. forces alone fired 19,269 guided weapons. The main weapons included 802 sea-launched BGM-109 TLAM, or Tomahawk cruise missiles, and 153 air-launched AGM-86 C/D CALCMs (conventional air-launched cruise missiles). They included 6,542 JDAM GPS (global positioning system)-guided bombs (GBU-31, GBU-32, GBU-53, and GBU-37) and 8,618 laser-guided bombs (GBU-10, GBU-12, GBU-16, GBU-24, GBU-27, and GBU-28). They also included 98 EGBU-27 weapons with both GPS and laser guidance. The United States fired 408 AGM-88 HARM high-speed anti-radiation missiles.

The United States delivered an extremely diverse mix of other guided weapons. These included 88 CBU-105 WCMD (Wind-Corrected Munitions Dispenser) sensor-fused cluster bombs. It also fired 818 CBU-103 and 2 CBU-107 WCMD cluster bombs, as well as lighter missiles such as 562 AGM-114 Hellfire and 918 AGM-65 Maverick anti-armor weapons, which sometimes were used against urban targets as well. The United States fired 4 longer-range AGM-130s, 3 AGM-84 SLAM ERs, and 253 AGM-154 JSOWs.

While some 68 percent of the weapons the United States fired were guided, the remaining 32 percent still added up to a massive total. The unguided weapons the United States delivered included 118 CBU-87 and 182 CBU-99 cluster bombs, 1,625 M-117 general purpose 750-pound bombs, and 7,202 Mark 82, 83, and 84 unguided bombs. The United States also made massive use of strafing, firing some 16,901 20-mm rounds and 311,597 30-mm rounds from the air.

The British classify the number of Tomahawks they delivered, but launched 27 of their new Storm Shadow stand-off attack weapons, 394 Enhanced Paveway II precision-guided bombs, 10 Enhanced Paveway III precision-guided bombs, 265 Paveway II laser-guided bombs, 38 Maverick anti-armored missiles, 47 ALARM anti-radar missiles, and 138 non-precision-guided and unguided munitions. This is a total of 919 munitions, of which 85 percent were precision-guided weapons.[20]

One of the most striking aspects of the coalition effort is how these sorties were allocated in terms of targets. The data that USCENTAF (United States Central Command Air Forces) has developed on the actual execution of sorties now use a weighted measure called "sortie equivalents" to take account of the different capabilities of different strike aircraft and their respective capability to hit multiple targets. If one uses these measures and counts only actual executed sortie equivalents, the coalition launched 15,592 sorties against Iraqi ground forces in killbox, interdiction, and close air support targets, or 79 percent of the total. It flew another 1,441 sortie equivalents to maintain air and space superiority (7 percent), 1,799 to suppress the Iraqi regime's ability to command Iraqi forces and govern Iraq (9 percent), 832 to suppress Iraqi theater missile and weapons of mass destruction delivery systems (4 percent), and 234 sorties to prevent noncombatant Iraqi forces from joining the battle or to compel the capitulation of forces actively involved in combat (1 percent).

These figures show the focus the coalition placed on defeating the regime and the Republican Guard versus any form of attacks on infrastructure and strategic targets outside the regime. It is also worth noting that many requests for attack sorties were rejected in the effort to limit the destructiveness of the air campaign. A total of 30,542 requests were made, measured in sortie equivalents, but only 25,240 got as far as the targeting list, and only 19,898 were executed—about 65 percent of those requested by component command.

Moreover, the United States had radically upgraded the targeting, data links, and avionics on its strike aircraft since the Gulf War and had honed its delivery techniques in the Balkans and Afghanistan. It had a monopoly of space assets and of greatly improved intelligence, targeting, surveillance, electronic warfare, and command and control aircraft. It had a near monopoly of unmanned aerial vehicles (UAVs) and far better systems.

The British Royal Air Force (RAF) deployed an additional 7,000 personnel and some 100 fixed-wing aircraft. These aircraft also included highly capable systems. The RAF used the E-3D Sentry aircraft for airborne command and control and 4 Jaguar GR3 fighters and Tornado GR4 bombers in reconnaissance mode. It used 14 Tornado F3 air defense aircraft with the newly integrated ASRAAM missile, and 30 Tornado GR4 bombers and 18 Harrier GR7 fighters to provide offensive capability, including precision-guided weapons. It also used 8 VC10 and TriStar air-to-air refueling aircraft and Hercules transport aircraft.

The RAF's Joint Helicopter Command provided helicopter support, consisting of 27 Puma and Chinook helicopters and about 1,100 personnel. RAF regiment units provided ground defense for the force. The British Army's 21 Signal Regiment provided communications support for the joint helicopter force.

The Royal Australian Air Force (RAAF) deployed another 2,000 personnel, a squadron of 14 F/A-18 Hornet fighter aircraft, three C130 Hercules transport aircraft, an Air Forward Command Element, and a small RAAF reconnaissance team.

The Coalition Application of Airpower

The fact that the United States and Britain had in many ways defeated the Iraqi Air Force in the air and had heavily suppressed the Iraqi land-based air defense system, even before the war began, allowed the coalition to suppress Iraq's air defenses with remarkable speed and to concentrate on strike/attack missions almost immediately. A monopoly of stealth and cruise missiles allowed the coalition to attack any static target in even the most heavily defended air space at any time in any weather. As the following chapter shows, the coalition leapt from air supremacy to nearly total air dominance.

No public battle damage assessment (BDA) data are available to assess the level of damage the coalition inflicted, and few data are as yet available on the effectiveness of individual aircraft and systems. Still, enough data are available from previous wars to show that a force ratio of over 18,000 well-directed precision-guided weapons to zero, plus thousands more unguided weapons, must have had a massive effect. It certainly makes conventional force ratio and order-of-battle comparisons largely meaningless.

Effects-based Bombing

More was involved than the ability to use airpower as a killing mechanism. The coalition could use precision-guided weapons and advanced U.S. com-

mand and control and targeting assets to limit collateral damage and civilian casualties. It could use new intelligence assets and targeting planning to severely limit the number of targets it had to strike and then carefully
match weapon accuracy and reliability, and the size and effect of the weapon,
to the right aim point necessary to destroy the function of a target without
imposing unnecessary destruction or risk to the target and target area.

This, in turn, allowed the United States and Britain to seek to paralyze
and destroy a regime, not bomb a country. It allowed them to avoid attacking most urban and populated areas unless there were time-urgent
regime targets or Iraqi forces that actively threatened coalition forces.

This issue of "time urgency" for a regime the coalition expected to survive for only weeks at most, and that it expected to lose control over most
of the country in days, was also critical. The coalition had no need to
bomb liberated or passive areas and Iraqi forces. It had no reason to strike
at economic targets unless there were actively hostile Iraqi forces in them
or a time-urgent risk that such targets could lead to the Iraqi use of WMD
or missiles. There was no need for extensive attacks on economic or infrastructure facilities, lines of communication, or most other civilian targets.

Anything but a Cakewalk

At the same time, "effects-based bombing" remained an art form and not a
science. One key problem, even with the targeting and intelligence assets
the coalition had available, was knowing how many fixed targets were
empty or no longer performed a critical function, and how many Iraqi
forces were able to disperse. Although no data are available on this aspect
of the Iraq War, some of those involved in battle damage assessment in
Desert Fox in 1998 feel the United States found that at least 20 to 30 percent of strikes hit largely empty buildings or facilities. Others indicate that
the coalition often struck at facilities simply because they were associated
with the military or had special security. In many cases, the United States
did not know the function of the facility before the war with any confidence and had no way to estimate the impact of such strikes.

The Iraqis had learned from the Israeli strike on Osirak in 1982 that
they should build the walls and roofs of structures before creating underground facilities and structures or putting in the final structure in terms of
floors and special features. They made increasing use of deep shelters and
tunnels whose character could be concealed from satellites and reconnaissance aircraft. They learned how to carry out activities where U.S. satellite
coverage was limited, and they exploited the intelligence the United States
gave them during the Iran-Iraq War to predict some of the limits to U.S.
sources and methods This learning process continued when Iraq aided

Serbia during the Kosovo crisis. The Iraqis had months to quietly prepare alternative sites, decoys, deception operations, and force dispersal.

Targeting was easier against conventional land, air, air defense, and naval forces that remained in or near their peacetime locations. The moment the war began, however, many Iraqi forces began to move, and the Iraqi force mix changed. U.S. and British intelligence also was far less capable in locating and characterizing people and vehicles that were or looked like civilian vehicles. As a result, it had major problems in dealing with infantry-dominated forces, light forces, and irregular forces like Saddam's Fedayeen. These problems were compounded by an inability to accurately characterize the warfighting capability of intelligence, security, Ba'ath Party, and paramilitary forces; and by the increasing intermingling of such forces with elements of the regular army and the Republican Guard as the war progressed.

As a result, U.S. targeting had to become dynamic and had to alter to hit at newly discovered or dispersed targets by the second day of operations. It then had to stay fluid and be shaped by the changing tactical situation, the discovery of new patterns in Iraqi military activity and dispersal, efforts to assess the damage done by previous air strikes and Iraqi engagements with coalition ground forces, and the concentration of the enemy near American and British forces. Events increasingly dictated targeting in ways that had to be based on less and less certain information as the battle became more dynamic, and these problems seem to have increased because of a relatively early breakdown in the battle damage assessment effort.

The dynamics of combat also affected the level of restraint the coalition could show. The allies still had to protect American, Australian, and British soldiers, their rear areas, and their flanks, and do so even in urban areas. Senior U.S. military officers said before the war that the coalition would hit whatever was necessary to do this, and that they still planned to use a total of 30 percent unguided weapons—although this total was around 10 percent in populated or sensitive areas.

The coalition flew extensive numbers of sorties where no central control could be exerted over the targets that were engaged. Aircraft flew in "kill boxes" and attacked targets of opportunity in the rear or provided close air support. There were many areas where the pilots of fixed-wing and rotary wing aircraft performed their own targeting on a target-of-opportunity basis, supported by their individual formation.

Targeting restraints had to be different in the case of known or suspected locations with chemical and biological weapon (CBW) or key related delivery systems. The United States and Britain could make maximum use of precision weapons and try to use the smallest weapon that could take out most CBW systems while limiting the risk of collateral damage. At the same time, the coalition had massive intelligence problems in locating and characterizing the targets involved, just as it had had during the previous Gulf War. It is now clear that many targets were hit that had little or no impact on any Iraqi capability to launch missiles or deliver either chemical or biological weapons. It was forced to bomb many targets simply because a successful Iraqi use of weapons of mass destruction on U.S., British, and Australian troops could have produced a massive increase in coalition casualties.

Once again, targeting was complicated by the fact that Iraq had every reason to try to disperse, use decoys, shelter in civilian areas and facilities, and use sensitive buildings and areas to limit American and British effectiveness. It had equal reason to exaggerate military and civilian casualties, religious and cultural destruction, and economic and infrastructure destruction for political purposes.

Urban and heavily populated areas presented a problem. Most urban areas were still open enough to allow the use of precision weapons. Many Iraqi regime facilities were surrounded by compounds and wide areas that allowed fighting to avoid densely populated areas, and civilians fled most adjacent areas or successfully took cover. Nevertheless, close-in urban fighting still happened in populated areas where the United States and Britain could not launch air or missile strikes without risking significant collateral damage, particularly in the cities. The coalition advanced through in the south and from Baghdad's outer defenses to the last core center of the regime. One senior U.S. military targeting expert called this kind of targeting "trying to have a fist fight in a really dark room." The United States, Britain, and Australia could not let soldiers engage in such fighting because of targeting constraints.

All of these issues meant that the United States and Britain had to react with rapid retargeting and bombing with progressively less information. There were also many real world constraints on "precision." Targeting and location errors were inevitable in such a massive campaign. The theoretical design accuracy of targeting systems, avionics, and precision weapons was also generally much higher than the real world performance of the delivery system and weapon in actual combat. Reliability problems and manufacturing errors meant many weapons did not achieve their design accuracy, significant numbers of misses occurred, and warheads or munitions misfired.

The United States, Britain, and Australia have not made any BDA data public that can be used to analyze how effectively the coalition air forces dealt with these problems. As has been touched upon earlier, some of the senior officers involved also indicate that the BDA analysis effort broke down early in the war and made it extremely difficult to assess "effects" on a timely basis. Moreover, even if some coalition member does publish public battle damage assessment data, these data may have uncertain value. Much of U.S. and British battle damage analysis is based on whether a strike destroys the desired part of the building or hits the correct area. There is no way to be sure who is in the building or shelter, or how much the strikes have hurt the functional capabilities of Iraqi forces. Similarly, the assessment of damage of major weapons systems often has to be probabilistic because universal sensor coverage is impossible, the full nature and cause of the damage done to a weapon is not clear from the sensor, and the use of multiple collection assets and pilot reports leads to dual counting. Despite all of the advances in technology, there often is still no way to reliably measure or verify lethality, and particularly to assess military and civilian casualties and the economic and function impact of collateral damage.

Nevertheless, the coalition did make extensive use of intelligence satellites, UAVs like Predator and Global Hawk, reconnaissance aircraft like the U-2, targeting aircraft like the E-8C JSTARS, helicopters, and Special Forces to maintain their targeting capability. It drew on U.S. resources that provided unprecedented intelligence assets, communications, and computer speed in acquiring, reviewing, and allocating targets. The fog of war must have remained, but it was certainly thinned.

The end result, at least from the evidence provided by media coverage to date, is that civilian casualties and collateral damage were remarkably limited and that postwar looting may actually have caused more damage than the coalition.

LAND-BASED AIR DEFENSES

The United States, several Gulf states, and Israel deployed the Patriot anti-aircraft (AA) and anti-tactical ballistic missile system, and used it in the defense of Kuwait. Israel deployed the Arrow ballistic missile defense system, but never had to use it. In practice, however, it was Iraq that had an effective monopoly of land-based air defenses in most of the fighting, and Iraq's land-based air defenses were its only potential counter to the coalition's monopoly of air power.

The Iraqi Air Defense Command

At the time the war started, the heavy surface-to-air missile forces of Iraq's Air Defense Command were still organized into one of the most dense defensive networks in the world despite the losses during the Gulf War and during the U.S. and British enforcement of the northern and southern no-fly zones.

USCENTCOM reported after the war that active Iraqi surface-to-air missile strength was a nominal 210 launchers and 150 early warning radars. No similar unclassified estimates are available of Iraq's missile holdings by type, but some sources indicate that Iraq still had a total inventory of 130 to 180 SA-2 launchers, 100 to 125 SA-3 launchers, 100 to 125 SA-6s, 20 to 35 SA-8s, 30 to 45 SA-9s, some SA-13s, and around 30 Roland VII and 5 Crotale surface-to-air missile fire units. Some of these systems were operated by the army. In addition, Iraq had some 2,000 man-portable SA-7s and SA-14s and some SA-16s.[21]

Iraq was able to maintain part of its battle control and management system, and many of its sheltered air defense and air force command and control centers remained operational. Iraq's French-supplied KARI air defense communications and data-link system had never been particularly effective, but Iraq had improved many of the sensor and command links, and made much heavier use of fiber optics.[22] It had an operational Headquarters Center, Air Defense Operations Center, and Air Defense Military Intelligence facilities in the Baghdad area, plus four Sector Operations Centers (SOCs) and an independent SOC to protect Saddam's palaces and key Republican Guard and security operations.

Iraq's heavy surface-to-air missile forces were backed by extensive low-altitude anti-aircraft guns and SA-8b, SA-11, and SA-13 short-and medium-range missiles. The Strela 2 and 10 (SA-7 and SA-10) were used for terminal defense of key buildings. Iraq learned to rapidly move its fire units and sensors, use urban cover and decoys, use "pop-on radar" guidance techniques, and use optical tracking.

Many radars and elements of Iraq's air defense C4I system were still operating, including the Soviet Spoon Rest, Squat Eye, Flat Face, Tall King, Bar Lock, Cross Slot, and Thin Skin radars. Iraq also had Soviet, Italian, and French jamming and electronic intelligence equipment. Some experts felt that many of Iraq's underground command and personnel shelters had survived the Gulf War and that at least 50 to 66 percent had survived the attacks made in enforcing the no-fly zones.

Iraq's ground-based defenses were concentrated around Baghdad, Basra, Mosul, and Kirkuk. Iraqi territory is too large to attempt territorial defense, and Iraq has always concentrated on defending strategic targets and deploying air-defense zones to cover critical land-force deployments. Iraq had redeployed some missiles during 1992 and 1993 to create surface-to-air missile "traps" near the no-fly zones. These traps were designed to attack aircraft with overlapping missile coverage when they attacked launchers deployed near the no-fly zones. Although the Iraqi efforts failed—and led to the destruction of a number of the missile launchers involved—it is not clear what portion survived or what other detailed redeployments Iraq had made before the war began.[23]

Unclassified estimates indicate that Iraqi air defenses were organized as follows:

- **The 1st Sector Operations Center** at Taji Military Camp in Northern Baghdad covered central and eastern Iraq and the greater Baghdad area. It seems to have had two missile brigades near al Dorah and at al Habaniah with a total of 10 SA-2 batteries and 6 to 9 SA-3 batteries, plus a range of independent batteries with SA-2s, SA-3s, SA-6s, Rolands, and possibly captured IHawks. It had four early warning radar regiments and an ECM unit.

- **The 2nd Sector Operations Center** covered western Iraq and was located near H-3 (al Waleed) Airbase near the Jordanian border. It covered the Syrian border, the Mosul area, and the northern Iranian border. It had a brigade with 4 SA-2, 6 SA-3, and some SA-6 batteries, a Roland battalion, ZSU-23-4 and other AA gun units, and an early warning radar unit.

- **The 3rd Sector Operations Center** covered southern Iraq and was located in Imam Ali Airbase near Nasiriyah. It covered the Saudi, Kuwaiti, and Jordanian borders and the southern Iranian border. It had at least one missile brigade and AA gun units, plus an early warning radar and control unit.

- **The 4th Sector Operations Center** was headquartered at Al Hurriyah Airbase near Kirkuk. It defended Mosul to the north, the Iranian border to the east, and the al Jazirah area in the west. It had at least 4 SA-2 battalions.

- **Iraq also had an independent SOC based in Baghdad** to defend the palaces, Republican Guards, and key security facilities. It had SA-2, SA-3, SA-8, SA-9, SA-11, and Roland batteries, plus SA-7s and SA-14s. The Special Republican Guard and Republican Guard each had independent air defense batteries that were not integrated into the SOC system used by the Air Defense Command.

The Weakness of Iraqi Air Defenses

Iraq's air defenses were anything but passive during the war. USCENTCOM estimates that there were 1,224 reports of Iraqi firings of AA guns,

1,660 reports of surface-to-air missile launches, and 436 instances of Iraqi radar emitters attempting to lock on to coalition aircraft. Once again, however, Iraqi numbers were not a substitute for effectiveness. The exact number of coalition aircraft lost to Iraqi enemy combat is still being clarified, but USCENTCOM puts the total at seven—4 AH-64D Longbow Apache attack helicopters, 2 AH-1W Cobra attack helicopters, and 1 A-10A Warthog attack aircraft. This is a negligible loss rate for the number of aircraft and sorties involved, and nearly twice as many aircraft—13—were lost to accidents and other causes.[24]

The systems design of Iraq's mix of SA-2s, SA-3s, and SA-6s was badly outdated, going back to the 1950s and 1960s. The coalition had shown it could suppress them during the Gulf War in 1991 and had had years of practice in dealing with Iraqi tactics and technology. It had long developed effective countermeasures it could use in most areas to launch strikes that avoided Iraqi defenses or penetrated them and then launched stand-off strikes from outside the range of Iraq's shorter-range air defenses, which were more difficult to suppress.

Iraq had lost much of its capability to carefully focused U.S. and British strikes on its air defense facilities during the time of the UN debate and particularly from March 1, 2003, to the start of the war. This "enforcement" of the no-fly zones effectively allowed the coalition to begin the suppression of enemy air defense (SEAD) phase of the war long before G-Day on March 19. During the struggle in the no-fly zones, the United States claimed it destroyed some 20 to 33 percent of the launchers and major radars Iraq still had.

Iraq had learned a great deal about land-based air defense operations from the Gulf War and more than 10 years of operations against the U.S. and British aircraft enforcing the no-fly zones. Iraq provided significant aid to Serbia in air defense tactics during the fighting in Kosovo, and helped Serbia make effective use of decoys, "pop-on" and remotely linked radar activity, various ambush tactics, and the use of deployments in civilian areas to limit NATO's ability to strike at such targets.

Iraq had developed some crude countermeasures to U.S. AGM-88 HARM anti-radiation missiles since the Gulf War, and had begun to get significant equipment through Syria. This may have included more advanced radar guidance kits for the 2K12 (SA-6 missile). It acquired equipment to jam the GPS guidance systems in U.S. aircraft and munitions and mounted some of its SA-3s on rotating launchers on trucks to give them some mobility. Deliveries of Czech and Ukrainian radar may also have occurred. In broad terms, however, the Iraqi forces were obsolete to obsolescent, having never recovered from the Gulf War, and had suffered from further attacks between 1992 and 2003.

Iraq had never shot down a U.S. or British aircraft in tens of thousands of sorties over Iraq. Iraq also still could not make any sustained use of its longer-range air defense systems with radar tracking and guidance without losing them. The coalition could strike effectively at most of Iraq's sheltered facilities, and it could use stealth and cruise missiles to penetrate deep into Baghdad and other defended areas and carry out SEAD missions. It could normally avoid dug-in short-range Iraqi defenses, and then systematically locate and kill them along with other key weapons systems when it engaged moving Iraqi land forces.

Iraq had developed contingency plans to move and disperse its land-based air defenses in the event of a major U.S.-led attempt to overthrow the regime. It planned to try to concentrate such defenses to protect the regime and try to use them to partially compensate for its lack of an effective air force. But it reacted too slowly. As with other plans, it could never execute a coherent defense.

Iraqi land-based air defenses were too old and too ineffective to counterbalance the coalition's air dominance or even degrade the quality of most coalition attack missions. Nevertheless, the sheer density of Iraqi defenses made them dangerous until the last stages of the fighting around Baghdad. Low-altitude penetration missions in close air support remained dangerous and sometimes fatal until the end of the war—particularly for helicopters.

IRAQI AND COALITION LAND FORCES

This near total lack of Iraq's capability for any aspect of joint warfare other than land combat makes the Iraq War unique and, again, makes any traditional comparisons of the strength of Iraqi and coalition land forces largely meaningless. This is particularly true in light of the relatively static nature of much of the Iraqi regular army forces during the war and the Iraqi leadership's failure to effectively exploit Iraq's strategic geography.

The ratio of total manpower was sharply disparate: Counting irregulars, Iraq had at least 390,000 men to the coalition's 250,000. However, it is warfighters that count in such comparisons, and quality is as important as force numbers. Iraq's army was a highly politicized conscript army organized into layers designed to prevent a coup more than to fight and equipped with weapons 15 to 25 years old. The U.S. and British forces were all-volunteer professional forces of men and women with extensive training and technical background. This reliance on professionalism gave the coalition de facto superiority in its force ratio even though it had a striking inferiority in force numbers.

Coalition Land Forces

The comparative strengths of coalition and Iraqi land forces in warfighting terms become far clearer from the history of combat in the next chapter than any static comparisons of force numbers can show. The full order of battle of the coalition land forces is also remarkably complex and involves a wide range of support and sustainment units and follow-on forces that cannot be discussed in detail.

In broad terms, however, the land forces on the coalition side of the military balance were asymmetric in several striking respects. First, the coalition had a much smaller number of actual combat troops on the ground. As has been noted, the total was much smaller than the coalition had originally planned, and senior officers in the Pentagon made it clear before the war that the total was small enough to significantly increase the risk if the coalition met unexpected opposition or if elements of the battle plan failed.

The total manpower strength of the combat troops in the U.S. Army 3rd Infantry Division, 82nd Airborne Division brigade, 101st Airborne Division (when deployed), 1st Marine Division, and supporting combat elements of V-Corps and the 1st Marine Expeditionary Force (1 MEF) probably totaled no more than 50,000 to 60,000 (although the total in the theater was much higher when support forces are included). USCENT-COM reported more than 115,000 U.S. troops in Kuwait at the start of the war with a total of some 57,500 army troops and 70,000 marines.

At the outset of the war, the United States had the following major land force elements ready in Kuwait. Additional forces arrived steadily during the battle, including the 173rd Airborne Brigade, which dropped into the Kurdish security zone in northern Iraq:[25]

- **Kuwait: U.S. Troops: 115,000+**[26]
  Coalition Forces Land Component Command (CFLCC) HQ
  Commander of all ground forces in Central Command: Army Lt. Gen. David D.
     McKiernan
- **Total Army Troops: About 55,000**
- **5th Corps (V Corps)**
  Command elements
  Troops: about 1,500
  Heidelberg, Germany
  Commander (of 5th Corps and all ground forces in Kuwait): Lt. Gen. William
     Wallace

- **3rd Infantry Division**
  "Rock of the Marne"
  Abrams tanks, Bradley Fighting Vehicles, Apache Longbow helicopters, Black
    Hawk helicopters
  Troops: about 18,000–20,000
  Fort Benning, Georgia
  Commander: Maj. Gen. Buford C. Blount III
- **2nd Brigade Combat Team of the 82d Airborne Division**
  Also known as the 325th Airborne Infantry Regiment
  "Falcon Brigade"
  Paratroopers
  Troops: about 4,000
  Commander: Col. Arnold Neil Gordon-Bray
- **101st Airborne Division**
  "Screaming Eagles"
  Light infantry, 275 Longbow Apache helicopters
  Army's only air assault division
  Troops: about 20,000
  Commander: Maj. Gen. Dave Petraeus
- **1st Marine Expeditionary Force and 1st Marine Division**
  Abrams tanks, Sea Knight helicopters, Sea Cobra helicopters, Super Stallion
    helicopters, Harrier jump jets
  Troops: about 60,000
  From the West Coast
  1st Marine Expeditionary Force
  15th Marine Expeditionary Unit
  Commander: Lt. Gen. James Conway
  From the East Coast
  2nd Marine Expeditionary Brigade
  Camp Lejeune, North Carolina
- **Navy**
  Special Warfare Unit 2

This meant the U.S. Army deployed a significant amount of its total strength overseas. The Congressional Research Service estimates that a large fraction of the army's 10 active-duty divisions and additional independent combat units were deployed or stationed outside the United States. Three divisions (the 3rd Infantry Division, the 101st Airborne Division, and the 4th Infantry Division), parts of two other divisions (the 82nd Airborne Division and the 10th Mountain Division) and one or two independent combat units (the 173rd Airborne Brigade and possibly the 2nd Cavalry Regiment) were deployed to Iraq, part of a division (the 82nd Airborne Division) was deployed to Afghanistan, two divisions (the 1st Armored Division and the 1st Infantry Division) were stationed in Germany, and most of another division (the 2nd Infantry Division) was stationed in Korea.[27]

The Marine ground force element was part of a Marine Air-Ground Task Force, or MAGTF, which included four infantry regiments, two artillery regiments, three light-armored reconnaissance battalions, two tank battalions, a force service support group, and three Marine aircraft groups with more than 400 aircraft. In addition, the Marines established a logistics command just to sustain the efforts of the MAGTF throughout the campaign in Iraq, and it obtained substantial support from the British while it supplied the U.S. Army with Marine close air support and airlift. Marine air assets were combined under the USCENTAF air component commander to provide deep air attack missions, hundreds of close air support missions, and airlift support to all coalition forces. Marine aircraft based aboard those amphibious ships launched nearly a thousand carrier sorties from their decks during the campaign to augment carrier-based aviation from the Arabian Gulf and the Mediterranean.[28]

Once again, this meant a large part of the Marine Corps total force was deployed overseas. The Congressional Research Service estimates that roughly 67 percent of the Marine Corps' operating forces were forward-deployed in Iraq and elsewhere, and almost 80 percent were either forward-deployed, forward-based, or forward-stationed. Two of the Marine Corps' three Maritime Prepositioning Ship (MPS) squadrons were committed to the Iraq War.[29]

The British Army provided another 26,000 men in the form of the British 1st (UK) Armored Division. This force included the 7th Armored Brigade, 16th Air Assault Brigade, 102nd Logistics Brigade, and various support units. The 7th Armored Brigade, nicknamed "Desert Rats," was a heavy armored unit equipped with Challenger 2 tanks and had been reinforced with additional combat elements. It included the Royal Scots Dragoon Guards (Challenger 2 tanks), 2nd Royal Tank Regiment (Challenger 2 tanks), 1st Battalion the Black Watch (Warrior infantry fighting vehicles), 1st Battalion Royal Regiment of Fusiliers (Warrior infantry fighting vehicles), 3rd Regiment Royal Horse Artillery (AS90 self-propelled guns), and 32 Armored Engineer Regiment.[30]

The 16th Air Assault Brigade had a combination of helicopter and parachute units. Its main combat elements included the 1st Battalion the Royal Irish Regiment, 1st Battalion the Parachute Regiment, 3rd Battalion the Parachute Regiment, 7 (Para) Regiment Royal Horse Artillery (105mm Light Guns), 23 Engineer Regiment, Household Cavalry Regiment (including one armored reconnaissance squadron), and 3rd Regiment Army Air Corps (Lynx and Gazelle helicopters).

The British division also had a number of independent support elements, including 30 Signal Regiment (strategic communications), the Queen's Dragoon Guards (reconnaissance), 1st Battalion the Duke of Wellington's Regiment (additional infantry capability), and 28 Engineer Regiment. It also included 102 Logistics Brigade.

Australia's contribution to the coalition, known as Operation Falconer, involved about 2,000 Australian defense force personnel. The Royal Australian Army deployed a Special Forces Task Group with some 600 to 700 men. Other elements included a Special Air Service squadron, CH-47 transport helicopters and personnel from 5th Aviation Regiment, troops from the newly established Incident Response Regiment (IRR), and a quick reaction support force drawn from the 4th Battalion Royal Australian Regiment (Commando) unit.

The Size and Capability of Iraqi Forces

There is no precise way to determine the combat manning of Iraqi forces or to make any clear one-on-one comparisons between armies with such different structures. In broad terms, Iraq remained the largest and the most effective military power in the Gulf at the start of the Iraq War, despite its defeat in the Gulf War and the loss of some 40 percent of its army and air force order of battle.

Iraq still had armed forces with around 389,000 full-time actives. Its army had some 350,000 actives, including some 100,000 called-up reservists (before it began a serious buildup in reaction to U.S. and British deployments), and an inventory of some 2,200 to 2,600 main battle tanks, 3,700 other armored vehicles, and 2,400 major artillery weapons.

This Iraqi force compares with total active U.S. tank holdings that probably did not exceed 850, and the number actively engaged was probably less. The U.S. Army 5th Corps had some 406 M-2 Bradley Armored Fighting Vehicles. One USCENTCOM source reported on March 17 that the 3rd Infantry Division had 200 M-1A1 tanks, 200 M-2 Bradleys, 50 M-109A1 Paladins, and 450 support vehicles. The U.S. forces also had inferior strength in other armored vehicles and artillery. Press reports indicate that the U.S. Marine Corps had roughly 150 M-1A1 tanks, 120 of which were actively deployed in the 1st Marine Division, and a similar number of lighter armored and tracked vehicles.[31]

The British forces added another 116 Challenger 2 tanks to the coalition total. This gave the coalition a total of around 1,000 tanks in comparison to Iraq's 2,200 to 2,600 tanks. British forces had something like another 290 armored vehicles, including 26 Challenger armored reconnaissance and recovery vehicles, 140 Warrior armored infantry vehicles (AIFVs), 26 Warrior command vehicles, 46 Warrior recovery and repair vehicles, 66 Scimitar tracked reconnaissance combat vehicles, and 12 Fuchs NBC vehicles. This gave the coalition about 1,000 other armored vehicles in comparison to Iraq's total of some 3,700 such vehicles.[32]

The British forces also had 36 AS90 155mm self-propelled guns and 39 105mm towed light guns. Their anti-tank weapons included 12 Striker armored vehicles with Swingfire anti-tank guided weapons. Air defenses included three Rapier Launchers and four Phoenix launchers, plus 24 Phoenix vehicles.

Coalition artillery strength seems to have totaled around 210 self-propelled and towed weapons—a far smaller total than Iraq possessed. Roughly similar disparities probably existed between Iraq's holdings of major land weapons and coalition holdings in other areas.

The United States did, however, have modern attack helicopter forces, and the Iraqis were unable to use their helicopters because of U.S. air supremacy. The U.S. Army 3rd Infantry division had 18 AH-64 Longbows. There were 72 additional AH-64s in the 101st Air Mobile Division and 60 in 5th Corps forces. The Marines also had 58 AH-1 Cobra attack helicopters and 8 AH-6s. The British army helicopter strength included 16 Gazelles, 18 Lynxes, 11 Chinooks, 7 Pumas, and 10 Sea Kings.[33]

By any traditional standard, Iraq's superiority in numbers made the coalition an inferior force, particularly because the British force had to be kept in the southeast to secure Basra and the area around it, to pin down the Iraqi regular forces near the Iranian border, and to secure the coalition's rear area. The U.S. Marines also did not have the same advanced armored infantry fighting vehicles as the U.S. Army forces in 5th Corps and relied on less advanced towed artillery weapons.

The coalition land forces would have been much stronger if the U.S. Army 4th Infantry Division and 3rd Armored Cavalry Regiment had been deployed in Turkey. The 4th Infantry Division also had more advanced versions of the M-1 tank and M-2 Bradley, had a significant attack helicopter force that included some 140 AH-64 Apache attack helicopters, and was the most "digital" division in the U.S. Army. In fact, senior U.S. military officers giving background briefings at the Pentagon before the start of the Iraq War noted that the lack of these forces increased the risk in executing the battle plan.

At the same time, the Iraqi land forces did have significant defects beyond the inept deployment and lack of effective strategic and tactical leadership discussed earlier.

The Iraqi Land Force Command Structure

The Iraqi command structure was highly politicized. Saddam Hussein was the supreme armed forces commander. The Special Republican Guard and Republican Guard reported directly to him and his younger son, Qusay, as did the President's Special Security Committee. Saddam chaired a defense council of key loyalists, including the minister of defense, minister of the interior, and armed forces commander.

Iraqi forces were under the command of loyalists to the regime. These included General Sultan Ahmad Tai, the minister of defense, and General Ibrahim Ahmad Abd Al-Sattar Muhammad al-Tikriti, the chief of staff. Saddam selected the chief of the General Staff, who was the head of the armed forces headquarters and combined service staff. Each of the four service headquarters was located in Baghdad, where it could be kept under tight control, as was the headquarters of the military intelligence elements. Each reported upward through the combined service staff, the armed forces commander, and the minister of defense.

Saddam Hussein had also set up a structure to maintain central control even if Baghdad could no longer be the source of such authority. He set up four regional commands at the time of Desert Fox in 1998, each of which was placed under one of his most dedicated supporters:

- **The Southern Region**, which included the governates of Basra, Dhikar, Misan, and Waset under Saddam's cousin General Ali Hassabn al Majid.

- **The Northern Region**, which was under Qusay and covered the three Kurdish governates of Sulaimaniya, Arbil, and Dohuk plus the northern governate of Mosul.

- **The Central Euphrates Region**, which was largely Shi'ite and included Karbala, Babylon, Najaf, Quadisiya, and Muthanna. It was commanded by Muhammed Hamza al Zubeidi, an RCC (Revolutionary Command Council) member and deputy prime minister.

- **The Central Region**, including Baghdad, Saladin, Anbar, and Diyala, under Defense Minister Ahmad Sultan.

Saddam Hussein created similar regional commands before the Iraq War and arranged to use the civil intelligence and security forces to attempt to hold on to each major urban area and region. Saddam must have known that even limited local resistance might help force the United States to disperse its forces, while successful urban resistance in a number of areas could confront the United States with much more serious problems in urban warfare. He also must have known that large elements of the Iraqi

Army might not be loyal if he did not maintain control over the key regions and towns and cities as long as possible.

The Iraqi Manpower Base

Part of the problem the Iraqi regime faced was the manpower base for its land forces. Iraq had a reserve pool of some 650,000 and a large pool of annual conscripts. The U.S. Central Intelligence Agency estimated that some 274,000 males entered military service each year. Iraq also could include more than 100,000 men from the security services and police forces in some military or paramilitary roles, and it had at least lightly armored combat elements in each of its three main civilian security and intelligence services. It also had the Fedayeen Saddam and a youth corps that received some form of military training.

Serious questions existed, though, about the effectiveness of any such mobilization. Iraq had small arms enough to equip several hundred thousand men for light infantry warfare and to play a limited role in urban warfare. It did not, however, have enough heavy weapons to properly equip such forces, and it rapidly became clear during the war that most Iraqi reserve and popular forces lacked the motivation to show up and fight.

Saddam Hussein had also spent the last decade dealing with repeated problems in his armed forces, and he had had to become more selective in the recruitment and promotion of the men in the regular army heavy divisions and Republican Guard. This was partly because Saddam and most of his close supporters were Sunnis from the area around Tikrit, and Iraq had deep ethnic divisions. The CIA estimated before the war that Iraq's current population was divided among the following: Arab, 75–80 percent; Kurdish, 15–20 percent; and Turkoman, Assyrian, or other, 5 percent. There were also major religious divisions: Muslim, 97 percent (Shi'a 60–65 percent, Sunni 32–37 percent), and Christian or other, 3 percent.

The fact that a relatively small Sunni Arab elite ruled oppressively over a majority of Shi'ites and Kurds (58–76 percent of the total population) led to ethnic clashes with hostile Kurdish and Shi'ite elements. Even the Sunni Arab portion of the population was divided. Saddam's main loyalists had a rural tribal rather than urban character in a largely urbanized country, and sometimes even "loyal" tribal elements turned against Saddam.

Saddam also faced serious Kurdish and Shi'ite uprisings after the Gulf War. Some 12 percent to 15 percent of Iraq's population was in the Kurdish security zone; and Saddam still had major problems in parts of the Shi'ite south. At the same time, no major Shi'ite or Kurdish conscript element of the regular army defected during the Iran-Iraq or Gulf Wars.

The Iraqi Land Force Order of Battle

The International Institute of Strategic Studies and Jane's Information Group estimate that in mid-2002 the Iraqi army could still deploy some 350,000 to 375,000 men, organized into seven corps, with two Republican Guard corps and five regular army corps. At the time of the war, these forces were divided into four major groups, each of which in some way watched the others:

- six Republican Guard divisions (3 armored, 1 mechanized, and 2 infantry);

- four Special Republican Guard brigades as part of a complex 14-battalion force structure designed to protect Saddam and the regime;

- a regular army with some 16 divisions (3 armored, 3 mechanized, and 11 relatively low-grade infantry); the regular army also had five commando and two Special Forces brigades; and

- a five-wing army aviation component with 2 fixed-wing and 21 helicopter squadrons.[34]

Iraqi combat units did not have standardized structures or levels of manning and equipment, and U.S. experts estimate that Iraqi divisions differed significantly by unit. In broad terms:

- Iraq had a total force at the start of the war of approximately 20 to 23 division-equivalents, versus 35 to 40 division-equivalents in the summer of 1990 and 67 to 70 division-equivalents in January 1991 (just before the beginning of the coalition offensives in the Gulf War).[35]

- Regular army divisions had an average authorized strength of about 10,000 men, although some sources indicate that about half of the 23 Iraqi divisions had manning levels of only around 8,000 men (less support forces) and "a fair state of readiness." Tank strength varied, but heavier divisions had some 175 to 250 tanks.

- Republican Guards divisions had an average authorized strength of around 8,000 to 10,000 men (less support forces) and averaged at least 80 percent of authorized strength. Brigades averaged around 2,500 to 3,2000 men.[36] Tank strength varied, but heavier divisions had some 175 to 300 tanks.

- The Special Republican Guard was organized into four brigades, but was more a force of specialized battalions than one of regular combat brigades.

Most units lacked modern training, and the regular army units depended heavily on conscripts. There were many reports of badly under-

THE FORCES ENGAGED 45

manned units.[37] Estimates that most divisions had 50 percent to 75 percent manning and substantial equipment shortages seem to have been accurate, and most Iraqi divisions were substantially smaller than they had been at the beginning of the Gulf War.

The Deployment of Iraqi Land Forces

Even a summary of the Iraqi order of battle shows the deep divisions between Iraq's three major types of forces and that Iraq's regular forces were spread out from north to south in a mix of regular and Republican Guard divisions.

The Iraqi regular army was organized into five major corps, with 17 main-force division equivalents and major bases at Baghdad, Basra, Kirkuk, and Mosul. Major training areas were to the west of Baghdad, near Mosul, and in the marsh areas in the south. The training area southwest of Basra had only limited use because of the no-fly zones.[38]

U.S. experts indicate that Iraqi land forces had a total of 14 divisions in the north, 3 divisions in central Iraq, and 6 divisions south of An Najaf. There were also four independent brigades: the 65th Special Forces Brigade, the 66th Special Forces Brigade, the 68th Special Forces Brigade, and the 440th Marine Brigade.

The Republican Guard had three armored divisions deployed in the vicinity of Baghdad—one near Taji, one near Baghdad, and one near As Suwayrah.[39] All Republican Guards divisions were located above the 32-degree line. Several additional Republican Guard divisions were located around Baghdad to play a major role in internal security. Several more Republican Guard divisions were located north of Baghdad closer to the Kurdish area.[40]

Although sources differ significantly over some of the details, unit designations, and unit locations, Iraq began the war with the following deployments:

Regular Army forces in Northern Iraq. The **1st Corps** was headquartered at Kirkuk and the **5th Corps** at Mosul. They guarded the Turkish border area and were deployed on the edge of the Kurdish enclave and the oilfields in the north. They had eight divisions, but only two were heavy mechanized divisions.

- **The 1st Corps** included the 2nd Infantry Division, the 5th Mechanized Division, the 8th Infantry Division headquartered, and the 38th Infantry Division.
- **The 5th Corps** had units defending the border area with Syria and Turkey as well as covering other parts of the north. It included the 1st

Mechanized Division, the 4th Infantry Division, the 7th Infantry Division, and the 16th Infantry Division.

Regular Army forces in Eastern Iraq. The 2nd Corps was deployed east of Baghdad to defend against Iran or any attack by Iranian-backed Iraqi opposition forces. It included the 3rd Armored Division headquartered at Jalawia, the 15th Infantry Division headquartered at Amerli, and the 34th Infantry Division headquartered near Khanaqin.

Regular Army forces in Southern Iraq. The army had two corps that played a major role in securing Shi'ite areas and suppressing Shi'ite dissidents. There were six divisions, two of which were heavy armored divisions:

- **The 3rd Corps** was positioned near the Kuwaiti border. It included the 6th Armored Division, the 11th Infantry Division, and the 51st Mechanized Division

- **The 4th Corps** defended the border with Iran. It included the 10th Armored Division, the 14th Infantry Division, and the 18th Infantry Division.

The Republican Guard. The Republican Guard—some 60,000 to 70,000 men—was under the supervision of Qusay Hussein and was commanded by Staff General Ibrahim Abdel Satter Muhammed al Tikriti. It had two corps and seven divisions:

- **The Northern or 1st Corps of the Republican Guard** could act to defend against Iran and Turkey, operate against the Kurds, and defend the greater Baghdad area and Tikrit. It included the 1st Adnan Mechanized Division, the Al Nida (Al Nedaa) Armored Division, the 2nd Baghdad Infantry Division, and the Al Abed (Al Abid) Infantry Division at Kirkuk-Khalid Camp.

- **The Southern or 2nd Corps of the Republican Guard** helped defend against Iran in the south, as well as against any U.S.-led attack, and acted as a deterrent force to suppress any Shi'ite uprising. It included the al Medina al Munawara Armored Division, the Nebuchadnezzar (Nabu Khuth Nusser) Infantry Division, and the Hammurabi Mechanized Division in the al-Taji area.

The Special Republican Guard or Al-Haris al-Jamhuri al-Khas. The third major element of the land forces included the four Special Republican Guard units, which were located largely within the Baghdad area and organized to defend the regime. The Special Republican Guard had four infantry/motorized brigades with 14 battalions, an armored brigade, and an air defense command with elements to secure Baghdad's ground-based air defenses against any coup attempt.

The Special Republican Guard was headed by Qusay Hussein, and its formal commander was Major General Kheir-Allah Wahees Omar al-Nassiri. It served as a praetorian guard, protecting presidential sites and escorting Saddam Hussein on travels within Iraq. It had a total active strength of about 12,000 to 15,000, but some sources claim it could mobilize to 20,000 to 25,000. It was the only force stationed in central Baghdad and in the Republican Palace, although there were light paramilitary brigades in the Special Security Service (SSS), the Iraqi Intelligence Service (IIS), and secret police.

Iraq's Irregular Forces

As has been noted earlier, the regime failed to attract broad support for its Popular Army, and many of the paramilitary forces in its order of battle never played a significant role in the fighting. The major exception seems to have been the Fedayeen Saddam, a force of 15,000 to 25,000 men.

The Fedayeen was founded by Saddam's son Uday in 1995 and started out as a force of some 10,000 to 15,000. The following year Uday was removed from their command, perhaps because of an incident in March 1996 when he transferred sophisticated weapons from the Republican Guard to the Fedayeen without Saddam's knowledge. Control passed to Qusay, further consolidating his responsibility for the Iraqi security apparatus.

During the Iraq War, these forces were widely reported to be the key element of the irregular forces that fought against U.S. and British forces in the south along with loyalists from the security services, intelligence services, and Ba'ath Party.

They may sometimes have been backed by the Lions of Saddam (Eshbal or Ashbal Saddam, a Hitler-youth-like paramilitary training structure for ages 10 to 16).

Another element that seems to have fought for Saddam was the Special Security Service, Special Security Organization (SSO), or Amn al Khass. Established in the mid-1980s, it too was controlled by Saddam's son Qusay and was intended to be an ultra-loyal force. It grew from a cadre of around 500 to a force of about 2,000 to 5,000 men recruited largely from loyal tribes around Tikrit, Hawuija, and Samarra, such as Saddam's own tribe, the Abu Nasr. It was headquartered in Palestine Street in Baghdad. According to most reports, it was the key security force for the regime and played a major role in controlling the actions of the Republican Guard and Special Republican Guard. It is also reported to have been in charge of the surveillance of Iraqi General Intelligence, Military Intelligence, Military Security, and General Security.

Iraqi Tank Strength

These layers of competing forces, each watching the others, were scarcely the basis for an effective modern army. They also relied on large numbers of combat-worn and obsolescent weapons. Only 1,800 to 2,000 of the inventory of 2,200 to 2,600 tanks seem to have been combat capable, and most were difficult to maintain. Like the rest of Iraq's equipment, they were worn and could not be sustained or repaired after an initial period of combat. About half of these tanks were obsolete T-54s, T-55s, T-59s, and T-69s. Iraq also had about 600 to 700 M-48s, M-60s, AMX-30s, Centurions, and Chieftains captured from Iran or obtained in small numbers from other countries.

Iraq had no modern tanks by U.S. and British standards, although it did have some 700 moderately capable T-72 tanks and 200 to 300 T-62s. But even the T-72s and T-62s had poor ergonomics. They were limited by lack of thermal vision and modern night warfare systems, and their sights and fire control systems could not approach the engagement range of coalition tanks. The 120mm gun on the M-1A1, for example, has a nominal maximum engagement range of about 3,000 meters. The T-72 can fire accurately out to about 2,500 meters but has far worse sights, fire control systems, and sensors. The older T-55 is limited to about 2,000 meters but has poor fire control systems and stabilization.[41] The coalition tanks could normally engage Iraqi tanks at 50 percent to 100 percent longer engagement ranges in open maneuver combat, and the coalition tanks had much better armor and mobility.

Iraq's efforts to upgrade the armor of its tanks had limited success. Iraqi armor had only limited functional capability to use overpressure and filters to deal with CBW threats. Iraq did retain more than 1,500 tank transporters and heavy vehicle trailers out of the several thousand it bought during the Iran-Iraq War, but it never made effective use of them during the fighting.[42] Iraq also had a poor history of field repairs for tanks, and had never made aggressive attempts to recover and repair tanks in battle.

Iraq's doctrine and tactics for using tanks was poor. Iraqi corps and division commanders often set personal standards for training and employing tanks.

Other Iraqi Armored Equipment Strength

The Iraqi army's other major weapons had similar problems. They included some 400 aging Soviet-bloc and French armored reconnaissance vehicles (AML-60/90s, BDRM-2s, EE-3s, and EE-9s). The army had some 1,200 BMP-1/2 armored infantry fighting vehicles, of which about 900

BMP-series seem to have been active. It had some 1,800 aging, worn, armored personnel carriers made up of 10 major types.

Iraq's lack of standardization in spare parts, and lack of common weapons and operating features, created major sustainability and cross-training/interoperability problems. Iraq faced a logistic and maintenance nightmare in supporting and providing combat and field repairs for so many types of vehicles with such different firepower, mobility, and endurance. Many were nonfunctional due to a lack of spare parts or otherwise limited operational capability. Furthermore, Iraq was forced to equip its divisions with different mixes of armor, with different maneuver capabilities and often with different training requirements for both the weapons crew and maintenance and support teams. It also had difficulties ensuring that its infantry could keep up with its tanks.

Iraq's tactical doctrine for using other armored vehicles varied with the major combat unit using a given mix of equipment. Some heavy Republican Guard units and regular army units used other armored vehicles much more effectively in supporting tanks than most of the Iraqi army. Iraq generally overrelied on tanks, however, and had not used its other armored vehicles aggressively in scouting or combat support operations. Its forces were best suited to defensive operations against relatively slow-moving mechanized infantry at short to moderate ranges.

Iraqi Artillery Strength

Iraq had some 200 to 250 active self-propelled artillery weapons—with Soviet 122mm 2S1s and 152mm 2S3s—largely in Republican Guard and a few elite regular army heavy divisions. The bulk of Iraqi artillery consisted of some 1,200 to 1,900 towed weapons, mostly 122mm, 152mm, and 155mm. Iraq had some 200 multiple rocket launchers—largely 122mm and 127mm systems but also some longer-range 400mm Ababil-100 systems. Iraq also had large numbers of 81mm, 120mm, 160mm, and 240mm mortars.

Iraqi artillery could fire chemical and possibly biological shells and rockets and had relatively long range. Iraq never demonstrated, however, that it could approach U.S. and British capability to rapidly target moving forces and switch fire. It relied heavily on mass fire and area suppression. Its ability to target beyond line of sight was limited, and sensor and command problems severely limited the ability to target maneuver forces at long ranges (although Iraq did have some RASIT artillery surveillance vehicles and French Cymbeline counter-mortar radars).

Iraq had more than 350 self-propelled mortars mounted on armored vehicles before the Gulf War. These do not seem to have been heavily committed to the Kuwaiti theater of operations, and Iraq probably still held several hundred after the conflict. Iraq also retained large numbers of 81mm and 120mm Soviet mortars. It had a total of more than 2,000 towed and crew-portable mortars.

Only a few Iraqi units had the radars, training, and organization to allow them to conduct effective counter-battery fire. Their targeting and observed fire was heavily dependent on forward observers, and it was often slow and unresponsive. Their ability to use UAVs and other techniques to acquire targets beyond visual range was limited, and artillery support of mobile Iraqi armored units had previously been consistently poor—even when the forward armored unit called in targets and requested support.

Iraq never demonstrated the ability to quickly shift fire and deal with rapidly moving armored forces. Its towed artillery was relatively slow moving and often road bound, unless sufficient time existed to support rear areas. Iraqi artillery units usually needed extensive time to deploy large amounts of ammunition into prepared rear areas in order to maintain high rates of fire, and had to pre-survey the battlefield to mass artillery fire effectively. Iraq also relied heavily on the "feed forward" of large amounts of ammunition, without prior request from the user unit, to make up for its slow-moving and unresponsive logistic and support system.

Iraqi self-propelled artillery units frequently had problems extracting themselves from prepared positions and moving rapidly under defensive conditions. Field repair and recovery of artillery systems were poor.

Other Iraqi Major Land-Force Weapons

Iraqi land forces had extensive stocks (2,000 plus) of relatively modern AT-3 (AM14), AT-4 (M136), Milan, and High-subsonic Optically Tele-guided (HOT) anti-tank guided weapons. Iraq also had significant numbers of obsolescent 85mm and 100mm anti-tank guns and 73mm, 82mm, and 107mm rocket launchers and recoilless rifles.

Iraq had rarely employed these weapons well in previous battles. During the Gulf War, it showed little understanding of the range at which modern Western armor could engage; the rate of advance and scale of maneuver of modern well-led armor; the limiting effects of night and poor-weather warfare on crew-served weapons without night vision aids; the need to rapidly maneuver crew-served weapons rather than rely on static positions; and the need to continuously conduct actual training firings of such equipment to develop and maintain proficiency. Iraq was also unprepared for the rapidly moving precision of coalition artillery and the ability of helicopters and tanks to bypass prepared defenses using such weapons.

Army Aviation

Iraqi Army Aviation had roughly 100 attack and 275 utility/transport helicopters, although many had little effectiveness or sustainability and a number were not operational at all. The armed helicopters included 12 Mi-25s, 20 SA-319s with AS-12 air-to-surface missiles, 10 SA-316s with guns, and 20 SA-342s with HOT anti-tank missiles. The transport and support helicopters include 20 SA-330Fs, 30 BO-105s, 10 Mi-6s, 30 Mi-8s, and 12 Mi-17s.

Iraq's combat helicopter performance was consistently poor to bad before the Iraq War. Training, operational readiness, and sustainability were all believed to be poor, and Iraq never demonstrated the ability to use these assets effectively against coalition forces.

Further, Iraq had to operate a fleet with 12 different types of helicopters of very different ages, using different technologies and sources of spare parts. The sensor and weapons mixes on Iraqi attack helicopters were at least 15 years old. Even those helicopters equipped with HOT guided weapons lacked the sensors and fire control systems to effectively use the missiles without closing to ranges that made the helicopter vulnerable.

Army Air Defenses

The army and semi-mobile elements of Iraq's 17,000-man Air Defense Command were capable of deploying large numbers of man-portable surface-to-air missiles like the SA-14 Strela 3, plus SA-7, SA-8, SA-9, and Roland vehicle-mounted surface-to-air missiles. Iraq is believed to have had an inventory of well over 1,000 such missiles, but the types are unclear. These systems had limited effectiveness against high-flying U.S.-UK fighters with standoff weapons but sometimes presented a significant threat at low altitudes.

Other Qualitative Problems

Each point in this analysis highlights reasons why the United States and Britain took far fewer chances in attacking with the level of ground forces they had ready on March 19, 2003, than is apparent in terms of force numbers, although some risks clearly remained. There were, however, additional factors that weakened the effective war-fighting strength of Iraqi land forces.

The Iraqi forces of March 2003 had lost most of the battle-experienced personnel of the Iran-Iraq War and Gulf War. They generally had had only low-level combat experience against the Shi'ite opposition in southern Iraq, and most forces had limited exercise training and had never mastered combined arms and joint operations by Western standards.

Saddam Hussein's regime had always given internal security against a coup much higher priority than military effectiveness per se. There were exceptions during the most threatening periods in the Iran-Iraq war. But many of the best officers were retired or shoved aside into positions of limited importance, and some suffered suspicious fatal accidents. Political control not only affected independence and initiative, but extended to limiting or preventing the use of ammunition in live-fire exercises, the scale of maneuver exercises, and forward stockpiling of ammunition and supplies that might be used in a coup.

THE PROBLEM OF FUTURE FORCE RATIOS

This analysis is not an argument that numbers are not important. It is an argument that force ratios must be fundamentally rethought in terms of joint warfare and force quality and the interactions between asymmetric kinds of force. The type of military analysis common in the order of battle analysis in World War I and II, or the force ratio analysis and war games used in the Cold War, assume roughly symmetrical forces in terms of structure, quality, and leadership. It is questionable whether that assumption has ever had more than limited validity. It is clearly invalid today.

The comparative strengths and weaknesses of the coalition and Iraqi forces allowed the coalition to attack with forces that seemed inadequate by any previous calculation of quantitative force strength. The coalition attack still involved carefully reasoned risks, and risks—by definition—make failure a possibility. As the next chapter shows, however, the coalition made a correct assessment of military capability in terms of a new era of high-technology joint warfare, and Iraq lacked the leadership to make effective use of older concepts of warfare and new approaches to asymmetric warfare.

The lessons for other developing or dated military forces are clear: They are to concede, proliferate, place vastly greater reliance on asymmetric warfare, or find some mix of all of these options. The lesson for the United States and Britain is that they have generally pursued an approach to coalition and joint warfare that gives them astounding strength in terms of traditional measures of force numbers.

At the same time, future opponents may not be as inept as the regime of Saddam Hussein and may make much better use of proliferation and asymmetric warfare. As the next chapter shows, when Iraq did use asymmetric warfare effectively, it had at least some success. The pace and lethality of the coalition attack never stopped the more dedicated elements of

Iraq's forces from fighting with skill and courage, in spite of the massive institutional and leadership problems imposed on them from above. The importance of every aspect of force quality is a lesson of the Iraq War. Hubris is not a lesson of any war.

Notes

[1] Many of the Iraqi war plan documents were captured but were not exploited at the time of this writing. See *Los Angeles Times*, April 25, 2003.

[2] Lt. General T. Michael Moseley, "Operation Iraqi Freedom—By the Numbers," USCENTAF (United States Central Command Air Forces), Assessment and Analysis Division, April 30, 2003. The reader should note that the data in this report are not based on an analytic review, but on a listing of facts as collected. The scope of this report is 0300Z 19 March 2003 (ATO M/D-Day) until 0259Z 18 April 2003 (ATOP1/D+29), a total of 720 hours inclusive. All numbers are reported to the nearest level of certainty. Members of all U.S. services, the United Kingdom, Australia, and Canada contributed to the collection and collation of this data. "Total" figures presented represent peak numbers employed in the operation. In some cases, multiple sensors or aircraft were used simultaneously in slightly overlapping areas or methods; this is represented by indicating "hours of coverage/24 hour period." In these cases, the "total coverage" could exceed 24 hours in a given day due to the number of sensors available during that time period.

[3] British Ministry of Defense, "Operations in Iraq: First Reflections" (London: Her Majesty's Stationery Office, July 2003), p. 7.

[4] The data on Iraqi forces are taken largely from Anthony H. Cordesman, *Iraq's Military Capabilities in 2002: A Dynamic Net Assessment* (Washington, D.C.: CSIS, September 2002). Also from the International Institute for Strategic Studies (IISS), *The Military Balance 2002–2003* (Oxford: Oxford University Press, October 2002), and the *Jane's Sentinel* series, online edition, accessed March 2003.

[5] Where possible, the data on U.S. force strengths and combat history are taken from the daily briefs of USCENTCOM at www.centcom.mil/, and from the data the U.S. Department of Defense makes available at Defense Link, www.defenselink.mil/.

[6] Coordinated by Ronald O' Rourke, "Iraq War: Defense Program Implications for Congress," Congressional Research Service, RL31946, June 4, 2003.

[7] The data on British forces in this chapter and the others in this book are taken largely from the British Ministry of Defense Web page on Operation Telic. See www.operations.mod.uk/telic/index.htm/. Also, see British Ministry of Defense, "Operations in Iraq: First Reflections," p. 7.

[8] The data on Australian forces in this chapter and the others in this book are taken largely from the Australian Ministry of Defense Web page on Operation Falconer. See www.defence.gov.au/opfalconer/.

[9] Moseley, "Operation Iraqi Freedom—By the Numbers."

[10] *Jane's Sentinel Security Assessment,* "Iraqi Air Force," online edition, accessed May 7, 2002.

[11] U.S. Central Command, *Atlas, 1996* (MacDill Air Force Base: USCENTCOM, 1997), pp. 16–18.

[12] *Washington Times,* September 5, 1996, sec. A, p. 1.

[13] USCENTCOM briefing by "senior military official." For further background, also see *Washington Times,* February 1, 1997, sec. A, p. 13; Reuters, September 4, 1996, 0911; *Jane's Pointer,* November 1994, p. 2; Associated Press, September 9, 1996, 0129; *Washington Times,* January 30, 1997, sec. A, p. 3, and February 1, 1997, sec. A, p. 13; IISS, *Military Balance 2002–2003,* and *Jane's Sentinel: The Gulf States,* "Iraq," online edition, accessed March 2003; Andrew Rathmell, *The Changing Balance in the Gulf,* Whitehall Papers 38 (London: Royal United Services Institute, 1996); Edward B. Atkeson, *The Powder Keg: An Intelligence Officer's Guide to Military Forces in the Middle East* (Falls Church, Va.: Nova Publications, 1996); Geoffery Kemp and Robert E. Harkavy, *Strategic Geography and the Changing Middle East* (Washington, D.C.: Carnegie Endowment/Brookings, 1997); and Michael Eisenstadt, *Like a Phoenix from the Ashes? The Future of Iraqi Military Power,* Policy Paper 36 (Washington, D.C.: Washington Institute for Near East Policy, 1993).

[14] The main source for these data is Moseley, "Operation Iraqi Freedom—By the Numbers." The U.S. Department of Defense has not published precise data in some of these areas. Some of the figures used are taken from Military City, www.militarycity.com/map/, and others from the *Washington Post,* April 20, 2003, sec. A, p. 20.

[15] The main source for these data is Moseley, "Operation Iraqi Freedom—By the Numbers."

[16] Ibid. Some adjustments have been made in the numbers to try to exclude allied aircraft, but the totals do not allow this to been done for some types.

[17] The main source for these data is Moseley, "Operation Iraqi Freedom—By the Numbers." These figures do not include special operations forces, U.S. army helicopter attack, and coalition sovereignty sorties.

[18] British Ministry of Defense, "Operations in Iraq: First Reflections," p. 48.

[19] Adapted from Moseley, "Operation Iraqi Freedom—By the Numbers."

[20] British Ministry of Defense, "Operations in Iraq: First Reflections," p. 48.

[21] The reader should be aware that these estimates are extremely uncertain and are based largely on expert estimates of the losses during the Gulf War. There is a sharp difference of opinion among some U.S. experts as to the size of Iraq's losses during the conflict. The U.S. Central Command listed 150 SA-2 launchers, 110 SA-3 launchers, 150 SA-6/SA-8 launchers, 30 Roland VII launchers, and 5 Crotale launchers in *Atlas, 1996,* pp 16–18. Also see the IISS, *Military Balance, 2002/2003,* and the *Jane's Sentinel* series, online edition, accessed March 2003.

[22] Cordesman, *Iraq's Military Capabilities in 2002*. Also, see Michael Eisenstadt, "The Iraqi Armed Forces Two Years On," *Jane's Intelligence Review* (March 1993), pp. 121–127; *Jane's Sentinel: The Gulf States*, "Iraq" (London: Jane's Publishing, 1997).

[23] USCENTCOM briefing by "senior military official"; IISS, *Military Balance, 2002/2003*, and the *Jane's Sentinel* series, online edition, accessed March 2003.

[24] Adapted from Moseley, "Operation Iraqi Freedom—By the Numbers."

[25] Based on work by Brian Hartman of ABC News.

[26] U.S. basing areas and facilities in Kuwait included: Ahmed Al Jaber Air Base—AF; Ali Al Salem Air Base—AF; Camp Arifjan—Army, Marines; Camp Commando—HQ, Marines; Camp Doha—CFLCC HQ; Failaka Island—82nd Airborne; Camp Matilda—Marines; Camp Grisley—Marines; Camp Shoup—Marines; Camp Peleliu—Marines; Camp Coyote—Marines; Camp New Jersey—3rd ID; Camp New York—HQ, Army 3rd ID; Camp Pennsylvania—3rd ID; Camp Virginia—3rd ID; Kuwait IAP—AF; LSAs [Several "Living Support Areas"]—Marines; Udairi Range.

[27] O' Rourke, "Iraq War: Defense Program Implications for Congress."

[28] Marine Corps Lt. Gen. Earl B. Hailston, Commander, U.S. Marine Corps Forces Central Command, "MARCENT Briefing from Bahrain," April 24, 2003, www.defenselink.mil/transcripts/2003/tr20030424-0124.html.

[29] O' Rourke, "Iraq War: Defense Program Implications for Congress."

[30] For further details, see British Ministry of Defense, "Operations in Iraq: First Reflections," pp. 45–46.

[31] *Washington Post*, April 20, 2003, sec. A, p. 20.

[32] Ibid.; *London Daily Telegraph*, March 17, 2001, p. 1.

[33] British Ministry of Defense, "Operations in Iraq: First Reflections," p. 46.

[34] Earlier estimates by U.S. Central Command (USCENTCOM) indicated that the Iraqi land forces had a total mobilizable strength of 700,000 personnel, including reserves. These estimates indicate that Iraq's major combat formations included 17 regular army divisions (6 heavy and 11 light), and 6 Republican Guard divisions (3 heavy and 3 light). USCENTCOM also estimated that the total Iraqi Army order of battle include 6 armored divisions, 4 mechanized divisions, 10 infantry divisions, 2 Special Forces divisions, 1 Special Republican Guard or Presidential Guard Division, 19 reserve brigades, 15 People's Army brigades, and 25 helicopter squadrons.

[35] Estimate first provided by USCENTCOM in June 1996, plus later interviews.

[36] USCENTCOM briefing by "senior military official."

[37] *London Daily Telegraph*, July 19, 2002, p. 1.

[38] Based on interviews; Cordesman, *Iraq's Military Capabilities in 2002*; and material in the *Jane's Sentinel* series on Iraq, online edition, accessed March 2003.

[39] Ibid.

[40] USCENTCOM briefing by "senior military official."

[41] Elliot Blair Smith, "Marine Tanks May Fire First Shots," *USA Today*, March 18, 2003, p. 5.

[42] These estimates are based primarily on interviews; Cordesman, *Iraq's Military Capabilities in 2002*; and material in the *Jane's Sentinel* series on Iraq, online edition, accessed March 2003.

CHAPTER FOUR

THE COURSE OF THE WAR AND
THE INTERACTION OF JOINT FORCES

One of the key lessons of every war is that the sheer complexity of war—
and of any effort to produce lessons without examining the history of the
fighting in some detail—can be dangerously misleading. This lesson is particularly applicable to the Iraq War, because the most important single lesson of that war is the success of the new form of complex, high-technology,
joint warfare that the United States has evolved since its defeat in Vietnam.

The United States and Britain used the capabilities discussed in the previous chapter to fight a kind of joint warfare different from any previous
conflict. Although the two countries certainly profited from the lessons
gained during the Gulf War of 1991 and the conflict in Afghanistan, a detailed day-by-day analysis reveals at least the outline of how air and missile
power, rapid and focused armored maneuver, the creative use of Special
Forces and air mobile forces, and sea power were combined to inflict a
massive and sudden defeat on a large traditional army.[1]

General Richard Myers, the chairman of the Joint Chiefs of Staff, described the "transformational" nature of the Iraq War as follows:

> …you're seeing a transformation of a sort. The equipment is the equipment
> we have had for years. But the difference is how well integrated all the capa-
> bilities of the services are in this case. All you have to do is look back, you
> can even look back at Afghanistan and see it's different than it was. Certain-
> ly look back at the first Gulf War.
>
> There, we were basically in a deconfliction mode. Here, between the var-
> ious capabilities the services bring to the table, we are in a mode of integrat-
> ing them in a way, and applying effects on the battlefield, thinking about the
> effects we want to have and being able to mass at the time and place of our
> choosing with very good command and control, intelligence, and surveil-
> lance and reconnaissance.

The fact we were tied together very well and had a pretty good picture of the battlespace allowed us to do some of the things we did very rapidly, very quick, and not put our forces in harm's way.

...Some of that is transformational in thinking, a lot of it is. Some of it is having commanders think in a more integrated way about how they employ their force. That's been our goal: to get to a level of joint warfighting where there is trust and confidence between the Army and the Air Force, the Navy, and Marines, the Coast Guard.

The organizational structures are not necessarily new. It's more the application and [USCENTCOM commander] General Tommy Franks' idea of how to use these forces in an integrated way. And having the eyes and ears and the command and control to be able to carry it off....Joint warfighting is the key to greater things on the battlefield.[2]

As the next chapter discusses, the issue of whether the Iraq War truly reflects a revolution in warfare, an evolution in warfare, force transformation, or a "new way of war" is an awkward and somewhat pointless cross between a word game and a theological debate. One thing is certain: the coalition attack in the Iraq War was certainly highly innovative in many dimensions. If the coalition attack did not meet all of the tests of "force transformation," or of the concept of "shock and awe" developed by analysts like Harlan Ullman and Jim Wade, it brought together a wide range of different combat elements to deliver a remarkable degree of speed, precision, and focus.

THE BEGINNING OF THE CONFLICT: THE DECAPITATION STRIKE AND INITIAL LAND ADVANCE

In some ways, the Iraq War began in late 2002, when the United States and Britain stepped up their attacks on Iraqi air defenses in ways that increasingly acted more as suppression of enemy air defense (SEAD) activity than punitive efforts to enforce the no-fly zones. From March 1 on, such attacks built to the point where Iraq could have had no doubt that it was losing its capability to maintain cohesive air defense and could be under attack within days. At the same time, it can be argued that the very reality of this threat should have persuaded Iraq to accept the U.S. and British ultimatum. These same air strikes destroyed much of the optical fiber communications systems Iraq relied upon for secure communications, forcing it to use high frequency radio communications that could be easily characterized and tracked and sometimes decrypted.[3]

Long before then, the United States and Britain had moved much of the supplies and equipment they needed into the theater by sea, and had created new basing and support facilities in Kuwait and other Gulf countries. These steps were critical because some 80 percent or more of all heavy equipment, weapons, and supplies had to move by sea, which took some six to eight weeks. Moreover, creating combat-ready bases allowed the rapid movement of personnel by air under conditions where they could quickly "marry up" with the necessary weapons, supplies, and facilities.

General Franks had deliberately exploited Turkey's decision to not allow the United States and Britain to base forces in Turkey by delaying the movement of the ships carrying equipment for the U.S. 4th Mechanized Division from the Mediterranean to the Gulf. Franks knew the division could not close quickly enough on Kuwait to be ready for the war. By acting as if the United States might still be able to move through Turkey, however, he created a deception plan that helped pin down most of the 13 divisions Iraq had deployed north of Baghdad.

Two special operations groups of CIA and Special Forces teams had long been present in the Kurdish zone in northern Iraq, and the CIA seems to have made an extensive effort to persuade or bribe Iraqi officers not to fight before the war started. More than 50 12-member U.S. Special Forces A teams had entered the Iraqi desert, along with British and Australian Special Forces. They prepared to take out Iraqi observation posts along Iraq's borders with Jordan, Kuwait, and Saudi Arabia; their preparations allowed them to take out 50 such posts on the first night of the war and 50 more on the second. Other Special Forces teams looked for Scud missiles and the deployment of chemical and biological weapons. British and Australian Special Forces were also present, but all details of their operations are classified.

The exact timing of the coalition attack came as surprise even to those in the theater. The press had already been quietly told that the war would not commence on the night of March 19. Yet, March 19 became "G-Day"—the day when the United States received indicators that its intelligence had located Saddam Hussein and his sons and that it might be able to launch a decapitating strike on Iraq's top leadership. The United States reacted within hours, launching a combined strike by cruise missiles and stealth aircraft as well as beginning to move troops into Iraq.

The attack came when the United States had only part of the forces included in its original war plan. It came before any of the forces from the U.S. Army 4th Infantry Division and 3rd Armored Cavalry Division could begin large-scale movement away from the Turkish theater where they had originally planned to fight toward the Gulf. The attack also began before the 101st Airborne Division could deploy most of its equipment.

The coalition also changed its war plan to delay plans to execute a massive preparatory air campaign of two to three days and some 3,000 precision strikes. Instead, U.S. and British ground forces drove into Iraq with little preparatory air bombardment because it was hoped that the decapitation strike on the regime would deprive its armed forces of leadership and the will to fight and that an air campaign of the scale that might interfere with nation building could be avoided. Roughly 24 targets were also removed from the prewar strike plan while waiting to see if the leadership had been killed, including sites with a high risk of civilian casualties and leadership sites and communications nodes that might be needed to disseminate the information that the regime has collapsed.[4]

General Myers, chairman of the Joint Chiefs, later responded as follows to a question about whether the war would have gone better with more forces on the ground:

> I think less well. If you look at the initial objectives—trying to have some modicum of tactical surprise at the time we had over 220,000 forces in the region—how do you achieve tactical surprise? Well, it's not by amassing 500,000 to 600,000 folks in Kuwait and Saudi Arabia. I think we were clearly inside the decision loop capability of the regime. We started the war first, before the air war.[5]

In retrospect, it is hard to argue with the coalition's level of military success. There are times to take well-reasoned risks, and victory is its own validation.

18/19 March: Prelude

Some key steps in the war began long before G-Day. The coalition had had more than a decade to improve its intelligence and targeting of Iraq. It had developed a basing structure in several of the southern Gulf states over several decades, had begun the sealift necessary to move heavy equipment and supplies nearly a year earlier, and had greatly improved its forward facilities in Qatar and Kuwait. It also transformed its patrols of the two no-fly zones in Iraq into the suppression of Iraqi air defense capabilities.

For example, Operation Southern Watch coalition aircraft used precision-guided weapons to target several Iraqi military targets in southern and western Iraq. The coalition executed these strikes after Iraqi forces fired anti-aircraft artillery at coalition aircraft patrolling the southern no-fly zone south of the 33rd parallel in Iraq. As a result, Iraqi air defense troops had fired either surface-to-air missiles or anti-aircraft artillery more than 170 times since the beginning of 2003.

The targets and locations included communication sites near Ash Shuaybah, Mudaysis, and Ruwayshid; long-range artillery near Az Zubayr; a mobile early-warning radar and an air defense command center at an Iraqi air base in western Iraq; long-range artillery on the Al Faw peninsula; a surface-to-surface missile system near Al Basra; and an air traffic control radar near Al Basra.

The coalition struck the communications sites and the early-warning radar because they enhanced Iraq's integrated air-defense system. The artillery was struck because it was a danger to coalition ground troops in Kuwait. The air traffic control radar was used to direct Iraqi anti-aircraft artillery fire at coalition aircraft.

Coalition aircraft dropped capitulation leaflets over suspected Iraqi troop locations. The leaflets gave detailed instructions about how the Iraqi troops could avoid being harmed by coalition forces in the event of military action. Although the coalition had dropped millions of leaflets over the past few months, March 19 was the first time that Iraqi troops had received capitulation instructions. The leaflets were dropped in an attempt to minimize Iraqi casualties if a military conflict occurred.

19/20 March: G-Day

Although some preliminary operations were conducted on March 19 against Iraqi air defense systems and missile systems that threatened coalition forces in Kuwait, the main attacks began early on March 20, some 20 minutes after the U.S. ultimatum demanding that Saddam leave Iraq expired. The war began with limited coalition attacks against selected military targets, including a leadership compound used by very senior members of the Iraqi regime.

These attacks were launched using Tomahawk Land Attack Missiles, or TLAMs, from six U.S. warships. Preliminary operations were also conducted against Iraqi air defense systems, surface-to-surface missiles, and artillery batteries to reduce the threat to coalition forces in Kuwait.

The aircraft included F-117 Nighthawks and F-15E Strike Eagles. The ships involved in the Tomahawk Land Attack Missile strikes were the USS *Milius* (DDG 69), USS *Donald Cook* (DDG 75), USS *Bunker Hill* (CG 52), USS *Cowpens* (CG 63), USS *Montpelier* (SSN 765), and USS *Cheyenne* (SSN 773).

Two Iraqi surface-to-surface missiles fired at coalition forces in Kuwait were reported as intercepted by air defenses. Another missile was reported to have landed near Camp Commando in Kuwait; no casualties were suffered.

The Patriot batteries successfully intercepted and destroyed two tactical ballistic missiles during an attack on Kuwait at approximately 12:24 p.m. and 1:30 p.m. (4:24 a.m. and 5:30 a.m. EST). Their guidance and control system locked onto the ballistic missiles, successfully engaging the targets with Hit to Kill PAC III and Guidance Enhanced Missiles (GEM). The land operation began on March 20, less than 24 hours after the first air strike.

INTENSIVE AIR OPERATIONS AND CONTINUING LAND ADVANCES

It will be interesting to see how military historians treat the next phase of the Iraq War once all of the data become available. The initial advance into Iraq quickly took the Al Faw Peninsula, largely as the result of a joint amphibious operation by 40 Commando and 42 Commando of the British Royal Marines, with the support of the Royal Navy. U.S. Special Forces secured Iraq's oil export terminals in the Gulf, and a combination of U.S. Marine and British forces secured much of the Rumaylah oil fields before Iraq could do more than sabotage a few wells. The 15th S. Marine Expeditionary Unit, under the command of the British 3 Commando Brigade Royal Marines, captured Umm Qasr within 48 hours.

At the same time, the main thrust of the U.S. Army and U.S. Marine forces advanced deep into southern Iraq with little initial opposition. Within four days, the U.S. Army was outside An Najaf, some 60 miles from Baghdad, and the U.S. Marines were in a position to move north through the area between the two rivers towards Al Kut.

Despite these initial successes, the first real fighting led some commentators to feel that the war plan might have failed. When the United States took high casualties on March 23 and the initial advance on Baghdad slowed down, some outside observers concluded that the pace of the U.S. land advance threatened to bog down for days or weeks because Iraq was making creative use of asymmetric warfare in attacking the U.S. lines of advance from the cities along the path of the 5th Corps advance on the western edge of the Euphrates. They also felt that the 1 MEF advance would have serious problems in moving rapidly through and beyond An Nasiryah.

That the population of southern Iraq did not rise up and welcome coalition forces as liberators was also seen as an ominous sign that the United States would meet massive resistance throughout Iraq, particularly in the areas of Baghdad and Tikrit, and would be forced to concentrate on a series of water-crossing and urban warfare actions that would make it vulnerable to Iraqi use of chemical weapons.

A great deal of the debate over the war plan discussed in the next chapter reflected the resulting fears. One was that the coalition lacked the ground forces to do the job. There was fear that the United States simply did not have the land forces to successfully attack Baghdad and would have to wait weeks or months for reinforcements to arrive before the Iraqi regime could be destroyed. Others argued that the United States had made a major miscalculation by not conducting a major air campaign before the land advance. These arguments were compounded when the main elements of the 5th Corps paused for several days to regroup, and the marines were seen to be involved in intensive fighting along the southern part of their line of advance on Al Kut.

The chronology that follows, however, gives a different picture. It shows that an intensive air campaign began. According to press reports, 2,500 missiles and bombs were dropped in the first 72 hours, and the air tasking orders (ATO) listed 11 missions. The missions are laid out in the chronology and included close air support for special operations forces in the north, west, and south; suppression and destruction of Iraq's air defenses; and aggressive combat air patrols and attacks on Iraqi air bases designed to keep Iraq's air forces on the ground.

The effect of the air campaign may not yet be measurable in the form of quantified estimates of battle damage. It certainly did much to disrupt and weaken Iraqi forces, however, and to destroy Iraq's ability to conduct cohesive command and control of its war effort early in the war.

Rather than pause for any extended period, the 5th Corps and 1 MEF also soon went on to fight a series of battles against Iraqi regular and then Republican Guard forces under conditions that shattered the cohesion of the Iraqi regular army in the south and forced the Republican Guards to deploy south in ways that exposed them to both air and land attack.

This does not mean the war plan was perfect. Iraq did have unexpected success in using combinations of regular and irregular forces like Saddam's Fedayeen to threaten U.S. and British forces. The United States was forced to commit much of the 101st Air Mobile Division and a brigade of the 82nd Airborne Division to securing its lines of advance and the rear areas in the south.

Lt. General William Wallace, the commander of the 5th Corps, later made it clear that this aspect of Iraqi operations came as a surprise:

> ...we had to adjust to his paramilitary (forces), which were more fanatical and more aggressive than we expected (them) to be. The adjustment that we made was to actually fight and have a presence in some of these urban areas that we had not really planned to do. We planned to bypass them. But we

found it necessary to establish a presence to stop these paramilitaries from influencing our operations.[6]

The coalition did misread the level of popular Iraqi support it had. The United States, in particular, missed the cumulative impact of (1) its failure to support the uprising in 1991, (2) its failure to conduct a meaningful public diplomacy campaign to explain that it was not responsible for the suffering of the Iraqi people under UN sanctions, (3) Iraqi and Arab hostility to the United States because of U.S. support of Israel and the Arab portrayal of the Second Intifada, and (4) the coalition's failure to convincingly rebut conspiracy theories that its goals were "neo-imperialist" and focused on seizing Iraqi oil.

The chronology of leaflet droppings that follows reflects what often seems to have been considerable success in those aspects of psychological warfare that helped cause Iraqi military inaction and expedite surrenders. At the same time, one of the key lessons of the war is that the United States and Britain failed to conduct a successful political, diplomatic, and psychological campaign at the tactical, strategic, and grand strategic level.

The fact remains, however, that there was far less of a military pause than a brief period of media panic—much of it coming from military analysts.

20/21 March

Iraq launched its first theater missile against Kuwait at 2009 Zulu time on March 20.

Coalition land forces pushed into Iraq. The 3rd Commando Brigade conducted an amphibious assault on the Al Faw peninsula, encountering light resistance. Casualties were inflicted on the enemy and prisoners taken. Oil infrastructure was successfully secured to prevent Saddam Hussein from attempting to release oil as an environmental weapon. Elements of 1(UK) Armored Division also entered Iraq along with other coalition forces, thrusting towards Basra.

U.S. Marines seized the port of Umm Qasr, and Royal Navy minehunters began work to clear the associated waterways of any mines.

The 3rd U.S. Infantry Division advanced north toward Baghdad. U.S. troops, supported by British specialist personnel, secured oil fields in the Basra area.

U.S. warships and Royal Navy submarines launched Tomahawk Land Attack Missiles at high-value targets, including command and control centers in Baghdad. Three U.S. ships and two British submarines that were part of the coalition forces maritime component launched TLAMs during the previous night's military operations to disarm Iraq. The ships included the Aegis guided-missile destroyer USS *John S. McCain* (DDG 56) in the Persian Gulf and two Los Angeles class submarines, USS *Columbia* (SSN 771) and USS *Providence* (SSN 719). The Royal Navy submarines that launched Tomahawks include the Trafalgar class HMS *Turbulent* and the Swiftsure class HMS *Splendid*.

Other Royal Navy vessels provided naval gunfire to support the advance of 3 Commando Brigade.

In the air, coalition aircraft, including RAF assets, were involved in a wide variety of operations. Tornado GR4s attacked key facilities, and Harrier GR7s provided close air support. Other aircraft, including tankers, provided invaluable support.

A U.S. Marine Corps CH-46 Sea Knight with 12 U.S. and UK personnel aboard crashed in Kuwait south of Umm Qasr, near Highway 801 in Kuwait; there were no survivors. Enemy action was not thought to have been the cause.

News sources reported that Iraq fired seven missiles at Kuwait, four of which were intercepted; the remaining missiles were allowed to land in unpopulated areas and caused no casualties after missile defense systems calculated that their point of impact was inconsequential and they should not be engaged.

Unconfirmed media reports stated that Iraqi forces moved missile launchers from the Basra area to Al Qurnah. The report quoted military sources as stating the missile attacks were not random launches and were aimed at U.S. positions in Kuwait. Iraq fired six Ababil-100 missiles at several targets in Kuwait, including the "Thunder Road" staging area for the 101st Airborne Division; Camp Doha, command center for coalition forces; Camp Udari, another staging area; the Ali Al Salem airbase; and Tactical Assembly Area Fox, a large marine logistics base. Of these six missiles, four were shot down, while the two launched against Tactical Assembly Area Fox missed their target. Additionally, Iraqi forces launched a CSS-C-3 Seersucker cruise missile at the headquarters of the 1 MEF at Camp Commando.

21/22 March

U.S. secretary of defense Donald Rumsfeld outlined the military objectives of Operation Iraqi Freedom:

- First, to end the regime of Saddam Hussein.
- Second, to identify, isolate, and eliminate Iraq's weapons of mass destruction.

- Third, to search for, to capture, and to drive out terrorists from that country.

- Fourth, to collect such intelligence as the United States and its allies can that is related to terrorist networks.

- Fifth, to collect such intelligence as we can related to the global network of illicit weapons of mass destruction.

- Sixth, to end sanctions and to immediately deliver humanitarian support to the displaced and to many needy Iraqi citizens.

- Seventh, to secure Iraq's oil fields and resources, which belong to the Iraqi people.

- And last, to help the Iraqi people create conditions for a transition to a representative self-government.

As ground forces continued to make good progress, the air campaign stepped up, aimed at several hundred military targets throughout Iraq. Coalition aircraft flew some 3,000 sorties in the air attack.

Sources differ over the scale of the air assault. USCENTAF reported that the air campaign of Operation Iraqi Freedom launched into high gear shortly before 1:00 p.m. EST on March 21, as hundreds of coalition aircraft and cruise missiles targeted select regime leadership and military targets in Baghdad and other various cities. Military command and control installations, structures, and buildings were the targeted sites. Other cities with military sites targeted were the northern towns of Kirkuk, Mosul, and Tikrit. More than 1,700 air sorties and 504 TLAM and CALCM cruise missiles were used.[7]

The USAF in the United States reported that the coalition flew 1,500 sorties, 700 of which were flown by strike aircraft. The rest were jammers, bomber escorts, surveillance, etc., during the 24-hour period that started March 21 at 1:00 p.m. EST.

The coalition launched a total of 600 cruise missiles—500 Navy sea-launched cruise missiles [Tomahawks] and 100 Air Force air-launched cruise missiles [CALCMs].

- The missiles were aimed at some 1,000 targets, also known as aim-points, throughout Iraq. Military command and control installations, structures, and buildings were the targeted sites. Other cities with military sites targeted were the northern towns of Kirkuk, Mosul, and Tikrit.

- Planes involved were B-52 bombers, B-2 stealth bombers, and F-117 stealth fighter-bombers. F-15s were used for air defense suppression.

Anti-aircraft fire was encountered, but no opposition from Iraqi aircraft.

■ The air campaign was adjusted in stride, as it was under way. Some planes hit the targets they had been tasked with upon departure; others had their targets shifted en route. Combined Force Air Component Commander Lt. General Michael Moseley, head of the air campaign, was described as "the quarterback of the operation, calling audibles in response to changing circumstances."

■ The early success of the air campaign allowed the coalition to further reduce its target list by hundreds of targets, including rail lines, bridges, power stations, and other facilities. It was clear that striking them was not necessary to support the land advance and they would have great value for nation building once the war was over.[8]

Tomahawk missiles were also launched from 30 U.S. Navy and coalition warships then assigned to the Naval Forces Central Command. The ships involved were the USS *Bunker Hill* (CG 52), USS *Mobile Bay* (CG 53), USS *San Jacinto* (CG 56), USS *Cowpens* (CG 63), USS *Shiloh* (CG 67), USS *Briscoe* (DD 977), USS *Deyo* (DD 989), USS *Fletcher* (DD 992), USS *Arleigh Burke* (DDG 51), USS *John S. McCain* (DDG 56), USS *Paul Hamilton* (DDG 60), USS *Milius* (DDG 69), USS *Higgins* (DDG 71), USS *Donald Cook* (DDG 75), USS *O'Kane* (DDG 77), USS *Porter* (DDG 78), USS *Oscar Austin* (DDG 79), USS *Augusta* (SSN 710), USS *Providence* (SSN 719), USS *Pittsburgh* (SSN 720), USS *Key West* (SSN 722), USS *Louisville* (SSN 724), USS *Newport News* (SSN 750), USS *San Juan* (SSN 751), USS *Montpelier* (SSN 765), USS *Toledo* (SSN 769), USS *Columbia* (SSN 771), USS *Cheyenne* (SSN 773), and two Royal Navy submarines, the HMS *Splendid* and HMS *Turbulent*.

The RAF's new Storm Shadow missile was successfully used for the first time in operations.

The U.S. 5th Corps secured bridges over the Euphrates in its rapid advance on Baghdad.

At Basra, the Iraqi 51st Mechanized Division surrendered as U.S. Marines and the UK's 7th Armored Brigade secured the area.

Coalition forces secured the port of Umm Qasr in southern Iraq at 4 p.m., laying the groundwork for the delivery of humanitarian assistance supplies. Forces from the 15th Marine Expeditionary Unit and the 3rd Commando Brigade Royal Marines were involved in the seizure of the port, one of the first objectives in Operation Iraqi Freedom. Securing the strategic port of Umm Qasr allowed international aid agencies to begin the much-needed work of getting humanitarian assistance to the Iraqi people.

At approximately 6 p.m., the 1st Marine Expeditionary Force secured the gas oil separation plants (GOSPs), crude oil export facilities, and oil wells in the Rumaylah oil fields. Although the oil infrastructure was confirmed to have been extensively booby-trapped, the installations were secured intact and U.S. and British troops began clearing the demolition charges.

U.S. Marines from the 1st Marine Division and UK Royal Marines combined their efforts to secure the critical Iraqi infrastructure. "Over half of the Iraqi oil production, approximately 1.6 million barrels per day produced by 1,074 Rumaylah oil wells, has been secured for the Iraqi people," said Lt. Gen. James Conway, commanding general of the 1st Marine Expeditionary Force.

Four GOSPs, a key pumping station at Az Zubayr, a manifold and metering station on the Al Faw peninsula, and the offshore crude oil export facilities were secured. These were critical nodes of the larger oil infrastructure in southern Iraq. These key facilities gave the Iraqi people the ability to preserve 85 percent of the function of those fields.

Special operations forces captured the Mina al Bakr export facility intact and in working order. Another facility, the Khor al Amaya export facility, was also occupied, but had been destroyed during the war between Iran and Iraq in the 1980s and was nonoperational. Both facilities are capable of handling 1.6 million barrels per day when operational.

Six major GOSPs, covering an area approximately 50 kilometers in length, included seven oil wells that had been sabotaged and were on fire. Oil fire fighting crews moved into the areas at a designated time to snuff out the fires. Flame trenches filled with oil were also deliberately set aflame by Iraqi troops. Some of the deserted plants were improperly shut down by Iraqis, causing oil pumping from the wells to overfill the pumping stations' oil tanks. The oil was seeping around the area and posed a threat of explosion if it reached the burning wells.

Three main missions were conducted. The first is safe shutdown procedures to properly shut down the facilities and keep the oil from pumping. Later, after the stations have been improved, they will resume pumping. The other main missions include spill containment and oil fire fighting, overseen by members of the UK forces; the U.S. Army, Navy, and Air Force; and civilian contractors.

Royal Navy and U.S. Navy minehunters continued clearance operations in the southern waterways to allow supplies to be shipped into Umm Qasr. In particular, the Royal Fleet Auxiliary Service's *Sir Galahad* stood by to deliver humanitarian aid.

Two Royal Navy Sea King Mk 7 Airborne Early Warning helicopters collided over the northern Arabian Gulf. None of the six British and one U.S. crew members aboard survived. Two U.S. Marines were killed in action in southern Iraq.

22/23 March

The air effort continues. In the 24-hour period starting at 06:00 (local Saudi Arabia time) on March 22, U.S. aircraft alone flew more than 1,500 sorties. Of those, 800 were "strike sorties," or bombing missions.

- There were about 500 aim points, or targets.
- The Navy reported launching more than 400 Tomahawk sea-launched cruise missiles to date.
- Pilots continued to report taking heavy anti-aircraft fire and sporadic launches of surface-to-air missiles.
- Targets included Iraqi Integrated Air Defense Systems (IADS), regime command and control, regime security, regime leadership, and weapons of mass destruction.
- The remaining sorties included intelligence, surveillance, and reconnaissance (IS&R); close air support; electronic jamming; air refueling; intra- and inter-theater airlift; combined search and rescue; and interdiction.
- U.S. Air Force jets bombed and destroyed two Ababil-100 missile launchers near Basra, only 30 minutes after one of them had launched a missile.
- On March 21, USAF F-117 stealth fighters "struck five strategic targets in Baghdad using a new precision-guided munition, the EGBU-27....the strike missions were able to precisely hit communication nodes and command bunkers."
- Sorties originated from as far away as Whiteman AFB in Missouri, the Indian Ocean, and the United Kingdom They were also flown from 30 other locations throughout the CENTCOM Area of Responsibility (AOR) and from five Navy aircraft carriers. The B-2s flew the longest missions (approximately 34 hours round-trip).

There were now more than 170,000 U.S. Army, U.S. Marine, and allied ground forces in Iraq.

The U.S. advance north continued but encountered stiffer resistance in some locations, including at An Nasiryah, where 12 U.S. troops were reported missing.

U.S. soldiers apparently captured by Iraqi forces were subsequently paraded on Iraqi state television.

Sporadic resistance continued at Umm Qasr. A prisoner of war camp was under construction in the area to properly accommodate the hundreds of Iraqi troops who had surrendered in the area. Work continued to make safe the booby-trapped oil installations in southern Iraq.

An RAF GR4 Tornado aircraft from RAF Marham, which was returning from an operational mission, was engaged near the Kuwaiti border by a Patriot missile battery. Both aircrew were killed.

In a late-night attack at Camp Pennsylvania in Kuwait, a soldier in the 101st Airborne wounded 10 senior division personnel, two of whom died later from their wounds.

USCENTCOM commander General Tommy Franks and General Vincent Brooks summarized combat operations to date as follows:[9]

General Tommy Franks:
The initiation of combat operations—we refer to that as D-day. The introduction of special operation forces—we refer to that as S-Day. The introduction of ground forces, G-Day. And the introduction of shock air forces, A-Day.

Additionally, a number of emerging targets have been struck along the way and will continue to be struck as they emerge. So the sequence you have seen up to this point has been S-G-A. That sequence was based on our intelligence reads, how we see the enemy, and on our sense of the capabilities of our own forces.

Brigadier General Vincent Brooks:
...I want to take a few minutes to brief you now on some of the operations that have occurred by the coalition over the last several days. The operation of course began on the 19th of March, and since that time, coalition forces have already achieved a number of several key mission objectives.

Our first effort is aggressive and direct attacks to disrupt the regime's key command, control, communications, integrated air defense and ballistic missiles using various targeting and methods that will achieve the desired effects....

Our second focus is on special operations. Coalition special operations forces entered Iraq at night, after destroying Iraqi military outposts. The special operation forces then began looking for Saddam Hussein's and the regime's weapons of mass destruction and their ballistic missiles that threaten their neighbors. Additionally, coalition special operations forces saved three key oil terminals that are used for export through the Gulf, and these terminals are key to the future of Iraq. By preventing certain destruction, the coalition has preserved the future of Iraq. This is the area where the three terminals were in southern Iraq, and in the Arabian Gulf. On these platforms we found a variety of things. We found weapons, ammunition, and explosives. These explosives are not meant for defenders.

Our coalition maritime forces have destroyed Iraqi naval forces, as the following video shows. This is a patrol boat being attacked from the air, and in a moment you'll see the secondary explosion completing its destruction.

They are also very active in ensuring that the waterways remain open and unmined so that Iraq is not cut off from the aid that is prepared to flow in…. Interdictions done by our coalition maritime forces and others over the last few days prevented, for sure, the release of 139 floating mines into the Khor Abdullah, which is an inlet that joins the Iraqi inland waterways with the Arabian Gulf.

Ground maneuver forces attacked to seize the key Rumaylah oil fields, simultaneously began an unprecedented combined arms penetration deep into Iraq. The attack continues as we speak, and has already moved the distance of the longest maneuver in the 1991 Gulf War in one-quarter of the time.

The oil fields were spared destruction that was intended by the regime because of the effectiveness of these attacks…wells were set afire on the 19th in the afternoon, before the coalition attack began. By the next day, the land component had already entered Iraq and had prevented any further destruction. And this is video from the entering forces. And the good news is only nine of the roughly 500 oil wells that are in the Rumaylah oil fields— only nine were sabotaged by the regime. The flame on the bottom shows where that location is. All the rest of them are okay.

I should add that the power of information has been key throughout this operation, and it is truly having the effect of saving lives—of the Iraqi people and military units who are choosing not to fight and die for a doomed regime. The leaders from several regular army divisions surrendered to coalition forces, and their units abandoned their equipment and returned to their homes, just as the coalition had instructed.

We know that there are other forces on the battlefield that we haven't even arrived at yet, and there are Iraqi units that are preparing to surrender even now as we speak. These are lines of roughly 700 Iraqi soldiers that we imaged in the desert away from their equipment, awaiting our arrival.

The coalition is committed to disarming Iraq. But the coalition is equally committed to bringing humanitarian assistance to the Iraqi people. Our humanitarian work in Iraq is only beginning. The U.S. military, coalition partners, and other civilian organizations from around the world have positioned millions of meals, medicines, and other supplies for the Iraqi people.

23/24 March

The "worst day of the war": Twenty-six soldiers died in combat. The coalition advance slowed and appeared to halt.

USAF planes continued to encounter heavy anti-aircraft fire, and some were returning to base riddled with bullet holes. The air campaign on March 23 focused mainly on providing close air-support for ground troops advancing in the southwest and in the north and on taking out Republican Guard targets in and around Baghdad.

U.S. aircraft flew about 2,000 sorties. Of those, 800 to 900 were strike runs. (This included the close air support mission). There were 500 preplanned targets.

There was still no action from the Iraqi Air Force.

Baghdad was hit by both cruise missiles and precision-guided bombs dropped from planes.

About 80 percent of the bomb drops were precision-guided, as close air support pilots dropped dumb gravity bombs on Iraqi ground forces.

Officials confirmed that two Tomahawk cruise missiles accidentally landed in Turkey; there were no injuries.

Cruise missile figures continued to be confusing and conflicting. The U.S. Navy said that they had fired more than 500 Tomahawks since the start of the war.

There have been "6 or 7" Tomahawk failures—duds that never left the tube and others that dropped in the water—out of all 500 Tomahawks.

U.S. forces advanced beyond An Nasiryah, while aviation forces attacked Republican Guard formations near Baghdad; one U.S. helicopter was lost.

In the north, U.S. forces reinforced their presence and targeted elements of regime support units and the Republican Guard. In and around Baghdad, they continued air and special operations activities with good success. In the south, air units continued the campaign toward Baghdad and continued to operate in and around the area in support of ground forces.

U.S. combat operations met resistance in a number of locations, the most notable of which was in the vicinity of An Nasiryah. U.S. Marines defeated an enemy attack there while sustaining 10 killed and a number of wounded in the sharpest engagement of the war thus far.

Also near An Nasiryah, a U.S. Army supply convoy was ambushed by irregular Iraqi forces. A number of U.S. service members were wounded in that action, and 12 are reported missing.

A U.S. Air Force MQ-1 Predator found and destroyed a radar-guided anti-aircraft artillery piece in southern Iraq Saturday at 5:25 EST, making it the first Predator strike of Operation Iraqi Freedom, defense officials announced. The Predator used one AGM-114K Hellfire II missile to strike an Iraqi ZSU-23-4 Mobile anti-aircraft artillery gun outside the southern Iraqi town of Al Amarah.

A Patriot firing battery successfully intercepted and destroyed an incoming Iraqi tactical ballistic missile (TBM) during an attack on U.S. and coalition forces in Kuwait at approximately 1:00 a.m. (5:00 p.m. EST). Two bright orange flashes were seen over Kuwait as the engaging Patriot missile destroyed the Iraqi TBM.

Mine clearance operations in the southern waterways made good progress, with half the route to Umm Qasr made safe. Logistic preparations continued to allow the shipping of humanitarian supplies once the route was cleared. The airport at Basra was secured.

Two British soldiers were reported missing after an attack on UK military vehicles in southern Iraq. In a separate incident, a British soldier was killed in action at Az Zubayr, near Basra.

24/25 March

Coalition air attacks continued against Republican Guard formations and regime command and control and military formations virtually all over the country with precision munitions and precision application of those munitions. On March 24, U.S. aircraft flew more than 1,500 sorties. Some 800 bombing sorties were flown against 500 preplanned targets.

During combat air operations at approximately 3:40 p.m. local time Monday, a U.S. F-16 fighter engaged a U.S. Patriot battery approximately 30 miles south of An Najaf. The F-16 pilot executed the strike against the Patriot while en route to a mission near Baghdad. No soldiers were injured or killed by the strike. The incident was under review to ensure the future safety of the Patriot crews and aircrews.

U.S. forces continued to advance north of An Nasiryah. British forces completed operations to secure Umm Qasr.

The Forward Command Element of the Military Coordination and Liaison Command, led by U.S. Marine Maj. Gen. Pete Osman, arrived in northern Iraq and began work. Osman then met with all primary and numerous other Iraqi opposition leaders in the region, conveying U.S. intentions and explaining U.S. plans and operations in northern Iraq. The MCLC's continued presence and activities in the region added stability to northern Iraq, as the organization fostered open communication and synchronized efforts among the various organizations operating there. The MCLC was established by the U.S. European Command to conduct liaison and coordination with military and humanitarian assistance organizations. Now under the operational control of U.S. Central Command, the organization's function was to provide a stabilizing effect in the northern region, coordinate international activities in northern Iraq, and support humanitarian assistance efforts.

British artillery destroyed Iraqi mortars and guns that had opened fire on Iraqi civilian areas in Basra. The 3 Commando Brigade, supported by helicopters and U.S. and UK aircraft, defeated a tank attack, destroying 19 T-55s.

A British soldier from the Black Watch was killed in action at Az Zubayr. In a separate incident, two more British soldiers were killed when their Challenger 2 tank was accidentally hit by another Challenger 2 during an engagement with Iraqi forces.

News reports stated that the Iraqis were using soldiers in civilian clothes as artillery spotters. Elsewhere, Iraqi forces continued to attack the coalition logistics train using mines and ambushes with RPGs and small arms.

THE CONTINUING ADVANCE FROM THE SOUTH

As the Iraq War proceeded, the most striking aspects of the war were not that the 5th Corps and 1 MEF forces sometimes had to pause to resupply and consolidate their positions, or that they had to deal with continuing threats to their lines of advance and communications. It was rather that their average rate of advance became so high and continued in the face of major problems with weather and sandstorms.

This continuous pressure from the land, coupled with air operations that continued in spite of major weather problems, moved far more quickly than Iraqi forces could deal with. One of the striking advances in coalition airpower was that the coalition's virtual air dominance allowed it to deploy otherwise-vulnerable slow fliers like the E-8C JSTARS forward nearer the battle space, along with refueling tankers. The Doppler radar of the JSTARS could locate Iraqi major ground weapons and maneuvers over an area of several hundred square miles, and the "fusion of intelligence" from other sources gave the coalition the ability to locate and target Iraqi forces under weather conditions they felt protected them from the air. Aircraft like the RC-135 Rivet Joint, for example, could characterize and locate the source of Iraqi military communications. The ability to refuel aircraft in forward areas greatly increases their "loiter" time and ability to find targets, and extend combat air patrol time.[10]

Fighter attack aircraft like the F-16 were able to locate targets, despite what the Iraqis thought was effective cover from the weather, and to even use laser-guided bombs. Less sophisticated aircraft like the A-10 were still able to use onboard sensors and binoculars to find and attack targets like Republican Guard units, and they were also given clearance to make use of cluster munitions like the GBU-87 to hit the units with area weapons. The Medina, Al Nida, and Hammurabi divisions of the Republican Guard were hit hard during this period.[11]

It is unclear just how much attrition took place and how much Iraqi forces suffered from the intense pace of ongoing air attack. It is equally unclear what level of attrition was necessary to severely degrade Iraqi warfighting capabilities, paralyze any cohesive command and control attempt at reorganizing and regrouping Iraqi defenses, and limit the willingness of much of the regular army to fight. In many cases, the weaknesses in Iraqi military leadership must have gravely compounded the impact of both the rapid U.S. land advance and precision airpower.

What is clear, however, is that from late March on, the Iraqi army ceased to fight as a cohesive force. Moreover, because Iraq's army was not prepared and in place to deal with the 5th Corps and 1 MEF advance, many elements of the Iraq regular army could not or would not move in any coherent pattern of maneuver. Iraq was forced to try to block the main thrusts of the coalition advance by committing its Republican Guards in a piecemeal form in maneuvers that made them vulnerable to air attack despite the weather, and that forced them to close on advancing coalition forces in what became a series of engagements in which coalition airpower could attack them as they closed and they were then outgunned and out-targeted by the 5th Corps and 1 MEF artillery and armor.

Saddam Hussein's regime stripped Baghdad and Tikrit of the shield of Republican Guard forces and possibly deployed elements of the Special Republican Guards as well. It may have calculated that this would result in enough U.S. casualties and delays to give the regime political support and time. The end result, however, was that the Republican Guards suffered steadily greater attrition and lost the force strength they needed to conduct a cohesive defense of Baghdad.

The Iraqi regime used up those elements of the regular army forces in the south that it could maneuver with little clear purpose, and it failed to achieve any major repositioning of the bulk of the regular army, which was deployed in the north. It failed to effectively blow up bridges and make use of water barriers. Although Iraq's regular forces could still fight in cities and could conduct raids along the U.S. line of advance and tie down British forces around Basra, this became more harassment than defense. It did not mean that Iraq could fight effectively in the more open areas that the United States used to the west of the Euphrates or that it could paralyze 1 MEF forces in their advance through much more densely populated areas. The 1 MEF did have to fight its way north, but it still advanced on Al Kut without having to encounter a coordinated in-depth defense by massed Iraqi land forces.

In contrast, the United States and Britain exploited many of the features of their war plan that had first become apparent months before the war began. The coalition advance focused on destroying the regime's center of power rather than on trying to defeat all Iraqi forces in detail. It did not attempt to occupy or secure rear areas, as distinguished from defeating and containing those forces that actively threatened the coalition's main line of advance.

The coalition used precision air and missile power to achieve the effect of disrupting and paralyzing enemy operations, rather than fighting the kind of battle of tactical attrition throughout the theater of operations fought in the 38-day air campaign in the Gulf War of 1991. At the same time, the coalition's focus on destroying narrowly defined active leadership targets, active C4I battle management facilities and systems, and the Republican Guard allowed it to achieve decisive "effects" without major attacks on population centers, infrastructure, industry, or lines of communication.

The coalition simultaneously made use of Special Forces, with the addition of the 173rd Airborne Brigade, to occupy air bases in the west, secure the Kurdish security zone, and conduct small operations in a wide range of areas in western and northern Iraq. While the details remain unclear, Iraq failed to put effective pressure on the Kurds, resist decisively in the west, and make effective use of what—on paper—was a decisive superiority in force numbers in units that were not under the 5th Corps and 1 MEF attack.

25/26 March

Weather had an impact on the battlefield, with high winds, some rain, and some sandstorms and thunderstorms throughout the country. Precision all-weather weapon systems, however, and an aggressive integrated operations plan by air and land components allowed the coalition forces to maintain and increase pressure on the regime on all fronts, even in the bad weather.

The air component flew more than 1,400 combat and combat-support missions over Iraq, paying particular attention to the Iraqi Republican Guard while attacking surface-to-surface missile systems in a time-sensitive fashion; these missile systems affected and threatened Kuwait and other neighbors in the region. The air component also focused on key regime command-and-control facilities. Command and control targets in Baghdad were attacked.

The U.S. Air Force reported that it flew more than 1,500 sorties on March 25, 700 of which were strike missions, and that it had about 100 pre-planned targets. The strikes focused on regime command and control, leadership and Republican Guard units in and around Baghdad.

The U.S. Air Force also flew extensive close air support in the south (Basra), north, and west. Aircraft supporting ground troops (mostly A-10 Warthogs) continued to take heavy anti-aircraft fire and were returning shot up. The air force said that the maintenance crews that keep these planes flying were the unsung heroes in the fighting.

The resulting combination of air operations, direct land-based attack, and precision special operations created a synergy that was key to the coalition strategy.

Coalition land forces continued to progress northward with engagements in the vicinity of An Nasiryah and Basra and with some casualties, but they inflicted more on the enemy and destroyed a number of Iraqi tanks, artillery pieces, and troop formations. The coalition lost one soldier, four marines, and two British soldiers in incidents throughout the country.

U.S. forces fought significant engagements near An Najaf and An Nasiryah. The Ba'ath Party headquarters in As Samawah was destroyed.

Iraqi tanks advancing out of Basra were engaged and destroyed.

The northern front opened on March 26 with the airlift of the U.S. Army 173rd Airborne Brigade.

British troops conducted effective raids against paramilitary forces in the Basra area. Engineering work to construct a fresh water pipeline from Kuwait into southern Iraq continued.

Reports in the news media also mentioned that U.S. forces using between 30 and 40 Apache and Apache Longbow attack helicopters attacked Republican Guard vehicles south of Karbala and came under very heavy fire, resulting in the loss of one AH-64D and the capture of its two crew. Pilots were shot at with small arms and RPGs from streets, roofs, and backyards. One pilot was quoted as saying, "They definitely had their air defense arrayed in different zones. That's what we were fighting against, plus some small arms." The tactics used by the Iraqis resembled helicopter ambush tactics first employed by North Vietnam in the late 1960s.

26/27 March

Sandstorms continued in Iraq, hindering fixed-wing and helicopter operations. According to media reports, Iraqi Republican Guard and Special Republican Guard units used the cover of the sandstorms to move units south from Baghdad. The Iraqi forces were hit by heavy air strikes and sustained estimated losses of hundreds of vehicles.

A U.S. Air Force B-2 Spirit bomber targeted and struck a major link in Iraq's national communication network. The communication link occupied a large tower on the east bank of the Tigris River in downtown Baghdad. The strike with two precision-guided munitions was to degrade the ability of the Hussein regime to command and control the actions of Iraq's military forces. Battle damage assessment was ongoing

U.S. airborne forces landed in northern Iraq. U.S. forces defeated attacks near An Najaf and An Nasiryah. One M-2 Bradley was reported destroyed in the fighting near An Najaf.

As for the land campaign, Michael Eisenstadt of the Washington Institute noted that

> U.S. forces heading to Baghdad had made remarkable progress, in one of the most rapid sustained armored advances in the history of warfare (averaging about 75 miles per day for the first four days). By avoiding major Iraqi military formations and skirting major population centers, U.S. forces racing to Baghdad have surpassed the achievements of the Germans in Russia (1941) and North Africa (1942), the Soviets in the Ukraine (1944) and Manchuria (1945), Israel in the Sinai (1967), and the United States in Iraq during Operation Desert Storm (1991).
>
> ...losses remain relatively light. A review of personnel attrition rates indicates that, after six days of battle, approximately 20 coalition soldiers have been confirmed killed in action (an average of about 3 per day), whereas more than 150 coalition soldiers were killed during the four-day air-land campaign at the end of Operation Desert Storm (for an average of nearly 40 per day).

A series of engagements occurred southeast of An Najaf over the period of about three to four hours. Coalition forces of the U.S. 5th Corps sustained a few damaged vehicles and in turn inflicted significant damage on the Iraqi force.

In particular, elements of the 3rd Squadron, 7th Calvary Regiment encountered Iraqi forces in a series of ambushes and were in repeated contact with Iraqi forces over 24 hours near As Samawah and Al Faysaliah. The regiment was attacked by heavy small arms and ATGM fire and lost two trucks, one Humvee, an M-2 Bradley IFV, and two M-1A1 tanks to enemy fire. Another M-1A1 tank and a fuel truck were lost in difficult terrain and could not be recovered. The M-1A1s were hit in the engine compartments.

In fighting throughout the region, Iraqi forces made use of harassing attacks and ambushes with mortars, anti-tank missiles, machine guns, and small arms. In many instances the Iraqi forces dug in along several-hundred-yard stretches along roads in an effort to halt the U.S. advance.

The lst Marine Expeditionary Force gained control of a hospital near An Nasiryah that was being used as a paramilitary headquarters, staging area, and storage area; 200 weapons, Iraqi military uniforms, one tank, 3,000 chemical protective suits, and nerve agent antidote injectors were found within the hospital.

Special operations forces continued to help prepare the advance of U.S. heavy forces by calling in close air support on military targets, including the destruction of the Ba'ath Party headquarters in As Samawah.

UK forces conducted aggressive patrols in the Al Faw area and in Umm Qasr to increase the security in those areas, and also conducted a raid that destroyed a Ba'ath Party headquarters in Basra. They continued to have success against the Iraqi regular army in the area.

Maritime forces began to clear the Khor Abdullah channel from the Gulf up to the Port of Umm Qasr.

Two mines were discovered at sea close to the swept channel leading to Umm Qasr. The arrival of the RFA *Sir Galahad*, carrying humanitarian supplies, was delayed to allow that part of the swept channel to be checked by Royal and U.S. Navy minehunters.

A squadron of the Royal Scots Dragoon Guards eliminated an Iraqi tank unit and infantry positions near Basra without suffering losses.

27/28 March

Sandstorms continued, slowing movement and hindering air operations.

U.S. forces defeated more paramilitary counterattacks north of An Najaf. The 3rd Infantry Division advanced beyond As Diwaniyah east of An Najaf, and an airborne brigade combat team (BCT) from the 173rd Airborne Brigade parachuted into an airfield in northern Iraq in the evening.

Coalition forces of the U.S. 5th Corps were attacked by vehicle-mounted irregulars east of An Najaf, where a significant number of approaching vehicles had been reported. The reports overestimated the size of the Iraqi force, but 5th Corps units defeated the attack, destroying most of the force.

In An Nasiryah, the lst Marine Expeditionary Force defeated an attack by irregulars, supported by armored personnel carriers, rocket launchers, and anti-aircraft artillery systems. The fight lasted for about 90 minutes. The marines did sustain some wounded but remained fully effective.

UK forces continued aggressive patrols and operations in the Al Faw and Basra areas, and they inflicted considerable damage on paramilitaries south of Basra and near Al Faw.

Maritime forces continued their efforts to expand the width of the cleared channel in Khor Abdullah. The channel was opened all the way up to Umm Qasr, and about 60 yards wide. As it was expanded to get to about a 200-yard-wide pathway, coalition forces identified some bottom-influenced mines. These are subsurface mines that can be programmed, if need be, to count the number of hulls that pass over them, and at a certain point, however programmed, they detonate.

Following further mine clearance operations, the RFA *Sir Galahad* arrived safely in Umm Qasr, delivering a major consignment of humanitarian aid.

A soldier from D Squadron, the Blues and Royals (Household Cavalry Regiment), was killed in an incident in southern Iraq.

28/29 March

The weather cleared; consequently, coalition forces increased the number of strikes on Baghdad and Republican Guard units. Ba'ath Party headquarters in nine locations were attacked by coalition air and ground forces.

Land forces consolidated territory gained over the last several days and conducted active security operations to eliminate identified terrorist death squads. The 1st Marine Expeditionary Force continued its advance beyond Kulat Sukhayr. The 5th Corps defeated paramilitary attacks north of An Najaf and continued to shape the battlefield for future operations.

U.S. forces captured a major Iraqi ammunition depot in central Iraq near Talil. Other coalition forces secured additional bridges across the Euphrates and launched offensives to isolate Iraqi forces holding out in the An Nasiryah and As Samawah areas. The 5th Corps bombarded the Republican Guard Medina division.

In the 3rd Infantry Division sector, soldiers from the 2nd Brigade Combat Team attacked and cleared the enemy from quarries to the south of Karbala. At one point, the brigade came under ineffective and uncoordinated enemy artillery fire, which was suppressed with radar-directed multiple launch rocket system (MLRS) counterfire from the corps' artillery.

The remainder of the 3rd Infantry Division attacked north throughout its zone to defeat small pockets of enemy forces. The attacks destroyed two 57mm air defense artillery systems, two armored personnel carriers, one artillery piece, nine technical vehicles, several enemy were killed in action, and approximately 30 enemy prisoners of war were taken.

The 101st Air Assault Division conducted patrols northwest and south of An Najaf, which resulted in the capture or defeat of one 120mm mortar, four weapons caches, several enemy killed in action, and approximately 20 enemy prisoners of war.

U.S. helicopters attacked the Republican Guard Medina division near Karbala. Apache attack helicopters from the 101st Airborne Air Assault

Division pounded the Republican Guards Medina Division during an early evening (March 28) deep strike in the vicinity of the city of Karbala. The deep attack was a deliberate, coordinated operation directed against an elite, well-entrenched Republican Guard division. In this attack, coalition forces used artillery and ATACMS rockets to attack suspected air-defense sites. Additionally, coalition helicopters called in fixed-wing aircraft to attack six more heavily defended targets. The tactics used in this attack seemed to be more effective in limiting damage to coalition forces. The initial battle damage assessment from the 101st Airborne Division reported the destruction of tanks, armored personnel carriers, an anti-aircraft artillery system, and a radar unit, in addition to numerous enemy personnel.

Outside of As Samawah, a pick-up truck attempted to crash through an 82nd Airborne Division checkpoint. One enemy was killed and three were wounded when paratroopers engaged the truck. No U.S. soldiers were wounded in the attack. In other action, the 82nd Airborne Division conducted several patrols around As Samawah that resulted in several enemy killed and the capture or defeat of numerous Iraqi wounded. These included approximately 20 enemy prisoners of war, two mortars, and two technical vehicles. As of March 27, soldiers from the 5th Corps had captured approximately 700 enemy prisoners of war.

UK forces succeeded in preventing any reinforcement of Basra while securing the southern oil fields and the key port of Umm Qasr.

In the north, coalition forces kept pressure on regime forces while maintaining stability in the Kurdish region of Iraq. Following bombardment by coalition aircraft, Iraqi forces pulled out of positions at Chamchal, near Kirkuk. Kurdish paramilitary forces later seized these positions. Elsewhere in northern Iraq, U.S. Special Forces and Kurdish fighters attacked and cleared several positions held by a Kurdish Islamist extremist movement, Ansar al-Islam, near Halabjah. It was estimated that 30 to 40 enemy troops were killed and two were captured.

Coalition special operations forces continued their actions throughout all of Iraq. An operation at night in An Nasiryah involving special operations aircraft destroyed two paramilitary headquarters.

Maritime forces cleared the mines found in the channel of Khor Abdullah, near buoy number 24. The waterway was reopened for the arrival of much needed humanitarian supplies.

USCENTCOM described missile defense activity as follows:

A total of about—a total of 12 missiles have been fired. We believe them to be in the Ababil-100 or Al-Samoud family, and those have been launched from within Iraq toward Kuwait. We're seeing a rate of about one per day at this point, and all of the threatening launches have been intercepted by Patriot missiles. Additionally, we have established combat air patrols near the areas where most of the launches are occurring. We have been successful in destroying a number of launchers before and after they're fired, and we're actively hunting for them.

U.S. airborne forces landed in northern Iraq.

British forces moved to interdict northern routes into Basra. The major oil refinery at Basra was secured. One British soldier died as a result of a friendly fire incident.

Two U.S. marines were lost in action in two separate incidents.

Iraqi forces conducted a successful airborne reconnaissance of 3rd Infantry Division staging areas by using an ultralight aircraft. The aircraft was successfully "acquired" visually by Linebacker air defense units, but they were unable to receive authorization to engage before the aircraft left the area.

29/30 March

Coalition aircraft attacked air defense, command and control, and intelligence facilities in the Baghdad area.

The 3 Commando Brigade launched an offensive near Basra that secured Abu al Khasib. A Royal Marine was killed in action on the Al Faw peninsula, and a Royal Signals noncommissioned officer (NCO) died in a road traffic accident in Kuwait.

An Iraqi suicide car bomber killed four soldiers from the 3rd Infantry Division near Najaf. Throughout the country, Iraqi forces continued their attacks on supply lines. Generally, Iraqi forces would lie in wait and ambush the rear of a supply column as it moved through built-up areas.

In the north, Iraqi forces withdrew from positions around Qush Tapa and Taqtaq. A battery of 105mm towed artillery was delivered to the Bashur airfield in northern Iraq to reinforce the 173rd Airborne Brigade.

An Iraqi CSS-C-3 Seersucker cruise missile was launched from southern Iraq and landed near a shopping mall in Kuwait. No injuries were reported.

A freshwater pipeline from Kuwait to Umm Qasr was completed, delivering 625,000 gallons of water per day.

30/31 March

General Franks defined current operational objectives as follows:

First, the coalition has secured the oil fields in the south from regime destruction, which they attempted, and this vital resource has been preserved for Iraq's future.

Second, we have air and ground freedom of action in western Iraq, working to protect Iraq's neighbors from potential regime use of weapons of mass destruction.

Third, our air forces work 24 hours a day across every square foot of Iraq. And every day the regime loses more of its military capability.

Fourth, we're now staging and conducting air operations from a number of Iraqi airfields that are now under coalition control.

Fifth, coalition forces have attacked and destroyed a massive terrorist facility in the last 48 hours in northern Iraq, and ground forces, as we speak, are exploiting the results of that strike.

Sixth, the entire coastline of Iraq has been secured and her ports stand today as a gateway for humanitarian assistance for the Iraqi people. As you know, the first humanitarian shipments have arrived in convoys, and additional shipments are on the way.

Seventh, the coalition has in fact introduced a very capable ground force into northern Iraq. These forces, along with large numbers of special operations troops, have prevented the rekindling of historic feuding which we've seen in years past between the Turks and the Kurds, and these forces do in fact represent a serious northern threat to regime forces.

Eighth, a large and capable ground force has attacked to within 60 miles of Baghdad on multiple fronts, and they currently maintain readiness levels of their combat systems above 90 percent mission capable. As we speak, elements of that ground force are continuing the attack. The regime is in trouble, and they know it.

Ninth, in the past 24 hours, I have received reports that coalition forces are working with local Iraqis in the city of An Nasiryah, and the death squads that operate—the squads of gangs, regime gangs that operate in that city—have come under fire. The Iraqis in and around An Nasiryah are helping us, once again as we speak, by providing records on Ba'ath Party officials and members of the regime attempting to operate in and around An Nasiryah. Similarly, we see from day to day Iraqis coming to our forces, linking up with free Iraqi forces, discussing the past, and wanting to discuss their future.

...this military campaign will be like no other before. We will attack the enemy, have and will continue to attack the enemy, at times and at places of coalition choosing. Sometimes simultaneously, sometimes sequentially.

Let me talk for just a minute about the road ahead. We'll continue to surprise the enemy by attacking at all times of day and night all over the battlefield. Coalition forces will continue to advance on Baghdad while the Iraqi regime will continue to lose control of the country. The regime will continue in the days ahead to locate military assets near civilians, near cultural sites, near hospitals, near schools. And the regime may well attempt to destroy the

Iraqi infrastructure. We'll do our best to protect the citizens of Iraq, while the regime does its best to use them as human shields. Our targets will remain the Iraqi regime, not the Iraqi people, and we will continue to provide humanitarian assistance, and we will continue to open the gateways in the south, and in the west, and in the north.

By 10:00 p.m. ET on March 30, the USAF had flown 1,800 missions over Iraq during the previous 24 hours. Of those, 800 were strike missions with 200 aim points or targets. The rest included 400 refueling tanker missions, 225 cargo or personnel airlift missions, and 100 command/control/intelligence/surveillance/reconnaissance missions.

U.S. forces dropped 1,200 precision-guided bombs and launched 14 Tomahawk cruise missiles. More than 80 percent of the strike missions were to support ground forces in the south, north, and west. Of those, 60 percent focused on degrading the capabilities of Republican Guard divisions around Baghdad. Other targets included command/control and leadership sites in and around Baghdad.

Moving through sandstorms and harsh terrain, soldiers from the Marine Corps' 3rd Infantry Division, 101st Airborne Division (Air Assault), and 82nd Airborne Division attacked the regular army, Republican Guard, and terror squad forces of the Iraqi regime.

The 3rd Infantry Division attacked and successfully seized a bridge over the Euphrates River near Al Handiyah, once again preserving Iraqi infrastructure that had been rigged for destruction. Engineers with the 2nd Brigade Combat Team cleared the explosives and reported that the bridge was in good shape.

Along with the 2nd BCT, soldiers from the division's 3rd Squadron, 7th Cavalry Regiment worked to deny enemy access to resupply routes in the sector. During the course of the day's operations, the division captured nearly 150 enemy prisoners of war and destroyed numerous enemy vehicles, air defense weapons, and small arms caches.

The 101st Airborne Division (Air Assault) attacked and seized the airfield at An Najaf in its continuing effort to isolate enemy forces in the area. The division destroyed two T-55 tanks, 15 technical vehicles, and a field artillery battery. More than 70 enemy soldiers were captured.

In operations in the vicinity of As Samawah, the 82nd Airborne Division used precision artillery counterfire to destroy an enemy D30 artillery system. The division continued operations to secure the corps' lines of communication. In total, corps units captured more than 230 enemy soldiers.

Coalition troops seized the Hadithah dam on the Euphrates to guard against deliberate flooding operations by the Iraqi regime.

A British soldier was killed during an explosive ordnance disposal operation in southern Iraq. A U.S. soldier was killed in action in fighting near Najaf.

31 March/1 April

Roughly 66 percent of the targets struck on March 31 were the Medina, Baghdad, and Hammurabi divisions of the Republican Guard. Another 20 percent were in support of ground operations in the south, west, and north.

On March 31:

- 2,000 total missions flown
- 800 attack missions
- 400 air refueling tanker missions
- 250 cargo airlift missions
- 125 command, control, intelligence, surveillance, and reconnaissance missions.

Since the start of the war:

- 18,000 sorties flown (40 percent during March 30–April 1)
- 8,000 precision-guided weapons dropped
- 70 percent of all bombs dropped precision-guided
- 20.1 million gallons of fuel pumped into planes on refueling missions
- 24,000 short tons of cargo moved by aircraft
- 27,000 passengers moved since October 2002
- 26 million leaflets dropped.

The status of Iraqi land forces was uncertain, but seemed to be as follows:

Regular army:

- The 4th Corps had one armored, and two infantry divisions. Its headquarters and key command, control, communications, and intelligence (C3I) facilities had been extensively hit from the air, as well as its armor and equipment in moving units. It was moving towards U.S. Marine forces, with elements deployed by Al Kut and Al Hillah and some near Karbala/An Najaf.
- The 3rd Corps had one armored, one mechanized, and one infantry division. Its headquarters in the An Nasiryah area had been captured. The 51st Mechanized Division was largely destroyed in fighting at Basra. The 11th Infantry Division was badly hurt by fighting at

An Nasiryah. The 6th Armored Division had clashed with marine elements and had been hit hard from air.

Republican Guard forces:

- The Southern or 2nd Corps of the Republican Guards was headquartered at Al Hafreia (Alsuwera Camp) and the Al Fateh al Mubin Command Center. Its facilities had been hit hard from the air.

- The Medina or al Medina al Munawara Armored was the major force challenging the advance of the 3rd Mechanized Division. It had three brigades: the 2nd and 10th Armored and the 14th Mechanized. Its headquarters and key C3I facilities had been hit hard from the air, as well as armor and equipment. The unit was estimated to have lost 35 percent to 65 percent of its effectiveness.

- The Nebuchadnezzar (Nabu Khuth Nusser) Infantry Division, normally at Al Husseinia-al Kutt, shifted west to defend against U.S. Marine advances. Its headquarters and key C3I facilities had been hit hard from the air, as well as armor and equipment in unit. Its loss of effectiveness was estimated to be between 10 percent and 20 percent.

- The 2nd Baghdad Infantry Division normally at Maqloob Maontin-Mosul had moved into the Al Kut area and was fighting U.S. Marine forces. Its headquarters and key C3I facilities had been hit hard from the air, as well as armor and equipment in unit. It seemed to have lost some 20 to 40 percent of its effectiveness.

- The Hammurabi Mechanized Division had moved out of the Al Taji area, and elements that guarded Tikrit were engaging the 3rd Infantry Division in the Karbala and An Najaf area as the Medina Division declined in combat capability. Its headquarters and key C3I facilities had been hit hard from the air, as well as armor and equipment in unit. Its loss of effectiveness was estimated to be between 10 percent and 20 percent.

The U.S. 173rd Airborne Brigade completed its deployment in northern Iraq. Air attacks continued on the Republican Guard divisions around Baghdad and Tikrit. The 5th Corps mounted simultaneous attacks at Al Hillah, Karbala, and As Samawah.

Since the beginning of Operation Iraqi Freedom's ground campaign 12 days earlier, the 5th Corps forces had traveled a distance roughly equivalent to the distance between New York City and Richmond, Virginia.

Fifth Corps actions included simultaneous, limited objective attacks near Al Hillah, Karbala, and As Samawah. These attacks were intended to create vulnerabilities in the Republican Guard defenses and also to isolate the remaining pockets of resistance. The attacks were effective and resulted in the capture of an Iraqi general, an airfield, and a training camp for regime death squads.

The 5th Corps engaged the Medina and Nebuchadnezzar divisions at Karbala, as well as continuing operations to clear paramilitary forces from An Najaf, where Iraqi forces were reported to be firing from the sacred Ali Mosque.

Attacks on Ba'ath Party headquarters continued, some assisted by the local population. The Black Watch battle group rescued two Kenyan civilians who had been taken prisoner by Iraqi forces at Az Zubayr. British forces also destroyed an armored force north of Basra.

A British soldier died in an accident involving a light armored vehicle.

The maritime component continued its work and was completing the clearance of the old portion of the port of Umm Qasr and was extending efforts to clear the newer part of the port to the north.

1/2 April

Coalition air forces attacked regime targets in Baghdad and areas throughout the country. Precision attacks against surface-to-surface missiles and Republican Guard forces also continued. Coalition air operations had struck more than 50 strategic regime targets in Baghdad on March 31. On April 1, they focused on killing Republican Guard targets and hitting strategic targets in Baghdad.

On April 1:

- 1,900 total missions flown total
- 800 attack missions
- 400 air refueling tanker missions
- 250 cargo airlift missions
- 150 command, control, intelligence, surveillance, and reconnaissance missions.

Since the start of the war:

- 20,000 sorties flown
- 8,000 precision-guided weapons dropped
- 70 percent of all bombs dropped precision-guided
- 22.3 million gallons of fuel pumped into planes on refueling missions
- 26,000 short tons of cargo moved by aircraft

- 27,000 passengers moved since October 2002

- 26 million leaflets dropped.

U.S. troops rescued a female soldier held prisoner by the Iraqis. At Al Hillah U.S. Marines captured two of the Al Samoud II missiles that contravened UN resolutions.

An attack by U.S. Marines drove back the Baghdad Division of the Republican Guard at Al Kut. The 1st Marine Expeditionary Force attacked the Baghdad Division near the town of Al Kut and crossed the Tigris River. The Baghdad Division was destroyed

The 5th Corps opened the gates to Baghdad with the destruction of the Medina Division of the Republican Guard in major offensive operations throughout the sector. The 3rd Infantry Division attacked to seize key terrain and devastate the Medina Division's forces. All three brigade combat teams combined overwhelming firepower and decisive maneuver to destroy multiple enemy combat systems, including 6 T-72 tanks, 13 enemy armored personnel carriers, and 15 air defense weapons. The division's engineer soldiers, working in conjunction with the 1st Brigade Combat Team, established control over numerous bridge and gap crossing sites.

Fifth Corps units also attacked to clear paramilitary forces in An Najaf. The attacking unit was welcomed by thousands of citizens. It was also met by fire from regime forces that had positioned themselves inside the Ali Mosque, one of the most important religious sites to all of Shi'a Islam throughout the world.

The 101st Airborne Division (Air Assault) continued offensive operations to liberate the city of An Najaf and isolate enemy forces in sector. Soldiers from the division destroyed 13 air defense and field artillery weapon systems along with 6 technical vehicles used by paramilitary forces.

The 82nd Airborne Division tightened its grip on enemy paramilitary forces in the As Samawah area, conducting a surprise attack on a platoon of paramilitary forces attempting to organize north of the city. The division's 2nd Brigade captured an enemy missile cache and additional enemy chemical protective gear.

Fifth Corps' long-range artillery units combined with close air support from the USAF to destroy more 60 enemy vehicles, including 5 tanks and 15 artillery systems. In total, the corps captured nearly 100 enemy prisoners, destroyed more than 100 enemy tracked and wheeled weapon systems, and eliminated numerous command and control facilities.

Coalition special operations forces continued to target regime concentrations with the aid of local populations. In An Nasiryah, aircraft con-

trolled by special operations forces destroyed numerous buildings and vehicles and five regime buildings, including the headquarters of the director of general security. In the western desert, two suspected Iraqi
intelligence service agents were captured at a special operations checkpoint.

The land component conducted operations throughout the zone of action that ran from Basra in the south to Al Kut in the east and Karbala in
the west.

There were several successful raids against regime death squad locations in Ba'ath Party headquarters. As with the special operations forces,
these raids were assisted by local populations, who were increasingly willing to provide information against the regime. One example involved the
1st Marine Expeditionary Force, which was conducting attacks near As
Diwaniyah and Ash Shatra, just north of An Nasiryah. Approximately
100 tribal men joined with coalition forces in these attacks, which resulted
in the capture of enemy prisoners of war and weapons, the destruction
of bunkers, and the removal of explosives from a bridge—with no
"friendly" casualties.

UK operations in the Basra area resulted in the destruction of a considerable number of Iraqi tanks and armored personnel carriers along Highway 6, north of the city. Operations there also resulted in the recovery of
two Kenyan men who had been held hostage near Az Zubayr, west of Basra. British troops destroyed Iraqi artillery and missiles near Basra.

UK forces continued to secure the Al Faw peninsula and the Rumaylah
oil fields while destroying any remaining resistance in the south. Among
their recent successes was the capture of five Styx cruise missiles near Ash
Shuaybah Airport. These missiles were designed for the Osa (patrol boats
sunk in the first days of the war). They could be fired into Kuwaiti territory or against ships in the North Arabian Gulf. UK forces remained firmly
in control of the northern approach to Basra.

UK forces captured a motorcycle courier. The motorcycle and crew
had maps in their possession that showed artillery positions. The UK forces went to find the artillery positions, found them, destroyed all the artillery, and also found three Ababil-100 missiles and destroyed them as well.

The maritime component handed over the port operations of Umm
Qasr to the land component today. A UK military port management unit
will take over the running of the port from the military side.

Representatives of the International Committee of the Red Cross visited Iraqi prisoners of war held by coalition forces in southern Iraq to confirm that their treatment was in accordance with the Geneva Convention.

2/3 April

The coalition air campaign focused on killing Republican Guard targets—the Medina, Baghdad and Hammurabi divisions—and hitting strategic targets in Baghdad.

The Combined Forces Air Component Commander reported daily and total sorties on April 2 as follows.

On April 2, the daily U.S. air effort totaled

- 1,900 total missions
- 900 attack missions
- 500 air refueling tanker missions
- 250 cargo airlift missions
- 100 command, control, intelligence, surveillance, and reconnaissance missions.

Since the start of the war, the U.S. forces had flown

- 21,000 sorties
- 8,000 precision-guided weapons dropped
- 70 percent of all bombs dropped precision-guided
- 24.7 million gallons of fuel pumped into planes on refueling missions
- 28,000 short tons of cargo moved by aircraft
- 36,000 passengers moved since October 2002
- 26 million leaflets dropped
- Two new weapons systems were used for the first time in an air attack by B-52s. One system was the Air Force's Sensor Fused Weapon, a smart submunition designed to attack tanks. This submunition was delivered using the new Wind Corrected Munitions Dispenser (WCMD). The designation of the WCMD carrying the Sensor Fused Weapon was the CBU-105.

The 1st Marine Expeditionary Force isolated the town of Al Kut and continued attacks west of An Numaniyah on the east side of the Tigris River. A road runs along the northern side of the river, and seizing that location and the space between it gave the 1 MEF commander the ability to attack toward Baghdad up the main road on the northeast side of the Tigris.

The 5th Corps penetrated the Karbala Gap, the narrow area between the town of Karbala and Lake Razzaza. It was defended by the Baghdad Division and elements of the Nebuchadnezzar Division. Most of those were arrayed further up to the northwest.

The U.S. 5th Corps drove back the Medina Division close to Baghdad and secured another crossing over the Euphrates. The U.S. forces began their attack on Saddam International Airport, west of Baghdad.

In crossing through the area, the 5th Corps forces were able to seize a bridge intact over the Euphrates River that was rigged for demolition. They were able to remove the demolition, cross the bridge, and continue the attack. At this point, 5th Corps began conducting a deliberate attack toward Baghdad. They were also continuing raids against identified regime pockets in places where the regime no longer has control.

The 101st Airborne Division (Air Assault) continued offensive operations to liberate the city of An Najaf and isolate enemy forces in sector. Soldiers from the division destroyed 13 air defense and field artillery weapon systems along with 6 technical vehicles used by paramilitary forces.

In northern Iraq, air strikes were called in against the Iraqi 15th Mechanized Division.

Coalition special operations forces in northern Iraq coordinated air attacks against the 15th Mechanized Division, a regular army unit. They had communication with Iraqi divisions along the "green line" separating the Kurdish-controlled enclaves in the north from the areas controlled by Saddam's regime, and provided information to them about the potential damage that would occur if they continued to fight. Special operations forces also moved into a number of positions to deny regime movement along the road that joined Tikrit and Baghdad. There were several skirmishes in those areas.

Special operations forces remained in control of the Hadithah Dam to prevent its destruction and the release of certain water flow that would affect the down-river areas, particularly near Karbala. The town of Hadithah was just to the south of the dam. The dam was a robust structure of 16 inside and underground floors. The top of the dam was seized in daylight. There were repeated artillery and mortar attacks against the coalition forces holding the dam by counter special operations units operating from Hadithah. The coalition forces were well-supported by close air support, which enabled them to hold the dam.

More special operations raids against key regime locations continued. Last night, a special operations element raided the Tharthar Palace, a residence known to be used by Saddam Hussein and his sons located approximately 90 kilometers, or 56 miles, outside of Baghdad. The forces took fire on entry from anti-aircraft artillery. The special operations helicopter put down near the entry point of the compound itself. Aerial gunships provided some support. The raid did not yield any regime leaders, but documents were taken that would be valuable for intelligence. The raiding force accomplished its mission, with no combat losses.

The maritime component continued its efforts to keep the waterways open. Patrolling along the Khor Abdullah remained a primary focus to ensure that humanitarian supplies could come in. They searched a small boat that was beached along one of the banks and discovered booby traps on it. They also found weapons caches in the surrounding area. A tunnel complex joined these different caches to one another. Small arms, grenades, rocket-propelled grenades and launchers, gas masks, and uniforms were found at these sites.

An F/A-18C was shot down, possibly by a Patriot missile battery. A UH-60 Blackhawk helicopter crashed in central Iraq; six soldiers aboard the helicopter were confirmed to have died.

3/4 April

The Combined Forces Air Component Commander reported daily and total sorties on April 3 as follows:

On April 3, the daily U.S. air effort totaled

- 1,900 total missions
- 850 attack missions—85 percent focused on "destroying Iraqi ground troops"
- 450 air refueling tanker missions
- 200 cargo airlift missions
- 100 command, control, intelligence, surveillance, and reconnaissance missions.

Since the start of the war (through Tuesday):

- 23,000 sorties flown
- 27.1 million gallons of fuel pumped into planes on refueling missions
- 31,000 short tons of cargo moved by aircraft
- 38,000 passengers moved since October 2002
- 26 million leaflets dropped.

Coalition forces struck Iraqi Air Force headquarters buildings in central Baghdad. The first fixed-wing coalition aircraft (A-10s) were based at Tallil Airport in Iraq on April 4.

The land component attacked further into the defenses of Baghdad, seizing key objectives. Concurrently, operations continued to eliminate paramilitaries and regime elements remaining in urban areas within the zone of attack.

The 5th Corps forces completed the destruction of the Medina Division April 3 and continued their march to Baghdad. The 3rd Infantry Division continued its attack through the Karbala Gap, with soldiers from 3rd Squadron, 7th Cavalry Regiment teaming with soldiers from the 3rd Brigade Combat Team to isolate Karbala and deny enemy forces freedom of maneuver. Soldiers from the 3rd BCT also rendered more than 30 enemy armor weapon systems inoperable in a military compound in their sector.

The 101st Airborne Division (Air Assault) completed the isolation of An Najaf, denying enemy paramilitary forces access to the city. The division was able to enlist the help of a local cleric to begin distributing humanitarian assistance supplies to the populace.

The 82nd Airborne Division conducted direct action missions against paramilitary and Iraqi intelligence service facilities in an effort to secure the As Samawah area. Soldiers from the division's 2nd Brigade established positions to ensure that coalition supply routes remained secure.

Coalition special operations forces in northern Iraq continued concentrated air attacks against regime military forces in northern Iraq, maintaining effective control of roads leading into and out of Iraq and roads between Baghdad and Tikrit. Special operations forces in key locations throughout the country were positioned to locate regime facilities or strategic systems and to direct precision fires to destroy them.

Operations were conducted to ensure resupply lines remained open, especially in As Samawah and An Najaf.

The U.S. 1st Marine Expeditionary Force continued its attack toward Baghdad, destroying remnants of the Baghdad Republican Guard division near Al Kut and elements of the Al Nida Republican Guard division between Al Kut and Baghdad. During the fighting near Al Kut, three marine tanks were hit by Iraqi fire. It was not known whether the tanks were disabled or destroyed. Additionally, CENTCOM relieved the commander of the 1st Marine Regiment of the 1 MEF, Colonel Dowdy. No further explanation of the dismissal was given.

Elements of the 1 MEF encountered foreign volunteers in fighting near Al Azizyah, southeast of Baghdad. Thought to be largely Syrian and Egyptian, these irregulars tended to be somewhat more steadfast than many of their Iraqi counterparts. The 5th Corps secured southern approaches to Baghdad and captured the Saddam International Airport to the west of the city.

Two marine pilots were killed in the crash of their AH-1W Super Cobra attack helicopter in central Iraq.

In the south, UK forces continued to expand the area influenced by the coalition and efforts to rid Basra of regime death squads. Aggressive patrols in the vicinity of Az Zubayr, just north and west of Basra, resulted in the seizure of a cache of 56 surface-to-surface short-range ballistic missiles and four missile launchers.

A suspected nuclear, biological, and chemical (NBC) training school in western Iraq was investigated by coalition forces.

THE "BATTLE OF BAGHDAD"

One of the most striking aspects of the climactic battles of the Iraq War is that the much-anticipated "Battle of Baghdad" involved a series of relatively small battles rather than a climactic encounter. By the time the battle began, coalition airpower had already inflicted massive damage on Iraq's Republican Guard and other units that had actively maneuvered or fought. It had destroyed much of Iraq's command and control capability and had shocked many units into ceasing to maneuver to fight or even into disbanding.

The coalition had also achieved an unprecedented degree of "air dominance" that allowed it to fly stacks of attack aircraft around the city with a wide range of different attack sensors and munitions that allowed on-call destruction of targets with minimal collateral damage. It was able to fly A-10s in low-altitude strafing missions and use attack helicopters for urban close air support. It could also operate normally vulnerable slow fliers like refueling tankers and sensor aircraft like the E-8C JSTARS in more forward positions where they could support the air battle.

The 5th Corps' successful push through the Karbala Gap, and the weakness of the remaining Republican Guard defense, opened up the defenses of Baghdad before the Iraqi regime could reposition its forces to the limited extent it could do so in the face of coalition airpower. It became apparent that the Republican Guard had been shattered outside of Baghdad, and the large numbers of regular army forces remaining either could or would not maneuver effectively against advancing coalition forces.

This was less true in the 1 MEF area. The Marine Corps line of advance pushed through significant concentrations of regular forces and was inherently more vulnerable to attack. Nevertheless, the marines advanced with remarkable speed, given the size of the remaining Iraqi ground forces.

The sudden drive by the 5th Corps into Baghdad's international airport exposed the overall weakness of the remaining Iraqi forces and divided them, and it enabled the coalition to launch deep armored penetrations and raids into Baghdad. These "thunder runs" showed that the coalition could defeat Iraq's remaining forces, and they proved to the Iraqi defenders that the regime's claims about coalition defeats were false.

Map 3
Baghdad

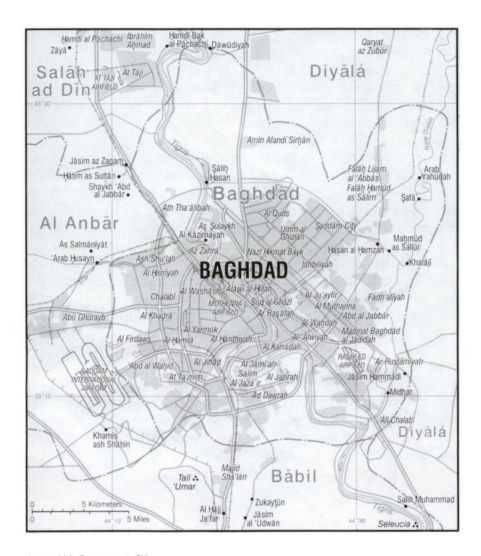

Source: U.S. Government, CIA.

They demoralized some of the defenders, further weakened the Iraqi regime's control over the city and the nation, and again forced the remaining elements of Iraqi forces into something approaching meeting engagements that made them far more vulnerable than a positioned and dug-in defense.[12]

The sheer speed of the 5th Corps and 1 MEF penetration into the regime's center of power in Baghdad, the permeating shock of continuing precision air strikes, and the operations of Special Forces and the 173rd Airborne Brigade largely paralyzed and then defeated most Iraqi resistance in the west and north as effective fighting forces.

More broadly, arms caches scattered throughout Baghdad and the country by the Iraqi regime indicated that the regime may have believed it could rely on the mass mobilization of the Iraqi people through the Popular Army. In practice, however, no such mobilization occurred. Cadres of regime loyalists did fight and presented a serious problem in terms of urban warfare in many cities in the south, but only as cadres—not as forces backed by large-scale popular support. The regime had similar cadres in Baghdad, but remarkably little popular support. Only relatively small elements of the Republican Guard and regular army forces made dedicated efforts to infiltrate back into the city to support its defense.

As a result, the regime of Saddam Hussein had little or no ability to conduct any kind of mass urban warfare throughout the city. The 5th Corps and 1 MEF were able to choose their areas and lines of attack with considerable flexibility and without encountering asymmetric tactics like mass suicide attacks or being dragged into house-by-house fighting. There was loyalist resistance, but it tended to disperse and melt away after initial defeats. The result was that the fighting inside the city became more of a pacification campaign than classic urban warfare.

One of the practical lessons of the conflict is that a tightly centralized dictatorship, with no convincing popular ideology and support, is inherently vulnerable to a strike at its center of power.

4/5 April

The air campaign continued on April 4. For the 7th straight day, the coalition bombed the Republican Guard "around-the-clock," and for the 16th straight day, it focused on "killing regime leaders" and knocking out command and control in Baghdad. Bombing priorities were "kill box interdiction"—meaning Iraqi ground troops in a particular area—and close air support for U.S. ground troops. Activity on April 4 included the following:

- 1,850 total missions flown
- 700 attack missions—80 percent focused on "destroying Iraqi ground troops"
- 400 air refueling tanker missions
- 350 cargo airlift missions
- 100 command, control, intelligence, surveillance, and reconnaissance missions.

Since the start of the war (through Wednesday):

- 25,000 sorties flown
- 29.6 million gallons of fuel pumped into planes on refueling missions
- 33,000 short tons of cargo moved by aircraft
- 43,000 passengers moved since October 2002
- 33 million leaflets dropped.

The 5th Corps attacked Iraqi forces on the approach to Baghdad and seized several key intersections on the south side of the city. The attack continued through the night, and by dawn the coalition had seized the Saddam International Airport. The airport was given a new name, Baghdad International Airport. U.S. forces began to make forays within the city boundaries.

Operations were conducted to ensure resupply lines remained open, especially in As Samawah and An Najaf. As coalition forces cleared those areas of regime presence, caches of weapons and ammunition were often found in residential areas. According to one report, the U.S. Army intelligence estimated that the Medina Division had been reduced to 18 percent of its prewar strength and the Hammurabi Division to 44 percent.[13]

The 1st Marine Expeditionary Force continued its attack toward Baghdad, destroying remnants of the Baghdad Republican Guard division near Al Kut, and elements of the Al Nida Republican Guard division between Al Kut and Baghdad.

British forces expanded the area of control northward from the main southern oil fields near Basra.

A patrol of UK forces near Az Zubayr, just outside of Basra, came upon two warehouses containing human remains in bags and boxes. Estimates indicated that the remains were of more than 100 persons. Some tatters of uniforms were in and among the remains, and in one warehouse there were pictures of executed soldiers. The remains were from some other conflict and appeared to significantly predate the current conflict. They were going to undergo forensic examination.

Major General Victor Renaurt of USCENTCOM provided a summary of the operational history to date at the USCENTCOM briefing on April 5:

As you know, we began building up forces some number of weeks ago, potentially months ago as we floated some forces in the early days of—or late days of last year with the 3rd Infantry Division. Those forces continued to build over time until we began combat operations on the 21st of March.

On the 21st, we began with an insertion of special operating forces and a strike in Baghdad by a number of Tomahawk land attack cruise missiles. Those targets were key leadership targets. We think the results were very favorable, and we're not exactly sure of the result of the leaders that were involved in that, but we continue to see disruption in the command and control of the regime.

Shortly after that, the 1st Marine Division crossed the line of departure, moved north out of Kuwait into the oil fields in the south, taking control of those oil fields and begin to secure them for the future of the Iraqi people. The key elements of those oil fields were the gas-oil separators, the individual wellheads themselves, and the objective was to be able to secure those before the Iraqi regime had the opportunity to destroy them. As many of you know, there were some wellheads that were destroyed. We have since been able to bring those well fires under control. We're down to two wellheads remaining to be secured and the fires put out. A joint Kuwaiti and coalition oil firefighting team is working on those. We hope to get the last two of those oil well fires put out within the next few days.

In addition to the oil heads that were damaged, we had a number of breaks in pipelines. Some of those were ignited. We have had a number of pools of oil that were let out on to the ground. Some of those were ignited as well. And we have since brought the majority of those under control, both securing the infrastructure in the oil fields and repairing those to be able to bring that back into operation.

[D]uring those first few days, we moved with the 1st Marine Expeditionary Force from south to north from Kuwait, and then with the 3rd Infantry Division moving from Kuwait's western, northwestern border to the northwest towards An Nasiryah, As Samawah, An Najaf, and then continuing on. The 3rd Infantry Division attacked to seize initially the Talil airfield, the town of An Nasiryah, and then to follow—with a follow-on objective of the town of As Samawah. We also seized key Highway 1 bridges in the vicinity of An Nasiryah to allow for the 1st Marine Division to then move forward to the north as they made the turn coming up out of the oil fields and continuing on towards Ash Shatra and Al Kut to engage a Republican Guard division in the vicinity of Al Kut.

I think the progress could be characterized as nothing short of superb. A lot was made about we were out there for three or four days—as you know, bad weather had challenged us a bit. A lot was made of bringing the supply lines along. I think what we've shown is that the plan was very smoothly executed, that logistics support, humanitarian assistance has flowed in behind the combat troops in a way that allowed the momentum of the fight to be carried to the Iraqis in a steady fashion with great results.

Over the five days from about the 27th of March until right at the end of the month, 5th Corps forces pressed north to the vicinity of Karbala, and the 1 MEF forces pressed from An Nasiryah towards Al Kut, As Diwaniyah, and the town of Ash Shatra, in each case, taking the time to reduce pockets of irregular forces in each of these locations, forces that were holding the local leaders of the towns and the populations of those towns hostage, if you will, and in some cases terrorizing them to the point of inactivity by any of the leaders in the town to resist.

The 1st UK Armor entered the battlefield also on the 27th of March, beginning to secure the area from south to north from Umm Qasr to Az Zubayr into the town of Basra. In addition, they expanded to the northwest to provide additional security for the southern oil fields.

And then in the north, on the 27th, the 173rd Airborne Brigade jumped into an area near Bashur in northern Iraq to provide additional combat power to the special operating forces that had already inserted themselves into Kurdish-held territory.

At the same time, combat operations were ongoing. Humanitarian aid— I mention this repeatedly because that is really one of the two great pillars of this combat operation—at the same time you're exerting combat power against a very focused enemy, you want to be able to infuse into that fight humanitarian assistance that will begin to normalize the lives of the people in the towns that you're liberating. And things like bringing in wheat to Umm Qasr, bringing in humanitarian aid over land from Kuwait—great support from the Kuwaitis to infuse that aid into the fight was noted as early as the second or third day after combat operations began.

The water pipeline was constructed and is completed now from Kuwait into Umm Qasr, up to Az Zubayr, and we now have a situation just a few days ago, a couple days ago, where water into Basra is almost completely restored. We have a few small areas [where] we're completing that infusion.

Those operations continued until the 4th of April, just yesterday, where we saw great operations conducted on a two-core front approach in towards Baghdad. The 3rd Infantry Division moved north from Karbala to the highway intersections of routes 1 and 8, just south of the city, about seven miles from the city center. In fact, you saw some of the forces that were at that intersection today driving through the inner city of Baghdad.

In addition, forces moved to the west, initially created a force to attack and then secure the Baghdad International Airport. Those forces have completed that operation and now hold the airport secure. And we are continuing to flow forces in there to reinforce and establish a main operating base.

At the same time, the 1st Marine Expeditionary Forces were attacking from the vicinity of As Diwaniyah and south of Al Kut to destroy the remnants of the Baghdad Division and then turn northwest along Highway 6 to the southeast corner of Baghdad, attacking remnants of a regular army division and a Republican Guard infantry division, destroying those forces as they moved north to establish an operating base on the southeast edge of Baghdad.

Continuing the great work in Basra and then moving further to the north, the 1st UK Armored Division has moved north through the oil fields to begin to secure more and more of those vital resources for the future, and we now have a substantial percentage of what we call the southern oil fields, the Rumaylah fields, the Qurnah fields, and some other smaller fields, Zubayr…under our safe control, and we continue to expand that UK lodgment position further north along Highway 6 to complete the destruction of the remnants, really, of four regular army divisions that began the fight in the vicinity between Al Amarah and Al Qurnah in the eastern portion of the country.

Finally, we've alluded to special operating forces throughout the operation, and I just want to spend a minute or two describing the intent of these very highly capable forces, the use of those highly capable forces around the country.

As we were beginning combat operations, special operating forces were infiltrated into western Iraq, into northern Iraq, and some areas in the south. The intent of these forces was to establish a relationship with leaders in the local area, to be able to call fires on theater ballistic missile launch sites in the west in order to protect neighbors in the region, other neighbors that were threatened by the Iraqi theater ballistic missile capability, to begin to set conditions to bring follow-on forces in to take advantage of the airfields in the west and in the north. In addition, to begin working in an unconventional warfare manner, engaging with Iraqi forces in the north that might be interested in laying down their arms and not continuing to fight. Those operations have been highly successful.

In addition to the unconventional warfare operations in the north, as many of you know, we attacked a terrorist base camp.…The intent here was to eliminate an al Qaeda and Ansar al-Islam based terrorist training camp and military facility, and potential chemical WMD processing or manufacturing plant. Those operations were very successful. It was a combination of U.S. Special Forces and Kurdish fighters, and those operations actually continue to eliminate small pockets of terrorist activity in extreme northeastern Iraq.

Finally, on a...note of success that was very visible to you all, the special operating forces, in coordination with conventional forces from the Marine Corps and the Air Force and the Army were able to successfully rescue Private First Class Jennifer [sic] Lynch out of a hospital and irregular military headquarters facility that was being used by these death squads in An Nasiryah and successfully return her to U.S. hands and on to medical care and a reunion with her family. I'll talk a little bit about that operation in just a little bit, so if you'll hold for that one just a second, I'll come back to it.

To continue to beat the drum of humanitarian assistance, we have worked to secure key bridges and infrastructure to maintain those for future use, and we begin—have begun to really accelerate the infusion of humanitarian assistance into the country.

Throughout all of these operations, we've encountered an enemy who has been determined. We have encountered an enemy who has chosen to use fear and terror and brutality as a means to push the people either to not support a change in their own communities, or even to the extremes to be used as shields to protect these fighters as they try to engage our forces. We've seen forces fighting in civilian clothes from vehicles we call technical vehicles, pick-up trucks with machine guns loaded on to them, SUVs. We've seen them stringing wire across roads that would be designed to decapitate people driving in trucks. We've seen them wearing uniforms that were U.S. or UK or Australia based equipment so that they might fit in. We've seen them using flags of truth—truce, I'm sorry—to gain a position of advantage on the battlefield, and on and on, from suicide bombings to other acts of terror on the field.

This has been an unconventional enemy, but not one we have not trained for. Through it all, we've seen prudent use of the military. We've seen professional performance by our soldiers, and they have been able to, in each case, defeat this enemy threat as we've moved on to each of our objectives.

Now, all of that happens because the people behind the scenes, the logisticians, ensure that we have the tools that we need to carry the battle forward on the field. Some of you have had a chance to listen to some of the logistics facts that we've used out there. And I won't go into lots and lots of them, but I do have a few tidbits of trivia that might be interesting for you.

The line of communication that we are maintaining open from Kuwait up to Baghdad is about 350 miles. On any given day out there on the battlefield, we've probably got 2,500 or more logistics support-related vehicles traveling on that road.

So if you can sort of imagine driving from L.A. to San Francisco, along the way there you'll see a whole—it's sort of like having a big old convoy of semi tractor-trailers running up and down that road, moving food and fuel and water and humanitarian assistance to our forces.

We've moved something on the order of 65 million gallons of fuel into the region in order to fill supply points around the area to allow our forces to continue operations unencumbered. If you throw that into a—well, I've got a little car, so I get about 20 miles to the gallon. If you throw that into my car, I could do an around-the-world trip about 52,000 times.

To fly the air tasking order that we have each day, the aircraft that are out there to support our operations, takes something on the order of about two and a half million gallons of fuel. And in that same car of mine, I could only make the trip around the world about 1,736 times.

So, to give you some perspective, the cost—the support required to keep these operations going continuously is substantial. And the work that is being carried out by our logistics experts in the field is nothing short of Herculean. There are some real superstars out there.

In order to keep our forces properly hydrated, we use about a million and a half liters of water a day. About 2 million tons of spare parts and support equipment is moved around the battlefield each day.

And then, finally, soldiers, as they say—you know, you feed the army; you have to maintain its ability to eat. And, you know, about a third of a million MREs [meals ready to eat] are consumed each day. So for that one marine out there that didn't get more than one that day, we've got some more out there coming to him and I think we've solved that problem.

5/6 April

Coalition aircraft struck the residence of Ali Hassan al-Majid, Saddam Hussein's cousin, in Al Basra, approximately 250 miles southeast of Baghdad. Notorious for ordering Iraqi forces to use chemical weapons on Kurds in northern Iraq, Ali Hassan al-Majid was infamously known as "Chemical Ali." Two coalition aircraft using laser-guided munitions struck the home at approximately 9:30 p.m. EST Friday.

U.S. forces consolidated their positions around Baghdad and at the international airport, establishing control of both the southwestern and southeastern approaches to the city, and entered Baghdad for the first time on April 5. Other operations continued at Karbala, An Najaf, and As Samawah to eliminate regime pockets of resistance.

The two-corps attack by the 5th Corps and the 1st Marine Expeditionary Force continued to isolate Baghdad, denying regime military forces reinforcements or any escape. The 5th Corps controlled the corridor from Karbala to Baghdad in the east. The 1 MEF controlled the corridor from Salman Pak to Baghdad.

The 3rd Infantry Division conducted aggressive offensive operations to secure the cities en route to central Baghdad. The 1st Brigade Combat

Team seized a palace believed to be a Special Republican Guard headquarters, while the 2nd Brigade Combat Team conducted a reconnaissance that led to enemy surrender. The three brigades combined secured key terrain, which led to the destruction of 30 military vehicles, 30 technical vehicles, three T-72 tanks, and three armored personnel carriers. During this operation an Iraqi RPG hit the track of an M-1 tank. The tank caught fire in the subsequent attempt to tow it away, and it was destroyed in place by U.S. forces.

The 101st Airborne Division (Air Assault) continued to isolate the city of An Najaf from enemy forces, allowing friendly forces to conduct stability and support operations. The division's fire power destroyed five mortars, two trucks, two weapons caches, and a host of other enemy combat systems.

The 82nd Airborne Division concentrated on conducting humanitarian assistance. The soldiers distributed 1,200 meals and worked to restore water and electricity in the city of As Samawah, making it a safer and more secure environment. Combined, the 5th Corps destroyed multiple enemy combat systems and took 30 enemy prisoners of war

A raid by the 1st Marine Expeditionary Force hit a training camp near Salman Pak. Coalition forces had learned from foreign fighters encountered from other countries, not Iraq, that the camp had been used to train these foreign fighters in terror tactics. It was destroyed.

Efforts to remove remnants of the regime from the areas of Basra, As Samawah, Najaf, and Karbala were ongoing. There were some encounters with regime forces in these areas, but the number of encounters went down appreciably while the support from the population increased. Work by UK forces in the vicinity of Basra clearly weakened the grip of the regime.

Coalition special operations forces in northern Iraq directed focused air support against regime forces in the north near Kirkuk. Some of those Iraqi forces from the lst Corps relocated approximately 10 kilometers to the south, away from what had been described as the "green line." The special operations teams, with Kurdish security elements, maintained contact with the lst Corps elements and moved forward in a portion of that 10-kilometer zone to observe the relocating Iraqi forces.

Special operations forces were positioned along several key roads, to prevent movement of ballistic missiles and deny free movement by regime forces or leaders.

British forces advanced further into Basra. A soldier from the Royal Regiment of Fusiliers was killed in action.

6/7 April

The coalition declared air supremacy over all of Iraq.[14]

Three U.S. service members were killed and five wounded in a possible friendly fire incident involving an F-15E Strike Eagle and coalition ground force.

The main focus of the land operation continued in and around Baghdad. The two-corps attack continued with the 1st Marine Expeditionary Force isolating Baghdad from the east along the Bialy River, and with the 5th Corps operating in the west and northwest and into the city of Baghdad itself. To the northwest, the attack prevented reinforcement by Iraqi forces north of the city and resulted in the destruction of an Iraqi unit composed of tanks, armored personnel carriers, other armored vehicles, artillery systems, and infantry.

Efforts to secure Baghdad International Airport continued from within the complex (where tunnels were found beneath it—some of them large enough to accommodate automobiles) and from without, where artillery systems able to range the airport were attacked, and the forward observer, in this case an Iraqi colonel, was taken into coalition control.

U.S. troops held positions in central Baghdad overnight, while U.S. Marines pushed into the city from the southeast, taking Rushed Airport. A USAF A-10 aircraft was downed by hostile fire near Baghdad International Airport; the pilot ejected safely.

Two soldiers and two civilian news media were killed and 15 soldiers injured in an enemy rocket attack south of Baghdad (April 7). The attack, against a 3rd Infantry Division unit, occurred at approximately 11:30 a.m. local time. The wounded were evacuated to a military medical treatment facility in Iraq.

In Baghdad, the 3rd Infantry Division took a suspected Special Republican Guard headquarters, while the 1st Marine Expeditionary Force consolidated its position to the east of the city. Iraqi military elements in the Baghdad area used mosques and hospitals as bases to conduct military operations. These locations included the "Mother of All Battles Mosque" in northwest Baghdad, and the Saddam Hospital, which remained on the coalition's no-strike list.

The 1st Marine Expeditionary Force attacked Iraqi forces resisting from inside populated cities. The force of nearly 85,000 U.S. servicemen and British troops have attacked enemy forces hiding in southeast Baghdad and inside the city of Basra, resulting in the discovery of five weapons caches consisting of more than 10 tons of ordnance, thousands of rocket-propelled grenades, thousands of aircraft bombs, 15 surface-to-surface

National Honors Society Gear

Women's Joggers

Quantity: _____

$31.00

S M L XL

**Navy blue w/ white letters

Men's Joggers

Quantity: _____

S M L XL 2XL

$35.00

See Women's Joggers for Image

Hoodie

Quantity: _____

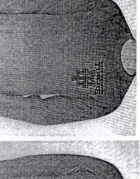

$32.00

S M L XL 2XL 3XL

Long-sleeve Shirt

Quantity: _____

Last Name: _____

**White with Navy blue sleeves; Navy blue letter

$19.00

S M L XL 2XL 3XL 4XL 5XL

**Grey with white letters

All orders due to Ms. Miceli by **Wednesday November 16**

NAME _____

TOTAL: $ _____

Checks payable to Holy Trinity High School

missiles, 13 surface-to-air missiles, 400 cases of mortar rounds, thousands of AK-47 assault rifles, and numerous crew-served weapons and ammunition. The force also destroyed, damaged, or captured 24 tanks, three artillery pieces, 31 armored personnel carriers, six fuel trucks, and six "technical" vehicles. The marines' aircraft wing flew more than 250 sorties in 24 hours while ground forces seized two of Saddam's palaces and a terrorist training camp. The force has captured more than 3,500 enemy prisoners of war since hostilities began. An Iraqi armored force was destroyed northwest of Baghdad

The 101st Airborne Division (Air Assault) continued to isolate the city of An Najaf from enemy forces, allowing friendly forces to conduct stability and support operations. The division's firepower destroyed five mortars, two trucks, two weapons caches, and many of other enemy combat systems. A Ba'ath Party headquarters at Karbala was destroyed. According to reports, one American soldier was killed and seven wounded in the two days of engagement at Karbala.

The towns of As Samawah, As Diwaniyah, and Najaf became more stable with coalition efforts against the regime. In Karbala, coalition forces destroyed a Ba'ath Party headquarters and fought against regime death squads to further reduce regime influence. U.S. troops remained in combat east of Karbala, while also conducting further humanitarian operations around As Samawah.

Coalition special operations forces continued with unconventional warfare in northern Iraq, southern Iraq, and central Iraq. These efforts were a key to facilitating operations by the air component in the north and in the west, and by the land component in the center and in the south of Iraq. More significantly, they represented the mechanism that made it possible for Iraqis to join in the fight against the regime.

Coalition special operations forces conducted direct action missions to secure the Hadithah Dam, to deny the regime the use of ballistic missiles, and to destroy regime headquarters locations whenever they were identified. They used a night raid to seize a training camp near Hadithah.

The lives of two critically wounded U.S. Army special operations soldiers were saved by a Combat Search and Rescue team that evacuated them from about five miles south of Baghdad; they were to be transferred later to a hospital in Kuwait.

British forces entered Basra in strength on April 6 despite the fact the original war plan did not call for the British to occupy the city. Their objective was rather to protect the right flank of U.S. forces as they advanced north by suppressing Iraqi resistance around the city, while monitoring the situation to make sure that the civilians in the city did not suffer. It became clear as time went on, however, that Iraqi civilians faced a growing threat from supporters of Saddam and the Ba'ath Party. As a result, Britain had already carried out a major intelligence effort and had carried out precision land and air attacks against the headquarters of the Ba'ath Party and its assembly areas. On April 6–7, they established control over a large part of the city of Basra. The old quarter, inaccessible to vehicles, was cleared on foot by the 3rd Battalion, the Parachute Regiment. Two British soldiers were killed in action.

RFA *Sir Percivale* made another large delivery of humanitarian aid supplies to Umm Qasr.

7/8 April

The main focus of air operations on April 7 was on "killbox interdiction"—continually bombing ground targets, close air support, command, control, intelligence, surveillance & reconnaissance missions. Intelligence flights focused largely on Baghdad to enable near-real-time strikes on emerging targets. Nearly one-fifth of the strikes focused on "ensuring the Iraqi military was unable to launch military aircraft."

The Combined Forces Air Component Commander reported daily and total sorties on April 7 as follows:

On April 7:

- 1,500 total missions flown total
- 500 attack missions
- 350 air refueling tanker missions
- 400 cargo airlift missions
- 175 command, control, intelligence, surveillance, and reconnaissance missions.

Since the start of the war (except where noted):

- 30,000 sorties flown
- about 12,000 strike missions since G-Day
- 14,500 precision-guided weapons dropped
- more than 750 Tomahawk cruise missiles fired from Navy ships
- 70 percent of all bombs dropped precision-guided
- about 6,200 tanker missions
- about 5,700 airlift missions
- more than 2,000 command, control, intelligence, surveillance, and reconnaissance missions

- 37 million gallons of fuel pumped into planes on refueling missions (through April 5)

- 40,000 short tons of cargo moved by aircraft (through April 5)

- 55,000 passengers moved (from October 2002 through April 5)

- 36 million leaflets dropped (from October 2002 through April 5).

A USAF B-1B attacked a leadership target in the Al Mansur district of Baghdad. It used precision-guided munitions—four 2,000-pound Joint Direct Attack Munitions (JDAMs)—to strike a suspected meeting of senior Iraqi regime leaders. The strike took place at 2:00 p.m. Qatar time (7:00 a.m. EST).

The main focus of the operation continued to be in and around Baghdad. In the east, the 1st Marine Expeditionary Force attacked across the Biyala River into the southeast corner of Baghdad. It encountered forces, including T-72 tanks, armored personnel carriers, other armored vehicles, surface-to-surface missiles, artillery pieces, and numerous technical vehicles, and destroyed them. The force proceeded on its attack to seize the Rashid Airport.

In the west, the 5th Corps remained in the center of Baghdad overnight and also continued attacks in the morning from the north and from the south, conducting operations inside the heart of Baghdad. The corps encountered a mixture of forces, including T-72 tanks, armored vehicles, technical vehicles, and artillery pieces. In one engagement at an interchange on Highway 8, resupply vehicles were caught in a fight with Iraqi forces, several of which were destroyed.

According to wire services, an Iraqi surface-to-surface missile struck the tactical operations center of the 2nd Brigade, 3rd Infantry Division killing two soldiers and two journalists and wounding 15 others. According to unconfirmed reports, 17 soft-skinned vehicles were destroyed in the attack.

Coalition forces near As Samawah continued to work in that area and the towns around it, eliminating any regime elements and transitioning into humanitarian actions. While water resupply networks were still being reestablished, military units operating in the area were providing As Samawah and Ar Rupa, located about 25 kilometers to the north, with purified water that they were generating from water purification systems.

In An Najaf and Karbala, operations continued increasing security in those areas and also eliminating any remaining regime elements. Combat operations were ongoing east of Karbala.

In Basra, coalition forces, under the leadership of the UK and supported by coalition special operations, succeeded in reducing the final remaining concentrations of Ba'ath Party officials and regime forces in Basra. The remaining pocket was in the old part of the city, and it was cleared by forces during the night. The capture of two more Ba'ath Party officials near the town of Az Zubayr, on the outskirts of Basra, reflected ongoing efforts to rid the entire southern region of regime presence and influence. Coalition special operations forces conducted special operations in the north, the west, the east, the south, and the center of Iraq. In the north, coalition special operations forces, in conjunction with Kurdish forces of northern Iraq, were maintaining pressure on the Iraqi military forces in that area while preventing their movement to Tikrit or Baghdad.

In one engagement near Arbil, in the north, special operations forces, in conjunction with close air support, destroyed a force of several armored personnel carriers, tanks, and infantry. In a similar engagement near Kirkuk, a special operations element defeated an armored counterattack, destroying several tanks, trucks, and armored personnel carriers.

In the west, coalition special operations forces continued to hold the important Hadithah Dam, denying freedom of movement to regime forces and also denying use of areas that could be used for ballistic missile launches. Unconventional warfare continued in other parts of Iraq.

Coalition maritime forces continued to take steps to maintain the flow of humanitarian assistance supplies into Iraq and to dredge the Khor Abdullah to create a deeper draft for larger ships to carry increasing amounts of humanitarian support and assistance into Umm Qasr.

Coalition forces continued to discover more weapons and ammunition stores.

8/9 April

The USAF reported that the top priorities for coalition air forces on April 8 were (1) 24/7 close air support in and around Baghdad; (2) killbox interdiction and close air support for coalition forces operating in the north around Mosul, Tikrit, and Kirkuk; and (3) close air support of special operations forces operating in the west.

About three-fourths of the strike sorties were focused on supporting coalition ground forces. The others were focused on the air component's strategic attack (regime leadership, command and control, and security targets) and counter-air (enemy aircraft and helicopters, runways, and surface-to-air missiles) missions.

Close air support in a heavily defended urban environment continued to be dangerous, and an A-10 was lost in Baghdad; some unconfirmed reports suggested that the plane was shot down by a French-made Roland surface-to-air missile. However, the coalition continued to provide close air support whenever and wherever coalition ground forces were in contact with the enemy.

The Combined Forces Air Component Commander reported daily and total sorties on April 8 as follows:

- Total sorties (April 8/since G-Day–March 19): about 1,700/almost 32,000
- Strike sorties (April 8/since G-Day–March 19): about 550/about 12,500
- Tanker sorties (April 8/since G-Day–March 19): about 325/about 6,500
- Airlift sorties (April 8/since G-Day–March 19): about 425/more than 6,000
- C2ISR sorties (April 8/since G-Day–March 19): about 100/about 2,150
- Munitions (total guided/total unguided/percent PGM): about 15,000/about 7,100/about 70 percent
- Aerial refueling offloads (through April 6): 270 million pounds (40 million gallons)
- Cargo moved (through April 6): almost 46,000 short tons
- Passengers moved (through April 6): almost 62,000
- Leaflets dropped (since G-Day–March 19/since October 2002): about 17 million/more than 36 million.

The first coalition fixed-wing aircraft landed at Baghdad airport on April 8.[15]

There was now no meaningful order of battle for Iraqi land forces. The Republican Guard had taken a massive hammering at every level and was now scattered and deploying somewhat erratically at the brigade level. There were strong indications that Iraqi forces had split up to fight by brigade and that the remaining elements of the Republican Guard were making major adjustments to defend Baghdad in small movements designed to minimize damage from the air. Some five Republican Guard divisions were said to have elements fighting in the south. Two—the Al Medina and Baghdad Divisions—were said to be crippled and to have lost well over 80 percent of their effectiveness.

On April 5, Lt. General Michael Moseley, Combined Force Air Component Commander, had described the status of Iraqi forces as follows from his headquarters in Saudi Arabia: "Republican Guard units outside of

Baghdad are now dead…we're not softening them up, we're killing them." Moseley said that the surviving Republican Guard soldiers were not operating in division formations or units anymore. "There are still some of them out there…we haven't killed all of them, but the ones that are still around are walking with a bit of a limp."

Moseley said the Iraqi military had been seriously degraded and that "the Iraqi defense" in terms of formations "doesn't exist any more." To date the Iraqi air force had not flown. "The airfields are still there" but "they are not flyable…we have killed a lot of them and done a lot of surface damage." If the Iraqis could get something in the air, Moseley said, it would not have a "strategic impact" because the coalition had air superiority. Moseley said he felt that many Iraqi air force members had "made a calculation in their mind that they will not survive."

USCENTCOM sources estimated on April 6 that the remaining four divisions of the Republican Guard had lost at least 50 percent of their effectiveness. The USCENTCOM briefing on the morning of April 7 announced that the Republican Guard units in the vicinity of Baghdad had been reduced to approximately 30 percent of their original strength. General Myers stated at the Pentagon briefing on the same day that the Republican Guards' original main battle tank strength had been reduced to the low dozens.

On April 8, Pentagon sources reported that elements of three Republican Guard divisions were fighting in small units scattered at the fringes of Baghdad. Of the 850 tanks the Republican Guard forces had started with, 19 remained. Of the 550 artillery pieces, they now had 40.

In steps that were considered unusual for Iraq, Republican Guard units were reported to have been reinforced by elements of forces from the regular army, many from units that had suffered major losses in the fighting in the south.

Iraq's regular army did seem to be dispersed but had been largely static in the north. As of April 4, it still acted as a buffer between the Kurds and Kirkuk—not a problem from the U.S. perspective—but some elements were pulling away from the Kurdish areas and toward Mosul or the Mosul-Tikrit-Baghdad area. If elements were reinforcing Baghdad, it was not clear what elements were involved or how large they were.

The regular army had no cohesive structure in the south, although substantial elements were still fighting or present in the area between the Tigris and Euphrates. They included elements of the 6th and 10th armored divisions. These forces had taken very serious damage from the air, but no damage estimates existed.

U.S. troops consolidated their control of much of Baghdad. The 1st Marine Expeditionary Force encountered minimal resistance from regular army units near Al Amarah. The marines also continued to push into southeast Baghdad. A counterattack across the Tigris that included some 50 soft-skinned vehicles and armored personnel carriers was defeated by elements of the 2nd Brigade, 3rd Infantry Division.

The coalition's operational maneuver consolidated gains in the areas south of Baghdad while continuing pressure against the regime and its remaining forces. Beginning in Basra, coalition forces transitioned to security and stability efforts. Coalition forces also continued expanding their area of influence north of Basra along the road between Basra and Al Amarah. Their efforts were focused on any remaining regime elements and transitioning to humanitarian assistance.

The 5th Corps continued operations in Baghdad and increased security areas beyond Baghdad to the west of the rivers. It also transitioned to humanitarian assistance.

The 1st Marine Expeditionary Force continued its attack near Al Amarah and in Baghdad. The marines met minimal resistance near Al Amarah from the 10th and the 14th divisions, two of the divisions that had originally been deployed on the eastern flank. These divisions had already abandoned their weapons and departed the battlefield after a period of air attacks and leaflet drops and following the liberation of Basra. Coalition forces now occupied the 10th Armored Division's headquarters and planned to transition to humanitarian assistance and civil military operations in the Al Amarah area.

As regime security forces were eliminated from populated areas, more information was provided by the liberated Iraqis. For example, after receiving information about a truckload of missiles, marines found a truckload of surface-to-air missiles southeast of Baghdad. The SA-6 surface-to-air missiles had been altered to add an infrared seeker to the nose of the missile.

In the metropolitan area of Baghdad, the 1st Marine Expeditionary Force continued its attacks across the Diyala River into the southeast corner of Baghdad and from there into the heart of Baghdad near key government facilities. The 1 MEF also proceeded along the west edge of the river into the northeast corner of Baghdad.

The 5th Corps forces continued to converge from multiple directions toward the center of Baghdad. The areas of convergence began in the north and towards the center of town. U.S. Army forces were already in position in the center of town, and both U.S. Army and U.S. Marine forces moved toward the center from the south. Large portions of the outskirts of Baghdad remained under coalition control, and the coalition was able to conduct operations with freedom of action in each of those areas.

The operations remained opportunistic and focused. There were some sporadic engagements in different areas, particularly in the vicinity of the bridges in the center of downtown Baghdad. U.S. forces were also able to enter some of Saddam Hussein's palaces on the western side of the city.

Baghdad International Airport had ongoing air operations.

Maritime operations allowed the arrival of ships carrying humanitarian supplies from the UK, Australia, and Spain. Large volumes of humanitarian supplies began to flow to the Iraqi people. The Spanish ship *Galicia* delivered humanitarian aid and a field hospital to Umm Qasr.

Two coalition airmen were missing after their USAF F-15E Strike Eagle aircraft went down in Iraq at approximately 7:30 p.m. EDT.

9/10 April

The regime in Baghdad effectively ceased to function on April 9.

The air campaign continued. The top priorities for coalition air forces on April 9 were (1) 24/7 close air support in and around Baghdad; (2) kill box interdiction and close air support for coalition forces operating in the north around Mosul and Tikrit; and (3) close air support of special operations forces operating in the west. About three-fourths of the strike sorties focused on supporting coalition ground forces in Baghdad, the north, and the west. The other quarter focused on the air component's strategic attack (regime leadership, command and control, and security targets) and counter-air (enemy aircraft and helicopters, runways, and surface-to air-missiles) missions.

The Combined Forces Air Component Commander reported daily and total sorties on April 9 as follows:

- Total sorties since G-Day–March 19): about 1,650/almost 33,000
- Strike sorties (today/since G-Day–March 19): about 550/about 13,000
- Tanker sorties (today/since G-Day–March 19): about 350/about 6,850
- Airlift sorties (today/since G-Day–March 19): about 375/more than 6,450
- C2ISR sorties (today/since G-Day–March 19): about 125/about 2,225
- Munitions (total guided/total unguided/percent PGM): about 15,500/about 7,500/about 70 percent

- Aerial refueling offloads (through April 7): 42.5 million gallons
- Cargo moved (through April 7): almost 48,000 short tons
- Passengers moved (through April 7): almost 65,000
- Leaflets dropped (since October 2002): more than 43.8 million.

U.S. forces secured all of the major routes leading into Baghdad, while continuing operations to eliminate resistance within the city. Coalition aircraft targeted a building near Ar Ramadi inhabited by Saddam Hussein's half-brother, Barzan Ibrahim Hasan al-Tikriti, a regime presidential adviser. The building was targeted with six JDAMs as part of the continuing effort to degrade the Hussein regime.

The outer cordon in the vicinity of Baghdad was completed. Elements of the 1st Marine Expeditionary Force and 3rd U.S. Division completed the cordon around, and cut the major routes in and out of, the city. This eliminated the opportunity for large forces to move in and reinforce and certainly complicated the problem of anyone trying to leave the city. By April 9, large crowds of Iraqis were free to pull down a massive statue of Saddam in the center of the city.

In the south, the first UK Armored Division conducted a number of operations in the Basra area and continued to move to the north to link up with elements of the 1st Marine Division in the vicinity of Al Amarah.

Coalition forces had now secured all of the southern oil fields and were moving through those oil fields to ensure they were secure. About 800 of the 1,000 wellheads had physically been inspected, and repair requirements had been determined for many.

Coalition forces did not bomb the Imam al-Adham mosque in Baghdad, contrary to news reports. Elements of the 1st Marine Expeditionary Force killed and captured enemy forces that were using the mosque as a fighting position. One U.S. Marine was killed in action and another 22 were injured in the fight.

Around Al Hillah, the U.S. 101st Air Assault Division continued operations against pockets of regime forces and liberated warehouses of food hoarded by the regime.

U.S. Marines from Task Force Tarawa secured the headquarters of the Iraqi 10th Armored Division, a nearby airfield, and an ammunition supply point at Al Amarah.

Elements of 1(UK) Armored Division pushed north from Basra toward the U.S.-held positions around Al Amarah. In the west of the country, the town of Ar Rutbah declared itself open to coalition forces.

Mine clearance work along the southern waterways leading to Umm Qasr having been accomplished, the focus of Royal Navy and

Royal Australian Navy clearance teams switched to the northern waterways leading to Basra.

THE END OF THE BATTLE OF BAGHDAD AND MOVEMENT TOWARD TIKRIT

By April 10 and 11, coalition forces had effectively defeated organized resistance in Baghdad and could begin to deploy elements of their land forces toward Tikrit. At that point, it was still not clear whether the U.S. 5th
Corps and 1 MEF forces would meet serious Iraqi resistance as they moved
north.

While U.S. intelligence estimated that most of the Republican Guard
had been destroyed, there were indications that up to one brigade of the
Republican Guard, along with Special Republican Guard forces, might be
digging in in the area of Tikrit. Many of the combat forces of the three Iraqi regular army corps in the north had been heavily bombed but had not
yet come under meaningful land attack, and at least some elements seemed
to be a potential threat.

Even so, most of the remaining 10 regular army divisions surrendered
or collapsed, and there seemed to be only elements of one brigade of the
Adnan Division of the Republican Guard left near Tikrit. Even before 22
days of bombing and attack, the Adnan Division was of only mediocre
quality by Guard standards, and a brigade would have had only around
50 to 60 tanks even at full strength.

Although no precise characterization of Iraq's remaining forces was
possible, Tikrit seemed to have had additional elements of the Special Republican Guard, even though these had no more strength than the equivalent of a few battalions. The heavy 4th Brigade does not seem to have
deployed its armor to Tikrit from Baghdad, but some reinforcement was
possible. Other elements of the Special Republican Guards that might
have been in Tikrit included:

- Survivors from the 2nd Brigade, which was normally headquartered
  at the Al Rashid military base and had combat elements outside
  Baghdad and in the Mosul area. Three battalions—the 11th, 14th, and
  15th—seemed reasonably well suited for urban fighting, and a few elements may have moved toward Tikrit. It was unclear whether any
  engaged the U.S. 3rd Infantry Division when it seized the airport on
  April 3/4 or the 1st Marine Division in the fighting of 4/5. The brigade
  may have taken serious losses—all forces had been hit hard from the
  air—and it probably had lost most major facilities and at least 70 to
  80 percent of its effectiveness.

- The 4th Battalion was a significant combat unit that protected Saddam's palace in Makhool in the Bayji area north of Baghdad. The 6th Battalion protected the palaces in the Mosul area. The 11th Battalion guarded the approaches to Baghdad from the direction of Taji. The 14th Battalion guarded the approaches to Baghdad from the direction of Salman Pak and Al Kut. The 15th Battalion was part of the western defenses of Baghdad.

- The 3rd Brigade was headquartered at Taji and had four combat battalions to defend Taji and the approaches to Baghdad. All forces had been hit hard from the air and had probably lost most major facilities and at least 70 to 80 percent of their effectiveness. The 3rd Battalion was a rapid reaction combat force. The 9th Battalion protected the palaces and road approaches in the Tharthar area. The 10th Battalion was a combat unit in Taji that protected Baghdad from the direction of north and northwest.

As for the regular divisions in the north, one of the great mysteries of the war is why Saddam left so many forces in place rather than rush them south the moment it was clear the 4th U.S. Army Infantry Division was not coming through Turkey. These divisions were in place near the Kurdish area and Iranian border, and they too were hit hard for 19 days.

The regular army forces were hit hard from the air during the initial weeks of the war. Kirkuk and Arbil had been liberated, and Mosul had surrendered. This had a major impact on the regular army forces that remained:

- The 1st Corps had one mechanized division and three infantry divisions. It had its headquarters at Khaleed Camp (Al Rashid Command Center) in Kirkuk City. It included the 2nd Infantry Division headquartered at Alrabee, the 5th Mechanized division headquartered at Shuwan, the 8th Infantry Division headquartered at Shuwan, and the 38th Infantry Division headquartered at Quader Karam. These forces were under significant air attack from D+3 on and then were under pressure from the land as well because of U.S. deployments in the north. Most units were believed to have broken up and disbanded by April 9. The full status was unknown.

- The 5th Corps had one mechanized division and three infantry divisions. It had its headquarters at Alsalamia Camp (Amouria Command Center) in Mosul. When the war began, it had units defending the border area with Syria and Turkey as well as covering other parts of the north. It included the 1st Mechanized Division headquartered at Makhmur, the 4th Infantry Division headquartered at Bashiqa Maonten, the 7th Infantry Division headquartered at Alton Kopri Castle, and the 16th Infantry Division headquartered near the Saddam Dam and Mosul. 5th Corps forces were under significant air attack from D+3 on and then under pressure because of U.S. land force deployments in the north. The corps commander surrendered on April 11. Most units were believed to have broken up and disbanded and the full status was unknown.

■ The 2nd Corps was headquartered at the Mansouria Alabal Camp (Al Yarmouk Command Center) in Deyala, and when the war began it was deployed east of Baghdad to defend against Iran or any attack by Iranian-backed Iraqi opposition forces. It included the 3rd Armored Division headquartered at Jalawia, the 15th Infantry Division head-quartered at Amerli, and the 34th Infantry Division headquartered near Khanaqin. These units too had been under significant air attack and recently under limited pressure because of U.S. deployments in the north. Some units of the corps had retreated and others had disbanded.

It is still unclear exactly why Iraqi forces collapsed so quickly. As the following chronology shows, the U.S. forces did not have to fight the expected battle of Tikrit and did not meet major organized resistance from other Iraqi forces. A combination of several causes—the fall of Baghdad, silence from the regime, weeks of precision air bombing, the breakdown in Iraqi command and control capability, and the sheer demoralization of a force that had lost cohesion and organized capability to resist—seem to have led to the rapid collapse of the remaining Iraqi force structure. In most cases, the regular forces were so shattered by airpower, and so defeated in political and psychological terms, that they ceased to fight.

Lt. General William Wallace, the commander of the 5th Corps, described the reasons for the fall of Baghdad as follows:[16]

> Three things stick in my mind as being important, right off the top of my head.
>
> One is the speed at which we were able to get into position to posture ourselves to come into Baghdad. The rapidity at which 3ID (the 3rd Infantry Division) was able to cross the desert and get into position—across the Euphrates and deep into Iraqi territory very rapidly—was significant, I think.
>
> The second thing that I think is significant (was), when it was clear the early regime collapse was not going to happen, the CFLCC commander (Lt. Gen. David McKiernan) placed the 82nd Airborne (Division) under my operational control. And that was significant in that it allowed us to extend our operational reach (to Baghdad) while still controlling the areas that we had already liberated.

And the third thing that comes to mind was when we simultaneously attacked (on March 31) to the east, north and west.

All those...simultaneous attacks were designed to establish our stance for the drive into Baghdad. We saw as a result of those attacks...that the enemy started repositioning into its final defensive sets in good weather under the eyes of the Air Force. And the Air Force was able to take advantage of that and do some great killing. That set the conditions for the decisive maneuver (on Baghdad), all of which occurred over the course of about two days, actually less than that, about 36 hours.

Lt. General Wallace did note, however, that the drive on Baghdad had not been without risk:[17]

I was concerned that we make sure that if (the enemy) changed his tactic that we could still continue to resupply; that if the enemy reacted to what he saw previously he might do something different than what we had seen.

As it turns out, (2nd Brigade Commander) Dave Perkins did great and wonderful work. Perkins recognized not only could he get in there but once he got in there, he was better off staying there from a security perspective than pulling out.

And so we had a very short conversation. (Maj.) Gen. Blount called me up and said, "I think we can stay" and I said, "Are you sure?" and he said "Roger. We've got all the intersections secured. We can run fuel tankers in. We can run ammunition resupply in. We've got good lines of communication. I recommend we stay." And I said, "Roger, out."

It also is again clear from the chronology that follows that Special Forces and the 173rd Airborne Brigade played a major role in deterring and paralyzing Iraqi operations in the north and the west, and that coalition airpower must also have had an effect.

10/11 April

Coalition air forces continued strikes in support of land forces, The top priorities for coalition air forces on April 10 were: (1) 24/7 close air support in and around Baghdad, with focus on the final destruction of the Republican Guard; (2) 24/7 close air support of special operations forces in the north, around Mosul and Kirkuk, and in the west; and (3) continued attacks on regime leadership, air force, and air defense targets. More than 80 percent of the strike sorties on April 10 focused on supporting coalition ground forces. The rest focused on attacking regime leadership and security targets in and around Baghdad, Mosul, and Kirkuk, and enemy aircraft, airfields, and surface-to-air missile assets.

The Combined Forces Air Component Commander reported daily and total sorties on April 10 as follows:

- Total sorties (today/since G-Day–March 19): about 1,750/about 35,000

- Strike sorties (today/since G-Day–March 19): about 550/about 13,500

- Aerial refueling sorties (today/since G-Day–March 19): about 350/about 7,200

- Airlift sorties (today/since G-Day–March 19): about 425/about 7,000

- C2ISR sorties (today/since G-Day–March 19): about 120/about 2,350

- Air and space supremacy sorties (today/since G-Day–March 19): about 275/about 4,700

- Combat search and rescue sorties (today/since G-Day–March 19): about 10/about 250

- Munitions (total guided/total unguided/percent PGM): about 15,950/about 7,750/almost 70 percent

- Aerial refueling offloads (through 8 Apr): 308 million pounds (45 million gallons)

- Cargo moved (through April 8): about 52,000 short tons

- Passengers moved (through April 8): about 71,600

- Leaflets dropped (since G-Day–March 19/since October 02): about 27 million/about 44 million.

Pockets of resistance remained, but USCENTCOM intelligence reported regime leadership and control systems had been broken through in most of the country. The deputy director of operations at the command noted: "There are increasing indications of regime-associated individuals attempting to escape the coalition by fleeing into other countries." Regime instruments were still available to the remaining elements, and the coalition continued efforts to find these instruments, as well as the regime elements, and destroy them.

In general terms, coalition efforts focused on increasing the conditions of security and stability in liberated areas and conducting focused combat operations in areas not yet liberated. The only significant combat in Iraq on April 10 was in the area of Tikrit, Army Brig. Gen. Vincent Brooks said. "The land component sent a U.S. Marine task force to attack from Baghdad to Tikrit," he reported, noting that the force met little resistance between the two locations. "The attack continued yesterday and its first efforts were to isolate Tikrit."

Coalition maneuver operations continued in Karbala and in Baghdad. A patrol from the 101st Airborne Division moved into the Karbala area by helicopter assault and proceeded to clear any remaining enemy resistance.

In Baghdad, operations continued to clear any remaining elements. There was still resistance inside of Baghdad in local pockets, and efforts were focused on increasing the conditions of stability and security in those areas. A vehicle explosion occurred in the northeast of Baghdad. That explosion, and the clearance of more than 350 mines from a minefield along Highway 8 served as reminders that Baghdad remained unsecured by both the 1st Marine Expeditionary Force units, on the east side of the Tigris River, and 5th Corps units on the west side.

The coalition began broadcasting world news television broadcasts in Arabic using existing military broadcast platforms. These were in addition to the radio broadcasts that continued 24 hours a day,

In Baghdad, coalition troops took the notorious Abu Gharib prison complex, which proved to be empty. Operations also continued to increase the security of Baghdad International Airport. At Karbala, the university was cleared of regime forces.

Soldiers of the 3rd Infantry Division conducted combat patrols in the Baghdad area, which reduced enemy obstacles and expanded the use of the airfield at Baghdad International Airport. The patrols also led to the capture of seven missiles and eight trucks with weapons and ammunition.

The 101st Airborne Division (Air Assault) encountered light enemy contact while conducting security operations in the cities of Karbala and Al Hillah. The soldiers also began clearing operations, which led to the destruction of two tanks.

The 82nd Airborne Division assessed the cities of As Samawah, Ar Rumaythah, and As Diwaniyah. The division continued to evaluate these cities to provide humanitarian assistance to the local populace as well as security to ensure freedom of movement.

Special Forces soldiers, members of the 173rd Airborne Brigade, and Kurdish Peshmerga militia entered Kirkuk to end any organized military resistance there. Other portions of the 173rd Airborne Brigade moved on to secure the Kirkuk oil fields and the military airport there.

A cease-fire agreement was brokered with the Iraqi regular army's 5th Corps near Mosul.

Unconventional warfare and direct action missions continued in all parts of the country. American and British special operations forces have been engaged for some time with an Iraqi garrison at Al Qaim, the site where Iraq enriched uranium for its nuclear weapons program in the 1980s.

In the west, special operations forces accepted the surrender of an Iraqi colonel who was responsible for the border control points at Highway 11, leading into Syria, and Highway 10. He turned over the keys to the border control point at Highway 11, giving the coalition control of that border crossing point. After a small firefight along Highway 1—the road running north of Tikrit to Bayji—coalition special operations discovered an area with five small airplanes covered with camouflage. These airplanes potentially might have been used by regime leaders to try to escape, or used for the delivery of weapons of mass destruction. All five aircraft were destroyed to prevent their use by the regime remnants.

Also in the north, a coalition special operations commander accepted a signed cease-fire agreement from the Iraqi 5th Corps commander, regular army, near Mosul. Discussions had been ongoing for some period of time and were brought to a degree of closure. This followed a period of bombing and close air support missions, and efforts to make contact.

Iraqi 5th Corps forces began to leave the battlefield—some leaving their equipment, and either returning to their garrison or simply proceeding with life as civilians out of uniform. Many Iraqi forces in the north removed their uniforms and left the battlefield to walk home without their equipment.

For the first time in combat history, a B-52 Stratofortress used a LITENING Advanced Airborne Targeting and Navigation Pod to target facilities at an airfield in northern Iraq at approximately 5:45 a.m. EST April 11. Using the LITENING system, the B-52 successfully dropped one laser-guided GBU-12 munition on a radar complex and one on a command complex at the Al Sahra airfield northwest of Tikrit.

A shipment of humanitarian aid from the Red Crescent and United Arab Emirates arrived in Umm Qasr.

11/12 April

The priorities and themes for air missions on April 11 were as follows:

- On-call close air support, SOF support, and persistent IS&R coverage.
- About 80 percent of strike sorties focused on 24/7 on-call close air support of coalition ground forces in Baghdad and throughout Iraq, ready to attack enemy forces instantly as required by coalition ground forces.
- About one-third of all strike sorties focused on supporting SOF forces in the north.

- The air component maintained persistent surveillance and reconnaissance operations over Iraq to locate and target enemy forces that were still resisting the coalition.

Coalition air forces maintained a constant close air support group over Baghdad and the north. The comparative daily and total air effort as of April 11 was as follows:

- Total sorties (today/since G-day): about 1,525/about 36,275
- Strike sorties (today/since G-day): about 375/about 14,050
- Air and space supremacy sorties (today/since G-day): about 260/about 4,900
- C2ISR sorties (today/since G-day): about 115/about 2,450
- Combat search and rescue sorties (today/since G-day): less than 5/about 270
- Aerial refueling sorties (today/since G-day): about 380/about 7,525
- Aerial refueling offloads (through April 9): 310 million pounds (46 million gallons)
- Airlift sorties (today/since G-day): about 400/about 7,100
- Cargo moved (through April 9): about 55,000 short tons
- Passengers moved (through April 9): about 76,000
- Aeromedical evacuation (AE) sorties (today/since G-day): about 5/about 110
- The number of urgent patients moved by AE sorties was less than five this day, and about 50 since the war had begun
- The number of total patients moved by AE sorties was about 150 on this day, and about 1,300 since the war had begun
- Munitions (total guided/total unguided/percent PGM): about 17,000/about 8,500/about 65 percent
- Leaflets dropped (since G-day/since October 2002): about 31 million/about 50 million.

These sortie and munition numbers include CFACC strike and strike support missions; they do not include CFSOCC sorties or munitions or CFLCC and CFMCC helicopter and small fixed-wing sorties.

These numbers do not mark the end of the war, but they do mark the point at which the United States had conducted a campaign that had effectively defeated all organized Iraqi conventional forces. To put such figures in perspective, the USAF Gulf War Airpower Survey counted the following sortie data for the 1991 Gulf War:

- Total strike sorties: 42,240
- Uncategorizable: 7,200—mostly against ground forces
- Against ground forces: 23,430
- Counterair: 4,990—11.8 percent
- 2,990 on air fields, 630 on air defense radars and C3I, and 1,370 on surface-to-air missiles
- Strategic—largely military: 3,790—9.0 percent
- Military industry: 970; nuclear/chemical/biological 990; against Scuds 1,460; against naval targets 370
- Strategic—largely civilian: 2,830—6.7 percent
- Leadership 260, electric power 280, oil/refinery/fuel 540, telecoms 580, lines of communication, 1,170.

Coalition land forces continued to secure and stabilize cities and thoroughfares around Iraq and to focus combat operations in areas where resistance continued. Coalition ground forces continued to clear and secure the remainder of Baghdad. Brigadier General Vincent Brooks reported: "The coalition is expanding areas of influence throughout the country and concentrating efforts on security and stability." Brooks stated that reports of looting in liberated areas had declined and that Iraqis were starting to work with coalition forces to provide security, to get critical infrastructure facilities back up and running, and to provide basic health and medical services. Coalition forces were receiving help from the Iraqi people in identifying foreign fighters who came into the country to fight for Saddam.

Coalition forces also worked on creating a climate of security and stability in liberated portions of the country. As deliberate operations continued in Baghdad, more information was made available to the coalition regarding remaining regime elements and also regarding the location of ammunition and equipment. The coalition received information from some of the Iraqi citizens about the location of some rockets; 5th Corps forces found five mobile launchers and one Al Samoud missile. Additional forces were added to the effort to clear Baghdad with the arrival of the 101st Airborne Division.

Coalition governments identified a list of 55 key regime leaders who must be pursued and brought to justice; the individuals could be pursued, killed, or captured.

The regime's presidential scientific adviser, Amir Hamudi Hasan al-Sadi, surrendered to coalition troops in Baghdad.

The land component continued its attack to defeat any remaining forces north of Baghdad. U.S. Marines encountered sporadic resistance on April 11 as they moved into Tikrit. The Marines entered the city easily and were extending their control. They secured the presidential palace and began the search for regime supporters. Coalition forces surrounded Tikrit to prevent Saddam's henchmen from escaping.

In the north, ground forces and Special Forces worked to secure Kirkuk and Mosul and degrade regime forces in and near Tikrit. This work included the beginning of securing the northern oil fields.

The situation in northern Iraq changed quickly as coalition forces, supported by Kurdish forces, moved into areas vacated by the Iraqi military. Significant increases in the number of Special Forces detachments in the area of Mosul in the North made it possible for U.S. military personnel to meet with local leaders and set additional conditions for stability. A neighborhood watch system went into effect in Mosul, and the presence of coalition forces there contributed to stability. Wholesale capitulations occurred, and effective military forces were not encountered in that area.

Coalition special operations forces and the 173rd Airborne Brigade continued efforts to increase the number of oil field structures that were secured. They were receiving assistance from local oil experts as these facilities were assessed.

Elements of the U.S. Army's 173rd Airborne Brigade and the 26th Marine Expeditionary Unit reinforced the special operations forces in the north. The 173rd was normally based in Vicenza, Italy, and the 26th at Camp Lejeune, North Carolina.

Coalition special operations forces expanded their contacts in the northern cities of Mosul, Arbil, and Kirkuk. Coalition forces completely secured the northern oil fields. Specialists checked the fields for regime sabotage and unexploded ordnance.

In the west, at Al Qa'im, coalition special operations forces continued their work in and around that area. They entered and searched a number of facilities, including a train station, an air defense headquarters, a phosphate plant, a cement factory, and a water treatment plant. They found two drones at the phosphate plant.

Coalition special operations forces also entered Al Asad Airfield. The airfield had been subjected to coalition attacks before, and 15 fixed-wing fighter aircraft were found hidden on the ground underneath camouflage and in what appeared to be undamaged condition.

At a checkpoint in the west, coalition special operations forces stopped a bus with 59 military-aged men traveling west. Among their possessions were letters offering financial rewards for killing American soldiers and

U.S.$630,000 in 100-dollar bills. The men and all of their possessions were taken into coalition control.

Coalition maneuver operations focused on increasing stability south of Baghdad to enable humanitarian assistance and on conducting combat operations to clear zones within Baghdad. The 5th Corps and 1 MEF forces expanded into new areas and there was a significant increase in the southern area because of the addition of one more unit—the 101st Airborne Division. Some pockets of resistance were encountered and were defeated.

In other areas, the coalition continued its operational maneuver in the area of Al Amarah in the east, where UK forces and coalition U.S. forces were moving toward one another to link up. There were still indications of a regime presence in the area of Al Kut, just to the northwest.

Coalition forces continued operations in Baghdad to improve security to allow humanitarian aid deliveries.

U.S. Marines discovered 310 suicide-bomber vests at an unspecified location in Baghdad on April 11. One hundred sixty of the vests contained ball bearings and were engineered with explosives. The remaining vests did not contain ball bearings. Sixty of the vests were made of black leather and were designed to be worn over clothing.

Coalition ground and sea forces maintained security on the Al Faw peninsula, the port at Umm Qasar, and in Basra and in the southern oil fields. 1(UK) Armored Division and U.S. Marines continued work to link the secured areas around Basra and Al Amarah.

Australian forces commenced Operation Baghdad Assist to help deliver medical supplies to the city.

12/13 April

U.S. and coalition troops searched for and eliminated pockets of Saddam-regime diehards while providing humanitarian relief to the Iraqi people. Marine forces in the Al Kut area searched for remaining Iraqi forces. U.S. and coalition troops continued attacks to defeat remaining enemy forces north of Baghdad, and U.S. troops combed the city for regime holdovers.

An Australian C-130 flew medical supplies into Baghdad International Airport.

In Basra, local police patrols resumed under the close supervision of British troops.

Members of the 1st Marine Expeditionary Force returned seven U.S. service members to the coalition. They were found in the vicinity of Samarra.

More countries provided humanitarian aid, such as a delivery of 50,000 tons of wheat to Umm Qasr by an Australian ship. The United Arab Emirates was providing 70 metric tons of food, water, and medical supplies. Assessments were ongoing throughout the liberated portions of Iraq to reestablish the country's infrastructure in partnership with the Iraqi people. For instance, efforts were under way in Umm Qasr to get the railway system back on track, as a rejuvenated Iraqi railroad was one of the ways to move supplies north toward An Nasiryah and beyond. U.S. and coalition battle plans had deliberately avoided destruction of Iraq's railroad system to ensure it would be ready for use after hostilities.

Coalition ships now had more than 60,000 men and women and 140 ships in the region. Aircraft flying from U.S. carriers had flown more than 7,000 sorties in support of Operation Iraqi Freedom as part of the air component command power projection mission. Maritime patrol aircraft, P-3s principally, had provided intelligence, surveillance, and reconnaissance of the battlefield forward into Iraq and over Baghdad. Since Operation Iraqi Freedom began on March 19, U.S. and UK ships had fired more than 800 Tomahawk missiles.

THE END OF THE CONFLICT AND FIRST EFFORTS AT THE TRANSITION TO NATION BUILDING

By April 13, the last remnants of organized resistance by main Iraqi units were fading and Saddam Hussein's regime had lost control over every major town in Iraq. It is not clear why no meaningful defense of Tikrit took place, but few cities in Iraq were more of a "free fire zone" for attack:

- Tikrit had a number of bunkers and a tunnel network. At the same time, it had been steadily bombed, and it had poor urban geography to defend.
- It was long and narrow, with little defensive depth.
- It had been given so much money that its streets were often wide and open.
- The main palace complex was totally outside the city with no defensive shield in terms of civilian areas. The palaces inside the city were wide open.
- There were three airports on the outskirts that had to be defended.
- It had many major equipment and storage centers and command and control facilities, but these too had been hit from the air.
- There were many major routes into the city or just north and south of it, and a bridge crossed the Tigris from the east in its center.
- A major four-lane bypass passed by the city on the west, allowing easy movement without entering the city.

■ The terrain was relatively trafficable off-road all around the city.

In any case, there was no formal regime surrender, and no smooth transition from war to peace. If anything, war with Iraqi forces faded into peacemaking duties and dealing with Iraq's divided factions while simultaneously attempting to deal with humanitarian concerns and nation building.

As was the case in the Balkans and Afghanistan, that transition proved much harder to make than the United States and its coalition allies had planned for. This in part was a result of the lack of manpower and force size that was forced upon the coalition by Turkey's decision not to base U.S. and British forces. In part it was also a result of calculations that estimated that far more of Iraq would see the coalition as a liberator and that more urban services and police forces would stay intact. And in part it was the result of a failure to plan for the need to simultaneously fight urban warfare and establish order and security.

13/14 April

Commanding General Tommy Franks said that no towns remained under Iraqi regime control: "Saddam Hussein's regime cannot exercise control over any portion of the country." This did not mean, however, that the fighting had ended. Franks stated he was not ready to declare victory, even though the Iraqi regime was destroyed. "We believe that there are a number of military objectives in this country," he said. "One of them for sure is to remove the regime. And we believe this regime is no longer in charge. In fact, it is an ex-regime."

"The United States still must find Iraqi weapons of mass destruction, root out terrorist cells, and then move to an 'end state' where the Iraqi people choose their government," Franks said. He noted that coalition forces, in their rush to Baghdad, bypassed a number of villages and cities that coalition forces must now go into and where there may be fighting by "dead-enders." "Resistance is spotty.…We have had our people in a number of places where they have had a hell of a fight. We have had our people go to other places where we were ready for a huge fight and been greeted by people saying all the regular army people have left."

Franks stated that Baghdad had been divided into 55 or 60 block zones, and that coalition forces could expect fighting in 10 to 15 of them. He said coalition forces had "a heck of a fight" around a mosque in eastern Baghdad. In some cases these fighters were members of the Iraqi Special Republican Guard and the Fedayeen Saddam. Foreign fighters, Syrians being the largest nationality represented among them, were also present. Franks reported that coalition forces had stopped people from coming into Iraq: "In some cases we have taken them as enemy prisoners of war, and in other cases we have sent them back on their way."

Franks said there were between 2,000 and 3,000 possible sites in Iraq where the regime may have weapons of mass destruction.

U.S. forces attacked Tikrit from the south, west, and north in what was the only significant combat action. After weeks of bombing, leafletting, a special operations raid, and direct talks with Iraqi officers, they met less resistance than anticipated. They secured the presidential palace, which was undefended.

Forces turned their attention to stability operations, moving to secure power stations, water facilities, and hospitals. Coalition engineers were meeting at all levels with Iraqi utility workers to restore services throughout Iraq.

Coalition forces secured all of the northern oil fields and worked with indigenous oil workers and firefighters on needed repair work. Northern fields were in better shape than those in the south. All fires in the south were out, however. One well in the north was still burning.

Village and city officials in some places worked with coalition forces to help restore their areas. For example, the Iraqis were helping coalition forces to identify the Saddam Hussein loyalists, and they were working to establish safety patrols. They were also working with civil affairs experts to fix electricity, water, and sewage systems.

USCENTCOM described Syrian and other foreign fighters as using terrorist tactics, stating that they "are at the very best mercenaries who have been paid to come into Iraq." There was no good estimate of how many of these well-armed and violent young men had made their way into Iraq. The greatest number were Syrians, however, and Iraqi intelligence services were believed to have recruited in Syria. Up to 80 suicide-bomber vests from the cache discovered on April 11–12 remained unaccounted for.

Joint patrols and about 200 police volunteers started patrolling Basra. In other areas, tribal leaders were establishing coalitions of tribes. In Karbala, a local police force had 200-plus volunteers, uniforms, and 10 marked police vehicles.

14/15 April

Major military operations ended on April 14. Pentagon spokeswoman Victoria Clarke stated, "The regime is at its end and its leaders are either dead, surrendered, or on the run." She gave a report on progress on the eight objectives set for the war:

- The first objective was to eliminate the regime of Saddam Hussein. "Most of the country is now free of the regime's influence," Clarke said.

- The second objective was to capture, kill, or drive out terrorists and terrorist organizations sheltering in Iraq. Clarke said that with the fall of Saddam, terrorists lost their largest state sponsor.

- The third objective was to collect intelligence on terrorist networks. Clarke said that as stability returned, Iraqis were coming to the coalition with information on those groups. Military intelligence personnel were also sorting through captured papers for information.

- The fourth and fifth objectives were to collect intelligence on weapons of mass destruction and to oversee their destruction. "We've begun the long process of exploring sites, sifting through documents, and encouraging Iraqis to come forward with information," Clarke said.

- The sixth objective was to secure Iraqi oil fields. Coalition forces secured the southern oil fields soon after entering the country on March 19, and coalition special operations forces, supported by conventional forces, secured the northern oil fields around Tikrit the previous week.

- The seventh objective was to end the UN sanctions against Iraq and begin sending humanitarian aid to the country. Clarke said President Bush and Prime Minister Tony Blair had asked the United Nations to rescind the sanctions imposed following the 1991 Gulf War. Clarke said aid from any number of countries was beginning to flow into Iraq.

- Finally, the eighth objective was to help the Iraqi people establish a representative government that does not threaten its neighbors. "We are working with clerics, tribal leaders, and ordinary Iraqis," Clarke said. "Many will meet tomorrow in An Nasiryah to discuss the future of Iraq and the Iraqi interim authority."

Coalition air sorties over Iraq had decreased over the last few days to about 700 to 800 sorties per day. Air forces had dropped less than 200 precision-guided munitions in the past 24 hours to support operations on the ground. April 14 was the last day that aircraft from all five carrier battle groups would fly missions into Iraq.

The marine task force that moved from Baghdad to attack Tikrit met little resistance in the town of Ba'qubah on the east side of the Tigris River and the town of Samarra along the Tigris River further to the west. The attack continued, and first efforts were made to isolate Tikrit from the south, from the west, and also from the north, as well as a key bridge in the center of town that crossed the Tigris River. The marine forces entered Tikrit, secured the presidential palace, and began the search for any remaining regime supporters. This was the only significant combat action that occurred within the last 24 hours.

Operations continued in northern Iraq to extend the area controlled by coalition forces around Arbil, Mosul, and Kirkuk. Emergency supplies of fresh water were delivered around Kirkuk, pending the recommissioning of water infrastructure. Special operations forces expanded contacts with local leaders throughout the country, particularly in the north and the west. Coalition presence in the northern areas of Mosul, Arbil, and Kirkuk was reinforced by the increasing commitment of the 173rd Airborne Brigade and also by the arrival of the 26th Marine Expeditionary Unit. Operations remained focused on locating regime leaders and searching key regime facilities.

Special operations forces and conventional forces expanded throughout the northern oil fields and secured all of them. Assessments continued with the active cooperation of Iraqi oil workers. The remaining fire in the southern oil field was extinguished, and all oil fields within Iraq now fell within areas secured by the coalition. One well fire was still burning in the north.

Special operations forces near Hadithah Dam, the location of intense combat in recent weeks, met with oil workers and fire fighters to organize an effort to extinguish an oil stabilization plant fire that was triggered by the regime over a week. Close cooperation between the coalition and Iraqis resulted in the fire being extinguished.

Electric power and water remained the key needs, and coalition forces continued to provide humanitarian support wherever possible. Coalition land forces actively engaged in setting the conditions for a stable Iraq. Among the challenges were disposing of all the matériel of war purchased and stored by the regime for use in the defense of Baghdad. As coalition forces moved to secure more power stations, water facilities, and hospitals in several zones of the city, they often uncovered or were guided to significant amounts of ammunition, weapons, aircraft, and vehicles used by the regime.

In one example, coalition forces found 12 surface-to-air missiles and six VIP helicopters near a Ba'ath Party headquarters building. Other examples included 51 Iraqi trucks loaded with ammunition and several buildings and bunkers loaded with many more truckloads worth of ammunition that needed to be moved and disposed of, including artillery ammunition, tank ammunition, and missiles.

In Baghdad, coalition experts examined the power plant that services all of western and southern Baghdad and also the water treatment plant in the south of Baghdad that provides safe water to the communities. Coalition military engineers met with senior Iraqi power industry officials and electrical engineers to find the best way to restore power to the city. Meetings like this happened at lower levels as well with military civil affairs teams or operational commanders throughout the country in places where the lack of power undermined the supply of water and put the population at risk.

The United States announced that two carrier battle groups centered around the USS *Constellation* and *Kitty Hawk* would leave the area. This left three carrier battle groups in the region: the USS *Nimitz, Harry S. Truman,* and *Theodore Roosevelt.* It was also announced that Gen. Tommy Franks was looking at ground-based air assets now that the need for strike aircraft had diminished, and that the mix of land forces would change: as more of the country became stable, more military civil affairs specialists, engineers, and military police would be needed.

Since the conflict began, 118 American service members had died.

15/16 April

Coalition forces in Iraq now totaled 143,000—122,000 U.S. troops and 21,000 British forces. U.S. officials said the number of ground troops was going to go up, although they were cutting back on the number of armored forces, which were no longer necessary.

Coalition air activities were scaled back on April 15 with 1,050 sorties, 275 being strike sorties. The only category to remain constant was airlift sorties, which numbered 425. Defense officials said these aircraft were carrying not only military supplies and personnel, but also humanitarian supplies; they also flew 10 aeromedical evacuation flights.

Elements of the 4th Infantry Division were heading north to take over responsibilities north of Baghdad, relieving the marines and special operations troops. In general, the U.S. Army was to assume responsibility for Baghdad and all territory north. The marines were to handle everything south of Baghdad. While ground troops were increasing, Air Force and Navy numbers were to be sharply reduced.

Coalition operations on April 15 focused on eliminating remaining pockets of resistance and looking for regime leaders as well as on increasing the military contributions to humanitarian assistance operations. The work of clearing sectors of Baghdad and Tikrit continued.

Coalition forces were still rooting out the remnants of the regime, most notably in Saddam Hussein's hometown of Tikrit. Maneuver operations focused on eliminating any potential remnants of the regime leadership or forces within Baghdad and the area north of Baghdad. Special operations forces in the Baghdad area supported the efforts of the land component as they continued their work. Numerous arms caches were recovered. A local police force was mustered in As Samawah, and police officers conducted joint patrols with U.S. forces in Baghdad.

The 1st Marine Expeditionary Force maintained the isolation of Baghdad along the eastern side of the city. The marines cleared additional zones in the center of the city and conducted joint patrols with Iraqis. The remaining areas in Baghdad that had not yet been cleared were all suspected to harbor armed regime loyalists. Other 1st Marine units continued to secure Tikrit.

Special operations forces were active in expanding security in the northern Iraq areas of Mosul, Arbil, and Kirkuk. All of the oil fields remained secure in the north, and the oil well fire reported the previous day had been extinguished. There were no burning oil wells in Iraq.

Cooperation by local populations enhanced the activities of special operations forces. In one case near Ar Rupa in the west, coalition forces were led to a group of three former regime death-squad members who had infiltrated into the area. The three were captured.

Direct action missions to locate regime leaders and to search former regime facilities were ongoing throughout the country. In a reconnaissance mission, special operations forces found 80 SA-2 or SA-3 surface-to-air missiles hidden in a revetment within a ravine.

Coalition maneuver operations remained focused on increasing security in urban areas throughout Iraq while assessing and addressing humanitarian needs. There was a steady decrease in looting and lawlessness as more communities organized themselves with coalition support.

The deliberate work of clearing sectors in Baghdad and Tikrit continued. Coalition forces regularly found large weapons and ammunition stockpiles with the assistance of the Iraqi people. Fifth Corps forces found a weapons cache with 91 cases of TNT and plastic explosives, six homemade bombs, and 23 cases of rocket-propelled grenades, and were then led by Iraqi people in the area to 10 smaller caches of ammunition and weapons in a different sector.

Coalition forces continued conversations with former regime commanders to seek any "final surrenders," but these were not large pockets of military resistance. The military capability throughout Iraq had been destroyed or had simply walked away.

In Ar Ramadi, an element of the 3rd Infantry Division accepted the capitulation of the 12th Armor Brigade, regular army, which was stationed in that area and had been defending the main road that leads from Jordan into Baghdad. The capitulation complied with the coalition instructions to move into some sort of formation that would clearly signal that the command wished to capitulate. This had been facilitated by special operations forces that had been in contact with the commander of the formation and by actions such as moving vehicles into administrative parking, reorienting their weapons away from coalition forces, and, in this case, the additional step of rendering some of the combat systems ineffective by removing batteries. Most of the force had already been released from service, but the commander had 40 soldiers who had remained to actually guard the equipment in the garrison. Although there could still be Ba'ath Party loyalists in Ar Ramadi, clearly the organized resistance there had come to an end.

U.S. forces stopped the flow of oil in a pipeline from Baghdad to Damascus, Syria, that was in violation of UN sanctions.

British forces secured oil facilities in the south and searched for the remnants of any irregular forces in the vicinity of Basra.

USCENTCOM announced that it was establishing a number of mechanisms to do the initial checking in its search for Iraqi weapons of mass destruction. Unit-level detectors and monitoring equipment would be used to give the first indication that there was an agent or weapon. At the next level, specialized military units would examine a sensitive site in detail, using the appropriate equipment to confirm an agent. If a confirmed agent were found, it would be examined further.

USCENTCOM had organized some units to do this sensitive site exploitation and had embedded the capability in other units. These included some special operations units and some forward operating units. An entire artillery brigade had been trained and devoted to performing site exploitations in small teams, a change from its normal mission of delivering fire support.

Coalition forces worked closely with emerging leaders and religious leaders in several areas to assist in the formation of local governmental structures. In As Diwaniyah, for example, local administrators worked to create a city council, get it started, and get under way with local government. Two former Iraqi generals in that same area had volunteered to organize a local police force, and their offer was being considered. In the town of Karbala, a local leadership council was formed. In As Samawah, a local police force was formed with more than 150 volunteers, selected from the 1,500 that showed up for consideration.

Maritime components continued efforts to expand access to the inland ports within Iraq to enable the flow of commercial vessels as well as humanitarian supplies. Work was under way to open the port of Az Zubayr, where efforts were ongoing to clear away 36 derelict vessels between that port and the port of Umm Qasr. Each case required the removal of any demolitions or unexploded ordnance, clearing for mines, and physically moving the vessel to clear the channel into Az Zubayr. A group of largely pro-United States Iraqi leaders met in An Nasiryah. The meeting included senior American diplomats Zal Khalilzad, the president's personal representative to Iraq, and Ryan Crocker, the former ambassador to Kuwait, as well as retired Lt. Gen. Jay Garner, the head of the Pentagon's Office of Reconstruction and Humanitarian Assistance. Iraqi opposition leaders from inside and outside Iraq were present.

The group issued a statement that included 13 points outlining how they would seek to establish a "federal system" under leaders chosen by the Iraqi people and not "imposed from outside." The gathering highlighted critical issues for continuing discussion such as "the role of religion in state and society." "Those who would like to separate religion from the state are simply dreaming," said Hussein Mussawi, a schoolteacher at the meeting. His view was echoed in the streets of southern Iraqi cities. Yet one Shiite cleric from An Nasiryah, Sheik Ayad Jamal al-Din, disagreed. "Dictators may not speak in the name of religion," he said, demanding a "system of government that separates belief from politics."

16/17 April

Coalition special operations forces continued to be a key ingredient of the coalition efforts to deny free movement to former regime members, to secure key facilities, and to enable other coalition operations.

In the first official reaction of Iran to the situation in Iraq and to the allegations against Syria, Iran's president Ali Mohammad Khatami said: "We will not recognize any administration in Iraq except for an all Iraqi government, but we are not seeking confrontations with anybody…we will not intervene in Iraqi internal affairs.…We will defend Syria, but this does not necessarily mean that we will engage in a military confrontation."

The 5th Corps continued to attack to cut off regime escape routes and also secured key Iraqi facilities. Other 5th Corps elements continued to secure population centers and key roads in central and southern Iraq and supported ongoing humanitarian assistance operations throughout the zone.

Direct action missions against regime leadership or terrorist interests were ongoing. On April 16, coalition special operations forces, supported by U.S. Marines, captured Barzan Ibrahim Hassan al-Tikriti, half-brother of Saddam Hussein and an adviser to the former regime leader with extensive knowledge of the regime's inner workings. There were no friendly or enemy casualties.

The 1st Marine Expeditionary Force maintained the isolation of Baghdad to the north along the eastern side of the city and also continued its operations within the center of the city, clearing additional zones and conducting joint patrols with Iraqis. The remaining areas in Baghdad that had not yet been cleared were all suspected to harbor armed regime loyalists. Other 1st Marine Expeditionary Force units continued to secure Tikrit. UK forces secured oil facilities in Al Qurnah and searched for the remnants of any irregular forces in the vicinity of Basra.

Coalition special operations forces were actively breaking the Iraqi links to terrorists. On the night of April 14, coalition special operations forces, supported by the 3rd Infantry Division of the 5th Corps, had conducted an operation in southern Baghdad to capture the Palestinian terrorist Mohammed Abbas, also known as Abu Abbas. Abbas was often described as the secretary general of the Palestine Liberation Front, or PLF, and was also a key planner of the *Achille Lauro* hijacking in 1985.

U.S. intelligence estimated that 800 to 1,000 hardcore regime supporters or non-Iraqi fighters were still operating in the Baghdad area in small two-man or three-man teams. Direct action missions went on throughout the country to locate former regime leaders and to search former regime facilities. An Iraqi intelligence service training facility was searched by coalition special operations forces and resulted in the seizure of information and materials.

The marines found an abandoned terrorist training camp, run by Iraq and the Palestine Liberation Front, where recruits had been taught how to make bombs. The troops found chemicals, beakers, pipes, and boxes of documents, as well as three men, who surrendered.

Special operations forces, reinforced with conventional forces, continued to expand security and set conditions for stability in northern Iraq. Power, water, and food were functional and adequate in most areas of the north. Four key cities—Dahuk, north of Mosul; Arbil; Kirkuk; and Sulaymaniyah, to the east of Kirkuk—were deemed "permissive security environments," which allowed humanitarian action to occur with much greater density and activity.

The United States acknowledged that marines shot civilians in Mosul after an angry confrontation. Special operations forces with civil affairs, and reinforced by some marines also operating in that area of Mosul, went into a location that they had selected to be used as a regional coordinating center, a place "where people could come and meet and do the business that's necessary for creating a stable environment." The building was a former government building, and it had a retaining wall around it, one of the reasons why it had been chosen.

After the first group entered, another group of marines joined them and encountered a very large crowd outside of the complex. The crowd was "violent" upon their arrival, throwing rocks at the marines, hitting them with their elbows and fists and spitting on them as they entered the complex. The marines entered the complex and took up their positions to secure the work that was ongoing inside of the complex.

The crowd later became more incensed and agitated. An ambulance arrived that had loudspeakers on it. The coalition also had a vehicle with loudspeakers, trying to calm the crowd. The ambulance arrived to incense the crowd. The crowd became more agitated, turned over a civilian vehicle, and set it on fire in the streets. The crowd's actions became increasingly violent.

The coalition special operations forces and marines observed men with weapons in and amongst the crowd who were firing in the air. It was not aimed fire. Warning shots were fired by coalition forces into a field beyond where the crowd was forming. Thereafter, aimed fire was directed at the marines and special operations forces in the complex. Aimed fire was returned against some of the demonstrators who were climbing over the wall of the compound. The attack occurred from two sides, and men with weapons were firing on the building during that time.

The U.S. military said it could confirm only 7 Iraqis killed; local residents said 10 were killed. The U.S. military version of the confrontation was as follows: A large crowd threw rocks and small arms fire came from within the crowd. The marines—after firing warning shots—returned lethal fire. This happened as they tried to secure Ba'ath Party headquarters. The situation at the end of April 16 was described as "relatively calm."

The United States was beginning to move on the last few Iraqi towns. Bequeath, east of Tikrit, was the largest of these.

The last organized unit in Iraq, the 12th Armored Brigade, "capitulated" near Ar Ramadi. Officials said, once the capitulation was negotiated, that they found there was little left of the unit.

Cooperation by civilians in the area of Al Kut led to the discovery of more than 2,000 mortar shells and several hundred rockets in the city.

The commander of the 101st Airborne estimated his troops would spend 75 percent of their time during the next two months searching for weapons, ammunition, and documents rather than enemy troops and leaders. By this time, the 101st Airborne had shot some 3,500 rounds of artillery, nearly 1,000 2.75-inch rockets and Hellfire missiles, 114 Army tactical missiles, and more than 40,000 rounds of Apache and

Kiowa machine-gun ammunition in close combat. It had also had 150 sorties of close air support and tons of other supplies. Three of its soldiers had been killed in combat and 79 wounded.[18]

The first elements of the high-technology 4th Infantry Division arrived north of Baghdad. The last elements were still arriving in Kuwait. The division was spread out over 300 miles. It included about 21,000 soldiers and was part of a larger Ironhorse Task Force that totaled about 30,000.

Civilian experts recruited by the United States to hunt for unconventional weapons in Iraq said bureaucratic confusion and infighting had delayed their efforts to a point that the search itself might be compromised. "They're going to blow it," one would-be inspector said. "That's the concern of a number of us."

At this point, all coalition land units were conducting humanitarian assistance assessments throughout their areas. Coalition forces reported that looting had been dramatically reduced throughout the area of operations.

Loudspeaker teams and radio broadcasts helped to discourage looting as well as reduce tolerance of looters. Emerging leaders joined in the call for looting to cease.

Coalition land component units continued several meetings with the Iraqi leaders regarding critical needs and issues. In a number of areas, control of infrastructure and the organs of governance were put back in the hands of the Iraqi people. In Al Amarah, for example, the local population was in control of most of the institutions, as was already the case in Arbil in northern Iraq.

Power remained the root issue for many humanitarian challenges within Iraq, whether for producing fresh water, or allowing hospitals to function at full capacity, or enabling certain types of infrastructure repair. The coalition continued to distribute water supplies and assistance in Iraq. The water system in Basra was functioning at about 60 percent of the needed capacity, as it was before the war, and work was ongoing to raise the system to 100 percent capacity in the coming weeks. In some other areas, like Az Zubayr, near Basra, 80 percent of the population had access to running water. In addition, humanitarian organizations were delivering bottled water and water by truck and in large bladders daily in that area. The water system in Kirkuk was functioning normally. Medical care and public health services received coalition support, and some facilities had already been restored to readiness.

Coalition countries and countries from outside the coalition committed health professionals, supplies, and facilities to provide assistance and relief. For example, a medical facility in Umm Qasr was being supplemented by Kuwait, by a Spanish field hospital, and by a ship-based hospital in the region. Insulin, children's vitamins, and bandages were being sent to the main hospital in As Samawah. Qatar had recently sent three pallets of medical supplies and 17 health professionals, including four doctors. A medical aid convoy and a Jordanian field hospital crossed into Iraq to provide assistance near Baghdad. Within Baghdad, water, fuel, pumps, and batteries were supplied to several medical facilities in cooperation with the ICRC.

The first humanitarian relief flight landed in Bushehr.

President Bush signed a supplemental budget bill giving the Department of Defense $62.4 billion for the Iraq War. The bill separated funding into major titles instead of giving the administration a free hand on how to spend the money:

- $31.2 billion for operations and maintenance
- $13.4 billion for military personnel
- $1.4 billion to support coalition partners
- $1.3 billion for procurement
- $502 million for Defense Health Program
- $81.5 million for research and development
- $15.7 billion for the flexible "Iraq Freedom Fund"—The report of the bill requires the Defense Department to notify Congress five days before transferring funds from the Iraq Freedom Fund. Advanced notification is also required before allocating funds for counterterrorism training activities and funds for Pakistan, Jordan, and other countries.

The Office of the Comptroller of the Office of the Secretary of Defense provided the Department of Defense with an estimate of the direct costs of the war to date:

- $19 billion to $21 billion total to date
- $2 billion a month
- $4 billion for personnel (including pay and benefits)
- $2 billion for personnel sustainment (food, clothing, etc.)
- $10 billion to $12 billion on operations (the fighting)
- $3 billion on munitions replacement
- $1.4 billion to reimburse allies (Pakistan and Jordan were at the top of the list. Pakistan was receiving about $70 million a month. The country sends receipts to CENTCOM; the U.S. Treasury sends a check.)

- $2 billion for "special pays" that service members received for serving in combat
- $2 billion to mobilize the reserves
- $1.2 billion a month for the entire global war on terrorism, without Iraq.

17/18 April

- U.S. dead at least 125: killed in action 96; noncombat 29
- U.S. missing 3
- British fatalities 31

Special operations forces captured another key member of the regime. Samir Abd al-Aziz al-Najim, one of the top-55 leaders of the regime, was handed over to coalition forces by Iraqi Kurds near Mosul in northern Iraq. He was a Ba'ath Party official, a regional command chairman for the Baghdad district, and was believed to have first-hand knowledge of the Ba'ath Party central structure.

Coalition special operations forces remained active throughout Iraq, gaining capitulations or surrenders in several areas, including Ar Rupa, Kirkuk, Al Amarah, Ar Ramadi, Mosul, and Al Qa'im.

Coalition maneuver forces continued clearing potentially hostile pockets while conducting assessments and aiding the delivery of humanitarian assistance. The arrival of the 4th Infantry Division into the land component operations area included a brief firefight in the vicinity of Taji Airfield north of Baghdad. In the engagement, the 4th Infantry Division forces killed and wounded a portion of the enemy force, destroyed some T-72 tanks, and captured more than 100 enemy fighters. The enemy force also had unmanned artillery pieces, armored personnel carriers, loaded multiple-rocket launcher systems, a surface-to-air missile warehouse, and a number of computers. The site and the materials were secured for further exploitation and examination. The coalition force reported the airfield clear of enemy forces and continued its attack to the north, encountering sporadic small-arms fire and snipers.

In the UK sector of southern Iraq, patrols were attacked by rocket-propelled grenades near a bridge in Basra. The patrols were still finding evidence of armed regime death squad members in the city, but Basra improved in stability and security.

An Iraqi-assisted discovery of five shallow gravesites near Az Zubayr was under investigation.

In other areas throughout Iraq, the coalition focused on improving the conditions necessary for a stable and free Iraq, particularly the restoration of power systems and the continuous availability of water and other services.

18/19 April

Prince Saud al-Faisal, Saudi Arabia's foreign minister, called on U.S. and British "occupation" forces to set up an interim government in Iraq—the dominant message from the first gathering of Arab leaders since the outbreak of the war: "So that they withdraw their forces as quickly as possible, we invite the occupation authority to set up an interim government and exert maximum efforts to reach this goal by establishing an Iraqi constitutional government based on the largest representation that would fulfill the ambitions and wishes of the Iraqi people in all their categories."

The Saudi foreign minister's call came during the opening of a conference in the Saudi capital Riyadh, that collected the foreign ministers of Iraq's neighboring countries—Kuwait, Syria, Saudi Arabia, Jordan, Iran, and Turkey—as well as Egypt and Bahrain. Egypt's foreign minister Ahmed Maher had earlier stated Egypt's support of Iraq's sovereignty and independence: "Egypt will not recognize any Iraqi administration unless it emanated from the free will of the Iraqi people....We look forward to allowing Iraqis to exercise their sovereign right and not to have anything imposed on them."

Coalition forces interdicted free movement by regime members or paramilitary elements by patrolling to maintain presence and security in selected locations along borders, along key routes, and in the vicinity of Baghdad.

Hikmat Mizban Ibrahim al-Azzawi, former deputy prime minister of economics and finance, was taken into coalition custody. He was captured by Iraqi police in Baghdad and turned over to the 1st Marine Division. He was number 45 on the U.S. Central Command Iraqi Top 55 list.

The building that was once the office of Dr. Riyadh Taha ("Dr. Germ") was now under U.S. Marine guard. Known officially as the National Monitoring Directorate, the building was considered by the United States to be the center of Iraq's biological weapons program.

The 10-story Ministry of Information building was in flames and apparently ignited by looters. A recording played over army loudspeakers warned people in Arabic to leave the area "immediately or there will be consequences."

Coalition maneuver forces adjusted their unit locations outside Baghdad and continued presence patrols in the other cities as well to increase security.

The 4th Infantry Division encountered paramilitary resistance along the route between Taji and Samara as it continued its move north. In the engagement, the coalition destroyed eight technical vehicles and captured more than 30 enemy prisoners. An armored unit of the division attacked an airfield north of Baghdad after images from an unmanned surveillance plane indicated that 20 to 30 paramilitary fighters were loading ammunition into pickup trucks. The fighters were presumed to be members of Fedayeen militia. No information on casualties was immediately available.

Australian commandos took possession of an airfield in western Iraq and discovered 51 undamaged combat aircraft and a quantity of weapons. The aircraft were well camouflaged and concealed; the base had not been bombed.

In Baghdad, six diesel-operated plants were on line and generating power, and the south Baghdad power plant had resumed operations In Hadithah, near the Hadithah Dam, power had been restored to the surrounding community. In the northern towns of Arbil, Dohuk, and Sulaymaniyah, there was sufficient fuel on hand to run electric power plants for more than 40 days.

The coalition assisted with medical care in Baghdad as well as in other areas. In some cases, this involved redistributing captured medical supplies. In other cases, it involved facilitating the delivery of supplies donated from other countries or from humanitarian organizations.

Coalition teams were active in discussions with emerging leaders throughout Baghdad and other areas. Discussions had occurred recently at a coalition civil-military operations center in Baghdad. The meeting covered a number of topics, including bringing some of the former police back to work and what uniforms these former policemen might wear to distinguish them as a new police force. Meetings like these were ongoing daily, and they identified interim public service employees for Baghdad and other cities.

U.S. officials predicted that Iraq's southern oil fields could be producing 1.1 million barrels a day within seven weeks. Damage to the southern oil fields from combat—or sabotage—proved comparatively light. The 1.1 million barrels would be about 40 percent of prewar levels. The prospects for Iraq's northern oil fields are less clear. Industry employees there said the widespread looting that followed the fall of the regime had affected production facilities, offices, and worker housing to the point it was unlikely oil would be flowing soon.

19/20 April

The Bush administration formulated plans to ask the UN to lift sanctions in phases. Administration officials told the *New York Times* that instead of a single Security Council resolution to lift sanctions on Iraq, the United States would seek three or four resolutions over several months. The step-by-step approach was described as a tactic to counter assertions by France, Russia, and other Security Council members that they would oppose lifting sanctions without a broader role for the United Nations than the one envisioned by Washington.

The Arab League issued a call to the "occupying power" that sanctions should be lifted once an Iraqi government was reestablished. "Now Iraq is under an occupying power and any request for lifting sanctions must come when there is a legitimate government which represents the people," said the Saudi foreign minister, Prince Saud al-Faisal, the host of the meeting.

The Arab League denounced U.S. pressure on Syria. Prince Saud said, "We reject utterly any accusations and threats against Syria; this will lead to a vicious cycle of wars and turmoil." Reading from the countries' nine-point declaration, he "expressed their countries' disagreements with allegations directed toward Syria" and "welcomed the news regarding the intention of the American Secretary of State to visit Damascus to discuss Syrian-American relations."

Syria banned Iraqis without visas from entering the country.

The U.S. Army began to take over from U.S. Marines in policing Baghdad. U.S. Army soldiers practiced crowd-control on hundreds of Iraqis swarming the Palestine Hotel in hopes of obtaining jobs with the transitional government. Shi'ites and Sunni Muslims protested against the U.S. military; about 500 people marched toward the Palestine Hotel, carrying such signs as "No to occupation."

Soldiers of the 3rd Infantry Division found $656 million in $100 bills in an exclusive Tigris River neighborhood where senior Ba'ath Party officials lived.

U.S. Marines in Baghdad guarded bank vaults blasted open by robbers using rocket-propelled grenades. One group of marines was equipped with machine guns and tanks.

Khala Khadr Al-Salahat, a member of the Abu Nidal terrorist organization, surrendered to the 1st Marine Division.

Abd al-Khalq Abd al-Gafar, Saddam Hussein's minister of higher education and scientific research, and 43rd on the U.S. list of 55 top Iraqi officials, was taken prisoner.

Six helicopters with about 58 Navy Seals and Polish Special Forces traveled 3 hours north from Kuwait to secure the Mukaraya Dam, one of the main hydroelectric dams in Iraq. Coalition forces were worried that Iraqi forces would damage the dam and flood Baghdad with up to two feet of water. There was no encounter with other forces or resistance, although there may have been some detainees.

Roland Huguenin-Benjamin of the ICRC said in Baghdad that "nothing works." "This country has collapsed. Nothing works—no phones, no electricity, no schools, no proper medical care, no transportation, nothing....It's more than bringing in food or tablets of aspirin. The basic services need to be restored and a new civil administration must be set up to answer people's needs."

British forces resumed train service from Umm Qasr to use it as an aid supply lifeline into the heart of Iraq. The train was to be a key link between Iraq's only major port, where thousands of tons of food aid was waiting, and Basra. British forces hoped the track beyond Basra would soon be secure up to Baghdad.

The United States sought to recruit an Iraqi as head of a board to jumpstart Iraqi oil operations.

Social services in An Nasiryah were slowly returning: The city's four water pumping and treatment stations were now functioning using generator power. Two hundred Iraqis were serving as police officers to guard critical facilities and provide traffic control, and the city's fire department was working and had responded to several fire calls. Marines assessed that two of three city hospitals were fully operational and another hospital was partially operational, needing structural repairs. Marines and locals devised a plan to restore administrative functions of the courts, including the issuance of marriage certificates and wills.

20/21 April

- U.S. dead at least 128: killed in action 94; noncombat 34
- U.S. missing   2
- British fatalities   31

The air campaign was winding down. The top priorities for coalition air forces were to (1) provide top cover for coalition ground forces, (2) support ongoing humanitarian operations, and (3) continue redeployment and reconstitution of forces.

Air operations in OIF were conducted on a much smaller scale, with strike missions limited to on-call close air support. Combat support missions continued but at lower sortie rates, while humanitarian assistance was ramping up.

Strike sorties were to focus on close air support of coalition ground forces through on-call CAS in stacks south of Baghdad and south of Tikrit.

The air component engaged in humanitarian operations in Iraq. So far, coalition air forces had flown six missions delivering approximately 125 tons of medical supplies to Baghdad and Tallil, two missions supporting the deployment of a Saudi hospital to Baghdad, and seven missions supporting the deployment of ORHA.

The air component was redeploying forces no longer required for OIF or OEF as rapidly as possible. The commander's goal was to reconstitute the force so the planes and people would be ready for whatever came next.

- Total sorties (April 22/since March 19): about 705/about 47,600[19]

- Strike sorties (April 22/since March 19): about 125/about 17,200

- Air and space supremacy sorties (April 22/since March 19): about 30/about 5,550

- C2ISR sorties (April 22/since March 19): about 60/about 3,400

- Combat search and rescue sorties (April 22/since March 19): about 10/about 280

- Aerial refueling sorties (April 22/since March 19): about 70/about 9,700

- Aerial refueling offloads (through April 21): 410 million pounds (60 million gallons)

- Airlift sorties (April 22 /since March 19): about 400/about 11,450

- Cargo moved (through April 21): about 81,570 short tons

- Passengers moved (through April 21): about 117,125

- Aeromedical evacuation sorties (April 22 /since March 19): about 5/about 190

- AE urgent patients moved (April 22 /since March 19): 2/about 80

- AE total patients moved (April 22 /since March 19): about 35/about 1,980

- Munitions (total guided/total unguided/percent PGM): about 19,050/about 9,750/about 66 percent

- Leaflets dropped (since March 19/since October 2002): about 41 million/about 60 million.

Two U.S. congressmen, Nick Rahall and Darrell Issa, met with Syria's president, Bashir Assad. Assad told them his government would not give asylum to Iraqis wanted for war crimes and would expel any Iraqis who cross into Syria. Issa said, "Assad went out of his way in being positive."

Marine Division elements in Baghdad were relieved by the U.S. Army's 3rd Infantry Division. The marines moved to new areas of operations in areas south of Baghdad. As part of the transition, the marines turned over the Civil-Military Operations Center (CMOC) at the Palestine Hotel in Baghdad. The CMOC directed civil-military operations in four major functional areas: electricity, law enforcement, water and sanitation, and medical care.

The Iraqi National Congress reported that they had taken custody of Jamal Nustafa Abdullah Sultan al Tikriti and were turning him over to coalition forces in Baghdad. He ranked 40th on the U.S. Central Command Iraqi Top 55 list. CENTCOM officials had no confirmation

In Al Harithiyah, the 2nd Brigade of the Army's 3rd Infantry Division discovered a primary school filled with weapons, ammunition, uniforms, new equipment, Iranian passports, flags, tents, food, and ID cards. Soldiers had been told by local residents about the weapons cache.

Sayyed Abbas Abu Ragif, a Shi'ite cleric, declared himself mayor of Al Kut and took control of the city hall in Al Kut. One American official in Al Kut said that this action was not significant because the real representatives of the city were convening there.

Ahmed Chalabi, the head of the Iraqi National Congress, called for U.S. troops to stay in Iraq until elections. "The military presence of the United States in Iraq is a necessity until at least the first democratic election is held, and I think this process should take two years."

Senate Foreign Relations committee chairman Richard Lugar, an Indiana Republican, said on NBC's *Meet the Press* that the political transition to a democracy in Iraq could take between four and five years.

Turkey, Italy, Bulgaria, and Denmark offered to help in reconstruction of Iraq. Turkish foreign minister Abdullah Gul said Ankara had agreed in principle to a U.S. request to send Turkish soldiers into neighboring Iraq for postwar peacekeeping duties. Other countries, including Italy, Bulgaria, and Denmark, offered to provide troops to help stabilize and reconstruct the country in the aftermath of the U.S.-led war.

NO CLEAN ENDING

Military victory did not mean political victory or grand strategic victory. In fact, military victory was always the prelude to a much more important struggle: winning the peace. Like the Afghan War, the Iraq War had no clean ending. Although President Bush declared the fighting was over in a speech on May 1, no senior official in the Iraqi regime surrendered.[20]

The problems of peace keeping and nation building began while the fighting still raged. Most Iraqi forces gave up, but not all. Large numbers of arms and munitions remained scattered throughout the country, and substantial cadres and cells of Ba'ath loyalists remained. Iraq's population was deeply divided along sectarian lines between Sunni and Shi'ite; along ethnic lines between Arab, Kurd, and Turcoman; along tribal lines; and between the supporters of the regime and those who had suffered under it. From the start, there was a threat of continued resistance from Saddam's supporters and those who opposed any outside or Western presence, as well as factional warfare.

These problems were compounded by the fact that U.S. and British forces were not manned and organized to occupy urban areas or to secure the country. This led to massive looting, which did far more civil and economic damage than the fighting. The United States and Britain also expected far more popular support as their forces advanced than they actually received, and they expected far more of the day-to-day operation of the Iraqi government and economy to continue than actually occurred.

The initial U.S. and British nation-building effort was badly under-staffed, and was organized far more for humanitarian emergencies than for the kind of security and economic reconstruction effort the Iraqis actually needed. Moreover, the jointness in military operations during the war did not lead to any effective coordination or "jointness" between the military forces still fighting against low-level threats and the new civil administrators of the nation-building effort. The coalition also failed to provide any clear set of goals and plans for nation building that could motivate and reassure the Iraqis before, during, and after the war. The result was to leave many Iraqis without physical or economic security, alienate many potential supporters, and fuel the many fears and conspiracy theories that Iraqis had about a U.S. and British occupation.

The nation-building effort began to gather momentum by July 2003, but serious resistance began to develop from pro-Saddam, pro-Ba'ath, and anti-U.S. factions. Low-level fighting threatened to replace the fight between the coalition and Saddam Hussein's regime. The problems in the U.S. and British peacemaking and nation-building efforts had helped lead to a state of violence that produced an average of nearly one American casualty a day and sometimes as many Americans killed per day as during the actual war. Iraqi civilian casualties also continued, although no numerical estimates were possible.

As is discussed in chapter 16 and chapter 17, "victory" had much of the character of "victory" in Afghanistan.[21] The enemy's main forces had been decisively defeated, but dispersed hostile elements remained. The inability to rapidly and decisively create nation-wide security gave hostile elements time to regroup and begin a level of hostile action that bordered on low-intensity conflict. At the same time, the lack of an effective nation-building effort created new centers of power, some of which were overtly or tacitly hostile. Months after President Bush declared "victory," it was not yet clear whether victory meant a successful transition to rebuilding Iraq or a transition to a military occupation that would have to try to create a new Iraqi political system and economy in the midst of an asymmetric war with cadres of Ba'ath loyalists and/or other opponents of the U.S. and British occupation.

Notes

[1] The details described in this section are taken largely from USCENTCOM daily briefings during the war and from online chronologies of the war provided by the British Ministry of Defense. Only minimal rewriting and editing has been carried out to keep the material as accurate as possible. One problem is that official sources sometimes did not distinguish clearly between Iraqi time and U.S. or British time. This has been corrected, where possible, but some details are not clear. In general, dates and times are shown in Iraqi time.

[2] "Interview: General Richard Myers," *Defense News*, April 14, 2003, p. 46.

[3] Much of this description of prewar activity is based upon Joseph L. Galloway, "Franks: We Held 25% of Iraq Before War," *Miami Herald*, June 20, 2003.

[4] Bradley Graham and Vernon Loeb, "An Air War of Might, Coordination, and Risks," *Washington Post*, April 27, 2003, sec. A, p. 1.

[5] "Interview: General Richard Myers," *Defense News*.

[6] Steven Komarow, "General Recounts Key Moments in Baghdad's Fall," *USA Today*, April 14, 2003, p. 5.

[7] Adapted from Lt. General T. Michael Moseley, "Operation Iraqi Freedom—By the Numbers," USCENTAF, Assessment and Analysis Division, April 30, 2003.

[8] Graham and Loeb, "An Air War of Might, Coordination, and Risks."

[9] USCENTCOM, Release Number 03-03-44, March 22, 2003.

[10] Graham and Loeb, "An Air War of Might, Coordination, and Risks."

[11] Ibid.

[12] For a good description of Iraqi attitudes and the combined impact of such runs and coalition air attacks, see William Branigan, "A Brief Bitter War for Iraq's Military Officers," *Washington Post*, April 27, 2003, sec. A, p. 25.

[13] Graham and Loeb, "An Air War of Might, Coordination, and Risks."

[14] Adapted from Moseley, "Operation Iraqi Freedom—By the Numbers."

[15] Ibid.

[16] Komarow, "General Recounts Key Moments in Baghdad's Fall."

[17] Ibid.

[18] Maj. Gen. David H. Petraeus, commanding general, 101st Airborne Division (Air Assault), "101st Airborne Division Commander Live Briefing from Iraq," May 13, 2003.

[19] The sortie and munition numbers shown here include CFACC strike and strike support missions; they do not include CFSOCC sorties or munitions or CFLCC and CFMCC helo and small fixed-wing sorties.

[20] David E. Sanger, "President Says Military Phase in Iraq Has Ended," *New York Times*, May 2, 2003, p. 1; Karen DeYoung, "Bush Proclaims Victory in Iraq," *Washington Post*, May 2, 2003, p. 1.

[21] See also Anthony H. Cordesman, *The Lessons of Afghanistan: War Fighting, Intelligence, and Force Transformation* (Washington, D.C.: CSIS, 2002).

CHAPTER FIVE

THREE DEBATES

WAR PLAN AND TRANSFORMATION, "POWELL DOCTRINE"
VERSUS "RUMSFELD DOCTRINE," AND THE "NEW WAY OF WAR"

The previous comparisons of U.S. and British forces with those of Iraq, and the history of the Iraq War, clearly reflect the transformational character of coalition forces. The outcome of the Iraq War both demonstrated the value of many such transformations and resolved a debate over one key set of lessons of the war that began even before the main battle for Baghdad.

As has been noted earlier, when the U.S. ground advance slowed in late March, a debate surfaced over charges that Secretary Rumsfeld had forced the U.S. military and USCENTCOM commander General Tommy Franks to accept much lower force levels than they originally had wanted. Some critics charged that this interference in the "war plan" had weakened coalition forces to the point where they were not large enough to win a decisive victory.

The speed and scale of the coalition victory speaks for itself. The coalition plan and force posture were not without risk, but the coalition did not need to meet traditional measures of force strength to win. At the same time, the outcome of the war does raise issues over the military doctrine the United States should use in future force planning and whether the United States can now plan to use a "new way of war" that need to be put in careful perspective.

THE WAR PLAN DEBATE

The full history of the evolution of the war plan used in the Iraq War remains a "black box." Few really know the details of how the coalition war plan evolved, and the options involved, beyond those directly involved in formulating and executing it. It is also a fact of life that virtually all war planning involves serious debates among the principals, that it is the duty of the military to advance the best possible military solution and it is the duty of the secretary of defense to ensure that the plan reflects political and resource constraints and the priorities of the president. A war planning process that did not involve such debates would reflect a dangerous passivity, if not outright incompetence, on the part of the officers and officials most responsible for the nation's security.

It is clear from personal conversations with some of the individuals involved in planning the Iraq War that some of the criticism of civilian interference in the war plan that emerged during late March 2003 had an element of truth. Secretary of Defense Donald Rumsfeld and his staff did challenge General Franks and the military planners early in the war-planning process and demanded that they examine military options that relied more on air power and relatively light ground forces. There were civilian and military clashes over the level of force required, the timing of major movements of troops and equipment, the size of the conventional ground forces involved, and the ability to rely on force elements like air power and special forces versus "traditional" elements of military power like heavy armor. At some points, serious tension did exist between the military officers in USCENTCOM and the Pentagon and Secretary Rumsfeld and his civilian staff.

The timing and nature of these debates remain unclear. Some press reports indicate that civilian officials were still pressing for force levels of 50,000 to 80,000 as late as August 2002 and that only eight major logistic ships were activated through the end of 2002, with the total raised to 42 in January 2003. Other reports claim that the ceiling was 150,000 and was raised earlier in 2002.[1] Still other reports have surfaced since the war that say the original plans called for a 20-day air war before the land war that was gradually cut to 10 days, 5 days, and then 3—only to have the land campaign begin before the massive air offensive.[2]

What is clear is that rather than present a single war plan, General Franks developed a number of options and that the debate over these options did include significant arguments over the relative balance of air and land power, the ability to rely on Special Forces and Iraqi opposition forces versus U.S. and allied heavy land forces, and the amount of logistic and sustainment resources that would be needed.

Senior officers present during these discussions note that these discussions sometimes were confrontational, but that much of the tension surrounding them had other causes. Some officers felt that Secretary Rumsfeld and his staff tended to be dismissive of military expertise. There was a heritage of tension that grew out of the secretary's plans for a major transformation of U.S. forces and various program and force planning discussions. This heritage was particularly strong in the case of the U.S.

Army, where at least some officers perceived Secretary Rumsfeld as having effectively sidelined the army chief of staff and as favoring the air force and space and precision warfare over heavy ground forces.[3]

Some officers were concerned about the force ratios and the amount of support force available at the time the war began. Measured by the planning standards of 1990 and the "Two Major Regional Contingency" studies that followed, the United States would have needed five to seven heavy divisions to deal with a force the size of the Iraqi Army, not one U.S. Army mechanized division, a Marine Corps Expeditionary Force with moderate armored strength, a British division that had armor roughly half the size of the armor in a U.S. heavy division, a relatively light 101st Air Mobile Division, and additional elements of light land forces from the United States, Britain, Australia, and Poland.

Traditional planning would have called for much stronger forces to secure the rear areas and flanks of the main land force thrusts and for more support forces of all kinds. This kind of force is still called for in the Time-Phased Forces Deployment List (TPFDL) that the Joint Staff uses for war planning. Secretary Rumsfeld repeatedly questioned the size and nature of the force called for by such planning methods, and did repeatedly press for cuts and changes in the early phases of the war plan.[4]

It is important to note, however, that this was scarcely a civil-military debate in which there was always a clear split between military and civilian views. A number of officers also questioned the need for traditional force levels and felt that some of the options in the initial planning were outdated. They felt some options called for too many forces and too slow an execution of the battle plan, and did not reflect advances in intelligence, surveillance, and reconnaissance (IS&R), precision air power, and the speed of ground force maneuver.

It may be unfair to talk about a "generation gap" within the military over such issues, as age seems to have little to do with support for change or tradition. What does seem fair to say is that at least some of the officers involved in the planning felt that the key elements in some options in the war plans the U.S. military advanced to Secretary Rumsfeld were outdated and tended to represent a lowest-common-denominator approach to military planning in which every service requested a larger force than it really needed. At least some civilians also felt that calls from some "neocons"—most outside the government—for an emphasis on air power and very limited ground forces were far too risky and based on ignorance of military realities.

It is also important to note that the war plan evolved in a climate where few had any illusions about the enemy's war-fighting capabilities, although no planner could dismiss the risk that Iraq would use weapons of mass destruction until the war was over. U.S. intelligence had clearly identified most of the comparative weaknesses in the Iraqi force structure outlined in chapter 3. While U.S. intelligence analysts saw Iraq as a potentially serious threat because of its large force numbers, they also saw grave weaknesses in virtually every aspect of Iraqi conventional forces, and their assessment did not provide a rationale for the kind of coalition force ratios that would be needed to defeat a more effective enemy.

Moreover, officers like the army vice chief of staff, General John M. Keane, had stated long before the war plan debate became public that precision air power and advances in armored maneuver capability and joint warfare created a situation where far smaller forces could be used to secure the flanks and rear, and where speed and precision of maneuver would be far more effective than a more traditional method of war fighting, General Richard Myers, the chairman of the Joint Chiefs, had made similar points.

Finally, war planning was certainly dominated by the United States, but Britain and Australia also played a role and their views had to be considered. The British Ministry of Defense described Britain's role in the planning process as follows in its report on the lessons of the war:[5]

> This was overwhelmingly a US shaped and led operation. The UK contribution was taken into the US plan where it could best complement and enhance US capabilities, both political and military. Most of what UK forces achieved took place under the umbrella of US dominance of every warfare environment. The coalition had naval and space dominance from the start, moved from air and information superiority to dominance and thereby quickly overcame Iraqi opposition on the ground. Coalition forces had technical superiority in virtually every area of combat and could operate through most conditions of visibility and weather and at night. In sum, the coalition dominated the political, diplomatic, military and economic levers. The operation was conducted at a time of its choosing, using unhindered lines of communication, without interference from Iraq at any stage up to the start of hostilities.
>
> While overall planning for the operation was led by the United States, the UK was fully involved, including through personnel embedded in US Central Command in Tampa and elsewhere. The plan evolved over time, and was sufficiently flexible to respond to changing circumstances. Since our aim was to achieve Iraqi compliance by diplomatic means if possible, it was impossible to know whether or when operations might need to begin. Despite these variables, the essence of the plan remained consistent, with the focus on mounting a rapid, synchronised and precise campaign to overwhelm Saddam Hussein's regime and its security forces and minimise the risk of civilian casualties or damage to Iraq's essential services.

Although the UK did not make final decisions on the composition and deployment of its force packages until early 2003, we were able to work closely with the US and influence the campaign from initial planning to execution through high-level political contacts and regular dialogue at official level, as well as by the presence of a significant number of embedded UK officers in key US headquarters.

THE POLITICAL FACTORS THAT MAKE THE "WAR PLAN" DEBATE LARGELY MOOT

Some of the serving officers who criticize Secretary Rumsfeld and his staff for an arrogant and confrontational approach to the military also note that it was General Franks who largely won the war plan debate. The fact that Turkey rejected U.S. and British basing of more than 200 more combat aircraft, roughly 70 to 100 more helicopters, and the U.S. 4th Infantry Division and 3rd Armored Cavalry Division had nothing to do with the debate over the war plan. The fact that the coalition went to war missing an entire and well-planned second front from the north had nothing to do with the war plan decisions made by Secretary Rumsfeld.

The same was true about most of the impact on force planning of the long UN debate over a Security Council resolution to authorize the use of force. That debate meant that the U.S. secretary of defense had to make political decisions to delay the movement of some troops and various sealift and airlift activities to avoid appearing to make the war a certainty before the UN had time to act. This same delay gave Iraq more time to prepare.

Finally, the decision to exploit a perceived opportunity to decapitate the Iraqi regime by striking at Saddam Hussein and the Iraqi leadership at the beginning of the war was a political decision that had nothing to do with tensions between Secretary Rumsfeld and the military. Neither did the decision to wait several days to begin the massive air campaign to see if Saddam was dead and the Iraqi regime would collapse.

THE PROBLEM OF NOT KNOWING THE DETAILED HISTORY AND NATURE OF THE "WAR PLAN"

Donald Rumsfeld thrives on confrontation and is not a man who solicits or stimulates much by way of sympathy and compassion. Nevertheless, his response to the war plan debate at the Department of Defense press conference on March 25 raises some basic issues about the fairness of the debate that are well worth noting:

First of all, I don't know how anyone outside of the government thinks they know what my views are, or what General Franks' views are, or what General Myers' views are. We've all been deeply involved, and the plan has been a plan that's been approved by all the commanders and by, needless to say, General Myers and General Pace and Don Rumsfeld and the president of the United States. And it is a good plan, and it is a plan that in four and a half or five days has moved ground forces to within a short distance of Baghdad. And forces increase in the country every minute and every hour of every day. And that will continue to be the case. There is a force flow that's been put in place weeks and weeks and weeks ago, where people were mobilized, people were trained, people were—equipment was loaded on ships, ships were leased, ships were sent over, ships moved into position, ships were unloaded, personnel were airlifted over to meet with their equipment. And every hour the number of U.S. and coalition forces in that country are increasing.

So I guess how I would respond to what you say are some folks who are concerned about that is that the people who are involved in this, the—General Franks and General McKiernan and General DeLong and General Abizaid and Admiral Keating, General Moseley, are very comfortable, as are the Joint Chiefs of Staff, who have met with the president twice in the last two days and discussed it.

…If you go back to the Afghanistan situation, it was only a few days into it that it was described by one of the newspapers here as a "quagmire." And it was a matter of days later that things looked quite good and, as I recall, Mazar-e-Sharif fell, and then the other cities began to fall.

I can't manage what people—civilians or retired military—want to say. And if they go on and say it enough, people will begin to believe it. It may not be true, and it may reflect more of a misunderstanding of the situation than an analysis or an assessment of it, but there's no way anyone can affect what people say. We have a free country. In Iraq, they can affect what people say because you get shot if you say something they don't like. We don't do that.

It is equally important to consider the response of Chairman of the Joint Chiefs Richard Myers to speculation on the war plan. General Myers gave the following response to questions on the issue during the same Department of Defense press conference on March 25:

…It's a plan that's on track. It's a plan everybody had input to. It's a plan everybody agrees to. I've been on public record that I think the plan as finally formulated and, as put together by General Franks with some help and some advice by his commanders, is a brilliant plan. And we've been at it now for less than a week. We're just about to Baghdad. Some of the biggest losses we've taken are due to Iraqis committing serious violations of the law of armed conflict in the Geneva Convention by dressing as civilians, by luring us into surrender situations then opening fire on our troops. So this is a plan that is very well thought out, and that will play out, I think, as we expect.

   …Well, I would say, given the fact that we're 200-plus miles inside Iraq at this time, on the doorstep of Baghdad, that we really haven't engaged on the ground the Republican Guard divisions. So—we've put helicopters against them, attack helicopters, we've put air against them, we've put some artillery against them, but we haven't engaged them in a classic battle. So their mettle has yet to be tested. We're going to have to find out.

Lt. General David D. McKiernan, the commander of the coalition Forces Land Component Command, made similar points at a briefing on April 23, once the fighting was over:[6]

This ground campaign to date has reflected itself in high-tempo continuous operations, decisive maneuver, extended logistical support, where I accepted some risk in the length of our lines of communication and our logistical reach, which—we have overcome that risk, and a execution of a plan that had several options in it but always remained focused on the enemy.

   …And I would refute any notion that there was any kind of operational pause in this campaign. There was never a day, there was never a moment where there was not continuous pressure put on the regime of Saddam by one of those components—air, ground, maritime, Special Forces, and so on.

   …there was no operational pause, when you have a tactical formation that is perhaps in the middle of very, very bad weather, which we had on about day three or four of this campaign, and they are stopped for a period of time to pull their logistics up to them, to get their formation back together after several fights, that might seem like a pause if you're sitting there with that unit that day on the ground. But at the same time, there is no let-up in aerial targeting, in attack helicopter operations, in other ground maneuver in other places on the battlefield, and in all the operations that our special operating forces did throughout Iraq.

   …Scott Wallace, a close friend of mine, what he would tell you if he was standing next to me here today, he would say that the fact that we ended up fighting a lot of paramilitary or death-squad formations that were coming out of urban areas in the southern part of Iraq was probably not the most likely enemy course of action that we war-gamed against, but it was certainly a course of action that we war-gamed against and it was one that we adjusted our plan that we had options built into our plan to adjust from, and his divisions were magnificent in making that adjustment.

Lt. Gen. McKiernan's reference to 5th Corps Commander Lt. General William (Scott) Wallace concerned a remark Wallace made during the temporary lull in the fighting to the effect that the Iraqi use of irregular forces was either "unexpected" or a "bit unexpected," and that it was "different from the one we war-gamed against."

Wallace was simply stating an obvious reality. The Iraqis did make several creative uses of irregular forces, and they did force the United States and Britain to adapt their tactics and force deployments in the south and along the main route of advance. As Wallace said in a postwar interview on May 7, 2003,

> I make no apologies for these comments....The enemy we fought...was much more aggressive than what we expected him to be, or at least, what I expected him to be. He was willing to attack out of those towns towards our formations, when my expectation was that they would be defending those towns and not be as aggressive. There was also a presence of foreign fighters that we subsequently discovered to be seeded within and cooperating with Saddam's Fedayeen, which were at least fanatical, if not suicidal. So all of those things led to that comment."[7]

The problem was not that Wallace was wrong in making his initial comments. In fact, the discovery of massive numbers of arms caches throughout Iraq indicates that the problems he addressed would have been much worse if Saddam's regime had been able to mobilize more than a small fraction of the Popular Army that it had created, attempted to train, and planned to equip.

The problem is rather that some commentators took Wallace's statement out of context during the worst period of the war and used it as an excuse to argue that the war plan had not been properly prepared and implemented. More generally, these same commentators did so in a way that implied that U.S. military should foresee all possible enemy tactics and actions in their original war plans, rather than be ready to adapt to the fact that war always involves the unexpected and enemies inevitably are creative and achieve at least limited surprise.

Lt. General Wallace made far more important points about the war plan, force strength, and surprise after the war. The following comments have been rearranged in chronological order from an interview by James Kitfield in the *National Journal*, and they not only put the whole war plan controversy in perspective, but serve as a short summary of many of the operational lessons of the war:[8]

> ...it's hard to argue with success. All of us would like more predictability in our lives and jobs. But we made this work—that's how I would phrase it. We had some very talented people who made it work. There are also advantages

to a "rolling start," because it allows you to get into the fight quicker. You gain some strategic as well as tactical advantages from that fact. The impression we have from talking to some Iraqi officers, for instance, is that some were expecting a Desert Storm-type campaign preceded by a long period of aerial bombardment. As you recall, instead we actually started the ground war before we started the air war. That decision was made for a number of different reasons, but I have to believe it surprised some Iraqi military officers who found themselves confronting U.S. tanks very early in the war.

...I would suggest to you that "tempo" can be fast or slow, either of which is OK as long as you are in control of the tempo and the enemy is not. When we slowed our forward progress and tempo, it was for a very deliberate, twofold reason. First, we wanted to build our logistics stance prior to moving into the battle for Baghdad. Second, even though we weren't moving forward, we were attacking the enemy every day. We had three fights going on nearly simultaneously around Najaf in that time frame, and a very serious fight down in Samawah. The fact that we weren't advancing through the Karbala Gap didn't mean that we weren't fighting. We continued to fight, we continued to secure our [logistics] lines, and we continued to kill a lot of bad guys.

...At the time, we simply couldn't discount the fanaticism with which those paramilitaries fought. I was not willing to ignore the threat it posed, or to expose my critical logistics train to it. In terms of forces to meet that threat, I had a very strong point of the spear with the 3rd Infantry Division. What I didn't have was a heavily mobile secondary force. The ability of the 101st Airborne Division to move itself around at that time was limited, quite frankly, because some of the trucks they rely on for mobility hadn't arrived in theater yet. So I was constrained in my ability to get one of the divisions around the battlefield. That led to some really tough calls on where to employ the 101st Division.

...Personally, the period during the dust storm was the low point of the entire campaign for me. That was definitely the hardest part and the low point of the war. You have to remember that the 3rd Infantry Division crossed the line of departure to open the war with about five days of supplies in terms of water, food, and ammunition. Then the dust storm hit on the fifth day of the fight, and lasted for most of three days. During that storm, our convoys took three to four days to reach our forward forces, and they were carrying two days of resupply. So the math didn't add up at that point, which concerned me. Not that we couldn't hold on to the ground we had gained, but we couldn't advance a lot further in our plans until we had solved the logistics issue. The period of the dust storm was also tough because we were fighting our tails off. There was all of this discussion on the lack of progress, but in actual fact, we were still maintaining a high operations tempo. We just weren't gaining ground. What we were doing was setting conditions for a decisive fight to follow.

We were surprised by the texture of the desert terrain. The dust problem in those areas was orders of magnitude worse than any of our terrain analysts had predicted. That caused us a number of problems. It caused us a problem in terms of convoy movement and in terms of aviation assets. Anytime anything moved out there, it kicked up a dust cloud. It was like driving through talcum powder.

…That [the fighting around Najaf and Karbala] may very well represent the single most significant adjustment we made in this entire war. We never had any intention of fighting in those southern cities, because we felt that would put us at a disadvantage; so we intended to bypass them.

As it turned out, the enemy was so aggressive in coming out of the cities and attacking us that we had to counterattack, first to secure our lines of communication, and second because the enemy was going to keep coming at us until we went into the cities and whacked him. So we had to make an adjustment to our battle plan and tactics to compensate for that aggressive tactic by the enemy.

I think Saddam's forces were trying to draw us into the cities, where they thought they had an advantage. Instead, we turned the cities into a disadvantage, with our armored raids taking out their heavy equipment, technical vehicles, and bunker complexes. Once we did that with our heavy armored forces, we switched to light infantry, backed by heavy reinforcements, to do the more detailed clearing operations. In the process of those fights, we not only secured our lines of communication and diminished the enemy's capabilities, but we also began to take control of population centers that we had anticipated addressing later, in Phase 4 stability operations. We just ended up confronting that issue earlier in the campaign than we anticipated.

…When we seized the bridge over the Euphrates River at what we called Objective Peach, at that point, I was pretty confident that we had Saddam by the balls. If we hadn't seized that bridge, we were prepared to put our own bridges in the water, but that probably would have added 24 hours to our operations. If he had the capability at the time—and it's not clear to me now that he did—he could have used that 24 hours to reposition forces and mass artillery, making life a lot harder for us. So when we got the main bridge across the Euphrates, I knew we were essentially home free.

…I'm about 95 percent convinced that when we crossed the Euphrates in a series of feints just after the dust storm hit, it forced the Medina to start repositioning its forces to counter an advance between the rivers that was never our main intent. We had beautiful weather with clear skies at that point, and we started getting reports of enemy armor moving on trucks, of

Iraqi artillery forces repositioning, and of attempts by Medina brigades to occupy what they believed would be optimum defensive positions. All that happened in the full view of the U.S. Air Force, and they started whacking the hell out of the Medina. So that was a pretty good feeling, knowing that the enemy felt he had to move his forces under conditions that were of great advantage to us as the attacker.

...For nearly a year, we had recognized collectively that once we were through the Karbala Gap, the fight would not be over until we seized the international airport in Baghdad. The entire fight from Karbala to the airport was considered as one continuous assault, because once we crossed through the gap, we were inside the range of all the artillery that was in support of Baghdad and all the Republican Guard divisions around Baghdad.

...We were also obviously worried about if and when Saddam would use chemical weapons. If you got 10 people in a room, you'd get 10 opinions on the subject, but clearly Karbala Gap was one of those choke points where Saddam could have used those weapons to some effect in terms of slowing us down. So the judgment I stated to my commanders was that once we crossed through the gap, we would be within Saddam's red zone in terms of defenses, and we had damn sure better be ready to continue the fight all the way to the encirclement of Baghdad.

THE "NEW WAY OF WAR" DEBATE

A far more relevant debate over the lessons of the Iraq War is the extent to which the war was the product of transformational warfare and reflected a new way of war. The answer in some ways is obvious. Much of the asymmetry between the U.S. and British forces and the Iraqi forces was the result of the fact that the United States was using a new mix of strategy, tactics, and technology and Iraq was not. As chapter 3 has shown, these changes affected virtually every aspect of force quality and, as chapter 4 has shown, they helped to accomplish a remarkably quick and decisive victory.

At the same time, any discussion of force transformation and a "new way of war" needs to be kept in historical perspective. There is a great work of military history still to be written on how the United States has transformed its forces since the beginning of World War II, the cycles of success and failure in this transformation, and the role that different military officers and civilians have played in the process. It is a process that has always involved civil versus military tensions as well as deep debates within the military. While the United States has benefited from many formal planning efforts, decisionmaking has always been dialectical and never Aristotelian.[9]

The Need to Remember the Past

Although much of today's transformation has its historical roots in World War II and the early period of the Cold War, the pace and nature of this transformation has been particularly striking since the American defeat in Vietnam, and it has gathered a unique momentum since the end of the Cold War.

This is not a casual point in analyzing the lessons of the Iraq War. It took nearly a quarter of a century under a wide variety of military civilian leaders to shape the U.S. forces that went to war in March 2003. They were the product of both victory and defeat, and virtually every element committed to battle was still in the process of ongoing transformation when it went into battle.

In broad terms, these forces had begun to practice a "new way of war" in the first Gulf War and had honed many of their techniques in the Afghan conflict. But many of the key weapons systems they used were shaped in Vietnam or previous conflicts. Certainly some of the most important lessons regarding readiness and leadership go back to the initial U.S. defeats in the Kasserine Pass and the shattering of Task Force Smith in the Korean War.

The discussion of comparative force strengths and weaknesses in chapter 3, the history of the war in chapter 4, and the discussion of the importance of military fundamentals in chapter 6 all illustrate the fact that any "new way of war" is built solidly on the past and the proper mix of new and old capabilities.

The New "New Way of War"?

The United States did implement many elements of a new "new way of war" as laid out in the force transformation documents and testimony issued by Secretary Rumsfeld and his staff. In one form or another, the course of the fighting described in chapter 4 can be said to have shown that the U.S. forces fighting in the Iraq War achieved each of the six goals laid out in the Quadrennial Defense Review:[10]

- First, to defend the U.S. homeland and other bases of operations, and defeat nuclear, biological, and chemical weapons and their means of delivery;

- Second, to deny enemies sanctuary—depriving them of the ability to run or hide—anytime, anywhere;

- Third, to project and sustain forces in distant theaters in the face of access denial threats;

- Fourth, to conduct effective operations in space;
- Fifth, to conduct effective information operations; and
- Sixth, to leverage information technology to give U.S. joint forces a common operational picture.

The conduct of the war also followed many of the military principles laid out in what some have started to call the "Rumsfeld doctrine," although press accounts differed on what that doctrine was thought to be.

One report described it as an emphasis on "Rapid Decisive Operations" that stressed[11]

- fast-moving, lighter forces, that can be moved quickly into battle;
- flexible decisionmaking, allowing field forces to react quickly to changes in the battle;
- joint operations involving army, navy, air force, and marines working together;
- use of strategic air power to attack simultaneously hundreds of targets; and
- use of high technology in smart bombs and battlefield intelligence gathering.

Another press account described the Rumsfeld doctrine as being based on the following:[12]

- civilian control of the war plan and its execution;
- speed and maneuver;
- flexibility in execution;
- heavy use of special operations forces, precision though massive air strikes, and unprecedented integration of the different service branches or "jointness"; and
- taking advantage of newer technologies, such as pilotless drones providing real-time pictures of the battlefield.

In an interview following the war, Secretary of Defense Rumsfeld's director of the Office for Force Transformation, Arthur K. Cebrowski, made no reference to any Rumsfeld doctrine." Instead, he summarized the initial lessons of the war in the following evolutionary terms:[13]

- the growing implementation of network-centric warfare and its role in shifting the balance of power through new forms of air-land battle and dynamics. Cebrowski termed this a long process driven by better sensors, good networked intelligence, high-speed decisionmaking, and the ability to exploit the noncontiguous battlefield—the battle-field without a front;

- the need for increased connectively in netcentric warfare;
- the increased use, interdependency, and effectiveness of all forms of indirect fire—artillery support, close air support, and aerial battle-field interdiction;
- a possible reduced dependence on helicopters on the battlefield for vertical lift;
- the increased value of Special Forces and the need for greater knowledge of regional factors, the ability to work with friendly local forces, and provide more SOF-like forces to support IS&R;
- the need for still further improvements in joint planning, particularly in codifying a clear doctrine for joint endeavors and the creation of a joint road map for force transformation;
- increased need for strategic mobility, possibly merging inter- and intra-theater lift, providing high-speed sealift, and possibly airships; and
- the need to accelerate the speed of command and control.

In fact, a little historical perspective shows that such reports of a "Rumsfeld doctrine" describe concepts and principles that derive in large part from military thinking that took place long before Secretary Rumsfeld became secretary of defense. One example is the series of Joint Vision strategy papers developed by the Joint Staff and perhaps best articulated in the Joint Staff study *Joint Vision 2020*, which was issued before the Bush administration came to office.[14]

Before one talks about civilian innovation and military conservatism, it is important to note that Joint Vision 2020 emphasized four concepts of operations that seem remarkably familiar in terms of both the war plan used in the Iraq War and the force transformation goals of Secretary Rumsfeld:[15]

- dominant maneuver,
- precision engagement,
- focused logistics, and
- full dimensional protection.

Other key concepts like "network-centric" or "netcentric" warfare emerged well over a decade before Secretary Rumsfeld came to office, as did the common use of the term "revolution in military affairs." The idea of using a wide range of synchronized forms of attack or "parallel warfare" was a key part of the war plan for the first Gulf War. Many of the ideas in "effects-based warfare" were used in Kosovo, and the emphasis placed on a "joint response force" in the force transformation study was laid out by officers like Admiral William Owens no later than the early 1990s. President Clinton's last secretary of defense, William Cohen, was a strong advocate of expanding the role of special forces, both as a senator and as secretary of defense.

The basic conceptual thinking in phrases like "rapid decisive operations" is as old as the art of maneuver warfare. The new military emphasis on "decision dominance" is simply a reminder of basic concepts of eighteenth-century European warfare and that era's emphasis on using combinations of military power, economic power, and political power to achieve war-fighting objectives—often without the use of war.

Even seen from the perspective of the Gulf and Afghan Wars, the Iraq War was more an evolution than a revolution. The dramatic speed of the coalition victory must also be measured against the weaknesses of Iraq as well as the strengths of the coalition, and one must always be careful about how "new" any new way of war ever is. The rubric of "rapid decisive operations" may be new, but the concept is as old as the writings on war. Concepts like "fighting fast and fighting light" would, after all, be familiar to Nathan Bedford Forest and Stonewall Jackson as well as Xenophon and Sun Tsu.

In short, new tactics and technology used in the Iraqi War, and projected for future force transformation, have taken decades to evolve. If U.S. progress over the last 10 years seems remarkably fast, at least part of the reason is that so many foreign armies have stood still or regressed and that so many Americans forget or never knew the past history of current developments. In practice, America's "new way of war" has been relatively conservative. The U.S. military services have never forced it to sacrifice proven force elements before the new ones were ready; the resulting process of change has mixed new and old methods of war fighting; and it has been measured and pragmatic.[16]

THE "POWELL DOCTRINE" VERSUS "RUMSFELD DOCTRINE" DEBATE

The speculation over the "Powell doctrine" versus the "Rumsfeld doctrine," that has become part of the war plan and force transformation debate seems to be more of a red herring. It had little do to with the actual details of military operations in Iraq, and was largely a debate over whether Powell favored decisive force using more conventional military means while Rumsfeld favored minimum force using high-technology weapons.

The debate again reflected the backlash from the more real debate between the U.S. military and Secretary Rumsfeld and many of his civilian advisors over how quickly force transformation should occur and the path it should take. It reflected tensions between the Rumsfeld civilians and the military on many other issues, including what the military often saw as an arrogant or abusive style and indifference to military opinion and what the Rumsfeld civilians often saw as an overbureaucratized military that was reluctant to face the need for change.

It also reflected a much broader political debate between those who supported Secretary Rumsfeld on a variety of issues that had little or nothing to do with the Iraq War and those who supported Secretary Powell. Washington infighting is Washington infighting, and grasping for headlines is grasping for headlines.

In practice, calling the war plan used in the Iraq War the result of a "Rumsfeld doctrine" made little sense for several reasons.

- First, as has been noted, the force levels involved were not the ones Rumsfeld had originally called for.

- Second, Secretary Powell had never expressed any public views on the war plan or any detailed views dissenting from the force transformation planning going on under Rumsfeld. Only Secretary Powell could have known whether he felt the war plan used in Iraq had insufficient force. It is hard to have a debate when most would-be spokesmen for the Powell doctrine quote themselves instead of the secretary and there is no "Powell doctrine" as stated by Secretary Powell.

  Furthermore, Secretary Powell had helped institute many of the basic changes in U.S. military technology and tactics that made victory in the Gulf War possible when he was chairman of the Joint Chiefs. He supported a war plan in 1991 that was also strikingly innovative. He had helped shape the major force cuts that followed the end of the Cold War, and he demonstrated quite clearly that he supported innovation and not a rigid adherence to doctrine.

- Third, there was no way that the Iraq War could have been fought with the kind of force transformation that Secretary Rumsfeld sought. That transformation had not yet been set forth in detailed future-year defense plans and was just beginning to be funded in the FY2004 defense budget. The transformational forces that Rumsfeld has sought will not be ready for at least five to seven years.

- Fourth, while the U.S. Air Force, Marine Corps, and Navy all have transformational concepts, they do not yet have detailed doctrines and force plans for long-term transformation that can be described as either following or opposing the undefined Rumsfeld plan.

- Fifth, although some of those discussing the so-called Powell doctrine associate it with the views of the U.S. Army's leadership, the army's plans are the most tenuous of all. The U.S. Army Stryker brigades—the first element in the army's effort to make its forces lighter and easier to project—were not fully ready for deployment in the Iraq War. Moreover, they were designed for combat against lighter forces than the tank-heavy Iraqi Republican Guard and had nothing to do with any "Powell doctrine" or the use or non-use of "decisive force."

The U.S. Army has so far failed to fully articulate a meaningful force plan for its Future Combat System that goes beyond a series of seemingly endless Power Point presentations to specific forces, equipment, and costs. Even according to its own presentations, the army's broad concepts of force transformation also could not be implemented until some undefined time frame between 2010 and 2020.

The issues surrounding the debates over a "new way of war" are serious, as are any major force-planning decisions. Personalizing a possible nondebate with no specifics around personal doctrines that neither Secretary Rumsfeld nor Secretary Powell have openly articulated in a contradictory form serves little purpose.

The Need to Redefine "Decisive Force"

As the previous chapter has shown, there also is a need to find new methodologies for calculating military effectiveness and force ratios. If one looks at the asymmetries in the coalition–Iraqi military balance outlined in chapter 3, it is clear after the fact that the United States and Britain did deploy "decisive" force relative to the weaknesses in Iraqi forces, Air dominance; superior intelligence, reconnaissance, and targeting; far more effective and survivable command and control; precision strike capability; far more rapid and adaptive cycles of decisionmaking; and far more rapid cycles of land maneuver were pitted against an incompetent enemy leadership whose forces had many deep structural weaknesses. At least in retrospect, to the extent that there were Rumsfeld and Powell doctrines, they can be said to coincide in terms of the actual course of the fighting and the outcome of the war and the balance of forces.[17]

At the same time, to return to some of the points made in chapter 2, far too little is yet known about the details of each battle to make sweeping judgments about what forces did or did not contribute to the outcome, and far too little is yet known about the detailed trade-offs within joint forces in terms of their impact on the enemy to suddenly go from the broad course of the fighting to sweeping statements about future require- ments and lessons for force transformation. Moreover, even if all of the necessary data were available, several key questions would still arise:

- First, what would have happened if Iraq had been able to fully execute its plans to call up massive irregular forces and make use of asymmet- ric warfare, and if it had used its conventional forces more effectively?

- Second, to what extent do the strengths and weaknesses of coalition and Iraqi forces in this war apply to other key contingencies like a war in Korea or across the Taiwan Strait, or a conflict with Iran, or— more importantly—an emerging power a decade from now that has acted intelligently on the lessons of this conflict and has developed effective and well-hidden means to use weapons of mass destruction both in direct war fighting and covert or proxy attacks?

- Third, do the United States and its allies really have a reliable mix of modeling techniques, operational analysis methods, and test and evaluation capabilities to properly use a single conflict like Iraq—or the broader patterns in recent conflicts—to analyze the real-world impact of sudden sweeping changes in forces, technology, strategy, and tactics in ways that allow them to make sweeping and rapid trade-offs? What risks can analysis really minimize in answering how much, what, and when is enough?

- Fourth, are there special risks in relying on "intangible" or "new" mea- sures of military effectiveness—like speed of military maneuver and action, improvements in IS&R and C4I/battlement management sys- tems, jointness, targeting, and effects-based operations—before the very real advantages of transformation in those areas are clearly es- tablished? Is it possible to go from choosing the proper vector for change to choosing a specific direction, and leapfrogging from cur- rent to transformational forces on the basis of what is known about the Iraq War and other recent conflicts?

- Fifth, how much slack is there in the existing force posture of the Unit- ed States and its allies? Being able to say that the coalition had decisive force in retrospect is not the same as saying it could have planned on being as decisive before the war. If one looks at actual major combat elements of force strength like combat battalions, combat-ready air- craft, and combat-ready ships, the United States has already cut its total deployable force strength by well over 40 percent since the end of the Cold War, while accepting growing de facto political con- straints on its ability to inflict casualties and collateral damage.

Even if one looks only at crude total force numbers, the army has cut its active force structure from 18 to 12 divisions and total active manpower from around 800,000 to 480,000. While it committed only some 12 combat brigades to the Iraq War versus 23 in Desert Storm, this was a total of 12 out of 32 combat brigades in the army's remaining force structure. The total cuts in combat ships and combat fighter and fighter attack aircraft have been even greater, and the marines had roughly half of its 170,000 personnel committed outside the United States at the peak of the fighting.

It seems clear that the United States did not have the worldwide assets during the Iraq War to effectively fight two major regional contingencies. Many U.S. military experts feel that U.S. forces are overdeployed and military personnel are being asked to make sacrifices that cannot be sustained. Force transformation cannot, in a democracy, ask those who risk their lives to defend their nation, while the vast majority of citizens take no risks at all, to assume either the peacetime or wartime burden of operating in a force structure that is either too small or involves too many transformational strains and risks.

- Sixth, even if all of these questions could be answered, does the United States or any other Western power have the tools in terms of program management, cost analysis, effectiveness analysis, and ability to deliver given technologies and weapons systems in fully trained and converted forces to make rapid shifts in force transformation, take risks in sharply reducing legacy forces before new forces are proven to be ready, and go from "evolution" to "revolution"?

- Seventh, in the process, can the United States and its allies establish a real-world balance between the ability to create new strategic and tactical concepts, as well as the technologies to implement them, on the one hand, and the ability to deal with the human factors inherent in making military forces effective and properly motivated, and with the need for the proper balance of recruitment and retention, training, basing, deployment cycles, and logistics and sustainment on the other hand.

- Eighth, how do the answers to all of these questions, particularly for the United States, affect the grand strategic posture of the nation involved in force transformation? How do they affect the motivation and interoperability of allies all over the world? How do they affect the nature of alliances? How are they perceived in terms of the political and military impact of forward presence and basing? To what extent do they deter and/or provoke potential enemies and neutral states? To what extent do they push opponents toward asymmetric warfare and terrorism, to proliferate or use terrorist movements as proxies?

It is worth noting in this respect, that it is far easier in theory than in practice to disregard the value of arms control treaties, the needs of NATO, the need for cooperation with the UN and EU, the value of NGOs and allies in peacemaking and nation building, the need for an effective regional presence and basing, and the need for interoperability with allies. The fact that the British Chief of Staff concluded that the most important British lesson of the war was that Britain needed to spend some two years without fighting another major conflict in order to give British forces time to recover and transform is only one of many warnings that American arrogance in force transformation can lead to American isolation in war fighting.

None of these questions mean that the United States and its allies should not pursue continued change and force transformation, or that Secretary Rumsfeld, the Joint Chiefs, and the military services should not push for change. Taking no risks in force transformation is also certain to be more costly and probably more dangerous than taking some risks. What they do mean is that any lessons coming out of the Iraq War are much more likely to provide useful insights in key areas than any basis for reaching radical conclusions about force transformation and military strategy. Put differently, it is precisely the kind of debates and open contention over strategy and force transformation that seems to have taken place before the Iraq War that should continue after it. Peacetime bureaucratic battles and interservice rivalries are far better than peacetime unity and wartime body bags.

The Dangers of American "Triumphalism"

Finally, there is much more important debate that U.S. strategic and defense planners should engage in. The success of U.S. arms in developing new ways of war and in winning the Iraq War is no excuse for any form of "triumphalism." The United States remains vulnerable to asymmetric warfare and terrorism. It has no good answer to nations that have successfully proliferated and where preemption or "first strikes" can provoke terrible regional conflicts.

Any definition of victory cannot ignore the war's cost in human lives, dollars, and property. It also cannot ignore the fact that Iraq was an enemy with all of the defects laid out in chapters 2 and 3. It is far from clear that the United States can plan for a world in which future opponents are equally weak.

The United States would face much more severe limits in any future war with North Korea or any confrontation with Russia or China. The United States' ability to wage and win wars is in no sense matched by its abilities to win a peace through peacemaking and nation building. Its status as the "world's only superpower" is heavily dependent on a network of regional allies and ultimately on sustaining a favorable balance of global political support.

One of the critical uncertainties still surrounding the Iraq War is how optional the war really was and whether containment and disarmament could have dealt with Saddam Hussein. The threat Iraq posed under Saddam Hussein does not seem to have been imminent, but it is not yet clear from the discoveries to date how much Iraq's success in retaining weapons of mass destruction made that threat so proximate that the United States and Britain had to attack. Saddam Hussein's long history of tyranny, aggression, and proliferation may well justify the Iraq War, but the war's timing may yet prove to be "optional."

As the later chapters on grand strategy show, the United States and Britain were also far less prepared for peacemaking and nation building than for war fighting. The United States in particular was initially unprepared to deal with any major aspect of conflict termination, and many U.S. policymakers had serious illusions about their ability to turn Iraq into a rapid example of the kind of state that might catalyze political and economic change in the Middle East. They also clearly failed to properly characterize the threat Iraq posed in terms of weapons of mass destruction, although the repeated discovery of mass graves made it all too clear that Saddam Hussein's regime was a vicious tyranny.

The advances in U.S. war-fighting capability do not mean America can wander off in search of enemies, or abandon the search to build stronger international institutions and to use diplomacy instead of force. The United States may have the ability to dethrone a series of the world's less powerful and more obnoxious leaders, but "can" is never a synonym for either "must" or "should." As Clausewitz notes,

> The first, the most far-reaching act of judgment that the statesman and commander have to make is to establish…the kind of war on which they are embarking, neither mistaking it for, nor trying to turn it into, something that it is not. This is the first of all strategic questions and the most comprehensive…."[18]

Ultimately, the United States must have the world's trust to underpin its structure of alliances and to reduce the risk that its actions will create a network of opposing military, political, and economic alliances. Trust is not earned by new ways of war, it is earned by justice and restraint.

Notes

[1] Mark Helprin, "Analyze This: Civilian Officials Only Reached a Point of Sufficiency Because They Were Pushed to It," *National Review*, May 5, 2003.

[2] Rowland Scarborough, "Decisive Force Now Measured by Speed," *Washington Times*, May 7, 2003, p. 1.

[3] The best discussion of this process to date can be found in Peter Boyer, "A Reporter at Large: The New War Machine," *New Yorker*, June 30, 2003, p. 54.

[4] For an anti-Rumsfeld critique, see Seymour M. Hersh, "Offense and Defense," *New Yorker*, April 7, 2003, pp. 43–45.

[5] British Ministry of Defense, "Operations in Iraq: First Reflections" (London: Her Majesty's Stationery Office. July 2003), pp. 19, 32.

[6] U.S. Department of Defense briefing on April 23, 2003, www.defenselink.mil/transcripts/2003/tr20030423-0122.html.

[7] Vernon Loeb, "Commander Defends Iraq War Comments," *Washington Post*, May 8, 2003, p. 18; Roland Scarborough, "General Tells How Cell Phone Foiled U.S. Attack in Iraq," *Washington Times*, May 8, 2003, p. 13.

[8] Interview with James Kitfield, "Attack Always," *National Journal*, April 25, 2003.

[9] There is no way to even begin to list all of the reports and studies over the years that helped shape the forces, tactics, and technologies used in the Iraq War and the current force transformation debate. Some recent works include Harlan K. Ullman and James P. Wade, *Rapid Dominance: A Force for All Seasons*, Whitehall Papers 43 (London: Royal United Services Institute, 1998); Douglas A. Macgregor, *Breaking the Phalanx* (Westport, Conn.: Praeger/CSIS, 1997); Stephen A. Cambone, *A New Structure for National Security Planning* (Washington, D.C.: CSIS, 1997); Hans Binnendijk, *Transforming America's Military* (Washington, D.C.: National Defense University, 2002); Tom Czerwinski, *Coping with the Bounds: Speculations on Nonlinearity in Military Affairs* (Washington, D.C.: National Defense University, 1998); Daniel Goure and Jeffrey M. Rankin, *Averting the Defense Train Wreck in the New Millennium* (Washington, D.C.: CSIS, 1999); and Michael O'Hanlon, *Technological Change and the Future of Warfare* (Washington, D.C.: Brookings, 2000).

[10] Taken from the testimony of Deputy Secretary of Defense Paul Wolfowitz to the U.S. Senate Armed Services Committee, April 27, 2002.

[11] This summary is adapted from Toby Harnden, "Fight Light Fight Fast Theory Advance," *Daily Telegraph*, April 14, 2001, p. 1.

[12] Brad Knickerbocker, "War Boosts Rumsfeld's Vision of an Agile Military," *Christian Science Monitor*, April 11, 2003. For a more general discussion of factors relating directly to the Iraq War, see Greg Jaffe, "Rumsfeld's Vindication Promises a Change in Tactics, Deployment," *Wall Street Journal*, April 10, 2003, p. 1.

[13] David A. Fulghum, "Fast Forward," *Aviation Week*, April 28, 2003, p. 34.

[14] See Chairman of the Joint Chiefs of Staff Vision Statement, *Joint Vision 2020* (Washington, D.C.: Government Printing Office, June 2000). Much of the work on force transformation also took place under the Clinton administration, and a key study shaping the later elements of the force transformation exercise was issued in June 2001. See Jim McCarthy et al., *Transformation Study Report: Transforming Military Operational Capabilities* (Washington, D.C.: Office of the Secretary of Defense, April 27, 2001).

[15] For a fuller discussion, see Merrick E. Krause, "Decision Dominance: Exploiting Transformational Asymmetries," *Defense Horizons*, no. 23 (February 2003), Center for Technology and National Security Policy, National Defense University, Washington, D.C.

[16] For some of the press debate over these issues contemporary with the Iraq War, see Vince Crawley, "Less Is More," *Army Times*, April 21, 2003, p. 18; Mark Mazzetti and Richard J. Neuman, "The Seeds of Victory," *U.S. News & World Report*, April 21, 2003; Toby Harnden, "Fight Light Fight Fast Theory Advance," *Daily Telegraph*, April 14, 2001, p. 1; and Vago Muradian and Riad Kahwaji, "War Puts Transformation to the Test," *Defense News*, March 24, 2003, p. 1.

[17] For some interesting early debates over the issues raised in this section, see Thom Shanker, "Assessment of Iraq War Will Emphasize Joint Operations," *New York Times*, May 1, 2003; Robert J. Caldwell, "Rumsfeld versus the Army," *San Diego Union Tribune*, May 4, 2003; Scarborough, "Decisive Force Now Measured by Speed," p. 1; Vernon Loeb, "Commander Defends Iraq War Comments," *Washington Post*, May 8, 2003, p. 18; Fulghum, "Fast Forward"; Seth Stern, "Military 'Transformation' May Not Mean Smaller Forces," *Christian Science Monitor*, May 7, 2003; Tom Bowman, "Rumsfeld Conducting War on Army," *Baltimore Sun*, May 7, 2003; Thom Shanker and Eric Schmitt, "Latest Mission for Forces: Analyze New Ways to Prepare for Conflicts," *New York Times*, April 30, 2003.

[18] The author is indebted for this quote to Merrick E. Krause, who used it in a different context in "Decision Dominance: Exploiting Transformational Asymmetries," p. 3. It is taken from the Michael Howard and Peter Paret translation of *On War* (Princeton: Princeton University Press, 1976), p. 88.

CHAPTER SIX

LESSONS ABOUT THE INTERACTION BETWEEN MILITARY FUNDAMENTALS AND NEW TACTICS AND TECHNOLOGY

Whatever the merits of any "new way of war" or "revolution in military affairs" may be, the Iraq War provides important lessons about the continued value of military fundamentals and the need for the successful integration of those fundamentals with new technologies and tactics. It is both easy and dangerous to focus on the "new." It is intellectually more exciting; it affects more shifts in key programs and resources; and it is far easier to assert that a future mix of strategy, tactics, and technology will solve current problems than it is to come to grips with troublesome realities.

The problem is that military fundamentals are not easy to deal with simply because they are familiar. Developing and maintaining a highly competent military that provides actual war fighters rather than uniformed bureaucrats has been a constant challenge from the start of civilization. Few countries have ever been able to sustain military professionalism and high levels of morale and motivation, and new tactics and technology almost inevitably increase the strains on military forces rather than reduce them. Innovation always means new problems in converting career structures, training, and support systems to make the most effective use of new tactics and technology, and it inevitably requires changes in the nature of combined arms, jointness, and interoperability. Moreover, the nature of war always pushes the use of new tactics and technology to the limits of the human operator, rather than reduces the strain on human factors—a problem that is compounded by efforts to make trade-offs and reduce costs that put even more pressure on war fighters to operate to the limit of their capabilities when they come into serious combat.

As the next chapter discusses, the search for broader ways of integrating military forces through jointness and netcentric warfare broadens the strain innovation places on individual elements of the force. So does the fact that innovation never occurs in balanced ways. There are always gaps and weaknesses in the process, and war inevitably exposes such imbalances in unexpected ways. Only a fool could believe that a highly structured and orderly Aristotelian concept of change could ever be imposed on reality. War inevitably requires war fighters to act in the face of continuing uncertainty and solve key problems in terms of dialectics.

THE VALUE OF TRAINING, READINESS, AND HUMAN FACTORS

No advance in jointness or technology would have mattered without truly professional men and women, trained as fighters, rather than garrison forces or military bureaucrats. The U.S., British, and Australian all-volunteer and professional military forces had a massive superiority in professional skills and unit cohesion. The United States, Britain, and Australia also could not have been half so successful if the coalition forces had not had the motivation and morale to fight under exhausting conditions, often in bad weather, and do so at unparalleled tempos of operation for periods that bordered on 24-hour operations for days at a time.

The value of training and readiness emerged in every aspect of U.S., British, and Australian operations. The low accident rates, the ability to sustain constant combat operations over some 20 days, the ability to manage extremely complex air operations, and the high quality of joint warfare and combined arms are all tributes to the quality of prewar training and readiness. U.S. aircraft and helicopters, for example, had better readiness rates in wartime than in peacetime, often averaging over 90 percent.[1] The coalition also benefited from reliance on all-professional active forces and the combat experience of the forces involved. For example, 70 percent of U.S. strike aircraft aircrews already had combat experience at the time the Iraq War began.

It seems certain that every commander on the coalition side would agree with the following comments of Lt. Gen. David D. McKiernan, the commander of the Coalition Forces Land Component Command:[2]

> I will tell you that why the coalition was so decisive in this campaign to date was because we have the military capability, training, leadership, and equipment that make us decisive. And I get very upset when I hear anybody say that this was so easy. There are 600-plus Americans who are dead or wounded in the course of this conflict, and it wasn't easy for them. And anybody that was here and anybody that traveled with those formations, I don't think you'll find anybody that says it was an easy fight. So if I sound a little emotional, I apologize, but there is nothing in wartime that's easy for that formation or for that pilot or for that ship when they're in harm's way.

The U.S. emphasis on realistic training, combined with the fact that the U.S. military is now one of the few military forces with wide and diverse combat experience, is a factor that is easy to discount, given the emphasis being placed on new technologies and new methods of war. In practice, however, changes in tactics and technology mean little unless they can be combined with training and readiness. Moreover, the United States learned the hard way in past wars that training must be as rigorous and realistic as possible; it must prepare forces to deal with enemy innovation and tactical defeat, and it must force them to realistically practice combined arms and joint warfare.

The British Ministry of Defense drew similar lessons regarding British forces in its assessment of the lessons of the war.[3]

> The Iraq operation showed once again why the UK's Armed Forces are regarded as among the best in the world. The high quality of their training and professional expertise was demonstrated in the skill with which they performed their roles. Above this, good discipline, motivation, resourcefulness, and courage were fundamental factors in their success. The tasks required of our Servicemen and women throughout the campaign and in the immediate aftermath of hostilities were numerous and complicated, and their impressive performance in achieving their military objectives so rapidly should not be underestimated.
>
> Our Armed Forces have unique experience of urban operations—in Northern Ireland and the Balkans in particular—developing valuable skills that have served them well in Iraq. These go beyond combat training and include having to manage sometimes hostile populations at a time of great uncertainty and turmoil. In Basrah, quickly gaining the trust and co-operation of the local people was of critical importance.
>
> …Overall, this operation confirmed the vision of the 1998 Strategic Defence Review (SDR) that the UK Armed Forces should evolve an expeditionary-based strategy, providing ready, balanced forces capable of applying decisive effect in scenarios of varying intensity, frequency, and character in an uncertain and unpredictable world. The SDR, and last July's SDR "New Chapter" based on analysis of the implications of 11 September 2001 and subsequent operations against terrorism, took into account the growth of asymmetric threat and the need to be able to operate with allies and partners.
>
> The operation confirmed that our war-fighting doctrine, broadly based on the tenets of maneuver warfare and decisive effect, was sound, albeit capable of further refinement. Similarly, despite some issues, our readiness posture had permitted a flexible, rapid response, coherent deployment and direct theatre entry into a hostile environment. Our equipment generally coped with the environmental demands and allowed us to maintain sufficient

firepower, mobility, protection, and technological advantage over the opposition. At the same time, our support infrastructure, although rigorously tested in fast moving combat, and with limited access to host nation support, sustained us in carrying out all assigned tasks.

Experience gained on other expeditionary operations, most recently in Afghanistan, was invaluable in Iraq. Beyond that, twelve years of enforcing the No-Fly Zones had conditioned coalition aircrews to the Iraqi environment. Exercise SAIF SAREEA II which took place in Oman was of particular benefit in rehearsing expeditionary operations in the Gulf area to practice real time land/air co-ordination. This underlines the need to train as realistically as possible.

Innovation and Initiative

It is important to note in this regard that U.S., British, and Australian forces were able to operate effectively even when they were in a protection mode against chemical and biological weapons and that they emerged with far better training for urban warfare than their Iraqi opponents. More importantly, detailed accounts of the fighting make it clear that it was the ability of junior officers, NCOs, and other ranks to innovate and adapt that compensated for a range of serious communications and other technical problems, particularly at the battalion level and below. In many cases, tactical communications were not adequate; orders from higher echelons did not keep up with the pace of combat; sensor and intelligence data were not available. In other cases, existing systems were not adequate to ensure the necessary cooperation between combat and support forces, the different elements of combined arms, or different services. Military personnel at all levels acted innovatively and exercised initiative, and the "human factor" was critical.

A number of officers who served in the Iraq War or helped to prepare for it have made clear in e-mails and personal commentary on the war that these problems not only validate the value of professionalism and training; they also show that much still needs to be done to find better ways to improve joint warfare both in terms of land-air operations and interservice cooperation. They feel that even within the U.S. military there are imbalanced advances in C4I and "digital" combat that complicate cooperation between the U.S. Army and the U.S. Marine Corps or complicate the deconfliction of armor, artillery, rotary-wing air, and fixed-wing air. They also feel that despite the success of U.S. forces in the Iraq War, there is a need for more demanding training for the command of large-scale joint operations. There is no way to put such feelings in perspective except to say that training and readiness are the foundations of all effective military operations and that each major step in force transformation almost inevitably creates the need for new and even more demanding forms of training and exercises.

Morale and Motivation

Morale and motivation are "intangibles" that are almost impossible to measure. The coalition victory did, however, involve more than training and readiness. U.S., British, and Australian forces had high morale and strong motivation as well as high professional capability. Iraq's forces generally did not. It is clear that some elements of Iraq's force structure continued to fight for Saddam Hussein through the first days of the Battle of Baghdad. The Republican Guard forces fought extensively, although after-action reports increasingly indicate a high desertion rate once they came under intensive air attack. Saddam's Fedayeen fought well in several urban clashes in the south. Iraq's regular army, however, showed only a limited willingness to engage, and efforts by the CIA to bribe regular army officers into avoiding combat clearly had an effect. The Iraqi Air Force played no role in the war, and the Popular Army essentially never showed up.

Morale and motivation are not things that the United States or its allies can take for granted. The United States learned this the hard way in Vietnam and, indeed, globally during the Vietnam era. It is also important to note that politics and propaganda generally have a more limited impact in shaping morale and motivation than do unit cohesion and loyalty and the extent to which military service is seen as a profession and as one that rewards those who serve. Those who emphasize technology and efficiency sometimes lose sight of this point. But it is clear at every level that the motivation and morale of coalition forces was a key factor leading to their willingness to sustain unequaled sortie and maneuver rates and to deal with problems like weather and the unexpected resistance of Iraqi regular forces.

Moreover, the retention rates that created such professional forces were partly dependent on the belief that their pay and privileges and their social status were adequate compensation. It was also clear long before the conflict that the U.S. force that went to war in Iraq had problems with the existing rate of deployments away from family and home base and that there were strains on the morale and motivation of the force. The need for a stable military career structure is scarcely a new lesson of the Iraq War. The danger is that the success of new tactics and technology may lead planners to ignore how important this lesson really is.

COMPETENCE, ADAPTIVENESS, AND FLEXIBILITY IN WAR PLANNING

The history of the Iraq War has already shown, in fact, that the United States, Britain, and Australia had an overwhelming advantage over the Iraqis in military professionalism and in dealing with the fundamentals of war. This advantage did as much as superior technology and new tactics did to overcome Iraq's advantages of fighting on the defensive, on home ground, and with internal lines of communication. The United States and UK began the fight with a war plan that relied on a northern front that did not exist for political reasons, and with significant elements of the deployments and supplies that were to be ready in Kuwait still in delivery because of delays resulting from the political sensitivies of dealing with the UN over a Security Council resolution approving the war.

This professionalism and adaptability in planning were greatly aided by major advances in joint warfare capability and its computerization and integration at every level. There is also a lesson in the fact that one of the most important skills in modern arms is not how to agree on a war plan, but how to change one when reality intervenes and—if necessary—abandon key elements of the plan with sufficient adaptiveness to win.

The "war plan" was flexible enough that the coalition could rapidly adjust its remaining elements. Adaptiveness and flexibility allowed the United States, Britain, and Australia to exploit precision airpower with extraordinary success. Precision airpower was used to paralyze many aspects of the Iraqi command and control structure, limit the maneuver capabilities of Iraqi regular army forces throughout the country, destroy many elements of those Republican Guard and regular army units that did move, and then conduct urban close air support operations. Seapower was exploited to use carriers and cruise missiles as a substitute for air bases, to use sealift to deliver equipment and logistic supplies over an extended period before the war began, and to provide secure access to ports in Kuwait.

Lt. General William Wallace provides a good description of coalition adaptiveness during the build-up and deployment phase: [4]

> ...I think we were right to characterize the fight to get here as a critical part of the equation. Certainly the fact that we only had a single airport and port through which our entire formation had to flow was a limiting factor in our operations. I think we did pretty well in adapting ourselves to that reality, but in hindsight, I might have made some different adjustments in terms of what flowed into the country, and when.

For example, early in the flow we were very concerned about fuel. There was a company's worth of 5,000-gallon tankers sitting in Kuwait, but the truck drivers weren't due into the theater for weeks. Ultimately we asked for and received permission to fly in truck drivers from V Corps [5th Corps] to fall in on that equipment, in order to get our truck companies moving. Those kinds of decisions and adjustments were being made virtually every day by our logisticians and leaders in the rear area. And ultimately, it worked.

The lack of many of the original land forces did not prevent the Coalition from rapidly adapting to a "land attack first" strategy based on the forces in the south. The Coalition adapted its plans to use of the British 1st Armored Division to secure Basra and the southeast, while U.S. V-Corps and 1 MEF forces drove through Iraq, exploited Iraqi strategic geography so the V Corps forces could largely avoid Iraqi towns and cities, and established relatively secure supply lines for a rapid advance on Baghdad through the desert areas west of the Euphrates.

In spite of political problems that made it impossible to execute many key aspects of the original war plan, adaptiveness and flexibility allowed its key elements to be implemented. This was particularly important during the advance of U.S. land forces. The 1 MEF (1st Marine Expeditionary Force) drive up between the Tigris and Euphrates from An Nasiryah to Al Kut allowed it to largely bypass towns, avoid the Iraqi regular army forces concentrated to the east, and then exploit the main road north of the Tigris. As both advances reached the area near Baghdad, they caught the Iraqi forces unprepared. The Republican Guards were forced to redeploy in the face of near-total coalition air dominance and then attack the 5th Corps and 1 MEF forces without the advantage of positioned and prepared defenses under conditions approaching those of a meeting engagement.

This pace of advance could not have happened without a high degree of adaptiveness and initiative at the battalion level and below in both the U.S. Army and U.S. Marine Corps, although combat diaries and accounts by individual soldiers make it clear that adaptiveness was of equally critical value in terms of altering attack helicopter, support, logistic, and C4I operations to support the land advance. Moreover, when some unexpected Iraqi actions did occur—particularly the use of irregular forces in the south and the lack of open popular support from Iraq's Shi'ites—the U.S. and British commanders adapted rapidly. When new Iraqi tactics and capabilities emerged, they responded.

This adaptiveness also extended beyond the level of planning and tactics. U.S. forces had to modify many aspects of the weapons and equipment they used during the war, and the role other ranks and technical personnel played in making such changes was critical in making such changes. So was the role of U.S. industry and private contractors in rushing forward the delivery of new equipment or making suitable modifications. The British Ministry of Defense made adaptiveness in meeting what Britain calls Urgent Operational Requirements one of its key lessons of the war.[5]

> For this operation, MOD approved over 190 UORs at a value of around £510M (a small number of additional UORs have since been progressed to support continuing UK operations in Iraq). In some cases, this meant that equipment had to be supplied by industry at extremely short notice, and we will wish in future to ensure that the balance of risk inherent in our readiness profile is accurately assessed and monitored. Some UORs involved accelerating existing programmes such as the procurement of the Temporary Deployable Accommodation and the Head Mounted Night Vision System. Others, in particular the measures to enhance interoperability with coalition allies, were new procurements made in short timescales. Industry responded magnificently to the surge of requirements in the build up to the operation, proving the value of the partnering approach that the MOD has developed over recent years. Although some long lead times presented significant challenges, most UORs that were procured were delivered and fitted before combat operations began. Despite units having had limited time in which to train and become familiar with the new equipment, our initial assessment is that they added valuable capabilities during the operation.

SYNCHRONICITY, SIMULTANEITY, SPEED, JOINTNESS, AND COMBINED ARMS

As has been discussed in the previous chapter, advances in synchronicity, simultaneity, speed, jointness, and combined arms all interacted to give the United States, Britain, Australia, and the other members of the coalition the equivalent of "decisive force." The history of the fighting also demonstrated that the United States had a major advantage over Iraq in terms of its ability to bring together land and air operations and support them from the sea and from friendly bases at very high tempos of coordinated operations and shift the mix of joint operations according to need over the entire theater of operations. The issue was far more than jointness per se; it was the coordination and sheer speed of operations at every dimension of combat.

Some might argue that such jointness should be seen as part of the new way of war rather than as a military "fundamental." Historically, it seems more valid to argue that synchronicity, simultaneity, speed, jointness, and combined arms have always been fundamentals of war, and that the difficulty has always been the willingness and ability to execute them as effectively as possible. The problems of coordinating cavalry, archers, and infantry are examples of the issues involved that are almost as old as civilization, not ones that began with the computer and modern communications. Certainly, the problem of coordinating air-land-naval operations is at least as old as World War I.

What is clear is that the United States, Britain, and Australia executed joint warfare and combined arms in ways that differed from the timelines and capabilities it had in even as recent a conflict as the first Gulf War. The Gulf War saw a 38-day air bombardment, much of which had to focus on suppressing the Iraqi Air Force and surface-based air defenses before the campaign could shift to attacking Iraqi forces in the Kuwait theater of operations, and it saw a massive diversionary effort to suppress Iraq's Scuds. The Iraq War began with air superiority and moved on swiftly to air dominance. Although comparable numbers are not available, in the first Gulf War the mission allocation of strike sorties was 55 percent of all sorties. In the Iraq War, the figures evidently exceeded 75 percent.[6]

Ground and air operations began on day one, but massive country-wide air and missile strikes against Iraqi leadership targets and ground forces began on Day 3 versus Day 7. In the first Gulf War, the ground advance forced Saddam to order the withdrawal of his forces from Kuwait on Day 41. In this war, U.S. forces had already moved the distance of the longest maneuver in the 1991 Gulf War in one quarter of the time. They advanced within 50 miles on Baghdad on Day 8, entered Baghdad International Airport on Day 16, and were in the center of Baghdad on Day 20.

Speed was critical during these operations, but "speed" could never have been effective if it has not been supported by maneuvers that exploited the enemy's weaknesses and bypassed enemy forces where possible. The speed of the ground advance was also made possible by air dominance and overwhelming superiority in firepower backed by far great situational awareness and a common operating picture (COP) among the U.S. military services and within coalition forces. The ability to use precision weapons throughout day and night and in virtually all weathers allowed the U.S. land forces to exploit their speed as well as reduced the need to take time to secure their flanks and rear areas. Superior sustainability and logistic support also made speed possible. Finally, the use of air and missile strikes against Iraqi leadership and communications centers further disrupted an already weak and heavily politicized Iraqi command and control system, and ensured that Iraq could not react in time to the speed of the U.S. advance.

The fact that the secretary of defense has given the main responsibility for developing the lessons of the Iraq War to the joint forces command is a valid indication of the value of joint task forces in modern war fighting, the progress jointness had made at the time of the Iraq War, and the value of integrating service plans at every level to create an even greater degree of synergy.[7] At the same time, detailed accounts of combat, as well as much of the reporting by U.S. combat forces on the lessons of the war, show that many problems in the U.S. approach to jointness remained and required constant workarounds and adaptiveness by the forces on the ground.

Although the United States and its allies did have the best common operating picture in military history, General Franks has been among the first to point out that the Iraq War was not fought by U.S. forces using a well-structured architecture for joint warfare, or a "system of systems" that efficiently cut across service lines in any integrated manner.[8] It was fought using a range of evolving C4I and training systems that were still heavily "service-centric," and many of the key systems within each service were in the process of rapid change and evolution. Linkages often had to be cobbled together or improvised, and workarounds had to be put in place during combat at every echelon of command. Many systems and aspects of communication had serious gaps and incompatibilities. The Iraq War occurred before the United States was able to fully act upon the lessons of Afghanistan or even lay out a detailed road map for a more advanced form of force transformation. This need to make further major improvements in jointness is reinforced by virtually every element of combat laid out in this chapter and the next, and it is clear that creating a truly effective structure for joint warfare will take at least another decade and possibly far longer.

Finally, nothing about the lessons of the Iraq War indicates that the broad roles and missions that currently define each U.S. military service are not valid or that the United States could gain from integrating its military services. It is also clear that improved jointness is scarcely the only priority. There also are many lessons that apply only to a single service or to ground, air, or sea operations.

SITUATIONAL AWARENESS, INTELLIGENCE, AND COMMAND AND COMMUNICATIONS

Once again, situational awareness, the value of intelligence, and the need for effective command and communications are fundamentals as old as the history of war. Once again, dramatic changes took place in the quality of their execution during the Iraq War. The United States had vastly improved every aspect of its intelligence, targeting, and command and control capabilities since the last Gulf War, in addition to having spent some 12 years in surveillance of Iraqi operations and military developments. Its combination of imagery, electronic intelligence, signals intelligence, and human intelligence was honed in Afghanistan, and improved communications and command and intelligence fusion at every level gave it near real-time day and night situational awareness.

It is again arguable whether these changes should be called an "evolution" or a "revolution" in military affairs. Much of the so-called transformational nature of U.S. forces is the result of trends that are now more than 30 years old and that were foreseen in the planning documents of the 1960s. It is clear, however, that the United States has made steady advances and that its capabilities are much more advanced than at the time of the Gulf War.

General Richard Myers, the chairman of the Joint Chiefs, described these changes as follows:[9]

> …Joint warfighting is the key to greater things on the battlefield. I think that's been clearly proven here. We have very good integration. The thing that enables that and eliminates gaps and seams is the C4ISR (command, control, communications, computers, intelligence, surveillance, and reconnaissance). I think such systems are performing as we thought—all the systems. I am trying to think of something that has not lived up to what we expected and I am hard pressed.

At the same time, as is the case with virtually every lesson of the war, U.S., British, and Australian success was heavily dependent on Iraqi failures and weaknesses. Fifth Corps commander Lt. General William Wallace makes the following comments about Iraq's performance:[10]

> We should be careful at this point, because wars are kind of like good wine, they tend to get better with age. But it seems to me that regardless of whether Saddam still had a command-and-control apparatus in place toward the end, it continually took Iraqi forces a long time—somewhere on the order of 24

hours—to react to anything we did. By the time the enemy realized what we were doing, got the word out to his commanders and they actually did something as a result, we had already moved on to doing something different. For a commander, that's a pretty good thing—fighting an enemy who can't really react to you.

The Scale of the IS&R Effort

Even if one looks only at the air campaign, some raw numbers highlight the importance of the intelligence, surveillance, and reconnaissance effort. Some 80 dedicated coalition aircraft flew more than 1,000 sorties on IS&R missions. They gathered some 42,000 battlefield images and provided 2,400 mission hours of SIGINT coverage, 3,200 hours of full mission video, and 1,700 hours of moving target indicator coverage.[11] The sheer scale of the battle management takes is indicated by the fact that the database for the command and control of the air battle involved some 1,800 airspace control measures, of which an average of 1,200 had to be implemented a day. During the war, battle management had to "deconflict"— take steps to ensure that coalition forces could safely operate in the same area—750 air and TLAM operations and 414 air and ATACMS operations.

Another measure of activity is the massive increase in communications activity that took place between the period before and after the war:[12]

Activity	Prewar	Wartime	Percentage of Change
Commercial SATCOM terminals	5	35	+560
Average commercial bandwidth (Mb)	7	10	+47
Military SATCOM terminals	20	44	+120
Average military bandwidth (Mb)	2	3	+68
Terrestrial links	11	30	+173
Average terrestrial bandwidth (Mb)	2	10	+444
Global broadcasting system (Mb)	24	24	0
Total terminals	36	107	+167
Total bandwidth (Mb)	113	783	+596

The Limits of IS&R Organization and Integration

At the same time, the United States still had major problems with many aspects of its IS&R systems. These problems inevitably also affected the British and Australian forces, which largely depended on the U.S. systems.

Some of these problems were procedural and long-standing. The United States was able to do a much better job of integrating the national intelligence effort by the CIA, NSA, NRO, and NIMA into the war-fighting effort, but coordination problems still remained, and war fighters note that overclassification, compartmentation, and restrictions on the release and dissemination of intelligence continued to present major problems. To put it bluntly, many actual users of intelligence in combat still see overclassification and dissemination as major problems and the security officer as much of a threat as the enemy.

Despite the increase in communications activity, there were still problems in handling the sheer scale of the IS&R effort. The volume of operational activity helped to contribute to the effective collapse of the effort to provide timely battle damage assessment data during the first few days of the war. The analysis and dissemination of IS&R data were much better than they had been in the Gulf War. However, each service still had a series of unique organizational, technical, and communications solutions to the circulation, processing, and dissemination of IS&R data, and this presented particular problems for both U.S. and allied ground forces.

For example, the U.S. 1st Marine Division headquarters did not have direct access to satellite primary imagery, although it did have access to satellite secondary imagery via image product libraries (IPL) and all-source product servers. This lack of direct access was not a matter of the Marine Corps not having the capability or of the NIMA/NRO withholding data. Rather, it resulted from a Marine Corps commander's decision based on prioritization of requirements and allocation of resources. Given the MEF's AOR, mission, prioritized requirements, and other factors, the commander opted to use the MEF's primary imagery receive assets (IntelBn's TEG-M and a dozen TEG-Es) to support the deep battle, employing them at the MEF Command Element (CE) and the Marine Air Wing (MAW). The commander allocated in direct support of the Marine Division 100 percent of his tactical UAVs (two Pioneer squadrons), TCDL receive suites for P3 AIP connectivity, and enough Trojan Spirits for Marine Division HQ and every RCT to use for secondary imagery reachback.[13]

Nevertheless, the analysis of the lessons of the war by the 1st Marine Division provides a powerful reminder that true netcentric warfare must get intelligence to the war fighter:[14]

The 1st Marine Division G2 did not have current, high-resolution, National imagery support during preparation or combat phases of the Operation. Baseline CIB was the only tool available to the Division—and used to great success—but was dated and incomplete. There were no successful National Imagery ad-hoc collections in support of the Division for the entire war.

Unlike the MEU, the Division did not have access to an organic TEG-E to download and exploit National Imagery. This was a weakness during planning, but a critical vulnerability during combat operations. There were issues with bandwidth, exploitation, and processes that caused this state of affairs, but the bottom line was no successful ad-hoc National imagery exploitation products during the entire war....

Once the Division crossed the line of departure, contact with the Intelligence Battalion was sporadic, and even this avenue was closed. It was frustrating to be desperate for current high-resolution imagery of Safwan Town (for example) and unable to receive it in response to a tactical unit's request, only to see perfect imagery appear in an NGIC assessment only days later. There was a broken link in this chain.

The only National imagery available to the Division was the 1m Controlled Imagery Base (CIB), and most of the Division's intelligence effort was based on products we built using this as a baseline. The NIMA provided Controlled Imagery Base (CIB1), though coverage area was large, did not provide the resolution required for detailed tactical planning. Some of the baseline coverage provided was also dated and misrepresented some areas that had changed over the last year.

If National level imagery products are to be of use to the tactical (Battalion) commander, the capability to request and follow through on National imagery collections must reside at lower echelons. The collections management hierarchy must be flattened. The Division must have the ability to download and exploit imagery organically, much like the MEU does now. Reliance on an external agency to anticipate requirements, know what is important to the supported commander, and be a full partner in the intelligence effort is not realistic.

Division should never enter planning or combat operations without complete baseline imagery coverage at no worse than 1m resolution. Baseline imagery must be reasonably current and have high enough resolution to be able to identify tactical terrain. It must also be geo-rectified and include elevation data to be used for thorough terrain analysis to support operational planning.

The same Marine Corps assessment of lessons learned notes several other intelligence problems that are both echoed by less formal reporting by sources in the U.S. Army and U.S. Air Force and generally all too familiar from the lessons of past conflicts:[15]

Lack of Organic Aerial Collection at Division and Regiment: After crossing the Line of departure, the Division received very little actionable intelligence from external intelligence organizations. The Division had to assemble a coherent picture from what it could collect with organic and DS [direct support] assets alone. The nature of the battlefield, the extreme distances, high operational tempo and lack of a coherent response from a conventional enemy all made it difficult for an external agency to know what was tactically relevant and required by the GCE commander. The Byzantine collections process inhibited our ability to get timely responses to combat requirements with the exception of assets organic to or DS to the Division. This made the Division almost exclusively reliant on organic or DS collection assets.

The Division found the enemy by running into them, much as forces have done since the beginning of warfare. The Pioneer worked great when the bureaucracy between the VMU and the Division G-2 could be negotiated, but the lack of a habitual relationship and adequate rehearsal time limited our ability to do so. A superb example of a successful UAV system was the Dragoneye, which was fielded to selected Battalions and allowed to collect against the commander's priorities, locations, and schedule without interference from higher headquarters. On a fluid high tempo battlefield, a highly centralized collections bureaucracy is too slow and cumbersome to be tactically relevant. The best possible employment option is to push more assets in DS to the lowest tactical level and increase available organic collections....Empower the lower echelons and decentralize the collection process.

Lack of Tactical Intelligence Collection at Division and Regiment: Generally, the state of the Marine Corps' tactical intelligence collection capability is well behind the state of the art. Maneuver units have limited ability to see over the next hill, around the next corner, or inside the next building. Supporting intelligence collectors (VMU, P-3AIP, ATARS, Theater, and National level assets) were great for developing deep targets, subject to the prioritization of higher headquarters (Division and higher.) Navigating the labyrinth of collection tasking processes proved too difficult in most cases to get reporting on Division targets, and certainly for Battalion-level collections. For the amount of money spent on an ATARS POD, could be handsomely equipped with a suite of motion sensors, digital imaging equipment with zoom lenses, laser range finders, small UAVs, thermal imagers, robotic sensors, and other tactically focused intelligence collectors.

The Marine Corps has a tremendous void in its intelligence collection capabilities at the echelon that needs it the most....Procure scalable family of tactical intelligence collection platforms, both ground and air, and make them organic to the Division and Regimental intelligence shops. Integrate them into an intelligence collections toolkit and make it the TO weapon for a Battalion S-2. Follow the model of the Radio Battalion Modifications program as an acquisition strategy. This program maintains modern equipment at tactical units by buying non-developmental systems and fielding them.

Information Inundation vice "Smart Push": Intelligence sections at all levels were inundated with information and data that had little bearing on their mission or Intelligence requirements. Information was not disseminated based on a proactive evaluation of what support commanders needed, it was just disseminated. There seemed to be little thought to tailoring information to specific MSCs or develop products that directly anticipated an MSC requirement. The concept of "smart push" (providing only the information, data, and intelligence that could support a given mission) was not used. It seemed that all data, information, and products were being pushed through overburdened communications paths with little thought to who needed what and when they needed it. The burden of sifting through tremendous amounts of raw data fell to each MSC's already overburdened intelligence section. Often, the MSC was forced to retrieve relevant collections reports directly from producing agencies or review the IOC journal to find relevant collections. Intelligence support to subordinate elements must be tailored to their current and anticipated future requirements. Too much time and bandwidth is wasted by employing the "information inundation" method....This applies to every echelon of command. Intelligence personnel at all levels, especially those in leadership positions, must be in tune with subordinate intelligence requirements, and guide a proactive effort to anticipate these requirements. Supporting intelligence agencies must proactively seek to know what their supported units require and seek to fill those requirements. This is a mindset and leadership issue, not a technical one.

Cumbersome Collections Bureaucracy: OIF [Operation Iraqi Freedom] presented the intelligence community with unprecedented robust collection architecture to support combat operations. Unfortunately it also presented the community and more specifically the tactical user with the equally unprecedented cumbersome collection bureaucracy. The existing hierarchical collections architecture, particularly for imagery requirements, is wildly impractical and does not lend itself to providing timely support to combat operations. Requesting imagery coverage required the use of a user-unfriendly PRISM system that was not readily accessible and provided the submitter of requests no feedback or other means of determining if his requirements were going to be met. There was no visible correlation between the submission of collections requests and actual collections conducted, nor does the current architecture provide any practical way to receive the results of user-requested collections from national or theater collection assets without conducting extensive and time- consuming database searches. The unwieldy nature of the automated system was further complicated by the need to work through multiple command layers in order to get tasking to a collection asset. All of this made for a collection management system that was too slow and cumbersome to provide meaningful support to the warfighter, particularly once operations had begun. This is not a technical issue, it is a human issue. The Byzantine labyrinth concocted to filter out collections requirements posed administrative hurdles too high for tactical users to leap. With few exceptions, such as the national support provided by NIMA, no meaningful or actionable imagery support to the GCE was provided by any collection asset not either attached to the Division or organic to it. [Need to] streamline collection request architecture. Modify existing PRISM system to provide automatic feedback to imagery collection requests and automatically route results of collections to requestors. Push more collection assets in direct support to maneuver units and field more and better tactical collections systems. Provide advocacy for MSC requirements at MEF and higher levels.

Problems with HUMINT: OIF presented the intelligence community with an extremely robust collection architecture. There was near comprehensive IMINT, MASINT, and SIGINT coverage of the battle space, but there was very little HUMINT [human intelligence] available to provide insight into the human dimension of the battlefield. Advances in technology and the mature collection environment in the theater made for a great profusion of intelligence on the enemy. We had an unprecedented level of resolution on the disposition of enemy equipment and near instant warning of activation of electronic systems or artillery fires. In many cases we maintained virtual surveillance of selected enemy forces. But, in spite of these capabilities we remained largely ignorant of the intentions of enemy commanders. While we were able to point with some certainty where their armor and artillery were deployed, we were largely in the dark as to what they meant to do with it. This shortcoming was especially critical as much of the war plan was either based on or keyed to specific enemy responses. When the enemy "failed" to act in accordance with common military practice, we were caught flat-footed because we failed to accurately anticipate the unconventional response. This was primarily due to a dearth of HUMINT on the enemy leadership. In trying to map out the opposition's reactions we were largely relegated to OSINT sources and rank speculation based on our own perceptions of the battlefield to make our assessments. There was no available intelligence on the opposition commanders' personalities, educations, decisionmaking styles, or previous experiences. Lacking this information, we were left with guessing what we would do in their place. This met with predictable results. In an effort to bridge the gap we did create an understudy program. Each Corps and Division Commander was assigned to a Marine Officer. The understudy then attempted to learn as much as possible about "his" commander, i.e., his training, history, decisionmaking tendencies, etc. This met with some success, but was limited to the amount of Intelligence and Open source information available.

Our technical dominance has made us overly reliant on technical and quantifiable intelligence collections means. There is institutional failure to account for the most critical dimension of the battlefield, the human one. As we saw demonstrated in OIF, the human aspect of the battle can be more important than the material one. Success on future battlefields requires that commensurate efforts be made to know the commander's mind as well as the disposition of his forces.... [We need to] focus national collection and analysis efforts on the idiosyncrasies of enemy leadership and work to build a national database that goes beyond basic biographical data to in-depth assessments on how potential enemy commanders think and behave. Information about Foreign Military Training curriculums and how this may influence their decisionmaking should be included.

HUMINT Representation on Division and Regimental Staffs: The 1st Marine Division G2 did not have sufficient HUMINT Representation at the Division Staff level and there was no HUMINT representation at the Regimental staff level. The HUMINT reps provided did yeoman's work trying to keep up with the tremendous demand, but were stretched thin. The HUMINT capabilities provided to the Division were incredibly valuable and highly effective. There is a definite need to have HUMINT representation down to RCT level. The planning, support, analysis, and employment of assets are dependent on knowledgeable representatives advising the commanders and staff. HUMINT assets were frequently improperly employed, inadequately tasked and supported at the Tactical level. There was insufficient HUMINT expertise at the staff level to do the planning in support of the unit's mission. There is also a lack of personnel to do analysis, it was not being done and pushed down from higher, and there was no one to do it at the unit level. Having a staff HUMINT officer at the Division level for planning and preparation phases of the operation would also be of great assistance. There needs to be staff representation at all levels for HUMINT. There needs to be a limited analysis capability down at the Regimental Level. Provide an Analysis and control cell down to the Division and Regimental Level, proportionate to the requirement. Ensure the expertise exists in the team to provide planning support to the commander and Analysis support for the supported S-2.

The Need for Improvisation and Tailoring IS&R Systems to a Given Conflict

Another Marine Corps report on the IS&R lessons of the war shows the degree to which each service had to improvise key elements of an IS&R system that was tailored to the specific needs of the Iraq War. At the same time, it provides a picture of a far more joint and effective tactical IS&R

effort than the United States had ever previously been able to employ in combat:[16]

1 MEF deployed an initial command element to Kuwait in October 2002 to prepare for the MEF main body to arrive and commence combat operations against Iraq. This culminated nine months of planning and preparation. It also marked a critical milestone in the progress of the Marine Corps Intelligence Plan adopted in 1994. The MEF ISR team eventually totaled nearly 3,000 Marines, Soldiers, Sailors, Airmen, and civilians.

...The pre-war IPB support was exhaustive. The MEF ISR team, coupled with MCIA direct support, as well as leveraged support from JICCENT and the national intelligence community, generated an unprecedented understanding of the battlespace and threat capabilities and intentions.... 1 MEF formed a Combat Intelligence Center (CIC) at Camp Commando in Kuwait that served as the intelligence "factory." The CIC formed around the Intelligence Operations Center (IOC) that provided current intelligence and reactive targeting support to the maneuver units. The MEF developed an all-source fusion center that included 1st Intelligence Bn analysts, Radio Battalion's OCAC, the 1st United Kingdom Armored Division's 245th Signals Battalion, an NSA cryptologic support element, a CIA Contingency Operations Liaison Team (COLT), and a NIMA quick response system for imagery and mapping support.

...1 MEF G2 knew that the tyranny of time and distance would preclude precise tactical intelligence flow from the MEF to the maneuver formations. Thus, the MEF constructed the ISR team to enable economy of force operations to hold enemy formations at bay on the flanks, shape the Republican Guard Divisions in the deep fight, while facilitating the success of the RCT S2 and Fire Support Coordinator in the close fight. The plan called for providing the RCT's with the ability to directly receive most of the signals from the theater and tactical sensors. By cutting out the middle men (MEF and the GCE's) the intelligence got to [the] using unit much faster and in time to have a chance to shape the local action. The concept of centralizing ISR planning and control while decentralizing execution control worked quite well. Communications limitations kept the maneuver battalions from fully participating in this bold concept. Extending that intelligence umbrella to the battalion commander is the next hurdle in the intelligence plan.

Decentralizing the ISR elements and sensor feeds enabled the RCT's to act as semiautonomous intelligence teams. Each RCT had a Trojan Spirit II to give it mobile SCI communications. The attached SIGINT Support Teams took full advantage of this by using these terminals to pass their collected intercepts. An imbedded Radio Reconnaissance Sub-Team accompanied most Force Reconnaissance Teams that were inserted into the deep battlespace. They provided threat warning to the recon teams and extended the

MEF's ground-based SIGINT collection baseline into the unreachable deep nooks and crannies of the MEF's battlespace. The HUMINT Exploitation Teams (HET's), located with each maneuver battalion, provided a treasure trove of real-time intelligence, even providing tips that enabled immediate cross-boundary fire support coordination with U.S. V Corps on the MEF's left flank. Moreover, the HET's developed the intelligence that led to the dramatic rescue of U.S. Army POW's in An Nasiryah and Samarra.

Imagery was used extensively to help shape the deep battle and decisively influence the close battle. The MEF's Intelligence Operations Center had a large imagery receive and exploitation capability. The IOC tasked, received, processed, and exploited imagery from national satellites, U2, F-14 Tarps, GR-4, ATARS, as well as full motion video from UAV's. The IOC produced literally hundreds of precision mensurated targets so that Third MAW aircrews could destroy large Iraqi formations with precision armament well before the GCE's could close on the enemy.

PIONEERS (UAVs) from VMU-1 and VMU-2 were among the stars of this event. These squadrons were placed in direct support of 1st Marine Division and Task Force Tarawa. They provided full motion video through direct downlink to the RCT's, helping pinpoint targets in both the close and deep fight. Their real-time support enabled MEF Fires while relieving the GCE's of this burden and thereby energizing the entire MEF Fires Process.

1st Force Reconnaissance Company deployed numerous ground mobile recon teams along the flanks and in the depths of the MEF's battlespace. These economy of force operations proved invaluable in freeing up larger maneuver formations or sections of F/A-18s that would otherwise have been absorbed in this critical flank security task. An interesting side note is that none of the MEF's ground reconnaissance elements used parachute operations as a means of insertion. All teams were inserted by either 3rd MAW CH-53E's or by their own HMMWV's or fast attack vehicles.

...The Marine Corps Intelligence Plan paved the way to...notable successes....However, Operation Iraqi Freedom revealed areas for continued growth to include

- a Marine Corps family of UAV's that cover the close fight through the deep fight;
- placement of the UAV squadrons in the MEF Command Element to ensure responsive command and control;
- complete review of the ATARS program to assure its relevancy in any future rapid, mobile warfare environment;
- continued aggressive decentralization of ISR to the maneuver battalion to enable semiautonomous ISR operations and facilitation of the targeting process; and

■ complete overhaul of the Marine Corps language program. It was inadequate to the tasks demanded of it. Marine Corps ISR has made incredible advances in the last twelve years. The last four years have seen an especially accelerated pace of change. 1 MEF took full advantage of this increased capability. It paid off with pinpoint, relevant, and focused intelligence, not only at the point of attack, but also throughout the expansive MEF battlespace.

It is clear from this description, as well as from similar reports from the other U.S. services and from discussions with British and Australian officers, that the Iraq War shows the need for significant advances in creating a standardized IS&R architecture—one that operates on a joint level for all the U.S. services, has suitable interoperability with key allies, and expands "jointness" to cover the entire U.S. intelligence community, including the CIA, NRO, NSA, and NIMA. At the same time, it is equally clear that any such "system of systems" must be extremely flexible and modular, must use technology and software that are mature enough to support high-intensity war fighting without strategic warning, and cannot substitute for dedicated single service systems and capabilities tailored to the needs of the war fighter at the combat level. As is the case with jointness, this describes a process of careful evolution that will almost certainly take a decade or more to mature.

The Limits of IS&R Capability

As General Tommy Franks noted in his first briefing to the Congress on the lessons of the Iraq War, the steady advances in IS&R systems and technology, and the expansion of analytic assets, have still left the United States with serious intelligence limits.[17] Some of these limits have already been discussed, and others are discussed in more detail in the chapters that follow. Still, the following key problems and shortfalls did emerge during the war:

■ The United States simply did not have enough area experts, technical experts, and analysts with language skills at any level to make optimal use of its sensors and collection. This was as true at the national level as at the tactical level, and collection overload was a problem in many areas.

■ As has been discussed, the United States had a far greater capability to target buildings than to characterize what went on in those buildings and the effects of strikes on most sets of structures. It could not measure the level of wartime activity in many cases (facilities with high emission levels were an exception), and this made the efforts at "effects-based" operations discussed in later chapters difficult and sometimes impossible. Moreover, estimates of the level and nature of underground and sheltered facilities and activity were generally highly problematic.

- The problem was compounded in many cases by an inability to establish clear parameters for operations in "strategic areas" like the value of potential leadership targets, degrading given C4I assets, attacking LOC facilities, or attacking military depots, facilities, and industrial activities. At least some experts feel the end result was that the U.S. IS&R effort mistargeted leadership facilities, exaggerated the importance of C4I strikes, and overtargeted fixed military facilities. It is, however, unclear whether the United States and its allies had any choice. Striking more targets in the face of uncertainty was probably better than striking only those targets where high confidence could be established as to the effect.

- The IS&R effort was not able to characterize and target the Iraqi weapons of mass destruction effort before or during the war, or to provide reliable warning of the tactical threat. It seems to have been somewhat better in dealing with potential delivery systems. But the level of improvement relative to the inability to locate the Iraqi chemical, biological, and nuclear effort is unclear.

- The IS&R effort often had to take a "worst case" approach to the potential role of Iraq's security forces, intelligence services, irregular forces like Saddam's Fedayeen, and unusual military formations like the Special Republican Guards. In fairness, however, it is difficult—if not impossible—to accurately characterize the war-fighting capability of forces that have never fought and that do not conduct open and realistic exercises.

- The IS&R sensor and analytic effort focused more on major combat forces, with heavy weapons, than on infantry or irregular forces. It could do a much better job of locating and characterizing weapons platforms and military emitters than of dealing with personnel and forces that relied on light vehicles. It was generally difficult or impossible to locate distributed forces in a built-up or urban environment until they were driven into some form of open military activity, and the United States often lacked the density of specialized assets like UAVs to carry out this mission even when open activity took place.

- The IS&R effort did much to reduce collateral damage and the risk of civilian casualties. It was neither organized nor capable, however, of assessing either civilian or military casualties.

- Improvements in C4I and the structure of the IS&R effort sharply reduced the time between the acquisition of targeting data and actual fire on the target, although many problems remained. The speed and intensity of the war do seem, however, to have led to a major breakdown in the battle damage assessment (BDA) process. Quite aside from the many gaps and uncertainties remaining in the BDA process, the IS&R system could not close the cycle in terms of target-shoot-assess on a timely and accurate basis, and this remains a critical challenge in creating true netcentric war.

None of these problems in analytic and collection capability can be called "intelligence failures." Rather, they are currently "intelligence impossibilities." Either the sensors and technology to collect the necessary information are lacking, or suitable analytic tools do not exist, or both. As is the case with so many other aspects of the Iraq War, however, it is important to understand that many major challenges and problems remain to be resolved.

THE IMPACT OF SPACE WARFARE

Space is scarcely a traditional fundamental of war. But it has been a fundamental ever since the United States first made use of satellites for intelligence purposes. In the Iraq War, the United States used space for battle management, for communications, to locate its forces and guide its weapons, and to perform a wide range of other missions. It built upon the lessons of the Gulf War and Afghan War and on progress in worldwide communications dating back to the days of Vietnam. At the same time, this was the first large-scale war in which the United States could fight with 24-hour continuing intelligence satellite and sensor coverage over the battlefield, as well as the first major conflict where it could take advantage of full 24-hour coverage by the global positioning satellite (GPS) system.

Overall Coalition Superiority

The United States and Britain did not have total dominance of space. Iraq had access to satellites for television transmittal during much of the war and was able to use friendly Arab satellite media to make its case. It had purchased large amounts of commercial satellite photography both directly and through various fronts before the war, and it could make commercial use of the global positioning satellite system.[18]

The coalition had so great a superiority in every area of space, however, that Iraq's capabilities were trivial in comparison. The United States was able to build upon the lessons of both the Gulf War and the war in Afghanistan, and although the strengths and weaknesses of its space-centered efforts may remain classified for years, it is clear that major progress was made. One press report indicates that the United States made use of more than 50 satellites during the war, including the two dozen satellites in the GPS system.

Space provided a wide range of intelligence, targeting, and battle damage assessment capabilities. It was the key to effective command and control and to netted global military communications. The range of space-based communications and sensor assets, and the vast bandwidth the United States could bring to managing global military operations, allowed it to achieve near-real-time command and control and intelligence collection, processing, and dissemination. At the same time, GPS allowed U.S. and British forces to locate friendly and enemy forces and both target and guide weapons. The United States also made use of satellites to locate missile launches, predict their target, and provide warning.[19] USCENTAF reports that U.S. infrared satellites detected some 26 Iraqi missile launches, 1,493 static events, 186 high-explosive events, 40 hook bursts, and 48 ATACMs events.[20]

Evolving Space into Jointness

At the operational level, a decade of command experience by U.S. Air Force, Army, and Navy commanders who stressed joint operations had helped transform the space operations community from a secretive scientific-based one to a specialized cadre integrated with air, land, and sea combat forces.

Some of this success may stem from organizational changes made in 2002. Previous commanders of the Air Force Space Command (AFSPC) also served as commander in chief of the U.S. Space and the North American Aerospace Defense commands, splitting their time among the three. On April 19, 2002, General Lance W. Lord was made a full-time commander of AFSPC. General Lord summarized the role of space in the Iraq War as follows: [21]

> During the Gulf War, milspace was in its formative stages. We only had 16–17 GPS satellites back then [for example]. That was a rudimentary capability compared to what we have now.... [Our] people are deployed throughout the Centcom [Central Command] Area of Responsibility...and are part of the Expeditionary Air Force, that's for sure.

One place you see [milspace] capabilities come to bear is in the Combined Air Operations Center at Prince Sultan AB in Saudi Arabia. We have a space team on duty round-the-clock in the CAOC, helping coordinate GPS, intelligence, surveillance, reconnaissance, weather, and communications—all the things "space" is capable of doing.

It makes sure "space" is fully integrated into any campaign planning and operations [now], and will be fully integrated into any future [war] operations.... I think they're growing, and we're out there, spreading the word that we're part of the team....We're really hitting our stride [now]. It's getting better all the time.

One article described the transformation as one from "space geeks" to "space-smart" officers in an environment where enlisted troops worked closely with traditional war fighters in Combined Air Operations Centers (CAOCs). Air strike planners regularly obtained advice and inputs from military space experts on how to ensure that a number of GPS satellites would be in view over a target area, particularly when GPS-aided weapons were to be delivered. The same was true of coordination in using satellite-derived weather information and imagery of target areas and in conducting network-centric operations and using space-based communication links.

These changes did much to break down the intelligence rivalries, compartmentation, and emphasis on "keeping the secrets" that badly hurt the space effort during the Gulf War—although preliminary conversations indicate that they scarcely solved the problem.[22] There is still a need to redefine "jointness" so that the entire Intelligence Community plays a suitable role in war fighting. Agencies like the CIA, NRO, and NSA may be civilian—and certainly have many other tasks and responsibilities—but they are also a critical part of modern joint and netcentric warfare. Good answers need to be found to fully integrating them into modern military operations and into joint commands. Moreover, field reports indicate that there are still too many barriers at every level in the chain to the proper flow and dissemination of information because of security classification. As one war fighter put it, "Security officers are supposed to be on our side, not on the side of the enemy."

The U.S. Army has also been slower than the U.S. Air Force to fully integrate space into its operations. It has updated some of its space policy as a result of the Iraq War, updating a policy dating back to 1994. It has been slow, however, to develop effective tasking arrangements for imagery satellites with the NRO, and some army experts believe it has been slow to seek more secure GPS technology.[23]

Space and Communications

The space effort in the Iraq War benefited from improved communications, integration, data processing, and analytic methods, and command and control at every level. National, theater, and tactical intelligence had much better integration, processing, and dissemination than during the Gulf War, building on the lessons of that conflict and Afghanistan. As in the Gulf and Afghan wars, however, space was particularly important to military communications. Work by the Marine Corps Systems Command (MCSC) on the lessons of the war illustrates just how vital space communications were to the coalition's success:

> Interoperability of various Communications equipment was an issue in all C3 vehicles and COCs (Tanks, LAR, AAVs). Marines were overwhelmed with the high number of varied communications equipment they were expected to use. Routinely, communicators, operations officers, and commanders found themselves in information overload as they received information over too many different networks (e.g., an LAV Marine was connected to the intercom via his CVC headset, receiving information on a personal intra squad radio (requiring him to remove his helmet to talk), while also (depending on the particular LAVs configuration) "working" 2–3 man portable radios to communicate with other units (PVC 5 for SEALs, PRC 148 for fellow Marines, etc.) and "monitoring" two laptops). This situation was exacerbated in C3 vehicles where I personally saw that every "shelf" was taken up by a radio and seat spaces and floor spaces were taken up with open computers for communications devices such as Blue Force Tracker, MDACT, or Iridium phones. Marines recounted numerous instances where units would call via radio to verify that a message was received over MDACT, while the receiving unit had just put the MDACT aside to monitor BFT since a previous unit had called asking about the receipt of a digital photo over BFT. Consolidation of communications assets/capabilities is an issue that requires review at the institutional level. Commanders want one box that provides multiple capabilities and that is simple and easy to use.
>
> Overwhelmingly, units were in agreement that communications architecture required an overhaul. There were too many different devices that provided redundant capabilities. Additionally, units never seemed to receive enough of *one* communications asset, forcing them to rely on a "hodgepodge" of assets that were not consistent throughout the force. (E.g., some units had only MDACT for digital communication while another unit had only Blue Force Tracker. These units could not talk to each other unless they went through a third party or used a courier system.) A specific case occurred between LAR S-2 and the Div G-2 while attempting to send pictures from the Dragon Eye to Division HQ G-2. The S-2 had BFT readily available while the

G-2 did not. The G-2 needed to "borrow" the commander's BFT to receive these messages or simply wait for a courier with a MEMOREX disk to arrive with the pictures. Time lost often rendered the pictures irrelevant in this fast-paced fight. As the Operations Officer from 1st LAR stated, "the communications architecture is broken and the interoperability of various communications assets is virtually non-existent."

...The only consistently reliable means of communication was "SAT-COM." In this fast-paced war, if a communications system was not functioning quickly, alternative methods were employed. This was a specific problem of the EPLRS radio (which relies on Line of Site [LOS]). With units constantly moving over various terrain, LOS was not possible. Accordingly, any system connected to the EPLRS radio proved unreliable (e.g., MDACT, AFATDS, etc.). The only systems consistently praised by the Marines were the Blue Force Tracker (SATCOM—though unsecure) and Iridium Phones (SATCOM). These systems provided reliable communications at all times. In many instances these systems were the sole means of communication.

Many Marines noted MDACT, which has a larger bandwidth and greater capability for sending electronic information, was marginalized by its dependence on the EPLRS (LOS) radio. As one commander stated, "Satellite Communications is simply the way of the future and the Marine Corps needs to start focusing on that." Rumor suggested the Army "gave" the Marine Corps satellite time [note: I believe the USMC contracted bandwidth prior to crossing the LD] in order to use the BFT; had this not been the case, the Marine Corps would have found itself fighting, in several instances, without tactical communication.

The Ongoing Evolution of Space

The United States and Britain made use of numerous communications satellites and about half a dozen electro-optical and signals intelligence satellites. A press report indicates that the National Reconnaissance Office (NRO) employed three advanced "KH-11"-type visible and infrared imaging satellites and 2 to 3 "Lacrosse"-type all-weather imaging radar satellites that proved especially effective in spotting armored movements and whose data were used in conjunction with data from the E-8C JSTARS. At least one of these satellites could image the battlefield every 2 to 3 hours, and they made some 12 passes per day. A total of some 33,500 personnel at 21 U.S. sites and 15 foreign locations were involved in the overall space support effort.[24]

Press reports, however, can only hint at the overall architecture and capabilities of U.S. space systems and how rapidly they are evolving. As a result, there is no way to quantify or describe recent and planned changes in U.S. space capabilities in detail. Unclassified discussions of the increase in satellite imagery (PHOTINT) coverage and capability simply cannot be grounded in reality, although the level of resolution and "24/7" persistence of coverage has clearly changed radically. The same is true of any effort to provide an unclassified analysis of the much more complicated problems of assessing the trends in space-based electronic intelligence (ELINT) and signals intelligence (SIGINT).

What is clear is that advances in data processing and the ability to develop complex "mosaics" of all forms of space intelligence are now being mixed in near-real-time with improved airborne platform coverage of imagery, ELINT, and SIGINT and processing of human intelligence (HUMINT), data from ground units like Special Forces, and open sources. The end result is a new form of space-centered joint intelligence that has led to a massive improvement in situational awareness and targeting capability that is one of the keys to precision warfare and rapid maneuver.

At the same time, those involved in operating and upgrading U.S. space systems are among the first to say that space warfare is still in its early days. Much of the ability to net, process, and utilize space capabilities remains relatively primitive compared to its potential; the human factors and ergonomics of space exploitation remain crude; and joint warfare is only beginning to exploit the potential of space-centered warfare.

The Importance of GPS

The importance of the global positioning satellite system is illustrated by the fact that when GPS was introduced into the U.S. Army during the Gulf War, there was a maximum of one receiver per company or 180 men. In the Iraq War, there were more than 100,000 Precision Lightweight GPS Receivers (PLGRs or "pluggers") for the land forces and at least one per nine-man squad. The marines had fewer units, but still had 5,400, or roughly one per platoon (3 to 5 squads.) Moreover, a number of marines carried their own civilian GPS units.[25] The British also had some units. These devices not only gave troops precise locations, but—as is described in the next chapter—allowed friendly forces to be automatically located and tracked as they moved.

These advances scarcely solved all military navigation and guidance problems. In one highly publicized incident near An Nasiryah, members of the U.S. Army's 507th Maintenance Company got lost and ran into an ambush. Eight servicemen were killed and six were taken prisoner. It is far from clear, however, that this was related to the capabilities of the GPS system.

In any case, the technology in future wars is likely to be much better. The PLGR now costs roughly $1,000 and weighs about 2.75 pounds, and it is accurate to within 10 yards versus 20 to 25 yards for civilian units. It does not, however, display maps, only location and velocity. In contrast, the new FBCB2 system introduced in U.S. Army combat vehicles during the war does allow broad electronic display of the battlefield and can track friendly forces using their GPS information and red forces using intelligence with GPS coordinates.[26]

The United States is also developing a new generation of hand-held GPS systems called the Defense Advanced GPS Receiver, or DAGR, which will be more accurate and more resistant to jamming. It also will have a mapping system that displays both red-blue forces and key terrain features and obstacles like minefields and rivers. The one-pound device can be plugged into military radios to communicate location data.

The GPS systems used by the land forces now run on the same 1,575 megahertz frequency as civilian systems, although the military system is encrypted. The new systems for land forces will use the much more secure military frequency of 1,227 megahertz that is used by combat aircraft, cruise missiles, and other airborne systems. They will be able to track all 12 GPS satellites in a given hemisphere at once, versus 5 for the current systems, and they will have classified technology to verify that the devices are reading only U.S. military signals and not jamming or deception signals from the enemy.

GPS Jammers and Countermeasures

Although Iraq had at least four jammers designed to jam the coalition GPS system although, these seem to have been destroyed early in the war and to have had little operational effectiveness. According to one press report, the jammers were successfully attacked by B-1Bs and F-117s; at least some seem to have been attacked with GPS-guided weapons.[27] The very fact such jammers existed, however, is a warning that eventually there is a countermeasure to virtually every tactic and technology. It is also a lesson that GPS modernization remains a critical priority.[28]

The GPS satellite signal is roughly equivalent to the light from a 25-watt bulb at a distance of 11,000 miles. The Russian firm Aviaconversia claims that its low-power 4-watt jammer can block a receiver from picking up signals up to 124 miles away if there is line of sight. One explanation is that military GPS signals are roughly 1,000 times stronger than civilian signals when they are locked into their military frequency and use the military P-code. As a result, a jammer with a potential jamming range of 100 miles against a civilian unit will only work for a few miles against a military unit. These counterjamming capabilities are also expected to increase strikingly in the near future when the United States deploys the G-STAR, a system designed to block the jamming signal and direct the GPS unit to use beam steering to look for other satellites. (Most GPS guided weapons have a fallback. For example, the JDAM defaults to inertial guidance, although its accuracy degrades from an average of around 40 feet to 100 feet.)

"OWNING THE NIGHT" AND "ALL-WEATHER WARFARE"

The value of all-weather capabilities has been critical ever since the end of the traditional military campaigning season, a development dating back in some ways to the end of the American Civil War and certainly at a broader level to World War I. The value of "owning the night" dates back to World War II and the first crude infrared searchlights and vision devices. U.S. and British forces had force-wide technical superiority in virtually every area of combat over an Iraqi force that had had only minimal modernization since the summer of 1990, and then only in the form of erratic deliveries of smuggled arms. One of the most critical areas, however, was one in which the U.S.-led coalition had a somewhat similar advantage in the Gulf War.

The Need for Improved Tactical Support Capabilities

U.S. and British forces could both fight and maneuver at night and largely in the dark. U.S. operations also continued despite major sandstorms, cloud cover, and rain. The value of this capability is indicated by the fact that 70 percent of Iraq was cloud free for only 30 percent of the war. The weather was clear or with scattered clouds at or below 10,000 feet, and with little or no dust impact, for only 17 days out of 31. As has been discussed earlier, coalition land and air forces kept fighting through three days of severe sand and dust storms. The coalition had to cancel only 4 percent of its sorties because of weather during the entire war; 65 percent of cancellations occurred during this three-day period of bad weather.

At the same time, accounts of combat make it clear that this capability was at least as much a matter of training and readiness as technology. In many cases, particularly for land forces and attack helicopters, sensors and night division devices had severe limitations and forces had to operate without adequate technology.

This was a critical aspect of logistics of combat forces. One possible lesson of the Iraq War that needs validation in the field is the need to provide better trackers, communications, GPS displays, and night vision systems to logistic and support forces—particularly if they are to move quickly through areas where the flanks and rear sections are not fully secured and also in combat, where the success of maneuver cannot wait on weather problems or night vision conditions.

The Need for Better Radar and Space Capabilities

There is another area where improvements may be needed. The dust storms in the Iraq War highlighted the value of radar imaging versus infrared and electro-optical imaging. The JSATS proved particularly valuable in tracking Iraqi land forces at a time when other sensors had severe limits. Aircraft and UAVs do, however, have limits in terms of coverage and the ability to provide continuous coverage on a "24/7" basis.

Although the programs involved are classified, the United States does not seem to have pushed forward with creating satellite capabilities to use radar imaging for ground tracking. The Department of Defense sought such a program, called Discover 2, in the late 1990s. It was cancelled by the House Appropriations Committee on the grounds of cost and because it was not integrated into an effective systems architecture and war-fighting concepts. Significant progress has been made in technologies like high-resolution synthetic aperture radars, however, and the Department has again requested funds for a space-based program.

The Iraq War is scarcely the only war in which weather has had a powerful impact on U.S. imaging capabilities, however, and it is just as important to "own the weather" as to own the night. As a result, there seems to be good reason why the United States should reevaluate the need for a robust radar satellite program.[29]

THE IMPORTANCE OF SUSTAINABILITY

Sustainability and logistics are more traditional military fundamentals, and their importance was critical at every level. Although the fact gets little attention, U.S. armored and mechanized forces are now the only armored forces in the world that can sustain long-range intensive air operations, support armored maneuver movements against hostile forces, and then conduct combat with sufficient combat and service support forces to maintain nearly 24/7 operations with minimal time for rest and regrouping, provide fuel and some 40,000 gallons of water a day, and supply some 300,000 MREs.

These capabilities are particularly striking for two reasons: the United States can project them virtually anywhere in the world, and even a force as professional as the British Army had serious problems providing reliable tactical supply in a location as close to Kuwait as the greater Basra area.[30] They are also a warning that without such capabilities, cosmetic NATO and EU power projection forces have little real-world war-fighting capability against a serious opponent. Any force that can move can be called a power projection force; only a force that can truly sustain long-range intensive air and armored maneuver warfare can truly project power.

Airborne Refueling

Once again, the ability to refuel in mid-air and in intense, complex missions proved absolutely critical to power projection and in theater air operations, substituting for aircraft range and payload and allowing long patrol and loiter times. As of April 11, the United States flew some 7,525 tanker sorties and delivered some 46 million gallons in aerial refueling.[31] If one looks at the entire period of the war, the USAF flew 6,193 tanker sorties, the USMC flew 454, the U.S. Navy flew 2,058, and the RAF flew 359, for a total of 9,064.[32] The British Royal Air Force flew 355 air-to-air refueling sorties. It dispensed 18.9 million pounds of fuel during its refueling operations, and more than 40 percent went to U.S. Navy and Marine Corps aircraft.[33]

However, this effort illustrates the need for depth in air space to allow such operations to be conducted outside the air battlefield, and the coordination problems in such efforts create a need for dedicated forms of air control management.

Vice Admiral Timothy Keating, commander of all maritime forces involved in Operation Iraqi Freedom, described these problems in a briefing on April 12, 2003:

> In the early days…there were some allocations challenges, certainly, that we worked through with Buzz Moseley. It didn't affect the overall campaign. We were able to move gas around tactically and operationally, if you will, near real time, and then make some accommodations in the air tasking order. You have to remember, and some of the guys you may know down from Oceania, for a fighter pilot, there's never enough gas airborne. They can always use more. So, you'll hear that beef from junior through senior fighter pilots of all services. There's never enough gas. There were some early growing pains, if you will, with the hundreds and hundreds of airplanes in the air simultaneously, but those problems were resolved very quickly, and it had no impact on the overall campaign.

General Tommy Franks also noted the need for both improved tanker availability, and improved strategic lift in his analysis of the lessons of the war. [34] Work is still under way on this aspect of the lessons of the war, but one preliminary conclusion seems to be that the United States will need to expand and modernize its tanker fleet for longer missions and longer-range power projection.[35]

Logistics and Power Projection

Advances in logistics allowed the United States to fight halfway around the world with an unparalleled tempo of operations. The ability to refuel aircraft, move fuel and water to maneuver units, maintain and repair equipment in the field, and rearm and sustain was critical to every aspect of operations. So were improvements at every level from support vehicles to new forms of packaging for shipping and transponder readable coding, plus half a century of practical experience in projection.

One striking change in the logistic systems in the Iraq War versus the Gulf War was the introduction of "three-dimensional" logistics in U.S. forces that allowed near-real-time tracking and characterization of shipments from origin to deployment. In the Gulf War, logistics management essentially broke down at the peak of U.S. deliveries because so many competing requests were made that it was impossible to properly track actual shipments and deliveries. In the Iraq War, much of what was shipped had small radio transponders with radio frequency identification (RFID) tags that broadcast a unique code for a given system or package. This allowed the rapid updating of on-line databases on a global basis, and the RFIDs were on the systems from factory to use in the field.[36]

The British also found the need for such a capability to be one of the lessons of the war.[37]

> ...[T]he logistic task is not complete once the equipment arrives in theatre. The complex process of distribution throughout the theatre of operations—often over hundreds of miles—then begins. The ability to track accurately the movement of stock, both whilst in transit and in theatre, is key to this process. MOD had identified the requirement for better stock visibility as an important lesson from previous operations. However, finding an affordable solution to meet this requirement has not proved easy. Elements of the US Total Asset Visibility (TAV) system were purchased as a UOR for the operation. Integrating this system into the UK's supply chain and providing sufficient training for operators in the space of three months was a challenging undertaking.

In the time available, only a limited capability was fielded. The system was not available for the early phases of the deployment, and full visibility of stores only reached as far as the entry point into Kuwait. With limited logistics information systems as well, it was therefore difficult to determine in theater the rate of consumption of critical spares (and thereby the need for reprovision) or to track down specific equipments. In the light of our experience, we need to examine the requirement for a common, robust tracking system to track equipment and stocks in fast-moving operations. However, the introduction of TAV did represent a substantial leap forward in capability and contributed to the logistic efficiency of later phases of the operation. Such efforts scarcely eliminated the challenges in logistics. Although mountains of unidentified supplies did not pile up as they did during the Gulf War, the radio transponders sometimes failed. There was little access to the RFID system at the company level that generally drew down on supplies in the field and allocated them from the rear. The allocation of lift remained a problem, and this created serious problems in providing just-in-time delivery. The army also fell short of trucks to sustain long-distance supply—a problem that is familiar to virtually every soldier concerned with supply in the field since World War II.[38] The sheer volume of the supply requirement is indicated by the fact that the coalition air forces alone used 195,753,818 gallons of jet fuel, 269,414 gallons of JPTS, 27,368 gallons of aviation gas, 2,147,248 gallons of diesel fuel, and 368,525 gallons of unleaded gasoline.

More generally, unit reports at the company and battalion level, and for detachments of helicopters, are filled with accounts of problems and delays in getting adequate supplies and in coordination between combat, support, and logistic elements. It is obvious that sufficient situational awareness did not always exist to properly synchronize the movement of logistic and support forces with the operations of combat forces. Logistic and support forces had to constantly work around these problems and were not fully equipped to adequately protect themselves. They were not properly organized or equipped to operate as the kind of highly independent elements needed to support high rates of combat unit maneuver and intense combat in an environment where the combat elements of U.S. land forces did not provide anything approaching the past level of effort to protect logistic and support forces by securing the flanks and rear areas of maneuver operations.

U.S. forces did an exceptional job of improvising and adapting. Tactical logistics need to be rethought, however, and improvements in training and equipment are needed to properly support the changes made in combat maneuver operations. Logistics and sustainment need to be better integrated into netcentric warfare, and, as discussed in the following chapters, more attention is needed to the quality of the net of communications, tracking, and force management capability at the battalion level and below. The current system overemphasizes "netting" at higher levels of combat organization at the expense of both battalion-level netting of combat elements and all aspects of logistics and sustainment.

The British also discovered an additional problem, and one that affects virtually every NATO ally to a worse degree. A heritage of constant efforts to cut the cost of logistics and supply had created a "just in time delivery" approach that worked in peacetime, but could not react to new and unanticipated demands in wartime. It is a historical reality in war that only too much is ever enough, and Britain is now reevaluating the role of its Defense Logistics Organization (DLO) to look at ways in which it could control the entire supply chain from industry to combat unit and speed orders and delivery. This may well help in reducing the lag in placing orders and between orders and delivery. It also can speed up orders and deliveries for the modification of equipment and new items that are in stock. What it cannot do is compensate for systematic underinvestment in sustainability and logistics systems—a problem that affects almost all nations in NATO as well as many other U.S. allies.[39]

Airlift and Sealift

U.S. and British ability to use sealift to move heavy cargo and equipment to the Gulf and Turkey during the months before the war, and to use Gulf ports, was critical to effective power projection. The combination of military and civil sealift and forward ports and bases made it possible to deliver virtually all equipment by sea and achieve a degree of tactical surprise, because Iraq focused on personnel movements rather than the equipment and logistic buildup.

Airlift was a natural partner in rapidly moving men and women without the lengthy delays inherent in sealift and in dealing with time-sensitive cargo and personnel movements. The United States deployed 120 C-130s and 7 C-17s full-time to the theater, plus large additional numbers of lighter transport aircraft. USCENTCOM reports that the United States flew 7,100 airlift sorties between G-Day and April 1, moved about 55,000 short tons, and deployed some 76,000 passengers between G-Day and April 9. During the full course of the war, the USAF flew 7,413 airlift sorties and Australia flew 263. The British RAF lacked the airlift to perform all of the necessary intertheater mission, but still used their four C-17 aircraft and other air transport assets to provide 50 percent of the personnel and stores that had to go by air.[40]

Intratheater mobility was also critical. The USAF flew 2,203 C-130 air mobility sorties, moving some 9,662 passengers and 12,444 short tons. It airdropped 954 personnel and performed 136 medevac missions for 1,572 patients. U.S. Marine Corps, U.S. Navy, and U.S. Air Force holdings of helicopters included 67 CH-46s, 11 CH-47s, and 54 CH-53s. The British RAF flew 263 intratheater airlift sorties.[41]

At the same time, as in the Gulf War and most previous conflicts, virtually all heavy equipment moved by sealift, as did most munitions, sustainment, and other support equipment. With the exception of light land forces, more than 90 percent of all combat unit logistic and equipment needs moved by sea. Sealift moved 18.6 million square feet of equipment for the U.S. Army and Marine Corps alone, and some 377 million gallons of fuel. The Military Sealift Command (MSC) employed nearly 80 percent of its fleet for this one contingency despite years of prepositioning. Its forces included 106 of 115 sealift ships, 33 of 40 prepositioning ships, 25 of 33 Naval Fleet Auxiliary Force vessels, and 3 of 25 special mission ships. The MSC chartered an additional 43 ships, but largely because some 40 ships carrying the equipment for the U.S. Army's 4th Infantry Division were kept in the eastern Mediterranean. Improvements in U.S. sealift would otherwise have largely eliminated the need to depend on non-U.S. ships, and the total was still far smaller than the 215 foreign charters that the MSC had to make during the Gulf War.[42]

This force included 19 of the large roll-on–roll-off ships built in the last decade to provide faster loading, sealift, and unloading. The ships can move at speeds up to 24 knots, and each is large enough to carry some 1,000 Bradleys or 3,000 SUVs. They can carry the equivalent of 140 C-5 or 240 C-17 sorties. The Royal Navy was able to obtain the delivery of four new roll-on–roll-off ships some 20 months earlier than originally planned, and they alone delivered some 11 percent (15,000 lane meters) of the equipment Britain needed. Britain depended heavily on chartered ships for the result of its build-up and supply effort.[43]

This again illustrates the fact that advances in air mobility in no way reduced the importance of sealift and of efficient and high-speed ships capable of rapidly deploying and offloading specialized military equipment. Sealift also was made more effective by the fact that ships were able to move at an average speed of 20 knots, versus 13 knots during the Gulf War, and that key ports, like Kuwait's Ash Shuaybah, could offload even the largest ships in 24 to 36 hours.

What is not clear is the extent to which experience during the Iraq War validated USAF and U.S. Navy calls for more airlift and sealift. US-TRANSCOM, for example, now has authority to buy 180 C-17s, but estimates that a minimum of 222 are required.[44]

THE ROLE OF THE RESERVES

Making the right trade-offs between active and reserve forces is another long-standing military fundamental, as important in its own right as the trade-offs between all-professional forces and conscript forces discussed in chapter 3. So far, the Iraq War has not produced the same kind of debate over the value and readiness of reserve forces that took place during and after the Gulf War in 1991. The United States did commit extensive reserve forces to Operation Iraqi Freedom. These included 10,686 in the U.S. Army Reserve, 8,866 in the Army National Guard, 2,056 in the U.S. Navy Reserve, 9,501 in the Marine Corps Reserve, 2,084 in the USAF Reserve, and 7,207 in the Air National Guard. These 40,400 reservists represent 9.5 percent of the total of 423,988 U.S. actives and reserves committed to Operation Iraqi Freedom. The Air National Guard deployed 236 aircraft and the Air Force Reserve deployed 70.[45]

The total number of reserves called up to serve in the U.S. military, however, reached a level of nearly 224,000 by late April. The Army Reserve and National Guard had more than 149,000, the Navy Reserve had nearly 12,000, the Air National Guard and Air Reserve had more than 37,000, the Marine Corps Reserve had more than 21,000, and the Coat Guard had more than 4,400. This total was surprisingly close to the 265,000 reservists that served in the first Gulf War.[46]

A study by the Congressional Research Service uses somewhat different figures, but notes that[47]

> from September 11, 2001, through April 25, 2003, the United States has involuntarily activated more than 286,000 reservists for federal service to support the ongoing global war on terrorism and more recently the Iraq war. In addition, at least 47,500 more reservists have been activated in other statuses—for example, to serve as members of the National Guard under state control, or as volunteers for active duty. Some reservists who were called up after September 11, 2001, were released from active duty and returned to civilian life prior to the start of the Iraq war. At the time of the Iraq war, roughly 220,000 reservists were on active duty. The call-up of reservists since September 11, 2001, represents the second largest reserve call-up since the end of World War II in 1945. Only the Korean War mobilization of 858,000 reservists in 1950–1953 was larger.
>
> …The role of the reserve components has undergone a dramatic shift since the Cold War effectively ended with the fall of the Berlin Wall in 1989. During the Cold War, the reserve components were primarily a force of last resort and were activated fairly infrequently—about once every 10 years—in response to a major war or crisis. In the post–Cold War era, however, they

have been activated much more frequently. Since 1990, there have been six involuntary activations of reservists, several of which are ongoing today. For most of these activations, affected reservists have been required to serve about 6 to 9 months before being released back to their civilian lives. Many reserves mobilized after September 11, 2001, however, have been required to serve on active duty for a year, and some may have to serve for two years. Call-ups can pose significant challenges for reservists. Some reservists suffer mobilization-related financial hardships due to income loss, increased expenses, or erosion of their professional practices.

So far, these call-ups have not led to major recruiting and retention problems. They did, however, force the Untied States to deploy 24 of its active combat duty brigades in 2003. The U.S. Army also still had 368,000 soldiers overseas in late July—nearly three months after the fall of Baghdad—and deployed in some 120 countries. This number included 232,759 full-time actives out of a total of 485,000, 74,551 National Guard out of a total of 352,000, and 61,590 reservists out of a total of 206,000.

The large reliance on this large a reserve force raises several issues. One key issue is equity. Reservists are being called up far more often and for longer periods, in part to compensate for a lack of national service. In practice, this often leads to massive disruption of their family lives and careers, but the pay and career protection they are given dates back to a much earlier era when national service was the rule. The current level of U.S. dependence on reserves—many of whom are now ex-serving military—raises serious questions about fairness, citizenship, and compensation.

There are force transformation issues as well. Only limited numbers of reserves can, in peacetime, maintain the speed of deployability and training levels necessary in rapid deployments and be ready instantly fight as fully ready members of a joint force team. The army in particular is over-dependent on reserves to provide such combat-ready elements as part of a "total force concept" for political reasons and because of congressional mandates. At least some of the army's problems in deployability are congressionally imposed and beyond its control. Furthermore, this dependence limits the ability to use reserves in homeland defense tasks for which they may be better suited and that impose fewer costs in terms of career and family.

Overdependence on reserves exacerbates the problems in overdeploying U. S. full-time active forces. Large numbers of U.S. active forces have been deployed away from their main base and homes for far larger than the active force structure is likely to be able to sustain and still recruit and retain the quality of the personnel it needs. By the end of the Iraq War, the

United States had much of seven out its ten active divisions deployed—leaving little reserve for new missions or a contingency like Korea. This resulted partly from the fact that there are political and practical limits to how many reserves the United States can call up and keep active in peacetime.

Work by Michael O'Hanlon of the Brookings Institution showed that the U.S. Army still had 185,000 men and women deployed in and around Iraq in July 2003, another 10,000 in Afghanistan, more than 25,000 in Korea, and roughly another 5,000 in the Balkans.[48] This total of some 250,000 deployed troops came out of a U.S. Army force structure of slightly more than 1.1 million, of which only 480,000 were active and only 320,000 were easily deployable. In contrast, another 550,000 were in the U.S. Army Reserve and National Guard. This meant that the United States either had to cut its mission requirements, extend the out-of-area deployments for its active forces even longer, call up more reserves, and/or deploy its reserves longer.

It is dangerous to say that the Iraq War provides some clear lesson about the need for the United States to carry out a major restructuring of its reserve forces. It may well be that the real answer is to recruit more active troops or find ways to obtain more allied support. At the same time, the need for continuing U.S. deployments after the Iraq War clearly raises the need to at least examine the current role of the reserves and their compensation. If the vast majority of Americans are to rely on active and reserve citizen-professionals for their defense and to make the resulting sacrifices, the rewards to those who do serve should be proportionate.

Notes

[1] Lt. General T. Michael Moseley, "Operation Iraqi Freedom—By the Numbers," USCENTAF, Assessment and Analysis Division, April 30, 2003.

[2] Department of Defense briefing, April 23, 2003, www.defenselink.mil/transcripts/2003/tr20030423-0122.html.

[3] British Ministry of Defense, "Operations in Iraq: First Reflections" (London: Her Majesty's Stationery Office,. July 2003), pp. 19, 28.

[4] Interview with James Kitfield, "Attack Always," in *National Journal*, April 25, 2003.

[5] British Ministry of Defense, "Operations in Iraq: First Reflections," pp. 22–23.

[6] Adapted from Moseley, "Operation Iraqi Freedom—By the Numbers," and Anthony H. Cordesman and Abraham R. Wagner, *The Lessons of Modern War*, vol. 4, *The Gulf War* (Boulder, Colo.: Westview, 1996), p. 443.

[7] Thom Shanker, "An Assessment of Iraq War Will Emphasize Joint Operations," *New York Times*, May 1, 2003; Major General Gordon C. Nash and Brigadier General Robert W. Cone, "DoD Briefing on Operation Iraqi Freedom Lessons Learned Process," news transcript, U.S. Department of Defense, June 3, 2003.

[8] Statement of General Tommy R. Franks, former commander of U.S. Central Command, before the U.S. Senate Armed Services Committee, July 9, 2003.

[9] "Interview: General Richard Myers," *Defense News*, April 14, 2003, p. 46.

[10] Interview with James Kitfield, "Attack Always."

[11] Adapted from Moseley, "Operation Iraqi Freedom—By the Numbers."

[12] Ibid.

[13] Stew Rayfield, "IMINT//Article on Marines and OIF National-Level Satellite Imagery," e-mail, June 25, 2003. An article entitled "Marines in Iraq Lacked Access to National-Level Satellite Imagery" (in *Inside the Navy*, June 16, 2003, p. 1) confuses a U.S. Marine Corps lessons report on the limits imposed by the marines' assets with a failure to obtain and use imagery data.

[14] Commanding General, "Operation Iraqi Freedom (OIF): Lessons Learned," Ref: (a) MEF FRAGO 279-03, 1st Marine Division, U.S. Marines, May 29, 2003.

[15] Ibid. Discussions with officers from other services indicate that similar problems occurred in those services, although the army and air force seem to have had somewhat better dissemination systems.

[16] Colonel Al Baldwin, USMC, "1 MEF ISR in OIF," Headquarters, U.S. Marine Intelligence Department, June 2003.

[17] Statement of General Tommy R. Franks, Senate Armed Services Committee.

[18] For a good discussion of many of the issues involved, see Lt. Colonel Peter L. Hays, *United States Military Space into the 21st Century* (Maxwell AFB, Ala.: Air University Press, September 2002). There are many earlier works outlining the possible uses of space the United States made in the Iraq War and illustrating the evolutionary nature of the changes taking place. For example, see Stuart E. Johnson and Martin C. Libicki, *Dominant Battlespace Knowledge: The Winning Edge* (Washington, D.C.: National Defense University, 1995).

[19] Vernon Loeb, "Intense, Coordinated Air War Backs Baghdad Campaign," *Washington Post*, April 6, 2003, p. 24.

[20] Adapted from Moseley, "Operation Iraqi Freedom—By the Numbers."

[21] William B, Scott, "Milspace Will Be Major Player in Gulf War 2," *Aviation Week & Space Technology*, January 12, 2003.

[22] Ibid.

[23] Jeremy Singer, "US Army Policy Spells Out Critical Space Capabilities," *Defense News*, June 16, 2003, p. 34.

[24] David A. Fulghum, "Offensive Gathers Speed," *Aviation Week & Space Technology*, March 21, 2003; Usha Lee McFarling, "The Eyes and Ears of War," *Los Angeles Times*, April 24, 2003, p. 1.

[25] Seth Schiesel, "On the Ground in Iraq: The Best Compass Is in the Sky," *New York Times*, April 17, 2003.

[26] Ibid.; Kim Burger, "U.S. Army Shares Radios to Avoid Fratricide," *Jane's Defense Weekly*, March 12, 2003.

[27] Stephen Trimble, "GPS Is Surviving Jamming Threat, Pentagon Says," *Aerospace Daily*, April 22, 2003; David Whitman, "Keeping Our Bearings," *U.S. News & World Report*, October 21, 2002.

[28] Whitman, "Keeping Our Bearings."

[29] James T. Hacket, "Tracking Targets from Space," *Washington Times*, July 8, 2003, p. 18.

[30] Michael Smith, "Frontline Troops Had Only Five Bullets to Defend Themselves," *London Daily Telegraph*, June 18, 2003.

[31] Henry Cunningham, "Airlift Capabilities Strained," *Fayetteville Observer*, November 17, 2002; David Wood, "U.S. Doesn't Travel Light in Going to War," Newhouse News Service, www.newhouse.com, October 10, 2002.

[32] Moseley, "Operation Iraqi Freedom—By the Numbers."

[33] British Ministry of Defense, "Operations in Iraq: First Reflections," pp. 14, 48.

[34] Statement of General Tommy R. Franks, Senate Armed Services Committee.

[35] Cunningham, "Airlift Capabilities Strained"; Terry Joyce, "War on Iraq Would Strain U.S. Airlift Capacity," *Charleston Post and Courier*, September 2, 2002, p. 1.

[36] Gopal Ratham, "War-Supply Tracker," *Defense News*, March 24, 2003, p. 25; Michael Shaw, "Computers Track Supplies for Buildup in the Gulf," *St. Louis Post Dispatch*, January 1, 2003, sec. B, p. 1.

[37] British Ministry of Defense, "Operations in Iraq: First Reflections," pp. 26–27.

[38] See Sean Naylor, "Logistics Still Tough Despite High Tech Help," *Defense News* March 24, 2003, p. 1.

[39] Andrew Chuter, "UK to Untangle Logistics Delivery Chain," *Defense News*, June 16, 2003.

[40] British Ministry of Defense, "Operations in Iraq: First Reflections," p. 26.

[41] Ibid., p. 48.

[42] This analysis is based on the data in Jason Sherman, "Logistic Success Built on Sealift," *Defense News*, May 12, 2003, pp. 33 and 34.

[43] British Ministry of Defense, "Operations in Iraq: First Reflections," p. 26.

[44] Kim Burger, "U.S. Build-Up Is Fast, But Not Fast Enough, *Jane's Defense Weekly*, March 19, 2003.

[45] Moseley, "Operation Iraqi Freedom—By the Numbers."

[46] Thom Shanker, "Guard and Reserve Members Likely to Begin Return Home," *New York Times*, April 25, 2003; "Guard, Reserve Plan to Be Ready Next Fall," *Aerospace Daily*, April 25, 2003.

[47] Ronald O'Rourke et al., "Iraq War: Defense Program Implications for Congress," Congressional Research Service, CRS RL31946, June 4, 2003.

[48] Michael O'Hanlon, "Breaking the Army," *Washington Post*, July 3, 2003.

INCREASED TEMPO OF OPERATIONS: SHOCK AND AWE VERSUS PRECISION AND FOCUS

The Iraq War certainly had an element of "shock and awe." U.S. air power may not have been applied in ways designed to maximize the psychological and political impact of U.S. air strikes. However, a combination of nationwide air and missile strikes and the speed and scale of the coalition land advance certainly had a powerful psychological impact on Iraqi forces and the Iraqi regime. The regime clearly was never able to respond coherently to the coalition attack—the shock of U.S. air power led many Iraqi units to disintegrate or largely avoid combat, and the shock of the land advance and initial U.S. land operations in the greater Baghdad area helped lead to the collapse of any last efforts at urban warfare.

At the same time, the coalition targeted with great restraint. As a result, it may be more accurate to describe the coalition campaign as having employed a new strategy of "precision and focus." This aspect of the war was largely air-dominated. A combination of new IS&R assets, new precision weapons, and much better avionics allowed all-weather precision strike operations with excellent targeting, with an emphasis on "effects-based" strikes and careful limitation of collateral damage. Not only did the United States use nearly ten times as many precision-guided weapons relative to unguided weapons as it had during the Gulf War, it was able to target them with far more focus and effect. As for sheer numbers, nearly 100 percent of the combat aircraft the United States deployed in the Iraq War carried precision weapons, versus some 15 percent of the aircraft in Desert Storm. The British made even more use of precision—85 percent of the total air munitions used—which compares with only limited British use of precision during the Gulf War and 25 percent of the munitions Britain used during Kosovo.[3]

The coalition fired some 19,948 precision-guided weapons in the less-than-four-weeks-long Iraq War versus 8,644 in the six-week Gulf War, and some 955 cruise missiles versus 300.[4] Unlike previous wars, the Iraq War also focused on defeating Iraqi ground forces rather than on a broad mix of strategic bombing, interdiction bombing, and close air support. According to one report, some 15,592, or 78 percent, of the weapons and aimpoints were chosen to provide direct support to some aspect of coalition ground forces.[5]

At the same time, land forces also had a new degree of precision and focus. The British essentially anchored the coalition position in the south while the main U.S. forces advanced directly on Baghdad, fighting only those forces that directly opposed their advance. Rather than try to defeat

CHAPTER SEVEN

LESSONS AFFECTING THE OVERALL CONDUCT OF THE WAR AND JOINT FORCES

There is never a clean break between the lessons of war that emerged long before the Trojan War, or in Thucydides and Sun Tsu, and the lessons that are specific to a modern conflict. This is particularly true of jointness, which the previous chapter has discussed in terms of fundamentals. On the one hand, the improvements in jointness are the result of a long process of evolution. On the other hand, the actual practice of jointness has changed radically even since the Gulf War of 1991.

The very term "jointness" took on a new meaning during the Iraq War in terms of speed of maneuver, tempo of operations, precision, lethality, intelligence, targeting, and battle management. In his March 22 USCENTCOM briefing on the course of the war, General Tommy Franks described the importance of these changes as follows:[1]

Let me begin by saying this will be a campaign unlike any other in history, a campaign characterized by shock, by surprise, by flexibility, by the employment of precise munitions on a scale never before seen, and by the application of overwhelming force.

Let me talk for a minute about our capabilities. The coalition now engaged in and supporting Operation Iraqi Freedom includes Army and Marine forces from the land component; air forces from several nations; naval forces, to include the Coast Guard, and Special Operations forces.

Our plan introduces these forces across the breadth and depth of Iraq, in some cases simultaneously and in some cases sequentially. In some cases, our Special Operations forces support conventional ground forces. Examples of this include operations behind enemy lines to attack enemy positions and formations or perhaps to secure bridges and crossing sites over rivers or perhaps to secure key installations, like the gas-oil platforms, and, of course, in some cases, to adjust air power, as we saw in Afghanistan.

Now, in some cases, our air forces support ground elements or support special operations forces by providing targeting and intelligence information, perhaps offensive electronic warfare capabilities. At other times, coalition airmen deliver decisive precision shock, such as you witnessed beginning last night.

At certain points, special operations forces and ground units support air forces by pushing enemy formations into positions to be destroyed by air power. And in yet other cases, our naval elements support air, support ground operations, or support Special Operations forces by providing aircraft, cruise missiles, or by conducting maritime operations or mine-clearing operations.

And so the plan we see uses combinations of these capabilities that I've just described. It uses them at times and in places of our choosing in order to accomplish the objectives I mentioned just a moment ago.

That plan gives commanders at all levels and it gives me latitude to build the mosaic I just described in a way that provides flexibility so that we can attack the enemy on our terms, and we are doing so.

For all the limits of jointness described in chapter 6 and in the detailed lessons in the chapters that follow, the different problems that emerge reflect a need for improved execution of jointness, and they in no way challenge the validity of the concepts the United States is now pursuing. In fact, in virtually every case, there is substantial interaction between lessons that affect jointness and individual lessons affecting the military services or key weapons and tactics.

LAND POWER–REINFORCED AIR POWER AND VICE VERSA

A case in point is the extent to which land power reinforced air power and vice versa. The Iraqi land forces were forced to expose themselves by the speed of land operations and then were hit hard from the air, which in turn sharply reduced the Iraqi threat to U.S. and British land forces. Jointness took on a new practical meaning.

These interactions between land power and air power may take some time to sort out. Nonetheless, there seems to be a significant contrast between the conduct of the Iraq War and the Gulf War. The long air bombardment in the Gulf War produced a focus on air operations that led some to concentrate on air power to the exclusion of land power and to claim that air power alone could be decisive. It also led some to claim that strategic bombing had a decisive effect. In reality, the USAF Gulf War Airpower Survey showed that General Horner, commander of the air effort during the Gulf War, was correct in totally rejecting initial plans to focus on strategic bombing at the expense of a proper balance of land forces. Similarly, the role of air power in Afghanistan against an enemy with vir-

tually no modern weapons led to similar claims about the decisive impact of air power by those whom General Horner came to call "airheads."

The irony in the Iraq War is that the delay in moving to a massive air campaign, the absence of any details about the air campaign during the daily press briefings, and the fact that so many reporters were embedded with ground forces led to a near reversal and a media focus on ground power to the partial exclusion of the largely "invisible" air and missile war. As shown in chapter 4, however, U.S. ground operations could not possibly have moved at the speed they did without the massive air effort that was under way, and it is clear from chapter 9 that air power could never have targeted and struck at Iraqi ground forces with anything like the impact it had on the course of the war had the Iraqis not had to maneuver to try to halt the advance of U.S. ground forces.

Time may provide a more exact picture of how much each element contributed to the outcome of the war. But the key lesson really seems to be that each advance in air capability also advances ground force capability and vice versa. Furthermore, even if one argues that the Iraq War shows that joint forces can rely on air power to reduce the need for ground troops, the "peace" that has followed has again shown that both asymmetric conflicts and peacemaking eventually tend to be dominated by the need for ground forces. In fact, if one compares the relative weight of ground and air forces in the Iraq War with that of the Gulf War, the main lesson seems to be that it is the ability to tailor new joint mixes of ground-air-sea power to the needs of a particular campaign that proves to be decisive.

This not only is a lesson that U.S. commanders have drawn from their experience during the war, but is one reflected in the British Ministry of Defense's report on the lessons of the conflict and in ways that illustrate how important U.S. progress in jointness can be to interoperability with its allies.[2]

> The overwhelming success of rapid, decisive operations in Iraq reflects the deployment of fast moving light forces, highly mobile armored capabilities and Close Air Support, which made use of near real-time situational awareness by day and by night. The US ability to combine land and air operations and support them from the sea and from friendly bases at very high tempo enabled the mix and impact of joint assets to be adjusted to operational need or events across the whole theatre of operations. This is likely to shape US doctrinal development and impact on potential partners. The implications of maintaining congruence with an accelerating US technological and doctrinal dominance need to be assessed and taken into account in future policy and planning assumptions.

the entire Iraqi force structure, or defeat the nation, U.S. armor concentrated on defeating the regime. At the same time, focused U.S., British, and Australian special operations forces allowed the coalition to strike at selected targets in the west, the north, and many other areas in Iraq—often combining special operations on the ground with the ability to call in air support to provide heavy fire power.

NETCENTRIC WARFARE, IS&R TECHNOLOGY, PROCESSING, INTEGRATION, AND NEAR-REAL-TIME INFORMATION FLOW AND TARGETING

As shown in chapter 5, many aspects of the C4I and IS&R systems used in the Iraq War reflected an evolution of past capabilities and problems. The coalition applied such systems, however, in a form of joint warfare that had an unparalleled degree of near-real-time situational awareness that shortened the "kill chain" in going from targeting to strike, and the sensors-to-shooter gap from days to hours in the Gulf War to hours to minutes in the Iraq War.[6] At this point, there is no way to analyze the relative role of space, UAVs, fixed-wing aircraft, SIGINT, ELINT, imagery, Special Forces, and human intelligence in detail. It is clear, however, that the resulting mosaic of intelligence and sensor data was far better than in the Gulf War, and was processed and disseminated far more quickly. The time-consuming and relatively rigid process of sortie planning and targeting that shaped the air traffic order in the Gulf War was replaced with a far quicker and more responsive system.

One senior officer described this process as follows:

All such offensive air operations, manned or unmanned, were coordinated with the USCENTCOM air component command headquarters. The types of targets were broad-ranging. Some of them were time-sensitive targets—where intelligence led the US to believe that a particular location was a valuable target. And so in a relatively brief period of time, particularly compared to the years past, the coalition was able to do the planning, get the missile loaded with its mission data, out of a submarine or—a British or American submarine or American ship—and down range and export on the target, or some rather more stationary and strategic targets, including missile defense facilities, to Republican Guard headquarters and some regime structures in and around Baghdad and all throughout the country....I think his degraded ability to command and control his formations meant that those Republican Guard formations had very little situational awareness on the battlefield of where to maneuver to, which played right into the decisive lethality that both the ground and the air component were able to put on him.

Lt. Gen. David D. McKiernan, the commander of the Coalition Forces Land Component Command, described the role of such assets, and net-centric warfare, as follows:[7]

> Network-centric warfare is an idea, a concept, and a reality that has been around now for some years. And to give you a good example, much of the command and control that this regime executed for its military was done through fiber optic cable and repeater stations. Through very, very good intelligence, and targeting and execution, that capability was consistently degraded to the point where we think he really had very little ability to command and control tactical formations before we closed with him with ground formations. And that's a reflection of network-centric warfare, of knowing where to go in that command and control network to take it out or degrade it so that he loses his ability to command and control his formations.
>
> ... the technology advances in our military today, compared to my experiences in Desert Storm, allowed me to talk via tactical satellite communications and other means across a battle space of hundreds of miles; to be able to conduct, when we need to, video teleconferences, where commanders can plot out where they're at and what decisions they need to do next; and all of that put together in a joint construct, where I could see where all the airframes were, where all the ships are, where my counterparts in the air and the maritime components can see where the ground formations are.
>
> When you put all that together, that allowed us to make decisions with situational awareness of where we were at, where the enemy was at, and our view of the terrain and the weather much, much faster than we ever could in the past and exponentially faster than our opponent could. So when you put all that together, it allowed us to make decisions and then execute those decisions faster than any opponent.

It is important to note, however, that many of the U.S. commands supporting USCENTCOM remained focused on the needs of a single service, and that many of the improvements in jointness were the results of improvising new approaches, rather than the result of a solid, well-established system for joint warfare. As one example, an Air Coordination Element, led by an air force major general supported by 18 airmen, was attached to the army's operations staff so that there would be closer cooperation in providing close air support and liaison with the USCENTCOM command staff in Qatar and the Combined Air Operations Center (CAOC) in Saudi Arabia. The manning of the CAOC was also increased from 672 personnel before the war to 1,966 during the conflict. Seven other teams, headed by a general or colonel, were assigned to each of the land force commanders to similarly improve operations, planning, and liaison. Britain had liaison officers attached to various U.S. elements to improve interoperability.

THE BROADER PICTURE: THE NEED TO RESTRUCTURE U.S. COMMAND AND CONTROL SYSTEMS AND THE POSSIBLE NEED TO RESTRUCTURE THEATER COMMANDS

These experiences raise broader questions about the need for an integrated common operating picture and interoperability, and the possible need to eliminate service-oriented subordinate commands in the theater. As General Franks has noted in his analysis of the lessons of the war, one key lesson of the war is the ability to exercise joint command over all U.S. services, and allied forces, at distances as great as 7,000 miles—the approximate distance from the theater to the USCENTCOM headquarters in Florida and the U.S. national command authority in Washington.

At a minimum, this requires the United States to keep developing the best common operating picture (COP) possible and to develop a truly integrated, user-friendly, tracking and command and control architecture that brings together the operations of all of the military services. It also requires the United States to design this system for information sharing with its allies.[8]

The report on the lessons of the Iraq War by the British Ministry of Defense reinforces the importance of this kind of advance in command and control as well as the importance of interoperability:[9]

> The UK has a wide range of communications and information systems performing different functions. These were not all compatible with each other or with US systems, which led to interoperability difficulties. As a result, reliable, secure, timely and effective communication between all stakeholders could not be guaranteed.
>
> The concept of Network Enabled Capability (NEC), introduced in the SDR "New Chapter," involves the integration of sensors, weapons and decision-makers in order to deliver rapid, controlled and precise military effect. Shortening the time between targeting decisions and execution…is a prime example of this. Many new capabilities introduced through the UOR process in this operation were designed to improve the passage and exploitation of information as first steps in the development of NEC.

The British report also notes the value of UK and U.S. special operations forces being able to track each other's locations, thus improving situational awareness at all levels of command. It notes that this led to more effective battle management and an increase in operational tempo in all weather conditions.

There may, however, be broader lessons for "jointness." It is clear from the U.S. experience during the Iraq War that all service-oriented commands should have strong teams from other services as part of their permanent organization and should train with such teams in peacetime. Some have argued that the need for jointness is so great that it requires a separate military profession. At a minimum, it requires that service-centric commands train and operate with joint elements at all times and that major changes take place in command post and field training exercises to ensure this.

The lessons of the Iraq War also, however, indicate that it may be time to restructure regional commands—such as naval, land, and air commands of USCENTCOM—into true joint force commands rather than having subordinate air, army, marine, and naval elements. The trade-offs between the continuing need for service expertise and jointness are difficult ones that will need careful examination, but jointness should not be a matter of one-time solutions or teams improvised before or during a conflict.

Areas for Improvement and Problems at the Battalion Level

As chapter 6 has already touched on, there are many other areas where U.S. and coalition operations in the Iraq War did not represent the future state of the art. At present, netcentric warfare is not a "system of systems" in any real world sense. It is rather a "systemless mix of systems" where many systems remain service-centric and where the command structure and coordination must be improvised around each new contingency. Almost inevitably, this improvisation works best between the highest levels of command and the major combat unit level. It is weakest at the level of the practical war fighter—particularly the war fighters involved in ground combat.

It is clear from discussions with some of the officers involved, as well as with technical experts in the Department of Defense, that "netcentric" warfare is in a rapid state of flux and that many further advances can be made. Methods and technology could be improved in many areas at every level, from communications in the field to basic procedures for integrating high-level decisionmaking. In case after case, the technology available during the Iraq War was also already in transition. In many cases, parts of U.S. forces were more advanced than other parts, or follow-on technology was already in development or procurement.

It is clear from talking to both general officers and more junior officers that the net was weakest at the battalion level and below. These problems were the result of technology and equipment, tactics, and training and not any one cause. But they limited jointness, and sometimes the commands from higher levels outpaced the ability of combat and logistic elements at lower levels to interact and coordinate. Such problems also do not seem to have been characteristic of any service or element of combined arms; they appear in virtually every after-action report from the field at lower levels of command.

These are problems that occurred for the British army as well as U.S. forces:[10]

> It has long been recognized that the Army's main tactical communication system, the ageing Clansman radio, suffers significant limitations. A new system, Bowman, will be introduced into service from 2004. As an interim improvement, Clansman was supplemented by the purchase of items such as lightweight tactical satellite communications systems, ensuring our forces had maximum operational flexibility. In addition, the Bowman Personal Role Radio, trialled in Afghanistan, was available to all combat troops for the first time. This short-range radio is designed to facilitate communications within small infantry teams. The US Marines have subsequently bought some 5000 sets.

One of the key realities of the war, and indeed of all efforts to create a netted or matrix approach to warfare, is that some parts of the net or matrix are always much more advanced than others, and some are critical weaknesses. There were still significant communications failures; battle damage assessment was still a major problem and so was the ability to "characterize" infantry and irregular land forces and the function and actual level of activity and capability in buildings. In fact, one army analysis of the problems in information technology during the war focused heavily on the need for improved energy sources to replace batteries.[11]

Some quotes from Joshua Davis, an embedded reporter from *Wired*, give a clearer picture of the reality of netcentric warfare versus the image:[12]

> The war was a grand test of the netcentric strategy in development since the first Gulf War. At least, that's the triumphal view from the Pentagon briefing room. But what was it like on the ground?…I tracked the network from the generals' plasma screens at Central Command to the forward nodes on the battlefields in Iraq. What I discovered was something entirely different from the shiny picture of techno-supremacy touted by the proponents of the Rumsfeld doctrine. I found an unsung corps of geeks improvising as they went, cobbling together a remarkable system from a hodgepodge of military-built networking technology, off-the-shelf gear, miles of Ethernet cable, and commercial software. And during two weeks in the war zone, I never heard anyone mention the revolution in military affairs.
>
> …A ruddy Texan sticks his hand out at me: "Lieutenant Colonel Caddell. Glad to meet you." Tymothy Caddell is in charge of wiring the JOC [joint

operations center]. He manages the 65 servers and 50 Army, Navy, Marine, and Air Force network administrators who keep the control center's generals connected to the war. "In October, this was an empty warehouse," he says. "It takes most big companies years to bring 65 servers online. We did it in three months."

Caddell leads the way to one of the shipping containers. Inside, two soldiers baby-sit three rows of Sun servers. "This is where the Global Command and Control System lives," Caddell says. GCCS—known as "Geeks" to soldiers in the field—is the military's HAL 9000. It's an umbrella system that tracks every friendly tank, plane, ship, and soldier in the world in real time, plotting their positions as they move on a digital map. It can also show enemy locations gleaned from intelligence. "We're in a whole different ball game from the last Gulf war," Caddell says. "We had a secure network back in '91, but the bandwidth wasn't there and the applications weren't there. Now they are."

The prime example, he says, is a portal called the Warfighting Web. Launched just nine months ago, it lets military personnel access key data— battle plans, intelligence reports, maps, online chats, radio transcripts, photos, and video. Caddell sketches out a typical scenario: A Special Forces unit in northern Iraq attacks an Iraqi irregular unit. The firefight is recorded with digital video, which is uploaded to GCCS via secure satellite. JOC intelligence officers fire up the Warfighting Web, click through to "Latest Intelligence," watch the fight, write a summary, and post follow-up orders to the unit. The soldiers either download the orders directly or receive them by radio from the nearest Tactical Operations Center, the most forward command post on the network.

We leave the GCCS container and head past a row of large refrigerated metal boxes. Caddell steps up to one and leans on a 3-foot metal lever. The thick front wall swings open, revealing two rows of Compaq servers. A blast of cool air hits me; the temperature here is about 20 degrees lower than in the warehouse. "Welcome to Siprnet," he says. GCCS runs over Siprnet—the Secret Internet Protocol Router Network—in the same way that Web applications run over the public Internet. The difference with "Sipper" is that it's basically a far-flung local area network. To maximize security, it doesn't connect with the Internet proper. But it links Centcom to the battlefield and, among other things, allows Franks to talk to Rumsfeld and President Bush via two-way videoconference every evening.

Caddell has one more important piece of Centcom to show me. "How would you like to see the JOC help desk?" he says, motioning me out of the container. We head toward the far end of the warehouse, where Specialist Adam Cluff—a heavyset, droopy-eyed kid from Utah—stands at attention when he sees Caddell. It looks like he'd been taking a nap. I ask him what he does here. "If a general has a problem with his Web browser, then I fix it," Cluff says. "How do you fix it?" I ask. "I consult Microsoft online help."

...The US Forward Command is a half hour due east of Kuwait City, approximately 75 miles from the Iraqi border. I've flown here from Qatar to learn more about the 11th Signal Brigade, the soldiers tasked with wiring the battlefield. They tote M16s, but their job is to jump out of helicopters and set up packet-based wireless networks. Their unofficial motto: Connecting the foxhole to the White House. Without these guys, Lieutenant Colonel Caddell's Warfighting Web would have no war to fight. For the 11th, the epicenter of the campaign is here at Satellite Park, where a dozen dishes are spread across a patch of dirt enclosed by razor wire. The operation is monitored by four men and a woman, each with a laptop and a secure digital telephone. They are the controllers. Each oversees the health of one of the brigade's five networks. That means all of the Army's battlefield communications flow through these five people.

Their laptops display icons representing a web of nodes and switches. When the icons are green, everything is running fine. But when a link turns red, panic sets in. "A link went red yesterday," says Sergeant Danny Booher, one of the controllers. "One of my guys came under mortar fire near Basra and the satellite got hit." Booher got on the phone with his nearest unit, and, minutes later, there was a humvee racing through the desert, towing a satellite dish on wheels.

Lieutenant Colonel Mims...chimes in. "If it's a question of the network going down, we get helicopters, air support, tanks—whatever we need," he says. As the brigade's intelligence chief, Mims is in charge of knowing where the enemy is and positioning forward signal units in secure locations. In the first Gulf war, Mims was a junior intel officer. "Signal has become a lot more complicated in the Internet age. We used to only have to worry about radios. Now it's about providing enough bandwidth to power streaming video and monitor real-time troop and vehicle movement."

The improvement in communications is the real innovation in this war, he explains. He grabs my notebook and a blue ballpoint pen and draws an obtuse angle. "When we attacked in the last Gulf war, we basically had our vehicles lined in a wedge," he says. "We had five divisions moving across the desert like that. As they went through, they'd sweep an area clear—if there's a problem, the other unit can see and hear it, and, more important, the unit is close by and can arrive quickly to help. In that model, once you move through, the rear zones are secure. There's not much left back there." Now Mims draws a bunch of small circles spread out on the page. This is Rumsfeld's theory of swarm tactics. Because technology allows soldiers to keep track of each other, even when they're out of one another's sight, they can now move in any formation. "We may not always know exactly where the enemy is," Mims explains, "but we know where we are. When the enemy engages us in this spread-out fashion, we send air cover to protect the unit until the support forces arrive."

Swarm theory holds that you move fast and don't worry about securing the rear. The benefits to this are many. First, you need fewer troops and less equipment. War becomes cheaper. Second, it's harder for the enemy to attack a widely dispersed formation. Third, units can cover much more ground—they aren't forced to maintain the wedge by slowing down to accommodate lagging vehicles. Fourth, swarming allows you to go straight for the heart of the enemy's command structure, undermining its support from the inside out rather than battling on the periphery. Swarm theory is also moving online—into chat rooms, an application Mims is pioneering for military purposes. When a problem develops on the battlefield, a soldier radios a Tactical Operations Center. The TOC intelligence guy types the problem into a chat session—Mims and his colleagues use Microsoft Chat—and the problem is "swarmed" by experts from the Pentagon to Centcom. Not only is the technology changing the way we maneuver, Mims notes, it's changing the way we think.

But the system is not without problems. Because anyone on Siprnet who wanted to could set up a chat, 50 rooms sprang up in the months before the war. The result: information overload. "We've started throwing people out of the rooms who don't belong there," Mims says. "What's funny about using Microsoft Chat," he adds with a sly smile, "is that everybody has to choose an icon to represent themselves. Some of these guys haven't bothered, so the program assigns them one. We'll be in the middle of a battle and a bunch of field artillery colonels will come online in the form of these big-breasted blondes. We've got a few space aliens, too."

…"When we were deployed from the States," says Lieutenant Marc Lewis—the commander of the convoy's 27 heavy equipment trucks—"they told us that we would be given encrypted, military-issue radios when we got here. When we arrived, they told us we should have brought our own." What Lewis brought was four Motorola Talkabouts, each with a range of about 1,000 feet. In the half-dozen convoy trips he's made since arriving in country, Lewis has taken to distributing a Talkabout to the first and last trucks. The other two go to vehicles at strategic points in between. It's hardly secure. Anybody with a radio could monitor the conversations.

Lewis is improvising as best he can. Before leaving the States, he bought a handheld eTrex GPS device, which he uses to track each of his forays into Iraq. In essence, he's created a map of Iraq's charted and uncharted freeways and desert roads. He just has no way to share it with anybody. But he is able to navigate as well as any of the tank or missile commanders he transported. I notice that at least four other soldiers in the convoy have brought their own store-bought GPS handhelds. These devices keep the convoys on track in lieu of having proper systems. "If we run out of batteries," Lewis says when showing me his map of Iraq, "this war is screwed."

Even in the case of fixed-wing air systems—which generally had the best and most digitized communications—there were many problems in interoperability, communications, and data flow as well as in procedures and computer support. These included a wide range of problems affecting the "sensor-to-shooter gap," time-urgent targeting, and dynamic targeting as well as deconflict and avoiding friendly fire.

The most serious problems, however, seem to occur at the level of the land war fighter, and some experts have even called this the "digital divide": a separation of the military above the division level into a largely digital force while most of the force below that level still relies largely on "analog" human beings.

The U.S. Army, the U.S. Marine Corps, and allied forces like the British Army all had different levels of "digitization." The U.S. Army was the most advanced land force, but its units had different levels of capability. Ironically, the 4th Infantry Division—the unit best equipped to use such capabilities—was not committed. It also is not clear just how much the United States was able to solve the coordination, processing, data allocation, and bandwidth problems exposed in Afghanistan or to deal with new capabilities to retarget aircraft in mid-flight. What is clear is that such technologies offer great promise and will rapidly evolve beyond the level of operations used in the Iraq War.

Target Characterization and Battle Damage Assessment

Two other areas are of critical importance in determining the efficiency of IS&R systems and of any concept of netcentric warfare. One is target characterization. As was discussed in chapter 6, the United States was far better equipped to target Iraq's armored and heavy ground forces, active land-based air defenses, and military emitters than it had been in past wars. The ability to strike at Republican Guard forces almost continuously during the conflict, even during sand and dust storms, is particularly impressive. The United States had far less capability, however, to deal with light irregular forces or to characterize the size and nature of asymmetric forces, particularly those that sheltered in urban or built-up areas. The ability to characterize armor versus other military vehicles seems to have remained a problem, as did the ability to find well-dispersed systems like aircraft and individual surface-to-air missiles or surface-to-surface missiles that were not actively moving or emitting.

As the British report on the lessons of the war notes, these targeting problems were compounded by the need to subject targeting to careful political review and to the need to minimize civilian casualties and collateral damage. As is the case in IS&R, jointness has become a civil-military requirement as well as a military one, and the political content of targeting has become an increasingly important issue for war fighting:[13]

> Planning for the air campaign included the development of a list of potential targets that would help the coalition to achieve its overall objectives. Over 900 potential target areas were identified in advance. All targets were derived from the campaign plan and were selected to achieve a particular military effect (such as the degradation of Iraqi command and control systems). Operating within parameters agreed by Ministers, Commanders taking targeting decisions had legal advice available to them at all times during the conflict and were aware of the need to comply with international humanitarian law, the core principles of which are that only military objectives1 may be attacked, and that no attack should be carried out if any expected incidental civilian harm (loss of life, injury or damage) would be excessive in relation to the concrete and direct military advantage expected from the attack.
>
> Extensive scientific support including detailed computer modeling was used in assessing potential targets. Strong coordination between the MOD, the Permanent Joint Headquarters (PJHQ) at Northwood and the in-theatre National Contingent Command helped ensure coherent target planning (a lesson from previous operations). The Department for International Development was also consulted on key humanitarian infrastructure issues. The process for approving all targets for UK aircraft, submarine-launched cruise missiles or for coalition aircraft using UK facilities was conducted with appropriate political, legal and military oversight at all levels. We also influenced the selection and approval of other coalition targets.

For all the advances in sensors, weather remained a problem. The United States was able to locate and target Iraqi forces during the dust storms in late March, but the storms still sharply degraded coverage and made battle-damage coverage of Iraqi ground forces almost impossible. General Myers, the chairman of the Joint Chiefs, has stated that the United States had no clear picture of how successful its air strikes were against the Republican Guards during the dust storms, and the fact that it had a high level of success could only be confirmed once the weather had cleared. As a result, the United States had to persist in its advance in spite of considerable uncertainty.[14]

The United States had problems in dynamic targeting of covered and sheltered facilities. UAVs and electronic intelligence assets, plus the use of

Special Forces, do seem to have given the coalition a better capability than the United States and its allies had during the Gulf War to know when buildings were empty and to locate new dispersed forces and facilities. The United States did not have enough of these needed assets to establish anything like full coverage, however, and is only beginning to learn how to best use them and fuse them into the overall IS&R process.

Moreover, each asset the United States does have has important limits. It still is impossible to see within buildings or shelters without men being physically present. In at least some cases, the United States actually struck at underground facilities or bunkers that postwar examination showed did not exist. These may even have included the "bunker" that the United States attacked on the first night of the war in an effort to kill Saddam Hussein and key elements of the Iraqi leadership.[15] It is generally impossible to characterize the nature of the equipment and operations in sheltered or covered facilities unless their purpose is clear from previous intelligence sources or their profile of activities is clear.

The issue of battle damage assessment (BDA) is a particularly important area of uncertainty. The data the United States (and Britain) have made public in the past on battle damage assessment have scarcely been reassuring. The data on so-called kills of large military weapons like armor and ground kills of aircraft and missiles have generally proved to be either exaggerated or uncertain. Data on attacks on command and control facilities, infrastructure targets, leadership targets, and industrial base and POL targets have often been able to show the damage to the building but were unreliable in assessing the effect—a problem that is progressively more important if the concept of "effect-based" operations becomes a key factor in war fighting. The long-standing reluctance of the United States to estimate enemy casualties ever since Vietnam seems to have compounded delays in finding ways to both target and assess battle damage to infantry and light forces, as well as paramilitary and terrorist forces, that are primarily people and not things.

The Iraq War showed that the United States and Britain had learned not to rush out with BDA statistics and estimates, although this may have been the result of the fact that the BDA process largely collapsed early in the war. Several U.S. and allied officers have also made it clear since the war that that the few estimates the coalition did issue on the level of equipment losses in the Republican Guard may simply have been broad estimates based on rough extrapolations from the improved imagery that became available after the dust storms ended, and could not distinguish battle damage with any accuracy or tell whether the breakup of

Iraqi combat capability was the result of physical damage to Iraqi weapons or desertions.

The United States and its allies simply do not yet have a fully effective and reliable set of sensors, processors, and methods to support netcentric warfare with reliable battle damage assessment or to provide such data quickly enough to support near-real-time allocation of force assets for either tactical or targeting purposes.

This does not mean that the U.S. and coalition forces did not make improvements in target characterization and in at least some aspects of battle damage assessment during the war. It does mean that there is no public evidence that they did so, or that they solved past problems. More generally, it is a reason for analysts to show caution in talking about advances in netcentric warfare and IS&R technology, processing, integration, and near-real-time information flow and targeting as if the key problems have been solved or there is a firm empirical base for making clear trade-offs or program decisions.

It is also valuable to remember the past. For most of the nineteenth century, well-equipped Western armies achieved quick and decisive victories—often at great odds—against ineffective opponents. These same armies, however, were generally unable to predict their capability to fight each other, or the actual war-fighting impact of the tactics and weapons that were felt to be "transformational" at the time. These problems became brutally apparent in the American Civil War and World War I. Furthermore, Britain found in South Africa and the Sudan, the French found in Vietnam, and the United States learned at the Little Big Horn that "transformation" cannot always compensate for numbers and overconfidence.

BANDWIDTH

The United States has found in every recent war that it did not have the communications density and capacity to carry out all of the existing aspects of netcentric warfare, much less the additional tasks that have already been discussed, and which are discussed in the following chapters. Secretary Rumsfeld and General Tommy Franks also raised the need for more capacity or "bandwidth" in their initial reports to the Congress on the lessons of the war.[16]

There almost certainly is a valid need for additional bandwidth. However, there are also serious dangers in assuming that this is a lesson that always ends in increasing the density and complexity of C4I/IS&R operations and the level of communications and processing density. "Bandwidth creep" threatens to become more and more demanding and expensive. It also tends to push information to virtually all potential users and to centralize decisionmaking and review in the process. It is far from clear that today's problems are truly bandwidth problems as distinguished from a failure to create efficient systems that limit the need for bandwidth, and it is equally unclear that there has been careful review of where the flow of information should stop, of how much information can really be used, and of the need to delegate and limit information flow.

Put simply, it is as important to limit bandwidth as it is to increase it. System efficiency is at least as important as system growth. Avoiding information overload is as critical as jointness. Avoiding overdependence on overcomplex and overvulnerable systems is equally important, as is avoiding overcentralization of review and command.

ASYMMETRIC WARFARE

One of the key issues shaping the war was the ability of U.S. and British forces to adapt to asymmetric warfare. In practice, these forces responded quickly and effectively to Iraqi tactics, whether in the form of covert mine warfare attempts, dealing with raids by "technicals," preventing suicide attacks, or coping with urban stay-behinds and diehards. U.S. and British forces demonstrated that they could adapt tactics and force postures to new and surprising uses of asymmetric warfare. The lessons of Somalia, Northern Ireland, and Afghanistan had been learned, and the value of improved training and organization for asymmetric warfare was clear.[17]

At the same time, the United States and UK benefited from the lack of large numbers of dedicated irregulars and martyrs. As General Wallace pointed out, Iraq did achieve surprise. There were serious battles involving mixes of regular and irregular forces near Al Hillah, and the situation might have been very different if Iraq had used chemical or biological weapons along with asymmetric warfare, or if it had been able to launch more than nine Al Samoud missiles and long-range tactical rockets.

U.S. and British success in the Iraq War also does not mean that the United States and its allies are ready for every asymmetric challenge. If one looks only at the fighting between March 19 and May 1, there are important "what ifs." One such "what if" is how the coalition would have fared if Iraq truly had been able to mobilize and use the large popular army it had created arms caches for throughout the country, particularly given the increasing need for powers like the United States and UK to reduce total casualties, civilian casualties, and collateral damage. Another is how different the war might have been if Iraq had been able to combine guerrilla or irregular warfare with the effective use of weapons of mass destruction and/or covert and terrorist attacks on the United States and British homelands. The Iraq War is only a limited warning of the kind of challenge a more effective opponent might pose.

The British Ministry of Defense report on the lessons of the war summarizes these challenges as follows:[18]

Clearly, despite their numerical advantage, the Iraqi armed forces could not expect to match the coalition in regular combat. Even so, the failure of Saddam's regime to employ its conventional military capabilities to best effect was striking. This may reflect the undermining of its command and control mechanisms early in the coalition campaign, as well as the reluctance of regular forces to fight in defense of an unpopular regime.

The full range of the Iraq experience will need to be reflected in future training and equipment provision. The Iraqi regular army put up stiff resistance in places, but mostly either surrendered or fled, abandoning their equipment and clothing. The greater threat to the coalition, particularly to lines of communication and rear areas, was from paramilitary and irregular forces closely associated with the Saddam regime. Such forces were also probably responsible for much of the resistance encountered from regular army units that did fight, whose soldiers in some cases appeared to have been coerced by threats against themselves and their families.

The Iraqis used suicide bombers in the attack on a checkpoint north of An Najaf, which killed four US soldiers. Combatants who were not in military uniform could not be distinguished from civilians, while others showed the white flag when still harboring intent to fire. While such tactics did not have a significant impact, they showed a disregard for the provisions of the Geneva Convention, put the Iraqi population at risk, and presented the coalition with a challenge as to how to respond. The UK's experience of asymmetric tactics in Northern Ireland proved invaluable and contributed to the early successes our forces enjoyed in southern Iraq.

However, the implications for, and limitations on, conventional forces fighting in urban environments will need to be considered—most training is conducted in clear, simple battle-space and needs better to reflect the complexity of modern engagement. Overall, it would appear that UK forces need to continue to be configured, trained and equipped to move from war-fighting to peacekeeping (which may include internal security duties). Above all, the operation highlights the value and potential of agile light forces in responding to asymmetric approaches.

Current and emerging asymmetric threats mean that the risk to coalition shipping needs assessing for all stages of transit. The RN committed significant resources to protect from potential terrorist attack some 60 UK chartered merchant ships bringing in over 95 percent of all UK military equipment, as well as 16 high value RN and RFA vessels, over a 5000 mile route. Over 50 percent of the deployable fleet was engaged in escorting duties in known threat areas and choke points.

Moreover, it has become all too clear that the fall of Baghdad and Tikrit, and the coalition victory over Iraq's conventional forces, did not put an end to the fighting. Instead, the United States, Britain, Australia, Poland, and the other allies involved in nation building found that this process at least had to begin in a climate of low-level asymmetric warfare. As has been the case in Afghanistan, as well as in so many other peacemaking efforts, armed opposition changes, and mutates, even dramatic military victory does not mean that the conflict is over.

In Iraq's case, this "post-conflict conflict" seems to have had a number of causes. They included the impact of the political vacuum and insecurity following the fall of a 30-year-long tyranny. They were the result of nationalism and the fears, anger, and conspiracy theories. As chapters 15 through 17 describe, they were caused by the coalition's failure to provide a quick and effective security and nation-building effort and to announce a clear plan for the future that can command popular support. Some of the violence was the result of religious and ethnic tensions in Iraq, and some was the result of Shi'ite and other Islamic resentment of what is felt to be a forced process of secularization.

Many of the attacks during the months following the war, however, came from Ba'ath loyalists, and their activity has certainly been encouraged by the coalition's failure to kill or capture Saddam Hussein and his sons. As was the case in Afghanistan, visibly destroying the leadership of a hostile regime is of major importance in reducing the level of support for that regime. There also are indications that Saddam Hussein's regime planned to fight a low-intensity conflict designed to confront the United States and its allies with a slow war of attrition in the form of constant low-level casualties and efforts to sabotage key elements of nation building even before the war. While the evidence is limited, the regime may have left cadres behind to try to fight and coordinate such a war after it collapsed.[19]

Even though President Bush declared an end to the major fighting on May 1, the coalition was forced to combine military and nation-building operations, and the United States had to conduct a series of military operations to deal with attacks on its forces and on the nation-building process. As of July 2003, these operations included Operation Peninsula Strike, Operation Desert Scorpion, and Operation Rattlesnake.[20]

The scale of these operations was significant. During Operation Desert Scorpion, which lasted from June 15 to June 28, the U.S. 4th Infantry Division and 1st Armored Division conducted a series of raids that detained some 1,330 individuals and confiscated some 497 AK-47s, 235 hand grenades, 124 rocket-propelled grenades, 22 machine guns, 130 pistols, 100 rifles, and 8,122 rounds of ammunition. The operation also confiscated U.S.$9.46 billion ,1.56 trillion Iraqi dinars, 1,071 bars of gold, and 52 vehicles.[21]

Coalition forces launched a new series of operations called Operation Sidewinder on June 29. It focused on rooting out various subversive elements attempting to undermine coalition efforts to restore basic infrastructure and stability in Iraq. On the day that Operation Sidewinder began, coalition forces conducted 1,317 day patrols and 1,053 night patrols. They also conducted 213 joint day patrols and 161 joint night patrols with the Iraqi police. The patrols, together with raids, resulted in 128 arrests for various criminal activities, including one murder arrest in Baghdad.[22]

At the end of Operation Sidewinder on July 5, the United States had detained 282 individuals and seized a variety of weapons. These included 96 AK-47 rifles, 3 heavy machine guns, 217 rocket-propelled grenades, 33 grenades, 200 60mm-mortar rounds, and other military equipment, documents, weapons and ammunition. In addition, U.S.$5,000 in cash and approximately 11 million Iraqi dinars, or about U.S.$6,000, were seized. Over the seven days of Operation Sidewinder and other supporting tasks, there were 30 casualties from Iraqi noncompliant forces and 28 coalition forces injuries.[23] No coalition force soldiers were killed during the seven days of the operation, but new attacks and casualties occurred immediately after the operation ended.

The U.S. operations also did not result in any early success in reducing the level of violence. The attackers made steadily better uses of sniping, ambushes, urban cover, mortars, bombs and sabotage, and there were growing questions as to whether some organized Ba'ath supporters in Iraq deliberately sought to break up the peace process and create enough casualties to drive the United States and its allies out of Iraq, and whether Saddam Hussein and his sons played some role in inspiring or directing the operation. By early July, casualties averaged nearly one U.S. casualty a day. One irony of this fighting was that the anti-U.S. Iraqi attackers in Baghdad were increasingly able to using sniping, RPG ambushes, and car bombs in a form of low-level urban warfare that could not confront U.S. forces directly, but that created a climate of uncertainty and fear that made nation building difficult and undermined public support in the United States and the West for a continued peacemaking and nation-building war.

In some ways, Saddam Hussein's supporters did a better job of fighting the peace than they did of fighting the war.

The patterns in U.S. casualties, which are shown in detail in table 7.1, make the cost of the fighting since the "end" of the war all too clear. Of the 199 U.S. deaths between March 19 and June 27, 138 occurred during the war (March 19–April 30). Of those, 89 were the result of hostile action, one was the result of illness, 28 were the result of accidents other than in helicopters, and 15 were the result of accidents in helicopters. Two occurred because a U.S. NCO shot several other soldiers in his unit (the "Camp PA" incident), and the remaining three were the result of known cases of friendly fire. "Postwar," there were 61 deaths between May 1 and June 27. Of those, 19 were the result of hostile action, 4 came from non-hostile action, 31 were the result of accidents other than in helicopters, 7 were the result of accidents in helicopters, and none were the result of known cases of friendly fire.[24] The situation also continued to deteriorate. As of July 8, a total of 29 Americans had been killed in combat since May 1, although noncombat deaths were still much larger. The United States had lost 43 men and women to accidents and other noncombat causes.[25] As a result, the United States had lost a total of 143 dead by early July, which compared with a total of 147 dead in the Gulf War.

There was also a risk that the scale of the fighting might broaden. Although the Shi'ite areas of Iraq remained more peaceful than the Sunni areas, six British military policemen were killed in one incident.[26] There also was low-level fighting in the north between Arabs and Kurds and at least one case of covert intervention by Turkish Special Forces. Iraqis who supported the nation-building effort were threatened, and significant numbers were killed, and there were growing numbers of sabotage attacks on key elements of the Iraqi economy like pipelines.

There is no way to predict whether future coalition nation-building and security efforts will bring an end to such violence. As of July 2003, the nation-building effort was only beginning to gather momentum, U.S. and British security operations were only in their early stages, the level of combat in Iraq was still very low, and accidents had been far more lethal than combat. At the same time, Iraq is a further lesson that the transition to peacemaking and nation building can also be a transition to asymmetric warfare. Afghanistan is scarcely the only precedent; Lebanon and Somalia are other examples of the fact that it "isn't over when it's over" and that that the conflict-termination process should be as much a matter of limiting or avoiding asymmetric warfare as creating a stable peace.

Table 7.1
Daily Patterns in U.S. Casualties, March 20 to June 27, 2003

| Date of Death | Total Deaths | Hostile Action | Non-Hostile | | Could be either ... depending on the Pentagon | | | Camp PA Incident |
			Other	Illness	Accident	Chopper Accident	Friendly Fire	
20-Mar-03	4					4		
21-Mar-03	2	2						
22-Mar-03	5				3	1		1
23-Mar-03	29	29						
24-Mar-03	4	4						
25-Mar-03	5	4						1
26-Mar-03	1				1			
27-Mar-03	1	1						
28-Mar-03	2	1			1			
29-Mar-03	7	6			1			
30-Mar-03	3					3		
31-Mar-03	2	1		1				
1-Apr-03	2	1			1			
2-Apr-03	10	1			2	6	1	
3-Apr-03	11	8			3			
4-Apr-03	10	6			3	1		
5-Apr-03	3	3						
6-Apr-03	2	2						
7-Apr-03	8	8						
8-Apr-03	6	6						
9-Apr-03								
10-Apr-03	2	2						
11-Apr-03	1	1						
12-Apr-03	2	2						
13-Apr-03	1				1			
14-Apr-03	6				4		2	
15-Apr-03								
16-Apr-03								
17-Apr-03	1				1			
18-Apr-03								
19-Apr-03								
20-Apr-03								
21-Apr-03								
22-Apr-03	4				4			
23-Apr-03								
24-Apr-03	1	1						
25-Apr-03	2				2			
26-Apr-03								
27-Apr-03								
28-Apr-03	1				1			
29-Apr-03								
30-Apr-03								
1-May-03	1				1			
2-May-03								
3-May-03	1				1			
4-May-03	1				1			
5-May-03								
6-May-03								
7-May-03								
8-May-03	1	1						
9-May-03	4				1	3		

Table 7.1 (continued)

Date of Death	Total Deaths	Hostile Action	Non-Hostile		Could be either ... depending on the Pentagon			
			Other	Illness	Accident	Chopper Accident	Friendly Fire	Camp PA Incident
10-May-03	1				1			
11-May-03								
12-May-03	2				2			
13-May-03	2	1			1			
14-May-03	1				1			
15-May-03								
16-May-03	1				1			
17-May-03								
18-May-03	2				2			
19-May-03	6				2	4		
20-May-03								
21-May-03	1				1			
22-May-03								
23-May-03								
24-May-03								
25-May-03	1				1			
26-May-03	5	1			4			
27-May-03	2	2						
28-May-03	2	1			1			
29-May-03								
30-May-03	3				3			
31-May-03								
1-Jun-03	1				1			
2-Jun-03								
3-Jun-03	1	1						
4-Jun-03								
5-Jun-03	1	1						
6-Jun-03	2				2			
7-Jun-03	1	1						
8-Jun-03	1	1						
9-Jun-03								
10-Jun-03	1	1						
11-Jun-03								
12-Jun-03	1				1			
13-Jun-03	1				1			
14-Jun-03								
15-Jun-03	1				1			
16-Jun-03	2	1	1					
17-Jun-03	2	1	1					
18-Jun-03	2	2						
19-Jun-03	1	1						
20-Jun-03								
21-Jun-03								
22-Jun-03	1	1						
23-Jun-03								
24-Jun-03	1		1					
25-Jun-03	1				1			
26-Jun-03	3	2	1					
27-Jun-03								
TOTAL	199	108	4	1	59	22	3	2

Source: E-mail from Michael R. Schreiber of ABC News, June 27, 2003.

Moreover, the United States and its allies must find solutions to the problem of asymmetric warfare during conflict termination, peacemaking, and nation building that avoid the trap that small hostile elements can potentially divide the United States from the people it is seeking to help by forcing the United States to concentrate on the security mission, alienating the U.S. military and the local population, driving both the U.S. military and the civilians involved in nation building into a fortress mentality where they become increasingly isolated, and sabotaging economic and political progress with relatively limited attacks and acts of sabotage.

For all of its conventional war-fighting strengths, the West is still vulnerable to even relatively low-level but persistent attacks during nation building. This is also a vulnerability that enemies are all too well aware of. Saddam Hussein and Iraqi intelligence cited the U.S. experience in Vietnam and Lebanon as examples of U.S. vulnerability long before the Gulf War. They saw a similar weakness in the U.S. approach to Somalia, Kosovo, and Afghanistan. At least some captured Iraqi documents described the option of a "postwar" asymmetric campaign against the United States.

Winning a peace may be anything but peaceful. The United States and its allies must be ready to deal with conflict termination and nation building as a new form of asymmetric warfare. They must be ready to deal with postwar power vacuums and a mutating enemy, to win hearts and minds, and to combine simultaneous political, economic, and security efforts.

FRIENDLY FIRE AND CASUALTY ISSUES

U.S., British, and Australian casualties were remarkably low during the war. As of April 12, the United States had lost 108 dead, 14 captured, and 399 wounded. This was about one casualty for every 480 soldiers, assuming some 250,000 forces engaged. It compares with 1 per 15 soldiers from World War I through Vietnam. As of April 20—at a point the coalition had clearly transitioned to peacekeeping and nation building—the United States had a total of 128 dead (94 killed in action and 34 killed in noncombat situations, largely accidents). The United States had 2 missing. The British had 31 dead.

On May 1, the day President Bush announced the end of the war, the United States had a total of 138 deaths: 114 from combat and 24 from other causes. The British had lost a total of 42 dead, 19 in accidents.[27] The highest daily level of fatalities was 29 on March 23. The average was just short of two a day, and the average due to hostilities was just over one a day. The average number of fatalities due to hostilities fell from four a day in March to about one and one-half a day in April.

This is an extraordinarily low rate of overall casualties. The United States lost an average of 211 combat deaths per day in World War II and 18 per day in Vietnam. The U.S. Marines lost 265 personnel in Lebanon during 1982–1984, including 241 who died in the attack on their barracks. The United States had a total of 613 casualties in the Gulf War: 146 service personnel were killed in action, including 35 killed by friendly fire, and 467 were wounded—72 by friendly fire.

The low casualty rate in Iraq reflects all of the strengths in the coalition's war-fighting capabilities and all of the Iraqi weaknesses mentioned earlier. A review of the casualties also indicates that the best-protected soldiers in combat were least likely to be casualties—a predictable point, but one that emphasizes the value of body armor and heavy armor.[28]

These casualty data do, however, reflect problems with fratricide or "friendly fire." The ABC analysis referenced earlier shows only confirmed wartime losses for the United States and does not include suspected cases or British losses. As a result, the total losses from friendly fire were only 3 dead as of June 27, versus 22 from helicopter accidents and 59 from accidents from other causes. If these data are correct, improving safety would be much more important for reducing deaths than dealing with the problems of friendly fire.

Another analysis, however, showed 10 U.S. combat deaths caused by friendly fire and another 10 incidents and 20 deaths under investigation.[29] The U.S. military has always been slow to analyze and confirm such cases, but it now seems likely that the United States and Britain lost more than a dozen personnel to friendly fire, and dozens more may have been wounded. The exact number of friendly fire cases remains uncertain, but they seem to include at least five major cases where air or ground forces attacked friendly forces. There may also be a sixth case.

Reports indicate that U.S. A-10s killed nine U.S. Marines on March 23, the day that the United States lost 29 personnel and that some analysts have called the worst day of the war.[30] These figures are much more consistent with the pattern of fratricide in the Gulf War, where 35 out of 147 combat deaths—some 24 percent—were the result of friendly fire. There is no way to put these cases in a broader historical perspective, because the historical data on this issue are so flawed that any trend analysis would have to be based on little more than statistical rubbish.[31]

If these levels of losses are accurate, they indicate that, in addition to improving safety, reducing friendly fire remains an important priority.

This includes dealing with such wartime issues as possible problems with the effectiveness of the IFF (identification of friend or foe) systems used, ranging from passive readout systems to transponders. For example, after an F-16CJ fired on a Patriot on March 24 the United States had to refine its IFF procedures during the course of the war and add a backup check using another system to lock the radar on suspected targets.[32]

At the same time, there are important limits to what can and should be done to reduce fratricide or friendly fire. Any major additional efforts to reduce friendly fire must be weighed against alternative uses of the same resources to determine which investment would produce the lowest net casualties and/or greatest increase in combat effectiveness. Similarly, more stringent rules of engagement could increase net casualties by slowing down the pace and lethality of operations and giving the enemy more opportunities to kill. It is also important to recognize that much more is involved than finding the right technology. Lt. Gen. David D. McKiernan, the commander of the Coalition Forces Land Component Command, described the problems during the fighting as follows:[33]

> What really makes all the difference in mitigating the risk of fratricide has nothing to do with technology. It has everything to do with the tactical discipline of units, of using the right fire support coordination measures, the right tactical graphics and the right weapons control status and discipline of formations. Technology does help mitigate it. The ability to use things like "identification friend or foe" technology or visual infrared reflective markers that help determine friendlies on the battlefield are all very important. All the services have made great strides since Desert Storm. Is there more that we can do? I believe there probably is, and I'm sure we'll address that as we look at resourcing future requirements.
>
> ...when you're fighting, for instance, in a dust storm at night in an urban area with special operating forces, conventional forces, air power, all operating in the same battle space, you are never, ever going to completely mitigate the risk of blue-on-blue fire. That's a danger we have in this profession that no amount of technology will ever completely erase.
>
> I don't know what the final numbers are going to look like, but my initial impression is that we have greatly reduced, given the tempo of these operations and the time of this campaign when you compare it to Desert Storm.

THE FORCE XXI BATTLE COMMAND BRIGADE AND BELOW (FBCB2) SYSTEM

U.S. forces in the Iraq War make good use of position-location-guidance radios linked with Precision Lightweight GPS Receivers called "pluggers."

These were given to platoon leaders and were paired with Force XXI Battle Command Brigade and Below, or FBCB2, software to provide the coordinates of forces down to the platoon level to the joint Global Command and Control System (GCCS) via satellites or radio frequencies. The GCCS could then retransmit the identification and location data to computers inside a company commander's vehicle.[34]

In previous wars, military operations had to be conducted by relying on commanders using radios to repeatedly call in their positions (and on the timeliness and accuracy of such methods). The new Blue Force Tracking, or BFT, system used in the Iraq War used Precision Lightweight GPS Receivers to provide that information in real time, and the software displayed it in the form of blue icons moving across a commander's screen to identify friendly forces. Commanders could also "click" on these blue icons to communicate with an unknown blue force even if it belonged to a Marine Corps or a British company.[35] This not only reduced friendly fire; it greatly improved situational awareness and the capability to carry out netcentric warfare.

This system has great growth potential. It should be noted that the Force XXI Battle Command Brigade and Below system—one of the key developments intended to improve situational awareness and solve the friendly fire problem—was not fully available. The system uses a mix of transponders, C4I/battle management systems, and display screens to keep track of both friendly and enemy forces. Its displays are highly sophisticated and can track movements even under complex maneuver conditions.

The army describes the role of the system during the fighting as follows:

Coalition situational awareness of US and UK ground maneuver forces was accomplished using the Force XXI Battle Command Brigade and Below (FBCB2) System over a commercial satellite-based communications network. The FBCB2 capability was installed onto selective US and UK command and control (C2) vehicles, logistical support vehicles, and rotary-winged aircraft based on a "thin fielding" concept. The fielding concept employed the FBCB2 capability down to the unit company commander level, or as required by the unit mission. The beyond line-of-sight satellite-based communications architecture provided on-the-move combat operations over extended ranges and during adverse weather conditions, e.g., sandstorms. In addition to real-time situational awareness the FBCB2 capability provided reliable e-mail messaging and battlefield maneuver graphics overlays on digitized maps.

The FBCB2 capability integrated coalition "blue force ground tracks" with the Joint Common Operational Picture (COP). Technically, FBCB2 equipped platforms automatically updated their Global Positioning System (GPS) locations onto Blue Force Tracking (BFT) primary and alternate database servers. The BFT situational awareness display was integrated into the Joint COP using the Global Command & Control System (GCCS). The GCCS further disseminated and digitally displayed the Joint COP. The Joint COP displays an integrated air, ground, and sea friendly forces against positively identified and suspected enemy force positions. The Joint COP enabled real-time battle command and control at all levels of command, e.g., Division, Corps, and Theater.

The US Army Central Command's (ARCENT) Coalition Joint Force Land Component Command (CJFLCC) Center was completely modernized with state-of-art digital large screen video and graphic displays. The digitalization of the CJFLCC enabled the battlefield visualization of the Joint COP including the BFT situational awareness.

One problem in using the system to its full effectiveness was that the 4th Infantry Division was the only U.S. Army unit fully equipped and trained to use the system before the war. This unit was originally supposed to be deployed through Turkey and had to be rerouted through the Gulf. As a result, it did not arrive in Iraq until the war was effectively over.

The command center at Doha in Qatar was equipped with suitable displays, however, and 10-inch mobile terminals and antennae were rushed into the field for the units that deployed to Kuwait. It is unclear how many systems went into the field, how they performed, and the extent to which they were used by both land and helicopter forces. One report states that 50 systems were delivered to the UK, that the U.S. Army had some 8,000 systems on hand, and that the U.S. Marine Corps bought some systems. Details are lacking, however, and only the 4th Infantry Division seems to have had a key feature in the form of the tactical Internet, a mix of elements including the Single-Channel Ground and Airborne Radio System and Enhanced Position Location System with line-of-sight radio transceivers. The others used satellite communications.[36]

Also unclear is the degree of netting the FBCB2 system will have with air units in the future.[37] The U.S. Army does have a developmental airborne command and control system (A2C2S), but the links to U.S. Air Force, U.S. Navy, and Marine Corps C4I, battle management, and air control and warning systems are unclear.[38] The USAF has, however, opened a competition for a Battle Management Command (BMC2) system that will perform some of the necessary functions. It will include a network to relay targeting data to manned and unmanned systems, space assets, and ground-based systems using common standards and an open architecture. As a result of the lessons of the Iraq War, it will also incorporate a joint system that tracks U.S. and allied personnel, building on the Blue Force Tracking system described in the following section.[39]

Blue Force Trackers

The United States has already taken steps to expand the use of the Blue Force Tracker and other systems that can both improve U.S. capabilities for netcentric warfare and reduce the risk of friendly fire. The army was not the only service to find this system extremely useful. The Marine Corps report on the 1st Marine Division's lessons of the war found the army system so effective that it recommended that it replace the Marine Corps system and be used not only for tactical purposes, but also to improve logistics and vehicle tracking and to correct the Marine Corps personnel system's inability to locate personnel accurately once they deployed to the theater:[40]

> During Operation Iraqi Freedom the 1st Marine Division used two distinct systems for Position Location Information (PLI). The MDACT program being fielded by MARCORSYSCOM was advanced to distribute over 319 MDACTs throughout the 1st Marine Division. The MDACT requires the line-of-sight transmission path provided by EPLRS radios and in order to function properly a significant amount of communications engineering is required to support radio channel spacing and IP addressing requirements. The MDACT/EPLRS system requires extensive operator and network engineer training to function properly. The BFT is a U.S. Army program that was advanced by CFLCC, V Corps, and I MEF to field 104 BFTs to the 1st Marine Division in order for CFLCC/V Corps to maintain PLI for Marine Units since the MDACT and BFT are not compatible systems. The BFT uses a commercial L Band Satellite communication system that is managed by the U.S. Army for the user and is basically an install and operate system but extensive behind the scenes coordination was required by the Army to make the BFT addressing and functioning transparent to the Marines of the 1st Marine Division. Operator training for the BFT is simplistic and the system is very operator friendly. Additionally the BFT provides a larger throughput capability for free text or formatted messages to any BFT throughout the world via satellite connection and the 1st Marine Division Marines found this capability very useful to maintain PLI and data text messaging "on the move" from the Division to RCT to Battalion Command Posts. For the 1st Marine Division, BFT was the overwhelming system of choice.
>
> *Recommendation:* That MCSC disestablish the MDACT program and establish a joint BFT program with the US Army that could support worldwide PLI for the Marine Corps from the MEU to the MEF. The new joint BFT program office needs to also establish a dismounted version of the BFT for

Infantry use (a similar concept to the Dismounted Data Automated Communication Terminal).

The British Ministry of Defense report on the lessons of the war reached similar conclusions:[41]

The ability confidently and quickly to distinguish between friendly and enemy troops is a vital but complex part of modern warfare, not least when operating in a coalition. Combat ID cannot be delivered by a single system or piece of equipment; it involves a combination of techniques, training and procedures (often operation-specific) reinforced by equipment.

The UK worked closely with the US to ensure that effective arrangements were in place, although the US did not decide which combat ID equipments they would operate until the end of 2002. A range of new equipment was procured to ensure that our capability was compatible, which primarily focused on equipment to allow recognition of forces from both ground and air and to enhance the situational awareness of UK forces.

The latter included some use of the US Blue Force Tracking system, which provides near real time tracking of assets deployed at unit level. By the start of operations, MOD had deployed 1861 vehicle-mounted and 5000 dismounted Combat ID sets. This was sufficient to meet the full requirement, although the scale of the equipment modifications required in theatre meant that some formations were still being fitted as the first units crossed the line of departure. In the air and at sea, extra "Identification Friend or Foe" (IFF) systems were procured to supplement those routinely fitted to all RAF aircraft and RN warships. This system is also used by the US. IFF systems are tested prior to each take-off and monitored during flight.

While no country has yet been able to field such a capability for land troops, the UK is actively involved in developing Battlefield Target Identification for ground-to-ground recognition in the future. Bowman will also improve situational awareness and, in turn, Combat ID.

While our aim is to provide UK forces with as effective a Combat ID system as possible, regrettably no system is 100 percent failsafe, no matter how sophisticated the technology. Sadly, a number of UK and US Service personnel were killed in so-called "friendly fire" incidents. These are still under investigation, but experience in this and previous campaigns indicate that we cannot relax our efforts or underestimate the importance of training, tactics and procedures in this vital area.

The United States intends to act upon these lessons. The army will lead the U.S. military services in an effort to create a strategy that will give every U.S. armored vehicle and aircraft a joint blue-force device to track other "friendlies" and give commanders the ability to instantly "message" any blue force that emerges as an icon on their displays or radar screens.

This effort is to include the development of faster and more sophisticated systems to improve "situational awareness" and reduce friendly fire incidents.[42]

According to press reports, on May 12, 2003, the Joint Requirements Oversight Council (JROC) approved the creation of an army-led integrated product team (IPT) that will report to U.S. Joint Forces Command (JFCOM). It will review currently fielded systems to track forces, find capability gaps, assess new technologies, and develop a joint BFT architecture and funding strategy to be implemented during FY2006–FY2011.

The U.S. Strategic Command has previously taken the lead in creating systems for "joint blue-force situational awareness" by transferring conceptual development activity to JFCOM, which is now tasked with developing a concept to outline joint priorities and help the army build a system architecture. The Senate Armed Services Committee has also called for a new acquisition strategy to develop a single interoperable blue-force tracking system to reduce the number of fratricide incidents, but the committee has questioned whether the level of involvement by other services and special operations forces matches the level of army activity. Recent U.S. Air Force plans to create improved jointness in the Air Force C2 system indicate that it will, but this will be part of a broad effort that will not be fully operation before 2013.[43]

The end result is that the United States is seeking several improved capabilities as the result of the lessons of both the Afghan and Iraq wars. It is seeking to reduce the time before blue-force positions show up in the satellite-enabled system. Aircraft were typically identified in one minute, whereas tanks were identified in four to five minutes. This reaction time is adequate for static ground forces, but not for vehicles maneuvering at speeds of up to 30 to 40 miles per hour. These delays, or "latency," need to be reduced to reduce fratricide. The new system will also build on another joint program, this one led by the air force, called the Family of Interoperable Operational Pictures (FIOP). This system is intended to integrate real-time land, air, and sea data into a single, Web-based mapping application. The army team will take the lead in creating a single integrated ground picture, the ground piece of the FIOP, which will include coalition combat ID technologies.

POSTWAR REVIEW OF FORCE PLANS, BASING, AND TRANSFORMATIONAL RESTOCKING

One obvious lesson of any major war is the need to make a comprehensive review of force plans and modernization plans to reflect the lessons of the war and to shape restocking plans to modernize and transform forces rather than simply replace past items with the same thing.[44] The Department of Defense is already acting on this lesson. Secretary Rumsfeld directed the Office of the Secretary of Defense and Joint Staff to develop such a "Post-War Defense Assessment" in mid-April 2003.[45]

As has been touched on earlier, a similar direction has been given to the U.S. Joint Forces Command. The Joint Forces Command had a 50-man lessons team assigned to the U.S. headquarters for USCENTCOM and each of its service components before the war began. They and an additional 20 service personnel stationed at the Joint Forces Command in Norfolk will produce a detailed examination of the lessons of the war.[46]

The United States also has commissioned a broader "Global Posture Study" to examine the adjustments the United States should make in its force posture and basing. Like the Afghan conflict, the Iraq War raises the question of how the United States can improve its mix of presence, basing, prepositioning mix, and use of prepositioning ships to best support rapid power projection and take advantage of the advances in joint warfare. No one war can do more than illustrate the value of the advances in U.S. capability in a single contingency, but it is clear that the role of air power is changing in many important ways, that the projection of land forces bear little resemblance to the needs of the Cold War and that the United States needs a force posture that can be as flexible and adaptive as possible.

THE BROADER IMPLICATIONS OF CUTTING ENEMY CASUALTIES AND COLLATERAL DAMAGE: A NEW DUAL STANDARD AND FORM OF ASYMMETRIC WARFARE?

More broadly, the United States and the West need to examine the long-term diplomatic and political implications of the effort to minimize casualties and rely on "effect-based" bombing, an effort that reflected a steadily growing potential for asymmetry between the Western approach to warfare and that of possible opponents.

Iraqi Civilian Casualties

As has been touched on earlier, there are no—and may never be—accurate estimates of Iraqi military and civilian casualties. The *Los Angeles Times* has estimated that 1,700 Iraqi civilians were killed and 8,000 were injured in Baghdad alone, and that the number of dead could reach 2,000. This estimate may include losses that occurred after the war, however, from Iraqis attacking Iraqis or from unexploded ordnance.[47]

As for the total number of civilian dead, Iraq made wartime claims of some 1,252 killed and 5,103 injured as of April 3. Some media simply rely on round numbers like 5,000 to 10,000 deaths. A more serious estimate made as of late June 2003 indicated that hospital records showed up to 3,240 dead civilians, including 1,896 in Baghdad, and the possibility of thousands more.[48] Another press estimate produced the range of 2,100 to 2,600, and one NGO produced a remarkably precise range of 4,065 to 5,223. The lowest estimate seems to be 1,100 to 2,355.[49] The most credible low-end estimate is 1,500 civilians dead.[50]

It is unclear, though, how many of the casualties counted in such totals were really civilians or were military no longer in uniform. It is equally unclear whether significant numbers of undocumented burials can be accurately reflected. As a result, the true number of casualties could either be substantially higher or substantially lower than the estimates made to date.

Iraqi Military Casualties

Any estimate of the number of Iraqi military casualties also can be little more than guesswork. The United States has not sought to make accurate estimates of such casualties and has no way of doing so. All it has said is that there were more than 2,320 dead as of April 8. As for press reports, one serious attempt at estimating casualties put the total at 2,320 military dead and 7,000 prisoners of war.[51]

The actual number of Iraqi military casualties could easily range from 5,000 to 20,000. There is no way to distinguish how many were the result of accidents, direct coalition action, or the problems caused once units disbanded or rushed into retreat. Some reports arbitrarily try to relate the number of precision-guided weapons used to probable casualties, and others exaggerate the extent to which crews abandoned their vehicles and deserted.

The Problems with Not Estimating Casualties in a World Seeking "No Casualty" Wars

The same problems with U.S. sensors, intelligence, and battle damage assessment methods that make it impossible to see into buildings or estimate the number of live military personnel in combat forces make it equally difficult to provide accurate estimates of casualties. The end result, however, is that the United States is seeking to reduce civilian casualties and collateral damage, as well as unnecessary enemy military casualties, without having any clear measures of effectiveness.

The U.S. military deliberately avoids developing better methodologies to make such estimates in part because of the difficulties involved, but also because of the certain public relations backlash from such estimates and the problems caused by the body counts of Vietnam. This, however, creates an analytic vacuum and a lack of any detailed substantive basis for target planning and effects-based operations. It also ensures that the issue of casualties becomes heavily politicized. Although some NGOs—such as Human Rights Watch—make an honest effort to establish the facts, many other NGOs, humanitarian organizations, and politicians tend to exaggerate probable casualties, sometimes to ideological extremes.

This inability and unwillingness to make estimates of casualties is not likely to remain an acceptable basis for war fighting in a world where Western powers face more and more pressure to minimize military and civilian casualties. As in Afghanistan, Kosovo, and the first Gulf War, the coalition not only made great efforts to minimize casualties; it faced growing domestic and international expectations it would do so. It had to fight in what in many ways was a dual standard: international expectations that casualties and collateral damage would be kept to an absolute minimum, yet without similar expectations about the conduct of Saddam Hussein's regime. It also had to operate in a climate where many of the interpretations of the laws of war called for both unilateral restraint and restraint to so great a degree that it could make military operations difficult to impossible.

The search to minimize casualties in limited wars also raises serious questions about future wars that are more existential in character. It is easy to show restraint against a weak and ineffective opponent. The situation could be totally different against a terrorist movement equipped with weapons of mass destruction, much less against a modern state. This is clearly an area where the Iraq War raises more legal, ethical, moral, and military questions than it answers.

Notes

[1] General Tommy Franks, USCENTCOM briefing, March 22, 2003, USCENTCOM Release Number: 03-03-44.

[2] British Ministry of Defense, "Operations in Iraq: First Reflections" (London: Her Majesty's Stationery Office, July 2003), pp. 19–20, 28.

[3] Ibid., p. 27.

[4] Adapted from Lt. General T. Michael Moseley, "Operation Iraqi Freedom—By the Numbers," USCENTAF, Assessment and Analysis Division, April 30, 2003; Anthony H. Cordesman and Abraham R. Wagner, *The Lessons of Modern War*, vol. 4,

The Gulf War (Boulder, Colo.: Westview, 1996), p. 477; and Stephen Budiansky, "Air War: Striking in Ways We Haven't Seen," *Washington Post*, April 6, 2003, sec. B, p. 1.

[5] General Hal M. Hornburg, "Air Support in Iraq," *New York Times*, June 3, 2003.

[6] For background on the planning and conceptual thinking behind some of these developments, see Daniel Gouré and Christopher M. Szara, eds., *Air and Space Power in the New Millennium* (Washington, D.C.: CSIS, 1997) and Stuart E. Johnson and Martin C. Libicki, *Dominant Battlespace Knowledge* (Washington, D.C.: National Defense University, 1995).

[7] Department of Defense briefing on April 23, 2003, www.defenselink.mil/transcripts/2003/tr20030423-0122.html.

[8] Statement of General Tommy R. Franks, former commander of U.S. Central Command, before the U.S. Senate Armed Services Committee, July 9, 2003.

[9] British Ministry of Defense, "Operations in Iraq: First Reflections," pp. 24–25.

[10] Ibid., p. 25.

[11] Joe Burlas, "G-6 Says OIF Validates Transformation Path," Army News Service, May 27, 2003.

[12] Joshua Davis, "If We Run Out of Batteries, This War Is Screwed," *Wired Magazine*, June 2003, www.wired.com/wired/archive/11.06/battlefield_pr.html.

[13] British Ministry of Defense, "Operations in Iraq: First Reflections," p. 5

[14] Rowan Scarborough, "Myers Says Annihilation of Iraqi Army Wasn't Goal," *Washington Times*, June 30, 2003.

[15] "No Bunker Found under Bomb Site," *New York Times*, May 29, 2003.

[16] Prepared testimony by U.S. Secretary of Defense Donald R. Rumsfeld, Senate Armed Services Committee, July 9, 2003; Statement of General Tommy R. Franks, Senate Armed Services Committee.

[17] For a technical explanation of some of the adaptations in helicopter tactics, see Robert Wall, "Guerrilla War," *Aviation Week*, March 31, 2003, pp. 24–25.

[18] British Ministry of Defense, "Operations in Iraq: First Reflections," p. 12.

[19] Paul Martin, "Iraqi Secret Plan Orders Mayhem," *Washington Times*, June 9, 2003, p. 1; Alexei Barrionuevo and Michael M. Phillips, "Mounting Troop Deaths in Iraq Raise Questions of U.S. Control," *Wall Street Journal*, June 25, 2003; Warren Vieth and Alissa J. Rubin, "Iraq Pipelines Easy Targets for a Saboteur," *Los Angeles Times*, June 25, 2003; Daniel McGrory, "Saboteurs Leave Cities Stifling in Dark," *London Times*, June 25, 2003; "Rumsfeld Downplays Resistance in Iraq," *New York Times* on the Web, June 18, 2003; Thom Shanker, "Pentagon Officials Say They See No Organized Iraqi Resistance," *New York Times*, June 15, 2003; Dave Moniz, "Official: U.S. Not Ready for Iraq Chaos," *USA Today*, June 11, 2003; Michael Slackman, "Carefully Planned Attacks Target U.S. Troops in Iraq," *Los Angeles Times*, June 11, 2003; Rowan Scarborough, "Rumsfeld Says Fate of Saddam Fuels Guerrilla Attacks," *Washington Times*, June 11, 2003; Paul Martin, "Scores of Saddam Backers Arrested," *Washington*

Times, June 30, 2003; "Rumsfeld Doesn't See Iraq Attacks as Guerilla Warfare," *Dallas Morning News,* June 28, 2003; Michael Elliot, "The War That Never Ends," *Time,* July 28, 2003, p. 28; James Gordon Meek, "US Calls Saddam Key to GI Killings," *New York Daily News,* June 30, 2003; Thomas E. Ricks, "Experts Question Depth of Victory," *Washington Post,* June 27, 2003; and Alexei Barrionuevo, "Resistance Groups Attack Iraqis Who Are Helping Coalition Forces," *Wall Street Journal,* June 27, 2003.

[20] "US Hunts Down Saddam Loyalists," BBC News, June 13, 2003, 21:01; US-CENTCOM Press Release, "Operation Desert Scorpion Begins Combined Combat and Humanitarian Action," USCENTCOM, Baghdad, Iraq, June 15, 2003; USCENTCOM Press Release, "Coalition and Iraqi Police Work to Make Iraq Secure," Release 03-06-78, June 24, 2003.

[21] USCENTCOM News Release, Release Number: 03-06-102, June 30, 2003.

[22] Ibid.

[23] Combined Joint Task Force (CTJF), "Operation Sidewinder Concludes—Net Results," CTJF Press Release, 030706b, July 6, 2003.

[24] Estimates differ as to the causes. According to the *Wall Street Journal,* the United States had lost 92 dead to enemy fire since Baghdad had fallen on April 9 in comparison with 102 during the war, and 52 Americans had been killed since President Bush had announced the formal end of combat action on May 1. Source: Alexei Barrionuevo and Michael M. Phillips, "Mounting Troop Deaths in Iraq Raise Questions of US Control," *Wall Street Journal,* June 25, 2003.

[25] Brian Hartman, ABC News, July 8, 2003.

[26] William Booth, "Six British Soldiers Killed in an Iraqi Town," *Washington Post,* June 25, 2003; James Hide, "US Deaths Rise," *London Times,* June 20, 2003.

[27] Neela Banerjee, "Violence in Iraq Spreads, 6 British Soldiers Are Killed," *New York Times,* June 25, 2003.

[28] For good reports on this issue, see Dennis Cauchon, "Why US Casualties Were Low," *USA Today,* April 21, 2003, p. 1; and Amy Goldstein, Jonathan Weissman, and Margot Williams, "Casualties Reflect Different War, Different Military," *Washington Post,* April 13, 2003, p. A25. The *Post* article provides an interesting breakout of rank and ethnicity, but the data do not reflect any particular lessons or reveal any pattern of discrimination.

[29] Peter Pae, "Friendly Fire Still a Problem," *Los Angeles Times,* May 16, 2003, p. 1.

[30] Ibid.; Tom Bowman, "Troop Deaths Laid to US Fire," *Baltimore Sun,* June 29, 2003.

[31] Pae, "Friendly Fire Still a Problem."

[32] Stephen Trimble, "Coalition Aircrews Add Procedure to Reduce Friendly Fire Incidents," *Aviation Week,* April 22, 2003.

[33] Department of Defense briefing on April 23, 2003, www.defenselink.mil/transcripts/2003/tr20030423-0122.html.

[34] Anne Plummer, "Army to Build System Architecture for Joint Blue-Force Tracking," *Inside the Army*, May 19, 2003, p. 1.

[35] Ibid.

[36] Frank Tiboni, "US, UK Troops Carry Force Trackers," *Defense News*, March 24, 2003, p. 6; Kim Burger, "US Army Shares Radios to Avoid Fratricide," *Jane's Defense Weekly*, March 12, 2003; Vernon Loeb, "Digitized Battlefield Puts Friend and Foe in Sight," *Washington Post*, March 3, 2003, p. 15; Frank Tiboni, "Force XXI Proves Mettle by Saving Lives in Iraq," *Defense News*, June 9, 2003, p. 42.

[37] Tiboni, "US, UK Troops Carry Force Trackers"; Burger, "US Army Shares Radios to Avoid Fratricide."

[38] Frank Tiboni, "US Army Seeks New Transports by 2008," *Defense News*, April 21, 2003, p. 22.

[39] Gail Kaufman, "USAF C2 Contest Gets Off Ground," *Defense News*, June 23, 2003, p. 18.

[40] Commanding General, 1st Marine Division, "Operation Iraqi Freedom: OIF Lessons Learned," Reference MEF Frago 279-03, May 29, 2003.

[41] British Ministry of Defense, "Operations in Iraq: First Reflections," p. 25.

[42] This analysis relies heavily on reporting by Plummer in "Army to Build System Architecture."

[43] Kaufman, "USAF C2 Contest Gets Off Ground."

[44] The United States did have an inventory capable of supporting two major regional contingencies. At the end of the Iraq War, the United States still had some 17,000 JDAMs, 25,000 laser-guided bombs, and 6,500 Wind Corrected Munitions. The war consumed roughly 30 percent of U.S. TLAM assets. *Inside the Air Force*, April 11, 2003, p. 3.

[45] Jason Sherman, "Restock and Rethink," *Defense News*, April 21, 2003, p. 1.

[46] Richard Whittle, "Military Mulls the Lessons of War," *Dallas Morning News*, April 22, 2003.

[47] Laura King, "Baghdad's Death Toll Assessed," *Los Angeles Times*, May 18, 2003, p. 1.

[48] Niko Price, "Tallying Civilian Death Toll in Iraq War Is Daunting," *Philadelphia Inquirer*, June 11, 2003.

[49] King, "Baghdad's Death Toll Assessed"; Peter Ford, "Survey Pointing to High Civilian Death Toll in Iraq," *Christian Science Monitor*, May 22, 2003, p. 1; Associated Press, May 15, 2003; Iraqbodycount.net.

[50] *Washington Post*, April 20, 2003, sec. A, p. 20.

[51] Ibid.

CHAPTER EIGHT

AIR, MISSILE, AND LAND–BASED AIR DEFENSE FORCES

While no set of lessons can be decoupled from the overall lessons regarding joint operations, there are a number of lessons that primarily affect air, missile, and air defense forces. These lessons reflect the fact that the Iraq War probably was the first major war in which air power could strike with near-real-time precision at many key tactical targets. At the same time, they also reflect the fact that air and missile tactics and technology continue to advance at an extremely high rate, and that future wars are likely to see even more effective use of precision, time-sensitive targeting and the integration of air and missile power into joint operations.

AIR DOMINANCE

As has been discussed in previous chapters, much of the air battle was conducted before March 19, 2003. The United States and Britain greatly intensified their attacks on Iraq's ground-based air defenses after November 2001, and they began an active campaign to suppress them in the summer of 2002 called "Southern Focus." The purpose of this "war before the war" was to prepare for the U.S. and British invasion to come. The impact of this is indicated by the fact the allies flew 21,736 sorties, struck 349 Iraqi air defense targets, and fired 606 munitions between June 2001 and March 19, 2003.[1]

Once the war began, the key missions for coalition air forces were to (1) neutralize the ability of the Iraqi government to command its forces, (2) establish control of the airspace over Iraq, (3) provide air support for special operations forces and the army and Marine forces that would advance toward Baghdad, and (3) neutralize Iraq's forces of surface-to-surface missiles and suspected caches of biological and chemical weapons.[2] The U.S., British, and Australian air forces had an unprecedented ability to execute these missions. The coalition's ability to paralyze Iraq's air force and the systematic suppression of Iraqi air defenses allowed coalition air forces to achieve nearly total air dominance shortly after the first air strikes on March 19—a level of air superiority the United States and its allies had never enjoyed in any previous major war.

The coalition allies employed some 1,800 aircraft to deliver approximately 20,000 strikes against Iraq, and no aircraft were lost to air-to-air combat in the process.[3] According to the USAF, seven aircraft were lost to Iraqi ground fire—one A-10, four AH-64s, and 2 AH-1Ws—although an additional F-15E and a UH-60 may also have been lost to such fire. This total is roughly half the number of aircraft lost to accidents and other non-combat causes. A total of 13 aircraft, including two fighters, were lost to other causes.[4] There were a total of 25 aircraft accidents: four serious Class A, five Class B, and 16 less serious Class C, and a total of 32 problems with near collisions or hazardous air traffic reports (HATRs).[5]

An analysis by Tom Cooper, the editor of the Air Combat Information Group, provides the following chronology of losses and damage during the course of the peak period of the fighting. This analysis is not official, but it seems accurate in indicating that accidents and friendly fire caused as much damage and as many losses as the Iraqi forces did:[6]

- 19 March
  — MH-53 Pave Low III, USAF; hard landing inside Iraq; helicopter destroyed, crew and passengers "self-recovered";
  — AH-64, 11th Aviation Brigade, U.S. Army; hard landing inside Iraq; helicopter and crew recovered; non-combat related accident;
  — CH-46, USMC; crashed in Kuwait, 12 KIA; non-combat related accident

- 20 March
  — 2 Sea King ASaC.Mk.7s; NAS 849; collided, 7 KIA;
  — AH-64, 11th Aviation Brigade, U.S. Army; hard landing inside Iraq; helicopter and crew recovered; non-combat related accident

- 23 March
  — Tornado GR.Mk.4 or GR.Mk.4A; shot down by U.S. Army PAC-3 Patriot SAM, 2 MIA

- 24 March
  — AH-64D 99-5135, 11th Aviation Brigade (C Company, "Vampires," 1-227 Attack Helicopter Battalion, 1st Cavalry Division), U.S. Army; damaged by RPG-7 and landed in the field near Karbala, Iraq; crew captured;

—AH-64D, 11th Aviation Brigade, U.S. Army; damaged by RPG-7 and SMAF; RTB, but probably w/o;

—AH-64, 11th Aviation Brigade, U.S. Army, damaged by RPG-7 and SMAF; RTB

- 26 March
  —Phoenix UAV, ZJ300, British Army; shot down near Basrah;
  —Phoenix UAV, ZJ393, British Army; shot down near Basrah

- 27 March
  —RQ-1B Predator UAV, 95-014, USAF; shot down over Baghdad

- 29/30 March
  —AH-64, unit unknown, U.S. Army; crashed in "brown-out" conditions, probably w/o; crew OK; non-combat related accident;
  —UH-60, U.S. Army; damaged by crashing AH-64; helicopter and crew fate unknown; non-combat related accident;
  —UH-60, U.S. Army; crashed in brown-out conditions; crew fate unknown; non-combat related accident;
  —OH-58 Kiowa Warrior, 11th Aviation Brigade, U.S. Army; damaged by SMAF;
  —OH-58 Kiowa Warrior, 11th Aviation Brigade, U.S. Army, damaged by SMAF

- 30 March
  —UH-1N, HMLA-169/MAG-39, USMC; crashed in southern Iraq; 3 KIA;
  —S-3B, VS-38/CVW-2, USN; rolled off deck after landing aboard USS *Constellation*; crew recovered; non-combat related accident;
  —AH-64, 1-3rd Aviation Regiment, 3rd ID (Mech), U.S. Army; crashed in "brown-out" conditions, w/o; crew... recovered; non-combat related accident

- 1 April
  —AV-8B, HMM-263 USMC; crashed during attempted landing aboard USS *Nassau*; pilot recovered; non-combat related accident;
  —F-14A, VF-154/CVW-5, USN; crashed due to engine malfunction during strike against enemy positions in southern Iraq; crew recovered; non-combat related accident;

- 2 April
  —UH-60A, B Company 2nd Battalion 3rd Aviation Regiment, U.S. Army; shot down by SMAF near Karbala; 6 KIA;
  —F/A-18C, CVW-5, USN; shot down by U.S. Army PAC-3 Patriot SAM over southern Iraq; pilot not listed MIA = probably recovered

- 4 April
  — AH-1W, HMLA-267/MAG-39, 3rd Marine Aircraft Wing, USMC; crashed in southern Iraq; 2 KIA …; non-combat related accident;
  — Phoenix UAV ZJ402, British Army; shot down over Basrah;
  — Phoenix UAV ZJ417, British Army; shot down over Basrah

- 7 April
  — F-15E, 336th FS/4th FW, USAF; shot down over Tikrit; crew MIA

- 8 April
  — A-10A, 173rd FS/Miss. ANG, USAF; shot down by MANPAD over Baghdad; pilot recovered;
  — A-10A, USAF; heavily damaged by SMAF and MANPAD over Baghdad; aircraft and pilot… recovered;
  — CH-46E, USN; crashed in Eastern Mediterranean during VERTREP-operation for USS *Truman*; crew recovered.

The Iraqi Air force never flew, and the Iraqi land-based air defenses failed to protect Iraqi forces in the field and eventually could not even defend Baghdad against urban close air support strikes by coalition forces.

What is uncertain is whether such a level of superiority can be achieved in the future. It may be possible with some developing countries, and even with nations with larger and more modern air forces that lack systems similar to the AWACS as well as a full range of specialized support and electronic warfare aircraft and modern IS&R and C4I assets. One great question will be the extent to which the deployment of advanced land-based air defense systems like the Russian S-300 and Patriot can offset the advantages of modern air power.

EFFECTS-BASED BOMBING: FUNDAMENTALLY CHANGING THE EFFECTIVENESS OF AIR POWER WHILE LIMITING CIVILIAN CASUALTIES AND COLLATERAL DAMAGE

Despite the problems in U.S. and allied IS&R and targeting capabilities described in previous chapters, improvements in these areas did allow the coalition to use a new approach to targeting. This approach is called "effects-based" bombing and involves the selective use of precision air power to strike at targets to produce effects rather than simply maximize physical damage.[7] Examples of such targeting include knocking out power, communications, and fuel supplies to Iraq military forces, rather than attacking major infrastructure facilities. Others include selectively bombing Iraqi regular army forces to paralyze or reduce their movement rather than destroy them by attrition, and using sensor platforms like the E-8C

JSTARS to attack actual military units in movement, rather than blow bridges and attack lines of communication.

Improved avionics and precision greatly reduced the need for multiple weapons to be used on a given target and for later restrikes. As one senior U.S. Air Force general put it, "Even in the Gulf War, the issue was always how many sorties it took to destroy a given target. In this war the issue is how many targets can be destroyed in a given sortie." Advances in precision also allowed the United States to reshape its targeting and choice of munitions to reduce civilian casualties and collateral damage. One irony behind the increased lethality of modern weapons and tactics is that they can be used to defeat the enemy with far fewer secondary costs. Improvements in laser-guided systems and the use of GPS allowed the use of smaller bombs and often allowed 500-pound bombs to be used instead of 2,000-pound bombs.

The United States made use of new targeting aids like the "bugsplat" program.[8] This allowed it to choose the munitions and angle of attack that could destroy the target to the point necessary to produce the desired effect, but to do so using the smallest munition and the angle and point of attack that would produce minimal risk to civilians and collateral damage.[9]

Understanding Effects-based Bombing

The USAF gave several briefings before the Iraq War that described these concepts in great detail, as well as the concepts behind the use of air power in the war plan.[10] One briefing in particular, by Col. Gary L. Crowder, the chief of Strategy, Concepts, and Doctrine of the Air Combat Command, provides an exceptional picture of the history of the changes in the U.S. approach to air power, as well as an explanation of the air portion of the coalition war plan. His briefing included what proved to be a remarkably prescient analysis of the impact of effects-based bombing during the war. The following text may be long, but it provides one of the best possible explanations of the lessons that drove the use of air power in the Iraq war and the lessons that have emerged from it.[11]

> In the first day of Desert Storm, we struck more targets than were struck in all of 1942 and 1943 by 8th Air Force during the combined bomber offensive. And we were able to do that because we took really a radically different approach in terms of how we wanted to prosecute a military operation....This is the capabilities that we had of advanced precision and stealth—gave the Air Force a little bit of a leg up in trying to move into this area of effects-based operations as we struggled to figure out how to do those types or exploit those capabilities to the greatest extent possible.

Over the course of the last decade, you have probably heard these terms, the term EBO or effects-based bombing, more and more often with each of the military services as each of the services has tried to…develop capabilities to more effectively and efficiently prosecute military operations.

The first piece, obviously, was the combination of stealth and precision. And I'll show you what that implication is for the conduct of air operations.

But the second thing is a different way of thinking about how we do—or what we want to achieve on the battlefield. Instead of a traditional attritional approach in terms of listing a bunch of targets and then go bombing targets, or finding where the enemy is and killing all the enemy, we really determined that what we wanted to do was in fact to achieve some sort of policy objective, and that you could, in fact, craft military operations to better achieve those policy operations in a more efficient and effective manner.

…First of all, it's important to understand the evolution and—or precision technologies since the Second World War. In the Second World War, the CEP of a B-17 was about 3,300 feet. And so if you wanted to destroy and have a high probability of destruction of a point target of about 6,500 feet, you'd need about 1,500 airplanes and about 9,000 bombs. That's a lot of stuff. And that's what drove those military operations and the destructiveness of the military air campaigns against both Germany and Japan…. precision is relative when you look at it today versus 1945.

By Vietnam, we had gotten significantly more accurate in the fact that these—a lot of these aircraft now [that] were doing the operations were fighter bombers, and dropping at a little lower altitude, we were able to be more precise. But still, it took a large number of airplanes to achieve the desired effect.

With the development of the laser-guided bombs, and specifically the laser-guided bombs on aircraft such as the F-111 and the F-117 in Desert Storm, we were able to hit two independent targets very precisely with about 10-meter CEP or 10-foot CEP from a single aircraft. When we added additional aircraft, such as the B-2, that capability is now to the point where we can hit multiple targets on a single pass.

Circular error probable or CEP is the probability that that weapon will—that 50 percent of the weapons will land inside that line. So, if what…if I say the CEP of a B-17 in World War II was 3,300 feet, that means there was a high likelihood that 50 percent of the bombs dropped landed inside 3,300 feet. Today it's a radius of 10 feet.

And it's important to understand that as we also develop Joint Direct Attack Munitions capability—these are these GPS-guided weapons—they also give us the ability for a large number of other aircraft besides just stealth aircraft to hit multiple weapons per targets. Navy F-18s are equipped with JDAM, as well as all the Air Force bombers. The B-1, for example, can carry

24 Joint Direct Attack Munitions in an internal payload that could be used against 24 separate targets.

…it's really important as well that what the capability of a Joint Direct Attack Munition has given to us, together with the integration of Global Positioning Systems on our aircraft is we are now able to achieve that near precision. And again, we have to understand that there is a difference between the precision of laser-guided weapons that are described here and the Joint Direct Attack Munition. The Joint Direct Attack Munition is not quite as accurate, although it is much accurate, we are finding in employment than we anticipated.

…But the addition of these capabilities gives us the ability to do a large number, an extremely large volume of fires or effects early in an operation in a very, very short period of time. And it really has been the evolution of about the last 20 years that has—from the earliest employment of laser-guided bombs in the Vietnam War, through Allied Force, Desert Storm and Enduring Freedom, that has given us this capability.

…It's also important to understand the role that stealth plays. We have an advantage in this conflict, in that the adversary has basically ceded most of his air—or about two-thirds of the country's air to us early, and so the extremely vicious fights that we had for air superiority—and even though we didn't lose a very large number of airplanes in Desert Storm and in Allied Force, those were sustained fights for air superiority....

But nevertheless, this is the size of the initial strike packages that went into Basra in January 1991. And if you look at all of the support aircraft that were required for that strike package, you basically had about 41 aircraft with only eight bombers. I mean, we had aircraft to do sweep and escort over the top to protect the air assets from enemy fighters. We had actually used drones to tickle the air defenses and to enable us to more effectively target the enemy surface-to-air missiles. You had a variety of SAM suppression airplanes, F-18s and F-4Gs, and you also had electronic attack planes, the Navy's Prowlers, EA-6Bs. And all of that to get eight bombers to a target. That was the way we had to do operations without stealth aircraft.

…If you look at the difference between the employment of the F-117s on the first night of the Gulf War, we literally had a significantly greater capability because they required a far fewer amount of support assets. Now, we don't throw 117s up by themselves. They like a lot of other people flying around with them and other stuff to get the volume of the radars down for everybody. But nevertheless, it is an almost independent capability, and its stealth qualities enable us to do a large number of things because we don't require all of the support assets necessary that would be used for this.

It's important to understand as well that the evolution of both the Air Force and the Navy and Marine Corps' combat aircraft will enable us to do even the left package or more conventional strike package with a far small number of support aircraft to bombers, just because we have much more dual-use capability in each of the Air Force's, Navy's and Marines' fighter aircraft as well as our bomber aircraft.

...in Desert Storm, the escort package for non-stealth was about 5-to-1...stealth required...a different approach. And I don't want to go into the specific details, but we used an area approach to support assets...the last thing we want—that F-117 or B-2 pilots want—is a bunch of wingmen out there that everybody can see. But it's important to understand that these were numbers, on the support side, from the first day of the war. As that operation proceeded, the support requirements obviously went down as we were able to erode the enemy air defenses. So again, this is not a—you know, a magic rule of thumb on how much support to conventional and stealth aircraft. But it is to understand that the stealth does give us some capabilities in addition to the precision and enables us to do a lot more stuff very early in a fight.

Now kind of to the meat, though I guess somebody had a lot of ideas here, but the old lightbulb chart. The—everybody is kind of familiar with how a series or a parallel circuit works. In a series circuit, you really talk about—I mean, as we put lightbulbs on a Christmas tree, you know, one bulb goes out and the whole thing is gone and you have to figure out which bulb was out. ...traditional military operations have taken kind of a serial approach, all the way back to time when it was a fact that you didn't have aircraft, so you had to take a linear approach to the battlefield and to defeat the enemy, you know, in turn.

But even with air assets, in terms of having to roll back enemy air defense, those types of things limited your ability to go after what you really wanted, because the air defense aren't the targets; the targets are the targets, and you have to go after the air defense to enable you to do other things, because once you can gain air dominance, then our surface combat forces have a significant greater—a significantly greater degree of flexibility in different things that they can do early in a fight.

And so, our ability to go after targets, if we had the ability to go after the entire target set from the—go after we wanted to instead of the air defenses, then go after the leadership, for example, early, or to go after industrial targets or whatever they may be, then that would actually provide us a significantly greater degree of leverage.

...in Desert Storm the traditional approach might have been to slowly roll that system back and to go after elements of the system one at a time. If we had a better way to do business, we might be able to go after that whole integrated air defense system. And that's, in fact, what we did in Desert Storm, is we were able to go right to the heart of the air defenses, take out the critical command and control early through creative use of Special Operations forces, Army

Apache helicopters. And so we were able to take down the air defense system or to attack the air defense system as a system.

....You have to kind of work it and look at each element of that system and figure out what its vulnerable points are. And if you had the ability to do stealth and precision to give you a higher volume of fire, then you could go and attack this system as a system....

If you had the ability to not only go after that target system that might be air defenses but also simultaneously go after a target that might be military or political leadership, that might be essential industries or transportation, you could actually now attack the enemy as a system and work towards trying to achieve systemic collapse. I really have to contend here that this is—and I've said it several times. What we have enabled ourselves to do through development of more complex and a better understanding in intelligence and analysis of adversary systems is we have an improved ability to go after adversary's systems. And I'll talk to you how we might go about doing this.

In a—I'm going to use an example here of electrical power. ... we used this approach in Kosovo, in the operation—the war in Yugoslavia. Electrical power is an easier system for us all to understand, because we all understand that they're all linked together and they talk to one another, and they are, in fact, an electrical power grid.

So if I had a target set—target system that might be an electrical power grid—... I would list all those targets—if I used a traditional attritional approach, I would list all those targets on my target list. And then I would go through and sequentially destroy each of those electrical power stations or power substations or generating plants, and when I got to the end of my list, I was complete.

But when the Air Force leadership was planning the Gulf War, they realized that it's not my objective to destroy electrical power stations. What is my objective? Well, electrical power is in fact a critical commodity that ties together air defenses, national leadership and a large number of other things, to enable a cohesive defense of a nation. So my real effect was to affect that, the adversary's ability to command and control forces and react, and one way I could affect that was to neutralize electrical power.

But if I neutralized electrical power by going after every station, it would take up all my assets to neutralize that electrical power. But the reality is, electrical power is in many ways a fairly fragile grid. When you look at what happens when we have a snowstorm and a couple of power lines go down and 30(,000) or 40,000 people are without electrical power—and so there you do not have to attack each element of that system to make the system not work.

An effects-based approach might look at that system and say, "If I looked and analyzed the enemy as a system in this particular case, I might only need to have to take out two of those power plants to enable me to go do that."

In such a way, I would prioritize, then, those targets by the manner in which they would enable me to achieve that effect of neutralizing the adversary's electrical power, and I would only have to…strike two targets.

Well, there's a good advantage of that. The first advantage is, one, you created a far less amount of destruction on the ground that you have to go and rebuild. Another advantage of that is that I now only have to attack two targets instead of 12. And so those assets that I was using to attack the other 10 I can now use to attack another system. And so this opportunity shows us ways in—to more effectively tie the specific effects for which we employ force or information on the battle space to military and political objectives.

But what if there's a problem? What if there's a problem and one of the targets is a no-strike target, because there is no way you can go after that power plant and not create unacceptable civilian casualties? Well, this opportunity—these analytical tools enable us…to find alternative methodologies. Maybe if you have to attack two additional targets, you can still neutralize the grid. The disadvantage, obviously, is you have more targets to strike, but the huge advantage is, you have achieved the same effect without creating significant collateral damage or civilian casualties.

Maybe there's an even easier solution. Maybe you go after power lines instead of power plants. An example is, in Allied Force, there were some—when we attacked the Yugoslavian electrical power system, there were some targets we simply could not take down to achieve the desired effect. As a consequence, the only way we could do that was to go after some of the power poles, or these 250-foot power towers. Difficult targets, and they're very difficult targets because they're designed to not have—weapons are designed with principally a blast effect, with mainly a blast effect. Well, power towers are designed not to be blown down, because that's their principal design characteristic. Nevertheless, we were able to neutralize those towers without civilian—or collateral damage, and neutralize the power system.

So there's a lot of different ways to do this. And oh, by the way, you don't even necessarily have to bomb anything. If you can pay somebody to turn the power grid off, that would be almost as effective…for example, in Desert Storm we frequently found instances where—after the fact, where electrical power plant operators knew they were going to leave their power plant off because if they turned it on, we'd bomb it. I had an instance—I flew in the Gulf War out of Turkey. I had an instance on the third night of the war where I flew a low-altitude mission into Turkey—or into Iraq from the north, and I saw the lights go out in a town all at once. The lights were there, and when approached the town, the lights went off. And so maybe just flying airplanes convinces these guys to turn the power off.

But the point here is, is that we don't have to attack everything, nor do you have to destroy everything. If we understood what the effect we desired on the battlefield, we could then figure out ways of creating that effect more efficiently, more effectively, striking less targets, using less weapons and, quite frankly, mitigating or easing potential concerns for collateral damage and civilian casualties.

That brings us back to how we got to enable us to do parallel warfare. By examining each one of those systems and understanding what the different target systems enabled us to do and what the specific political effect that we—and military objective we desired, we were able to attack a far greater amount of those target systems, creating a greater effect on each individual system, and that, in turn, started to collapse the system from the inside.

Again, I really need to caution that we are not talking about, hey, turning a computer on and finding out the answer to war. But it does provide us methodologies to more efficiently and effectively carry out military operations to achieve fairly clearly defined political and military objectives in ways that mitigates the potential negative side of casualties and collateral damage.

And that actually drives us to one of the principal issues here. The military forces in the Persian Gulf are doing some of the most, quite frankly, sophisticated planning that any military anywhere has ever done. Each of the component commanders and the Central Command planning staff under General Franks, are actually driving us to how in fact we do effects based operations across the military services. A good example of the effects based operations you see going on every day are the leaflet operations. In the '40s or '50s you might have said, Hey, if I—to defeat the enemy I have to defeat the enemy's army. No, I have to neutralize the enemy's army. And if the enemy's army decides to surrender because I used leaflets and convinced them that there was a better alternative than trying to fight me, then that's somebody I don't have to neutralize. And so there's an advantage here, and what we are trying to do with not only air operations but air and ground operations is really focus on what the desired political and military effect are, and then shape those desired effects on the battlespace.

But it only really truly works if you understand how each event that you do, everything that you do, how that ties back to the specific military and policy objectives that have been established for the commanders. And we do this fairly robustly in the Air Force. And I don't mean to belittle either of the other—any of the other services, but Desert Storm caused us to try to think about this. And so we literally come up with a high heaven objective—what are my tasks that I have to come—build to achieve that objective, what are the effects that I need to create on the battlespace, and then what are the things that I need to do, what targets I need to hit, things I need to jam, information I need to corrupt on the battlespace to achieve those desired effects. So in many ways every single thing I do has to be shown to tie back to a political objective or I'm going to take it off the list of things to do, because we have too many things that we have to do to do things that are either not appropriate or not in line with the political or military guidance.

But the system that we develop in terms of developing both desired effects, examining capabilities and desired concepts of operation to achieve those effects doesn't work in isolation. The thing about war is it's against two humans. It's a human against a human, and the adversary is thinking, and he's trying to do something against you. And so, every concept of operations or idea, or capability that you have, you must then vet that against what the adversary is going to do, or what you anticipate the adversary is going to do. In doing that, you can evaluate the enemy as target systems, or as systems of systems. And that will help you understand how those different things interrelate and where the vulnerabilities between, perhaps, an integrated air defense system and communications systems might lie to enable you to more effectively prosecute those operations.

From an air perspective, this is how this is wrapped up and brought together on an air tasking order. We look at the CONOPS, we look at the desired effects we want to create on the battlespace, we look at the available assets. And quite frankly, we have one ATO in this war. And everybody's on the ATO, everybody's integrated and working off that single air tasking order so there's common command and control architecture for all the air players that are involved. And so, it's a critical element in—we think we learned that lesson a little bit the hard way in Operation Allied Force. But then we evaluate the target sets that we need to do, that—those effects that we need to create on the battlespace, we bring those together into a integrated plan, and the integrated air and ground and maritime plans are, in fact, that. They clearly have separate elements, but these plans have been more integrated than we have ever seen them in the U.S. military history. The—one could say that we fought side by side as services in Desert Storm, which that would be a fairly close description. But we didn't fight in an integrated manner.

The Air Force has sent a major general to work at the combined force land component commander's headquarters to enable a significantly greater degree of interaction between air and surface operations to better integrate these plans. But we build those things together and then you come up with something that looks like an air tasking order or a piece of paper, and you send it out to the troops and they execute. It's not quite that easy, but it's—it is, quite, frankly, I think a significant achievement on all the men and women who are out in the Persian Gulf at this point in terms of bringing all those different effects from each of the capabilities of each of the services together to achieve the best result possible.

There clearly are going to be opportunities to better do this in the future. We have emerging operational concepts. Joint Forces Command has been tasked to develop and further evaluate these. We have emerging capabilities, both in terms of munitions, in terms of aircraft, in terms of information capabilities, that we simply have scratched the surface on. But what in the end we hope to do with concepts such as effects based operations are to fight more effectively, efficiently and to make conflicts shorter because we can attack the adversary more completely as a system in a shorter period of time as opposed to a sequential series of attritional-type operations.

As for the concept of "shock and awe,"…it actually gets right back to some of the discussion on effects operations—effects based operations. You don't win a war by not intimidating an adversary. The—I think General Franks—I don't want to put words in his mouth, but I think the effects that we are trying to create is to make it so apparent and so overwhelming at the very outset of potential military operations that the adversary quickly realizes that there is no real alternative here other than to fight and die or to give up. And so, they really are trying to kind of ensure that everybody in Iraq understands what's coming. Because if they understand what's coming in a macrosense, I think that there will be a greater likelihood that they might choose not to fight for the regime.

…what will happen is the great unknown. And the—we could speculate all we want, and there's a million answers and everybody's probably got an opinion on that. But quite frankly, we really have little clear understanding of exactly what will happen when we step across that line. I think there's going to be a wide variety of different reactions by the Iraqi people and the Iraqi military forces.

…One of the issues I think that routinely comes up is for folks who are not involved in military operations and have not been involved in the extensive planning is to understand the difficult and really comprehensive process we use to mitigate collateral damage….

First, there is—we all have to understand that there is—the term "collateral damage" is often misused. From a military sense, collateral damage means or by definition is that damage that can be expected from the reasonable occurrence from attacking a system or attacking a target. For example, if I looked at a target and I examined—I was going to put a 2,000-pound bomb on it, and windows broke across the street, I can plan for that. And that is collateral damage. It is the anticipated effects created by the employment of force.

In collateral damage calculations, we try to make an assessment of human casualties. And you saw, perhaps, a lot of that take place in Allied Force, where targets were struck and timed specifically to minimize the potential for civilian casualties….It includes both structural damage and civilian casualties.

Now that is different from unintended damage, and it is different both philosophically and from a practical manner. Unintended damage is when something goes wrong. Either a fin breaks on a weapon and the weapon goes off course—and everything we drop is a mechanical device, and as like as we would that these things be perfect, they are in fact not. Mechanical devices that we employ can fail....

We will also have some degree of intelligence failure. We don't have perfect information. The Al Firdos bunker example or the Chinese Embassy are examples, perhaps, of intelligence failure. But it is what happens when something goes wrong. And it's really important to understand these two distinctions. And it's important because we can do a great deal to plan for and mitigate collateral damage. We can do a great deal to mitigate the potential for unintended damage, but there is very little we can do to plan for or substantially eliminate unintended damage because it is, by definition, something went wrong.

Let me talk a little bit about how we do this.... first of all, there's not a target that we would strike that is not specifically struck to achieve a desired effect. And so we look at that target and we say, what do we want to do to that target? I want to neutralize or I want to destroy this bunker. And then I examine what munitions I might use to destroy that bunker.... When we do that, we do an analysis not only of the target, the size and the capabilities of the munition designed to create the right effect, but we also do an analysis of the surrounding area to understand what the use of that munition on that target might do to structures outside the facility or to create either collateral or—I mean, civilian casualties or collateral damage.

...If, however, in the course of dropping that bomb, a laser-guided bomb, for example, a fin breaks off the laser-guided bomb and the thing goes spiraling 3,000 feet away from the target, there was really no practical way for me to plan for that. That is not collateral damage; that is unintended damage, and if there are civilians killed, they are unintended civilian casualties. I don't mean to kind of draw a fine legal line between the two, but it's important to understand that as we plan these things, there are a great deal of things we can do to mitigate collateral damage and in fact have potential to mitigate some unintended damage, but these things, again, are mechanical devices and some will fail. And so if somebody has a hope that we're going to go into a conflict and nothing is going to happen in terms of collateral damage, unintended damage or civilian casualties, I think you should absolve yourself of that hope because that probably is not a realistic expectation.

...we like to use the term "fast CD," but the—we do have an improved capability. It is designed principally for kinetic weapons; that is true.

...We have developed planning tools that are at our air operation centers to enable us to more effectively project the potential explosion of an armament as it hits a particular structure.

...An example: When we were doing operations in Afghanistan, I think that we all need to hire the Afghan workers to build our walls, because we would blow some—a house up inside a wall, and it seemed like—that that wall protected all the structures around it. But the reality was—is when we drew our circle to examine potential collateral damage, we didn't take into consideration that there was another building there, or there was a wall, or that I was hitting one side of the building and the size of the—and the direction of the explosion that takes place on the ground is in fact not a circle. It's more like a butterfly effect.

...And so by using that tool, you can better understand the environment and the immediate neighborhood of where you're dropping that munition, and then you can do an examination of various things that might include changing the size of the weapon; changing when the weapon fuses, to perhaps fuse the weapon underground, to mitigate that explosion even more; or even changing the direction of your attack axis, because if you attack from one way, you might completely mitigate all effects, if things work properly, but if you attack from another, there might be no way.

...So it is one of a series of planning tools that we have incorporated into our air operations centers and out on the carriers as well, to examine different alternatives on—to better employ the right weapon and the right target in the right way.

...effects-based operation and collateral damage are fairly well—closely tied together, because the best way to mitigate collateral damage is to only strike the stuff that you need to strike—or affect the stuff that you need to affect.

...from a[n]...Air Force targeteer viewpoint, there are probably 50,000 targets in Iraq, maybe more. But you know, that's only in a development effort. In other words, as we examine a country—and we know Iraq pretty well—we look at every bridge, every power station, every military infrastructure, every air defense site, and we catalogue and develop a requirement of what that potential target might look like and what I might have to do to neutralize that target.

...Nevertheless, what happens is, as we go through that planning process of defining clearly established political objectives, military objectives, determining the desired effects I want to create and then examine the target sets that I need to attack, I come up out of that 50,000 with some list of targets that I need to examine. Every one of those targets is examined for collateral damage. We first look to ensure that the target is directly tied to an objective. We then ensure that we do—we know enough about the target so that we can create the desired effect. You don't always know enough about the target, but to the degree that we can, we will try to understand what we need to do to that target to affect it. We choose the right weapon to create the desired effect. We then do a clear examination not only of the collateral damage potential, but also of law of armed conflict potential, and those types of issues, the legal implications of striking that target. And then we do everything we can do in the planning factor in adjusting the weaponeering and providing the tasking to air crews to enable us to most effectively achieve the desired effect with the minimum damage—minimal potential collateral damage for civilian casualties.

...But the reality is, is that these are very, very tough decisions that the senior military leadership has to make. There is no magic number that says five is acceptable, six is not. There is no magic way to determine when I do something whether the potential of civilian casualties is five or 10 or 20. We do have some ballpark assessments based on the population of an area, of who might be living in that area, whether it's a residential or commercial area, and the time of day you might strike that. But there is simply no way that I can say there is an easy answer.

...But in each case where civilian—the potential for civilian casualty exists, potential for collateral damage, those targets are all reviewed by the senior commanders.

...in most instances..., most of the targets that we are striking are—actually have very low potential for collateral damage because they're military targets that are generally military installations of that sort.

Nevertheless, there are going to be targets in which a closer evaluation needs to be made and some sort of determination by the commanders in the field of what is an acceptable number, or what we anticipate an acceptable range might be. And there's no one answer. Each target, you look at what the—for example, if you had a nuclear or a biological weapon sitting on top of a Scud missile that was surrounded by civilians, and that thing had the potential to go off and hit Kuwait or Israel, then I would probably be willing to accept a greater degree of civilian casualties because of the consequences of not acting on that target. If, on the other hand, it was a Scud missile without a warhead parked in a barn, then I probably wouldn't be willing to take as much risk to go after that target. But in each instance, the commanders will look at what the specific effects are, what they intend to achieve and whether or not that desired effect and military worth is worth that trade-off in terms of potential civilian casualties.

...We are finding that our—both our effects and accuracy with Joint Direct Attack Munition was significantly higher than we anticipated in Enduring Freedom in Afghanistan. However, for both laser-guided weapons—especially laser-guided weapons and Joint Direct Attack Munitions, we have to understand that a large percentage—perhaps the highest in modern history—a large percentage of the missions flown were doing something like time-sensitive targeting, and they took off without the target, and somebody gave them that target airborne. As a consequence, that is a little bit higher risk, because there's a lot of other things that can go wrong if I don't know what the picture of the target looks like. Nevertheless, solid preplanning improves our ability to do this.

...I can't give you a specific number on a specific weapon. But Joint Direct Attack Munition—the beauty of that weapon is that once it's gone from the airplane, it's going to where it's going—actually, the highest percentage of the time it's going to where it's going and I don't have to worry about a pilot trying to keep a laser spot on a target or worrying and maneuvering to do that.

...We have to understand that doing CAS out of a B-52 was not anything any of our tactical air control parties or B-52 crews practiced before Afghanistan. Additionally, we—many of them got that equipment for the first time when they were out in the field. But we have—the Air Combat Command has spent literally millions of dollars over the last year to get the best possible equipment to our combat controllers in the field so that they have the opportunity not only to have the best equipment but to train with that equipment well prior. So, we have worked on solutions to those challenges, yes.

...it's important to understand that the collateral damage assessment doesn't stop at an air operations center. Each of our—each of the—what we call them is JTACs, Joint Terminal Air Controllers, which are personnel from the Air Force, Army, Navy and Marines who are fully qualified as terminal controllers. In the Air Force we call them ETACs. Generally they're enlisted personnel in the United States Air Force.

As well as our airborne forward air controllers and our ground forward air controllers, each of these men and women have been trained to specifically make collateral damage assessments as they are airborne to try to ensure that they can mitigate that. Is that as good as using cosmic analytical tools back at the air operations center? No, it's not. But, it—literally, every pilot, when they drop a bomb, or every combat controller who—or terminal air controller who's calling a bomb in is trying to make all the right—make those decisions based upon the availability of the weapon, using the right weapon on the right target. I mean, working in Enduring Freedom, at the operations center it was absolutely amazing to me that after about a month we could have a conversation with the terminal air controller on the ground, an Air Force staff sergeant who might be 25 years old, and we tell him exactly the different types of airplanes that are available to him, and he will then say, all right, I'm using these weapons off this airplane against these targets, the F-18s with their laser-guided bombs are going to be more accurate so I want to use those weapons on these targets. So all of our personnel, most of our aircrews and most of our terminal air controllers are trained specifically to make those assessments. Is the airborne assessment as good as a complete analytical assessment in an

AOC? No. But I think that these people are about as well trained as we can get them. They are some very, very talented individuals.

...In the Gulf War we had effectively 98 precision-guided munitions, we had 36 F-117s, we had 62 F-111Fs, and then we had a number of E/A-6s on the carriers. Today—and oh, by the way, most of those aircraft, other than 117s, most of the 111s would go after a single target or maybe two targets.

...Today, virtually every aircraft of the—I think the number is around 600-odd aircraft—every combat aircraft in theater has the capability of precisely striking multiple targets, and most of them can do it simultaneously. I mean, F-18s can carry a number—two to three JDAM, depending upon their anticipated targets. As I said, B-52s can carry 12 JDAM, plus an internal configuration that might be conventional munitions or cluster munitions. B-2s—most of the airplanes are out there. So if I have about half the number of airplanes, but each of the airplanes is capable of striking multiple targets on a single day—on a single mission, and in many cases much more than just two or three, then the numbers of desired impact points—because each target we have to understand is actually a set of desired—a set of items. For example, a SAM radar site might be the radar itself, as well as each of the missiles, as well as perhaps a command and control facility. And so when I say an order of magnitude higher, I think we would literally see an order of ...we struck approximately 125—well, on the first day of the Gulf War, if you looked at it, we probably included somewhere on the number of 400 to 600 precision-guided weapons—or 300 to 400 precision-guided weapons. I think that number was going to be significantly higher.

...I just want to touch...on some of these...myths about collateral damage. I mean, first of all, it cannot be avoided. When you employ military force, collateral damage is going to incur, unintended damage is going to incur, and unfortunately, and as tragic as it might be, civilians who have no business in the operation and who are not targets will be killed in the operation.

...We also must assume that we—we can't assume that intelligence is perfect. We clearly understand that it's not, and there will be some degrees or lack of complete information on targets that is going to cause us to do things that we would have done differently, had we known more information.

...Weapons don't always work. I'd like to give you a perfect answer on a mathematical percentage, but that simply isn't possible. ...we do have some historical data on weapons effectiveness and accuracy and reliability, but I think that we just have to understand that these are mechanical devices. Mechanical devices will fail on occasion. We have improved the reliability. We have improved the efficiency, with Joint Direct Attack Munitions. We have improved the ease of delivery, to make it far easier for aircrews to get that weapon to the right place and then release it, to get it to the target by itself. But still, weapons will in fact malfunction to some degree.

…Not all damage and not all collateral damage is caused by friendly fire. And clearly, our adversaries in the past, Milosevic, Hussein as well, have taken advantage of collateral damage or damage that has been a consequence of adversary fire, And you simply have to ask a question; all those bullets going up into the sky, they come down someplace. And the missiles go up that miss targets; they come down some place and they cause damage as well. So we just have to be cautious about assuming that if something happened, it necessarily was a consequence of direct coalition activity.

…There is a great myth about high altitude and accuracy. The argument that I have to be low-altitude to hit a target is false. It is patently false. Joint Direct Attack Munition actually is far more accurate at high altitude than it is at low altitude, because it has more time to get to the target.…depending upon the weather; if I have cloud decks, then laser-guided munitions can create some problems. But altitude, when you see air crews up at 15,000 or 20,000 feet, in most instances, or even higher, that is not affecting in the vast majority of cases their ability to create the desired effect on a desired target.

…And the other thing I think we need to be cautious about: we're going into an operation, a surface combat operation if we potentially go into Iraq, which we have not seen in a very long time in this country. We have seen and we have developed fairly established and critical procedures to mitigate collateral damage using air operations. And quite frankly, as much as airmen have chafed—airmen of all the services have chafed under those rules and restrictions, we have learned a very great deal in how to do our jobs better. We have not had as much experience in these issues on the ground.

…We…have provided our air crews—or our personnel who are doing the planning for these military operations a set of tools that have simply not existed before. Some are collateral damage mitigation tools, some are the ability to sit at a single computer.

I had the ability even in Enduring Freedom to sit at a computer and go from a one to a million scale map using a track ball, go all the way down to a one to 250,000 scale map and then five-meter imagery and one-meter imagery, all with a track ball on a computer. And that capability gave a lieutenant that was working for me in collateral damage—he could come up with a collateral damage assessment in some cases in minutes by just—by attack P reporting a target at an area just with a set of coordinates.

So, some of these tools—if you add to that our fly-out capabilities that we have and things like Power Scene, that I think Fox News just showed on TV the other day, which gives the ability for air crews as well as ground forces to go through a mission and rehearse a mission to see what they expect to see.

…We have improved munitions. As I mentioned, the Joint Direct Attack Munition…is working and it is working better than we ever anticipated.…That is a significant capability in enabling more efficient and effective operations, because now, most of my platforms can go after multiple targets in a single pass.

Sensor Fused Weapon will probably be employed for the first time in this operation. Sensor Fused Weapon is an anti-armor personnel which has a triple-redundant dudding mechanism if, in fact, it fails to find a target that it wants to employ. It's a great capability and actually is a far more accurate munition that can get—destroy enemy vehicles, enemy armored forces, even if they're widely dispersed....I believe F-16s and A-10s both carry them, but F- 15E—the good news about that weapon is that it's a—the only thing that we changed was the insides. And so it can—basically, anybody who could carry a—or, what we call a tactical munitions dispenser or those cluster munition canisters can be carried—can carry that weapon.

...the way the system works is that it will operate at a—well, we actually have Sensor Fused Weapon with a Wind Corrected Munitions Dispenser, which is the fourth one. Wind Corrected Munitions Dispenser are INS-guided cluster munitions to enable us—cluster munitions were notoriously inaccurate (sic) from 30,000 or 40,000 feet. But these weapons actually get the weapon to the exact point in space that we want it to open up. When that happens with Sensor Fused Weapon, there are 10 internal canisters inside that weapon, each with four munitions. Those canisters deploy, and they have a parachute that slows the rate of descent of the canister and then those four independent munitions pivot out. And those munitions can then independently seek adversary armored vehicles. But if the weapon fails to detonate in the air and it lands on the ground, after a fairly short period of time, each of the submunitions will disarm itself. And at that point, about the only way to make it go off is a blasting cap.

...But those are the types of capabilities that we're fielding. The Navy's improved both their inventories and the capabilities of the Tomahawk since Desert Storm dramatically. And so all of these I think are a fairly good news story.

...I talked about air crew training, things like Power Scene. Again, air crews from all of the services have had to live with and understand the issue of collateral damage over the last decade. And it's improved in our training programs, it's improved in our documentation, in how we train those air crews from the ground up as well as, as I mentioned, all of the Joint Terminal Air—TAC Controllers and all the services who do controlling from surface combat operations.

...We have improved weapons assessment and tracking. We now have the ability basically to track every weapon as it's released, or reported back to the air operations center so we can build a detailed map of expenditures post-conflict, which is a really good thing to do if I—because, in fact, we used this capability in Allied Force. The Germans were going into a destroyed Serbian military camp to set up as their point of operations when they moved the peacekeepers into Kosovo, and we were able to give the Germans a detailed map of expected munitions that we expended and the potential duds that might be in that area. Very helpful if one talks about post-conflict and post-conflict clean-up.

...we've done some tremendous effort in this area. It's not perfect. It's not going to make wars bloodless. But I think that the capabilities that the Air Force has fielded, that the other services have fielded, what we've done in training has also dramatically improved.

...When you start trying to target individuals, the world gets really complicated really fast. And quite frankly, your ability to do something like that is—especially with an adversary who has specifically made it hard for his own people to target him, it becomes very difficult. But I think—my point would be, is that because we now have the ability to go after these target systems as a whole, I can now go after what I want to attack as opposed to going after all the air defenses.

...every bomber we have in the inventory can kill multiple—in many cases, it least 12-plus targets, 12 to 24 targets, every bomber in the inventory. Every—or the majority of the Navy's F-18s have the ability of using joint direct attack munitions to kill two, three or four targets in a single mission. Our F-15s and -16s likewise have a similar capability.

So—and everybody out there, if you're not dropping PGMs, you're probably not close to the fight. I mean, there are a few airplanes that are a little bit less capable, but the vast majority of the Air Force and Navy's inventories are PGM-capable weapons either through laser-guided munitions or joint direct-attack munition. And so, we have to remember, in the Gulf War, only 9 percent of the munitions dropped were precision-guided. As well, only 2 percent of the sorties—the 117s flew only 2 percent of the sorties, yet they struck 53 percent of the targets in the target deck.

And so if we examine that capability, this—if that capability that was resident or perhaps airplanes that were only 2 percent of the sorties, 36 airplanes, and with the hundreds we have now, my capability is dramatically—and I cannot underscore that—it is dramatically improved over the (percent?) I had in the Gulf War.

...the weapons are tracked in this system—since we don't have right now—I would like to have a networked weapon that told me where it hit. That would be really a perfect world. And then it gets right back over the datalink architecture into the air operations center, and then two seconds after it hit, I knew what happened. We're still a few years away from that. But I think that they could probably make that assessment fairly quickly.

Most of those assessments initially are going to be done through air crew reporting upon when they come back from MISREP, and then we have to calculate those numbers and try to make those complete assessments.

But again, I think that even over the end of Allied Force, and even over Enduring Freedom, the capabilities and tools we've given to the men and women in the air ops centers, as well as the connectivity and interconnectivity we have between the land and maritime and air components—commands, has given us a lot greater degree of flexibility where somebody in General MacEwen's (sp) headquarters—"I need some information"—and—(snaps fingers)—we can get it to them quickly.

...ACC is the air component—or we provide forces through 9th Air Force to Central Command. And we work—since the majority of our 9th Air Force under General Moseley, is the air component to Central Command. We are there, what we call an Air Force forward—or the commander of the Air Forces—General Moseley commands all U.S. Air Force personnel in the region. And we provide complete support to him and his planning and Central Command planning efforts.

So that there's a lot of stuff that takes place at Tampa, but there's also a lot of specific challenges that General Moseley asks for some help on, and then we at Air Combat Command have put together some really, really talented people into some dark rooms and wouldn't let them out until they came up with some solutions. So we are at this point supporting General Moseley and supporting General Franks in anything that they need.

...The first question, the strike package I showed you earlier that went into Basra that had the 41 aircraft that went to Basra. I mean, they were SA-6s and SA-2s and SA-3s and Crotales and Rolands. And not much of that stuff is alive at Basra anymore. We have—I mean, having lived over the no-fly zones for the last 12 years, it is a significantly less hostile place than it was in northern and southern Iraq on the opening night of the Gulf War. And that simple fact will make the jobs of our men and women, the air crews that are out there doing this, a whole lot easier. And, and it's important to note, that control of the skies that we will have almost from the outset over the southern and northern regions of the country enable our surface combat forces to exploit more quickly, more effectively, more rapidly.

The Pattern of Effects-based Bombing during the War

When the war actually took place, the coalition used some 1,800 aircraft to deliver some 20,000 strikes. One key to the way in which effects-based bombing was implemented is that coalition targeting capabilities had improved to the point where they could target and strike Iraqi ground forces in near real time. This allowed coalition forces to concentrate on Iraq's military forces, particularly the Iraqi Republican Guard forces, while they were maneuvering outside populated areas.

U.S. and British official sources differ slightly as to the number of strike sorties flown during the Iraq War, although the general scale and nature of these strikes is consistent from source to source. In an analysis, Lt. General T. Michael Moseley, the commander of coalition air operations during the war, stated that some 1,800 aircraft delivered some 20,000 strikes, and that 15,800, or 80 percent, of these were directed against Iraqi ground forces versus 1,800 (9 percent) against Iraqi government targets; 1,400 (7 percent) against Iraqi Air Force and Air Defense Command targets; and 800 (4 percent) against suspected sites, forces, and installations that might have weapons of mass destruction or surface-to-surface missiles.

Lt. General Moseley did confirm that there were serious problems in the battle damage assessment process and differences between U.S. Air Force and U.S. Army officers over how to best plan the strikes. This limited the ability to develop a truly joint doctrine for effects-based bombing in the target category where the coalition carried out 85 percent of its strikes, and, as noted elsewhere, it meant that the coalition could not accurately assess the effect of its strikes on these targets.

These problems were at least as serious in the case of the other targets. While no quantified data are yet available, it is clear from interviews that many of the strikes against Iraqi government targets did not do the damage originally estimated during the war, or they hit targets whose nature and value to the Iraqi war effort had not been accurately estimated, or they hit targets that had been largely evacuated.

The data on the allies' ability to characterize and achieve the necessary damage against Iraqi Air Force and Air Defense Command targets are more uncertain, but a number of strikes have proved to have been directed against low-value or empty targets. As is discussed in chapter 12, the allies were able to locate and hit some surface-to-surface missiles. But it has been confirmed that virtually all of the suspect chemical, biological, and nuclear targets had no weapons and did not provide an imminent threat. It is also clear that unless a target involved high levels of visible activity or radio frequency emission, there was little way to assess even the broad impact of the "effect" of strikes on these targets.

Civilian Casualties and Collateral Damage

If one looks at the bombing patterns by target category, a maximum of 10 percent to 12 percent of the sorties were delivered against targets that are normally close to populated areas. [12] In practice, the number that risked civilian casualties and collateral damage was far smaller, in part because of both high-level policy and joint coalition review.

Lt. General Moseley also stated that all strikes that the allies estimated would put more than 30 civilians at risk had to be approved by U.S. secretary of defense Donald Rumsfeld. According to Moseley, only around 50 such strikes were proposed, and all were approved by Secretary Rumsfeld. British and Australian senior officers add, however, that the United States did propose additional strikes during command discussion and that they were "redlined" by the British and Australians.

As is discussed in chapter 7, there are no reliable estimates of casualties for the war. It is clear from the range of estimates to date, however, that the United States and the UK inflicted negligible civilian casualties and collateral damage in comparison with previous wars. As has been noted, an estimate made in late June stated that hospital records indicated up to 3,240 dead civilians, including 1,896 in Baghdad, and the possibility of thousands more.[13] Again, the lowest estimate seems to be 1,100 to 2,355.[14] The most credible low-end estimate is 1,500 civilians dead.[15]

These are still tragic losses. But they are remarkably small for so intensive an air campaign in a country of some 24 million people, and they compare with Iraqi claims of some 2,278 civilians dead in the Gulf War of 1990, where the United States did not invade Iraq, and there was no fighting in Iraqi cities. They also include casualties from Iraqi anti-aircraft fire, Iraqi fire directed at coalition troops, and all other causes and do so despite the fact that Iraqi forces made extensive use of civilian facilities to shelter Iraqi military forces and equipment.

TRUE PRECISION AIR-STRIKE CAPABILITY

While no battle damage data are publicly available, and reliable battle damage data may never be available, it is clear from the history of the war that the evolution of precision air strike technology greatly improved coalition capabilities in carrying out these strikes. Even in the Gulf War, only a small number of aircraft like the F-117, F-111, and F-15E were properly equipped for advanced precision strike missions. In the Iraq War, virtually all U.S. aircraft had the avionics necessary to make use of a wide variety of precision weapons by acquiring targets, illuminating them when necessary, using GPS guidance, and acquiring targeting coordinates from the ground. To put these differences in perspective, only one out of five strike aircraft could launch laser-guided bombs in the Gulf War; all strike aircraft could launch laser-guided bombs in the Iraq War.[16]

The onboard sensors and computer systems on these aircraft were much more capable both in executing preplanned strikes and in the dynamics of acquiring and killing. The integration of intelligence assets into target planning and the speed of execution made precision strikes more effective. All-weather coverage was better, and while the term "all-weather" will probably always seem at least somewhat ironic in air combat, field reports so far indicate that it was a far more realistic description in the Iraq War than in previous conflicts.

A combination of UAVs and better sensor aircraft, systems like the E-8C, and improved infrared and radar sensors interacted with better command and control to allow the effective use of both better delivery platforms and better precision weapons. For example, experimental use was made of the E-8C JSTARS to target Iraqi armor even under sandstorm conditions. Dust and sand did present problems in some cases. Still, the widespread dissemination of laser illuminators to ground forces and special operations forces units allowed them to call in precision close air support, as did giving them GPS targeting capability.

Understanding the True Meaning of Precision

This does not mean that the air and missile campaign achieved anything approaching "perfect war." Detailed BDA data are lacking, but enough pilot and post-strike reports are available to show that precision is still relative despite all of these advances. The U.S. and British briefings shown during the war provided television footage of weapons that virtually all hit the correct target. In practice, however, there are still major problems in the IS&R effort, and significant numbers of targets were mischaracterized.

The British Ministry of Defense report on the lessons of the war describes the following range of issues involving targeting:[17]

> Planning for the air campaign included the development of a list of potential targets that would help the coalition to achieve its overall objectives. Over 900 potential target areas were identified in advance. All targets were derived from the campaign plan and were selected to achieve a particular military effect (such as the degradation of Iraqi command and control systems). Operating within parameters agreed by Ministers, Commanders taking targeting decisions had legal advice available to them at all times during the conflict and were aware of the need to comply with international humanitarian law, the core principles of which are that only military objectives1 may be attacked, and that no attack should be carried out if any expected incidental civilian harm (loss of life, injury or damage) would be excessive in relation to the concrete and direct military advantage expected from the attack.
>
> Extensive scientific support including detailed computer modeling was used in assessing potential targets. Strong coordination between the MOD, the Permanent Joint Headquarters (PJHQ) at Northwood and the in-theatre National Contingent Command helped ensure coherent target planning (a lesson from previous operations). The Department for International Development was also consulted on key humanitarian infrastructure issues.

Targeting for submarine-launched cruise missiles or for coalition aircraft using UK facilities was conducted with appropriate political, legal and military oversight at all levels. We also influenced the selection and approval of other coalition targets.

...The campaign also showed that coalition aircraft needed to be able to identify and target mobile, camouflaged, and underground assets and facilities and to achieve discrimination in urban areas. This requires improvements in data transfer, tactical reconnaissance, and high definition imagery systems to deliver shorter sensor to shooter times for time-sensitive and 'find and destroy' missions. The operation also highlighted that the integration of Close Air Support aircraft requires further refinement and practice. It demonstrated the advantages of multi-role aircraft and long-range, high payload platforms. Unmanned Aerial Vehicles have the potential to play an increasing role in the joint battle, both for surveillance and strike and may offer opportunities against time sensitive targets.

...Future targeting work will concentrate on improving precision and reducing the time taken to guide weapons on to targets including weapons fired from the sea and long-range, indirect land systems.

It is also important to note that the accuracy of precision weapons quoted in most technical sources is based on the average distance from the target hit by 50 percent of the weapons fired—assuming a perfect target location, a perfect launch, and perfect functioning of the weapons system through the final guidance phase. In the real world, this means that roughly half of the weapons fired are less accurate, but there is no statistical definition of their accuracy. Data on the real-world average performance of weapons under operational conditions are sometimes available, but are generally classified.[18] Moreover, the combination of perfect targeting, perfect launch, and perfectly functioning weapons assumed in producing such accuracy data is rarely possible.

The United States and its allies compensated for this reality by establishing rules of engagement that sought to prevent the launch of weapons under uncertain conditions, particularly when they might produce collateral damage. Nevertheless, "precision" did not mean that many weapons were not fired at the wrong target, or selected in ways where the munition had the wrong effect, or launched under the wrong conditions, and/or that they did not fail in some way in flight. There also are enough pilot and combat reports to show that major failures of the control surfaces on guided weapons sometimes resulted in the weapon striking far from its intended target, regardless of the target coordinates used to launch the weapon and the potential accuracy of its guidance system. To put this in perspective, it often took several weapons to achieve a kill or the required level of damage—rather than the one kill per weapon generally shown in official briefings.

Yet, it is also clear that the real-world targeting, launch, and weapons performance of precision weapons was generally much more accurate than it had been in Kosovo or the Gulf War. It is also important to note that briefings and battle damage assessment tend to focus on achieving catastrophic damage or enduring functional kills of the target. The coalition often did achieve these effects, but they are only part of the impact of precision warfare.

The psychological impact of near misses and of watching precision kills on other nearby targets is extremely high. It is quite clear from postwar Iraqi accounts that it is not necessary to achieve the desired degree of damage to have forces evacuate a building or desert their equipment. Moreover, the high levels of attrition sometimes claimed against targets like the major weaponry in Republic Guard units—50 percent, 70 percent, and even 90 percent—are scarcely necessary to force the disintegration of the unit as a functioning war-fighting entity. Losses of only 15-20 percent have been enough to achieve such results in previous wars, although the level of damage required varied sharply by military force and unit. The fact that BDA cannot quantify the impact of precision on morale, desertions, and the willingness to fight does not mean that even "misses" are not of vast importance in terms of their real-world military effects.

The Scale and Nature of the Coalition Effort

As has been discussed in chapter 4, the coalition dropped a ratio of 19,948 precision-guided weapons, plus nearly 9,251 unguided weapons, to none.[19] While sources disagree on the exact number and the precise period that should be used to make the count, U.S. forces alone fired at least 19,269 guided weapons. Precise comparisons of these totals with those of the Gulf War and Afghan War are again difficult because the counts vary according to source even within the individual military services, and because guided weapons differ sharply by type. For example, some counts put the total number of guided weapons fired by the coalition in the Gulf War at 10,468, while others are in the 9,000 range; and the USAF Gulf War Airpower Survey provides detailed annexes that only list 8,644.[20]

If the Gulf War Airpower Survey data are used, 5.8 percent of the weapons dropped by the United States in the Gulf War were precision-guided, versus 68 percent in the Iraq War. However, most estimates indicate 8 to 9 percent of the munitions in the Gulf War were precision-guided versus 70 percent for the Iraq War.[21] Again, sources vary. The munitions involved were very different. The USAF Gulf War Airpower Survey states that 4,086 laser-guided bombs were used in the Gulf War. This compares with 8,618 in the Iraq War plus 6,542 of the new JDAM GPS-guided weapons. However, the United States used 3,065 Hellfires in the Gulf War versus only 562 in the Iraq War, and it used 5,296 Mavericks in the Gulf War versus 918 in the Iraq War.

What is even more striking are anecdotal reports on the extent to which the air effort focused on the support of ground forces. One report from a U.S. Air Force general claims that of the 19,948 precision weapons used against Iraqi aimpoints, 15,592, or 78 percent, were used in direct support of coalition ground forces.[22] Once again, counting methods make it difficult to verify such figures or compare them with previous wars. But the Gulf War Air Power Survey indicates that the figure for the Gulf War would only be 55.5 percent—although this was a total of 23,340 strike missions out of a wartime total of 42,420.[23] The data NATO provided on the war in Kosovo indicate that NATO flew 987 strike missions by D+50 and that a maximum of 30.7 percent were flown against Serbian ground forces.[24] (The data for the Afghan conflict are lacking, but the target base other than ground forces was very limited. As a result, the percentage of strikes against Taliban and Al Qaeda ground forces was almost certainly extremely high.)

In any case, such numbers tell only part of the story. What is truly important is that the coalition was able to combine a broad reliance on precision-guided weapons with major advances in avionics, IS&R, and command and control capability and (1) conduct an "effects-based" campaign directed primarily at Iraq ground forces in a joint operation with coalition ground forces; (2) strike at other targets like the Iraqi leadership, Iraq's command and control assets, its potential weapons of mass destruction and delivery systems, and its air force and surface-to-air missiles; and (3) use such assets to allocate fighters and helicopters to perform on-call missions using precision weapons.

IN-FLIGHT AND RAPID TARGETING AND RETARGETING: TIME-SENSITIVE STRIKES

While the technical details are unclear, the United States seems to have flown some 156 time-sensitive missions against leadership, missile, and WMD targets that involved rapid retargeting in periods from minutes to two hours. According to USCENTAF, these strikes were allocated as follows:[25]

Location	Terrorist	Leadership	WMD	Total
South	2	40	66	108
West	0	2	19	21
North	2	8	17	27
Total	4	50	103	156

A special Time Sensitive Target cell in the Combined Air Operations Center (CAOC) in Saudi Arabia used intelligence data to "find, fix, track, target, engage, and assess" such strikes: to direct attacks with laser- or GPS-guided weapons, analyze battle damage, and integrate time-sensitive operations with other air operations.

It helped plan the rapid strikes on Saddam Hussein and the Iraqi leadership on March 19/20 and April 7.[26] The strike on March 19/20 took about three hours from the intelligence report to an execution that involved two F-117 fighters firing 2,000-pound bombs and four ships launching 40 Tomahawk missiles. This included approval from Washington of what one commander called a "pop up" target.[27] The target cell also made the first use of the EGBU-27 one-ton penetrating bomb, which uses a mix of GPS and inertial guidance.

The aim point for the underground shelter that was attacked was not a visible structure, and intelligence had to rapidly estimate a point some 100 to 200 feet from the nearest structure. As a result, all four bombs dropped were spread out in an effort to hit and destroy the underground structure in something approaching a square with points at 50-foot intervals. The attack had been considered for several days but only in an "on again, off again" kind of contingency planning. When the order came, detailed strike planning was authorized at 1:30 a.m. and executed by 5:30 p.m. A planning effort that would have taken some four hours during the Gulf War took 30 minutes in the Iraq War. Total mission preparation took two hours and execution two more.[28]

The Time Sensitive Target cell also directed a strike by F-16s using 500-pound laser-guided bombs on the home of General Ali Hassan al-Majid ("Chemical Ali") on April 4. On April 7, it took about 45 minutes from intelligence to strike for a B-1B raid that dropped four 2,000-pound GPS guided bombs on a building where intelligence indicated that Saddam Hussein and his sons might be meeting, and 30 minutes on April 10 to call in a B-1B to drop JDAMs in an attempt to kill Hussein's half brother, Barzan Ibrahim Hasan al-Tikriti.

This rapid retargeting capability enabled the United States to respond to active intelligence rather than bomb predetermined or fixed targets by the numbers. For the first time, it deprived enemy leaders of the sanctuary they had enjoyed in terms of the slow response time between acquiring intelligence indicators and actually being able to strike.

Numerous other missions included the growing use of Special Forces to confirm and illuminate targets that could be struck with precision weapons, or to identify high-priority targets that led to the retargeting of aircraft as they approached the battlefield.

The coalition also launched some 686 additional strikes at "dynamic targets." These included high mobile and otherwise important targets using "reroled" airborne aircraft. There were 243 such strikes in the south, 271 in the west, and 172 in the north.[29]

This ability to rapidly target and retarget can be improved significantly in the future with better communications, procedures, software, and equipment. The Marine Corps, for example, has developed procedures to allow forces on the ground to see the spot that aircraft are targeting with the LITENING, and to verify the image of a target captured by an aircraft's avionics. Such advances may well change retargeting to add a new degree of both precision and protection against friendly fire. The ability to retarget cruise missiles in flight will add another dimension to such capabilities.

At the same time, at least the Marine Corps found serious problems in the overall timeliness of the targeting and sortie allocation process. Although its lessons reports note advances in time-sensitive strikes and find that the "kill box" system ensures the availability of on-call air support, at least one report—the report on the lessons of the war by 1 Marine Division—finds that much still needs to be done:[30]

> …Target tracking and assessment was extremely difficult during OIF. There was no reliable and responsive process or means to determine whether Air Interdiction (AI) targets on the PTL were serviced and successfully attacked during and after ATO execution. The impact was that targeting personnel/ LNOs could not consistently and reliably provide the necessary feedback to MSC commanders that their AI target nominations were being serviced or not. Further, there was no consistent or reliable method for the MSCs and Force Fires to track their target nominations on the DS ATO. Ostensibly due to system constraints, TBMCS would not accept the MEF Target Reference Number from the PTL. Hence when the ATO was published there was no easy way to associate the target reference number (TRN) with the assigned aircraft mission number on the ATO. The customer would have to cull through the

ATO searching for other data elements like BE number, location or target description that matched the TRN. Often the ATO did not consistently list the BE numbers, locations and/or target descriptions.

…The system constraint and inability of TBMCS to accept and record a MEF TRNs needs to be corrected. If this system issue can't be corrected then an alternative consideration is to allow the MEF to assign aircraft mission numbers from a block of pre-designated mission numbers. These mission numbers would link each target number on the PTL and would serve as the common data element that all levels could track and monitor, from target nomination through assessment.

During OIF the 72-hour deliberate targeting process did not keep pace with the dynamics of the battlefield. The key reason was due to the fact that the planning to execution cycle was too long and the process did not react quickly enough to changes in the scheme of maneuver. As a result, the AI shaping effort often did not focus on the enemy forces I MEF would actually fight in 48 hours.[31] Another factor that caused the 72-hour targeting cycle to lag execution was the speed at which the Division executed its scheme of maneuver. This speed of execution was never really appreciated or understood by the MEF future planners. Hence the maneuver briefs provided at the targeting boards and other forums were typically lagging by at least 24 hours (sometimes 48 hours.) Finally, the Synchronization Working Group conducted each evening did not sufficiently address changes in the SOM as we attempted to validate the Prioritized Target List (PTL). The expectation at the SWG was that the SOM and the results of the Intelligence collections effort would drive the validation /update of the PTL. If this was the purpose and intent of the SWG, it never really happened.

Shorten the 72-hour Targeting Cycle. Pushing the targeting planning cycle closer to execution will help keep the PTL more current and relevant during ATO execution.[32] Require the MSC Liaison Officers to brief their respective schemes of maneuver in detail at all of the Targeting forums vice the MEF Future Operations planner. The LNOs through their constant dialogue with their G3 and FSCs have the most current information /changes….new target nominations may need to be added to the PTL that were not approved on the Battle Field Shaping Matrix (BSM)(briefed 48-72 hours earlier), but clearly need to be serviced.

STEALTH

Both the B-2 and F-117 played an important role in the Iraq War, although the value of stealth per se remains uncertain. For example, the 12 F-117 stealth strike fighters based at Al Udeid Air Base in Qatar flew 80 of the roughly 17,000 to 20,000 sorties classified as strike missions. While the numbers were limited, all of those missions were against heavily defended targets in the greater Baghdad area and struck at key targets like the air defenses, important headquarters, and radio relay stations.[33]

For the first time, these missions were able to use GPS-guided weapons. Unlike the laser-guided weapons used in the first Gulf War, the GPS-guided weapons could not be obscured by clouds or smoke.[34] Problems still emerged because of the long time needed to enter targets into the ATO. But the use of time-sensitive targeting and kill boxes allowed Iraqi forces to be targeted at the last moment, greatly cutting down on the "kill cycle" in the Gulf War and also freeing the pilot to concentrate on the mission.

This rapid decision cycle also allowed the F-117 strikes to be coordinated with the cruise missile strikes launched against Saddam Hussein and the Iraqi leadership on the first night of the war—as well as rapid arming with EGBU-27s that had just arrived in theater the day before, and planning support sorties from F-16CJ anti-radar fighters, EA-6B electronic warfare aircraft, and KC-135 tankers. About one-third of the F-117 missions came in the first three days of the war, when Iraqi air defenses were most effective. One interesting aspect of their missions is that a shortage of refueling tankers forced two-thirds of the F-117 missions flown during the first major night of strikes to cancel their mission before they launched their weapons. This is another demonstration of the value of range-payload in bombers like the B-2 or in new stealth-like aircraft like the FB-22.

At the same time, cost remains a critical issue. Whatever the potential value of stealth aircraft, they are extremely expensive and have a long history of escalating in procurement and operating costs. The F-16 also proved to be highly effective in the Iraq War, as did the A-10 within its mission limitations. The F/A-22 Raptor has increased in cost by 128 percent since its development started in 1986, and the GAO claims the program has encountered some $20 billion in overruns. The planned buy of the F/A-22 has shrunk from 750 aircraft to around 276, and the procurement cost of the smaller number has risen to $42.2 billion in spite of a congressionally imposed ceiling in 1998 of $36.8 billion.[35]

This experience is not unusual for a new major weapons system. It illustrates, however, the broader risks in force transformation touched upon in chapter 5. At the same time, the F-16 is largely a sunk cost and the more advanced models have recently had a unit cost of roughly $38 million—somewhat similar to the cost of the late model production runs of the F-15. In contrast, the air force's current estimate of the unit cost of the F/A-22 is $133.6 million and the GAO puts the cost at over $200 million. The new Joint Strike Fighter, or F-35, also has some stealth features and an estimated unit cost of between $37 million and $47 million, and the U.S. Navy is seeking to buy some 548 F/A-18 E/F Super Hornets.[36]

Like many other possible "lessons" of the Iraq War, these facts show the danger of generalizing from combat experience without explicitly analyzing cost-benefit and cost-risk, the value of alternative uses of money, and the risks inherent in giving up current force capability or force numbers for as yet unproven and uncostable systems.

CLOSE AIR SUPPORT

In spite of all the progress the United States and Britain made in jointness, both forces still believe significant improvements can be made in organizing and supporting the close air support mission, and in training for this mission. For example, the British Ministry of Defense concluded that, "The operation…highlighted that the integration of Close Air Support aircraft requires further refinement and practice."[37]

This message has been reinforced by a recent study by the General Accounting Office, although the study preceded the Iraq War. The study found that troops were not properly trained for close air support, and that the USAF continued to focus more on longer-range interdiction missions. It also found that a joint interservice steering committee still has made only limited progress in standardizing procedures and equipment.[38] Both British and Australian officers report a similar need to standardize if forces are to be properly interoperable.

One key challenge is to integrate fixed-wing, attack helicopter, artillery, and land-based air defense operations. The United States seems to have done much better in the Iraq War—partly as a result of lessons learned from Operation Anaconda in the Afghan War—but much of this improved was improvised on an ad hoc basis and much can still be done. It is also clear from the Iraq War that every advance in IS&R, communications systems, and digital management of the battlefield both increase the capability to carry out close air support and the need for tighter integration, better training, and more standardized procedures and equipment.

URBAN CLOSE AIR SUPPORT: A REALITY UNDER THE RIGHT CONDITIONS

The United States conclusively showed that modern air power can target and strike even in cities with great effect and minimal collateral damage.[39] The United States effectively set up urban "kill boxes" over Baghdad with strike aircraft on 24/7 patrols armed with a variety of munitions. It used a variety of UAVs for surveillance and targeting, including the Predator and high-flying Global Hawk. This allowed strikes to be called in with munitions suited to the precision and warhead size needed for such attacks.

The use of 500-pound bombs and cement bombs reduced collateral damage in strikes on "sensitive" targets near civilians or key civilian facilities. Bombers provided the endurance and high payloads necessary to ensure rapid response and the ability to deliver multiple strikes. Close air support aircraft and attack helicopters like the A-10, Harrier, and AH-1W provided low-altitude coverage over both Baghdad and Basra, and could provide better angles of attack using weapons like Hellfire and TOW and could also strike with lower-yield weapons that inflicted less collateral damage.[40]

New fuses on "bunker buster" weapons like the GBU-27 and GBU-28 ensured that the weapons exploded underground. Having men on the ground illuminate and verify targets helped. It is not clear how pure kinetic weapons were used, if at all, but accuracy has improved to the point where a cement warhead can be used to demolish key walls and barriers.

At the same time, the war did expose limits. The coalition was able to move key aircraft forward, such as tankers and the E-8C JSTARS, only because it had gone far beyond air superiority to air dominance. This also allowed it to use aircraft like the A-10 in low-attitude strafing runs at 2,000 to 3,000 feet and to keep "stacks" of different aircraft with different mixes of munitions safely on call near the greater Baghdad area.

The coalition found that its initial targeting constraints and rules of engagement were too restrictive. They sometimes forced restrikes or failed to accomplish their mission, forcing additional combat without reducing collateral damage. As a result, the coalition increased the intensity and concentration of some types of strikes against urban targets, inevitably increasing collateral damage.[41]

Many air munitions could not be used in areas with buildings closely placed together because they could not be launched with the proper angle of attack. In several cases, a target could be attacked only if ground troops were present to illuminate it, but the troops could not remain in the conflict area long enough to allow the aircraft to come in or the laser could not be read because of urban dust and complex visual angles. More flexible munitions may be needed, along with systems like robotic reconnaissance and illuminators to allow ground troops to conduct targeting without being exposed to combat.

THE VALUE OF EXPEDITIONARY AIR POWER AND PROBLEMS IN ALLIED READINESS, INTEROPERABILITY, AND MODERNIZATION

The U.S. military has long recognized the need for expeditionary air power. Carriers provide it by definition, all Marine Corps aviation is expeditionary, the U.S. Army is increasingly making its helicopter forces expeditionary, and the U.S. Air Force has steadily converted to a lighter posture and one where power is easier to project. As a result, the USAF has divided its aircraft into 10 sets called Air Expeditionary Forces (AEFs) that are designed to deliver a full mission-capable mix of aircraft in pairs of AEFs that can be deployed for 90 days. Four full AEFs were sent to the war in Iraq, along with parts of four others. In addition, the USAF has worked with the U.S. Navy to develop synergistic packages where scarce special purpose aircraft with similar functions—such as the RC-135 and EP-3—can either reinforce or replace each other. The U.S. Navy and Marine Corps, in turn, are developing a Fleet Response Concept to allow U.S. Navy and Marine Corps aircraft to deploy more quickly and in greater numbers, to allow carriers to stay longer on station by rotating crews, to use amphibious ships as light carriers, and to improve Marine Corps aviation capability to act as an expeditionary force off ship.[42]

During the Iraq War, USAF Expeditionary Combat Support (ECS) was critical to U.S. success. USAF ECS units built and supported 12 new bases (including 5 in Iraq) while expanding capabilities at 10 established sites. At the same time, they maintained, loaded, and launched the Combined Forces Air Component Commander's air force.

During the actual operation, ECS units did the following:

- launched more than 46,000 sorties with a maintenance effectiveness rate of 98 percent;
- issued more than 1 million gallons of JP-8 per day (five times the typical rate) at three bases in the region, with a high at one base of 1.8 million gallons in one day;
- offloaded 344 different munitions commodities from ships and strategic airlifters with no sorties lost to weapons availability and 21.5 million pounds of ammunition delivered;
- served more than 111,000 hot meals each day and positioned 2.7 million MREs in support of combat operations in and around Iraq;
- positioned 91,000 JSLIST chemical warfare suits, 2,100 gas masks, 1,000 flak vests, and 7,200 weapons in-theater to outfit the force after unit reporting instructions changed on the fly;

- formed the "Red Tail" express with leased Kuwaiti trucks to transport CFACC combat power deep into Iraq when the need outpaced the availability of coalition trucks;

- ensured combat readiness at one location by contracting for bare-base support, including site preparation, building the large expeditionary shelters, and putting up billeting tents for 375; and

- made purchases off the Iraqi economy to support deployed forces during ongoing combat operations.

The ability of Special Forces, the U.S. Army, the U.S. Marine Corps, and the U.S. Air Force to rapidly restore airfields or create ones large enough for C-130 operations was another important aspect of expeditionary air power. So was the ability of the C-130 and C-17 to operate off of short and unimproved runways.[43]

The British Royal Air Force converted to a far more effective expeditionary posture between 1990 and 2003. It was able to rapidly adapt basing and support plans focused on deployment to Turkey to allow operations in the Gulf. Like similar changes in the USAF and U.S. Marine Corps to support more rapid forward basing and expeditionary operations, the RAF demonstrated that effective power projection planning and equipment are a critical part of effective air power. It also was able to help the U.S. Navy because RAF tankers use refueling drogues, rather than a piloted boom, and can refuel U.S. Navy aircraft—an example of allied interoperability that helped the United States.

The RAF also moved away from an outdated reliance on low-altitude penetration using unguided weapons in 1991 to the use of precision-guided weapons and aircraft with avionics capable of targeting and firing such weapons (rather than needing to bring in Buccaneers to illuminate the target for Tornadoes), and it introduced new weapons like the Storm Shadow stand-off cruise missile, which has a range of up to 300 nautical miles.[44] Britain also introduced the use of the Enhanced Paveway II GPS-guided bomb and Maverick AGM-65 by its Harrier G7 attack aircraft, and it made use of the Enhanced Paveway II and III GPS-guided bomb on its Tornadoes.

The British Ministry of Defense cited the success of this expeditionary approach to air power as one of the lessons of the war.[45] It also recommended that, "Further investment is required in Expeditionary Campaign Infrastructure, Temporary Deployable Accommodation and personal equipment, which should be designed to support expeditionary air operations.[46]

Although the Royal Australian Air Force provided only a limited number of aircraft, it too demonstrated the value of designing an air force for power projection and tailoring combat aircraft for interoperability with larger air forces like those of the United States. Australia had learned from deployments during the Gulf War, East Timor, and Afghanistan, and it had acquired new aerial refueling tankers, Airborne Early Warning and Control (AEW&C) aircraft, improved air-to-air missiles, and standoff air-to-surface weapons. It had also upgraded the avionics on its F-18 fighters to make them interoperable with U.S. and British forces by taking steps like replacing their APG-65 radars and fire control systems with APG-73s.

There is, however, a much grimmer lesson here for most European air forces, as well as for NATO and the European Union. There is no "western" advantage in air power. Most European air forces lack sustainability, modern technology, and effective readiness and training. Most also lack the capability either to act as independent expeditionary air forces or to be fully interoperable with the United States. To be blunt, their civilian masters have allowed them to decay into aging, heavily bureaucratic forces that often modernize in ways better suited to the politics of the European defense industry than to effective war fighting.

There are good reasons why most European governments furnish virtually no meaningful transparency into the readiness of their air forces and the effectiveness of their modernization plans. In most cases, their five-year plans are simply a cosmetic façade hiding a steady decay in force strength and/or readiness and drift toward high-cost technological obsolescence. This is not helped by NATO and EU force plans that similarly paper over real-world problems, set meaningless or unmet goals, and are triumphs of institution building over military reality.

CHANGES IN AIR COMBAT PACKAGES

No data have been published on the kind of mixes or "packages" of different aircraft types the United States and Britain assembled to carry out given missions in the Iraq War. It is clear, however, that substantially fewer air defense and electronic warfare escorts were needed and that the number of electronic intelligence aircraft dedicated to given packages could be reduced because of superior netting, intelligence platforms, and multipurpose aircraft. On the other hand, there are some indications that the number of refueling missions went up because coalition aircraft had fewer bases near Kuwait, flew longer mission distances, and loitered longer.

HARD-TARGET KILL CAPABILITIES

It will take some time before the United States and Britain can clearly evaluate the effectiveness of their attacks on hard targets and deep underground shelters. At least one preliminary report indicates, however, that
the United States failed at least sometimes to kill critical underground facilities. A reporter who walked through one shelter in Saddam Hussein's
Abu Ghurayb Palace produced the following report:[47]

> The bunker, toured several days later by a reporter, withstood the palace's de-
> struction by at least two satellite-guided bombs. The bombs left six-foot
> holes in the reinforced concrete palace roof, driving the steel reinforcing rods
> downward in a pattern that resembled tentacles. The subsequent detonation
> turned great marble rooms into rubble. But the bunker, tunneled deep below
> a ground-floor kitchen, remained unscathed. The tunnel dropped straight
> down and then leveled to horizontal, forming corridors that extend most of
> the breadth of the palace. Richly decorated living quarters were arranged
> along a series of L-shaped bends, each protected by three angled blast doors.
> The doors weighed perhaps a ton. In a climate-control room, chemical weap-
> ons filters and carbon dioxide scrubbers protected the air and an overpres-
> sure blast valve stood ready to vent the lethal shock waves of an explosion.
> And a decontamination shower stood under an alarm panel designed to flash
> the message "Gas-Gaz."

Other reports raise more serious issues. At least some of the targeting
assumed the existence of bunkers or tunnels that did not actually exist.[48]
This proved to be true, for example, of the attack on a supposed bunker in
the Dora Farms area near Baghdad on the first night of the war. It was this
"bunker" that coalition planners hit in an effort to kill Saddam Hussein
and other top members of the Iraqi leadership. In practice, the information proved to be from an inaccurate Iraqi source, and postwar examination showed that there was no bunker at the site.[49]

More generally, discussions with U.S. targeteers and analysts indicate
that despite more than a decade of intense analysis, the United States still
has no clear basis for estimating what was in most hard and soft shelters,
whether they had been evacuated before the war began, and what the effect of destroying or damaging the building or facility was on Iraqi war-
fighting capability. In this sense, "effects-based bombing" usually is limited
by the fact the United States cannot see into a black box either on the surface or underground.

In short, the hard target problem is not simply one of hard target kill,
but one of hard target characterization. This involves the existence of the
target, its physical nature, its function, whether it is actually occupied and

used in wartime, and the effect of any given level of damage. This is a critical problem both in IS&R terms and in the ability to implement a full range of effects-based and netcentric operations. It is also an important caveat regarding the use of very large conventional or small nuclear weapons to kill hard targets. The issue is not simply one of ensuring that the target can be destroyed; it is ensuring whether the target exists and should be destroyed at all.

The problem is also certain to grow with time. While U.S. and allied IS&R coverage is increasing in scope and persistence, the ability of developing countries to create closed structures and then create hardened facilities in or near those structures in ways that are not detectable by imagery is also growing. So is the understanding of both governments and extremist groups that rapid dispersal, the creation of covert dispersal facilities, and the exploitation of natural features like caves present major challenges in terms of both targeting and physical attack.

CRUISE MISSILES

The United States used a total of 153 bomb-launched CALCMs and 802 BGM-109 TLAM Tomahawk sea-launched cruise missiles in the Iraq War. These cruise missiles proved far more effective in the Iraq War than in the Gulf War, in large part because the addition of GPS guidance and improved reliability allowed them to be much more accurate and to fly a much wider range of attack profiles. The operational range of the system also increased from "500 miles plus" to "more than 1,000 miles," and missiles could be programmed in hours rather than over a period of three days. [50] At the same time, the relatively small warhead size of the Tomahawk limits the range of targets it can attack, and the performance of the CALCM, with a heavier warhead and hard target penetrator option, remains uncertain.

The CALCM has a nominal range of around 600 nautical miles and flies at high subsonic speeds. Some estimates put its warhead at 1,500 to 2,000 pounds. Other sources put it at 3,000 pounds. Two versions seem to have been used in the Iraq War.

■ The Block IA CALCM uses a third-generation GPS receiver along with advanced navigation software and a GPS anti-jam electronics module and antenna for a significant increase in jamming immunity. To increase its effectiveness against a wider spectrum of targets, it has a capability for shallow to near-vertical dive angles from any approach reference point. Flight software improvements include a large-state Kalman filter for optimizing GPS accuracy, including code and phase measurement data, pressure and temperature measurements, and wide-area GPS enhancement to reduce system errors.[51]

- The AGM-86D Block II program is the Precision Strike variant of the CALCM. It incorporates a penetrating warhead, an advanced guidance package coupling GPS and inertial guidance, and a modified terminal area flight profile to maximize the effectiveness of the warhead. The penetrating warhead is augmented with two forward shaped charges. To maximize the warhead's effectiveness against hardened targets, the Block II will maneuver and dive onto its target in a near-vertical orientation. The updated guidance system is supposed to have obtained a less than 5 meter CEP.

The navy's BGM-109 Tomahawk Land Attack Missile, or TLAM, cruise missile also demonstrated a steadily increasing accuracy, reliability, and lethality. It now combines jam-resistant GPS guidance with its earlier terrain contour matching (TERCOM) radar guidance that compares a stored radar map against the radar signature of the terrain to navigate and optical Digital Scene Matching Area Correlation (DSMAC) to home in on its target by comparing the image to the actual target. The GPS guidance allows the Block III and later version of the TLAM to fly a wide range of attack profiles, making its direction of attack less predictable, and the system can be programmed more quickly. Its improved performance was first demonstrated in Bosnia in 1995, and then demonstrated in depth during some 70 attacks on Taliban and Al Qaeda targets in the Afghan conflict in 2001. The BGM-109 Block III has both unitary and cluster warheads with combined effect submunitions. Its nominal payload is 1,000 pounds. Its speed is about 550 miles per hour and its range is about 600 nautical miles.

Thirty-five of the 140 vessels the U.S. Navy had in the Persian Gulf, Red Sea, and Mediterranean were capable of firing the missile. They had a total inventory of roughly 1,500 missiles, and approximately 800 were fired. Vice Admiral Timothy Keating, commander of all maritime forces involved in Operation Iraqi Freedom, described the role of cruise missiles as follows in a briefing on April 12, 2003:

> Since we began Operation Iraqi Freedom on the 19th of March, United States and United Kingdom ships have fired over 800 Tomahawk missiles in support of General Franks' campaign. Sailors and ships... we coordinate all those targets with the Air Force. As I think you all talked last week with General Buzz Moseley, he is the air component commander, and so all offensive air operations, manned or unmanned, are coordinated with—through Buzz Moseley's targeting shops. So, any target that we're assigned and told to

prosecute, that is vetted with Buzz Moseley's air component command headquarters.

The types of targets were broad-ranging. Some of them were time-sensitive targets—that is to say that we had intelligence that led us to believe that this particular location was a valuable target. And so in a relatively brief period of time, particularly compared to the years past, we were able to do the planning, get the missile loaded with its mission data, out of a submarine or—a British or American submarine or American ship—and down range and export on the target, or some rather more stationary and strategic targets, including missile defense facilities, to Republican Guard headquarters, and some regime structures in and around Baghdad and all throughout the country.

…when TLAM were first introduced into the Navy arsenal, it was a matter of not hours, not even days, but several days for all of the planning to take place. And so it took quite a while from determination of target, through mission planning, to prosecution of the targets. These days it can be measured in hours, due principally to—well, one reason, we have better computers these days. Another reason, more important, we have smarter kids doing it these days. And third, the fusion of intelligence and operations and our ability to communicate over secure lines worldwide. All of those factors contribute to a dramatic reduction in the time required from determination that's the target we want to hit to Tomahawk impacting the target.

…You know, as do I, that a few of our missiles have been found in Turkey and Saudi Arabia. We've shot over 800 and we've found less than 10 in—that didn't get to the target, if you will. That is a very low percentage, as you no doubt know—1-over-80, or 0.1 to 1.25 percent. As for the effectiveness of those Tomahawks and the effectiveness of each individual piece of ordnance, I couldn't tell you right now, but I would say, hazarding a guess, that the dramatic success that General Franks and everybody working for him that we've enjoyed is likely due to our ability to prosecute specific targets throughout the entire country of Iraq, and again, prosecuting with remarkable, in our view, remarkable flexibility and this very pinpoint precision so as to be able to, in the aggregate go very quickly around areas where we didn't want to fight or didn't need to fight and get to the heart of the Iraqi regime leadership and topple that leadership in very short order.

The claimed failure rate for the Tomahawk cruise missile in the Iraq War was about 2 percent as opposed to more than five times that percentage in the Gulf War. The 800 missiles launched compares to 288 in 1991. The time for targeting at the CAOC was reduced to hours and sometimes minutes in comparison with an average of several days during the Gulf War.[52] For the first time, U.S. command and control could also closely coordinate air and cruise missile strikes, as it did in the attack on Saddam Hussein and the Iraqi leadership on March 19.

At the same time, the cost of some 800 missiles approaches $500 million to $1 billion—depending on the costing method used; the U.S. Navy budgets some $600,000 per missile, but the Congress still appropriates roughly $1 million.[53] Some missiles also went off course in politically embarrassing ways over such countries as Saudi Arabia and affected U.S. overflight rights. The need to cost-engineer cruise missiles to much lower prices and find some form of self-destruct remains a lesson of this war, as it has in every war since the Gulf War.

THE USE OF PRECISION AIR MUNITIONS

Only minimal data are available on how given air munitions were used in different aspects of the battle, the precise targets chosen, and their battle damage impact. At the same time, the U.S. Air Force has provided significant data on the overall patterns in the use of precision munitions. These patterns provide some important insights and lessons.

Laser-guided Bombs and the JADM

The key precision weapons the coalition used in its missile and air strikes included 802 sea-launched BGM-109 TLAM (Tomahawk) cruise missiles and 153 air-launched AGM-86 C/D CALCMs. They included 8,618 laser-guided bombs (GBU-10, GBU-12, GBU-16, GBU-24, GBU-27, and GBU-28). They also included 98 EGBU-27 weapons with both GPS and laser guidance. They fired 6,542 JDAM GPS-guided bombs (GBU-31, GBU-32, GBU-53, and GBU-37) and 408 AGM-88 HARM high-speed anti-radiation missiles.

These figures reflect the fact that the development of inexpensive strap-on kits for laser and GPS guided weapons made mass strikes far more affordable and cost effective, and enabled the United States to allow strike aircraft to operate outside of the effective range of most current light air defense systems. It is important to note that while the JDAM got most of the publicity, the United States delivered 30 percent more laser-guided bombs than GPS-guided weapons, in part because laser illumination is more rapid and accurate in dynamic targeting.

The GBU-12 Paveway laser-guided 500-pound bomb was the most commonly used precision weapon in the war. Some 7,114 were used. The weapon has a maximum range of about eight miles and an accuracy of around nine meters. That a 500-pound weapon could be used so often relative to heavier systems is an indication of improvements in both preci-sion and the ability to execute "effects-based" strikes. In contrast, the Unit-ed States used 236 GBU-10s with 2,000-pound conventional or penetrating warheads. It used 1,233 GBU-16s with 1,000-pound war-heads; 23 GBU-24 Paveway IIs with 2,000-pound conventional or pene-trating warheads and improved maneuverability; 11 GBU-27s, which are 2,200-pound weapons specially modified for delivery by the F-117; and 1 GBU-28 5,000-pound bunker buster.

The JDAM was the second most-used precision weapon in the war. The JDAM is essentially a cheap GPS guidance strap-on kit for regular bombs that allows all-weather and night operations in even the worst weather.[54] The strap-on kit costs $18,000, and the weapon can be launched up to 15 miles from its target and use GPS to strike within 10 to 20 feet of its target. Although much of the force planning before the Afghan conflict focused on expensive guided weapons, the JDAM made up some 4,600 out of the 7,200 precision weapons used during the Afghan conflict.[55]

The United States delivered 5,086 GBU-31 2,000-pound bombs during the course of the war. It is notable that the JDAM was generally delivered as a much heavier, 2,000-pound weapon than the laser-guided bomb, which was generally delivered as a 500-pound weapon. The United States also delivered 768 1,000-pound GBU-32s, 675 1,000-pound GBU-35 ther-mally protected bombs for carrier use, and 13 GBU-37s, which are special 2,000-pound bombs with special guidance links to the B-2's GPS naviga-tion and Synthetic Aperture Radar (SAR) capabilities.

Other Guided Weapons and the CBU-105

The United States delivered a diverse mix of other guided weapons. These included 88 CBU-105 WMCD (wind-corrected munition dispenser) sen-sor-fused cluster bombs. The CBU-105 is potentially an important new system because it can be employed at low altitude using level or shallow dive delivery angles from altitudes of 200 to 20,000 feet and at speeds up to 650 knots, as well as at altitudes of up to 40,000 feet and ranges of 12 miles. It contains sensor-fused submunitions for attacking armor using the SUU66/B Tactical Munitions Dispenser (TMD), with 10 BLU-108/B sub-munitions, and 40 cylinder-shaped (3.5" high by 5" wide) skeet armor penetrating with infrared sensors.

There are two versions of the weapon—the CBU-105A/B baseline weapon and the enhanced CBU-105B/B weapon, which was used in Iraq. Each baseline weapon can cover an area of about 15 acres; the enhanced version can cover 30 acres.[56]

After release from the aircraft, the TMD opens and dispenses the 10 submunitions, which are parachute-stabilized. Each holds four armor-penetrating projectiles with infrared sensors to detect targets for the A/B weapon and an additional laser rangefinder to profile targets in the B/B weapon. At a preset altitude sensed by a radar altimeter, a rocket motor fires to spin the submunition and initiate an ascent. The submunition then releases its four projectiles, which are lofted over the target area. The projectile's baseline version sensor detects a vehicle's infrared signature, and an explosively formed penetrator fires at the heat source. The enhanced projectile adds an active laser system to also detect the target's profile, and allow a more varied target capability. If no targets are detected after a period of time, the projectiles automatically fire to self-destruct. The enhanced version has an additional self-destruct feature that detects low altitude if it has not detected a target. The weapon is most effective when employed at low altitude from level flight attitudes in a non-countermeasured environment. It proved effective in more than 100 live fire tests before the beginning of the Iraq War. However, no details are available on its effectiveness during the war.

The United States made use of its new wind corrected munitions delivery system to fire 818 CBU-103 and 2 CBU-107 WCMD cluster bombs. The United States also delivered lighter missiles such as 562 AGM-114 Hellfire and 918 AGM-65 Maverick anti-armor weapons, which sometimes were used against urban targets as well. Systems like the Hellfire proved very effective in urban warfare, and a version of Hellfire with a thermobaric warhead allowed attacks on individual floors in individual buildings, as well as attacks on caves and shelters.[57]

The AGM-130, SLAM, and JSOW

What is striking in view of much of the focus on high-cost long-range missile systems during the early 1990s is that the United States used only 260 such systems. The United States fired 4 longer-range AGM-130s, 3 AGM-84 SLAM-ERs, and 253 AGM-154 JSOWs. Little is known about the effectiveness of these systems, but their technical features illustrate the range of different precision strike techniques that the United States can use:

- The AGM-130 is a powered air-to-surface missile designed for high- and low-altitude strikes at standoff ranges against a variety of targets. It has two variants, based on the warhead: a MK-84 blast/fragmentation warhead and a BLU-109 penetrator. The AGM-130 is equipped with either a television or an imaging infrared seeker and data link. The seeker provides the launch aircraft with a visual presentation of the target as seen from the weapon. During free flight this presentation is transmitted by the AXQ-14 data-link system to the aircraft cockpit monitor. Range and speed are classified. The range is believed to be over 40 miles.

- The U.S. Navy SLAM-ER, or Stand-off Land Attack Missile–Expanded Response, is an upgrade of the SLAM. It is a day/night, adverse weather over-the-horizon, precision strike missile with an over-the-horizon in excess of 150 nautical miles (277.95 km) and high subsonic speeds. It uses ring laser gyro Inertial Navigation System (INS) guidance, with multichannel GPS; an infrared seeker for terminal guidance; man-in-the-loop control data link from the controlling aircraft; and Automatic Target Acquisition (ATA).

- The AGM-154 JSOW, or Joint Stand-off Weapon, is a family of air-to-surface glide weapons in the 1,000-pound class. It provides stand-off capabilities from 15 nautical miles (low-altitude launch) to 40 nautical miles (high-altitude launch). It is a launch-and-leave weapon that employs a coupled Global Positioning System (GPS)/Inertial Navigation System (INS) capable of day/night and adverse weather operations. It uses inertial and global positioning system for midcourse navigation and imaging infrared and datalink for terminal homing. It has unitary warheads, anti-personnel cluster weapons, and anti-armor cluster weapons.[58]

British Use of Precision Weapons

The British RAF dropped a total of 919 air munitions out of what it estimates was a coalition-wide total of 41,400 air munitions used during the war. A total of 85 percent of these weapons were precision-guided weapons. These munitions included 27 new Storm Shadows, 394 Enhanced Paveway II precision-guided bombs, 10 Enhanced Paveway III precision-guided bombs, 253 Paveway II laser-guided bombs, 38 Maverick anti-armor missiles, and 47 ALARM anti-radiation missiles.[59] The RAF was able to mount two ALARM missiles on the Tornado, rather than one as the result of a modification made in preparation for the war.[60]

The British Ministry of Defense report on the lessons of the war described the value of precision weapons as follows:[61]

The air campaign began in earnest on the evening of 21 March, with precision strikes using cruise missiles and guided bombs on several hundred military targets throughout Iraq. Precision strikes continued at lower intensity for several weeks, whilst direct support to ground forces became an increasing proportion of the overall air effort. The combat power of the Republican Guard Divisions defending Baghdad was considerably reduced by precision air attack before they were engaged by coalition ground forces. Up to 700 sorties per day were flown against Iraqi ground forces, with the RAF making a major contribution.

A guiding principle of the coalition air campaign was to achieve maximum effect with minimum force. The use of precision-guided weapons was key to this. The value of cruise missiles had previously been demonstrated in Afghanistan, Kosovo, and the 1991 Gulf Conflict. But whereas in the 1990s it took days between identifying a target and attacking it, by this operation the improvements in our systems reduced the time to a matter of hours, enabling time-sensitive as well as fixed locations to be targeted precisely. UK submarines played a key role in Iraq by firing Tomahawk cruise missiles which again offered a particularly useful long-range, stand-off, precision capability, the firing of which was unconstrained by weather and basing issues. This operation also saw the first use of the Storm Shadow standoff, precision, air-to-ground cruise missile, carried by Tornado GR4 aircraft. Storm Shadow has a range of over 230km and can be deployed by day or night in all weather conditions to destroy a wide variety of high value targets. The missile navigates by digital terrain profile matching and Global Positioning System (GPS) with a terminal seeker to achieve exceptional precision and thus minimize the risk of collateral damage. Early analysis of its performance suggests it will provide a step-change in the RAF's standoff attack capability.

Following operations in Kosovo, MOD acted quickly to enhance the RAF's precision attack capability in air-to-ground munitions by procuring anti-armor Maverick missiles and Enhanced Paveway bombs that can hit targets using GPS guidance. The number of Tornado GR4s and Harrier GR7s capable of carrying such weapons was also increased. This built on MOD's existing laser-guided bombing capability provided by Paveway bombs. Around 85 percent of air-launched weapons used by UK forces in Iraq were precision guided, compared to about 25 percent in Kosovo. This helped achieve the coalition's objectives more quickly, while minimizing civilian casualties and the risk to our own personnel. Precision weapons also included inert Paveway II bombs for use against targets in densely populated areas, where the aim was to destroy single targets while leaving neighboring buildings intact.

...However, precision weapons were not appropriate in all circumstances. Weapons such as cluster bombs also played an important role against dispersed military targets in the open. RAF aircraft dropped a total of 70 cluster bombs during the operation, mainly in the vicinity of Baghdad against troops and armor in the open. In addition, the UK fired some 2000 artillery-delivered extended range bomblet shells, mostly around Basrah. Without these weapons, disproportionately powerful munitions would be needed to achieve the same effect, increasing the devastation caused.

Dumb Weapons and Strafing

Anyone looking at the lessons of the war should be careful to remember that 32 percent of the munitions remained unguided, and that the United States dropped some 9,251 conventional bombs. Similarly, the British RAF dropped 138 unguided conventional bombs, or a total of 15 percent of 919 munitions.[62] Precision is not the solution to every problem, and the value of "dumb" weapons should not be ignored. This is particularly true when weapons have to be used against area targets for either killing or disruptive effect.

Moreover, a great deal of military analysis tends to ignore the value of strafing and air-delivered gunfire. Historically, prisoner of war interviews indicate that such fire often had a major tactical effect. The United States fired 16,901 20-mm rounds and 311,597 30-mm rounds. The 30-mm round is particularly lethal against armored and other vehicles.[63] Available after-action reports from attack helicopter and A-10 pilots on the use of such munitions are anecdotal and cannot be tied to battle damage assessment data, but virtually all stress the value of gun and cannon fire.

THE PROBLEM OF CLUSTER MUNITIONS

The problem of cluster munitions dates back to the Vietnam War. Despite U.S. efforts to reduce civilian casualties and collateral damage in the Iraq War, once again U.S. cluster munitions acted as mines, killing civilians in urban areas like Baghdad long after they were dropped.[64]

There were good reasons for using such weapons, as General Myers, the chairman of the Joint Chiefs, stated after the war:[65]

Coalition forces dropped nearly 1,500 cluster bombs of varying types during Operation Iraqi Freedom. Most were precision-guided. An initial review of all cluster munitions used and the targets they were used on indicate that only 26 of those approximately 1,500 hit targets within 1,500 feet of civilian neighborhoods. And there's been only one recorded case of collateral damage from cluster munitions noted so far.

We used cluster munitions against surface-to-surface missiles, radar sites, air defense sites, surface-to-air missiles, regime mobile communications, aircraft, armor, artillery, troops, and other select military targets. Because the regime chose to put many of these military assets in populated areas, and then from those areas fired on our forces, in some cases we hit those targets knowing that there would be a chance of potential collateral damage.

Coalition forces used cluster munitions in very specific cases against valid military targets, and only when they deemed it was a military necessity. These are tough choices. And it's unfortunate that we had to make those choices about hitting targets in civilian areas, but as we've said before as well, war is not a tidy affair, it's a very ugly affair. And this enemy had no second thoughts about putting its own people at risk. Indeed, multiple civilian casualties were clearly a high priority for the regime so as to put pressure on the coalition. Now they will not be able to do that any longer.

Cluster munitions were particularly useful in attacking Iraqi armor when it attempted to use the cover of sandstorms to move and the use of precision-guided weapons was difficult to impossible.

Nevertheless, the failure to deal with the inadvertent sowing of cluster munitions as mines is now some three decades old. Some form of deactivation timer is clearly needed once such munitions are released. Similarly, the failure to precisely map where the submunitions were delivered has much the same impact as failing to precisely map a minefield, particularly when bomblets change in shape, as was the case with the new BLU-108 puck-shaped bomblets used in the Gulf War. The more familiar BLU-97 is a yellow soda can-sized weapon and the KB-1 is the size of a grenade. Ironically, the BLU-108 is supposed to be a more modern, self-destruct weapon, but this feature does not seem to have functioned reliably. It also often buried itself and was so small that demolition teams could detect it only if its parachute was visible in the area.[66]

It is also important to note that the United States has recognized this problem to the extent that more modern "smart" cluster munitions, such as the Sensor Fused Weapons, are designed to self-destruct after a fixed time if no target is detected. The original version was designed to inactivate by depleting its battery energy; the more modern CBU-105B/B, which was the weapon used in Iraq, has a triple redundant feature that causes the projective to self-destruct at a predetermined altitude before it reaches the ground if it cannot find a target.[67]

THE BOMBER AND THE ADVANTAGE OF RANGE-PAYLOAD

The Iraq War will eventually produce detailed lessons for virtually every aircraft used in it, just as it will for virtually every other land or air system. In the case of aircraft, initial pilot reports make clear that virtually every attack fighter benefited from the improvements in sensors, avionics, and precision-guided weapons delivery capability. This affects the A-10,

AV-8B, F-14, F-15, F-16, F-18, and Harrier, as well as future designs. Some of these lessons are discussed throughout this book. Many, however, require detailed operations analysis that may take a year or more to complete.

The Continuing Role of the Bomber

Among the general lessons that are already available, the changes in the role of the bomber are particularly striking. As in the Afghan War, the B-1, B-2, and B-52 all demonstrated the value of the bomber as a precision strike system with stealth penetration or stand-off delivery capability to hit large numbers of aim points or targets with precision weapons in a single sortie. The B-2B stealth bomber, for example, had the capacity to carry 16 2,000-pound bombs like the JDAM or up to 70 500-pound guided bombs on a single sortie and fire each at a separate target.

The B-52 and B-1B could also carry large numbers of precision weapons like the JDAM, as well as use the Wind Corrected Munitions Dispenser and strike at different targets on each sortie. The use of precision-guided weapons allowed these bombers to strike from outside the range of all but the most heavily defended areas, and the steady upgrading of their electronic warfare capabilities improved their survivability. One press report indicates that the B-52 and B-1B delivered two-thirds of the bombs dropped during the war; another credits the B-1B alone with dropping half of the JDAMs. These numbers may well be exaggerated, but there is no doubt that these legacy systems played the same kind of critical role in terms of total tonnage dropped that they did in Afghanistan.[68]

The B-52 was the long-established workhorse of the U.S. bomber fleet. The USAF showed that a bomber as old as the B-52 could be given new life by improving its precision-guided weapons targeting and launch capabilities like the LITENING forward-looking targeting pod, its electronic countermeasures, capability to retarget in mid-flight, and reengining. [69]

USCENTCOM estimates that bombers flew roughly 555 sorties between March 19 and May 1, with the B-2 flying 50 combat sorties, the B-1B flying 225 sorties, and the B-52 flying 280. This was only 1.7 percent of the 32,850 USAF sorties flown during this period. USCENTCOM also estimates that fighters flew some 17 times more sorties than bombers. The B-1 and B-52, however, delivered a surprisingly high percentage of the total tonnage and precision-guided weapons delivered, and many of these strikes were flown against time-sensitive targets. In many ways, this repeated the experience of bombers in Operation Enduring Freedom in Afghanistan, where bombers flew only 20 percent of the sorties in the first three weeks of the fighting but delivered more than 76 percent of the tonnage.[70]

The impact of the B-1B Lancer. The B-1B's mission readiness rate had improved strikingly during the year before the Iraq War, in part because one-third of the fleet had been deactivated in August 2001 to allow the remaining bombers to improve their readiness rates and reduce "cannibalization" in the form of taking parts from other aircraft. The B-1B had not flown in the first Gulf War because it could not carry precision-guided weapons. Giving it such a capability after the war allowed it to fly 74 sorties during Operation Allied Force in Kosovo. Eight B-1Bs were deployed to support operations in Afghanistan.[71] According to press reports, they flew only 5 percent of the sorties during the first three weeks of the Afghanistan war, but delivered 28 percent of the tonnage and ultimately delivered nearly two-thirds of the total number of JDAMs used in the conflict.[72]

In the Iraq War, reports indicate that the B-1B flew only 2 percent of the total sorties but dropped as much as 44 percent of all JDAMs. One press report indicates that B-1 bombers flew 6 to 7 sorties a day and delivered a total of more than 2,100 bombs and a payload of more than 4 million pounds. Another indicates that the B-1Bs and B-52s combined flew more than 432 sorties and delivered more than 2,250 tons of bombs. Each B-1B could carry 24 1-ton weapons, and most used a mix of bombs fused to delay for 25 milliseconds to penetrate their targets and to explode on contact. The aircraft could loiter for up to 8 hours over the battlefield, with refueling. In one strike on April 7, for example, a B-1B was called in to deliver four weapons against a site near a restaurant in downtown Baghdad where Saddam and his sons were thought to be meeting and then went on to hit 15 additional targets (6 in Baghdad and 9 in Tikrit).[73]

The future mix of B-1Bs and B-52s. The United States does not have enough B-1s to equip its 10 air expeditionary forces, and the USAF must use a mix of six B-1s and six B-52s for each force. This helps explain the continued upgrading of the B-52. Similar upgrading is taking place with the B-1B. There are 67 to 69 B-1s available, and virtually all of the 96 remaining B-1s would have to be operational to rely on the B-1. The USAF is also considering providing full Link 16 and Fully Integrated Data Links to transmit more complicated targeting and command and control data digitally to the aircraft. At present, all four crew must verify voice signals.

Other possible upgrades include providing a more reliable communications link to ground forces to eliminate a problem in communications when the B-1B is banking or turning. Another is improving the resolution of the radar from 10 feet to one foot, providing cheaper and more effective electronic countermeasures, and adding a forward-looking infrared system to provide better night and laser-guided bomb targeting such as the

Litening II pod being installed on some B-52s. Equipping the aircraft to use the 250-pound smart bomb would also allow its revolving launcher to carry between 96 and 144 guided weapons.[74]

The Impact of Range-Payload on Fighter Attack Aircraft and the F/A-18E/F

High-range payload fighter-attack aircraft like the F-15, F-16, F-18, and Tornado demonstrated a similar capability to make far more effective use of air power. The ability to retarget aircraft to use precision weapons on an on-call basis demonstrated the value of range-payload in increasing loiter time as well. So did the F-16C/D, which had had a massive upgrade in its avionics and capability to deliver precision-guided weapons since the Gulf War, and had a far greater range-payload than the original F-16A/B The improved IR sensors in a number of U.S. strike attack fighters allowed them to target Iraqi armor far more effectively than in the past, sometimes in dust storms.

The United States also made combat use of the new F/A-18EF Super Hornet for the first time. The F/A-18E/F aircraft are 4.2 feet longer than the F/A-18C/D. They have a 25 percent larger wing area and carry 33 percent more internal fuel. This increases their mission range by 41 percent and endurance by 50 percent. The nominal mission radius is increased from 369 miles to 520 miles, and the recovery payload from 5,523 pounds to 9,000 pounds.

They also incorporate two additional weapon stations that provide increased payload flexibility by mixing and matching air-to-air and/or air-to-ground ordnance, including "smart" weapons like the JDAM JSOW. The F/A-18 E/F also has some stealth features. Although the more recent F/A-18C/D aircraft has incorporated some low observables technology, the F/A-18E/F was designed from the outset to optimize such features. It also has a new Advanced Targeting Forward-Looking Infra-Red (ATFLIR), the baseline infrared system pod that features both navigation and infrared targeting systems, incorporating third-generation midwave infrared (MWIR) staring focal plane technology.[75]

Vice Admiral Timothy Keating, commander of all maritime forces involved in Operation Iraqi Freedom, described the range-payload advantages of the new F/A-18E/F as follows in a briefing on April 12, 2003:

> We've had the introduction of the F-18 E and F, our new Super Hornet, which has longer legs. It can fly further, it can carry more ordnance. It has some very sophisticated radar and electronic improvements, so it has proven—and it can also, by the way, carry a tanker store to pass gas to other airplanes

airborne, which goes back, I think, to Dale's question about gas airborne. We've been able to flex a little bit with the F-18 E/F and...accomplish even more missions than we could in 1991.

The Issue of Survivability in Future Wars

Once again, questions must be asked as to whether bombers and heavily loaded strike fighters would have been as able to survive as well against an enemy with better air defense or land-based air defense systems. At the same time, few nations have such capabilities, and the USAF has shown that bombers can be steadily modified and upgraded.[76] It is clear that strike-fighter range-payload and the ability to carry and deliver large numbers of precision-guided munitions and either fire at standoff ranges or use stealth is a key aspect of fighter performance. Moreover, it is perhaps one that is gaining importance relative to advanced air combat maneuver capability in a world where so few air forces have anything like peer capability in air combat, and where air-to-air encounters increasingly occur at ranges beyond "dogfight" direct maneuver encounters. The Iraq War at least raises the possibility that trade-offs may been needed between an air superiority fighter like the F-22 and new strike-attack fighters like the JSF and FB-22.[77]

The Role of the E-8C JSTARS

There are no combat operations data available in a form that makes it possible to precisely define the role of sensor aircraft like the E-8C JSTARS, or Joint Surveillance and Target Attack Radar System. It is clear, however, that extensive use was made of JSTARS. The coalition's air dominance allowed it to be deployed forward and nearer the battle space, where it could track Iraqi armored and vehicle movements over hundreds of square miles, and it was used to cover the greater Baghdad area. The "fusion of intelligence" from the E-8C and other sources enabled the coalition to locate and target Iraq forces under weather conditions the Iraqis felt protected them from the air. Aircraft like the RC-135 Rivet Joint, for example, could characterize and locate the source of Iraqi military communications.[78]

The evolving capabilities of JSTARS. The Joint Surveillance and Target Attack Radar System is also a symbol of the rapidly evolving role of jointness in the air-land battle. A technical description of the aircraft is in many ways a technical description of the new IS&R, C4I, and battle management techniques that shape the evolving U.S. approach to war.

JSTARS is a joint development project of the U.S. Air Force and U.S. Army that provides an airborne standoff range, surveillance, and target

acquisition radar and command and control center.[79] It was used experi-
mentally in the Gulf War. In September 1996, JSTARS was approved for
full-rate production for 14 aircraft, the last of which was delivered in August 2002. The first of three more aircraft was delivered in February 2003,
and the USAF plans to acquire a total of 19.[80] The fully operational
JSTARS was used for the first time to support peacekeeping operations in
Bosnia-Herzegovina and during the Kosovo crisis.

The aircraft provides ground situation information through communication via secure data links with air force command posts, army mobile
ground stations and centers of military analysis far from the point of conflict. It provides a picture of the ground situation equivalent to that of the
air situation provided by AWACS. JSTARS is capable of determining the
direction, speed, and patterns of military activity of ground vehicles and
helicopters. The aircraft has a flight endurance of 11 hours or 20 hours
with in-flight refueling.[81]

The radar system uses a 24-foot antenna installed on the underside of
the aircraft, which is mechanically swiveled and pointed to scan in elevation, and scans electronically in azimuth to determine the location and
heading of moving targets. The main operating modes of the radar are
wide-area surveillance, fixed-target indication, synthetic aperture radar,
moving target indicator, and target classification.

JSTARS aircraft have 17 operations consoles and one navigation/self-
defense console. A console operator can carry out sector search focusing
on smaller sectors and automatically track selected targets. Fixed high-
value targets are detected through synthetic aperture radar (SAR). Signal
processing techniques are implemented through four high-speed data
processors, each capable of performing more than 600 million operations
per second. Processed information is distributed via high-speed computer
circuitry to tactical operators throughout the aircraft.

JSTARS has secure voice and datalinks to the army's ground command
and communications stations and to the U.S. Air Force command centers.
Voice communications systems include 12 encrypted UHF radios, 2 encrypted HF radios, 3 VHF encrypted radios with provision for Single
Channel Ground and Airborne Radio System (SINCGARS), and multiple intercom nets.

The digital datalinks include a satellite communications link (SAT-
COM), a surveillance and control datalink (SCDL) for transmission to mobile ground stations, and Joint Tactical Information Distribution System
(JTIDS). The JTIDS provides tactical air navigation (TACAN) operation
and Tactical Data Information Link-J (TADIL-J) generation and processing. The Cubic Defense Systems SCDL is a time-division multiple-access

datalink incorporating flexible frequency management. The system employs wideband frequency hopping, coding, and data diversity to achieve robustness against hostile jamming. Uplink transmissions use a modulation technique to determine the path delay between the ground system module and the E-8C aircraft.

The aircraft will become significantly more effective in the future. The U.S. Air Force has awarded a contract to develop the next generation JSTARS as part of the Radar Technology Insertion Program (RTIP). The new, much more powerful radar will be an electronically scanned 2-D X-band active aperture radar that will have a helicopter detection mode and inverse synthetic aperture (ISAR) imaging capability, as well as MTI (moving target indicator) mode, allowing real-time imaging of moving objects.

In 1997, the U.S. Air Force awarded two contracts for a computer replacement program to take advantage of the latest commercial off-the-shelf technology (COTS). The program integrates new Compaq AlphaServer GS-320 central computers that are significantly faster than the original system. The programmable signal processors will be replaced and a high-capacity switch and fiber-optic cable will replace the copper-wired workstation network. The Computer Replacement Plan (CRP) has completed EMD testing and the first upgraded aircraft was delivered in February 2002.

Integrating JSTARS into joint warfare. There are many accounts in informal reports from U.S. Army and USAF forces in the theater as to the value of JSTARS during the Iraq War. The best formal account comes from the report on the lessons of the war by the 1st Marine Division:[82]

> The presence of a JSTARS CGS at the Division had a tremendous positive effect for integrating this information into a comprehensive intelligence picture. The ability for the Div G-2 and Army CGS operators to work side-by-side allowed us to use the system in unconventional ways with tremendous tactically useful results. There was a critical requirement to monitor the potential movements of these enemy divisions in order to allow the 1st Marine Division move deep into the enemy battle space quickly.
>
> No other collection asset provided the wide area all weather coverage of the battle space that the JSTARS did with the MTI radar. Critical to our ability to use the capabilities of the JSTARS was the interface provided by the JSTARS Common Ground Station. The equipment allowed us to interact in real time with the collection platform and focus on our critical requirements and process the collection data into usable and actionable intelligence products. The soldiers who operated the system proved equally as critical as the equip-

ment in processing, interpreting, and translating operational requirements to the collection platform. Because they were close to the point of decision, these JSTARS operators shared the sense of urgency and 'can-do' attitude. They worked aggressively to find ways to answer questions instead of deflect them. When other platforms failed or were unavailable the CGS JSTARS combination ensured that we were not blind on the battlefield. JSTARS showed us enemy traffic over allegedly "no go" terrain, gave us estimated speeds of advance for our own forces by evaluating enemy speeds over that terrain, proved which bridges supported traffic, etc.

The Marine Corps needs to invest the JSTARS MTI system and trained operators for provision down to the Division level…The Marine Corps needs to invest in the development of doctrine to request and employ the JSTARS MTI system. Need to acquire CGS systems and trained operators for provision down to the Division level with appropriate adjustment to the Division T/O and T/E.

It is noteworthy that the Marine Corps report again stresses the need for trained personnel, and for an effective tactical interface to make use of IS&R assets. It is much easier to improve collection and sensor platforms than it is to integrate their output into effective war-fighting capability.

UNMANNED AERIAL VEHICLES (UAVS)

While no sortie data are available on the coalition's use of UAVs, the nature and importance of the data they collected, or the specifics of the role they played in joint operations, it is clear that they had a major impact. The coalition used more than a dozen types of UAVs in the conflict, building on the U.S. success in using such systems in Afghanistan.[83]

The UAVs included larger systems like the Predator, Global Hawk, and the Pointer, the three systems the United States used in Afghanistan. The United States had used the Pioneer in the Gulf War. In the Iraq War, the coalition also made use of new tactical systems like the U.S. Army Hunter and Shadow, the Marine Corp's Dragon Eye, and the USAF Force Protection Surveillance System. The change was particularly important in the case of field commanders, who had only one type of UAV available in the Gulf War but had 10 types available in the Iraq War.[84] Both the U.S. military services and the Britain Ministry of Defense concluded that the value of these UAVs was one of the major lessons of the war.[85]

The Predator

The upgraded RQ-1 Predator UAV carries the Multispectral Targeting System (MTS) with inherent AGM-114 Hellfire missile-targeting capability, and integrates electro-optical, infrared, laser designator, and laser illuminator into a single sensor package. The Predators cannot carry MTS and a synthetic aperture radar, or SAR, simultaneously. The aircraft can carry and employ two laser-guided Hellfire anti-tank missiles with MTS.

The Predator has a cruise speed of around 84 mph (70 knots), and a maximum speed of up to 135 mph. It has a range of up to 400 nautical miles (454 miles), a ceiling of up to 25,000 feet (7,620 meters), and a payload of 450 pounds (204 kilograms). Its ability to loiter for up to 24 hours at altitudes of up to 15,000 feet also allowed it to support the ground battle and to be used to call in systems like the AC-130 gunship, A-10, and Tornado.

The Predator was flown to support virtually every major mission in the war, providing imagery day and night of a quality that under optimal conditions allows the user to distinguish between military civilian personnel at distances up to three miles. Some 15 Predators flew during the war, roughly one-third of the total fleet, and they flew more than 100 missions. These included joint missions such as using an RC-135 Rivet Joint electronic warfare aircraft to locate the area of an Iraqi surface-to-air missile and then sending a Predator to find the target and send back its precise coordinates. Even when not armed with Hellfire missiles, the Predator served as an effective means of improving targeting and strike reaction times.

An armed version of the Predator, the MQ-1, fired more than 12 Hellfire missiles against Iraqi targets during the course of the war.[86] The United States also equipped some Predators with Stinger air-to-air missiles. It did so because a Predator had also flown a mission several months before the war in which an Iraqi MiG-25 fired two air-to-air missiles and shot it down. The Predator had, however, been able to fire two Stinger air-to-air missiles in response and transmit video images of the engagement. Although this encounter showed that the Predator was vulnerable in spite of its relatively small visual and radar profile, it also showed that unmanned aerial combat vehicles (UCAVs) could be given a limited self-defense capability.[87]

The Global Hawk

The Global Hawk Unmanned Aerial Vehicle (UAV) provides joint battlefield commanders with near-real-time, high-resolution intelligence, surveillance, and reconnaissance imagery. It cruises at extremely high altitudes and can survey large geographic areas with pinpoint accuracy to provide information about enemy location, resources, and personnel. Once mission parameters are programmed into the Global Hawk, the

UAV can autonomously taxi, take off, fly, remain on station capturing imagery, return, and land. Ground-based operators monitor UAV health and status and can change navigation and sensor plans during flight as necessary.

The aircraft has a wingspan of 116 feet (35.3 meters) and is 44 feet (13.4 meters) long. It can range as far as 12,000 nautical miles, at altitudes up to 65,000 feet (19,812 meters), flying at speeds approaching 340 knots (about 400 mph) for as long as 35 hours. During a typical mission, the aircraft can fly 1,200 miles to an area of interest and remain on station for 24 hours. Its cloud-penetrating Synthetic Aperture Radar/Ground Moving Target Indicator electro-optical and infrared sensors can image an area the size of Illinois (40,000 nautical square miles) in just 24 hours, and it can image some 200 to 300 sites on a single sortie. Through satellite and ground systems, the imagery can be relayed in near-real-time to battlefield commanders.[88]

The Global Hawk operated at higher altitudes than the Predator, and its radar imagery allowed it to function even during sandstorms. One aircraft was deployed, and it flew missions every day of the war. It operated out of the United Arab Emirates (UAE) and was controlled from Beale Air Force Base in California. It was used for time-sensitive targeting, which was coordinated through the CAOC in Saudi Arabia. The synthetic aperture radar proved to be particularly useful in targeting even static ground forces, like elements of the Medina Division that were still in revetments.[89]

The Dragon Eye

The Dragon Eye is another small UAV designed to provide threat detection for small units. The marines deployed 20 Dragon Eyes and 10 ground stations with the 1st Marine Division, and the U.S. Army used the Hunter in a similar role with the 5th Corps.[90] The Dragon Eye is a fully autonomous, back-able, hand-launched UAV that can provide an "over-the-next-hill or building." Its operating altitude is between 300 and 500 feet, and it has a video-link range in excess of five kilometers. The payloads are capable of real-time high-resolution day color and low-light black/white imaging. Its electric motors provide a low noise signature, and its small wingspan makes it very difficult to detect. The air vehicle's battery provides up to 60 minutes of flight time and has a flight weight of approximately five pounds. It can be assembled and launched by a two-man team in approximately 10 minutes. The aircraft is programmed via a seven-pound ruggedized handheld computer that is capable of flight planning, flight monitoring, and storage of air vehicle-transmitted video. The aircraft's flight profile is GPS waypoint guided, each waypoint allowing for various linear and orbiting search patterns and altitudes. The aircraft's flight profile can be updated or changed in flight.[91]

Marine Corps Lt. Gen. Earl B. Hailston, the commander of the Marine Forces in USCENTCOM, described the role of Dragon Eye and other UAVs as follows:[92]

> I would tell you right off the bat...that things that we were most pleased with are...intel on the battlefield, ready intel to the commander, so that he can see over the hill in front of him and then control—have more control, anyways, on his future.
>
> We were very, very pleased with the capability of the Predator, on how it worked across the field, across the area. We had very, very good success with ATARS on the F-18s. And we enjoyed the same success with the Harrier and its Lightning pods.
>
> And as far as Dragon Eye, this is a very good story in that we launched the—our VMU units were running artillery strikes for us. We could get over the top of forces out in front of our lead elements and actually control artillery strikes onto the enemy.
>
> So I think those that allowed us better command and control on the battlefield really worked out exceedingly well. We were also doing much better in our communications in that we've recently put into the field the Smart-T comm [communication] suite, which has kept us in solid comms across the battlefield, from some of our headquarters that still were in Kuwait and here, and certainly within Iraq.

The value of the Dragon Eye is illustrated by an incident on April 4, when an aircraft spotted a large Iraqi Army formation moving out of Baghdad under the cover of darkness. The data were passed to the Marine Combat Operations Center, which displayed them as a real-time stream of information, It provided grid coordinates that were passed on to Marine F/A-18s and AV-Bs, which attacked the Iraqi formation in a virtual "turkey shoot." BDA later claimed some 80 vehicles destroyed.[93] As the same time, a field report by the Marine Corps Systems Command illustrates the problems inherent in introducing a new system into the field and makes clear that small UAVs with "soda straw" coverage were scarcely the answer to every tactical problem:

> *Dragon Eye* ~ Division HQ G-2's Dragon eye was used for a week, prior to crossing the LD. However, prior to crossing the LD the computer went down and there was no maintenance plan in place. *(note: there was a maintenance plan in place. It is not clear, however, how much of this plan the operators were aware of).* Thus, the HQ G-2 did not utilize the system. However, the week that the Dragon Eye was used it received favorable comments. Extensive

analysis and feedback was received from 1st LAR's S-2 section on the Dragon Eye. They used this system daily throughout the war. *Overall the system was highly regarded and the S-2 section was extremely happy* to have it as a tool for their intelligence gathering.

The system's outer shell was characterized as "flimsy" and not durable enough. The harsh sandy environment immediately caused excessive wear. The rubber bands used for launch of the system consistently broke. Users stated that at least 10-15 extra launching bands were needed to be fielded with the system. There was no maintenance plan in case of an item breaking. CLS was discussed and immediately disregarded. Contracted civilians were not desired in the battle-space. Training for the Dragon Eye was minimal and all Marines desired more detailed training. They hoped that this training would be incorporated at the schools and throughout the fleet.

Batteries were a critical vulnerability of the dragon eye. Not only did the battery run out, but finding a replacement battery in a timely manner was nearly impossible. The battery used was company specific. Marines desired a rechargeable battery or as a second choice a battery that was easily purchased on the open market.

Night use of the dragon eye was poor. An infrared camera would be a usable addition to the dragon eye. Also, some kind of infrared strobe would be helpful, especially in locating the dragon eye upon landing. Marines had trouble finding the small "plane" when it returned from a mission, especially at night.

The range of the dragon eye was acceptable, but as always, more was desired. A desire for retrans was voiced in order to extend the range. Overall, a recurring concern was communication from the ground with the system. The operators found that the signal received on the computer often "cut out" and no video feed was received. At times the operator desired to abort the mission; however, he could not "contact" the Dragon Eye. When the system was up and running the video resolution was very clear and easy to read/decipher. However, Marines found the 10km range somewhat insufficient; ideal would be a range of 20km. The current altitude of the system was also found to be insufficient. For clearer pictures and easier deciphering the Marines desired the system to be capable of being flown as low as 100ft. Flight duration (currently 1 hour) was also insufficient; ideal desired time would have been 2 hours.

Finally, the laptop had a few features that could have been a bit more "user friendly." The method of looking at numerous pictures at one time was very cumbersome and needs to become more "user friendly" (i.e., double click on one icon to open a picture vice filtering through various tool bars). Also, the laptop needs to be plugged in; a rechargeable battery option would be good for an infantry Marine in the field. On a "positive note," the size and weight of the Dragon Eye were considered ideal. If given the choice of keeping the current capability and thus maintaining size and weight or increasing the capability/technology with the result of a dramatically heavier and larger machine the Marines overwhelmingly would choose the former.

The Shadow and the Raven

The U.S. Army also made added use of UAVs. The army used a small short-range UAV called Pointer at the unit level. The Pointer is designed as a tactical reconnaissance vehicle with onboard camera (color, or IR day/night vision). It relays live video images to the pilot and mission navigator, to a video recorder, or even to other remote ground receivers. It has GPS in its standard version, and some seem to have had chemical and biological weapons detection sensors. It has a flight duration of 1.5 hours, an airspeed of 29-80 km/hour (22 to 50 mph), and a patrol radius of 8 km (5 miles).[94]

The army may also have made use of the Raven, a six-pound, smaller version of the Pointer that was rushed into service for the first time for use in Afghanistan.[95]

The army did introduce a new UAV called the Storm Shadow 200 at the brigade level. It was used after the 4th Infantry Division deployed, and flew 800 hours worth of missions during the Iraq War. It also used a large UAV called Hunter at the corps level. The Hunter is being modified as a UCAV as a result of the lessons of Afghanistan and Iraq. It will be adapted to fire the BAT or brilliant anti-tank munition, Hellfire, Stinger, and possibly the 2.75-inch rocket.[96]

The UAV Tactical User Interface

As with most other transitional systems, there were important issues in making effective use of UAVs. Informal U.S. Army and USAF reporting tends to concentrate on a lack of adequate assets and problems in the user interface. The report on the lessons of the war by 1 Marine Division provides a more detailed perspective, and the need to develop more effective forces becomes particularly clear when several of the lessons drawn are examined together:[97]

> After crossing the Line of departure, the Division received very little actionable intelligence from external intelligence organizations. The Division had to assemble a coherent picture from what it could collect with organic and DS assets alone.
>
> The nature of the battlefield, the extreme distances, high operational tempo and lack of a coherent response from a conventional enemy all made it

difficult for an external agency to know what was tactically relevant and required by the GCE commander. The Byzantine collections process inhibited our ability to get timely responses to combat requirements with the exception of assets organic to or DS to the Division. This made the Division almost exclusively reliant on organic or DS collection assets. The Division found the enemy by running into them, much as forces have done since the beginning of warfare. The Pioneer worked great when the bureaucracy between the VMU and the Division G-2 could be negotiated, but the lack of a habitual relationship and adequate rehearsal time limited our ability to do so. A superb example of a successful UAV system was the Dragoneye, which was fielded to selected Battalions and allowed to collect against the commander's priorities, locations, and schedule without interference from higher headquarters.

On a fluid high tempo battlefield, a highly centralized collections bureaucracy is too slow and cumbersome to be tactically relevant. The best possible employment option is to push more assets in DS to the lowest tactical level and increase available organic collections.

…Generally, the state of the Marine Corps' tactical intelligence collection capability is well behind the state of the art. Maneuver units have limited ability to see over the next hill, around the next corner, or inside the next building.

Supporting intelligence collectors (VMU, P-3AIP, ATARS, Theater and National level assets) were great for developing deep targets, subject to the prioritization of higher headquarters (Division and higher.) Navigating the labyrinth of collection tasking processes proved too difficult in most cases to get reporting on Division targets, and certainly for Battalion-level collections. For the amount of money spent on an ATARS POD, could be handsomely equipped with a suite of motion sensors, digital imaging equipment with zoom lenses, laser range finders, small UAVs, thermal imagers, robotic sensors and other tactically focused intelligence collectors.

The Marine Corps has a tremendous void in its intelligence collection capabilities at the echelon that needs it the most.

…Despite heavy focus and planning for Visual Aerial Reconnaissance (VAR) and numerous attempts to request support during the war, the actual output of the process was disappointing.

The G-2, 3d MAW produced an outstanding VAR plan and methodology. In execution, however, it was clear that the Wing operators and aircrew did not have an appreciation for how important their efforts were in driving the Division's efforts and saving lives. More training and rehearsals of this concept would likely improve the collections. This should be routine for aircrews to assist the GCE by providing much-needed aerial perspective. The DASC could have facilitated ad-hoc VAR requests on an individual sortie basis, by ensuring collection of the VAR NAIs based on their knowledge of an aircraft's position in the battlespace. An entire intelligence function was left out by the DASC and its capabilities to route conventional air platforms over areas of interest in the Division battle-space.

Understanding and advocacy for GCE requirements greatly diminishes outside the shouting radius of the GCE commander. More work has to be done to institutionalize the VAR process in the MAGTF in order for it to live up to its potential.

1st Marine Division successfully employed the Pioneer Unmanned Aerial Vehicle (UAV) in the role of fire support sensor. Success in this area was limited only by competition with the UAV's primary mission as a collections asset.

The UAV proved to be a very valuable observer, facilitating the proactive attack of enemy high payoff targets. It's ability to loiter on station and "adjust" fires real time ensured desired effects on target and provided real time Battle Damage Assessment (BDA). In what may have been the best example of the Division's employment of the UAV in the aerial observer role, the Division Target Information Officer coordinated with G-2 Collections to have the UAV confirm the locations of the Division's preplanned targets for one of the artillery preparations on G-day. The mission flew within 2 hours of fire support plan execution and four targets in the plan were refined. UAV was again overhead as the preparation was fired before being re-tasked in Direct Support (DS) of one of the Regimental Combat Teams (RCTs). While the UAV was still in DS of the Division, the TIO was able to observe secondary explosions confirming the destruction of at least one of the targets in the fire plan.

The UAV was not employed to refine preplanned targets prior to the execution of subsequent fire support plans, largely due to competing requirements for employment of the asset. To employ the UAV effectively as a fire support acquisition platform requires dedicated UAV sorties. OIF experience argues for a robust capability that can provide 24-hour coverage to both the Division and one Regimental Combat Team (RCT) (the Main Effort).

Tactics, techniques, and procedures (TTPs) for the employment of UAVs as a fire support sensor have not been formalized. The Division's experience in OIF suggests that:

- The TIO should be the interface between Fires and the UAV payload operator. The payload operator is the observer.
- Remote Receive Terminals (RRTs) are required at both the Division and RCT.
- A direct communications link is required between TIO and UAV payload operator. In OIF, this was accomplished using Internet chat.

...As the Marine Corps acquires a replacement for the Pioneer UAV, it should buy enough systems to dedicate platforms to target acquisitions as

well as to collections. In the interim, I MEF should support training opportunities that allow the Division to integrate UAV into live fire training and
afford VMU's payload operators opportunities to adjust fires onto targets.

Some of these issues have been discussed in chapter 6, and it is not clear
just how much the U.S. Army and allied ground forces suffered from the
same problems as the Marine Corps. There are enough anecdotal reports
to suggest, however, that providing effective imagery to the actual war
fighter remains a major problem and that there is a tendency to favor
higher echelons of command even if the requirement is less time-sensitive
and tactically oriented.

As a result, broad examination may be needed of the extent to which
war-fighting intelligence is tailored to meet the time-sensitive needs of the
user on the ground, and UAVs offer a potential way of providing cost-effective direct support to ground combat units. Certainly, the Marine
Corps analysis reiterates many other comments that indicate that jointness and netcentric warfare become much less effective at the battalion level and lower.

UAV Procurement and the UAV Road Map

The success of UAVs is indicated by the fact that the United States issued a
new UAV "road map" on March 18, 2003, just before the Iraq War. The
road map laid out the development and use of unmanned aerial vehicles
and unmanned air combat vehicles over the next 25 years based on the lessons of Afghanistan. The road map called for significant advances in UAVs
in dealing with missions like the suppression of enemy air defenses. It
called for better interoperability and standardization, for improved ability to manage air corridors and deconflict the use of UAVs/UCAVs (unmanned combat aerial vehicles, and for more rapid advances in UCAVs.[98]
The road map also called for an increase in the number of UAVs supporting global military operations from around 90 in 2003 to 350 by 2010.[99]

After the Iraq War, the United States issued plans to increase funding
for UAVs from $1.3 billion in FY2003 to $1.7 billion in FY 2004,and to $2.5
billion in FY2005. [100] This includes funding for 16 faster and better-armed
Predator Bs—a procurement justified by experience in Afghanistan as
well as in Iraq—and about $500 million for the development of much
larger versions of the Global Hawk, including a maritime surveillance
version. The goal is to have 27 Global Hawks by 2007 and to eventually
create a total force of 51, at an average cost of $57 million each. At the
same time, the United States is stepping up its research effort in creating
much more advanced unmanned combat aerial vehicles.

THE STRENGTHS AND WEAKNESSES OF THE A-10

Both attack helicopters and the A-10 played effective and important roles in the fighting, as they did during the Gulf War. The USAF reports that the A-10s had a mission-capable rate of 95.7 percent in the Gulf War, where they flew 8,100 sorties and launched 90 percent of the AGM-65 Maverick missiles. While no similar data or quantified estimates of BDA are available for the Iraq War, the A-10 clearly was able to operate effectively in sandstorms, using binoculars and sensors in some cases and cluster weapons in others to attack the Republican Guard. It patrolled 30-square-mile kill boxes in both the forward and rear areas, helping to secure U.S. lines of communication.[101]

The A-10 operated effectively over Baghdad during the battle for that city, even dropping down to 2,000-3,000 feet for strafing runs. Several A-10s were hit hard by enemy fire, including one that returned to base with nine hits. Only one A-10 was lost to enemy fire, when it was hit by a man-portable surface-to-air missile on April 8.[102]

The avionics on the current A-10 also illustrate the advances in U.S. avionics even in relatively "simple" strike aircraft. Thunderbolt IIs have Night Vision Imaging Systems (NVIS), goggle-compatible single-seat cockpits forward of their wings, and a large bubble canopy that provides pilots with all-around vision. The avionics includes inertial navigation systems, fire control and weapons delivery systems, target penetration aids, and night vision goggles. Their weapons delivery systems include heads-up displays that indicate airspeed, altitude, dive angle, navigation information, and weapons aiming references; a low-altitude safety and targeting enhancement system (LASTE), which provides constantly computing impact-point freefall ordnance delivery; Pave Penny laser-tracking pods under the fuselage; and the Global Positioning System.

The A-10 also illustrates the merits of good protection and the ability to operate effectively as part of an expeditionary force. The A-10/OA-10 has excellent maneuverability at low air speeds and altitude, and it can loiter near battle areas for extended periods of time and operate under 1,000-foot ceilings (303.3 meters) with 1.5-mile (2.4 kilometers) visibility. Its wide combat radius and short takeoff and landing capability permit operations in and out of locations near front lines, and it can conduct missions during darkness.[103]

The aircraft can survive direct hits from armor-piercing and high-explosive projectiles up to 23mm. Its self-sealing fuel cells are protected by internal and external foam. Manual systems back up its redundant hydraulic flight-control systems, which permits pilots to fly and land when hydraulic power is lost. Many of the aircraft's parts are interchangeable left and right, including the engines, main landing gear, and vertical stabilizers. The Thunderbolt II can also be serviced and operated from bases with limited facilities near battle areas. This, and the fact that the coalition seized the air facilities at Tallil near An Nasiryah, allowed the aircraft to refuel there and gain an extra hour of mission time.[104]

THE STRENGTHS AND WEAKNESSES OF THE A-64 APACHE AND OTHER ATTACK HELICOPTERS

Attack helicopters like the AH-64, AH-64 Longbow, and AH-1 also played an important role in air support. There is, however, some debate over their performance and whether the war shows the need for new technical characteristics or for new tactics.

The Apache and Apache Longbow

The AH-64D allowed the attack helicopter to use fire and forget air-to-surface missiles for the first time. The AH-64D Longbow is fitted with the Longbow millimeter wave fire control radar and the AGM-114D Longbow Hellfire air-to-surface missile, which has a millimeter wave seeker that allows the missile to perform in full fire and forget mode. The range is 8km to 12km. The Apache has been equipped with air-to-air missiles (Stinger, AIM-9 Sidewinder, Mistral, and Sidearm) and 2.75-inch rockets. The Longbow Apache can carry 16 Hellfire missiles on four 4-rail launchers and 4 air-to-air missiles in the close air support role.[105]

The Longbow fire control radar incorporates an integrated radar frequency interferometer for passive location and identification of radar-emitting threats. An advantage of millimeter wave is that it performs under poor visibility conditions and is less sensitive to ground clutter. The short wavelength allows a very narrow beamwidth that is resistant to countermeasures.

The Longbow Apache can carry out an attack in thirty seconds. The radar dome is unmasked for a single radar scan and then remasked. The processors determine the location, speed, and direction of travel of a maximum of 256 targets. The Longbow Apache uses the Target Acquisition Designation Sight (TADS) (AN/ASQ-170) and the Pilot Night Vision Sensor (PNVS) (AN/AAQ-11). The turret-mounted TADS provides direct-view optics, television, and three fields of view forward-looking infrared (FLIR) to carry out search, detection, and recognition and has a laser rangefinder/designator. PNVS consists of a FLIR in a rotating turret located on the nose above the TADS. The image from the PNVS is displayed in the monocular eyepiece of the Honeywell integrated Helmet And Display Sighting System, HADDS, worn by the pilot and copilot/gunner.

The Apache is equipped with an electronic warfare suite consisting of AN/APR-39A(V) radar warning receiver; AN/ALQ-144 infrared countermeasures; AN/AVR-2 laser warning receiver; AN/ALQ-136(V) radar jammer; and chaff dispensers.

The AH-64 benefited from the fact that the army rushed in rapid upgrades from the Block 3 modernization program just before the war. These upgrades included an air transportability kit that allowed the Apache to deploy without dislodging the rotors and radar dome, and it can be made combat-ready within 20 minutes after unloading from a C-17 or C-5 rather than two hours. The upgrades also included an internal auxiliary fuel system that added 100 gallons of fuel and extended flight time by an average of 50 minutes, although at the cost of reducing the 1,200-round 30mm magazine to 300 rounds.[106]

A Need for Changes in Tactics and/or Technology?

The success of the AH-64 in Afghanistan may have been a factor leading the U.S. Army to decide to retain it as a long-term part of its Objective Force and to upgrade it with new computer systems (although the decision to cap production of the RAH-66 Comanche attack-reconnaissance helicopter at 650 aircraft has been a major driving factor). [107]

The Iraq War, however, raised questions about the vulnerability of low-altitude fliers like the Apache and AH-1W.[108] One Apache was shot down by small arms fire and its two-man crew was captured. Press reports indicate that another 30 had small arms hits. The U.S. Army also had to pull back from long-range attack missions after it sent 34 AH-64Ds from the 11th Aviation Regiment to attack elements of the Republican Guard Medina Division near Karbala on March 24. Instead of ambushing Iraqi tanks by penetrating in undetected low altitude attacks, the helicopters encountered heavy small arms and light anti-aircraft fire before they closed on the Iraqi armor, and they had to retreat back to base after doing minimum damage.[109] Reports from marines in the field show that they also had to restrict the operations of their AH-1 attack helicopters to avoid using them against Iraqi land forces with heavy short-range air defenses.

At the time, USCENTCOM spokesman Brigadier General Vincent Brooks noted that only one aircraft was lost and that all the other helicopters involved in the March 24 mission did accomplish their mission and return safely to base. General Tommy Franks also stated, "We know that they were very effective in their mission."[110] However, General Richard

Myers, the chairman of the Joint Chiefs, described the relative roles of the A-10 and the Apache in the Iraq War as follows:[111]

> The A-10 is doing good. Always has done good. But it needs kind of a moderate environment or less to operate. It's had that where its been operating. It's a good machine.
>
> The Apache Longbow system has also done extremely well. Of course, the Longbow is a fairly new modification, but it has done very well.

Lt. General William Wallace, the commander of The 5th Corps, also both praised the Apache and noted that it was vulnerable when it flew long penetration missions into areas with heavy short-range air defenses. He too stated that changes in tactics were needed to use it most effectively:[112]

> The...adjustment that we had to make during the course fight was the techniques we used for the employment of the Apache helicopter. It's because everybody in this country has a weapon. And if they all shoot them up in the air at the same time at every helicopter that flies over, it becomes a very lethal environment for a low-flying aircraft.
>
> The attack helicopter doesn't have the luxury of flying at 25,000 feet as the Air Force does. So in order to effectively employ the Apache we had to make adjustments to our tactics. The tactic that we settled on was first of all focusing on close support of ground forces with the Apache, which is called "over the shoulder." It's not really over the shoulder but is close cooperation with ground maneuver and air maneuver. That has proven to be very effective.
>
> The other tactic that we have come to employ very successfully is using the Apache doing armed reconnaissance—for example, what the 11th (Aviation) Regiment has been doing the last three days, in areas that we had driven through to engage the enemy but we're not absolutely certain of the degree to which the area was cleared.
>
> So we've been using the attack helicopters as a reconnaissance platform and as a platform that goes out to see if there's an enemy in a particular area...in some of the less contested areas, to insure that those areas are secure and free of air defense and enemy formations, that sort of thing. And that has proven to be very successful.

General Wallace later commented more broadly on the role of army aviation and drew the following conclusions:[113]

> Our attack aviation performed a significant role during the fight, but I must admit it didn't perform the same role that I had envisioned for the attack aviation. The attack of the 11th Aviation on the Medina Division did not meet the objectives that I had set for that attack. We found out, subsequent to the

attack, based on some intelligence reports, that apparently…both the location of our attack aviation assembly areas and the fact that we were moving out of those assembly areas in the attack was announced to the enemy's air defense personnel by an Iraqi observer, thought to be a major general, who was located someplace in the town of An-Najaf using a cellular telephone. In fact, he used it to speed- dial a number of Iraqi air defenders. As our attack aviation approached the attack positions, they came under intense enemy fire.

Interesting also that as we approached the attack positions, based on our pilot reports and after-action review after the aviation attack, the entire power grid in the area went blank; the entire town, the entire area, went black for about three seconds and then came back on…in what we believe to be a signal to the air defense gunners using small arms and aimed tracer fire to engage our attack aviation. Thankfully, all our attack aviation, save one aircraft, returned from that fight. And also, thankfully, the two downed pilots from that aircraft, the two POWs, have returned safely back to Fort Hood, Texas.

As a result of that experience, we conducted an after-action review with the pilots and commanders involved in the attack, and we altered our use of our attack aviation based on that information.

Two nights later, we conducted a successful deep operation using the attack aviation of the 101st Division into an area just north of the city of Karbala.

We also have used the Apache a number of times in armed reconnaissance missions, one in particular where I used the 11th Aviation Regiment to do an armed recon of the corps' right flank. As you might recall, during the campaign, based on the maneuver of the corps up to Baghdad and the maneuver of the 1st Marine Expeditionary Force toward al Kut and subsequently to the right flank at Baghdad, there was a significant area in between the two corps formations that had not been cleared by any ground forces, and I had a great deal of concern that there might still be enemy artillery that could engage us from that wedge that was in between the two formations. So I used the 11th Aviation Regiment to go out there and clear that area. And in fact they found enemy air defense [short audio break from the source]—they found a large [amount] of abandoned enemy equipment. They did not find any substantial enemy artillery formations out there, which gave me a degree of security and…a sense of security, at least, associated with our right flank.

Most significantly, though, what we used our attack aviation for, which we trained for prior to crossing the line of departure, was in what we refer to as close combat attack, close support of our ground forces. When the 3rd Infantry Division attacked through the Karbala Gap and subsequently to Baghdad, they attacked with their own Apache battalions, plus I placed an attack aviation squadron of 21 Apaches from the 11th Attack Helicopter Regiment under their operational control. So they had in excess of 30 Apaches that were available to provide close combat attack or close support of ground forces 24 hours a day during that attack.

...to summarize, I would suggest to you that we learned from our mistakes, we adjusted and adapted based on what we learned, and we still used the Apache helicopter in a significant role during the course of the fight. I will tell you also that the pilots that I talked to have gained a tremendous appreciation for the fightability and the survivability of the Apache based on their experience.

This discussion scarcely indicates that the AH-64s had critical mission limitations. It does indicate that the restrictions on their operations may have occurred because it was already clear that the United States could win this particular war without taking major losses. It also has become clear that one reason the 11th Aviation Regiment ran into so many problems on March 24 was that it happened to overfly an Iraqi position where the end objective of their attack was clearly predictable and the Iraq commander used a cell phone to alert the Medina Division. One key question is whether the loss of tactical surprise was a freak incident or more typical of what can be expected of an alert enemy in the future.

Major General David H. Petraeus, commanding general of the 101st Airborne Division (Air Assault)) indicated that relatively limited changes in tactics allowed the Apache to be effective on many other occasions:[114]

Our Apaches did a great job for us. We did in fact change our tactics from nightlong deep attack operations, for two reasons. After a successful deep attack, but one in which we crashed a helicopter in a night dust landing on return, and also had problems on take-off—so we had two problems.

One was that night dust landings at—southwest of An Najaf, where we were, and all throughout the area, where we originally began these operations, about 400-plus kilometers into Iraq, were very, very difficult, and it's despite soldiers who had flown in Afghanistan, spent quite a bit of time with environmental training in Kuwait, had no problems there, and so forth.

The other problem, frankly, was that the Iraqis dispersed very early on and moved their tanks and fighting vehicles and artillery away from the avenues of approach that the 3rd Infantry Division, in particular, was going to use. And so they...weren't massed in the way that we want usually for Apache operations. We did, as I say, have one quite successful deep attack operation, had reasonable BDA. But it was not the kind that we had hoped to with the, frankly, you know, 100-plus tanks, tracks, artillery and air defense systems.

Following that, when we could not get the target definition that we needed, we went to daylight, deep armed reconnaissance operations and conducted a number of very successful operations of that type. I don't think they were given the publicity, in part because, frankly, exciting offensive operations were being conducted against Karbala, some of the stuff we were doing in Najaf, Karbala, and Al Hillah. And the BDA in some cases was not huge, although they did knock out very significant targets on a number of occasions, and did have one or two that did have very substantial BDA, on the order of several batteries of D-30 artillery, a number of air-defense pieces, and so forth.

We packaged these operations with ATACMS missiles, and as I mentioned, we shot — or we called for 114 of these. Each of these clears an entire grid square. They're massive munitions. We had a direct line between the shooters and the Apaches. We also had JSTARS supporting them, to direct them; AWACS, EA-6 jammers, and close-air support all packaged together with HARM shooters. And that package went down range; we could identify the target at up to eight kilometers. And then, depending on how much fuel the Apache had, if he had a lot of fuel, would bring in close air support, ATACMS, and save his missiles and rockets for later. And then, as he got toward the end of his time on station, find a target, use his munitions, be relieved in place by another platoon or company of Apaches, and do the same thing again and again and again.

We also had considerable success with attack helicopters operating in close support of our infantry soldiers. The one operation in which we actually ran into a substantial fight with the Republican Guards, and one of the few cases that I'm aware of where the Republican Guards employed combined arm operations was the morning that the V Corps attacked with an armed recon by our Apaches to the northwest of Karbala, the lake; the 3rd Infantry Division attacked into the Karbala Gap, both in the west and the east of the city; and then, of course, really never stopped from there.

We attacked into south Al Hillah, where we encountered a dug-in Republican Guard battalion with a tank company, with artillery and with air defense, and it fought very, very effectively. We had a very heavy fight there, lost our first soldier. The tank battalion commander attached to us received a Silver Star for his actions already. The Apache company in that operation fought very, very hard, and eight helicopters take some degree of fire. All of them made it safely back, another sign that the Apache can get hit and just keep on flying, as it showed in Afghanistan as well, in close combat.

In that fight, we destroyed that Republican Guards battalion. We destroyed the tank company. We destroyed two D-30 artillery battalions, destroyed an artillery battery and a number of other systems. We never again saw a Republican Guard unit stand and fight and employ combined arms like that.

We also employed our Kiowa Warrior cavalry squadron attack helicopters directly over cities, with enormous success. That squadron commander, in fact, also will receive a Silver Star and a Distinguished Flying Cross and a Bronze Star with "V" for actions in three different fights. He had two helicopters shot up underneath him. Each of them made it back safely. And again, they were very, very effective in their role as well.

We tended to use the Kiowas over the cities, where they flitted around a bit, were hard targets to hit generally, and could take the doors off and look directly down through the palm trees and into the city streets where the regular army and militia and Fedayeen were hiding their systems, and then using the Apaches around the edge of the city and occasionally bringing them in for really robust attacks. That, again, worked quite successfully.

So the Apaches did great for us. But I would say that I'd like to think that we were flexible and adaptable in the way that we used them when we encountered both the problems with night dust landings and the problems with the enemy massing his systems, as he would have had to actually stop an enemy attack up the route through Karbala on the way to Baghdad.

The Need for Joint Fixed-Wing and Rotary-Wing Attack Operations?

Some experts think that the army might have been able to carry out longer-range strikes more successfully if it had realized that the nape-of-the-earth and pop-up tactics it used to try to reduce helicopter vulnerability would not work in heavily defended areas. They argue that long-range attack helicopter strikes and operations in heavily defended areas could still be effective if they were carried out as joint operations with the air force, where aircraft suppressed ground-based air defenses and small arms fire while the helicopters attacked armor. [115]

There are reports of a later joint operation by both AH-64s and the A-10 where the helicopters again went against the Medina Division and encountered heavy fire, allowed the A-10s to suppress the Medina Division's air defenses and small arms, and then reentered and destroyed a large number of Iraqi tanks. It also seems clear that the A-10 was more effective in other ways than in the Gulf War because of improvements in its avionics and precision strike capability. The end result may be that attack helicopters and close air support aircraft are another part of the joint arms team.

Nevertheless, other commentators like General Merrill A. McPeak, the former chief of staff of the USAF, argue strongly that the AH-64 and other attack helicopters should have their operation restricted to short-range missions directly in combat support of land force commanders. General McPeak argues that nothing can give attack helicopters the stealth and speed necessary to survive, and that aircraft like the A-10 and fighters using standoff precision weapons are far more effective in the mission.[116] Short of a major exercise in joint test and evaluation, there is no clear way to resolve this debate.

Balancing Lessons from AH-1 Operations

At least some marines also think that their experience with the AH-1 indicates that attack helicopters benefited from support from the combined arms team. Like most reports from AH-64 pilots, however, they chronicle a wide range of operations, in terms of both forward combat and protection of rear areas and lines of supply.

One Marine aviator has provided a particularly good report of what it was actually like to fly a combat helicopter in the Iraq War. His report tracks closely with those of many other attack helicopter pilots. Excerpts help put the use of attack helicopters in perspective as well as broadly refute any lingering impression that fighting in the war was some kind of cakewalk. They also describe the real-world nature of joint warfare and the limits of sensors and netcentric warfare, and they give a sense of both the strengths and vulnerability of the attack helicopter and other combat systems in intense combat:[117]

> As I reflect back on the past month that I spent in Iraq fighting the war, I'm amazed at what we accomplished. On a personal level, I'm astonished I'm alive. On the micro level, I'm truly overwhelmed at what my squadron achieved. We flew nearly 3,000 combat hours with 27 helicopters and we did not lose a single Marine to an accident or to the Iraqis. On the macro level, I'm astounded at the intensity with which the Marine Corps fought....
>
> ...I was lucky enough to be designated the division lead for a flight of four Cobras that were tasked to destroy Iraqi border posts that could send a warning to other Iraqi military units of our pending invasion. The mission was to be executed at night.
>
> ...Living in the sand for the first time, we realized that even the lightest of winds caused quite a bit of the sand to turn into dust in the air. With ten knots of wind or more, visibility could quickly be reduced to next-to-nothing. Something that would definitely affect us later.
>
> ...the first day of the war. Now remember, we were planning on executing our first mission at night. That's key for a couple of different reasons. First, you can take advantage of the cover of darkness: the Iraqis wouldn't be able to see us. Second, the squadron's schedule is set by the launch time of the aircraft. Maintenance crews need to have advance notice to prepare the aircraft for flight. Pilots have to get the required amount of rest, and then prepare for the mission. On this day, no less than five times, the word changed on what time they wanted us to launch. It ranged from, "GO RIGHT NOW!" to "Go 8 hours from now." It was a mental roller coaster.
>
> Around dinnertime, the word to launch finally comes, ...My flight of four is supposed to be the lead flight out of the airfield, but our timing is all screwed up. The winds have picked back up, and visibility is less than a mile.

In the confusion, another flight of Cobras departs the airfield ahead of us. Oops. Lots of talking on the radios to sort it out. For those of you who haven't looked through a pair of NVGs (Night Vision Goggles), they are built for use in darkness. If there is too much light, then they don't work correctly. The worst time to fly on the goggles is right after sunset. And of course, that's when we had launched. The sand in the air is something that we hadn't dealt with too much in training.

In accordance with our peacetime training rules, if visibility is poor, you don't fly. Common sense—safety. But in war—when American lives are at stake, sometimes you have to push the edge of the envelope and deal with conditions that you're not normally accustom [ed to]. With the reduced visibility and lack of moon that night, I can say that that was the darkest night I've ever flown in my life. Now mind you, I've been a Marine for almost 15 years. I've been flying Cobras since 1990. I've got a fair amount of experience. But this was dark. Seat-cushion-clenched-in-your-butt dark. Not only did the sand hang in the air to minimize horizontal visibility, but also the desert that we were flying over was completely smooth and lacked any detail. You couldn't tell, from two hundred feet above ground level (AGL), how high you were. No depth perception. You couldn't see obstacles until you were right on top of them. That's a bit nerve-wracking.

…Upon arrival, Kujo is working the FLIR (Forward Looking Infrared) sensor to find our assigned targets. Unfortunately, the target area photos didn't quite display all the surrounding terrain features that were in the FLIR's field of view. What seemed like hours for Kujo to pick out the right targets, actually only took about a minute or two…Kujo locates the targets—three missiles away. Border post destroyed.

…After the initial border post strikes, my section proceeds to a FARP (Forward Arming and Refueling Point) that had been set up only hours prior near the Iraq/Kuwait border. None of us had been there before. The FARP was located on an asphalt road—but there were power lines and sand all over the place. Just to land for gas took me four attempts. I kept having to wave off because of the lack of visibility. Not being able to land because of visibility had never happened to me before. I'm fighting panic and despair. We're just about out of gas. Finally with Kujo's help, we make it safe on deck. After refueling, we shut down and assumed a strip alert.

…On my second flight of the war, the fear factor is pretty high. Not because of the Iraqis—it's the lack of visibility. We can't see in front of us. I can only see a road underneath us, so Kujo navigates us down the roads, making turns at intersections—and we pick our way back up to the front. Once there, the Grunts are starting to push across the border. They're taking sporadic mortar fire. Because of the reduced visibility, we couldn't find the enemy for them. Low on gas. Time to head home. As we travel back toward our original sand-and-tent base, I can no longer keep tabs on where the ground is. There are tall radio towers and power lines everywhere that we can't see. I jerk back on the stick once, when I saw that a radio tower that was less than fifty feet from our aircraft. I'm starting to get vertigo. Kujo bails me out. Flying right down the highways and roads, we pick our way back to our base. Aeronautical navigation charts were worthless that night.

...My next flight in the war was in the vicinity of Basrah. We launched off the ship and proceeded to the FARP for gas about an hour prior to sunset. We pushed up north to work with the British. In the dwindling daylight, I came to realize that although the Brits and I are both speaking English, we aren't speaking the same version of the language. I just can't figure out what they want me to do—and where they want me to go. Just after sunset, I had flipped down my NVGs, which have two independent battery packs for power. Battery set one dies immediately. No problem, switching to number two. Dies. Great. I can't see anything. My dash two that night, "Murph" and "Kramer," make a desperate call on the radio to avoid traffic. In the haze and darkness, another section of Cobras had some how intermingled with my section. One of the Cobras passed right in between my aircraft and Murph's. Near mid-air collision. Great. Spent the whole night searching for work.

Frustrating. The oil fields in Rumaliyah that the Iraqis set on fire light up the sky. You couldn't even look in that direction with your NVGs because the intensity of the light degraded the abilities of the NVGs to the point where they were basically useless. Sent to search for Iraqi troop movements to the north of a river. Can see some Iraqis on the FLIR, but cannot tell if they are soldiers or not. Can't engage them. Felt like we were missing out on the action. We recovered back aboard the ship after first light, having not fired a single round.

The weather turned bad. Sandstorms throughout the entire region clobbered the skies. Even at sea, visibility was reduced down to less than a hundred yards or so. It continued for three days. During that time, frustration grew amongst the aviators. ...Watching your brother Marines in combat, and being unable to go out and provide support for them, was one of the most exasperating things I've ever had to deal with. Finally, the weather cleared. We get another chance to help out with the effort.

...We launch off the ship and head up to a FARP about one hundred miles deep into Iraq. From there, we launch up north to the city of An Nasariyah. While we were on the ship during the bad weather, we had seen on TV the intense action going on in that city. This was my first real flight during the daylight hours. Approaching the city, I felt completely naked. At night, the darkness hides you from the Iraqis, but in the daytime, you're there for everyone to see. Really makes you feel vulnerable. We make our way around the west side of the city, avoiding the built up areas. On the north side, a Marine unit has just crossed the river, and is waiting to continue up the road.

Approaching their location, we get directed to engage an enemy mortar position that is located on the river's bank. We roll in with rockets and guns. Holding back over friendlies (where it is relatively safe), Kujo spots enemy anti-aircraft artillery (AAA) and regular artillery just to the Marine unit's west. After receiving clearance from the FAC (Forward Air Controller), we engage. Back over friendlies again. Looking down, we notice that there are two Marine LAVs (Light Armored Vehicles) that had been hit prior to our arrival. We had heard on the news that some of our Marines had died in that ambush. Sobering. Out of gas.

…The Marines have resumed their movement up the road to the north. Now we're escorting their convoy along the roads. Military gear and trucks all along the roads. We engage a truck with ammunition in the back. Secondary explosions. A few kilometers to the north, we spot some Iraqi soldiers in a ditch waiting to ambush our vehicles when they get close. Huddled in the trench, they began to move, undetected by the Marine convoy, toward the road with their weapons. Up to this point, we had destroyed a lot of military equipment, and smashed military buildings. This was the first time we'd be specifically rolling in against another human. This attack definitely had a different feel to it. I put the aircraft into a dive and strafed the trench with the cannon. We continued escorting and shooting as the Marines marched to the north. We race back to the FARP for more gas and reloads.

… It's dark now. The Marine vehicles are parked in a coiled formation— so that each individual vehicle can fire in a specific direction to protect the rest of the vehicles in the coil. Each tank and LAV is assigned a particular sector of fire. As we approached, we could see that they were in a pretty decent firefight. As we moved to get over their position, fire is going out in every direction from the coil. TOW missiles, 25mm chain gun, M-1 tank main gun, and heavy machine gun fire. We were so low over them that the firing of the machine guns made your teeth rattle. Every couple of minutes, a FAC would give me a rollout heading, and I'd either ripple a pod of rockets, or blast away with the cannon. Everything was danger close.

When you're a brand-new Second Lieutenant in the Marine Corps, you begin your career by going to The Basic School (TBS) at Quantico. During your six-month tenure at TBS, one thing they demonstrate to you is called the "Mad Moment." In this demonstration, they essentially show you what it looks like with machine guns shooting, artillery shooting, tanks shooting, and aircraft shooting, all at the same time. The demonstration lasts about 5 minutes. Up north in Nasariyah that night, the mad moment lasted for hours. Except now there were bullets flying in all directions.

The tactics that the Iraqis used this night were a sign of the times to come. Using the cover of darkness and small guerilla-type teams, they'd attempt to sneak up within RPG (Rocket Propelled Grenade) range of the Marines.

Often, they'd drive vehicles with their headlights off at a high rate of speed right into the Marines' position, with the hopes of killing as many Americans as possible. This particular night, I saw the Iraqis drive a Greyhound-style bus at full speed with its lights off right at the Marines. An M-1 tank main gun round slammed into the bus just as it reached the Marines' perimeter.

A Brit GR-1 Tornado jet checks in with the FAC, and is going to work in conjunction with my flight to protect the coil. Much like my first encounter with the Brits, the FAC was having a difficult time describing to the jet crew exactly where the Iraqi targets were. After talking the pilot onto the target by using a large fire as a checkpoint, the Tornado begins his target run. As the jet passes over the city of Nasariyah, all hell breaks loose. Large caliber AAA and SAMs (Surface to Air Missiles) begin to race through the sky in every direction. 100-millimeter AAA rounds looked as though they were in slow motion as they arced up into the sky and exploded. Low trajectory shots angled through the darkness around us. This was the first time we'd been shot at. It was absolutely terrifying—and nearly made me freeze on the controls…it was petrifying. Out of gas. Avoid the city.

…After shooting again, we proceed back to the FARP. We shutdown the aircraft and sleep for 2 hours. It was freezing cold. No cots or tents; no sleeping bags. We slept on the ground next to the aircraft. Long transit back out to the ship at first light.

…"Howdy", who's my wingman, and I are tasked to screen north of the city (Basrah) to check out suspected sites where the Iraqis are waiting to ambush British ground forces. We depart the Brit headquarters and fly to the north side of the city, where we begin conducting armed reconnaissance. As soon as we began our search, Kujo locates military equipment bunkers where the Iraqis had stockpiled ammunitions and weapons for their troops. The bunkers are everywhere. To describe the bunkers, they are basically about the size of a two-car garage. There is no roof. And the walls are large dirt berms that a bulldozer has made. They are good to protect against ground fire, but essentially worthless against aircraft.

As we size up the weapons cache, Kujo spots an AAA piece with large stashes of ammunition at the ready near it. Kujo engages with a TOW missile. Rolling off target, I spot Iraqi tanks in bunkers. They're T-62 tanks, which are exports from the Former Soviet Union. One by one, we begin to pick off the tanks with our TOWs and Hellfires. Finally running out of missiles, we race back to the FARP for reloads. As we arrive at the FARP, I spot a Marine truck convoy departing the airstrip. Our ordnance team had gotten word to leave the FARP and proceed up to the north to the next base. Without the ordnance men, we won't get any reloads. Trying to flag them down from the air, I finally decide that the only way to get them to stop is to land on the road in front of them. Once I landed the aircraft, Kujo jumped out and ran over to tell the convoy commander that we need them to go back to the airfield. Thankfully, they complied. We race back up to the north.

…Launching out again that evening in support of the Brits, they had tasked us to attack a suspected covert meeting site that the Fedeyeen forces had been using. Following that, we were to attack the Ba'ath Party headquarters in Basrah. Lastly, we would fly up and conduct visual reconnaissance for some of the Brit infantry units.

Upon launching, we realized that the Iraqis had started some oil fires in the outskirts of Basrah. What they would do is dig a large trench with a bulldozer, and then fill the trench with oil. To obscure visibility for aircraft, they'd light the trenches on fire, which would put up a thick black smoke into the air. That night, the smoke was hanging in the air from 350 feet to about 1,000 feet.

Working our way around the southern side of Basrah, so that we can find the Fedeyeen meeting site, we begin to take a heavy amount of small arms fire. We could see the muzzle flashes on the ground as the Iraqis were trying to shoot us. The volume of fire is enough that we have to turn around and move back to the western side of the city. From there, we move to the firing position we had selected to engage the Ba'ath Party headquarters. Finding the three buildings on the FLIR, Kujo begins to pump Hellfire missiles into the buildings. "Mookster," who is Howdy's copilot, begins to shoot TOW missile sat maximum range into the buildings. It was quite a sight watching all these missiles going down range.

…The next mission cycle I flew in was to support the Marines as they moved up the highways between An Nasariyah and Al Kut. We launched in the early afternoon to head up north. Upon reaching the front lines, the FAC that we were to support had his unit stopped along a road while they reconnoitered a small village up ahead. On arrival, we were tasked to check out the village. Not fully aware of the threat, we pushed north along the highway to check out the village. As we moved around the western side of the small town, large black puffs started appearing around our aircraft. After a pregnant pause, loud booms were heard. Someone in the village was firing large caliber AAA at us. Screaming to break left into the radio, our flight turned hard and moved back to friendlies. Kujo, ever the wizard, lased the AAA battery and got a location. Passing that location to the FAC, Marine artillery put salvo after salvo of high explosives on the enemy site, which was most impressive. Would hate to be on the receiving end of that.

Pushing toward Al Kut and Baghdad, the next mission cycle was supporting the Marines as they blocked the Republican Guard from retreating from Al Kut to Baghdad. Meeting up with the Grunts near a river, we began to conduct reconnaissance forward of the friendly lines. To their north, we located an Iraqi artillery position. At the same time, the FAC wanted us to return to their position to engage some Iraqis that had camouflaged themselves near a large ditch embankment. Racing back to the Marines, we engaged the Iraqis with rockets and guns. Hit the trench line and a truck. Back up at the artillery site, Kujo begins to shoot the missiles at the artillery tubes. We destroyed 5 guns and 2 trucks. One of the trucks was carrying fuel and when hit by Kujo's missile, disappeared in a high order explosion.

...Our assignment was to screen forward of their nightly position, in anticipation of the massive movement toward the capital. Looking forward of our friendly lines, we spotted an Iraqi unit that had dug in around a mosque. All around the yard surrounding the religious facility, the Iraqis had put their military trucks, command and control vans, and weapons in the tree line surrounding the mosque, thinking that we wouldn't be able to engage them for fear of hitting the church. Kujo and I opened up with Hellfire missiles. "Wally" and "Tinkle," my wingmen, engaged the targets as well...I spotted a fuel truck in the tree line. Hit it with a rocket from 3 kilometers. Massive explosion. And not a scratch of damage to the mosque.

...That night, I was flying overhead cover for Sideshow's unit. His armored vehicles were moving toward Salman Pak, which had a large contingent of Iraqi army troops. The night prior, a West Coast Cobra had crashed in this area. It had apparently hit a set of large power lines. Around Baghdad, the power lines were about 350 feet high. The wires and the stanchions are tan in color... so they are next to impossible to see during the day... and you almost never see them at night.

About 11:00 p.m., we were orbiting just to the west of Salman Pak, looking into the city with our infrared sensors and our night vision goggles. After several reconnaissance sweeps, we detected an Iraqi military compound in the center of the town, and it contained a surface to air missile battery and other military hardware that the Iraqis were using to defend the town. I maneuvered the flight to the west, and I rolled my aircraft in to the target so that we could shoot the missile battery with one of our missiles.

As Kujo was lining up the shot, I noticed two flashes from my right side. Looking over, I saw two heat-seeking missiles racing up toward our aircraft. Rolling the aircraft into a violent nose-down maneuver and expending decoy flares, we screamed for the ground to break the lock that the missiles had on our aircraft. We had started out at 800 feet or so above the ground, and I pulled the nose up around 100 feet. After bottoming out of the dive, we had descended all the way down to 50 feet, and had successfully broke lock with the missiles. As we recovered back up to a higher altitude, we realized that high-power tension lines surrounded us.

Two miracles occurred that night. First, we managed to not get hit by the missiles; and second, we somehow managed not to hit these large powerlines, which were like spaghetti all over the ground in that area...Seemed like an eternity. But in reality, the whole engagement was over in about 4 seconds or so. Those heat-seeking missiles travel at about Mach 2.5 (about 1,700 MPH). Not a lot of time to react... and not enough time to be scared.

...On another day mission, we're working the highway that connects Al Kut to Baghdad...Checking in on station at the same time is a section of Air Force A-10s with the call sign Eager 31 and 32. Giving them my coordinates, I directed the A-10s to my position. Simultaneously, I cleared Wally, who was my wingman, to start engaging the Iraqi tanks. With the A-10s overhead, I began to talk their eyes onto the various tank targets. Clearing them to use their 30-millimeter cannon, they roll in from above and begin to strafe the tanks. Their cannon is so loud that I can hear it from 2 miles away in my aircraft. It was quite an awesome sight. That day, we destroyed eight T-72 tanks.

As the battle for Baghdad was in full swing...We receive a launch order to proceed to Baghdad. Evidently, there was a large fight building in the downtown area of the city. Arriving at the suburbs of the city at first light, we begin to hold in an area that we felt was relatively safe. Down on the ground, urban Iraqis were outside of their houses watching us flying around. It made you nervous—you couldn't tell who was friendly, and who wanted to harm you. Something as simple as watching men looking up at you while talking on a cell phone made you wonder just who they were talking to on the other end of the phone. Traveling as a light division (3 AH-1Ws), we continue to hold and try to sort out what is going on in the city before we stick our noses in. Howdy is one of my wingmen. He takes a small caliber round into his engine door. The fight in the city was too hot. Without the specific approval of the commanding general, we can't go in to provide fire support. Frustration mounts because the FAC wants us to come into the city to conduct reconnaissance; but the volume of fire coming up out of the city is too high. Out of gas, we start our trek back to Jalibah.

As the fight for Baghdad concluded, the Iraqi forces that still wanted to resist moved up north to Hussein's hometown of Tikrit. Needing to relocate to be closer to the fight, a portion of the MAG moved up to an abandoned airstrip outside of Salman Pak.

My first day flying out of Salman Pak, we were directed to escort a Marine ground unit that was working its way north out of Baghdad...Talking to the lead vehicle in his large column, we begin to give steering commands to the drivers: turn right—take your next left by the two-story building. Out in front of Sideshow's unit, we located Iraqi artillery waiting for the Marine unit to come within range. Setting up with Wally, we begin to engage the artillery battery. After destroying it, Sideshow's unit proceeds. Running out of gas, we race for Salman Pak, and we meet up with one of our UH-1N Hueys, flown by "Friar". He joins my section. We proceed back up to Sideshow's location and continue escorting his column into the night. Upon our return to Salman Pak for the night, our mechanics discovered bullet holes in one of my rocket pods. Good thing they didn't penetrate and set off the ordnance hanging on my aircraft.

…Launching out … as a hunter-killer team (2 AH-1Ws and 1 UH-1N), we're directed to a landing zone located in the city of Baghdad. Proceeding to their location, we fly overhead and see that the Marines are located in a soccer stadium in the city. We land at their location. Hundreds of Iraqis are standing out in the streets watching us land. Feel extremely vulnerable—again. Climbing out of the aircraft, I tell Kujo, who is staying in the Cobra, that if he starts taking fire, to take off and get the aircraft to safety. Conducting a face-to-face brief with the FAC, our understanding is that they want to use the Huey as a command and control platform, but they won't need them for another couple of hours.

…Launching out of Salman Pak as a hunter—killer team, we proceed toward Tikrit, where the last Iraqi resistance is still standing. One of the Iraqi airfields outside that city was being used as a FARP. Approaching the FARP and contacting them on the radio, we're informed that they are taking artillery fire from the Iraqis. With plenty of gas remaining, my flight begins to conduct reconnaissance to the southeast of the FARP, in hopes of finding the Iraqis who were firing on the Marines at the FARP. Flying over a date tree grove, we find what we're looking for: Iraqi artillery and surface-to-surface rockets. As the sun is setting, we await permission from the command and control system to engage. As the sun sets, we are given approval to attack. Rolling in from the north, we begin to engage the Iraqi artillery. Rockets and 20-millimeter cannon fire hit the tree lines…After multiple passes with our cannons, rockets and missiles, the Iraqi artillery and rockets are destroyed and burning.

…From my perspective of being an attack helicopter pilot, the war was not something that just took up part of the day—it was a 24/7 mindset. Unlike a jet squadron, whose pilots are only flying for a couple of hours each day, and get to return back to their creature comforts in Kuwait or on the aircraft carrier, a light/attack helicopter squadron is always on the move with the infantry. In order for us to keep up with their movement to the north, we were constantly repositioning our squadron to provide the best fire support available to them.

Although jets played a key role in the outcome of the war by bombing strategic and tactical targets before our ground forces arrived, it was the Cobra that the Grunts wanted for close air support. When Marines are in contact on the ground and the enemy is close, a jet just can't hit the target without fear of hitting friendlies— even with all the precision guided munitions that were touted in the news during the war. Close air support is our bread and butter— and that was our motivation and purpose throughout the war—to provide close in fire support to the ground combat element—whether that be killing the enemy at arms length—or doing it up close and personal.

THE U.S. MARINE CORPS AV-8B HARRIER

The U.S. Marine Corps has had a troubled history with the AV-8B. At one point much of its fleet was deadlined, and detailed data are not yet available on the AV-8B or Harrier's performance in the Iraq War in either U.S. or British forces. However, Marine Corps Lt. Gen. Earl B. Hailston, the commander of the Marine Forces in USCENTCOM, noted after the war:[118]

> …we had the Harriers, both shore-based and sea-based. The vast majority of them were sea-based, over 50 aircraft out to sea. They flew over a thousand sorties from off the decks out there. And the shore-based Harriers have an equal percentage of ordnance carried and sorties flown.
>
> We did move them ashore, used forward arming and refueling points where we took the carriers in so they wouldn't have to return to the ship to refuel. And that worked exceedingly well. They've kept the airplanes overhead our Marines 24 hours a day, ready to support anything that they needed.
>
> The airplane certainly, especially now with some upgrades and carrying new technology and sophisticated pods, became the envy of pilots even from my background. I happened to fly the Hornet. And there's an awful lot of things on the Harrier that I've found the Hornet pilots asking me [for]….
>
> So we couldn't have asked for a better record. It flew as much as anybody else. We had absolutely no incidents with it. It's always been an airplane that's performed well. But in this environment, it performed exceedingly well.

According to one Marine Corps source, the corps was able to base AV-8Bs on its light amphibious carriers, which gave the coalition 60 more jets in theater than it otherwise would have had, due to lack of space to base, and which supported 60 of the 76 AV-8s in theater on amphibious carriers.

The corps claims the Harriers had 85 percent aircraft availability and that there were Harriers in the air over Iraq 24 hours a day, seven days a week. The AV-8Bs rearmed and refueled out of An Numaniyah airfield 60 miles southeast of Baghdad. MALS-13 logisticians kept the flow of repairables and consumables moving to the 76 MAG-13 Harriers.

In 25.5 days of combat, AV-8Bs flew more than 3,400 hours and 2,000 sorties. They dropped or fired over 1,400 weapons, 900 of which were laser-guided bombs (LGBs). Marine Corps officers claim that the use of the Litening II targeting pod achieved a better than 75 percent kill effectiveness on target with GBUs, and that laser-guided bombs killed the target seven times out of ten. In one wave alone, Harriers operating off of the USS *Bonhomme Richard* inflicted heavy damage on a Republican Guard Baghdad Division armored tank battalion in advance of the MEF's push on Al Kut.

The AV-8Bs normally flew in close support of tanks, mainly using Hunter/Killer tactics where the lead AV-8B (Hunter) was configured with the Litening pod and one GBU-16. Dash 2. The Killer was configured with two GBU-12s and occasionally MK-82 with VT fusing or Rockeye on Stations 1 and 7.

This was the first time the corps had had so many sea-based AV-8Bs (plus 16 in Kuwait) under a Marine Group commander, and they flew combat missions both day and night from both the *Bonhomme Richard* and *Bataan*, where 48 of the 60 sea-based Harriers were located. The aircraft routinely flew missions off the ships, attacked their targets, went to a land base or forward operating base, or FARP, refueled, rearmed, flew back out for another mission to attack targets for the MAGTF or coalition forces and then recovered back to the LHD/LHA amphibious ships.

Not surprisingly, the corps argues this performance strongly reinforces the need to procure the F-35B Joint Strike Fighter for the Marine Corps. The corps also has drawn the conclusion, however, that the range-payload and endurance limitations of the AV-8B may have a different solution. The report on the lessons of the war by the 1st Marine Division suggests that many of the problems in using the AV-8B could be solved by procuring the AC-130 gunship:[119]

> In OIF, distances between the Forward Line of Troops (FLOT) and Wing Forward Operating Bases (FOB) were such that the Wing found it difficult to support the CAS requirement with assets with significant FLIR capability and sufficient time on station. The AV-8B with the lightning pod has a significant FLIR capability, but usually had just 15-20 minutes of time on-station, which could be extended with tanker support. Once the target was located, the Harrier only has the ability to drop 500 pound or 1000 pound bombs (it can strafe with a limited number of rounds if a gun pod is mounted). By contrast, the AC-130 has the capability to loiter in excess of 6 hours and combines a first-rate sensor suite, including unequalled FLIR capability, with an impressive and scaleable array of armament: 105mm howitzer, 2x 20mm (or 25mm) chain guns, and 40mm cannon.
>
> In future as in recent conflicts, the Marine Corps will fight in a permissive airborne threat environment because the coalition has secured air supremacy early. In this environment, the Marine Corps needs an organic AC-130 capability. Current USMC C-130 maintenance capability, both at the "O" Level (Operations) and "I" Level (Intermediate), does not extend to mainte-

nance of some AC-130 avionics and ELINT equipment, so an upgrade to capability would be required. However, the cost and increased burden on C-130 maintenance support would easily be justified by the overwhelming combat capability the AC-130 brings to the fight.…With the introduction of the C-130J, buy two of the admittedly expensive AC-130 variants in order to enhance MAGTF firepower

THE U.S. MARINE CORPS V-22 OSPREY

The Iraq War did not provide clear lessons for dealing with one of the U.S. Marine Corps' most critical force-planning and resource decisions: the merits of the V-22 Osprey. Some marines feel that the war showed that the CH-46 was too limited in range and speed of deployment to keep up with the forward elements of 1 Marine Division, and that this affected missions like casualty evacuation. At least some of these problems, however, seem to have been primarily problems in vulnerability—a factor that some reports indicate also limited the use of the Cobra.

Without considerably more data and a clearer picture of how the V-22 would have affected a wide range of operations, along with data on the tradeoffs necessary to buy and deploy the V-22, any attempt to draw lessons would have to be even more speculative than most of the preliminary conclusions presented in these chapters.

SUPPRESSION OF ENEMY AIR DEFENSE (SEAD)

The United States and Britain had some four years of operational experience in suppressing Iraqi air defenses and were able to use the no-fly zones to sharply reduce Iraqi capabilities before the war began.[120] Operation Northern Watch enforced the no-fly zone north of the 36th parallel in Iraq and monitored Iraqi compliance with United Nations Security Council resolutions 678, 687, and 688.

The United States and the United Kingdom provided about 45 aircraft and more than 1,400 personnel to support the operation. Operation Southern Watch enforced the no-fly zone south of the 33rd parallel in Iraq and monitors compliance with UN Security Council Resolutions 687, 688, and 949. The United States and the United Kingdom provided about 150 aircraft and 6,000 men and women to support the operation. During the period from December 1998 onward, the two no-fly zones became the scene of a long series of duels between U.S. and UK air forces and the Iraqi land-based air defenses, with occasional probes and challenges by the Iraqi air force. The Iraqis lost all of these duels and suffered a steady attrition of their land-based defense capabilities. It must have also become apparent that the Iraqi air force could not successfully challenge U.S. and British forces in air combat.

The sheer scale of the no-fly zone effort was impressive long before the United States and Britain began to carry out a major effort to suppress the system. By August 2002, the United States and UK had already flown near-ly 300,000 flights in the zones. These included 265,000 sorties in the south-ern zone since 1992 and 33,000 in the northern zone since 1997. They involved packages of air defense suppression planes like the F-16CJ and EA-6B, strike fighters like the F-16C and F-15E, refuelers, and AWACS air controllers.

The United States and Britain began to step up their operations against Iraqi air defenses as early as November 2001. During the first four months of 2002, however, the United States and UK struck targets in the northern and southern no-fly zones only six times. It was in the summer of 2002 that they began to strike at Iraqi air defenses with the deliberate goal of sup-pressing them in the event of a U.S. and British invasion, and to hit at key command and control targets in the Iraqi air defense command and con-trol system like the repeater stations necessary to allow its buried optical fiber communication system to function.

Sources differ over the scale of this effort. Some sources report that U.S. and British aircraft struck roughly 48 times from October through No-vember 2002. They also report that these strikes both intensified and struck deeper and harder at the entire air defense system in December, in-cluding targets around Al Kut, An Nasiryah, Amarah, Basra, and the Tal-lil air base. Iraq charged that U.S. and British aircraft entered Iraqi air space 1,141 times between November 9 and December 6, while the United States and Britain said that Iraq had fired on their planes more than 470 times since the beginning of 2002. [121]

These same sources report that the duels stepped up after UN Security Council Resolution 1441 was passed on November 8, 2003, Iraqi forces fired on U.S and British pilots 264 times before the war began on March 19. In addition to actual firings, Iraq "painted" coalition aircraft with ra-dars far more often. The United States and Britain responded with stepped-up air strikes on Iraqi air defenses that concentrated on destroy-ing their command centers, main fire units, and the optical fiber networks that connected them. After March 1, U.S. forces flew large numbers of sor-ties that largely carried out the key phase of the SEAD mission before the war began on March 19.[122]

A postwar briefing by Lt. General Moseley, the commander of coalition air forces during the war, indicated that U.S. and British strikes had been intensified in both the northern and southern no-fly zones in November

2001 in reaction to increased Iraqi efforts to shoot down a U.S. or British aircraft. The air strikes were further intensified in the summer of 2002 as part of operation Southern Focus, which was designed to suppress Iraqi air defense capability in the event of a U.S. and British invasion. Moseley stated that the allies struck 349 Air Defense Command targets in southern Iraq and fired 606 munitions between June 2001 and March 19, 2003.[123]

The wartime suppression of Iraqi air defenses was carried out remarkably well. It did not interfere with an immediate shift to other offensive missions, and it both rolled up the Iraqi defenses in key areas and attrited their numbers to the point they lost much of their low-altitude air defense effectiveness.

According to *Aviation Week*, the United States also made effective use of deception in dealing with SEAD and was even able to use the effort for additional forms of targeting.[124] *Aviation Week & Space Technology* reports that Iraqis shown on television during the war who thought they were shooting at a crashed U.S. fighter and its pilot were actually shooting at a downed USAF drone sent up as a decoy to draw out Iraq's defenses. According to this account, the plane flew undetected until it ran out of gas and crashed:

> One clue to clandestine U.S. activity came from television footage shot early in the conflict of Iraqi soldiers combing the banks of the Tigris River in Baghdad and shooting into stands of reeds. The hunt for downed coalition pilots was triggered by two over-age U.S. Air Force Predator UAVs that had been stripped of equipment and flown into the city's airspace to probe its air defenses. Intelligence officials also monitored Iraqi communications during the search to see what was left functioning of Iraq's military command and control system.
>
> The unmanned aircraft were never shot down and finally ran out of fuel, which doubtlessly told analysts something about the state of Iraq preparations. Baghdad was the zone of the country's most concentrated air defenses. One Predator plunged into the Tigris and the second into a lake. The UAVs were referred to as "chum" because they served as bait for the anti-aircraft defenses.

Aviation Week also reports that the destruction of secure communication links forced Iraqis to talk on more easily intercepted channels, which helped lead to the opening strike of the war:

> "We spent a lot of time taking out SAMs and radars and breaking open fiber-optic vaults, trying to make [Iraqi] command and control more difficult and visible to us so we could hear what they were saying and suck up the information that we needed," said a senior Air Force official. That effort resulted in the

tip-off about Saddam Hussein's whereabouts that launched the conflict with a raid on Iraq's senior leadership. "Within 4 hr., we had four bombs down in the bunker."

At the same time, the SEAD mission should not be seen as easy. As has been discussed in chapter 3, USCENTAF estimated that some 210 surface-to-air missile launchers and 150 early warning radars were still active when the war began. The United States deployed a massive electronic warfare effort as part of its air order of battle. It planned some 2,374 sortie equivalents to maintain air superiority and executed 1,441. It fired 408 High Speed Anti-Radiation Missiles. The United States would also have faced a very different set of mission requirements if it had not been able to hit Iraqi defenses before the war began, or if Iraq had been able to modernize its air defenses and/or had properly organized them. The SEAD mission would be very different, for example, against a defense based around versions of the Russian S-300 or S-400 missile system or around the most modern European short-range missile air defenses.[125]

THE ROLE OF THE PATRIOT

USCENTCOM claims that the Patriot Pac 2 GEM and PAC-3 intercepted 9 of the 12 Al-Samoud 2 and Ababil-100 missiles fired at Kuwait during the conflict. Two intercepts were by Kuwaiti Patriot PAC-2w, and seven were by U.S. PAC-2s and PAC-3s (Only two of the Patriot missiles fired were PAC-3 because such missiles were in limited deployment when the war began.)[126] This performance is striking because the Patriot borders near Iraq had only 2 to 3 minutes from rocket or missile launch to intercept the target versus 10 to 12 minutes in the Gulf, where the missiles were fired from much further away. It compares with estimates by the GAO that only 9 percent of the Patriots fired during the previous Gulf War hit their target, and they hit only 1 of the 39 Scuds that Iraq fired at Israel.

The performance of the Patriots was also a further demonstration of the value of space because of the warning of launch and missile vector provided by the infrared detection and tracking satellites in the Defense Support Program (DSP), and it seems to have validated the use of the Joint Tactical Air-to-Ground System (JTAGS) that the army deployed to Jordan. The definition of intercept is unclear, however, in terms of warhead kill, as is the decision to not fire at systems that appeared to head into the Gulf or empty desert.[127] The Patriot also failed to detect an Iraqi CSSC-3 Seersucker cruise missile attack on Kuwait on March 20 and what seems to have been a Silkworm cruise missile attack on March 29, although the

Seersucker is a low-flying sea/land skimmer that the Patriot's radar is not designed to detect.[128]

The Patriot firings also exposed a problem with identification of friend or foe (IFF). This problem may have occurred because pilots often turn off their transponders to avoid location by enemy surface-to-air defenses, or it may have been the result of a fault in the IFF system in the British Tornado. However, it may also have been the result of problems in the Patriot's IFF detection system and the need for almost instant response to a missile attack that were exposed in Patriot trials in Georgia as much as three years earlier.[129] There are also some indications that two Patriot units were placed too closely together, and that the electromagnetic radiation from one unit disrupted the operation of the other.[130]

Several different kinds of incidents are involved. Patriots shot down a British Tornado on March 22 near the Iraq-Kuwaiti border, and two British aircrew were killed. The Patriot locked on an F-16 south of Najaf on March 24, and the F-16 fired a HARM missile that destroys the Patriot radar. In this case, the Patriot crew was taking shelter from enemy artillery fire and had placed the system in the automatic mode. The F-16 may have mistaken the automated radar activity for an Iraqi preparation to fire. The Patriot is suspected of shooting down an F-18 near Karbala on April 2 and killing the pilot. In both cases, the aircraft failed to show up on the Patriot control screens despite their identification of friend and foe (IFF) systems.[131]

At this writing, there are no clear statements on the causes, and it should be noted that the coalition flew some 15,800 sorties over areas covered by the Patriot and any problems were limited in scope. Lt. General Ronald Kadish, head of the Missile Defense Agency, said later that the incidents might have been the result of a combination of flaws in both missile and aircraft IFF procedures and systems. General Myers, the chairman of the Joint Chiefs, responded to a question on the issue by saying that "procedures and electronic means to identify friendly aircraft…broke down somewhere."

Lt. Gen. David D. McKiernan, the commander of the Coalition Forces Land Component Command, described the performance of the Patriot as follows:[132]

> …there have been some blue-on-blue incidents. We take every one of those extremely seriously. Every one is investigated individually. And it's premature for me to comment on any of them, because, to my knowledge, none of those investigations have been completed. There were a couple that involved Patriot, but I would tell you on balance that every surface-to-surface missile that was fired that Patriot engaged was destroyed. Some of them we didn't

engage because they landed out in places in the desert where it wasn't a threat or they landed out in the North Arabian Gulf. But I will tell you the Patriot's been a big winner over here in our theater missile defense plan…every one of these blue-on-blue incidents is investigated in great detail. And when those investigations are complete, I'm sure all the services and CENTCOM will have comments on all of them.

No Iraqi missiles were fired at Israel, and the Arrow and Patriots deployed there were not fired in defense.

Notes

[1] Michael Gordon, "US Attacked Iraqi Air Defenses Starting in 2002," *New York Times*, July 20, 2003; Bradley Graham, "US Moved Early for Air Supremacy," *Washington Post*, July 20, 2003.

[2] Ibid.

[3] Ibid.

[4] Lt. General T. Michael Moseley, "Operation Iraqi Freedom—By the Numbers," USCENTAF, Assessment and Analysis Division, April 30, 2003.

[5] Ibid.

[6] The data and analysis quoted here are taken from Tom Cooper, "Documented Coalition Losses in the III Persian Gulf War, as of 11 April 2003, Air Forces and Air Arms," www.orbat.com/site/agtwopen/iraq_equipment_losses.html.

[7] For a more detailed discussion of effects-based bombing, see David A. Deptula, *Effects Based Operations: Change in the Nature of Warfare* (Arlington, Va.: Aerospace Education Foundation, 2001).

[8] Bradley Graham, "Military Turns to Software to Cut Civilian Casualties," *Washington Post*, February 21, 2003, p. 18.

[9] The details of these efforts are described in U.S. Central Command, "Target and Collateral Damage," March 5, 2003 (background briefing), and Senior Defense Official, "Background Briefing on Targeting," Department of Defense News Transcript, March 5, 2003.

[10] For an excellent book-length study of the subject, see Edward R. Smith, *Effects Based Operations: Applying Network Centric Warfare in Peace, Crisis, and War*, Department of Defense Command and Control Research Program (CCRP), Washington, D.C., November 2002.

[11] Department of Defense, Transcript, Col. Gary L. Crowder, Chief, Strategy, Concepts and Doctrine, Air Combat Command, "Effects Based Operations Briefing," March 19, 2003, www.defenselink.mil/news/Mar2003/t03202003_t0319effects.html. The author has edited this briefing to remove all questions and references to slides and to greatly shorten the briefing. The words quoted, however, are Colonel Crowder's.

[12] Gordon, "US Attacked Iraqi Air Defenses Starting in 2002"; Graham, "US Moved Early for Air Supremacy."

[13] Niko Price, "Tallying Civilian Death Toll in Iraq War Is Daunting," *Philadelphia Inquirer*, June 11, 2003.

[14] Laura King, "Baghdad's Death Toll Assessed," *Los Angeles Times*, May 18, 2003, p. 1; Peter Ford, "Survey Pointing to High Civilian Death Toll in Iraq," *Christian Science Monitor*, May 22, 2003, p. 1; Associated Press, May 15, 2003; Iraqbodycount.net.

[15] *Washington Post*, April 20, 2003, sec. A, p. 20.

[16] Rowan Scarborough, "Myers Says 'Annihilation of Iraqi Army Wasn't Goal,'" *Washington Times*, June 30, 2003.

[17] British Ministry of Defense, "Operations in Iraq: First Reflections" (London: Her Majesty's Stationery Office, July 2003), pp. 5, 21.

[18] A fully accurate analysis would require a complex analysis of all of the sources of error, or an "error budget," for a given mix of targeting data, given launch conditions, and a given mark or model of a weapon. For obvious reasons, this would be a mathematical nightmare, even if suitable test and evaluation methods could be developed and funded.

[19] Adapted from Moseley, "Operation Iraqi Freedom—By the Numbers."

[20] Anthony H. Cordesman and Abraham R. Wagner, *The Lessons of Modern War*, vol. 4, *The Gulf War* (Boulder, Colo.: Westview, 1996), pp. 476–477.

[21] Arnaud de Borchgrave, "War by Remote Control," *Washington Times*, April 28, 2003, p. 17.

[22] See General Hal. M. Hornburg, "Air Support in Iraq," *New York Times*, June 3, 2003,

[23] The reader should be aware that 7,200 strikes could never be characterized by mission. See Cordesman and Wagner, *The Lessons of Modern War*, vol. 4, *The Gulf War*, pp. 442–443.

[24] See Anthony H. Cordesman, *The Lessons and Non-Lessons of the Air and Missile Campaign in Kosovo* (Westport, Conn.: Praeger, 2001), pp. 151–153.

[25] Adapted from Moseley, "Operation Iraqi Freedom—By the Numbers."

[26] Tony Capaccio, "US Launched More Than 50 'Time Sensitive' Strikes in Iraq," Bloomberg News, April 14, 2003.

[27] David A. Fulghum, "Offensive Gathers Speed," *Aviation Week & Space Technology*, March 21, 2003; David A. Fulghum, "Opening Night in Baghdad," *Aviation Week & Space Technology*, March 21, 2003.

[28] Fulghum, "Opening Night in Baghdad."

[29] Adapted from Moseley, "Operation Iraqi Freedom—By the Numbers."

[30] Commanding General, 1st Marine Division, "Operation Iraqi freedom (OIF): Lessons Learned," MEF-FRAGO 279-03, May 29, 2003.

[31] The initial analysis conducted by CNA (April 2003) indicated the close fight could not be predicted 48 to 72 hours in advance and that shaping often did not focus on the primary objective laid out in the targeting process.

[32] A plan to implement a 48-hour targeting cycle was approved by the DCG on April 23, 2003. Also, the real key to ensuring the PTL remains relevant and accurate is contingent on the efficacy of the intelligence collections effort, which is addressed in a separate topic.

[33] This compares with a total force of 42 F-117s that flew 1,300 missions in the Gulf War.

[34] Eric Schmitt, "High Tech Fighter Pilots Recount Exploits," *New York Times,* April 25, 2003.

[35] David Montgomery, "Critics: Iraq War Shows New Jets Aren't Needed," *Miami Herald,* May 5, 2003.

[36] Ibid.

[37] British Ministry of Defense, "Operations in Iraq: First Reflections," p. 21.

[38] Christian Lowe, "Joint US Training Vital to Close Air Support," *Defense News,* June 16, 2003, p. 38.

[39] For a more detailed discussion of the issues involved, see Peter C. Hunt, *Aerospace Power in Urban Warfare: Beware the Hornet's Nest,* INSS Occasional Paper 39 (Boulder, Colo.: U.S. Air Force Academy, May 2001).

[40] Eric Schmitt, "Baghdad Air War Shifts with GI's in the City," *New York Times,* April 6, 2003; Vernon Loeb, "Intense, Coordinated Air War Backs Baghdad Campaign," *Washington Post,* April 6, 2003, p. 24; Christian Lowe, "Urban Combat Role Grows for Airstrikes," *Defense News,* April 21, 2003, p. 19.

[41] William M. Arkin, "The Price of Precision Bombing," *Los Angeles Times,* April 6, 2003.

[42] Thom Shanker and Eric Schmitt, "Latest Mission for Forces: Analyze New Ways to Prepare for Conflicts," *New York Times,* April 30, 2003.

[43] For examples, see Robert Wall, "Foss Field," *Aviation Week,* March 22, 2003, and David Hughes, "Heavy Lift as War Looms," *Aviation Week,* March 9, 2003.

[44] Douglass Barrie, "Storm Trials," *Aviation Week,* March 31, 2003, p. 25.

[45] British Ministry of Defense, "Operations in Iraq: First Reflections," p. 21.

[46] Ibid.

[47] Barton Gellman, "Frustrated, U.S. Arms Team to Leave Iraq: Task Force Unable to Find Any Weapons," *Washington Post,* May 11, 2003, sec. A, p. 1.

[48] "No Bunker Found under Bomb Site," *New York Times,* May 29, 2003.

[49] Gordon, "US Attacked Iraqi Air Defenses Starting in 2002"; Graham, "US Moved Early for Air Supremacy."

[50] Scarborough, "Myers Says 'Annihilation of Iraqi Army Wasn't Goal.'"

[51] This description is adapted from www.fas.org/nuke/guide/usa/bomber/calcm.htm.

[52] Tony Capaccio, "Raytheon Tomahawks Miss Few Iraqi Targets, Navy Says," Bloomberg News, April 12, 2003.

[53] Dan Morgan and Walter Pincus, "High Cost of Defense Plan Gets Little Discussion," *Washington Post*, May 26, 2003, p. 2.

[54] The Joint Direct Attack Munition (JDAM) is a guidance tail kit that converts existing unguided free-fall bombs into accurate, adverse weather, "smart" munitions. With the addition of a new tail section that contains an inertial navigational system and a global positioning system guidance control unit, JDAM improves the accuracy of unguided, general-purpose bombs in any weather condition. The navigation system is initialized by transfer alignment from the aircraft that provides position and velocity vectors from the aircraft systems.

The JDAM uses the 2,000-pound BLU-109/MK 84, 1,000-pound BLU-110/MK 83 warhead, or new MK-82 500-pound warhead as the payload. JDAM enables employment of accurate air-to-surface weapons from fighter and bomber aircraft against high-priority fixed and relocatable targets.

Once released from the aircraft, JDAM autonomously navigates to the designated target coordinates. Target coordinates can be loaded into the aircraft before takeoff, manually altered by the aircrew before weapon release, and automatically entered through target designation with onboard aircraft sensors. In its most accurate mode, the JDAM system will provide a weapon circular error probable (CEP) of 13 meters or less during free flight when GPS data is available. If GPS data is denied, the JDAM will achieve a 30-meter CEP or less for free flight times up to 100 seconds with a GPS quality handoff from the aircraft.

JDAM can be launched from very low to very high altitudes in a dive, toss and loft, or in straight and level flight with an on-axis or off-axis delivery. JDAM enables multiple weapons to be directed against single or multiple targets on a single pass. JDAM is currently compatible with B-1B, B-2A, B-52H, F-16C/D and F/A-18C/D, the A-10 F-15E, F-22, F-117, AV-8B, F-14A/B/D, F/A-18E/F, S-3, and the Joint Strike Fighter.

Desert Storm highlighted a shortfall in air-to-surface weapon capability. Adverse weather conditions limited employment of precision-guided munitions. Unguided weapon accuracy was also degraded when delivered from medium and high altitudes. Research and development of an "adverse weather precision guided munition" began in 1992. The first JDAMs were delivered in 1997 with operational testing conducted in 1998 and 1999. More than 450 JDAMs were dropped during testing, recording an unprecedented 95 percent system reliability while achieving a 9.6-meter accuracy rate. JDAM and the B-2 made their combat debuts during Operation Allied Force. The B-2s, flying 30-hour, nonstop, roundtrip flights from Whiteman Air Force Base, Mo., delivered more than 600 JDAMs during Allied Force. The Navy is currently studying the effects of adding enhancements such as improved GPS accuracy, a precision seeker for terminal guidance and additional warheads. Source: www.af.mil/news/factsheets/JDAM.html.

[55] de Borchgrave, "War by Remote Control."

[56] Letter from Robert P. Buckley, senior vice president, Textron Systems, June 17, 2003; www.fas.org/man/dod-101/sys/dumb/cbu-97.htm; www.globalsecurity.org/military/systems/munitions/cbu-105.htm; and http://news.bbc.co.uk/1/hi/world/americas/2911327.stm.

[57] "Rumsfeld Touts Value of Missile Used in Iraq," *Washington Times*, May 15, 2003, p. 10.

[58] Adapted from www.globalsecurity.org/military/systems/munitions/agm-154.htm.

[59] British Ministry of Defense, "Operations in Iraq: First Reflections," p. 48.

[60] Andrew Chuter, "UK Weapons Debut in Iraq," *Defense News*, May 12, 2003.

[61] British Ministry of Defense, "Operations in Iraq: First Reflections," pp. 13, 22–23.

[62] Ibid., p. 48.

[63] Adapted from Moseley, "Operation Iraqi Freedom—By the Numbers."

[64] Carol Rosenberg and Matt Schofield, "Bombs Sow Rage in Baghdad," *Philadelphia Inquirer*, April 16, 2003; Laura King, "Bombing Ends But Not Danger," *Los Angeles Times*, April 22, 2003, p. 1; Paul Watson, "Lack of Data Slowing Cluster Bomb Cleanup," *Los Angeles Times*, April 27, 2003.

[65] Department of Defense, Transcript, Press Briefing, Secretary Rumsfeld and General Myers, April 25, 2003, www.defenselink.mil/transcripts/2003/tr20030425-secdef0126.html.

[66] Rosenberg and Schofield, "Bombs Sow Rage in Baghdad"; King, "Bombing Ends But Not Danger."

[67] Textron comments on prior drafts of this analysis, dated June 17, 2003.

[68] William M. Arkin, "It Ain't Broke after All," *Los Angeles Times*, April 27, 2003; David A. Fulghum and Robert Wall, "Baghdad Confidential," *Aviation Week*, April 28, 2003, p. 32.

[69] Gail Kaufman, "B-52 Gets Refits for New Roles," *Defense News*, March 24, 2003, p. 18.

[70] Lance M. Bacon, "Back in the Big Game," *Air Force Times*, June 16, 2003, p. 14.

[71] Gail Kaufman, "B-1B to Deliver Unique Weapons Combination," *Defense News*, October 14, 2002, p. 19.

[72] Bacon, "Back in the Big Game."

[73] Arkin, "It Ain't Broke after All."

[74] Fulghum and Wall, "Baghdad Confidential."

[75] Adapted from www.globalsecurity.org/military/systems/aircraft/f-18ef.htm.

[76] Kaufman, "B-52 Gets Refits for New Roles."

[77] Gail Kaufman, "USAF to Speed Long-Range Strike by 2012," *Defense News*, April 7, 2003, p. 20.

[78] Bradley Graham and Vernon Loeb, "An Air War of Might, Coordination, and Risks," *Washington Post*, April 27, 2003, sec. A, p. 1.

[79] This description is adapted from the USAF database at www.airforce-technology.com/projects/jstars/.

[80] The 116th Air Control Wing operates the JSTARS aircraft at Robins Air Force Base in Georgia. The 116th is a new "blended wing" with both Air Force and Air National Guard personnel.

[81] On a standard mission the JSTARS aircraft has a crew of 21 with 3 flight crew and 19 system operators. On a long endurance mission the aircraft has a crew of 34, with 6 flight crew and 28 system operators. The Boeing 707-300 series aircraft is the JSTARS airframe. The aircraft are remanufactured at Northrop Grumman in Lake Charles, Louisiana, then transferred to the Battle Management Systems Division in Melbourne, Florida where the electronics are installed and tested. The propulsion system of the JSTARS aircraft consists of four Pratt and Whitney JT3D-3B turbojet engines, each providing 18,000 pounds of thrust.

[82] Commanding General, 1st Marine Division, "Operation Iraqi freedom (OIF): Lessons Learned."

[83] Eric Schmidt, "In the Skies Over Iraq, Silent Observers Become Futuristic Weapons," *New York Times*, April 18, 2003; Marc Selinger, "US Using More than 10 Types of UAVs," *Aerospace Daily*, April 22, 2003.

[84] Scarborough, "Myers Says 'Annihilation of Iraqi Army Wasn't Goal.'"

[85] British Ministry of Defense, "Operations in Iraq: First Reflections," p. 21.

[86] The RQ-1 Predator is a medium-altitude, long-endurance unmanned aerial vehicle system. It is a Joint Forces Air Component Commander-owned theater asset for reconnaissance, surveillance, and target acquisition in support of the Joint Force commander. It is a system, not just aircraft. A fully operational system consists of four aircraft (with sensors), a ground control station (GCS), a Predator Primary Satellite Link (PPSL), and 55 personnel for continuous 24-hour operations. The basic crew for the Predator is one pilot and two sensor operators. They fly the aircraft from inside the GCS via a C-Band line-of-sight data link or a Ku-Band satellite data link for beyond line-of-sight flight.

The first aircraft were equipped with a color nose camera (generally used by the aerial vehicle operator for flight control), a day variable aperture TV camera, a variable aperture infrared camera (for low light/night), and a synthetic aperture radar (SAR) for looking through smoke, clouds, or haze. The cameras produced full motion video and the SAR still-frame radar images. The three sensors were carried on the same airframe but could not be operated simultaneously. The upgraded Predator carries the Multispectral Targeting System (MTS) with inherent AGM-114 Hellfire missile-targeting capability, and integrates electro-optical, infrared, laser designator, and laser illuminator into a single sensor package. These Predators cannot carry MTS and the SAR simultaneously. The aircraft carry and employ two laser-guided Hellfire anti-tank missiles with MTS.

Each Predator aircraft can be disassembled into six main components and loaded into a container nicknamed "the coffin." This enables all system components and support equipment to be rapidly deployed worldwide. The largest component is the GCS, and it is designed to be rolled into a C-130. The air-transportable PPSL consists of a 6.25 meter Ku-Band satellite system mounted on a trailer. It provides communications between the ground station and the aircraft when it is beyond line-of-sight and is a link into secondary intelligence dissemination networks.

The RQ-1B system needs 5,000 feet by 125 feet (1,524 meters by 38 meters) of hard-surface runway with clear line-of-sight to each end from the GCS to the air vehicles. The RQ-1B includes an ARC-210 radio, an APX-100 IFF/SIF with Mode 4, an upgraded turbo-charged engine, and an ice mitigation system. Source: www.af.mil/news/factsheets/RQ_1_Predator_Unmanned_Aerial.html.

[87] Gordon, "US Attacked Iraqi Air Defenses Starting in 2002"; Graham, "US Moved Early for Air Supremacy."

[88] Source: www.af.mil/news/factsheets/global.html.

[89] Fulghum and Wall, "Baghdad Confidential."

[90] Jonathan Finer, "With the Dragon Eye," *Washington Post*, March 7, 2003, sec. A, p. 14.

[91] Adapted from www.globalsecurity.org/intell/systems/dragon-eye.htm.

[92] Marine Corps Lt. Gen. Earl B. Hailston, Commander, U.S. Marine Corps Forces Central Command, "MARCENT Briefing from Bahrain," April 24, 2003, www.defenselink.mil/transcripts/2003/tr20030424-0124.html.

[93] Graham and Loeb, "An Air War of Might, Coordination, and Risks."

[94] Source: www.aerovironment.com/area-aircraft/prod-serv/pointer.html.

[95] Gail Kaufman and Frank Tiboni, "US Army Lays Out UAV Plans," *Defense News*, June 16, 2003.

[96] Ibid.

[97] Commanding General, 1st Marine Division, "Operation Iraqi freedom (OIF): Lessons Learned."

[98] Department of Defense, www.defenselink.mil/news/Mar2003/t03182003_t0318uav.html.

[99] See www.defenselink.mil/news/Mar2003/n03182003_200303186.html.

[100] Walter Pincus and Dan Morgan, "Defense Bills Expected to Pass Quickly," *Washington Post*, May 19, 2003.

[101] See www.af.mil/news/factsheets/A_10_OA_10_Thunderbolt_II.html.

[102] Graham and Loeb, "An Air War of Might, Coordination, and Risks."

[103] See www.af.mil/news/factsheets/A_10_OA_10_Thunderbolt_II.html.

[104] Graham and Loeb, "An Air War of Might, Coordination, and Risks."

[105] Some 232 AH-64Ds are in service with the U.S. Army, and Boeing is upgrading 269 U.S. Army AH-64A Apaches to AH-64D standard by 2006. The technical description has been adapted from http://www.army-technology.com/projects/apache/.

[106] Stephen Trimble, "Apache Upgrades Rush to Units in Kuwait, Iraq," *Aerospace Daily*, April 22, 2003.

[107] Scott Calvert, "Army's Apache Gunships Carry Potent Sting," *Baltimore Sun*, March 17, 2003, Frank Tiboni, "US Army Seeks New Transports by 2008," *Defense News*, April 21, 2003, p. 22.

[108] Richard Whittle, "Military Mulls the Lessons of War," *Dallas Morning News*, April 22, 2003

[109] Rowan Scarborough, "Apache Operations a Lesson in Defeat," *Washington Times*, April 22, 2003, p. 1.

[110] Rowland Scarborough, "General Tells How Cell Phone Foiled US Attack on Iraq," *Washington Times*, May 8, 2003, p. 13.

[111] "Interview: General Richard Myers," *Defense News*, April 14, 2003, p. 46.

[112] Steven Komarow, "General Recounts Key Moments in Baghdad's Fall," *USA Today*, April 14, 2003, p. 5.

[113] Lt. Gen. William Scott Wallace, "Fifth Corps Commander Live Briefing from Baghdad," May 7, 2003, www.defenselink.mil/transcripts/2003/tr20030507-0157.html.

[114] Maj. Gen. David H. Petraeus, commanding general, 101st Airborne Division (Air Assault), "101st Airborne Division Commander Live Briefing from Iraq," May 13, 2003.

[115] For a discussion of some of the issues involved, see David A. Fulghum, "Not So Fast: Battle of Baghdad Delayed," *Aviation Week*, March 31, 2003.

[116] Merrill A. McPeak, "Leave the Flying to Us," *Washington Post*, June 5, 2003, p. 33.

[117] Major Jamie Cox, USMC, "MILINET: A Cobra Pilot's Eye-View of Iraqi Freedom," May 10, 2003, available at www.grunt.com/forum.

[118] Marine Corps Lt. Gen. Earl B. Hailston, Commander, U.S. Marine Corps Forces Central Command, "MARCENT Briefing from Bahrain."

[119] Commanding General, 1st Marine Division, "Operation Iraqi freedom (OIF): Lessons Learned."

[120] See David Fulghum, "Info Warfare to Invade Air Defense Networks," *Aviation Week*, November 30, 2003, p. 30; "US, Britain Double Dailey flights over Southern Iraq," *Baltimore Sun*, March 6, 2003; Eric Schmitt, "Air Patrols Shift Targets in Iraq, Clearing the Way for Attack," *New York Times*, September 17, 2002, p. 1; "Strikes in the No Fly Zones," *International Herald Tribune*, October 2, 2002, p. 4; "No Fly Zone Pilots to Benefit in Case of War with Saddam," *Washington Times*, August 27, 2002, p. 7; Hugh Pope and Christopher Cooper, "Iraqi Fire in No Fly Zones Provokes Divisions at UN," *Wall Street Journal*, November 20, 2002; Peter Baker, "Casualties of an Undeclared War," *Washington Post*, December 22, 2002, sec. A, p. 1; Rowland Scarborough, "US Offers Proof of Iraqi Defiance," *Washington Times*, October 1, 2002, sec. A, p. 1; Todd Zeranski and Tony Capaccio, "US, UK Strike No Fly Target in Iraq," Bloomberg.com, September 9, 2002.

[121] USEUCOM and USCENTCOM briefings. One report says 4,000 sorties between March 1 and 19; see Marj Mazzetti and Richard J. Newman, "The Seeds of Victory," *U.S. News & World Report,* April 21, 2003.

[122] Ibid.

[123] Gordon, "US Attacked Iraqi Air Defenses Starting in 2002"; Graham, "US Moved Early for Air Supremacy."

[124] For the full *Aviation Week* text, see www.aviationnow.com/avnow/news/channel_awst_story.jsp?id=news/04213iraq.xml.

[125] Adapted from Moseley, "Operation Iraqi Freedom—By the Numbers."

[126] Riad Kahwar, "Kuwaiti, US Patriots Found Success against Iraqi Missiles," *Defense News,* June 23, 2003.

[127] Andrea Stone, "Patriot Missile: Friend of Foe to Allied forces," *USA Today,* April 15, 2003, p. 6; Glenn W. Goodman, "New Questions Surround Patriot Missile System," *Defense News,* April 7, 2003, p. 8.

[128] Jon R. Anderson, "Army Stands behind Patriot Missile System as Critics Question Its Value," *Stars and Stripes,* May 6, 2003.

[129] Charles Piller, "Vaunted Patriot Missile Has a Friendly Fire Failing," *Los Angeles Times,* April 21, 2003, p. 1; Marc Selinger, "Kadhish, Christie Pleased with Patriot Performance," *Aerospace Daily,* April 22, 2003.

[130] Anne Marie Squeo, "Radiation May Impair Patriot Missile System," *Wall Street Journal,* May 23, 2003.

[131] Bradley Graham, "Radar Probed in Patriot Incidents," *Washington Post,* May 8, 2003, p. 21; Jon R. Anderson, "Army Stands behind Patriot Missile System as Critics Question Its Value," *Stars and Stripes,* May 6, 2003.

[132] Department of Defense briefing on April 23, 2003, www.defenselink.mil/transcripts/2003/tr20030423-0122.html.

CHAPTER NINE

LESSONS AFFECTING ARMY LAND FORCES

Once again, no set of lessons can be decoupled from the overall lessons regarding joint operations. The commander, Third U.S. Army and U.S. Army Forces Central Command and the Coalition Forces Land Component Command—Lt. Gen. David D. McKiernan—made this clear when he summed up the campaign at a briefing on April 23, 2003:

> This has been a joint campaign. We have applied on a continuous basis the power of the air component, of the land component, of the maritime component, of special operating forces and information operations.
>
> My intent for this ground portion of the campaign was basically to put continuous pressure on the regime of Saddam Hussein, and my mission was to remove that regime and search for, and find, and be part of the process of disarming weapons of mass destruction.
>
> This ground campaign to date has reflected itself in high-tempo continuous operations, decisive maneuver, extended logistical support, where I accepted some risk in the length of our lines of communication and our logistical reach…we have overcome that risk, and a execution of a plan that had several options in it but always remained focused on the enemy.
>
> Most of our combat vehicles have driven in excess of a thousand miles to date. They have not run out of fuel. Our maintenance status is in good shape. Our logistics has been sustained and will continue to be sustained.
>
> And I would refute any notion that there was any kind of operational pause in this campaign. There was never a day, there was never a moment where there was not continuous pressure put on the regime of Saddam by one of those components—air, ground, maritime, Special Forces and so on.
>
> But most importantly, the battles that have been won by the ground component have been won by individual soldiers and Marines and small-unit tactical skill.
>
> It has not come without price. It has been a tough fight. And to date, we have suffered over 600 casualties in this fight. We have not suffered the last casualty.

And today, D plus 35, where we sit is in a blurred transition between combat operations and post-hostilities operations. We're still fighting pockets of resistance throughout Iraq, and we're still dealing with paramilitary forces.

...There are some places where we continue to find pockets of regime resistance. We had some fighting last night in the Tikrit area. We'll have some fighting in other places as we continue to expand our control of the battle space. There's a second category of paramilitaries—some of those, many of those are not Iraqi, they've come in from other countries—they will continue to have to clear and deal with. And then there is a continued threat of protecting the force from suicide bombers or any other lethal threats that our forces might face. So I would say that the large combat decisive operations are probably coming to a close, but there are still pockets of resistance that we're having to deal with.

We have found probably very small numbers of mechanized or wheeled Iraqi vehicles that are being used, and we also continue to find some that have been abandoned and many that have been destroyed.

...And we're still expanding the ground component battle space. Today we have elements of the 101st Air Assault in Mosul. We have elements of the United States 5th Corps extending out into the western part of Iraq. We're securing—continuing to secure Baghdad, Tikrit, other urban areas. But rapidly we are transitioning to a focus on civil military operations and an effort to restore basic services to the Iraqi people that are either at or better than their prewar standards.

My commanders have the authority across Iraq to work with local Iraqi workers, clerics, political figures, bureaucrats, to get Iraqis back into the workplace and back in control of their destiny. And at my level, I am teaming very hard with Jay Garner and ORHA, the Office of Reconstruction and Humanitarian Assistance, as we together try to bring civil administration back on line here in Iraq and get the basic services and businesses and economy back on line.

I would tell you that all of us can be very proud of our service members—all services. They have all participated and all been vital to the success of this campaign to date. You can be proud of our military capability and that of our coalition partners.

...we are more of a joint military organization than we ever have been. And the ability and the coordination between air, maritime, ground, special operating forces has been to a degree that I have—in over 30 years, I've never witnessed before. It's never perfect—no military operation is perfect, but jointness has been huge in this campaign. I would also tell you that our training and our training doctrine that is both service-related and joint-related has been—and I'd kind of like to think I was part of that; that we've been working very hard for the last decade—paid off in spades in this military operation.

Abrams and $258.8 million for the Bradley because of their performance in the Iraq War.[5]

The British Ministry of Defense too has concluded that the war demonstrated the value of the British Challenger tank, as well as of Britain's armored self-propelled artillery:[6]

> In addition to the quality of our people, the reliability, mobility, and protection offered by Challenger 2, Warrior and AS90 contributed to the coalition's success on land. The operation confirmed that protection is vital when an enemy (regular or irregular) is using direct or indirect weapon systems.
>
> ...Challenger 2, Warrior, and AS90 all proved to be battle-winning equipment and achieved very high availability levels. Dust mitigation measures for Challenger 2 were effective, and overcame the difficulties reported during Exercise SAIF SAREEA II. The low level of UK casualties is a reflection of the outstanding protection afforded by our armored vehicles.

This does not mean that the U.S. Army and other forces cannot find new, lighter combat systems to replace the 70-ton M-1A2. It does indicate, though, that interim systems such as the Stryker could not be an effective substitute for heavy armor in major regional contingencies. An even more serious problem is the extent to which the conversion of systems like the Abrams, with weights of nearly 80 tons, to developmental systems such as 20-ton weapons with similar war-fighting capabilities or to robotic weapons can actually take the place of heavy armor.

The U.S. Army has awarded Boeing a limited contract to design and test new forms of tanks and armored warfare systems for the army 's Future Combat Systems (FCS).[7] The resulting "mounted combat system" is designed to produce a family of armored vehicles in the 22- to 24-ton range, with optional add-on armor, that could provide protection against most threats other than a direct hit by a tank round or advanced anti-tank guided weapon.[8] It would also include a new form of 155-mm self-propelled cannon using the same basic chassis. The army has never, however, been able to develop a major weapon on time, at the projected cost, and with the projected efficiency, or to deploy a combat-ready system without years of follow-on modification based on practical experience with troops and in different types of combat and areas of the world.

The first FCS brigade would not be deployable as a test force before 2012 at the earliest even if its component weapons met their schedule and had the proper effectiveness. But the plans so far have been poorly defined and subject to constant revision. A service with a zero historical success rate in meeting its own cost, performance, and scheduling goals for major

Nevertheless, there are a number of lessons that do primarily land forces.

THE VALUE OF MAIN BATTLE TANKS AND HEAVY FIREPOWER AND ARMOR

For all the talk of force transformation, the accounts of fighting by bo the 3rd U.S. Army Infantry Division and 1st Marine Division make it clea that the M-1A1 Abrams Main Battle Tank, and its combination of protec tion and firepower, played a critical role in ensuring that Iraq's forces could not bring tanks to bear at engagement ranges that allowed them to be effective, and that the superior protection of the M-1A1 greatly re- duced losses and casualties. The 120mm gun on the M-1A1, for example, has a nominal maximum engagement range of about 3,000 meters. The T- 72 can fire accurately out to about 2,500 meters but has far worse sights, fire control systems, and sensors. The older T-55 is limited to about 2,000 meters and has poor fire control systems and stabilization.[1] The protec- tion and firepower of the M-2A3 Bradley proved to be equally important in dealing with irregular forces like Saddam's Fedayeen and other "techni- cals" and suicide attacks.[2]

General Richard Myers, the chairman of the Joint Chiefs, described the role of armor in the Iraq War as follows:[3]

> I don't think anybody has ever said that as you transform the force, and you try to become more easily deployable, you want to get rid of everything old. The Army's Future Combat System, which will eventually replace the M-1 tanks, is meant to have as much lethality and survivability on the battle- field, but be different than trying to do it by adding more and more ar- mor to something.
>
> But, it was never said that things like the M1 tanks and M2 Bradley Fight- ing Vehicles are not required. That's never been part of the discussion. Some of these systems have a lot of value and will have a lot of value for a long time to come.

Legacy versus Future Combat Systems

The Iraq War demonstrated the value of heavy armor, at least in terms of firepower and force protection. There are some indications that as a result of the lessons of the Iraq War, the U.S. Army is already rethinking some of its plans to cut armor modernization.[4] Similarly, the House Armed Ser- vices Committee has approved $726.8 million to upgrade elements of U.S. armor such as the Abrams tank and Bradley, with $24 million for the new combat systems is not in a position to learn from this war that a tank in the bush is worth more than one at hand.

It is equally important that the army have a real-world picture of just how much more rapidly it can deploy sustainable FCS for future major regional contingencies than it can its existing force. If such forces still have to move largely by sealift and still require secure major ports and extensive deployments of ammunition, supplies, and fuel, the fact that individual systems are smaller and lighter may not have as significant an impact on total force deployability as equipment comparisons would indicate. Equipment-versus-equipment comparisons are not force-versus-force comparisons, and only the latter are relevant in measuring war-fighting capability.[9]

Tank Losses, Causes, and Lessons Learned

Questions do arise, however, about what would have happened if Iraq had had large numbers of more modern anti-tank guided weapons like the Russian-designed Kornet. Iraq's anti-armor inventory—like that of most of its weapons—had been largely frozen in time since the UN embargo on Iraqi arms imports in August 1990. No official data are currently available on the exact details of M-1 and M-2 losses during the Iraq War, but it may be that they would have provided less protection against a force with more modern weapons. At the same time, other questions arise as to whether the U.S. Army can justify light AFVs to replace heavy ones when casualties would have been much heavier in Iraq had light AFVs been used.

At this point, unofficial sources disagree sharply over the source of M-1A1 losses and their implications. One source, Col. David Hackworth, reports that a total of 151 M-1A1 tanks were hit, that three were destroyed by AT-14 Kornet ATGMs, and that 12 were damaged beyond economical repair. He also reports that Iraqis destroyed 16 AFVs and seriously damaged 35 more, and that a total of 23 M-113 APC and 53 trucks were destroyed. Almost all of these hits were the result of RPGs that could potentially defeat the Stryker.[10] Colonel Hackworth charges that the Department of Defense has failed to address the fact such hits occurred because it wants to convert from heavy armor to a 20-ton family of AFVs that can be transported rapidly by air (an estimated ability to transport four AFVs versus one M-1 in a C-5B; two to three AFVs versus one M-1 in a C-17; and one AFV versus none in a C-130).

Another source—Tom Cooper, the editor of the Air Combat Information Group—has reported that no coalition vehicles are known to have been lost to strikes by AT-14 Kornet ATGMs, although Syria delivered 200 rounds and 12 launchers to Iraq in the autumn of 2003. One M-1A1 fell into the Euphrates River after the driver was shot while crossing the bridge, but no M-1s had yet been destroyed by enemy fire.[11] All combat losses of M-1A1s initially occurred because of RPG-7/16 hits into the engine compartment, open turret hatches, or fuel cells. In most cases, the tanks then had to be abandoned and left to burn out. In one case, an M-1A1 was set afire and then hit by a coalition air strike to deny it to the Iraqis. Cooper reports that Iraqis probably captured a total of seven M-1A1s—of which only three were intact—but lacked the time and equipment to tow them away. One burned-out M-1A1 that was initially captured by the Iraqis ("Cojone EH") was later recovered by the U.S. Army.[12]

Cooper reports the following total losses of armored vehicles by cause:

- U.S. Army
  - 1 M-1A1 Abrams by Hellfire from USMC AH-1W near Basrah; recovered
  - 3 M-1A1 Abrams 3-7th Cavalry by Iraqi RPG-7 shots from the rear near Karbala; fate unknown
  - 1 M-1A1, probably 3-7th Cavalry, U.S. Army; captured almost intact; date and place unknown (video released by Iraqi TV after the same battle near Karbala in which 3-7th Cavalry lost three M-1A1s, and together with the video of the M-9 captured intact)
  - 2 M-1A1s of 3rd BCT/3rd ID (Mech) on April 3; some 10km south of Baghdad; fate of crews unknown
  - 1 M-1A1 "Cojone EH," 2nd BCT/3rd ID (Mech), on April 6, during the raid into Baghdad downtown; set afire after RPG-7-damage to a fuel cell; wrecked by coalition air strike; wreck recovered
  - 1 M-113A-3 (fitter's vehicle) of 3rd ID (Mech), on April 3; fate of crew unknown
  - 1 M-109A6 Paladin by ammunition explosion; burned out
  - 1 M-9 (captured together with three M-1A1s of the 3-7th Cavalry)
  - claims for up to five M-2 and M-3 Bradleys lost during the fighting so far, but none were confirmed by photographic evidence.

- USMC
  - 2 AAV-7s by Iraqi RPG-7 shots in An Nasiriyah; both destroyed; number of casualties unknown (several other AAV-7s got bogged down in the mud or fell into irrigation ditches, but all were recovered)
  - 1 AAV-7 of USMC on April 1 or 2, place unknown; one KIA
  - 1 AAV-7 of 3-4 Marines on April 7 near Baghdad; one KIA
  - 1 M-1A1 fell from bridge when driver was shot by Iraqis; crew KIA; not recovered

— 2 M-1A1s on April 5, four kilometers south of Baghdad; two crew KIA, several injured
— 1 M-1A1 2nd Tank Battalion/1st MARDIV near Sayyid Abd, on April 6; disabled, crew fate unknown
— There are rumors about one LAV-25 of the USMC being destroyed as well; there is no confirmation except this blurred picture, which seems to be showing the "fitter's vehicle" version that fell into a ditch (and was certainly recovered).

- British Army
  — On March 25 a Challenger 2 from C Squadron, Queen's Royal Lancers (part of the Royal Regiment of Fusiliers Battle Group) had the turret and glacis severely damaged when another Challenger 2 attached to the Black Watch Battle Group mistakenly engaged it in the middle of a series of night contacts with Iraqi forces along the Shatt-al-Basra canal. The driver and tank commander were killed, but the gunner and loader, while seriously injured, are recovering.
  — On March 28 a Scimitar CVR(T)s from D Squadron of the Household Cavalry Division (attached to 16th Air Assault Brigade) was destroyed in a daylight blue-on-blue engagement by a USAF A-10 on a road along the Shatt-al-Arab, northwest of ad-Dayr. One British soldier was killed and four wounded.
  — A picture of a Challenger 2 with a damaged track was published, and there are also reports about a Warrior or Scimitar AFV damaged after driving over an unexploded 60mm mortar shell.

Cooper also reported that the U.S. Army and USMC lost between 25 and 30 Hummer "jeeps" (including at least five by RPG-7s), as well as up to 20 different trucks so far. Also damaged was an U.S. Army Patriot fire-control radar; this was hit by an AGM-88 HARM, fired from an USAF F-16C on a patrol over southern Iraq, when the radar established a lock-on on the fighter.

Still another source, "Strategy Page," reports a series of far more detailed lessons, many of which are supported by e-mails from the U.S. Army 3rd Infantry Division. These reports indicate that 14 tanks were damaged and 2 were destroyed:[13]

There were no catastrophic losses due to Iraqi direct or indirect fire weapons:
- several tanks were destroyed due to secondary effects attributed to enemy weapon systems;
- majority of losses attributed to mechanical breakdown and vehicle either being stripped for parts or severely vandalized by Iraqi people;
- no reported case of an AGTM being fired at any U.S. Army vehicle;
- no Kornet missiles found in country.

Two M-1A1s may have been knocked out by friendly fire in a night battle outside Najaf on March 24–25. The evidence indicates a hit on the rear by eight rounds from the 25mm gun on a Bradley, rather than an Iraqi weapon.

The M-1A1's frontal turret and hull armor continues to provide excellent crew protection, but its top, side, and rear armor remains susceptible to penetration:

- documented instances where 25mm AP-DU and above ammunition disabled a tank from the rear;
- left- and right-side non-ballistic skirts repeatedly penetrated by anti-armor RPG fire;
- cosmetic damage only when struck by anti-personnel RPG rounds;
- no reported hits on ballistic skirts;
- no reported instance of tank hitting an anti-tank mine.

The turret ammunition blast doors worked as designed:

- documented instance where turret ready rack compartment hit and main gun rounds ignited. Blast doors contained the explosion and crew survived unharmed except for fume inhalation;
- externally stored items highly vulnerable to small arms fire;
- in some instances, catastrophic losses resulted from burning EAPU material and/or packaged POL products dripping down into the engine compartment catching the engine on fire;
- many instances where TA-50 lost or damaged due to enemy fire or secondary effect.

It was only a fear of vehicle/technology compromise that led to decisions to destroy abandoned tanks:

- tanks repeatedly shot by friendly fire; however they *never* catastrophically destroyed the tanks except in one instance;
- took one thermite grenade, one sabot in turret ammunition compartment, and two Maverick missiles to finally destroy the tank. Ended up compromising the SAP armor package during the destruction process.

The individual protective equipment worked well:

- JLIST suits are much better than the old NBC suits;
- CVC's *will* stop a 7.62 mm round.

In terms of firepower:

- very little SABOT was used, but had devastating effects when used;
- heat and MPAT ended up being the preferred main gun round, and were effective against buildings and bunkers;
- crew served machine guns ended up being weapon of choice in numerous engagements;
- target-rich environment;

- Iraqis hid in fighting positions until tanks were very near before attacking, thus negating the use of the main gun.

There is no way yet to resolve these differences or verify the accuracy of these data. Clearly, however, armored protection remains a critical capability on the battlefield. On the subject of reports that the director of force transformation in the Department of Defense had said the Iraq War showed that heavy tanks are no longer needed, one analyst commented informally as follows:

The Navy gave up its battleships over a decade ago. Except for the CVNs, Navy ships have virtually no armor—if they get hit, they are seriously damaged or sunk. VADM Cebrowski now wants the Army to follow suit and give up its main battle tanks. The problem is that in a naval environment, one can keep the enemy at a considerable standoff because sensor ranges are generally many miles out, thus buying time for defenses and countermeasures to work. In land warfare, an ATGM can fly as fast as an anti-ship cruise missile, but thanks to terrain and "cultural features" it may be fired from only a kilometer or two away. A tank main gun round is much faster, and can travel several kilometers, and is even less susceptible to countermeasures. In both cases, the tank has only a very narrow window in which to defend itself or employ countermeasures, and the effectiveness of those countermeasures is likely to be much lower.

Before we try to go from a 70-ton to a nominal 35-ton tank, we need to ascertain the full extent of the changes in doctrine, tactics, equipment, and training that will entail, and whether breakthroughs in armor technology, weapons, active protection suites, power systems, etc. will be able to "deliver the goods." While Russian and French tanks are smaller and lighter than U.S. tanks, it is unclear that they are as lethal, survivable, and reliable/maintainable as U.S. tanks. It is also worth considering that even with an advanced hybrid turbo-diesel-electric drive instead of a fuel-slurping gas turbine, U.S. tanks are expected to have a greater unrefueled range than most foreign tanks, and fuel weights.

Stryker Brigades do not give tactical airlift-delivered light infantry a useful level of protection or firepower. While better protected than Armored HMMWVs, they are more susceptible to hostile fire than the M113 upgrade known as the MTLV, just as vulnerable, while providing less firepower. They are also much harder to squeeze into a C-130. The Stryker's only advantage is for on-road speed/fuel economy. Forces in STRYKER Brigades are still light infantry, albeit motorized light infantry. They must still fight dismounted, since the vehicles provide no protection against RPGs, anti-vehicle mines, or automatic weapons over 14.5mm. The MGS cannot fit into a C-130, and there is still no 120mm mortar variant.

A serious medium force would be based upon the proven, thoroughly developed M2/M3 Bradley, which has ample firepower to overmatch anything short of a tank, and with Javelin ATGMs can handle that threat, too. Of course, this would require the politically unpopular move of replacing the Air Force's C-130s with C-17s on a one-for-one basis if the force were to be at least initially emplaced by air, and deploying more fast sealift (both intertheater and intratheater) for maritime deployment where feasible. But Afghanistan and Iraq demonstrated both the current forces' impressive capabilities for difficult (though largely uncontested) entry, and their sustainment limitations over extended overland LOCs.

"PRECISION ARTILLERY" AS A PARTNER TO "PRECISION AIR POWER"

As is the case with the use of air power, there are no battle damage assessment data on artillery. There also is no way to determine the importance of artillery relative to air power, or the relative usage and effectiveness of given artillery weapons. Some advances are clear. The flow of intelligence and targeting data to artillery units was better than in previous wars, and artillery was more maneuverable and quicker to react. It took eight minutes to set up the standard M109 155mm howitzer in the Gulf War. It took 30 seconds to set up the army's Paladin 155mm howitzer in the Iraq War. [14]

Some preliminary reports indicate that the United States was able to use long-range artillery and artillery rockets such as the ATACMS to strike at Iraqi forces long before they could close on U.S. forces and also to compensate for the problems air power experienced in flying attack and close air support missions during sandstorms. At the same time, other reports state that F-15s used targeting data from the E-8C JSTARS to launch GPS-guided bombs during the sandstorm and were the dominant weapon damaging Iraqi armor. [15]

Major General Buford C. Blount, the commander of the U.S. army 3rd Infantry Division, described the role of artillery in a briefing on May 15, 2003. He stated that long-range artillery was of major value, although he indicated that the army was not ready to issue battle damage assessment data: [16]

...Let me address the last piece first. It's the first time we've used the SA-DARM in combat, and it worked very well. We had several opportunities to use that, with two or three of our new systems, one being the LRAS, which gave our reconnaissance elements a capability to look out seven or eight kilometers and lase to a target and get a 10-digit grid, [it] really enhanced the capability of our munitions from our artillery systems to be lethal against armored targets. And so we're very happy with that link-up and the success that we had using that....you know, we had a lot of counter-battery fire. We received a lot of artillery and mortar fire, and are very pleased with our radar acquisitions, our ability to acquire the mortars and artillery shooting at us. And then we used various means for counter-battery, used artillery, used MOS rockets, and we also made good use of CAS, which was readily available. So we had basically three systems that we could use to take down his artillery, his mortar systems as he engaged us, as we conducted our movements. And that worked out very well.

...We're not going to at this point release our numbers of BDAs on tanks, personnel, et cetera. We are compiling that still. I can tell you that we engaged multiple divisions and defeated multiple divisions on the battlefield, from the 11th Division—(Inaudible.)—division, multiple Republican Guards divisions plus the Special Republican Guard units, and multiple elements of the Fedayeen. So it was a real combination of forces that we took on in each fight as we attacked in the multiple cities that we fought through.

...Some of our new equipment worked very well.... one is our friendly force tracker system, which enabled the leadership to command and control on the move, and we did that from a new command and control vehicle that we had, [the] C2V. So in the C2V we had the friendly force tracker system, which enabled us to see all of our leadership on the battlefield, plus we could see where the MEF was, and the 101st, and any element in the theater that had their systems on. So that gave us a situational awareness from where we were on the battlefield.

...And then our communications, our ATACS communications, which is a new system to us, enabled us to talk over extreme distances....[As] an example, in one day we had the division over about a 230-kilometer front and we were attacking and fighting in basically three separate fights, and we were able to command and control that, divert resources or fix priorities, be able to talk to each commander, be able to see where his forces were and what was happening on the battlefield, and do all that while we were moving....[This was] just a tremendous capability, a tremendous success for the Army. And that's just one or two of several of the systems that we have. I mentioned one, the LRAS, which is a night observation—or day/night observation sight for our reconnaissance elements, just a tremendous success.

The MLRS/ATACMS

Television coverage showed that the 3rd Infantry Division made heavy use of tube artillery and the MLRS/ATACMS during sandstorms, at night, and in clashes with Iraqi forces in better weather and where attack helicopters and attack fighters were present. The marines also made extensive use of their towed tube artillery, even though it involved much longer set-up and emplacement times.

Major General David H. Petraeus, commanding general of the 101st Airborne Division (Air Assault), stated that his division used 114 ATAC-MS and used them in conjunction with both attack helicopters and in forces whose combined arms elements made equally good use of anti-tank guided weapons as precision artillery:[17]

> First, the ATACMS were tremendous. You obviously have to have a large area to fire them into. Needless to say, we didn't use them anywhere near built-up areas or civilian targets. We did use them, again, very, very effectively out in the desert, both west of Karbala and northwest of Karbala, packaged with our Apaches for both suppression of enemy air defenses en route to battle positions and then once our Apaches were in those positions. As I mentioned earlier, those missiles clear a grid square, a square kilometer. And so, those are incredibly lethal. And they were absolutely devastating against those enemy targets in which we employed them....

> I don't know how many Javelins we used, and I'll probably have to research that. I do know that we used Javelins and TOW missiles on a number of occasions, and also the SMAW-D, the squad medium anti-tank weapon, which is a very good bunker buster....we used these against buildings typically in the outskirts of cities and then inside when we encountered fire.

> One of my battalions [that] went in with 3 ID to the airport and cleared the airport terminal, and later fought a very, very substantial fight at the east gate of the terminal—I believe that they also used the Javelin quite effectively that night that they were attacked, along with a lot of close air support, and again, the TOW ITAS system, which proved very, very effective for us.

> The FLIR and the TOW ITAS in particular, was the hero of the battlefield. It enabled us to see the enemy way, way out before he could even believe we could see him. And that night outside the airfield, for example, our TOW gunners could see the enemy and bring in either close air support or artillery before the enemy even realized he was being seen. Same with, of course, the tank FLIR or the Avenger FLIR.

The Potential Impact of SADARM

U.S. artillery forces will have acquired considerably more lethality if the use of the SADARM proves to have been effective. The new M898 SADARM is the artillery's first fire-and-forget multisensor munition. It can be fired from any 155mm howitzer and delivers two separate submunitions with one projectile. It is an indirect fire munition intended primarily to counter enemy artillery, and it is fired after counter-battery radar, such as the Q37 Firefinder, locates enemy artillery. It can also attack other armored vehicles and air defense systems.[18]

When it nears the indirect fire impact area, the two submunitions are released from the SADARM projectile and slowed by ram-air inflated devices. Next, a parachute-like vortex ring puffs out and rotates the submunition to make it arm. In a complex internal sensors communication scenario, which takes only milliseconds, the munition "determines" its altitude and scans for threats. Once the munition detects a target, internal sensors and a processor validate it, make a decision to select it, and destroy the target by firing an explosively formed penetrator into it.

The device is exceptionally "smart." Using active and passive millimeter wave and infrared sensors, it locates a target and verifies its signature—its unique size, shape, and relationship to its background. SADARM then uses this information to select a real target from a group of potential real and false targets. For example, it will not confuse a heated aluminum shed with a howitzer, or a small building with an air defense system.

At the same time, press reports of numerous other incidents make a strong case for better communications and control and for the improvements the "digital army" is intending to make in communications, targeting, and situational awareness that will allow more effective use of artillery. Targeting was often a problem, and ground troops could not coordinate precisely with artillery units to target fires quickly and accurately at the highest-priority targets. This was a particularly severe problem in urban areas but also affected combat in the field. It is clear from this experience that the reaction times involved could still be improved to provide better time-on-target capability.

It seems likely that the availability of the sensor-fused weapon would have helped in artillery attacks on armor in some cases, and guided artillery projectiles would have helped in others. In short, important improvements in artillery capability currently in development probably would have made artillery significantly more effective in the Iraq War if they had already been fielded.

One lesson that the Iraq War does not support is trade-offs between artillery, rotary-wing attack helicopters, and fixed-wing attack aircraft. The data to date indicate that Iraqi forces could rarely close on U.S. Army and Marine Corps forces in sufficient strength to put a major strain on air attack resources. Some have suggested that this makes systems such as the MLRS and ATACMS less important. It seems doubtful, however, that many wars against major regional opponents can be fought with a similar degree of air supremacy, and one key to the ability of U.S. ground forces to maneuver so quickly and aggressively is their ability to bring firepower to bear in an emergency. It is dangerous to propose trade-offs based on an opponent that may be unique in many ways without far clearer data in terms of the actual killing power of air and artillery systems, and without full consideration of the risks imposed in terms of maneuver warfare.

SPECIAL FORCES AS AN ELEMENT OF JOINT WARFARE

Special Forces and Ranger forces played a major role throughout Iraq. The new interactions between Special Forces, precision air power, and advanced IS&R systems demonstrated during the Afghan conflict are redefining the role of Special Forces. There are reports that General Tommy Franks found Special Forces to be so effective during the fighting in Afghanistan that he deployed some 9,000 to 10,000 personnel in similar roles in Iraq.[19] Some estimates put the total at 8 percent of the forces actually engaged in combat.

Special Forces were generally employed in teams of 12 or smaller and had numerous special purpose aircraft, including a peak strength of 8 AC-130 gunships, 8 HC-130s, 8 EC-130s, 14 MH-47s, 31 MH-53s, 7 MH-6s, and 18 MH-60s. They were employed in joint operations with small elements of armor and the forces of the 173rd Airborne Brigade, and with strike aircraft. Improvements in communications and command and control allowed commanders and other forces to locate Special Forces units with far more accuracy than in the past and to communicate with them in near real-time in missions like the time-sensitive targeting of strike aircraft.

The Tactical Role of Special Forces

As chapter 4 made clear, U.S., British, and Australian Special Forces were involved in a wide range of missions and were employed in much of Iraq before the war formally began on March 19. It is also clear that they performed a wide range of missions ranging from securing Iraq's offshore oil export terminals to combined arms operations with tanks during the advance on Tikrit.

These missions often played a critical role in working with friendly Iraqis such as the Kurds in the north, in finding and illuminating targets for air attack, in searching for Iraqi missiles and weapons of mass destruction, in securing Iraqi facilities in the west, in other operations in the north and in Baghdad, and in securing Iraqi oil facilities and export terminals in the Gulf.[20] The role of the CIA has had only limited public discussion.

However, at least two Special Operations Groups were in place in Iraq in the Kurdish enclave weeks before the war began, one with Barazani and one with Talibani, and other teams were probably involved. The CIA teams seem to have had Special Forces seconded to them or working closely with them.

The exact role the Special Forces played in the west is unclear, but they seem to have allowed the United States to maintain a significant presence with limited forces, assisting in the capture of Iraqi airfields like H-2 and H-3. The relative static character of Iraqi forces and their lacks of sensors and communications allowed Special Forces to operate and maneuver with considerable freedom in the open desert areas of the west. Their ability to help cover large amounts of space in missions such as the search for Iraqi missiles and weapons of mass destruction seems to have improved significantly since the Gulf War. This is in part because of better communications and links to U.S. intelligence assets and airborne sensors, and in part because commanders in the rear could do a much better job of locating Special Forces, communicating with them, and providing air support.

Technology

It seems clear from press reports and discussions with those involved that the ability of Special Forces to call in air strikes and either illuminate targets or provide GPS coordinates compensated in at least some cases for their lack of heavy weapons and firepower. Their ability to use secure communications and displays, and their use of new systems such as the individual transponders or "Blue trackers," also gave them a new degree of situational awareness and allowed them to coordinate more closely with other ground forces and operate in ways where higher echelons of command could do more to coordinate their operations.

The two-pound transmitters were about the size of a small Walkman and sent codes every 5 minutes to 10 minutes identifying the units and their GPS coordinates. This allowed the Special Forces to be fully coordinated in battle plans where their location could be mapped relative to friendly armored forces and threat data, and allowed for far more effective coordination on fluid battlefields. The U.S. Special Forces Command has purchased some 1,680 transmitters and 27 aircraft-mounted receivers. The transmitters were developed in cooperation with the National Reconnaissance Organization (NRO) and U.S. Space Command, and they can be read by U.S. satellites. Representatives of Special Forces at the CAOC helped coordinate the effort to use the data for battle management purposes.[21]

"Snake Eaters" with Master's Degrees

U.S. Special Forces also seem to have been one of the few combat elements with the language skills and area training needed to work closely with opposition forces like the Kurdish Pershmerga and to make effective use of the volunteers from external Iraqi opposition groups who were trained to act as liaisons between U.S. forces and the Iraqi people. One of the almost constant problems in U.S. operations during the war was that U.S. units had far too few local Arabic speakers and far too few experts on Iraqi religious and cultural practices, with the result that they were not prepared to deal with Iraqi civilians or Iraqi military who attempted to communicate with them.

This deficiency was not critical during battles with Iraqi Republican Guards or conventional forces or in firefights. But there was a clear and vital need for units trained in asymmetric warfare and equipped with language skills and area training in the north and the west. The Iraq War also demonstrated the natural synergy between the Special Forces of Australia, Britain, and the United States and intelligence operations by organizations such as the CIA. Special Forces have evolved beyond the mythos of combat elements like Delta Force and the sheer drama of sudden assaults on terrorists by the SAS.

The special training and tactics of special operations forces still give them the war-fighting capabilities of "snake eaters." However, special operations forces now do far more than carry out covert operations and dramatic raids. They now often are high-technology "snake eaters" with master's degrees. They are forces that have special area and language training, and that carry out a variety of specialized intelligence missions. They are also forces that employ lasers, new radar sensors, computers, UAVs, and the kind of netting that makes use of GPS, computers, and new communications links for joint warfare.

It is already clear that at least the United States has drawn the lesson that such forces are so valuable that they need significant expansion, a better-defined role in joint warfare, and higher priority for investment in new equipment. One key question that emerges from both the Afghan and Iraq conflicts, however, is how the structure and composition of special operations forces should change in the process, and whether standards should change to create more specialists in intelligence and civil action even if this means less demanding training and requirements for qualification as war fighters. Another equally important question is how special operations forces should be commanded and integrated into joint war fighting. The current thinking seems to emphasize placing larger elements of special operations forces more directly under joint command, but the nature of such reforms is unclear.

Tactics of Improved Jointness

Lt. Gen. David D. McKiernan gave Special Forces the following praise for their role in the battle:[22]

> ...I'm not the right one to comment on the special operating forces, because I don't command those. But I will tell you that their effects were felt before D-Day and are still felt today, that they have been a huge combat multiplier in this joint campaign to topple this regime.

It seems likely that Special Forces are becoming a critical new element of joint warfare in an era of asymmetric warfare. The history in this book can only hint at the details, however. It is also clear that there were occasions when the light weaponry of Special Forces presented serious problems in challenging Iraqi regular forces, particularly when air support was not immediately available. Task Force Red Devil, for example, encountered such problems in dealing with Iraqi artillery in an operation near the Kurdish security zone.[23]

As is the case with most of the lessons of the Iraq conflict, and the Afghan conflict as well, it is also important to consider the quality of the enemy. U.S. light forces are almost certain to be more successful when the enemy lacks leadership and motivation, and the definition of "light" is relative when it includes massive amounts of air support with precision-guided weapons.

There may well be a reason to seek to provide Special Forces with new transformational weapons and even better means of calling in air and missile support. However, most of the presently programmed improvements in U.S. Special Forces have grown out of the Afghan War, and it is too soon to estimate how the Iraq War will change these requirements.[24]

URBAN LAND WARFARE

Much of the past concern about urban warfare has centered on house-by-house or street-by-street fighting and on the risk that this kind of warfare commits Western forces in ways that severely limit their technological advantages and that can produce high casualties. As discussed in chapters 3 and 4, Iraq had some limited success in engaging U.S. and British forces in urban warfare. But it was never able to force them into intensive urban combat; it had lost most of its most effective forces before the battle of Baghdad began; and it was never able to mobilize an effective popular resistance. This makes it difficult to generalize about the lessons of urban warfare based on this experience.

Maneuverability Rather Than Fighting on Traditional Terms?

The U.S. Army and Marine Corps did demonstrate, however, that it is possible to use the new degree of situational awareness provided by modern IS&R assets to help overcome the enemy's superior knowledge of terrain and to move into the open areas of modern cities to conduct armored patrols with helicopter and air support.

Contrary to doctrine, armor often moved swiftly through modern cities in Iraq without forward screening by infantry patrols. It was able to find relatively open routes and exploit the longer fields of fire provided by major streets and boulevards. It could bypass crowded and narrow, packed areas, and it either had sufficient protection to survive limited clashes or could dismount infantry once the encounter began.

The United States showed that it could divide cities using key routes and areas of concentration rather than seeking to occupy large areas, and that it could "take a city" by focusing on seizing key symbols and centers of regime power.

Lt. Gen. William Wallace, commander of the 5th Corps, offered the following comments about urban warfare in Baghdad:[25]

> You have to go back to the battle of Najaf to understand our actions at that point, because that's where we learned we could do better. We learned that armor could fight in the city and survive, and that if you took heavy armored forces into the city—given the way Saddam was defending the city with technical vehicles and bunker positions—we could knock all of those defenses out and survive. As a result of Najaf, I think our soldiers also gained an extraordinary appreciation for the survivability of their equipment. So Najaf made decisions associated with being more aggressive when we got to Baghdad a hell of a lot easier.
>
> In fact, we found that the positioning of our forces around the palace downtown was actually more defensible than our positions on the outside of town, because the parks and broad plazas in the city gave us good fields of fire, and we were in a place where he couldn't mass his artillery on us because we were in the middle of his artillery forces....all of that added up to making our decision to stay in downtown Baghdad a good one. Third Infantry commander Maj. Gen. Buford Blount called me up and said, "Well, we control all the intersections, and I recommend we stay, because if we stay, we have the city." I agreed.
>
> One day our troops are kicking down doors, and the next they're passing out Band-Aids. And in some cases, they're kicking down doors without really

knowing if they are going to have to pull a trigger or pass out a Band-Aid on the other side. And it's really a remarkable tribute to the mental acuity of our soldiers that they are able to do that.

The U.S. experience in Al Hillah and An Nasiryah shows that these tactics might be much less effective against better-organized defenses. It also seems likely that the outcome would have been different if the Republican Guards had been organized into a cohesive, prepared urban defense and had not been committed piecemeal to combat outside urban and built-up areas. Accordingly, the lessons of urban warfare could be very different if future enemies are more cohesive and have time to organize.

Force the Defender to Maneuver and Move Outside of Cities

One possible lesson is also to force the enemy to move forward and to engage outside the urban area. The fact that the Republican Guard was forced into meeting engagements helped to ensure that Baghdad could not be defended effectively. If maneuver warfare can prevent reliance on urban defenses, and indeed static defenses of any kind, it greatly increases the effectiveness of every element of joint warfare.

Postwar Urban Warfare

At the same time, the losses the United States has taken to Iraqi attacks since the Iraqi Army ceased resistance in late April 2003 show that urban warfare can be serious even in what is supposed to be peacetime. As described in chapter 7, the U.S. Army has taken serious casualties as a result of irregular attacks since the war supposedly ended. Many have been in urban areas, where sniping, rocket-propelled grenades, bombing, and mortar attacks have posed a serious threat to U.S. forces and friendly Iraqis and where economic sabotage has also been an issue.

Urban warfare in Iraq has proved a peacemaking and nation-building problem, not simply a war-fighting problem. Moreover, this form of urban warfare has had to operate under different rules and in a highly political context where it may be impossible to use air power and where pushing the United States into the use of excessive force may be a major goal for an enemy. Similarly, it may be possible for an enemy to defeat the United States by alienating U.S. troops from the local population, and vice versa; by isolating the U.S. military and civilian presence by pushing it into an emphasis on protection; by blocking progress in the nation-building effort because NGOs and civilians will only take limited risks; and by creating a constant flow of low-level casualties whose political effect is congressional and popular calls for a U.S. withdrawal.

This highlights the need to see urban warfare in peacemaking and nation-building terms and the need to develop suitable tactics, training, and equipment.

RESEARCH AND RE-RESEARCH ON LOCAL WEATHER AND OPERATING CONDITIONS

No military forces in the world have more experience in operating in a wide range of climates and areas than U.S. military forces, or do more to adapt their equipment to global conditions. At the same time, every theater of operations places new and unexpected demands that have to be considered in going to war. These demands make forward area operations research critical, as well as careful research into weather and other factors that may alter the battlefield.

The United States was not surprised by sandstorms during the Iraq War; their effects had been studied in some detail. Nevertheless, the reality was more challenging than U.S. forces expected. Lt. Gen. Wallace, commander of the 5th Corps, made the following points about the impact of sandstorms and desert terrain after the fighting:[26]

> I was certainly happy with the way our forces handled the terrain. We captured a map that an Iraqi reconnaissance battalion commander in the Republican Guards was carrying, and it showed they were anticipating our forces to go exactly where we decided not to go, largely because the terrain between the Euphrates and Tigris Rivers was so difficult for maneuver forces.
>
> Having said that, we were surprised by the texture of the desert terrain. The dust problem in those areas was orders of magnitude worse than any of our terrain analysts had predicted. That caused us a number of problems. It caused us a problem in terms of convoy movement, and in terms of aviation assets. Anytime anything moved out there, it kicked up a dust cloud. It was like driving through talcum powder.
>
> Personally, the period during the dust storm was the low point of the entire campaign for me. That was definitely the hardest part and the low point of the war.

THE PROBLEM OF ALLIED POWER PROJECTION, INTEROPERABILITY, AND ALLIED WAR-FIGHTING CAPABILITY

More generally, the coalition experience in land warfare provides the same grim lessons for most European land forces, as well as for NATO and the European Union, as it did for air forces and does for sea forces. Britain is now the only European power with meaningful experience in modern land warfare, a high degree of combat readiness and professionalism, and serious power projection capability. Even Britain, however, cannot sustain heavy forces in long-distance combat maneuvers at long power projection ranges.

Although it may not be polite to say so, the European members of NATO and the European Union threaten to create cosmetic power projection forces at a time when they are becoming a coalition of the incapable. In the case of far too many European air and naval forces, there is no "Western" advantage in air power. Most European land forces lack sustainability, modern technology, effective readiness and training, and the capability either to act as independent expeditionary forces or to be fully interoperable with the United States. Once again, the lack of a central focusing threat and the absence of missions that go beyond limited combat and peacemaking have led their civilian masters to allow them to decay into aging, heavily bureaucratic forces that often modernize in ways better suited to the politics of the European defense industry than to the requisites of effective war fighting.

As is the case for air forces and sea forces, there are good reasons why most European governments provide virtually no meaningful transparency into the readiness of their land forces and the effectiveness of their modernization plans. In most cases, their five-year plans are simply a façade hiding a steady decay in force strength and/or readiness and drift toward high-cost technological obsolescence. And, once again, the situation is not helped by NATO and EU force plans that similarly paper over real-world problems, set meaningless or unmet goals, and are triumphs of institution building over military reality.

The ability of the United States to find ways to work around the broad incapacity of European forces and find some selected elements that can be of value in given contingencies is not effective interoperability. Neither is the U.S. ability to separate out forces with inadequate capability and interoperability and give them some token mission for political purposes. Something is better than nothing, but this is not likely to be a particularly beneficial lesson of war.

Notes

[1] Elliot Blair Smith, "Marine Tanks May Fire First Shots," *USA Today*, March 18, 2003, p. 5.

[2] For some of the debate over this issue, see Robert J. Caldwell, "Rumsfeld versus the Army," *San Diego Union Tribune*, May 4, 2003; and Robert Little, "Abrams Heavy Tank Proves Its Mettle in Iraq Campaign," *Baltimore Sun*, April 10, 2003.

[3] "Interview: General Richard Myers," *Defense News*, April 14, 2003, p. 46.

[4] Frank Tiboni, "U.S. Army Rethinks Armor Cuts," *Defense News*, April 7, 2003, p. 22.

[5] Walter Pincus and Dan Morgan, "Defense Bills Expected to Pass Quickly," *Washington Post*, May 19, 2003.

[6] British Ministry of Defense, "Operations in Iraq: First Reflections" (London: Her Majesty's Stationery Office, July 2003), pp. 20, 27.

[7] Renae Merle, "Boeing Wins Contract for Army Modernization," *Washington Post*, May 16, 2003, sec. E, p. 1.

[8] See Frank Tiboni, "U.S. Army's Future Tank Features New Look," *Defense News*, June 9, 2003, p. 40.

[9] Thom Shanker, "New Armored Vehicle Is on the Path to Approval," *New York Times*, May 22, 2003.

[10] Col. David Hackworth, writing in *Military.com*, May 24, 2003.

[11] The data and analysis quoted here are taken from Tom Cooper, "Documented Coalition Losses in the III Persian Gulf War, as of 11 April 2003," *Air Forces and Air Arms*, www.orbat.com/site/agtwopen/iraq_equipment_losses.html.

[12] See www.acig.org/phpBB/viewtopic.php?topic=2103&forum=7&7.

[13] See www.strategypage.com/gallery/default.asp?target=abrams2.htm&source=abrams_lessons_learned. Also, Sean D. Naylor, "Friendly Fire Hit Abrams in the Gulf," *Defense News*, June 9, 2003, p. 42.

[14] Rowan Scarborough, "Myers Says 'Annihilation of Iraqi Army Wasn't Goal,'" *Washington Times*, June 30, 2003.

[15] Richard T. Cooper and Peter Pae, "Battle for the Military's Future Unresolved," *Los Angeles Times*, April 12, 2003.

[16] Department of Defense News Transcript, May 15, 2003, www.defenselink.mil/transcripts/2003/tr20030515-0184.html.

[17] Maj. Gen. David H. Petraeus, commanding general, 101st Airborne Division (Air Assault), "101st Airborne Division Commander Live Briefing from Iraq," May 13, 2003.

[18] The technical description of SADARM is adapted from www.dtic.mil/armylink/news/Mar1997/a19970303sadarm.html.

[19] For some background on the use of such capabilities in preparing the war, see Douglas Walters, "The CIA's Secret Army," *Time*, February 3, 2003; and Thomas Ricks and Peter Slevin, "US Confirms Presence of Personnel inside Iraq," *Washington Post*, January 30, 2003, p. 14. For wartime action, see James Dao, "War Plan Drew US Commandos from the Shadows," *New York Times*, April 28, 2003, p. 1.

[20] For a good preliminary discussion of some of the forces and methods involved, see Richard Whittle, "Military Mulls the Lessons of War," *Dallas Morning News*, April 22, 2003; Evan Thomas and Martha Brant, "The Secret War," *Newsweek*,

April 21, 2003; and Linda Robinson, "The Men in the Shadows," *U.S. News and World Report*, May 19, 2003.

[21] Tony Capaccio, "US Commandos Wore General Dynamics Transmitters," Bloomberg.com, April 30, 2003; Dao, "War Plan Drew US Commandos from the Shadows."

[22] Department of Defense briefing on April 23, 2003, www.defenselink.mil/transcripts/2003/tr20030423-0122.html.

[23] See Steve Voegel, "Far from Capital, A Fight That US Forces Did Not Win," *Washington Post*, April 10, 2003, p. 38.

[24] Jason Sherman et al., "Rising Profile Profits U.S. Special Forces," *Defense News*, April 21, 2003, p. 30.

[25] Interview with James Kitfield, "Attack Always," *National Journal*, April 25, 2003.

[26] Ibid.

CHAPTER TEN

LESSONS AFFECTING MARINE CORPS LAND FORCES

Many of the lessons relating to the U.S. Marine Corps are described in other chapters of this book. This is because the Marine Corps has provided extensive data on the lessons that it has drawn from its operations that apply to both U.S. Army and U.S. Marine Corps operations or to the entire war. There are, however, a number of more detailed lessons that apply primarily to the corps, and it seems useful to put these lessons in the context of the corps' overall role in the war. Lt. Gen. James Conway, commander of the 1st Marine Expeditionary Force, described this role as follows:[1]

> From the outset, the Marine Expeditionary Force was a supporting attack. We had to cross one, two, three—arguably, four rivers. We had an avenue of approach that Marine and Army planners both agreed was essentially a brigade-size avenue of approach, and we were putting, essentially, a reinforced division over it.
>
> I asked my people in the end how many Iraqi divisions did we engage, and it's arguably somewhere between eight and 11. We always knew that An Nasiriyah was going to be a critical point on the battlefield; that our supply lines, up Highway 7 and across Highway 1, both cross the Euphrates River at An Nasiriyah. And we simply had to take that place and hold it in order for the 1st Marine Division to be able to sweep north, as it finally did.
>
> It involved some close combat. And we saw that, I think, repeatedly as we attacked north; that we knocked out great formations of Iraqi armor, but the forces that we had come up against us were pretty much in the villages and towns along the single avenues of approach that we had that led into Baghdad. It was close-quarter fighting, in some cases hand-to-hand fighting. And I just think that a combination of things, that nature of close-in combat and the number of forces that we had to face on secondary avenues of approach to get to Baghdad, have led us to those numbers of casualties.

And let me tell you, we felt every one of them. I think based upon some of the equipment that we now have in the force, we're fortunate that they were not worse. We tried to ensure that every marine had what we call a SAPI [small arms protective inserts] plate, an armor plate that goes on the front of the flak vest. It covers the vital parts of the upper torso. And we compute that we had somewhere between 25 and 30 strikes 762 or larger…on the SAPI plates and they worked. And we think that they truly save lives.

THE MARINES: BOTH "POST-AMPHIBIOUS" AND "POST-LITTORAL" FORCES

In the process of carrying out this role, the U.S. Marines proved that they remain true expeditionary forces that can carry out heavy armored combat at long ranges from sea. The danger in this lesson is that it can blur the need for a specialized combat arm trained and organized to work with the U.S. Navy and trained and equipped for the kind of littoral warfare that is critical in military operations along the world's sea coasts.

At the same time, the Iraq War shows that the role of the marines in joint warfare should continue to include training, equipping, and organizing for heavy armored warfare. It is also a warning against making trade-offs in force planning that preserve the size of the Marine Corps active combat force structure at the cost of reducing such capabilities. The Marine Corps did, for example, have to fight the Iraq War without self-propelled artillery and using light armored vehicles designed primarily for amphibious warfare and vertical envelopment.

It might well be worth reexamining the force plans of the Marine Corps in light of the Iraq War to see if they adequately preserve the dual role of the Marine Corps in both littoral warfare and traditional land combat missions. It is also worth reexamining the overall balance of funding within the defense budget to see if a larger percentage of total funding should be shifted to the corps to enable it to preserve this mission, particularly in view of what seems to be at least a decade-long delay in the U.S. Army's ability to convert to a force structure it can deploy rapidly. Current army plans still leave many combat elements that take months to prepare and move.

Such trade-offs will be complex and uncertain. The U.S. Marines could not have sustained their operations without support from the U.S. Army. The marines are, and should remain, light enough to be an expeditionary force. As one U.S. Army officer points out,

the Marines (and the Army for that matter) are able to maneuver their "heavy" forces only because they are plugged into a largely Army support infrastructure at echelon above division, echelon above corps, and theater level. The theater infrastructure is necessary for the successful maneuver and support of the Land Component, regardless of whether it is made up of expeditionary forces from the Army or USMC or both.

DETAILED LESSONS FROM MARINE FORCES: FRICTION AND THE CONTINUING FOG OF WAR

Like the other services, the marines in the field have produced a number of reports on the lessons of the war, as well as anecdotal field reports from officers and other ranks about the course of combat and the lessons learned during the advance of U.S. Marine ground forces. The principal report is the one from the commanding general of the 1st Marine Division to the commanding general of the 1 MEF that has been referenced in previous chapters.[2] Many of the lessons in that report are highly technical or service specific. Others, however, help illustrate the reality that the battle put nearly continuous stress on troops, that the fighting was often hard, and that the "friction of war" was present at every level, from command and communications to the stress placed on the individual marine.

Several such lessons again illustrate the endemic problems in communication, battle management, and IS&R systems that still occur in spite of netcentric warfare, particularly at the level of the division war fighter and below:

Battlespace Geometry/Zone Management: OIF experience demonstrated that zone management must be a collaborative effort between fires and maneuver. Operational planning must produce battlefield geometry that "works," and orders transition must incorporate Tactics, Techniques, and Procedures (TTPs) to verifiably ensure that Major Subordinate Elements (MSEs) receive, understand, and implement their zones of responsibility. The solution is a Fires Planning SNCO at the Division Fire Support Coordination Center (FSCC).

As the Division rapidly advanced to Baghdad, fragmentary orders were often given verbally, backed up by written documents that at times reached the Division combat operations center (COC) staff and MSEs only hours before execution. This was a friction point for the Division FSCC, which had to build, disseminate, and verify receipt of battlefield geometry to permit the coordination of fires in support of the scheme of maneuver. The task required 3 hours to accomplish under the best of circumstances but was frequently complicated by a number of factors:

Incompatibility between G3 Plans products produced using Command and Control Personal Computer (C2PC), and Advanced Field Artillery Tactical Data System (AFATDS), the FSCC's tool for execution. Differences between fires- and maneuver-oriented concepts of battlespace deconfliction: i.e., maneuver needs linear boundaries between adjacent units; fires need two-dimensional zones that clearly assign responsibility for coordinating air-and surface-delivered fires throughout the entire Division area of operations (AO). Confusion caused by multiple versions of C2PC overlay files or human error in the preparation of planning products.

The requirement to pass coordination measures grid by grid over radio voice nets, tactical phone or other communication means to units incapable of receiving digital AFATDS communications or SIPRNET email (the principal reason it took a minimum of 3 hours).

The requirement to fight the current fight while preparing for future operations (the FSCC only had enough marines to operate one AFATDS, which was used to coordinate fires and process fire missions as well as to manage the target list and build fire support plans, zones, and fire support geometry for the coming phase of operations).

Recommendation: The solution is add a Fires Planning SNCO to the T/O of the FSCC. Unlike the Assistant Fire Support Coordinator (AFSC), who participates in planning but also supervises the current fight, the Fires Planning SNCO would be a full-time planner. While advising and assisting the G3 Plans Section, the Fires Planning SNCO would ensure that battlefield geometry and planning products were compatible with automated fire support systems and fire support coordination methods.

Battle Tracking and Common Tactical Picture Management: The 1st Marine Division G2 created its own Common Tactical Picture by producing periodic overlays with the assessed enemy situation. The data on MIDB was often untrustworthy. Other track management systems did not appear to function at all.

There were a number of technical and management issues with the CTP. Perhaps more significantly, the enemy did not conform to our expectation of a conventional line and block organization for combat. Since there was little confidence in the automated CTP databases based on exercise experience, the Division created its own methodology of disseminating C2PC overlays every 2–3 hours with the current assessed enemy picture. The Division deliberately chose a periodic quality-controlled product over real-time erroneous information. This process also was flexible enough to handle the non-standard nature of the enemy. The CTP architecture management responsibility has been largely abdicated to contractors. Although they are a talented and dedicated bunch, the fact that this process has to be contracted out is indicative of the fact that it is not usable by operational commanders in its current configuration. Track management seems to work well to track enemy airplanes or submarines, but is not flexible enough to reflect ground organization for combat at tactically usable levels. Trying to use the CTP "hammer" on a problem that is not a "nail" creates training and credibility issues at lower echelons. There seems to be little functionality for the COP/Common tactical picture as currently managed.

Recommendation: Need to revamp system and TTPs for CTP management, to include getting commanders back in the driver's seat. CTP as currently practiced is useful at Division and higher only, and a secondary mechanism, such as the overlay system used during 1MARDIV during combat, is required. Need the ability to customize for different enemy models or to create symbols to track incidents and events.

Communications T/E And T/O of the Marine Division: The Division communications T/E modernization the last decade has weeded out obsolete equipment and injected more reliable digital equipment (SINCGARS, TACSAT, Telephone Switches). Yet despite the modernization of some equipment the Marine Infantry Division is still using a "Vietnam Era" T/E in that all units are heavily dependent on Line of Site Communications equipment for coverage of only about 20 miles or so vice the equipment needed for communicators to support maneuver warfare over greater distances. Additionally, the quantity of equipment replaced has not been 1 for 1 in all cases. This has made Division units "to do more with less" while at the same time maneuver warfare has called for the Marine Division to move farther and faster exceeding the pace of communications equipment fielding to keep up. An additional concern is the reduction of communicators within the Division over the years leaving fewer communicators to install, operate, and maintain (IOM) all types of communications equipment despite not being school trained to IOM the equipment (i.e., Data Systems, TACSAT Radios). Some new equipment has also shown to be less capable than the equipment it replaced (i.e., power out and distance coverage for SINCGARS Line-of-Sight Radios is less than the equipment it replaced). High power HF equipment has not changed in 20 years and desperately needs to be modernized. A High power HF on the move capability needs to be fielded. UHF Tactical Satellite radios are key to battlefield command and control providing a secure voice and data capability over extended distances. To support maneuver warfare that requires units to move quickly over long distances, TACSAT Radios allow commanders the opportunity to seize and maintain momentum without concern for losing LOS communications or limitations of current HF radio mobility. When combined with the vehicular mounted OS-302 antenna, TACSAT capability significantly enhances command and control and needs to be fielded throughout the Marine Division in significantly more numbers than they currently are.

MRC Vehicles of all types are of primary concern. During Operation Iraqi Freedom the 1st Marine Division required augmentation of 26 MRC vehicles from the Command Element of the two MPSRONs that were only allocated after extensive negotiations at the RSO&I conference. 4th Marine Division Communications Company augmented the Division with over 250 Marines and an additional 18 MRC vehicles.

To adequately support a Division Support Area, a Division Main CP, a Division Forward CP, a Division Jump CP, a minimum of 2 retransmission teams, and multiple liaison officer requirements the 1st Marine Division required the full Division T/E with significant augmentation from 2 MPSRONs and the 4th Marine Division Communications Company. The same shortfalls existed at the Regiment and Battalion levels as well. The Division and each MSC deployed a Fly-In or Sail-In Echelon with their full T/E of MRC vehicles and a duplicate allowance of their T/E from MPSRON for 2 of the 3 RCTs. Hence the 1st Marine Division MRC vehicle communications assets were augmented at levels of 100 percent to 150 percent above T/E for Operation Iraqi Freedom.

Recommendation:

- Conduct a complete review of each Division T/E major communication end items such as MRC vehicles and TACSAT Radios down to the Battalion level.

- A 50 percent T/E increase of AN/MRC-145s for each Infantry/Artillery Battalion.

- A 100 percent T/E increase of AN/MRC-145s for each Regiment and the Division Communications Company.

- Replace all AN/PRC-104s and AN/PRC-138A & B with AN/PRC-150s and increase the Infantry Battalion allowance by 100 percent.

- Develop and field a replacement for the HF Radio AN/MRC-138s with a new vehicular HF radio vehicle (compatible with AN/PRC-150) that can operate while on the move.

- A 100 percent T/E increase of AN/MRC-138s for each of the Infantry, Artillery, and Separate Battalions.

- A 60 percent T/E increase of MRC-138s for Regimental Headquarters.

- A 50 percent T/E increase of MRC-138s for the Division Communications Company.

- Establish a T/E of 5 UHF TACSAT radios for each Infantry Battalion, each Artillery Battalion, and for the Division AAV Battalion.

- A 100 percent T/E increase of UHF TACSAT for Regimental Headquarters, the Division Reconnaissance Battalion, the Tank Battalion, and the LAR Battalions.

- Establish T/E of 2 OS-302 vehicle mounted antennas for each Regiment, Infantry Battalion, Artillery Battalion, separate Battalion and the Division Communications Company to enable TACSAT use while on the move.

Personal Role Radios (PRRs): The idea for the procurement of PRRs for the 1st Marine Division was to support the marine infantryman in the urban fight expected in Iraqi cities and especially for any fighting required in Baghdad. Commanders at all levels called for a reliable, lightweight, and durable radio that could be fielded rapidly in support of the marines of the 1st Marine Division. The British-made PRR was the radio recommended by the Infantry Battalion Commanders and the Division G-6. This radio provides a headset that fits under a helmet and a rifle-mounted push to talk system to easily operate the radio even during a firefight. The PRR radio is designed to be a low probability of intercept and detection with a range of 500 meters to support marines at the tactical level, especially for communications within the Infantry Squad and Platoon. The PRRs were especially effective in urban areas but were also widely used for security force operations, and convoy support. The Division received and distributed 3443 PRRs throughout the Division to include 2nd Marine Division attachments. This system received the universal acclaim of the marines who used them.

Recommendation: That PRRs be issued to each marine infantryman in each Infantry Battalion and Regiment of the Marine Division. There should be no attempts to "add on" to the PRR by any program manager. The PRRs are to be used for the "last 500 meters" by Marines up close and personal with the enemy. No requirement for increased range nor for crypto needs to be pursued. The radio should be procured and used especially by the Infantry Marines within each Infantry Division.

Iridium Phones: The 1st Marine Division G-6 began the procurement of Iridium Telephones (at approximately $4000 per phone to include the secure sleeve) in the summer of 2002. Initially 6 Iridium phones were procured to support the CG, ADC, 1st, 5th, 7th, and 11th Marine Commanding Officers. Over the next several months many more phones were procured to the point that the 1st Marine Division (Rein) had 77 Iridium Phones in use to support of the Division. These phones were instrumental in augmenting tactical communication support. At times, due to the limitations of tactical equipment not being able to operate on the move (i.e., SMART-T, UHF TACSAT, and HF Radio Communications), Iridium phones and Blue Force Tracker were the only available means of communications until units stopped and had the time to set up their tactical communications equipment.

Recommendation: All Iridium Phones procured by the Division Commands should have locally assigned TAMCNs for accounting on a CMR and with the EKMS Custodian (due to secure sleeves). Commands will be responsible for coordinating funding support for the monthly reoccurring costs or for suspending phone services not required to support training operations. The Iridium Phones and the Secure Sleeves need to be maintained within the Division Commands for future use as required. Iridium Pagers (also procured by the Division) were used for text messages during Operation Iraqi Freedom. In the future the Division will use Iridium Pagers to receive off-line encrypted brevity code text messages via NIPRNET messaging. This will provide yet another means of secure communications for the Division to pass along Commanders Intent down to at least the Regiment and Battalion Level—a capability that will be trained to in future.

Instant Text Messaging Capability for Intelligence I&W: Intelligence professionals at all levels were crippled in their ability to provide timely intelligence of a time-sensitive nature due to communications challenges. Newly fielded systems like Iridium pagers and Blue Force Trackers have the ability to do limited instant text messaging.... There is currently no way to reliably pass data down to the Battalion level or to the Regiment while on the move. There are times it took days for email messages to reach Div/Regiments due to server queues or some such. Although on the surface a communications issue, the impact on timely, actionable intelligence is severe. Chat rooms were not much better at RCT level...There is no secure, quick, reliable way to pass I&W to Regiments and Battalions.

    Recommendation: Need to procure and field a reliable, secure responsive Intelligence System that allows text messaging for Intelligence I&W. For example, there may be merit in fielding an Iridium pager text messaging capability as an Intelligence system. This would provide a significant enhancement to I&W capabilities.

Other lessons illustrate the need for innovative mixes of light forces to supplement the role of main force combat units, along with the continuing need to adapt to the special conditions of asymmetric warfare:

Light Armored Regiment And Battalion Organic to the Marine Division: During OIF, nimble, hard-hitting LAR units proved themselves highly versatile and employable across the spectrum:

- in advance guard, screening, covering force missions;
- put together under the ADC, three LAR Battalions executed a 150-mile attack beyond Baghdad to Tikrit and Bayji; and
- dominating in stabilization operations.

They can be the most lethal, versatile force on the battlefield if we

- add the best FAC suite equipment available; and
- add an assault gun/120mm mortar.

    We should also consider use of the Army Stryker vehicle to defray R&D costs/lower unit cost.

Recommendation: 7th Marines become an LAV Regiment to work in co-operation with a DS towed artillery battalion and tank battalion. One independent LAR Battalion remains to source MEUs and provide the Division Commander with his own GS LAR capability.

Use of Reconnaissance Battalion in a Non-doctrinal Role: The Division used the 1st Recon Battalion in non-doctrinal roles during OIF. The Battalion was provided enough mobility assets to become a separate maneuver unit and be attached to one of the Regimental Combat Teams. They were used as a battalion to screen the Division's flank, as an attack force to capture the Qalat Sikar airfield, a blocking force in Al Kut, and a raid force in Baqubah. These different mission capabilities provided versatility to the Division and Regimental Commanders and were a tremendous force multiplier.

Recommendation: Rewrite the mission statement of the Division's Reconnaissance Battalion to include the non-doctrinal roles performed in OIF.

LESSONS FROM THE COMBAT ASSESSMENT TEAM REPORT FOR THE MARINE CORPS SYSTEMS COMMAND

Another source of Marine Corps reporting is a three-man Combat Assessment Team that made a preliminary field study for the Marine Corps Systems Command (MCSC):[3]

Dust abatement. Remains a high priority for the MEF and affects units throughout the battlespace. My personnel experience suggests that this type of materiel needs to come into theatre ASAP. Dust in certain areas is greater than 6" deep and very much like a fine talcum powder. Foot and vehicle traffic, along with ever-present winds, can reduce visibility to less than 50' feet in a matter of moments. Convoy operations become exceedingly difficult, air operations come to a halt and living conditions for marines become intolerable. A bigger concern is that commanders in the field are faced with a Catch-22 situation of spraying oil on the ground (hazmat, environmental issues in a "win the hearts and minds environment") vs. functioning.

Logistics trains. CSSG resupply trains were fired upon. However, their technology and armor was inferior to that of the divisions. Marines without SAPI plates in soft skinned vehicles were the norm. "Rear area" units have elements that routinely operate on the "front lines." Though CSSGs did not face the same intensity and threats of Division units, they received fire and worked in a very hostile environment. As the tempo of the modern fight will cause differences between the front lines and rear areas to blur, Advocate level consideration needs to be given to more equitable fieldings of equipment. FSSG units need to be outfitted with more Blue Force Trackers, more high tech radios, and better-armored protection (SAPI plates, armored HM-MWVs, etc).

Low-cost receiver. This system proved very easy to use, was lightweight and "Marine Proof." The system never failed to work and was used to push information around the battlefield and every unit wanted one of these systems.

Forward Air Controller (FAC) Suite/GLTD II. Operators who used the designator found that it performed acceptably. Operators in vehicle platforms (to include AAVs and tanks) would like to have a stabilized vehicle mounted variant. The FAC suites were not issued as requested in the UNS. The fielding team only issued the GLTD II laser designator suite. The PEQ-4 laser illuminators/markers and AN/PRC-7C night vision goggles went directly to Division and were distributed before the fielding team arrived in country *(note: as the crossing of the LD became imminent, it was decided to field components as they came in, IOT some capability vice no capability. The GLTD II literally "just made it" and was the last item fielded before the LD was crossed).* Units already have assets to communicate with the aircraft (PRC-113), night vision devices (AN/PVS-7s, AN/PVS-14s) to spot the laser illumination, and AN/PVS-17C to give the GLTD II a "night sight capability." The AN/PVS-17C has a maximum effective range of 500m at a point target in ideal/perfect conditions. This distance is within the "danger close" area, and therefore doesn't give the system a night capability. Units didn't reallocate the AN/PVS-17's for the designators as the capability gained is far less than what is lost by taking them off they intended weapon platforms. Operators would like to be able to see the laser "splash" on the target from a piece of gear mounted to the designator. They were unable to do this with the gear available. They also requested having a thermal site attached or mounted.

Operators were very impressed with the AN/PEQ-4 Laser Illuminator; which was used extensively. It was the primary tool used by the FAC's, especially when working with Cobras. They illuminated the target and once the pilot spotted it, he was able to control the mission. Many would like these issued beyond the FAC's. Often, smaller units (platoons, squads, teams) don't have a school trained FAC with them but need the capability. Users would prefer ISLD 1000 vice AN/PEQ-4 for increased capability; however, the PEQ-4 "answers the mail."

AN/PVS-14 Night Vision Equipment. "Great piece of gear, need more." Some infantry units have one per man, (combined AN/PVS-14 and AN/PVS-7 assets), others, one per squad. Operators are asking to have one set of Night Vision Goggles (NVG's) per fire team; one per man is preferred. Units who received the M16A4 with ACOG scope/site would like to mount the NVG in front of the ACOG to give them a night shooting capability. For those who did this, they found the capability worked well. Some units couldn't mount the AN/PVS-14 on the 1913 RAIL (unknown if they had a different model, were missing parts, or lacked training). They taped the NVG on and had limited success. Actual mounting would be better.

Long-range Thermal Imager (SOPHIE). Operators were amazed by the capability. They would like more of the capability but would like to see it in a smaller and lighter package that is vehicle mountable and stabilized. Operators needed more extensive training. They didn't really know what they were seeing.

AN-PAS 13 Thermal Weapon Sight. "Amazing, need more." Many operators were able to see clearly to "10+ kilometers" under good conditions. In mild dust, they were also impressed since they could see "almost as far, 8+." Most reports were that they worked very well in all but the most extreme dust storms. Highlighted the need for thermal avanced visual identification AFVID USMC wide! If PAS-13 gets wide distribution, infantry units will need rigorous AFVID training. Currently, Tanks, LAV, Tow, and Air train to such standards. The proliferation of numerous hand held thermal devices without proper training could prove problematic. In addition, infrared can be viewed. Passing lanes proved problematic for some LAR vehicles that relied on thermals. Passives had to be used to spot IR chem.-lights. Thermal chem.-lights or beacons can prove costly.

M249 Squad Automatic Weapon (SAW). The SAW's are worn out and apparently beyond repair. They have far exceeded their service life. Many marines are duct taping and zip tying the weapons together. Reconnaissance units were requesting parasaw, infantry units requesting collapsible buttstock.

5.56mm vs. 7.62 Lethality. 5.56mm "definitely answered the mail" and "as long as the shots were in the head or chest they went down" were typical quotes from several marines; many who were previously very skeptical of 5.56mm ammunition. Most of the interviewed marines who reported targets not going down and/or could still fight were referencing non-lethal shots to the extremities. There were reports of targets receiving shots in the vitals and not going down. These stories need not be described, but are of the rare superhuman occurrences that defy logic and caliber of round. Some marines did ask about getting the heaver-grained 5.56mm rounds, up to 77 grain if possible.

TOW 2. Operators are extremely happy with the performance. Several operators reported tank (T-72) catastrophic (K) kills. TOW 2B caused some concern when shooting over any metal (such as around the oil fields) and around "friendlies" because of the one sensor. The operators already knew these factors. The TOW 2A had no such concerns. The one downside comment (a constant theme by all interviewed), had to do with training. For gunners trained on the newer sight, they are great. For the untrained on the new system, gunners are unable to identify and range targets, etc. Many operators are also having a tendency to follow the rocket with the sight when the rocket rises above the gun-target line, instead of leaving the site on target. This causes the rocket to go higher and higher as the operator follows the rocket. Sometimes they recover and hit the target, most of the time they don't. Additionally, the TOW sites are being successfully used for surveillance purposes. Operators are impressed with the capabilities the site offers in this area.

SMAW Thermobaric (New) Round. Only received reports of two shots. One unit disintegrated a large one-story masonry type building with one round from 100 meters. They were extremely impressed. However, another unit tried to breach a wall of a similar masonry building after being unsuccessful at trying to mechanically breach a door. "The round just bounced off the wall." They were not so impressed.

Enemy Engagements. Almost all interviewed stated all firefight engagements conducted with small arms (5.56mm guns) occurred in the twenty to thirty (20-30) meter range. Shots over 100m were rare. The maximum range was less than 300m. Of those interviewed, most sniper shots were taken at distances well under 300m, only one greater than 300m (608m during the day). After talking to the leadership from various sniper platoons and individuals, there was not enough confidence in the optical gear (Simrad or AN/PVS-10) to take a night shot under the given conditions at ranges over 300m. Most marines agreed they would "push" a max range of 200m only.

LMT (Lightweight Mobile Tactical) Water Purification System. There were several complaints about the "flimsy" construction of the LMT. Most components were made of easily breakable plastic. Also, the purification of the LMT was not enough to purify the fresh water from the Euphrates River; its effectiveness and usefulness was questioned. A small system was a "good concept" however, the purification capability needed to be greater.

3000 gallon Water Bladders. Marines in the Utilities field admired the 3000 gallon water bladders used by the Seabees. These bladders were very effective as a sealed water storage capability. The current 3000-gallon "onion skins" were good for raw water storage, but not purified water. Also, the 500-gallon pods were not a large enough storage capability for purified water.

SAPI (Small Arms Protective Insert). To no surprise this item was worth its weight in gold. SAPI plates saved lives. In five separate incidents at 2D Tank Battalion the SAPI prevented death or serious injury. In the words of Capt. David Bardorf, 2D Tank Bn., "SAPI is God's gift to the Marine Corps." Marines were hoping that the future could bring a lighter version that was slightly wider in the front, but these requests for modification were minimal and insignificant compared to the positive feedback and effectiveness of the plates.

LAVs. The LAV community had favorable comments about the LAV. However, the concern was raised that LAVs are getting old, requiring increased maintenance. A replacement was desired for the near future.

Combat ID Panel. These were highly desired and utilized. However, they were obtained by borrowing panels from the Army as well as fabricating panels prior to crossing the LD. Several marines emphasized that Combat ID panels are a necessity for war; the USMC needs to field these critical fratricide prevention devices.

Phrase-later. This was another small open purchase item that was purchased through unit funds. It consists of a small "palm pilot" size computer system that translates phrases into the desired language. This was used on numerous occasions to ask simple questions of locals and EPWs (with heavy usage at checkpoints). Recommend C4I or CESS look at providing to deploying units. The system is manufactured by Maine Acoustics.

Iridium Phones. There was a lot of positive feedback on the Iridium phone. Due to its ability to be used when not in Line of Site, these phones were often used for communication. It was a highly reliable means for the forces to continually be in contact with one another.

AAV as Tank's C3 vehicle. A concern was raised with respect to the comparatively lightly armored AAV being the C3 vehicle and thus employed with the Tank battalion. Those in the AAV felt vulnerable to enemy fire when engaged in a battle with the Tank Battalion.

D9 Dozer. These bulldozers received highly favorable reviews from all that benefited from their use. They were seen clearing a row of buildings effectively within an extremely short period of time. Also, they were used in quickly clearing a highway for use and constructing hasty combat roads. Marines stated that the D9 can do the equivalent of approximately (4) D7 dozers. They would like to see this Dozer employed in more operations in the future.

Mine Detectors. These received poor reviews. They were labeled "flimsy" and "inaccurate." The marines of the Combat Engineer Battalion recommended a review of the ANPSC-12 (in Albany). They desired to test these to see if they would be more effective.

Anti-Personnel Obstacle Breaching System (APOBS). Each compound is too heavy and the range is considered ineffective. The range of approximately 25 meters was questioned. As one Marine stated, "Why should I lug a 50lb piece of gear around that only clears 25 meters when I can just mark it

386 THE IRAQ WAR: STRATEGY, TACTICS, AND MILITARY LESSONS

for EOD and walk around the obstacle?" The Bangalore torpedo was still a preferred breaching system for obstacles.

Imagery. Imagery from various systems did not make it to the HQ G-2 level on numerous occasions due to a lack of bandwidth and electronic imagery transferral means. BFT did not possess the bandwidth for larger files and MDACT was unreliable as a communications means due to its limitation on Line of Site communication with the EPLRS radio.

Full-width Mine Plows (FWMP) "The Pearson Plow." In my earlier report I wrote, "Of the 20 plows procured, only 11 went forward. Of this 11, I saw 3 on the highways of Iraq. Presumably cut lose as units went forward, it appears the plows are now combat losses. The 3 I saw were laying in the highway; burned out." Apparently, the weld mounts on the plows did not hold and broke from the body of the tank. This may account for the 3 I saw on the high-way. The fielding team observed an incidence of this during the application of the hardware and repaired. The 5-ton trucks used to transport the FWMPs broke down. At no time did 2D Tank Battalion employ its FWMP or Track Width Mine Plows. Even though 2D Tanks did not use the FWMPs, Lt. Col. Oehl, the battalion commander, stated the item had its merits. It "did not drastically reduce the effectiveness of the tank" as implied by junior marines in 2D Tank Bn. He noted it would have been a valuable asset had the mission called for breaching a minefield. Lt. Col. Oehl also supported the FWMP for use on the Armored Breacher Vehicle (ABV).

Blue Force Tracker (BFT). The Blue Force Tracker proved very popular with marines from both LAR and 2D Tank Battalion. The 5.1 MB download capability proved to be very useful. Real-time information transfer and satellite imagery was mission critical on several occasions. BFT was considered "very responsive" due to instant messaging capability. Most of the commanders agreed that the pace of the battle required a device similar to Blue Force Tracker. Units were, at times, unable to maintain VHF over distance due to the inability to establish retransmission sites. Potential retrans sites would be forecasted to be located in unsecure areas. In the absence of communications, BFT provided units with responsive message traffic. Tanks and LAR used it in the absence of radios. It was, at times, the only means of communication for dispersed units. BFT was considered very reliable for providing friendly situation reports. Many officers and senior enlisted felt that the Scout Platoon and Alpha and Bravo commands needed this capability. It was recommend that at least 24 systems should be fielded per battalion, two tanks at the platoon level.

MDACT. Comments suggest that it was a highly unreliable due to the system's reliance on having the server up constantly. The system was marginalized when an active server hub went down. There were reported instances of units showing up in the "wrong" country. Some units appeared miles away from their known locations. This effected confidence in the system. Some marines claimed it was too complicated to use. Windows pull down menus on a small screen made accessing information time consuming and difficult under combat conditions. This feature was also cumbersome while traveling at high rates of speed over difficult terrain. Transmission with the 56K modem took four to five minutes to send out a message. Other concerns included the screen being too small and not being user friendly. The MDACT system was noted to have great capabilities and was considered a "good concept" however, on the user level it was not employed due to its unreliability. BFT was preferred and MDACT was ignored.

Firepower Enhancement Program (FEP) Raytheon/DRS. Comments on the FEP include the following: Position location capability and the ability to range a target and get a ten-digit grid were considered very useful. It proved valuable in fire missions and situation awareness. The fifty-magnification sight needs better resolution but proved useful. Thermal Bloom (washout in the TIS sites from fire trenches and burning vehicles) took one to three minutes of recover. Raytheon FEP site engaged vehicles in excess of 2300m. Was used by Bravo Company to Identify Snipers in buildings. Used as land navigation tool during road marches. Worked well in open terrain and built-up areas. One criticism of the Raytheon FEP was that it took four minutes for the Far Target Locator to align. It was the opinion of the experienced crews that it was impractical to sit idle for that period of time in the combat environment. On several occasions, the crew rolled without FTL alignment due to time constraints. The crew then had no option but to fight the tank in degraded mode. They recommend a 30 second alignment process. In static positions the FEP site was used to provide over watch for the tank company and to friendly infantry patrolling forward of lines. Crews recommended retaining the binocular site at the gunner's station. The ability to see in both day and night with the GPS and binocular site was very popular and useful to tank gunners.

M88A2 Hercules Tracked Recovery Vehicle. The M88A2 was rated as an excellent recovery asset. However, the general comment was that there were not enough of them. The original quantity of two M88A1 was reduced to one M88A2 for each tank company on the T/O. The long trek into Iraq resulted in many self-recovery operations (tank towing tank) due to the lack of recovery assets. This tied up needed combat power. Recommend USMC revisit the T/O of tank battalions to add at least two additional M88A2s per battalion on MPF. Some units used M88A2 as an armored ambulance. Cpl. Myhre, Company A. 2D Tank Bn modified one M88A2 with a loaders M240 7.62mm machine mount from an M1A1 tank. This modification gave the M88A2 another weapons station in addition to its .50

M2 Machine gun. Recommend more tow bars for tank units (*note: there are not of enough tow bars of all types to support all equipment in the operating forces. The USMC needs to revisit this issue and invest in acquiring more of these assets*). Number of self-recovers demonstrated this requirement. Need vehicle power source to recharge laptop computers containing Technical manuals for the maintenance crews. The pace of the advance did not allow for time to recharge the set with field generators. Track continued to snap on left side. CWO3 Dan Wittcop speculates possible problem is the torque caused by the more powerful engine of the Hercules. Track would simply "pop." It is recommend at least exploring a sturdier center guide for the track. Winch fragility was also addressed. Some recoveries required off angle approaches outside the recommend 20-degree angle. Recommend that an update to the TM include a reference to use a floating block in recoveries. One snapped cable was repaired in the field. However, at the time of this report a recovery was not attempted with that cable. Skirts on the M88A2 design made it difficult to do rapid track maintenance. During combat operations, removing bolts proved problematic. Recommend exploring a vehicle modification to allow for better access. A Battle Damage Repair (BDR) should, if possible, be developed for fixing cables on M88A2.

Armored Vehicle Launched Bridge (AVLB) AVLB. Not employed to any great extent during operations. However, many in the 2D tank battalion cited the need for an improved AVLB variant. Throughout operations, the AVLB was slow, achieving speeds of only 20mph. It was recommended that HETs be used to transport AVLBs. AVLB is at the end of its life cycle. Spares were difficult to get. AVLB track was in short supply. AVLB track was repaired with SL-3 on vehicle. Once that ran out, track from non-operational AVLBs was used. Only two of the battalion's AVLBs made it to the site at Ad-Diwaniyah at the time of this interview. It is recommended that MCSC should coordinate with Requirements and the Advocate IOT POM for a variant that can keep pace with the M1A1. LAR Marines offered some unique perspectives based on their mission experiences. One Marine suggested that AVLB assets were needed forward with LAR. They proposed a lightweight "LAR" MCL Bridge variant or a faster tracked MCL 70 ton variant.

LESSONS FROM FIELD REPORTING FROM THE 1ST MARINE DIVISION

Other, less formal field reporting is available from individuals within the 1st Marine Division. Any such lessons can only be suggestive at this point. Like similar reports mentioned in chapters 8 and 9, there is no way to put most into a broad context that can validate whether the reporting represents individual views that others do not share or atypical combat experiences.

Some quotes from these reports do, however, seem representative enough to mention. They provide a useful picture of the fact that the perspective of those actually in combat was very different from one of ease and the ability to rely on technology:

- War commenced prematurely due to information received from CIA regarding the presence of Saddam in Baghdad. Likewise, CIA liaison at 1 MARDIV HQ was off the mark. Reports of up to 90 T72s advancing towards border pre-D Day forced Div Comd to change plan that had been in place for 6 months. After having changed F15E confirmed report in fact incorrect, tanks were same 6 tanks that had been present since D-20 days. Plan back to the original plan. Sufficient flexibility and training within the organization to make changes at short notice.

- On the commencement of the war first discovered none of the T62s and T72s was occupied which was a bit of a concern. All lined up neatly in tactical formation with Iraqis standing next to them surrendering holding out wads of cash to the marines. There were competitions being held between the tanks (2nd Tanks led the advance) as to who could get the longest-range tank kill. Longest recorded was 4,100 meters.

- Iraqis feared Tanks and LAR more than anything. However, the fanatics were quite happy as long as they didn't have to deal with dismounted infantry. The weather had huge effect on both operations and morale. But the force kept moving on regardless albeit confined to the hardball.

- The Iraqis had made extensive defensive preparations around all towns. The works had been well planned and sited with engineer input. The trenches were where marines conducted the majority of fighting around the towns.

- Iraqis would always camp under palm trees and therefore that was where the majority of contact was joined. The Republican Guard were surrendering on masse, however because of the speed of the advance the marines usually ignored them due to not wanting to take on the burden of EPWs. So we guess they just walked home.

- Fedayeen tactics fell apart the moment marines dismounted and cleared through the buildings. Their tactics were far more comfortable with dealing with vehicles and marines that remained mounted.

- The planning cycle was way behind the execution being conducted by the forward commanders. Div HQ was still producing lengthy OPLANS and FRAGOs that were too late for the commanders, as they had already stepped off. Staffs are adhering to the training and requirements they are taught by MSTP for CAX.

- Force Recon suffered from a lack of employment. Their employment was considered far too high risk.

- Nighttime was for driving not operations. Night vision devices were put to very good use for night driving, however only one night attack was conducted by 3/7.

- There was a lack of common intelligence picture throughout the Div. Points that were being picked up as a result of one Battalion's action about the enemy were not being passed up the chain for other units to take not of. Lack of comms had some bearing upon this, in addition personnel are not trained to take note of what will be important both up the chain and laterally to neighboring units.

- Battle preparation, maintenance and prep for the next day was poor. Marines were exhausted by day four with little sleep and rest. Commanders in particular were making questionable decisions due to lack of rest. There was continued implementation of the stand to / stand down procedure, which was compounding the lack of rest for the marines. Some companies took it upon themselves to remedy the situation such as Fox 2/5 who modified this procedure to allow the marines to get more sleep.

- About half of our guys who were wounded or killed came from accidents...picking up unexploded ordnance, run over by vehicles, negligent discharges, etc. Much of it was because guys were exhausted and simply got careless.

- Confusion continues between U.S. Marines and Army in particular around the vicinity of Nasiryah where Army re-supply columns were being ambushed. Marines were not aware in many instances of their presence and were tasked at one stage to go back and rescue bulk fuel tankers and their crews who were hiding in the scrub after one contact. Having said that communication within the marines, in particular 1 MARDIV and Task Force TARAWA did not exist due to not having the same fills. Personal face-to-face comms was the only means of coordination between the two forces.

- Nasiryah saw the culmination of this confusion over MOUT. Commanders were not prepared to go in and clear a town no bigger than Victorville. This was an initial hesitation that eventually subsided to some outstanding MOUT ops later in the action by 5th and 3rd Marines south of Baghdad.

- MOUT continues to be point of contention between U.S. Army and Marines. Army plan was always to isolate and conduct limited raids, Marine intention was to penetrate and hold key terrain within the towns and cities. The actions in Baghdad were primarily a result of the actions of Comd 1 MARDIV.

- There was an operational pause. JFLCC imposed a 4-day OP PAUSE prior to final assault on Baghdad.
- Cobras were employed more as IS&R than CAS and suffered from resulting ground fire.
- Mech/Infantry work and protection requires more work. A lack of understanding of how the parts work together to form a team protecting each other's vulnerabilities. There needs to be a clear understanding between a convoy and a tactical movement. 5th Marines line of advance was approx 100km long.
- LAVs rule the desert. Use them if you have them.
- Fire discipline was poor at times with one weapon system opening fire, which led to all weapon systems opening up.
- UAVs were used down to Battalion level and were [of] great value. They need to [be] incorporated into Marine training.
- SMAW thermobaric rounds are awesome. Javelins performed very well in combat too. The M1A1 MPAT rounds are devastating…blow the turrets right off of T-72s. MDACT is a piece of shit.
- On the SAPIs, it's give and take. When it gets hot or you are moving significant distances, the SAPI will wear you out and can be counterproductive. However, the stuff works great when you need it. We had a lot of guys shot at close range with AKs and the SAPI saved them. The day a suicide bomber came up and detonated himself at one of our checkpoints was a great example. The marines all had shrapnel in their arms and legs, but their torso and vital areas were untouched and it saved them. Conversely, we had a guy bleed out from his stomach after catching two rounds in an ambush. Doc thinks if he had his SAPI on he would have lived, but he chose to take it out for the patrol (and he was the PL). I certainly recommend them for MOUT and short duration ops for sure. See if you can make them lighter and everyone will be happy.
- Commanders knew there would be only three supply routes during the war: two for the marines one for the Army. Commanders knew they would be long and choked; therefore they took everything with them, which made the supply routes even longer. The long supply lines could not be controlled by the MPs because they were not included in the forward echelons, and due to choked routes could not get to the forward echelons to clear the choke points.

- Logistics drove operations. Ask the 4 before you do any event. We made some long moves, as long as 15 hours on the road at a time. Plan your supplies. Fuel was the key more than water. There is always room for some chow.

- Big convoy on the hardball? At night? Turn the lights on ansd go fast as the slowest vehicle. Point a few dozen machineguns outboard and drive like hell. LAV's and 7 tons can do 65 at night on the hardball. Tell your marines to stay off the roads at night. Convoys will go by on short notice. It's better to be going fast and being able to see than trying to have 75 vehicles going 20 MPH on NVG's.

- A combat load is heavy on the marines and the vehicles. Take only what you need.

- Study convoy operations. If you have CAAT, JAV, or LAR, put them in charge and have them run the convoy. You may be senior but they know how to do this and this lets commanders worry about the bigger picture. Brief your convoys. Never "just drive away." Give each vehicle a number, from 1 to the very end. Some convoys were big. We went from 1 to 75. Know the senior man in each vehicle. Know what is in you convoy. An avenger has FLIR. Use everything to your advantage. Forget call signs. Use the vehicle numbers. It worked! Plan for vehicle recovery and brief it. Get more tow bars. Use tow straps. Spread [your] MT Métis all over the BLT. These guys saved us every day.

- Strip everything off your vehicles that you don't need. Sandbag your vehicles. Carry as much ammo as you can. Strip highback vehicles down. Hang the packs on the sides and get as many rifles pointing left and right as you can. Take the doors off everything except hardbacks and FAV's. Never let the a-driver attach the handset to his helmet strap. You need to be able to get out of the vehicle fast. Pistols suck. Bring and use every weapon. Shotguns are great at close ranges.

- PM everything as time permits. Our vehicles never ran better because the marines did not want to get stuck on the side of the road. If a vehicle goes down in a convoy give them 5 minutes and after that tow it. If several go down plan for multiple tows. If the situation is bad plan to grab mission type gear and radios and blow the vehicle. You can get another vehicle if it prevents a fire fight.

- CASEVAC was predominantly by road through the Battalion Doctor and aid station. Air was at least 45 minutes away. The CH46 did not have the legs to keep up with the advance and therefore the marines saw very little air other than Cobras.

- Comd 1 MARDIV commanded the Div via one HUMVEE and two aides who remained with him throughout. One aide kept the batteries in his

Iridium up; the other rubbed out red icons on the map. He commanded via the Iridium and the map on the side of the HUMVEE. He was usually no less than 100-200 meters behind the lead Battalion or main effort. He would talk to Regt Comds on the insecure Iridium using veiled speech only. Nothing else!

- Most marines used commercial GARMIN GPS rather than military issued GPS. Personal preference.

- Communications were particularly poor; one Battalion managed to be out of comms for up to 6 hours, VHF was not the answer and did not perform well in this operation.

- Rumor-spreading was rife in particular over the most secure means the SIPRNET. People were using it as a chat room and making unsubstantiated allegations and claims on this means. Commanders lost faith in the SIPR and chose direct voice comms as the best means. It also created confusion and fear amongst marines that was unnecessary.

- Rumor control again caused a negative effect upon the operations. Marines were hearing negative reports of Iraqi actions and were therefore displaying a negative attitude towards the Iraqi population.

- PRR is invaluable and marines can't see how they will work without it in the future. Some range problems and comms interference in some buildings but not in others. Otherwise great piece of gear.

- Every Marine was seeking ACOG. Squad leaders were taking it for themselves for reasons unknown, probably for ease of targeting. They all wanted it.

MARINE CORPS ARTILLERY

Few Marine accounts are available on the impact of artillery. According to one press report,

the Marines' 155-millimeter howitzer is effective at a range of more than 15 miles. With its computerized targeting, it can hit an object the size of a 50-gallon drum. In one 30-minute barrage, 400 rounds were fired at Iraqi positions. So many shells were in the air at once that computers and satellite imagery were used to keep projectiles from colliding: "It's like being an air traffic controller in Los Angeles," said Gunnery Sgt. Will Villalobos of the 1st Marine Division.

The report of the commanding general of the 1st Marine Division on the lessons of the war states that the Marine Corps has had continuing design problems with its M198 towed 155-mm howitzer:[4]

Fractures of the travel lock for the M198 have been an issue for a very long time. In fact, the travel lock is designed to fail under certain conditions. Normally, the fractures are welded and the gun is placed back in service. However, the issue has worsened since the Division began towing the M198 with the new MTVR. The fractures are spreading to the hinges and on to the cradle and the barrel itself. These types of fractures require at least 48 hours to correct, during which time the gun cannot be used. During analysis, the Division has observed two contributing factors to the problem. First, a normal pressure reading for the M198's tires during off-road driving should be 85 psi. In many cases, the tire pressure was found to be around 110 psi. This causes the M198 to bounce a lot. Second, the new MTVR has a different feel than the old 5-ton trucks. Drivers tend to forget about the loads that they are pulling. This leads the drivers to exceed the maximum 15-kph speed limit when pulling the M198 off the hardball road.

FRIENDLY FIRE

Although the problem of friendly fire has been discussed in detail in previous chapters, Lt. Gen. James Conway, commander of the 1st Marine Expeditionary Force, has provided some interesting additional insights into the Marine Corps' perspective on the problem:[5]

...(friendly fire) is probably my biggest disappointment of the war, and that is the amount of blue on blue, what we call blue on blue, fratricide in a lot of instances, that occurred.

I spoke to every formation before we crossed the line of departure, I spoke separately to the officers and I emphasized a number of things, but among them were the fact that our weapons are so accurate, are so deadly, that anymore, that when it goes off the rail or it goes out the tube, it's probably going to kill something. And so you've got to make certain that what you're shooting at is indeed the enemy.

We did have a large number of wounded at An Nasiriyah, based upon a friendly fire incident. Fortunately, no killed came out of that...particular engagement. There is another one that's under investigation where we think that there may have been an air strike roll in on our forces, and there were other incidents.

... One [device we used in this war] was called Blue Force Tracker. It gave us position locations and identification on major units. It helped some, I think, with location and identification of friendly forces.

But what we truly need is something that can identify a friendly vehicle—it either squawks or beeps or emits some sort of power source that tells a shooter—an airplane or a tank or whatever—that they're looking at a friendly piece of equipment....[W]e've been trying to develop that now ever since the Gulf War, without success, I might add. And the man that invents that, I think, will be very rich, indeed. Because it continues to be something that we see happen in the U.S. military, and it's really something that we've got to stop.

MARINE CORPS SUPPLY AND LOGISTICS

Both the U.S. Army and the U.S. Marine Corps had problems with logistics in the field, as well as broader tactical problems. They both were affected by weather and by attacks by Iraqi irregulars in the field. Moreover, the sheer tempo of operations and speed of maneuver created supply problems and led to continuing coordination problems between forward combat elements and combat support, service support, and logistics forces. These problems were exacerbated at the battalion level and below by tactical and rear area communications problems and by the fact that neither the U.S. Army nor the Marine Corps had advanced digital systems capable of displaying and managing force elements, including logistics.

Lt. Gen. Conway, commander, 1st Marine Expeditionary Force, described the problems with the logistics system as follows:[6]

> I am so proud of my logisticians that I can probably not convey it in words. The Marine Corps is not designed or organized to go 600 miles deep into enemy territory. Our logistics are simply not built that way. We have tremendous reliance on our shipboard logistics. We essentially say that we come from the sea. That said, that was not the CINCs [Commanders in Chief] or the CFLCC's [Coalition Forces Land Component Command] plan in this case, and so we were asked to execute something that was in excess of what we were built to do. With Army augmentation, however, and with, I think, some wise planning that tied our logistics to airfields along the avenues of approach, we made it work.
>
> Now, if you ask me if every Marine went into the attack with a full tank of gas in his tank and three MREs in his pack and all the water that we might like to have, the answer is absolutely not, because we certainly stretched the rubber band. But that said, I think there was a level of comfort in the marines in the combat units that as they crossed the line of departure in the morning, they could look over their shoulder and see a supply convoy arriving that would have those things for them by the end of the day.
>
> So logistics never truly halted the attack, but based upon those supply lines that we faced, even doing the best job we could with emergency resupply via air and so forth, we were never rich in supplies. That was a conscious risk that we were willing to accept, and one in this case, I think, proved itself to be

worth the risk. We felt that through speed, we could save lives. And we weren't willing to sacrifice that speed for the sake of full tanks and full packs.

...As you all will recall, there was a halt, an operational halt, that allowed us to build supplies. We were well up Highway 1 at that point, still south of the Tigris River, at that point really making a feint on the underbelly of Baghdad. And we held forces in place for two or three days, allowing that rubber band to maybe become a little less taut, and to get some supplies built up to the point where we were comfortable that we weren't experiencing extreme risk.

While that was happening—and you have to understand, I guess, some[thing] about how this MEF fights. But we have a tremendous air arm that was able to put about 300, 320 sorties a day on our enemies out in advance of our ground troops. So while we were stationary, we were, in fact, attacking with our air, taking maximum advantage of intelligence, surveillance, and reconnaissance capabilities to determine what the enemy was that we faced.

And quite frankly, again, we weren't fully topped off with the supplies that we might like, but every indication that we had was that the enemy had been significantly pounded by our air, and our intelligence resources were telling us that he was not there in large numbers. So those two things combined told me, and I suspect my superiors, that it was a risk that was manageable and a risk that we could take, again, in order to generate the speed that we did.

The 1st Marine Division report on the lessons of the war contained far more serious criticisms:[7]

...There is no such thing as a supply system in the Marine Corps. I MEF uses SASSY and ATLASS I. II MEF uses ATLASS II. Blount Island Command uses another supply system for MPF equipment. The field warehouse system used by MLC at the start of the operation had to be scrapped because of its inability to perform. None of these systems provide an interface with an in-transit visibility system at either the operational or tactical level. The supply system architecture planned for use during Operation Iraqi Freedom was a "workaround" combination of systems and methods. The workaround never permitted visibility at the Battalion level of a requisition from inception to receipt. Problems were directly attributable to the incompatibility of these systems, lack of training in their use, lack of a standard method of passing supply requisitions from MEF units through an MLC, lack of a dedicated logistics communications architecture, and the lack of an interface with an in-transit visibility system. In general, the supply officers were not familiar with the system. Although they were familiar with using ATLASS I to induct requisitions, they did not understand how their requisitions were being handled by the supporting CSSBs and MLC. Due to an absence of NIPRNET connectivity at the Battalion level there was no means for Battalion Supply Officers to pass requisitions and get the feedback data necessary for their management and by exception reports. As a result, they lost faith in the processes established, started using workarounds, and gave up on any type of established supply management.

Field reports from individual units and soldiers in the U.S. Army reflect very similar problems. The field logistic effort could not be properly coordinated with forward combat elements; communications between combat and logistic forces were a serious continuing problem; the data management system was inadequate at the data level; and, like the Marine Corps, the U.S. Army often had to improvise.

In an ideal world, this situation would lead to the creation of a common management and communication system that could deal with the problems of both the Marine Corps and U.S. Army in every contingency and in ways that allowed a coordinated joint logistic effort with the U.S. Navy and U.S. Air Force. In practice, such a system may not be feasible for a decade or more, if ever. Steady improvement is possible as both the Marine Corps and the U.S. Army become digital forces. It simply is not clear that any system architecture can ever eliminate the need for improvisation, workarounds, local unit-to-unit arrangements, and flooding supplies forward in anticipation of need. Creating overambitious systems and solutions could result in costly failures or in an over-rigid "joint" effort that becomes more of a problem than a solution.

Notes

[1] Lt. Gen. James Conway, commander, 1st Marine Expeditionary Force, "Live Briefing from Iraq," May 30, 2003, www.defenselink.mil/transcripts/2003/tr20030530-0229.html.

[2] Commanding General, 1st Marine Division, "Operation Iraqi Freedom (OIF): Lessons Learned," MEF FRAGO 279-03, May 29, 2003.

[3] These quotes cover only selected areas of general interest. The full report is much longer and includes many technical issues of interest only to the Marine Corps.

[4] Commanding General, "Operation Iraqi Freedom."

[5] Conway, "Live Briefing from Iraq," May 30, 2003.

[6] Ibid.

[7] Commanding General, "Operation Iraqi Freedom."

CHAPTER ELEVEN

LESSONS AFFECTING NAVAL FORCES

Some of the most important lessons regarding seapower have been discussed in the previous chapter. These include the critical importance of being able to protect air and land power using sealift, access to friendly ports, and substitutes for land bases. The importance of cruise missiles and of improving the range-payload of carrier-based aircraft has also been discussed.

Iraq was a negligible seapower, and it could not make effective use of its land-based anti-ship missiles or mines. It did use irregular forces like Saddam's Fedayeen to help delay the coalition's access to its port cities, and its tactics in using ships to help block shipping channels may well be used by other powers.

There are several other lessons that seem worth considering.

AIRCRAFT CARRIERS

U.S. carriers again demonstrated that they are critical substitutes for air bases that can now be supplemented with cruise missiles. Vice Admiral Timothy Keating, commander of all maritime forces involved in Operation Iraqi Freedom, noted in a briefing on April 12, 2003 that

> [s]ince the 20 of March, aircraft flying from our carriers have flown over 7,000 sorties—7,000 sorties in support of Operation Iraqi Freedom as part of the air component command power projection mission. Maritime patrol aircraft, our big-wing P-3s principally, have provided valuable intelligence, surveillance, and reconnaissance of the battlefield forward into Iraq and over Baghdad as we speak in support of ground and sea assets.

The U.S. carriers made combat use of the F/A-18E/F Super Hornet for the first time. They also could make effective use of large inventories of laser- and GPS-guided weapons that were not available to the U.S. Navy in the Gulf War. In fact, the carrier aircraft enforcing the no-fly zone as part of Operation Southern Watch enforcement actions had already been using nothing but guided weapons, and the navy had recently increased the number of aircraft able to drop JDAMs.

At the same time, the need to deploy five carriers for one major regional contingency validates the U.S. Navy's emphasis on new carrier designs that can hold more aircraft and sustain higher sortie rates. It also, however, is another reason to give Marine Corps amphibious ships a dual role as light helicopters and to consider how they can be used to project Special Forces as well as Marine Corps units.

Another challenge for the carrier forces is keeping a large number of aging aircraft flying. Despite the arrival of the F/A-18E/F, most carrier aircraft are old and have steadily more demanding maintenance and logistic burdens. The F-14s and S-3s are aging systems, and the E-2Cs and EA-6Bs have high maintenance requirements and engine maintenance problems. It is clear that new aircraft like the Joint Strike Fighter are badly needed.

JOINTNESS IN NAVAL AIR OPERATIONS

The level of "jointness" was much greater in the Iraq War than in the previous Gulf War. Major advances have been made in integrating carrier air wings with land-based air and land operations. In the Gulf War, the daily air tasking order (ATO)—a document some 800-pages thick that specified aircraft mission assignments—was physically transported to the carriers. This added delays and coordination problems to an already over-rigid and time-consuming ATO process, and even then there was poor integration. In the Iraq War, the ATO was sent digitally by secure Internet from the air-planning cell in the Combined Air Operations Center (CAOC) to the carriers. Moreover, each carrier had representatives at the CAOC to help ensure that the ATO assigned the right missions to the carrier air wings.[1]

Aboard the carrier, the ATO was now handled using modern computer hardware and software, and there were programs to allow the air wing and squadrons to search the document for relevant sections, eliminating the need to study the entire order.[2]

The navy has sought to further increase coordination with improved joint training and assignments, and it is seeking to improve its information sharing. It is creating a Joint Fires network and Cooperative Engagement Capability (CEC) system to allows ships to share radar data and to fire missiles based on another ship's information and on data from aircraft like the E-2C Hawkeye airborne command and control aircraft. Joint Fires is a U.S. Navy version of the U.S. Army's sensor-fusion Tactical Exploitation System (TES) that allows a carrier to receive imagery from airborne collectors and other sensors. TES can also overlay signals intelligence from USAF RC-135 Rivet Joints. A smaller version of the TES, called the Remote Terminal Capability (RTC), is on other large ships. The navy is trying to determine if it should buy the TES or the less costly RTC.

JOINTNESS IN C3, IS&R, AND "OPEN ARCHITECTURE"

Like the other services, including the U.S. Marine Corps, the U.S. Navy is evaluating ways to improve its C3 and IS&R systems. This is part of a broader effort to establish an open architecture for U.S. Navy information systems, many of which were designed on a ship-by-ship or platform-by-platform basis and, in some cases, decades ago. The submarine fleet and naval air operations have modernized significantly more quickly than the surface fleet, but it is clear that the navy needs to make advances in these areas if it is to properly support amphibious and littoral operations and match the USAF's advances in developing joint "digital" communications, control, targeting, and data systems with U.S. and allied land forces.[3]

CRUISE MISSILE SHIPS

As has been noted in chapter 8, the coalition made heavy use of sea-launched cruise missiles in the Iraq War. This raises issues regarding the need for cheaper and more cost-effective cruise missiles and ones with a wide range of lethality and the ability to attack a broader target mix. More generally, it raises questions about the cost-effectiveness trade-offs between sea- and air-launched platforms in an era where relatively inexpensive air-launched platforms like the JDAM can be so effective.

At the same time, the value of precision-strike capability is so high that questions arise as to what would happen in environments less permissive than Iraq, such as North Korea. In contrast to Iraq, where highly "visible" slow flyers like the B-1B and B-52 were able to loiter and provide time-sensitive strikes, there might well be a need for some form of "arsenal ship" that could supplement naval aviation with massive long-distance strike power, preferably without major escort forces.

MINE WARFARE AND NAVAL RAIDS

The use of special operations forces to seize Iraq's offshore oil export terminals, as well as British Royal Marine and SBS operations in coastal areas, provides yet another illustration of the broad value of such forces in modern warfare. Although the Iraq War did not involve amphibious operations, it is clear that control of local waters and even small littoral operations can have high payoffs.

The Iraqis failed to use mines and suicide boats effectively against coalition naval forces and ships, but did succeed in blocking the channels to Iraq's ports. It is clear that the anti-mine and ship protection mission remains critical.

More broadly, Iraq did retain anti-ship missile capabilities. It is clear that asymmetric warfare remains as much a threat at sea as it does on land and in the air.

VALUE OF SEALIFT AND MARITIME PRE-POSITIONING SHIPS

As has been discussed in chapter 6, the United States and Britain could not have fought the war in the way they did without relying on sealift to provide most of the supplies, heavy equipment, and heavy weapons that were needed. The timing of the war was also critically dependent on the ability to carry out this sealift process from a beginning in the spring of 2002 to a peak just before and during the war.

The United States also drew heavily on the use of maritime pre-positioning ships (MPS). The army, marines, and air force all benefited heavily from maritime and land pre-positioning and access to forward bases. Lt. Gen. James Conway, commander of the 1st Marine Expeditionary Force, described the value of pre-positioning ships, and the lessons to be learned, as follows:[4]

> …we have always felt in the Marine Corps that the MPS concept, Maritime Prepositioning Ship concept, is a real success story. It proved to be so during the last Gulf War, to the extent, I think, the United States Army saw the value in it and it created a very similar capability, at least here in Southwest Asia.
>
> This time through, it performed magnificently. We brought 11 ships in from two separate MPS squadrons, and the estimate was somewhere between 20 and 25 days for the off-load. We did it in 16. And we're extremely proud of our Marines and the process that allowed that to happen, because it gave us two full brigade sets of equipment on deck. And that did not include the Amphibious Task Forces, East and West, sailing with additional Marines, armor, helicopters, fixed-wing aircraft and those types of things. So, this Marine Expeditionary Force truly arrived from the sea.
>
> …an important component of that is the support that we get from the United States Air Force in that they fly over large numbers of Marines, both with Air Force air and contract air, to link us up with that equipment and

then move it into tactical assembly areas. But suffice it to say that we brought in about 60,000 Marines in about 45 days, once the Department of Defense and the administration decided that it was time to prop the force and make it ready.

Where we go from here is, I think, an interesting question. I will tell you that our planners at Headquarters Marine Corps are looking at even more efficient ways to organize the ships, and I think the commandant has made the decision that that will happen. What it basically involves is like types of ships in like squadrons. But I've got to tell you, this is a pretty tremendous capability right now, and I think any tweaking that we do will be pretty much on the margins, because now in two successive conflicts, it has truly proven its value.

THE VALUE OF ALLIES

The British Ministry of Defense drew the same general lessons about the value of seapower as the United States. It also highlighted the value of the long history of close cooperation between the British and U.S. navies and the value of "jointness" defined in international terms:[5]

> The operation confirmed the flexibility of sea-borne forces for maneuver and for the application of combat power, theatre entry and power projection, in the form of sea-based aviation, cruise missiles, amphibious forces and Naval Fire Support. It also showed the possibilities of afloat support for sea-based sustainment of joint forces.
>
> The performance of UK maritime forces in successfully meeting their objectives demonstrated the development of the RN's joint and expeditionary credentials since the SDR. Our forces showed linkage with the US in virtually every maritime warfare discipline, and we expect to draw a number of lessons from the U.S. experience in using large carriers and powerful amphibious groups in both the pre-combat and combat phases of the operation.

The interoperability of U.S. and British naval forces, and those of Australia as well, is not a new lesson of the Iraq War. This does not, however, make the lesson any less important.

Notes

[1] Rowan Scarborough, "Myers Says 'Annihilation of Iraqi Army Wasn't Goal,'" *Washington Times*, June 30, 2003.

[2] This discussion is based largely on Robert Wall, "Waging War Precisely," *Aviation Week*, March 16, 2003.

[3] See Jason Sherman, "US Navy Seeks Open Info Architecture," *Defense News*, June 23, 2003, p. 18.

[4] Lt. Gen. James Conway, commander, 1st Marine Expeditionary Force, "Live Briefing from Iraq, May 30, 2003," www.defenselink.mil/transcripts/2003/tr20030530-0229.html.

[5] British Ministry of Defense, "Operations in Iraq: First Reflections" (London: Her Majesty's Stationery Office, July 2003), p. 20.

CHAPTER TWELVE

LESSONS RELATING TO INTELLIGENCE AND WEAPONS OF MASS DESTRUCTION

A number of the lessons of the Iraq War affect intelligence, the ability to deal with weapons of mass destruction, and psychological warfare. Although these lessons cannot be fully separated from the analysis of intelligence, surveillance, and reconnaissance (IS&R), targeting, and conflict termination in other chapters, several issues merit detailed examination.

INTELLIGENCE STRENGTHS AND WEAKNESSES

The coalition had overwhelming overall superiority in the intelligence aspects of IS&R. It also had the advantage of experience and a vast range of intelligence collection and analysis to build upon. The United States had used space and other intelligence assets to study and target Iraq for more than 12 years, from the summer of 1990 to the beginning of 2003, and it had had to prepare for war several times after 1991.

The United States and Britain had carried out major strikes during Desert Fox in 1998, and they repeatedly flew reconnaissance missions and strikes over Iraq to enforce the no-fly zones during 1998–2003. This combination of intelligence effort and combat experience provided a unique degree of situational awareness before the war began. At the same time, it is important to temper any lessons about the advantages of U.S. intelligence assets with the understanding that similar experience and knowledge may not be present in future contingencies.

The Iraq War is a warning that even the world's most advanced intelligence systems and more than a decade of intensive intelligence collection and analysis could still leave major gaps and serious intelligence problems. As has been discussed throughout much of the preceding analysis, the United States and its allies still had serious problems in the following aspects of intelligence collection and analysis:

- The United States and Britain were never able to establish a credible picture of Iraqi links to terrorist organizations, including Al Qaida. Many charges were made, but none were substantiated.

- The United States did not have enough area experts, technical experts, and analysts with language skills at any level to make optimal use of its sensors and collection of data. This was as true at the national level as at the tactical level, and collection overload was a problem in many areas.

- The United States had a far greater capability to target buildings than to characterize what went on in the buildings and the effect of strikes on most sets of structures. It could not measure the level of wartime activity in many cases (facilities with high emission levels were an exception), and this made the efforts at "effects-based" operations discussed in later chapters difficult and sometimes impossible. Moreover, estimates of the level and nature of underground and sheltered facilities and activity were generally highly problematic.

- The IS&R effort mistargeted leadership facilities, exaggerated the importance of C4I strikes, and overtargeted fixed military facilities. It is unclear, however, that the United States and its allies had any other choice. Striking more targets in the face of uncertainty was probably better than striking only those targets where a high confidence could be established about the effect.

- The IS&R effort often had to take a "worst case" approach to the potential role of Iraq's security forces, intelligence services, irregular forces like Saddam's Fedayeen, and unusual military formations like the Special Republican Guard. In fairness, however, it is difficult—if not impossible—to accurately characterize the war-fighting capability of forces that have never fought and that do not conduct open and realistic exercises.

- The IS&R sensor and analytic effort focused more on major combat forces, with heavy weapons, than on infantry or irregular forces. It could do a much better job of locating and characterizing weapons platforms and military emitters than of dealing with personnel and forces that relied on light vehicles. It was generally difficult or impossible to locate distributed forces in a built-up or urban environment until they were forced into some form of open military activity, and the United States often lacked the density of specialized assets like UAVs to carry out this mission even when open activity took place.

- The IS&R effort did much to reduce collateral damage and the risk of civilian casualties. It was neither organized nor capable, however, of assessing either civilian or military casualties.

- The speed and intensity of the war seem to have led to a major breakdown in the battle damage assessment process. Quite aside from the many gaps and uncertainties remaining in the BDA process, the IS&R system could not close the cycle in terms of target-shoot-assess on a timely and accurate basis. This remains a critical challenge in creating true netcentric war.

- The IS&R effort was not able to characterize and target Iraq's weapons of mass destruction effort before or during the war, or to provide reliable warning of the tactical threat. It seems to have been somewhat better in dealing with potential delivery systems, but the level of improvement relative to the inability to locate the Iraqi chemical, biological, and nuclear effort is unclear.

THE NEED FOR BETTER ASSESSMENT, CHARACTERIZATION, AND LOCATION OF WEAPONS OF MASS DESTRUCTION AND KEY DELIVERY SYSTEMS

The most controversial failures in intelligence lay in the area of weapons of mass destruction. It may be months or years before it will be possible to locate and analyze the data the war makes available on Iraq's history of proliferation, its imports and domestic programs, its capabilities at the time of the war, and its goals or objectives.

It has become clear that the U.S. and British governments had only a tenuous understanding of the threat they faced from Iraqi weapons of mass destruction—and that they were unable to characterize the scale of the Iraqi effort they described as a key motive for the conflict—during the period before the war began.[1]

It is also clear from the previous chapters that coalition commanders had little intelligence on Iraq's WMD programs and war-fighting capabilities as they advanced. A wide range of reports during the war show that there were many false alarms—when elements of the advancing forces thought they had found weapons of mass destruction or the facilities to produce them; when coalition forces donned chemical protection gear they later turned out not to need; or when coalition commanders, lacking the tactical intelligence support that would give them a clearer picture of the risks involved, had to ignore the risk that Iraq might use such weapons.

Key Points in the U.S. and British White Papers

President Bush, Prime Minister Blair, and many U.S. and British officials made numerous charges before the war that Iraq was actively developing weapons of mass destruction that it had probably deployed combat-ready chemical and biological; weapons; that it had an active nuclear weapons program; and that it was developing new delivery systems, including missiles and UAVs. The British government issued two white papers on Iraq, and the United States issued one. U.S. officials like Deputy Secretary of Defense Paul Wolfowitz made additional charges, and Secretary of State Colin Powell presented a detailed briefing to the United Nations setting forth additional U.S. charges against Iraq.

Most of the attention since the war regarding the prewar charges against Iraq has focused on the fact that both British and U.S. speeches and briefings included unvalidated statements that Iraq had sought uranium ore and was ready to use weapons of mass destruction; that the British paper on WMD stated that Iraq could deliver such weapons with only 45 minutes warning; and that one of the British white papers paraphrased unattributed material from a graduate student.

In reality, U.S. and British intelligence made a long series of complex charges, only some of which were properly qualified. To understand the true scale of the intelligence problems involved and the need for improvement in this intelligence, it is necessary to understand that the charges issued in the British Joint Intelligence Committee and CIA white papers involved the following detailed points: [2]

Summary Conclusions

British Summary

Intelligence shows that Iraq is preparing plans to conceal evidence of these weapons, including incriminating documents, from renewed inspections. And it confirms that despite sanctions and the policy of containment, Saddam has continued to make progress with his illicit weapons programs.

As a result of the intelligence, we judge that Iraq has:

- Continued to produce chemical and biological agents;
- Military plans for the use of chemical and biological weapons, including against its own Shia population. Some of these weapons are deployable within 45 minutes of an order to use them;
- Command and control arrangements in place to use chemical and biological weapons. Authority ultimately resides with Saddam Hussein. (There is intelligence that he may have delegated this authority to his son Qusai);

- Developed mobile laboratories for military use, corroborating earlier reports bout the mobile production of biological warfare agents;
- Pursued illegal programmes to procure controlled materials of potential use in the production of chemical and biological weapons programmes; tried covertly to acquire technology and materials which could be used in the production of nuclear weapons;
- Sought significant quantities of uranium from Africa, despite having no active civil nuclear power program that could require it; recalled specialists to work on its nuclear program;
- Illegally retained up to 20 al-Hussein missiles, with a range of 650km, capable of carrying chemical or biological warheads;
- Started deploying its al-Samoud liquid propellant missile, and has used the absence of weapons inspectors to work on extending its range to at least 200km, which is beyond the limit of 150km imposed by the United Nations;
- Started producing the solid-propellant Ababil-100, and is making efforts to extend its range to at least 200km, which is beyond the limit of 150km imposed by the United Nations;
- Constructed a new engine test stand for the development of missiles capable of reaching the UK Sovereign Base Areas in Cyprus and NATO members Greece and Turkey), as well as all Iraq's Gulf neighbors and Israel;
- Pursued illegal programmes to procure materials for use in its illegal development of long range missiles;
- Learnt lessons from previous UN weapons inspections and has already begun to conceal sensitive equipment and documentation in advance of the return of inspectors.

U.S. Summary

Iraq has continued its weapons of mass destruction (WMD) programs in defiance of UN resolutions and restrictions. Baghdad has chemical and biological weapons as well as missiles with ranges in excess of UN restrictions; if left unchecked, it probably will have a nuclear weapon during this decade.

- Baghdad hides large portions of Iraq's WMD efforts. Revelations after the Gulf war starkly demonstrate the extensive efforts undertaken by Iraq to deny information.
- Since inspections ended in 1998, Iraq has maintained its chemical weapons effort, energized its missile program, and invested more heavily in biological weapons; most analysts assess Iraq is reconstituting its nuclear weapons program.
- Iraq's growing ability to sell oil illicitly increases Baghdad's capabilities to finance WMD programs; annual earnings in cash and goods have more than quadrupled.

- Iraq largely has rebuilt missile and biological weapons facilities damaged during Operation Desert Fox and has expanded its chemical and biological infrastructure under the cover of civilian production.
- Baghdad has exceeded UN range limits of 150 km with its ballistic missiles and is working with unmanned aerial vehicles (UAVs), which allow for a more lethal means to deliver biological and, less likely, chemical warfare agents.

Although Saddam probably does not yet have nuclear weapons or sufficient material to make any, he remains intent on acquiring them.

- How quickly Iraq will obtain its first nuclear weapon depends on when it acquires sufficient weapons-grade fissile material.
- If Baghdad acquires sufficient weapons-grade fissile material from abroad, it could make a nuclear weapon within a year.
- Without such material from abroad, Iraq probably would not be able to make a weapon until the last half of the decade.
- Iraq's aggressive attempts to obtain proscribed high-strength aluminum tubes are of significant concern. All intelligence experts agree that Iraq is seeking nuclear weapons and that these tubes could be used in a centrifuge enrichment program.
- Most intelligence specialists assess this to be the intended use, but some believe that these tubes are probably intended for conventional weapons programs.
- Based on tubes of the size Iraq is trying to acquire, a few tens of thousands of centrifuges would be capable of producing enough highly enriched uranium for a couple of weapons per year.

Baghdad has begun renewed production of chemical warfare agents, probably including mustard, sarin, cyclosarin, and VX. Its capability was reduced during the NSCOM inspections and is probably more limited now than it was at the time of the Gulf war, although VX production and agent storage life probably have been improved.

- Saddam probably has stocked a few hundred metric tons of CW agents.
- The Iraqis have experience in manufacturing CW bombs, artillery rockets, and projectiles, and probably possess CW bulk fills for SRBM warheads, including for a limited number of covertly stored, extended-range Scuds.

All key aspects—R&D, production, and weaponization—of Iraq's offensive BW program are active and most elements are larger and more advanced than they were before the Gulf war.

Iraq has some lethal and incapacitating BW agents and is capable of quickly producing and weaponizing a variety of such agents, including anthrax, for delivery by bombs, missiles, aerial sprayers, and covert operatives, including potentially against the U.S. Homeland.

- Baghdad has established a large-scale, redundant, and concealed BW agent production capability, which includes mobile facilities; these facilities can evade detection, are highly survivable, and can exceed the production rates Iraq had prior to the Gulf war.

Iraq maintains a small missile force and several development programs, including for a UAV that most analysts believe probably is intended to deliver biological warfare agents.

- Gaps in Iraqi accounting to UNSCOM suggest that Saddam retains a covert force of up to a few dozen Scud-variant SRBMs with ranges of 650 to 900 km.
- Iraq is deploying its new al-Samoud and Ababil-100 SRBMs, which are capable of flying beyond the UN-authorized 150-km range limit.
- Baghdad's UAVs—especially if used for delivery of chemical and biological warfare (CBW) agents—could threaten Iraq's neighbors, U.S. forces in the Persian Gulf, and the United States if brought close to, or into, the U.S. Homeland.
- Iraq is developing medium-range ballistic missile capabilities, largely through foreign assistance in building specialized facilities.

Developments since 1998

British Summary of Developments since 1998

Iraq has a useable chemical and biological weapons capability, in breach of UNSCR 687, which has included recent production of chemical and biological agents.

Saddam continues to attach great importance to the possession of weapons of mass destruction and ballistic missiles that he regards as being the basis for Iraq's regional power. He is determined to retain these capabilities.

Iraq can deliver chemical and biological agents using an extensive range of artillery shells, free-fall bombs, sprayers, and ballistic missiles.

Iraq continues to work on developing nuclear weapons, in breach of its obligations under the Non-Proliferation Treaty and in breach of UNSCR 687. Uranium has been sought from Africa that has no civil nuclear application in Iraq.

Iraq possesses extended-range versions of the SCUD ballistic missile in breach of UNSCR 687, which are capable of reaching Cyprus, Eastern Turkey, Tehran, and Israel. It is also developing longer-range ballistic missiles.

Iraq's current military planning specifically envisages the use of chemical and biological weapons.

Iraq's military forces are able to use chemical and biological weapons, with command, control, and logistical arrangements in place. The Iraqi military are able to deploy these weapons within 45 minutes of a decision to do so.

Iraq has learnt lessons from previous UN weapons inspections and is already taking steps to conceal and disperse sensitive equipment and documentation in advance of the return of inspectors.

Iraq's chemical, biological, and nuclear and ballistic missiles programmes are well funded.

CIA Estimate of Developments since 1998

Since December 1998, Baghdad has refused to allow UN inspectors into Iraq as required by the Security Council resolutions. Technical monitoring systems installed by the UN at known and suspected WMD and missile facilities in Iraq no longer operate. Baghdad prohibits Security Council-mandated monitoring overflights of Iraqi facilities by UN aircraft and helicopters. Similarly, Iraq has curtailed most IAEA [International Atomic Energy Agency] inspections since 1998, allowing the IAEA to visit annually only a very small number of sites to safeguard Iraq's stockpile of uranium oxide.

In the absence of inspectors, Baghdad's already considerable ability to work on prohibited programs without risk of discovery has increased, and there is substantial evidence that Iraq is reconstituting prohibited programs. Baghdad's vigorous concealment efforts have meant that specific information on many aspects of Iraq's WMD programs is yet to be uncovered. Revelations after the Gulf War starkly demonstrate the extensive efforts undertaken by Iraq to deny information.

Limited insight into activities since 1998 clearly show that Baghdad has used the absence of UN inspectors to repair and expand dual-use and dedicated missile development facilities and to increase its ability to produce WMD.

Chemical Warfare Program

UK: Chemical Warfare

Since the withdrawal of the inspectors the JIC has monitored evidence, including from secret intelligence, of continuing work on Iraqi offensive chemical and biological warfare capabilities. In the first half of 2000 the JIC noted 17 reports of intelligence on Iraqi attempts to procure dual-use chemicals and on the reconstruction of civil chemical production at sites formerly associated with the chemical warfare programme.

In mid-2001, the JIC assessed that Iraq retained some chemical warfare agents, precursors, production equipment and weapons from before the Gulf War. These stocks would enable Iraq to produce significant quantities of mustard gas within weeks and of nerve agent within months. The JIC concluded that intelligence on Iraqi former chemical and biological warfare facilities, their limited reconstruction and civil production pointed to a continuing research and development programme. These chemical and biological capabilities represented the most immediate threat from Iraqi weapons of mass destruction. Since 1998 Iraqi development of mass destruction weaponry had been helped by the absence of inspectors and the increase in illegal border trade, which was providing hard currency.

In the last six months the JIC has confirmed its earlier judgments on Iraqi chemical and biological warfare capabilities and assessed that Iraq has the means to deliver chemical and biological weapons.

Subsequently, intelligence has become available from reliable sources which complements and adds to previous intelligence and confirms the JIC assessment that Iraq has chemical and biological weapons. The intelligence also shows that the Iraqi leadership has been discussing a number of issues related to these weapons. This intelligence covers:

Confirmation that chemical and biological weapons play an important role in Iraqi military thinking: intelligence shows that Saddam attaches great importance to the possession of chemical and biological weapons which he regards as being the basis for Iraqi regional power. He believes that respect for Iraq rests on its possession of these weapons and the missiles capable of delivering them. Intelligence indicates that Saddam is determined to retain this capability and recognizes that Iraqi political weight would be diminished if Iraq's military power rested solely on its conventional military forces.

Iraqi attempts to retain its existing banned weapons systems: Iraq is already taking steps to prevent UN weapons inspectors finding evidence of its chemical and biological weapons programme. Intelligence indicates that Saddam has learnt lessons from previous weapons inspections, has identified possible weak points in the inspections process and knows how to exploit them. Sensitive equipment and papers can easily be concealed and in some cases this is already happening. The possession of mobile biological agent production facilities will also aid concealment efforts. Saddam is determined not to lose the capabilities that he has been able to develop further in the four years since inspectors left.

Saddam's willingness to use chemical and biological weapons: intelligence indicates that as part of Iraq's military planning Saddam is willing to use chemical and biological weapons, including against his own Shia population. Intelligence indicates that the Iraqi military are able to deploy chemical or biological weapons within 45 minutes of an order to do so.

When confronted with questions about the unaccounted stocks, Iraq has claimed repeatedly that if it had retained any chemical agents from before the Gulf War they would have deteriorated sufficiently to render them harmless. But Iraq has admitted to UNSCOM to having the knowledge and capability to add stabilizer to nerve agent and other chemical warfare agents that would prevent such decomposition. In 1997 UNSCOM also examined some munitions which had been filled with mustard gas prior to 1991 and found that they remained very toxic and showed little sign of deterioration.

Intelligence shows that Iraq has continued to produce chemical agent. During the Gulf War a number of facilities which intelligence reporting indicated were directly or indirectly associated with Iraq's chemical weapons effort were attacked and damaged. Following the ceasefire UNSCOM destroyed or rendered harmless facilities and equipment used in Iraq's chemical weapons programme. Other equipment was released for civilian use either in industry or academic institutes, where it was tagged and regularly inspected and monitored, or else placed under camera monitoring, to ensure that it was not being misused.

This monitoring ceased when UNSCOM withdrew from Iraq in 1998. However, capabilities remain and, although the main chemical weapon production facility at al-Muthanna was completely destroyed by UNSCOM and has not been 19 rebuilt, other plants formerly associated with the chemical warfare programme have been rebuilt. These include the chlorine and phenol plant at Fallujah 2 near Habbaniyah. In addition to their civilian uses, chlorine and phenol are used for precursor chemicals that contribute to the production of chemical agents.

Other dual-use facilities, which are capable of being used to support the production of chemical agent and precursors, have been rebuilt and re-equipped. New chemical facilities have been built, some with illegal foreign assistance, and are probably fully operational or ready for production. These include the Ibn Sina Company at Tarmiyah (see figure 1), which is a chemical research centre. It undertakes research, development and production of chemicals previously imported but not now available and which are needed for Iraq's civil industry. The Director General of the research centre is Hikmat Na'im al-Jalu who prior to the Gulf War worked in Iraq's nuclear weapons programme and after the war was responsible for preserving Iraq's chemical expertise.

Parts of the al-Qa'qa' chemical complex damaged in the Gulf War have also been repaired and are operational. Of particular concern are elements of the phosgene production plant at al-Qa'qa'. These were severely damaged during the Gulf War, and dismantled under UNSCOM supervision, but have since been rebuilt. While phosgene does have industrial uses it can also be used by itself as a chemical agent or as a precursor for nerve agent.

Iraq has retained the expertise for chemical warfare research, agent production and weaponization. Most of the personnel previously involved in the programme remain in country. While UNSCOM found a number of technical manuals (so called "cook books") for the production of chemical agents and critical precursors, Iraq's claim to have unilaterally destroyed the bulk of the documentation cannot be confirmed and is almost certainly untrue. Recent intelligence indicates that Iraq is still discussing methods of concealing such documentation in order to ensure that it is not discovered by any future UN inspections.

Almost all components and supplies used in weapons of mass destruction and ballistic missile programmes are dual-use. For example, any major petrochemical or biotech industry, as well as public health organizations, will have legitimate need for most materials and equipment required to manufacture chemical and biological weapons. Without UN weapons inspectors it is very difficult therefore to be sure about the true nature of many of Iraq's facilities.

For example, Iraq has built a large new chemical complex, Project Baiji, in the desert in north west Iraq at al-Sharqat. This site is a former uranium enrichment facility that was damaged during the Gulf War and rendered harmless under supervision of the IAEA. Part of the site has been rebuilt, with work starting in 1992, as a chemical production complex. Despite the site being far away from populated areas it is surrounded by a high wall with watchtowers and guarded by armed guards. Intelligence reports indicate that it will produce nitric acid, which can be used in explosives, missile fuel and in the purification of uranium.

Iraq has a variety of delivery means available for both chemical and biological agents. These include: free-fall bombs: Iraq acknowledged possession of four types of aerial bomb with various chemical agent fills including sulphur mustard, tabun, sarin and cyclosarin; artillery shells and rockets: Iraq made extensive use of artillery munitions filled with chemical agents during the Iran-Iraq War. Mortars can also be used for chemical agent delivery. Iraq is known to have tested the use of shells and rockets filled with biological agents. Over 20,000 artillery munitions remain unaccounted for by UN-SCOM; helicopter and aircraft borne sprayers: Iraq carried out studies into aerosol dissemination of biological agent using these platforms prior to 1991. UNSCOM was unable to account for many of these devices. It is probable that Iraq retains a capability for aerosol dispersal of both chemical and biological agent over a large area; al-Hussein ballistic missiles (range 650km): Iraq developed chemical agent warheads for al-Hussein. Iraq admitted to producing 50 chemical warheads for al-Hussein that were intended for the delivery of a mixture of sarin and cyclosarin. However, technical analysis of warhead remnants has shown traces of VX degradation product which indicate that some additional warheads were made and filled with VX; al-Samoud/Ababil-100 ballistic missiles (range 150km plus): it is unclear if chemical and biological warheads have been developed for these systems, but given the Iraqi experience on other missile systems, we judge that Iraq has the technical expertise for doing so; L-29 remotely piloted vehicle programme : we know from intelligence that Iraq has attempted to modify the L-29 jet trainer to allow it to be used as an Unmanned Aerial Vehicle (UAV) which is potentially capable of delivering chemical and biological agents over a large area.

The authority to use chemical and biological weapons ultimately resides with Saddam but intelligence indicates that he may have also delegated this authority to his son Qusai. Special Security Organization (SSO) and Special Republican Guard (SRG) units would be involved in the movement of any chemical and biological weapons to military units. The Iraqi military holds artillery and missile systems at Corps level throughout the Armed Forces and conducts regular training with them. The Directorate of Rocket Forces has operational control of strategic missile systems and some Multiple Launcher Rocket Systems.

CIA: Chemical Warfare

Iraq has the ability to produce chemical warfare (CW) agents within its chemical industry, although it probably depends on external sources for some precursors.

Baghdad is expanding its infrastructure, under cover of civilian industries, that it could use to advance its CW agent production capability. During the 1980s Saddam had a formidable CW capability that he used against Iranians and against Iraq's Kurdish population. Iraqi forces killed or injured more than 20,000 people in multiple attacks, delivering chemical agents (including mustard agent1 and the nerve agents sarin and tabun2) in aerial bombs, 122mm rockets, and artillery shells against both tactical military targets and segments of Iraq's Kurdish population. Before the 1991 Gulf war, Baghdad had a large stockpile of chemical munitions and a robust indigenous production capacity.

Although precise information is lacking, human rights organizations have received plausible accounts from Kurdish villagers of even more Iraqi chemical attacks against civilians in the 1987 to 1988 time frame—with some attacks as late as October 1988—in areas close to the Iranian and Turkish borders.

UNSCOM supervised the destruction of more than 40,000 chemical munitions, nearly 500,000 liters of chemical agents, 1.8 million liters of chemical precursors, and seven different types of delivery systems, including ballistic missile warheads. More than 10 years after the Gulf war, gaps in Iraqi accounting and current production capabilities strongly suggest that Iraq maintains a stockpile of chemical agents, probably VX,3 sarin, cyclosarin, and mustard.

Iraq probably has concealed precursors, production equipment, documentation, and other items necessary for continuing its CW effort. Baghdad never supplied adequate evidence to support its claims that it destroyed all of its CW agents and munitions. Thousands of tons of chemical precursors and tens of thousands of unfilled munitions, including Scud-variant missile warheads, remain unaccounted for.

UNSCOM discovered a document at Iraqi Air Force headquarters in July 1998 showing that Iraq overstated by at least 6,000 the number of chemical bombs it told the UN it had used during the Iran-Iraq War—bombs that remain are unaccounted for.

Iraq has not accounted for 15,000 artillery rockets that in the past were its preferred means for delivering nerve agents, nor has it accounted for about 550 artillery shells filled with mustard agent.

Iraq probably has stocked at least 100 metric tons (MT) and possibly as much as 500 MT of CW agents.

Baghdad continues to rebuild and expand dual-use infrastructure that it could divert quickly to CW production. The best examples are the chlorine and phenol plants at the Fallujah II facility. Both chemicals have legitimate civilian uses but also are raw materials for the synthesis of precursor chemicals used to produce blister and nerve agents. Iraq has three other chlorine plants that have much higher capacity for civilian production; these plants and Iraqi imports are more than sufficient to meet Iraq's civilian needs.

Of the 15 million kg of chlorine imported under the UN Oil-for-Food Program since 1997, Baghdad used only 10 million kg and has 5 million kg in stock, suggesting that some domestically produced chlorine has been diverted to such proscribed activities as CW agent production.

Fallujah II was one of Iraq's principal CW precursor production facilities before the Gulf war. In the last two years the Iraqis have upgraded the facility and brought in new chemical reactor vessels and shipping containers with a large amount of production equipment. They have expanded chlorine output far beyond pre-Gulf war production levels—capabilities that can be diverted quickly to CW production. Iraq is seeking to purchase CW agent precursors and applicable production equipment and is trying to hide the activities of the Fallujah plant.

Biological Warfare Program

UK: Biological Warfare

Since the withdrawal of the inspectors the JIC has monitored evidence, including from secret intelligence, of continuing work on Iraqi offensive chemical and biological warfare capabilities. In the first half of 2000 the JIC noted intelligence on Iraqi attempts to procure dual-use chemicals and on the reconstruction of civil chemical production at sites formerly associated with the chemical warfare programme.

Iraq has claimed that all its biological agents and weapons have been destroyed. No convincing proof of any kind has been produced to support this claim. In particular, Iraq could not explain large discrepancies between the amount of growth media (nutrients required for the specialized growth of agent) it procured before 1991 and the amounts of agent it admits to having manufactured. The discrepancy is enough to produce more than three times the amount of anthrax allegedly manufactured.

Iraq had also been trying to procure dual-use materials and equipment that could be used for a biological warfare programme. Personnel known to have been connected to the biological warfare programme up to the Gulf War had been conducting research into pathogens. There was intelligence that Iraq was starting to produce biological warfare agents in mobile production facilities. Planning for the project had begun in 1995 under Dr Rihab Taha, known to have been a central player in the pre-Gulf War programme. The JIC concluded that Iraq had sufficient expertise, equipment and material to produce biological warfare agents within weeks using its legitimate biotechnology facilities.

In mid-2001, the JIC concluded that intelligence on Iraqi former chemical and biological warfare facilities, their limited reconstruction and civil production pointed to a continuing research and development programme. These chemical and biological capabilities represented the most immediate threat from Iraqi weapons of mass destruction. Since 1998 Iraqi development of mass destruction weaponry had been helped by the absence of inspectors and the increase in illegal border trade, which was providing hard currency.

In the last six months the JIC has confirmed its earlier judgments on Iraqi chemical and biological warfare capabilities and assessed that Iraq has the means to deliver chemical and biological weapons.

Subsequently, intelligence has become available from reliable sources which complements and adds to previous intelligence and confirms the JIC assessment that Iraq has chemical and biological weapons. The intelligence also shows that the Iraqi leadership has been discussing a number of issues related to these weapons. This intelligence covers:

Confirmation that chemical and biological weapons play an important role in Iraqi military thinking: intelligence shows that Saddam attaches great importance to the possession of chemical and biological weapons which he regards as being the basis for Iraqi regional power. He believes that respect for Iraq rests on its possession of these weapons and the missiles capable of delivering them. Intelligence indicates that Saddam is determined to retain this capability and recognizes that Iraqi political weight would be diminished if Iraq's military power rested solely on its conventional military forces.

Iraq has claimed that all its biological agents and weapons have been destroyed. No convincing proof of any kind has been produced to support this claim. In particular, Iraq could not explain large discrepancies between the amount of growth media (nutrients required for the specialized growth of agent) it procured before 1991 and the amounts of agent it admits to having manufactured. The discrepancy is enough to produce more than three times the amount of anthrax allegedly manufactured.

We know from intelligence that Iraq has continued to produce biological warfare agents. As with some chemical equipment, UNSCOM only destroyed equipment that could be directly linked to biological weapons production. Iraq also has its own engineering capability to design and construct biological agent associated fermenters, centrifuges, sprayer dryers and other equipment and is judged to be self-sufficient in the technology required to produce biological weapons.

Almost all components and supplies used in weapons of mass destruction and ballistic missile programmes are dual-use. For example, any major petrochemical or biotech industry, as well as public health organizations, will have legitimate need for most materials and equipment required to manufacture chemical and biological weapons. Without UN weapons inspectors it is very difficult therefore to be sure about the true nature of many of Iraq's facilities.

Experienced personnel who were active in the programme have largely remained in the country. Some dual-use equipment has also been purchased, but without monitoring by UN inspectors Iraq could have diverted it to their biological weapons programme. This newly purchased equipment and other equipment previously subject to monitoring could be used in a resurgent biological warfare programme. Facilities of concern include:

- The Castor Oil Production Plant at Fallujah: this was damaged in UK/U.S. air attacks in 1998 (Operation Desert Fox) but has been rebuilt. The residue from the castor bean pulp can be used in the production of the biological agent ricin;
- The al-Dawrah Foot and Mouth Disease Vaccine Institute: which was involved in biological agent production and research before the Gulf War;
- The Amariyah Sera and Vaccine Plant at Abu Ghraib: UNSCOM established that this facility was used to store biological agents, seed stocks and conduct biological warfare associated genetic research prior to the Gulf War. It has now expanded its storage capacity.

UNSCOM established that Iraq considered the use of mobile biological agent production facilities. In the past two years evidence from defectors has indicated the existence of such facilities. Recent intelligence confirms that the Iraqi military have developed mobile facilities. These would help Iraq conceal and protect biological agent production from military attack or UN inspection.

Iraq has a variety of delivery means available for both chemical and biological agents. These include:

- free-fall bombs: Iraq acknowledged to UNSCOM the deployment to two sites of free-fall bombs filled with biological agent during 1990–1991. These bombs were filled with anthrax, botulinum toxin and aflatoxin;
- artillery shells and rockets: Iraq is known to have tested the use of shells and rockets filled with biological agents. Over 20,000 artillery munitions remain unaccounted for by UNSCOM;
- helicopter and aircraft borne sprayers: Iraq carried out studies into aerosol dissemination of biological agent using these platforms prior to 1991. UNSCOM was unable to account for many of these devices. It is probable that Iraq retains a capability for aerosol dispersal of both chemical and biological agent over a large area;
- al-Hussein ballistic missiles (range 650km): Iraq told UNSCOM that it filled 25 warheads with anthrax, botulinum toxin and aflatoxin;
- al-Samoud/Ababil-100 ballistic missiles (range 150km plus): it is unclear if chemical and biological warheads have been developed for these systems, but given the Iraqi experience on other missile systems, we judge that Iraq has the technical expertise for doing so;
- L-29 remotely piloted vehicle programme : we know from intelligence that Iraq has attempted to modify the L-29 jet trainer to allow it to be used as an Unmanned Aerial Vehicle (UAV) which is potentially capable of delivering chemical and biological agents over a large area.

CIA: Biological Warfare

Iraq has the capability to convert quickly legitimate vaccine and biopesticide plants to biological warfare (BW) production and already may have done so. This capability is particularly troublesome because Iraq has a record of concealing its BW activities and lying about the existence of its offensive BW program.

After four years of claiming that they had conducted only "small-scale, defensive" research, Iraqi officials finally admitted to inspectors in 1995 to production and weaponization of biological agents. The Iraqis admitted this only after being faced with evidence of their procurement of a large volume of growth media and the defection of Husayn Kamil, former director of Iraq's military industries.

Iraq admitted producing thousands of liters of the BW agents anthrax, 6 botulinum toxin (which paralyzes respiratory muscles and can be fatal within 24 to 36 hours), and aflatoxin (a potent carcinogen that can attack the liver, killing years after ingestion), and preparing BW-filled Scud-variant missile warheads, aerial bombs, and aircraft spray tanks before the Gulf war.

Baghdad did not provide persuasive evidence to support its claims that it unilaterally destroyed its BW agents and munitions. Experts from UNSCOM assessed that Baghdad's declarations vastly understated the production of biological agents and estimated that Iraq actually produced two-to-four times the amount of agent that it acknowledged producing, including Bacillus anthracis—the causative agent of anthrax—and botulinum toxin.

The improvement or expansion of a number of nominally "civilian" facilities that were directly associated with biological weapons indicates that key aspects of Iraq's offensive BW program are active and most elements more advanced and larger than before the 1990-1991 Gulf war.

- The al-Dawrah Foot-and-Mouth Disease (FMD) Vaccine Facility is one of two known Biocontainment Level-3—facilities in Iraq with an extensive air handling and filtering system. Iraq admitted that before the Gulf war Al-Dawrah had been a BW agent production facility. UNSCOM attempted to render it useless for BW agent production in 1996 but left some production equipment in place because UNSCOM could not prove it was connected to previous BW work. In 2001, Iraq announced it would begin renovating the plant without UN approval, ostensibly to produce a vaccine to combat an FMD outbreak. In fact, Iraq easily can import all the foot-and mouth vaccine it needs through the UN.

- The Amiriyah Serum and Vaccine Institute is an ideal cover location for BW research, testing, production, and storage. UN inspectors discovered documents related to BW research at this facility, some showing that BW cultures, agents, and equipment were stored there during the Gulf war. Of particular concern is the plant's new storage capacity, which greatly exceeds Iraq's needs for legitimate medical storage.

- The Fallujah III Castor Oil Production Plant is situated on a large complex with an historical connection to Iraq's CW program. Of immediate BW concern is the potential production of ricin toxin. Castor bean pulp, left over from castor oil production, can be used to extract ricin toxin. Iraq admitted to UNSCOM that it manufactured ricin and field-tested it in artillery shells before the Gulf war. Iraq operated this plant for legitimate purposes under UNSCOM scrutiny before 1998 when UN inspectors left the country.

- Since 1999, Iraq has rebuilt major structures destroyed during Operation Desert Fox. Iraqi officials claim they are making castor oil for brake fluid, but verifying such claims without UN inspections is impossible. In addition to questions about activity at known facilities, there are compelling reasons to be concerned about BW activity at other sites and in mobile production units and laboratories. Baghdad has pursued a mobile BW research and production capability to better conceal its program.

UNSCOM uncovered a document on Iraqi Military Industrial Commission letterhead indicating that Iraq was interested in developing mobile fermentation units, and an Iraqi scientist admitted to UN inspectors that Iraq was trying to move in the direction of mobile BW production.

Iraq has now established large-scale, redundant, and concealed BW agent production capabilities based on mobile BW facilities.

Nuclear Warfare Program

UK: Nuclear Warfare

Since 1999 the JIC has monitored Iraq's attempts to reconstitute its nuclear weapons programme. In mid-2001 the JIC assessed that Iraq had continued its nuclear research after 1998. The JIC drew attention to intelligence that Iraq had recalled its nuclear scientists to the programme in 1998. Since 1998 Iraq had been trying to procure items that could be for use in the construction of centrifuges for the enrichment of uranium.

It is clear from IAEA inspections and Iraq's own declarations that by 1991 considerable progress had been made in both developing methods to produce fissile material and in weapons design. The IAEA dismantled the physical infrastructure of the Iraqi nuclear weapons program, including the dedicated facilities and equipment for uranium separation and enrichment, and for weapon development and production, and removed the remaining highly enriched uranium. But Iraq retained, and retains, many of its experienced nuclear scientists and technicians who are specialized in the production of fissile material and weapons design. Intelligence indicates that Iraq also retains the accompanying programme documentation and data.

Intelligence shows that the present Iraqi programme is almost certainly seeking an indigenous ability to enrich uranium to the level needed for a nuclear weapon. It indicates that the approach is based on gas centrifuge uranium enrichment, one of the routes Iraq was following for producing fissile material before the Gulf War. But Iraq needs certain key equipment, including gas centrifuge components and components for the production of fissile material before a nuclear bomb could be developed.

Following the departure of weapons inspectors in 1998 there has been an accumulation of intelligence indicating that Iraq is making concerted covert efforts to acquire dual-use technology and materials with nuclear applications. Iraq's known holdings of processed uranium are under IAEA supervision. But there is intelligence that Iraq has sought the supply of significant quantities of uranium from Africa. Iraq has no active civil nuclear power programme or nuclear power plants and therefore has no legitimate reason to acquire uranium.

Intelligence shows that other important procurement activity since 1998 has included attempts to purchase:

- vacuum pumps which could be used to create and maintain pressures in a gas centrifuge cascade needed to enrich uranium;
- an entire magnet production line of the correct specification for use in the motors and top bearings of gas centrifuges. It appears that Iraq is attempt-

ing to acquire a capability to produce them on its own rather than rely on foreign procurement;

- anhydrous hydrogen fluoride (AHF) and fluorine gas. AHF is commonly used in the petrochemical industry and Iraq frequently imports significant amounts, but it is also used in the process of converting uranium into uranium hexafluoride for use in gas centrifuge cascades;
- one large filament winding machine which could be used to manufacture carbon fiber gas centrifuge rotors;
- a large balancing machine, which could be used in initial centrifuge balancing work.

Iraq has also made repeated attempts covertly to acquire a very large quantity (60,000 or more) of specialized aluminum tubes. The specialized aluminum in question is subject to international export controls because of its potential application in the construction of gas centrifuges used to enrich uranium, although there is no definitive intelligence that it is destined for a nuclear programme.

In early 2002, the JIC assessed that UN sanctions on Iraq were hindering the import of crucial goods for the production of fissile material. The JIC judged Iraq's long-standing civil nuclear power programme is limited to small-scale research. Activities that could be used for military purposes are prohibited by UNSCR 687 and 715.

Iraq has no nuclear power plants and therefore no requirement for uranium as fuel.

Iraq has a number of nuclear research programmes in the fields of agriculture, biology, chemistry, materials and pharmaceuticals. None of these activities requires more than tiny amounts of uranium, which Iraq could supply from its own resources.

Iraq's research reactors are non-operational; two were bombed and one was never completed.

...while sanctions remain effective Iraq would not be able to produce a nuclear weapon. If they were removed or prove ineffective, it would take Iraq at least five years to produce sufficient fissile material for a weapon indigenously. However, we know that Iraq retains expertise and design data relating to nuclear weapons. We therefore judge that if Iraq obtained fissile material and other essential components from foreign sources the timeline for production of a nuclear weapon would be shortened and Iraq could produce a nuclear weapon in between one and two years.

CIA: Nuclear Warfare

More than ten years of sanctions and the loss of much of Iraq's physical nuclear infrastructure under IAEA oversight have not diminished Saddam's interest in acquiring or developing nuclear weapons.

Iraq's efforts to procure tens of thousands of proscribed high-strength alu-minum tubes are of significant concern. All intelligence experts agree that Iraq is seeking nuclear weapons and that these tubes could be used in a cen-trifuge enrichment program. Most intelligence specialists assess this to be the intended use, but some believe that these tubes are probably intended for conventional weapons programs.

Iraq had an advanced nuclear weapons development program before the Gulf war that focused on building an implosion-type weapon using highly enriched uranium. Baghdad was attempting a variety of uranium enrich-ment techniques, the most successful of which were the electromagnetic iso-tope separation (EMIS) and gas centrifuge programs. After its invasion of Kuwait, Iraq initiated a crash program to divert IAEA-safeguarded, highly enriched uranium from its Soviet and French-supplied reactors, but the on-set of hostilities ended this effort. Iraqi declarations and the UNSCOM/IAEA inspection process revealed much of Iraq's nuclear weapons efforts, but Baghdad still has not provided complete information on all aspects of its nuclear weapons program.

- Iraq has withheld important details relevant to its nuclear program, in-cluding procurement logs, technical documents, experimental data, ac-counting of materials, and foreign assistance.
- Baghdad also continues to withhold other data about enrichment tech-niques, foreign procurement, weapons design, and the role of Iraqi secu-rity services in concealing its nuclear facilities and activities.
- In recent years, Baghdad has diverted goods contracted under the Oil-for-Food Program for military purposes and has increased solicitations and dual-use procurements—outside the Oil-for-Food process—some of which almost certainly are going to prohibited WMD and other weapons programs. Baghdad probably uses some of the money it gains through its illicit oil sales to support its WMD efforts.

Before its departure from Iraq, the IAEA made significant strides toward dismantling Iraq's nuclear weapons program and unearthing the nature and scope of Iraq's past nuclear activities. In the absence of inspections, however, most analysts assess that Iraq is reconstituting its nuclear program—unrav-eling the IAEA's hard-earned accomplishments.

Iraq retains its cadre of nuclear scientists and technicians, its program documentation, and sufficient dual-use manufacturing capabilities to sup-port a reconstituted nuclear weapons program. Iraqi media have reported numerous meetings between Saddam and nuclear scientists over the past two years, signaling Baghdad's continued interest in reviving a nuclear program.

Iraq's expanding international trade provides growing access to nuclear-related technology and materials and potential access to foreign nuclear expertise. An increase in dual-use procurement activity in recent years may be supporting a reconstituted nuclear weapons program.

The acquisition of sufficient fissile material is Iraq's principal hurdle in developing a nuclear weapon. Iraq is unlikely to produce indigenously enough weapons-grade material for a deliverable nuclear weapon until the last half of this decade. Baghdad could produce a nuclear weapon within a year if it were able to procure weapons grade fissile material abroad.

Baghdad may have acquired uranium enrichment capabilities that could shorten substantially the amount of time necessary to make a nuclear weapon.

Problems in Collecting Data on Iraqi and Other Country WMD Capabilities and Delivery Systems

Even a cursory review of this list of U.S. and British charges about Iraq's WMD capabilities shows that point after point that was made was not confirmed during war or after the first few months of effort following the conflict. Despite all of the advances in their IS&R capabilities, the United States and Britain went to war with Iraq without the level of evidence needed to provide a clear strategic rationale for the war and without the ability to fully understand the threat that Iraqi weapons of mass destruction posed to U.S., British, and Australian forces. This uncertainty is not a definitive argument against carrying out a war that responded to grave potential threats. It *is* a definitive warning that this intelligence and targeting are not yet adequate to support grand strategy, strategy, and tactical operations against proliferating powers or to make accurate assessments about the need to preempt.

It is difficult to put these problems into perspective without access to classified material. Past declassified U.S. intelligence reporting on proliferation has made it clear, though, that proliferation presents very serious problems for intelligence collection and analysis. UNSCOM and UN-MOVIC reports show that Iraq was well aware of these problems and how to exploit them:

- Iraq and other powers sophisticated enough to proliferate are also sophisticated enough to have a good understanding of many of the strengths and limitations of modern intelligence sensors, the timing and duration of satellite coverage, and the methods used to track imports and technology transfer. They have learned to cover and conceal, to deceive, and to create smaller and better disseminated activities.

- Intelligence collection often relies heavily on finding key imports and technology transfers. Such reports, however, usually cover only a small fraction of the actual effort on the part of the proliferating country, and the information collected is often vague and uncertain. This occurs in part because importers and smugglers have every incentive to lie and are also familiar with many of the ways to defeat intelligence collection and import controls. When information does become available, it is often impossible to put in context, and a given import or technology transfer can often be used in many different ways, often other than proliferation. Import data can hint at the character of a proliferation effort, but may give no picture of the overall character of the activity.

- Even when data are available on given imports or technology transfers, they generally present three serious problems. One is that there is no way to know the end destination and use of the import and how it is integrated into the overall effort. The second is there is no way to know if it is integrated into an ongoing research and development effort, a weapons production effort, being procured or stockpiled for later use, or simply an experiment or mistake that is never further exploited. The third is that many imports have civilian or other military uses. These so-called "dual-use" imports may have legitimate use.

- The very nature of arms control agreements like the Nuclear Non-Proliferation Treaty (NNPT), Biological Weapons Convention (BWC), and Chemical Weapons convention (CWC) encourages proliferating nations to lie and conceal as effectively as possible. The same is true of supplier agreements like the Missile Technology Control Regime (MTCR) and Australia List, and any form of sanctions. Arms control only encourages compliance among non-proliferators and non-sellers, and current enforcement efforts are too weak to be effective while their provisions effective license technology transfer to those nations who succeed in lying or concealing.

- The technology of proliferation generally permits the research and development effort to be divided up into a wide range of small facilities and projects. Some can be carried out as legitimate civil research. Others can be hidden in civil and commercial facilities. As proliferators become more sophisticated, they learn to create dispersed, redundant and parallel programs, and mix high secret covert programs with open civil or dual-use programs. Chemical, biological, and cruise missile programs are particularly easy to divide up into small cells or operations. However, this is increasingly true of nuclear weapons centrifuge programs, plutonium processing and fuel cycles, and the testing and simulation of nuclear weapons that does not involve weapons grade materials. Many key aspects of ballistic missile R&D, including warhead and launch system design fit into this category.

- Iraq and most other proliferators have, in the past, focused on creating stockpiles of weapons for fighting theater conflicts against military forces. These stockpiles require large inventories, large-scale deployments, and generally mixes of training and war-fighting preparations that create significant intelligence indicators. There are, however, other strategies and many proliferators may now be pursuing them. One is to bring weapons to full development, and to wait until a threat becomes imminent to actually produce the weapon. A second is to follow the same course, but create large dual-use civil facilities that can be rapidly converted to the production of weapons of mass destruction. These can include pharmaceutical plants, food-processing plants, breweries, petrochemical plants, and pesticide plants, but key assembly lines can be concealed in a wide range of other commercial activities.[3] Weapons production facilities can be stockpiled for a later and sometimes sudden breakout. A third is to focus on creating as few highly lethal biological or nuclear weapons to attack key political or civilian facilities in a foreign country, rather than its military forces. Highly lethal non-infectious or infectious biological agents are one means of such an attack, biological weapons directed at crops or livestock are another.

- Countries can pursue very different strategies in dealing with their past inventories of weapons. They can disclose and destroy them, knowing they do not face an urgent war-fighting need, better weapons are coming, and this suits current political objectives. They can claim to destroy and hide the remaining weapons in covert areas known only to a few. They can claim to destroy, or lie, and disperse weapons where they can be used for war-fighting purposes. In many cases, intelligence collection may not be able to distinguish between such strategies, and a given proliferator like Iraq can pursue a mix of such strategies—depending on the value of the weapon.

- In many cases, there is no clear way to know whether a program is R&D, production and weapons deployment, or production capable/breakout oriented. The problem is further complicated by the fact that Iraq and other countries have learned to play a "shell game" by developing multiple surface and underground military facilities and dual-use facilities and to create relatively mobile mixes of trailer/vehicle mounted and "palletized" equipment for rapid movement. Large special-purpose facilities with hard-to-move equipment often still exist, but they are by no means the rule. Intelligence collection takes time and may often lag behind country activities.

- Unless a country keeps extremely accurate records of its programs, it is often far easier to estimate that maximum scale of what it might do than provide an accurate picture of what it has actually done.

- In most cases, it is impossible to know how far a given project or effort has gotten and how well it has succeeded. The history of proliferation is not the history of proliferators overcoming major technical and manufacturing problems. It is the history of massive management and systems integration problems, political failures, lying technical advocates and entrepreneurs, project managers who do not tell their political masters the truth, and occasional sudden success. Short of an intelligence breakthrough, it is rarely possible to assess the success of a given effort, and even on-the-scene inspection can produce very wrong results unless a given project can be subjected to detailed technical testing. For example, UNSCOM and the IAEA found that virtually all of their preliminary reporting on Iraq's nuclear effort in 1992-1993 tended to exaggerate Iraqi capabilities once they had had the time to fully assess the efficiency of key efforts like the Calutron and centrifuge programs.

- The only definitive way to counter most of these collection problems is to have a reliable mix of redundant human intelligence (HUMINT) sources within the system or as defectors. The United States, however, has never claimed or implied it had such capabilities in any proliferating country, and the history of U.S., British, UNSCOM, and UNMOVIC efforts to deal with Iraq makes it painfully clear both that such transparency was totally lacking in Iraq and that most Iraqi defectors and intelligence sources outside Iraq made up information, circulated unsubstantiated information, or simply lied. Breakthroughs do occur, but HUMIMT is normally inadequate, untrustworthy, or a failure, and these shortcomings cannot generally be corrected with data based on other intelligence means. Either inside information is available or it is not. When it is, imagery and signals intelligence generally do far more to indicate that HUMINT is wrong or suspect than to reveal the truth.[4]

- In many cases, even the leaders of a proliferating country may not have an accurate picture of the success of their efforts, and most probably do not have a clear picture of the accuracy, lethality and effects, and reliability of their weapons. U.S. and British research efforts have long shown that even highly sophisticated technical models of the performance and lethality of chemical, biological, and nuclear weapons and delivery systems can be grossly wrong, or require massive levels of human testing that simply are not practical even for closed authoritarian societies. No declassified intelligence report on any proliferation effort in any developing country has yet indicated that Iraq or any other proliferator has sophisticated technical and testing models in these areas. Intelligence cannot collect data that do not exist.

Problems in Analyzing Iraqi and Other Country WMD Capabilities and Delivery Systems

Many of the resulting problems in the analysis of the WMD capabilities of Iraq and other countries are the result of the previous problems in collection. The details of U.S., British, and allied intelligence analyses remain classified. At the same time, background discussions with intelligence analysts and users reveal the following additional problems in analyzing the WMD threat:

- The uncertainties surrounding collection on virtually all proliferation and weapons of mass destruction programs are so great that it is impossible to produce meaningful point estimates. As the CIA has shown in some of its past public estimates of missile proliferation, the intelligence community must first develop a matrix of what is and is not known about a given aspect of proliferation in a given country, with careful footnoting or qualification of the problems in each key source. It must then deal with uncertainty by creating estimates that show a range of possible current and projected capabilities—carefully qualifying each case. In general, at least three scenarios or cases need to be analyzed for each major aspect of proliferation in each country—something approaching a "best," "most likely, " and "worst case."[5]

- Even under these conditions, the resulting analytic effort faces serious problems. Security compartmentation within each major aspect of collection and analysis severely limits the flow of data to working analysts. The expansion of analytic staffs has sharply increased the barriers to the flow of data, and has brought large number of junior analysts into the process that can do little more than update past analyses and judgments. Far too little analysis is subjected to technical review by those who have actually worked on weapons development, and the analysis of delivery programs, warheads and weapons, and chemical, biological, and nuclear proliferation tends to be compartmented. Instead of the free flow of data and exchange of analytic conclusions, or "fusion" of intelligence, analysis is "stovepiped" into separate areas of activity. Moreover, the larger staffs get, the more stovepiping tends to occur.

- Analysis tends to focus on technical capability and not on the problems in management and systems integration that often are the real world limiting factors in proliferation. This tends to push analysis toward exaggerating the probable level of proliferation, particularly because technical capability is often assumed if collection cannot provide all the necessary information.

- Where data are available on past holdings of weapons and the capability to produce such weapons—such as data on chemical weapons feedstocks and biological growth material—the intelligence effort tends to produce estimates of the maximum size of the possible current holding of weapons and WMD materials. While ranges are often shown, and estimates are usually qualified with uncertainty, this tends to focus users on the worst case in terms of actual current capability. In the case of the Iraq War, this was compounded by some 12 years of constant lies and a disbelief that a dictatorship obsessed with record keeping could not have records if it had destroyed weapons and materials. The end result, however, was to assume that little or no destruction had occurred whenever UNSCOM, UNMOVIC, and the IAEA reported that major issues still affected Iraqi claims.

- Intelligence analysis has long been oriented more toward arms control and counterproliferation rather than war fighting, although DIA and the military services have attempted to shift the focus of analysis. Dealing with broad national trends and assuming capability is not generally a major problem in seeking to push nations toward obeying arms control agreements, or in pressuring possible suppliers. It also is not a major problem in analyzing broad military counterproliferation risks and programs. The situation is very different in dealing with war-fighting choices, particularly issues like preemption and targeting. Assumptions of capability can lead to preemption that is not necessary, overtargeting, inability to prioritize, and a failure to create the detailed collection and analysis necessary to support war fighters down to the battalion level. This, in turn, often forces field commanders to rely on field teams with limit capability and expertise, and to overreact to any potential threat or warning indicator.

- The intelligence community does bring outside experts into the process, but often simply to provide advice in general terms rather than cleared review of the intelligence product. The result is often less than helpful. The use of other cleared personnel in U.S. laboratories and other areas of expertise is inadequate and often presents major problems because those consulted are not brought fully into the intelligence analysis process and given all of the necessary data.

- The intelligence community does tend to try to avoiding explicit statements of the short comings in collection and methods in much of its analysis and to repeat past agreed judgments on a lowest common denominator level—particularly in the form of the intelligence products that get broad circulation to consumers. Attempts at independent outside analysis or "B-Teams," however, are not subject to the review and controls enforced on intelligence analysis, and the teams, collection data, and methods used are generally selected to prove given points rather than provide an objective counterpoint to finished analysis.[6]

More broadly, the users of intelligence are at best intolerant of analysis that consists of a wide range of qualifications and uncertainties even at the best of times, and the best of times do not exist when urgent policy and war-fighting decisions need to be made. Users inevitably either force the intelligence process to reach something approaching a definitive set of conclusions, or else they make such estimates themselves.

Intelligence analysts and managers are all too aware of this fact. Experience has taught them that complex intelligence analysis—filled with alternative cases, probability estimates, and qualifications about uncertainty—generally goes unused or makes policymakers and commanders impatient with the entire intelligence process. In the real world, hard choices have to be made to provide an estimate that can actually be used and acted upon, and these choices must be made by either the intelligence community or the user.[7]

The Politics of Characterizing and Targeting Iraqi WMD Capabilities and Delivery Systems

All of these points have obvious importance in assessing the political and policy-level use of intelligence during the Iraq War. It is easy to focus on the extent to which the intelligence that the United States and Britain provided before the war was or was not "politicized" as part of the effort to make the case for the war. Yet, far broader issues are involved that are scarcely specific to the Iraq War. Rather, these issues are almost certain to apply to future crises and conflicts. The same problems that limited U.S. and British intelligence capabilities during the Iraq War—and which will limit them for the foreseeable future—necessarily apply to other countries and to any international organizations.

There also are no peers with superior capabilities. No other state can compete with the United States in intelligence collection and analysis resources, although a growing number of states do have significant satellite and other technical means and any state can score a human intelligence breakthrough. Organizations like the UN have no independent intelligence collection capability other than the reporting and inspection provisions provided by international agreements. UNSCOM and UNMOVIC showed during their inspection efforts in Iraq that direct inspection can often provide important discoveries. But such search techniques also provide only limited and time-consuming coverage and cannot function effectively without intelligence data and analytic inputs from other countries.

No one who focuses on the specific case of the Iraq War can afford to ignore the fact that future threats of proliferation posed by states or terrorist movements may again seem so great that it may not be possible to wait to take military action until many key uncertainties are resolved. Moreover, it is difficult to see how leaders can lead if they communicate all of the uncertainties involved in the intelligence assessment of most proliferating countries.

In practical terms, any political effort to try to communicate the true level of uncertainty and probable outcomes inherent in most estimates of proliferation seems almost certain to make it difficult or impossible to gain a political consensus for timely and effective domestic or international action. Communicating uncertainty may be a good way of arguing against action, but only because its impact is to create nearly endless discussion and debate on any policy that requires broad political agreement on a single course of action or the use of military force. In practical terms, the United States and its allies may again have to act on the basis of something approaching "worst case" assumptions. This is a risk that proliferating nations and extremist movements may have to learn they take when they proliferate.

Dealing with a proven proliferator. It is also necessary to put any politicization of intelligence by the British or the Americans in context. Whatever mistakes may have been made in the intelligence assessments before and during the war, Saddam Hussein's regime was clearly proliferating. During the period of 1991–1998, UNSCOM found that Iraq had concealed major chemical, biological, and nuclear programs, and it continued to lie about them until it expelled UNSCOM. These lies affected many detailed aspects of the Iraqi nuclear and missile program. They also, however, succeeded in concealing the existence of a biological weapons program until 1995—four years after the Gulf War was over and a massive inspection effort was under way. And they succeeded in concealing a major VX nerve gas weaponization program until 1997–1998—seven years after the war was over.

Iraq clearly failed to meet the requirements of the UN Security Council's Resolution 1441 that established the ground rules for the resumption of UN inspections under UNMOVIC. Iraq's declaration to the UN did virtually nothing to resolve immense uncertainties about the remaining scale of the Iraqi proliferation effort, which could still have involved massive stocks of chemical and biological weapons. UNMOVIC found that Iraq continued to try to conceal major violations of the ceasefire limits on the development of long-range missiles, and it was anything but forthcoming in making its scientists available for interviews and in implementing most other aspects of cooperation with the UN. When it did improve its cooperation, it almost always did so because the threat of U.S. and British military action had become more imminent.[8]

Outstanding issues concerning Iraq's compliance with the UN effort. Whatever the problems in the U.S. and British statements and white papers may have been, virtually all of the reports on the material, weapons, and equipment that Iraq had not accounted for were taken from reporting by UNSCOM during the period between 1991 and 1998. Interviews with French, German, Russian, and other experts before the war also indicate that few Western nations did not think that Iraq was actively proliferating, and most Western intelligence agencies saw similar risks—although some felt that Iraq's war-fighting capabilities were lower and its production capabilities were much more uncertain.

Hans Blix—the executive chairman of UNMOVIC before and during the war and a man who disagreed with many of the U.S. and British assessments of Iraqi capabilities issued to make the case for war—expressed serious concerns in his reports to the UN during 2003 about Iraq's failures to comply with UN Security Council Resolution 1441 as well as about the U.S. and British assessments of the Iraqi WMD threat. The UNMOVIC report to the Security Council of January 27, 2003, stated as follows:[9]

- Resolution 687 (1991), like the subsequent resolutions I shall refer to, required cooperation by Iraq but such was often withheld or given grudgingly. Unlike South Africa, which decided on its own to eliminate its nuclear weapons and welcomed inspection as a means of creating confidence in its disarmament, Iraq appears not to have come to a genuine acceptance—not even today—of the disarmament, which was demanded of it and which it needs to carry out to win the confidence of the world and to live in peace.

- As we know, the twin operation "declare and verify," which was prescribed in Resolution 687 (1991), too often turned into a game of "hide and seek." Rather than just verifying declarations and supporting evidence, the two inspecting organizations found themselves engaged in efforts to map the weapons programs and to search for evidence through inspections, interviews, seminars, inquiries with suppliers, and intelligence organizations. As a result, the disarmament phase was not completed in the short time expected. Sanctions remained and took a severe toll until Iraq accepted the Oil for Food.

- While Iraq claims—with little evidence—that it destroyed all biological weapons unilaterally in 1991, it is certain that UNSCOM destroyed large biological weapons production facilities in 1996. The large nuclear infrastructure was destroyed and the fissionable material was removed from Iraq by the IAEA.

- One of three important questions before us today is how much might remain undeclared and intact from before 1991; and, possibly, thereafter; the second question is what, if anything, was illegally produced or procured after 1998, when the inspectors left; and the third question is how it can be prevented that any weapons of mass destruction be produced or procured in the future.

- For nearly three years, Iraq refused to accept any inspections by UNMOVIC. It was only after appeals by the secretary general and Arab States and pressure by the United States and other Member States, that Iraq declared on 16 September last year that it would again accept inspections without conditions.

- It would appear from our experience so far that Iraq has decided in principle to provide cooperation on process, notably access. A similar decision is indispensable to provide cooperation on substance in order to bring the disarmament task to completion through the peaceful process of inspection and to bring the monitoring task on a firm course. An initial minor step would be to adopt the long-overdue legislation required by the resolutions.

- In this updating I am bound, however, to register some problems. Firstly, relating to two kinds of air operations.

- ...I am obliged to note some recent disturbing incidents and harassment. For instance, for some time farfetched allegations have been made publicly that questions posed by inspectors were of intelligence character. While

I might not defend every question that inspectors might have asked, Iraq knows that they do not serve intelligence purposes and Iraq should not say so.

- On a number of occasions, demonstrations have taken place in front of our offices and at inspection sites.
- The other day, a sightseeing excursion by five inspectors to a mosque was followed by an unwarranted public outburst. The inspectors went without any UN insignia and were welcomed in the kind manner that is characteristic of the normal Iraqi attitude to foreigners. They took off their shoes and were taken around. They asked perfectly innocent questions and parted with the invitation to come again.
- Shortly thereafter, we receive protests from the Iraqi authorities about an unannounced inspection and about questions not relevant to weapons of mass destruction. Indeed, they were not. Demonstrations and outbursts of this kind are unlikely to occur in Iraq without initiative or encouragement from the authorities. We must ask ourselves what the motives may be for these events. They do not facilitate an already difficult job, in which we try to be effective, professional and, at the same time, correct. Where our Iraqi counterparts have some complaint they can take it up in a calmer and less unpleasant manner.
- Paragraph 9 of resolution 1441 (2002) states that this cooperation shall be "active." It is not enough to open doors. Inspection is not a game of "catch as catch can". Rather, as I noted, it is a process of verification for the purpose of creating confidence. It is not built upon the premise of trust. Rather, it is designed to lead to trust, if there is both openness to the inspectors and action to present them with items to destroy or credible evidence about the absence of any such items.
- On 7 December 2002, Iraq submitted a declaration of some 12,000 pages in response to paragraph 3 of resolution 1441 (2002) and within the time stipulated by the Security Council. In the fields of missiles and biotechnology, the declaration contains a good deal of new material and information covering the period from 1998 and onward. This is welcome.
- One might have expected that in preparing the Declaration, Iraq would have tried to respond to, clarify and submit supporting evidence regarding the many open disarmament issues, which the Iraqi side should be familiar with from the UNSCOM document S/1999/94 of January1999 and the so-called Amorim Report of March 1999 (S/1999/356). These are questions that UNMOVIC, governments and independent commentators have often cited.
- While UNMOVIC has been preparing its own list of current "unresolved disarmament issues" and "key remaining disarmament tasks" in response to requirements in resolution 1284 (1999), we find the issues listed in the two reports as unresolved, professionally justified. These reports

do not contend that weapons of mass destruction remain in Iraq, but nor do they exclude that possibility. They point to lack of evidence and inconsistencies, which raise question marks, which must be straightened out, if weapons dossiers are to be closed and confidence is to arise.

- They deserve to be taken seriously by Iraq rather than being brushed aside as evil machinations of UNSCOM. Regrettably, the 12,000 page declaration, most of which is a reprint of earlier documents, does not seem to contain any new evidence that would eliminate the questions or reduce their number. Even Iraq's letter sent in response to our recent discussions in Baghdad to the President of the Security Council on 24 January does not lead us to the resolution of these issues.

- When we have urged our Iraqi counterparts to present more evidence, we have all too often met the response that there are no more documents. All existing relevant documents have been presented, we are told. All documents relating to the biological weapons programme were destroyed together with the weapons.

- However, Iraq has all the archives of the Government and its various departments, institutions and mechanisms. It should have budgetary documents, requests for funds and reports on how they have been used. It should also have letters of credit and bills of lading, reports on production and losses of material.

- In response to a recent UNMOVIC request for a number of specific documents, the only new documents Iraq provided was a ledger of 193 pages which Iraq stated included all imports from 1983 to 1990 by the Technical and Scientific Importation Division, the importing authority for the biological weapons programme. Potentially, it might help to clear some open issues.

- The recent inspection find in the private home of a scientist of a box of some 3,000 pages of documents, much of it relating to the laser enrichment of uranium support a concern that has long existed that documents might be distributed to the homes of private individuals. This interpretation is refuted by the Iraqi side, which claims that research staff sometimes may bring home papers from their work places. On our side, we cannot help but think that the case might not be isolated and that such placements of documents is deliberate to make discovery difficult and to seek to shield documents by placing them in private homes.

- Any further sign of the concealment of documents would be serious. The Iraqi side committed itself at our recent talks to encourage persons to accept access also to private sites. There can be no sanctuaries for proscribed items, activities or documents. A denial of prompt access to any site would be a very serious matter.

- When Iraq claims that tangible evidence in the form of documents is not available, it ought at least to find individuals, engineers, scientists and managers to testify about their experience. Large weapons programmes are moved and managed by people. Interviews with individuals who may have worked in programmes in the past may fill blank spots in our knowledge and understanding. It could also be useful to learn that they are now employed in peaceful sectors. These were the reasons why UNMOVIC asked for a list of such persons, in accordance with resolution 1441.
- Some 400 names for all biological and chemical weapons programmes as well as their missile programmes were provided by the Iraqi side. This can be compared to over 3,500 names of people associated with those past weapons programmes that UNSCOM either interviewed in the 1990s or knew from documents and other sources. At my recent meeting in Baghdad, the Iraqi side committed itself to supplementing the list and some 80 additional names have been provided.
- In the past, much valuable information came from interviews. There were also cases in which the interviewee was clearly intimidated by the presence of and interruption by Iraqi officials. This was the background of resolution 1441's provision for a right for UNMOVIC and the IAEA to hold private interviews "in the mode or location" of our choice, in Baghdad or even abroad.
- To date, 11 individuals were asked for interviews in Baghdad by us. The replies have invariably been that the individual will only speak at Iraq's monitoring directorate or, at any rate, in the presence of an Iraqi official. This could be due to a wish on the part of the invited to have evidence that they have not said anything that the authorities did not wish them to say. At our recent talks in Baghdad, the Iraqi side committed itself to encourage persons to accept interviews "in private", that is to say alone with us. Despite this, the pattern has not changed. However, we hope that with further encouragement from the authorities, knowledgeable individuals will accept private interviews, in Baghdad or abroad.

The International Atomic Energy Agency report of January 27, 2003, noted the following:[10]

Little progress has been made in resolving the questions and concerns that remained as of 1998. On the question of external assistance to the past nuclear programme, Iraq has provided a letter that summarizes information provided by it during earlier discussions and which reiterates Iraq's previous statements that it had never followed up on offers of such assistance. On the issue of the abandonment of the programme, Iraq has indicated its intention to adopt, as required in paragraph 34 of the OMV Plan, laws prohibiting the conduct of proscribed activities in Iraq.

Blix reported a more favorable situation to the UN on February 14 in his last report before the war began. He also warned that the intelligence provided to UNMOVIC had been found to be flawed in some aspects:[11]

> International organizations need to analyze such information critically and especially benefit when it comes from more than one source. The intelligence agencies, for their part, must protect their sources and methods. Those who provide such information must know that it will be kept in strict confidence and be known to very few people. UNMOVIC has achieved good working relations with intelligence agencies and the amount of information provided has been gradually increasing. However, we must recognize that there are limitations and that misinterpretations can occur.
>
> Intelligence information has been useful for UNMOVIC. In one case, it led us to a private home where documents mainly relating to laser enrichment of uranium were found. In other cases, intelligence has led to sites where no proscribed items were found. Even in such cases, however, inspection of these sites was useful in proving the absence of such items and in some cases the presence of other items—conventional munitions. It showed that conventional arms are being moved around the country and that movements are not necessarily related to weapons of mass destruction.

The presentation of intelligence information by the U.S. secretary of state suggested that Iraq had prepared for inspections by cleaning up sites and removing evidence of proscribed weapons programs. I would like to comment only on one case, which we are familiar with, namely, the trucks identified by analysts as being for chemical decontamination at a munitions depot. This was a declared site, and it was certainly one of the sites Iraq would have expected us to inspect. We have noted that the two satellite images of the site were taken several weeks apart. The reported movement of munitions at the site could just as easily have been a routine activity as a movement of proscribed munitions in anticipation of imminent inspection. Our reservation on this point does not detract from our appreciation of the briefing.

Nevertheless, UNMOVIC's last report to the Security Council before the Iraq War, which was published on February 28, 2003, noted that UNMOVIC had found a small stock of mustard gas and some surviving bombs designed to carry weapons of mass destruction. The report also confirmed that Iraq had developed and deployed two missiles—the Al Samoud 2 and Al Fatah—in violation of UN Security Council resolutions:[12]

> UNMOVIC experts have found little new significant information in the part of the declaration relating to proscribed weapons programmes, nor much new supporting documentation or other evidence. New material, on the oth-

er hand, was provided concerning non-weapons-related activities during the period from the end of 1998 to the present, especially in the biological field and on missile development.

The part that covers biological weapons is, in UNMOVIC's assessment, essentially a reorganized version of a previous declaration provided by Iraq to the United Nations Special Commission (UNSCOM) in September 1997. In the chemical weapons area, the basis of the current declaration was a declaration submitted by Iraq in 1996 with subsequent updates and explanations. In the missile field, the declaration follows the same format, and has largely the same content as Iraq's 1996 missile declaration and updates.

...As there is little new substantive information in the weapons part of Iraq's declaration, or new supporting documentation, the issues that were identified as unresolved in the Amorim report (S/1999/356) and in UNSCOM's report (S/1999/94) remain. In most cases, the issues remain unresolved because there is a lack of supporting evidence. Such supporting evidence, in the form of documentation, testimony by individuals who took part in the activities, or physical evidence, would be required.

...Under resolution 1284 (1999), Iraq is to provide "cooperation in all respects" to UNMOVIC and the IAEA. While the objective of the cooperation under this resolution, as under resolution 1441 (2002), is evidently the attainment, without delay, of verified disarmament, it is the cooperation that must be immediate, unconditional and active. Without the required cooperation, disarmament and its verification will be problematic. However, even with the requisite cooperation it will inevitably require some time.

...During the period of time covered by the present report, Iraq could have made greater efforts to find any remaining proscribed items or provide credible evidence showing the absence of such items. The results in terms of disarmament have been very limited so far. The destruction of missiles, which is an important operation, has not yet begun. Iraq could have made full use of the declaration, which was submitted on 7 December. It is hard to understand why a number of the measures, which are now being taken, could not have been initiated earlier. If they had been taken earlier, they might have borne fruit by now. It is only by the middle of January and thereafter that Iraq has taken a number of steps, which have the potential of resulting either in the presentation for destruction of stocks or items that are proscribed or the presentation of relevant evidence solving long-standing unresolved disarmament issues.

Blix made the following points about the problems in assessing Iraq's WMD programs in his last report to the UN, after the Iraq War was over.[13]

...the Commission has not at any time during the inspections in Iraq found evidence of the continuation or resumption of programmes of weapons of mass destruction or significant quantities of proscribed items—whether from pre-1991 or later. I leave aside the Al Samoud 2 missile system, which we concluded was proscribed. As I have noted before, this does not necessarily mean that such items could not exist. They might—there remain long lists of items unaccounted for—but it is not justified to jump to the conclusion that something exists just because it is unaccounted for.

...we note that the long list of proscribed items unaccounted for has not been shortened by inspections or Iraqi declarations, explanations or documentation. It was the task of the Iraqi side to present items unaccounted for, if they existed, or to present evidence—records, documents or other—convincing the inspectors that the items do not exist.

If—for whatever reason—this is not done, the international community cannot have confidence that past programmes or any remaining parts of them have been terminated. However, an effective presence of international inspectors will serve as a deterrent against efforts aimed at reactivating or developing new programmes of weapons of mass destruction.

Although during the last month and a half of our inspections, the Iraqi side made considerable efforts to provide explanations, to begin inquiries and to undertake exploration and excavations, these efforts did not bring the answers needed before we withdrew. We did not have time to interview more than a handful of the large number of persons who were said by Iraq to have participated in the unilateral destruction of biological and chemical weapons in 1991. Such interviews might have helped towards the resolution of some outstanding issues, although one must be aware that the totalitarian regime in Iraq continued to cast a shadow on the credibility of all interviews.

The report before you gives details of the Commission's supervision of the destruction of 50 Al Samoud 2 missiles out of the 75 declared deployed and of other items in the missile sphere....Fifty percent of the declared warheads and 98% of the missile engines remained intact. Also, there was no time to assess whether the Al Fatah missile programme stayed within the range allowed by Security Council resolutions.

In the context of destruction of proscribed items, I should like also to draw the attention of the Council to the information...that the *weapons* that were destroyed before inspectors left in 1998, were in almost all cases declared by Iraq and that the destruction occurred before 1993 in the case of missiles, and before 1994 in the case of chemical weapons. The existence and scope of the biological weapons programme was uncovered by UNSCOM in 1995 despite Iraq's denials and concealment efforts. As to items, only a few remnants of the biological weapons programme were subsequently found. A great deal—Iraq asserts all—was unilaterally destroyed in 1991.

Thus, in the main, UNSCOM supervised destruction of actual weapons and agents took place during the early years of the Commission, and had regard mainly to items declared by Iraq or, at least, found at sites declared by Iraq. Subsequent UNSCOM disarmament activities dealt almost exclusively with the destruction of equipment and facilities for the production of weapons connected to past programmes. In addition, of course, UNSCOM was able, with great skill, to map large parts of Iraq's WMD programmes.

While we are all aware of the large amounts of proscribed items, which still remain unaccounted for, we should perhaps take note of the fact that for many years neither UNSCOM nor UNMOVIC made significant finds of weapons. The lack of finds could be because the items were unilaterally destroyed by the Iraqi authorities or else because they were effectively concealed by them. I trust that in the new environment in Iraq, in which there is full access and cooperation, and in which knowledgeable witnesses should no longer be inhibited to reveal what they know, it should be possible to establish the truth we all want to know.

Before one places too much blame on the United States and Britain for faulty intelligence, it is important to note that Iraq could have resolved the issues involved simply by complying with the UN Security Council resolution. The United States and Britain may have been wrong, but Saddam Hussein played an almost suicidally stupid game in failing to immediately declare Iraq's true holdings and comply with UNSCR 1441's demand for immediate and comprehensive compliance. As Rolf Ekeus, executive chairman of UNSCOM from 1991 to1997, pointed out after the war, Iraq never gave up the basic core of its chemical, biological, or nuclear weapons efforts or the effort to find dual-use and other production equipment.[14]

The Costs of Politicizing Intelligence

That said, one key lesson of the Iraq War is still that it is dangerous to overpoliticize intelligence and to not provide a picture of the threat and reasons for war fighting that is properly qualified. Overselling the threat before a war leads to overreacting during a conflict and to major credibility problems in the aftermath of the conflict that can interfere with nation building and limit domestic and international support in future conflicts.

It is now all too clear that the United States and Britain did not find the right balance of persuasion and objectivity in their public analyses of the threat before the war and in their arguments in favor of the conflict. The fact that no evidence surfaced during or soon after the war that tracked with the previous U.S. and British intelligence assessments—evidence showing that Iraq had the capability to use weapons of mass destruction in war fighting, or indicated that it had active programs for the production of weapons of mass destruction that were creating an imminent threat—has

been a source of major embarrassment for the Bush and Blair governments, as well as for allied governments like Australia. It also seriously
undermines U.S. and British credibility in dealing with future cases of proliferation.

Postwar reports and interviews make it clear that the United States and
Britain presented worst-case estimates to the public and the UN without
sufficient qualification. They also make clear that their intelligence communities came under serious political pressure to make something approaching a worst-case interpretation of the evidence, and to interpret
the inability to account for missing weapons of mass destruction, delivery
systems, and production capabilities as meaning that Iraq had something
approaching matching inventories of deployed weapons.

As has been mentioned, there are also many indications that the U.S.
intelligence community came under pressure to accept reporting by Iraqi
opposition sources that had limited credibility and, in some cases, a history of actively lying to exaggerate their own importance or push the United
States toward a war to overthrow Saddam Hussein.

In the United States, this pressure seems to have come primarily from
the Office of the Vice President and the Office of the Secretary of Defense.
The vice president and his assistant, Lewis Libby, seem to have made repeated personal efforts to intervene in the intelligence process and push
for the selection of material that would make a case for war. President
Bush's deputy national security adviser, Stephen J. Hadley, ignored key
CIA warnings that reports Iraq had sought to buy uranium from Niger
were incorrect.[15]

There also are reports that the Office of Special Plans (OSP) within the
Office of the Secretary of Defense assembled a staff with strong biases in
favor of war who sifted through intelligence data and pushed for the
"worst case" interpretation of the data on Iraqi weapons of mass destruction and possible Iraqi ties to terrorist groups like Al Qaeda. In what bore
a striking resemblance to similar worst-case interpretations of the global
threat from the proliferation of ballistic missiles under the Rumsfeld
Commission, U.S. policymakers seem to have pushed for the interpretation that would best justify military action and to have focused on it as if it
were a reality rather than a possibility.[16] The Bush administration as a whole
sought intelligence that would support its case in going to war, and this had a
significant impact on the intelligence community from 2002 onward.[17]

There are at least two cases where charges were made that should never
have been made public. One such charge was the assertion by both the U.S.
and British governments that there was evidence that Iraq had imported
uranium from Africa. This assertion was made when the key source relat-

ing to Niger was already known to be fraudulent, and there was no credible evidence of supply by the Congo or Somalia.[18] Part of the problem may have arisen because British and U.S. intelligence did not share all of the data they had on this possibility.[19] However, the key cause was political choices about the way in which uncertain indicators and warnings of forgery that overrode the recommendations of intelligence professionals note to use the material. Similarly, British claims that Iraq was able to deploy chemical and biological weapons within 45 minutes, including against its own Shi'ite population, later turned out to be based on a single unvalidated report from an Iraqi officer of very uncertain credibility.[20]

Senator Carl Levin, however, provided a much broader indictment of the U.S. analysis in a speech to the Senate on July 15, 2003:[21]

Last week, CIA Director George Tenet accepted responsibility for having gone along with the African uranium statement in the President's State of the Union address. His acknowledgment that it should not have been included in the address and his acceptance of responsibility were appropriate. But his explanation of the CIA's acquiescence in allowing the use of a clearly misleading statement raises more questions than it answers, and statements by other administration officials, particularly National Security Adviser Condoleezza Rice, compound the problem.

Even more troubling, however, is the fact that the uranium statement appears to be but one of a number of several questionable statements and exaggerations by the Intelligence Community and Administration officials that were issued in the buildup to the war. The importance of objective and credible intelligence cannot be overstated. It is therefore essential that we have a thorough, open and bipartisan inquiry into the objectivity, credibility and use of U.S. intelligence before the Iraq War.

First, relative to the uranium issue: the President in his State of the Union message said that the British government had learned that Iraq recently sought to purchase significant quantities of uranium from Africa. The sole purpose of that statement was to make the American people believe that the American government believed the statement to be true and that it was strong evidence of Iraq's attempt to obtain nuclear weapons. But the truth was that, at the very time the words were spoken, our government did not believe it was true. Condoleezza Rice's effort to justify the statement on the grounds that it was "technically accurate" doesn't address the heart of the matter, which is that the statement was calculated to create a false impression. It is simply wrong to make a statement whose purpose is to make people believe something when you do not believe it yourself.

It is all well and good that the CIA has acknowledged its role in caving in to pressure from the National Security Council to concur in something which it did not believe. But Director Tenet's acknowledgment raises further questions of who was pushing the false impression at the National Security Council. The NSC should not misuse intelligence that way. The President's statement that Iraq was attempting to acquire African uranium was not a "mistake." It was not inadvertent. It was not a slip. It was negotiated between the CIA and the NSC. It was calculated. It was misleading. And what compounds its misleading nature is that the CIA not only "differed with the British dossier on the reliability of the uranium reporting."

To use Director Tenet's words, but the CIA had also "expressed [its] reservations," again using Director Tenet's words, to the British in September 2002, nearly five months before the State of Union address. Furthermore, the CIA pressed the White House to remove a similar reference from the President's speech on October 7, 2002, and the White House did so—nearly four months before the State of the Union address.

The uranium issue is not just about sixteen words. It is about the conscious decisions that were made, apparently by the NSC and concurred in by the CIA, to create a false impression. And it is not an isolated example. There is troubling evidence of other dubious statements and exaggerations by the Intelligence Community and Administration officials.

Aluminum tubes: In a speech before the UN General Assembly on September 12, 2002, President Bush said "Iraq has made several attempts to buy high-strength aluminum tubes used to enrich uranium for a nuclear weapon." In fact, an unclassified intelligence assessment in October acknowledged that some intelligence specialists "believe that these tubes are probably intended for conventional weapons programs," and on February 5, 2003, Secretary of State Colin Powell told the UN Security Council that "we all know there are differences of opinion," and that "there is controversy about what these tubes are for." The International Atomic Energy Agency, after conducting an inquiry into the aluminum tubes issue concluded they were not for uranium enrichment.

Iraq-al Qaeda connection: On September 27 of last year, Secretary of Defense Donald Rumsfeld described the Administration's search for hard evidence for a connection between Iraq and al Qaeda. He said, "we ended up with five or six sentences that were bullet-proof. We could say them, they are factual, they are exactly accurate. They demonstrate that there are in fact al Qaeda in Iraq." While Secretary Rumsfeld later went on to say, "they are not beyond a reasonable doubt," he did not say there was considerable uncertainty in the Intelligence Community about the nature and extent of ties, if any, between Iraq and al Qaeda. It was certainly never a "bullet-proof" case.

Nuclear reconstitution: Last Sunday, Ms. Rice said, "we have never said that we thought he [Saddam] had nuclear weapons." But Vice President

Cheney said on March 16 "we believe he [Saddam] has, in fact, reconstituted nuclear weapons."

Certainty that Iraq possesses chemical and biological weapons: On August 26, 2002, Vice President Cheney said: "Simply stated, there is no doubt that Saddam Hussein now has weapons of mass destruction. There is no doubt he is amassing them to use against our friends, against our allies, and against us."

On September 26, 2002, President Bush said, "The Iraqi regime possesses biological and chemical weapons." On March 17, 2003, President Bush told the nation that "intelligence gathered by this and other governments leaves no doubt that the Iraq regime continues to possess and conceal some of the most lethal weapons ever devised." And on March 30, 2003, Secretary of Defense Donald Rumsfeld said, "We know where they [weapons of mass destruction] are. They're in the area around Tikrit and Baghdad and east, west, south and north somewhat." The fruitless search to date for Saddam Hussein's weapons of mass destruction during and after our entry into Iraq suggests that our intelligence was either way off the mark or seriously stretched.

Mobile biological warfare labs: On May 28, 2003, the CIA posted on its website a document it prepared with the Defense Intelligence Agency entitled "Iraqi Mobile Biological Warfare Agent Production Plants." This report concluded that the two trailers found in Iraq were for biological warfare agent production, even though other experts and intelligence community members do not agree with that conclusion, or believe there is not enough evidence to reach such a conclusion. None of these alternative views were posted on the CIA's web page.

White House Web Site Photos: On October 8, 2002, the White House placed three sets of satellite photos on its web site, with the headline "Construction at three Iraqi nuclear weapons-related facilities". Although one of the facilities was not nuclear-related, the captions of the photos gave the impression that Iraq was proceeding with work on weapons of mass destruction at these facilities, although UNMOVIC and IAEA inspections at these facilities found no prohibited activities or weapons. For the Al Furat Manufacturing Facility, the caption notes that "the building was originally intended to house a centrifuge enrichment cascade operation supporting Iraq's uranium enrichment efforts," and that after construction resumed in 2001, "the building appears operational."

So the misleading statement about African uranium is not an isolated issue. There is a significant amount of troubling evidence that it was part of a pattern of exaggeration and misleading statements. That is what a thorough, open and bipartisan investigation should examine.

Finally, Mr. President, again relative to the uranium statement, I am deeply troubled by Ms. Rice's continuing justification of the use of the statement in the President's State of the Union address. She repeatedly says it was "accurate," despite the fact that its clear aim was to create a false impression. Her statement and Director Tenet's statement raise more questions than they answer. Here are some of those questions:

1. Who in the Administration was pressing the CIA to concur in a statement that the CIA did not believe was true, and why did they do so even after the CIA objected to the text?
2. Who at the CIA was involved in pressing the White House to remove the similar reference from the October 7 speech, and what reasons did they give for removing it?
3. Who in the White House was involved in removing a similar reference from the President's speech on October 7, nearly four months before the State of the Union speech?
4. Who at the CIA knew about the decision to tell the British intelligence service in September, 2002 of CIA's "reservations" about the inclusion of references to Iraqi efforts to obtain uranium from Africa in the British intelligence service's September 24 dossier?
5. Given the doubts of the U.S. Intelligence Community, why didn't the President say in his State of the Union speech not only that "The British government has learned that Saddam Hussein recently sought significant quantities of uranium from Africa," but that "our U.S. Intelligence Community has serious doubts about such reporting"?
6. How and when did the U.S. government receive the forged documents on Niger, and when did it become aware that they might be bogus?
7. What role did the Office of the Vice President have in bringing about an inquiry into Iraq's purported efforts to obtain uranium from Africa? Was the Vice President's staff briefed on the results of Ambassador Wilson's trip to Africa?

These and many other questions underscore the critical importance of a thorough, open and bipartisan inquiry into the objectivity and credibility of intelligence concerning the presence of weapons of mass destruction in Iraq immediately before the war and the alleged Iraq-al Qaeda connection, and the use of such intelligence by the Department of Defense in policy decisions, military planning and the conduct of operations in Iraq.

Like many similar speeches by members of the Australian and British Parliaments, Senator Levin's speech clearly had the motive of politicizing the politicization of intelligence. Both the issues and questions that Senator Levin raised were valid, however, even if they did focus on politics rather than the problems in intelligence analysis and capability. They also illustrate the "backlash" effect that is almost inevitable when short-term political priorities ignore long-term consequences.

In Britain, much of the political character of what was said came as the result of more direct interference in the reporting of the British intelligence community by the Prime Minister's office, and particularly by Alastair Campbell and other special advisors to the Prime Minister who sought to create the strongest possible political case. A report by the House of Commons Foreign Affairs Committee noted enough problems in the way the British estimate of Iraqi capabilities were generated to call it the "dodgy dossier." [22]

The report cleared Campbell of a direct role in British claims that Iraq could use weapons of mass destruction with only 45 minutes notice, but noted deep concerns about the fact this claim was ever made and the way in which the British government made and defended claims relating to Iraq's attempts to purchase Uranium ore. It also noted that Alastair Campbell chaired intelligence meetings for which he had no background or qualifications, and that placing the review of the data under Campbell and the Iraqi Communications Group he chaired, and the Coalition Information Centre, "were contributory factors to the affair of the 'dodgy dossier.'" [23]

The British reporting on the Iraqi threat presented further problems because the intelligence report presented by the British government copied text from the work of a graduate student.[24] The House of Commons Foreign Affairs Committee report stated: "We conclude that it is wholly unacceptable for the Government to plagiarise work without attribution and to amend it without either highlighting the amendments or gaining the assent of the original author." [25]

Moreover, a detailed comparisons of the British and CIA reports shows that the British document often implied that intelligence had more certainty than the U.S. document, although both governments shared virtually the same intelligence. It is clear from the investigation by the British parliament that this was partly because the British report had a much heavier degree of editing by the Prime Minister's office.

In general, political spin artists and public relations experts have zero background in the details of intelligence, and are among the last people who can ensure the credibility of the product. This is a lesson confirmed by less serious problems in the speeches on the subject by President Bush, Secretary Powell, National Security Advisor Rice, and Deputy Secretary Wolfowitz.

THE NEED FOR RAPID AND RELIABLE CHARACTERIZATION OF CHEMICAL AND BIOLOGICAL AGENTS AND THE COALITION INTELLIGENCE EFFORT

The problems in the intelligence efforts of the United States and other coalition members affected war fighting as well as the politics of the war. Despite all of the advances in IS&R capabilities, and despite more than a decade of additional intelligence collection and targeting experience, the United States and its allies were just as unable to characterize and target Iraq's capabilities to use, produce, and deliver weapons of mass destruction during military operations as they had been during Desert Storm and Desert Fox. If anything, the United States was more successful in the Gulf War, although many of its limited successes during that war were more the accidental result of hitting secondary targets than the product of intelligence analysis and military planning.

Each of the military services had to plan before and throughout the Iraq War for the risk that Iraq would use weapons of mass destruction. General John P. Abizaid, General Franks' deputy during the war and the new commander of USCENTCOM, described the situation as follows to the Senate Armed Services Committee:[26]

> Intelligence was the most accurate I've ever seen on the tactical level, probably the best I've ever seen on the operational level, and perplexingly incomplete on the strategic level with regard to weapons of mass destruction. It is perplexing to me…that we have no found weapons of mass destruction, when the evidence was so pervasive that it would exist…I can't offer a reasonable explanation….

Lt. Gen. James Conway, commander, 1st Marine Expeditionary Force, describes the problems created by such uncertainties as follows:[27]

> …we were… not hit with weapons of mass destruction—I think we had four triggers that we were prepared to defend ourselves against—different times when we thought that the regime might try to employ the weapons of mass destruction against us. And we truly thought that they were distributed—not to everybody, not to the regular army divisions that we saw in the south. But my personal belief was that they probably did reside in the Republican Guard units, and we encountered, arguably, three, maybe four, Republican Guard divisions on the way to Baghdad. But my personal belief was that the Republican Guard corps commander probably had release authority, and that we might well see them when we started to encounter his force or enter his area.
>
> It was a surprise to me then, it remains a surprise to me now, that we have not uncovered weapons, as you say, in some of the forward dispersal sites. Again, believe me, it's not for lack of trying. We've been to virtually every ammunition supply point between the Kuwait border and Baghdad, but they're simply not there. Now, what that means in terms of intelligence failure, I think, is too strong a word to use at this point. What the regime was intending to do in terms of its use of the weapons, we thought we understood or we certainly had our best guess, our most dangerous, our most likely courses of action that the intelligence folks were giving us. We were simply

wrong. But whether or not we're wrong at the national level, I think, still very much remains to be seen.

It is important to note that from an operational point of view, no commander could know whether weapons of mass destruction could or would be used until the end of the war. There were many cases where units had to use protective gear, and the speed of maneuver involved significant potential risk in the face of any sudden Iraqi escalation to the use of such weapons.

In many cases, more sophisticated and quicker reacting detectors and grids could have reduced the strain on U.S. and British forces. It is also clear from the results of the search for weapons of mass destruction during and after the war that current field equipment cannot rapidly and accurately characterize some chemical and biological threats and can produce serious false alarms. In case after case, units encountering suspect facilities and weapons produced false positive findings that could be disproved only after further testing in the rear.

Problems also still exist in using protection suits in combat. While reporting to date is anecdotal, several field reports indicate the equipment produced significant fatigue and interfered in operations. One typical field report states:

> We had guys tripping over their floppy MOPP boots trying to attack trench lines. One guy tripped, fell into a trench, and found himself fighting with a Republican Guardsman. Shot him in the head, by the way, and then took his MOPP boots off and tossed them out of frustration. Regardless of what people say, you can't do fire and movement effectively in the shit for extended periods.

This point is further illustrated in the report on the lessons of the war by the commanding general of the 1st Marine Division:[28]

> During the planning phase for offensive operations in Iraq, it became apparent that the Division had insufficient decontamination capability to free us from contamination without siphoning off combat capability. The doctrine for NBC decontamination states that the NBC section needs augmentation from combat engineers, motor transport, and other Division elements. We assigned this task to 3rd AA Battalion along with the additional task of traffic management control. The Division NBC Platoon augmented the battalion to provide expertise and support. Decontamination sites were placed by water sources because the Division does not have the organic capability to transport the volume of water necessary to conduct decontamination operations.
>
> *Recommendation:* ... Adopt the doctrinal roles of operational decontamination and traffic management and control. The Division possesses a more

robust capability, in both personnel and equipment, to achieve the ability to conduct decontamination at the rate of one company per hour. CSS assets should be tasked with providing the water for the decontamination site to keep the location independent of local water sources.

Assessing proliferation is not simply an intelligence or policy problem, it is an operational problem. The greater the uncertainty, the greater the operational dilemma in choosing between protective and defensive measures and in maintaining the tempo and focus of combat. If the Iraq War provides a lesson in this area, it is that the United States and its allies have no reliable way as yet to reduce this dilemma, reduce the risks involved, or reliably deal with this aspect of asymmetric warfare.

ORGANIZED SEARCHES FOR WEAPONS OF MASS DESTRUCTION IN PROLIFERATING COUNTRIES: THE SEARCH DURING AND AFTER THE WAR

The Iraq War provides important lessons about the need to search for possible weapons of mass destruction and sensitive facilities during a war, and the need to secure such facilities as soon as possible. The United States did carry out an ongoing effort to find and secure Iraqi weapons of mass destruction and related facilities as it advanced. But this effort had limited manning and uncertain intelligence support, and could provide only limited coverage. The United States lacked an effective plan and coordinated effort to secure Iraq's WMD and missile facilities as U.S. forces advanced, and some—including nuclear facilities—were looted as a result.

The United States was so convinced that it would find large stocks of Iraqi weapons and/or major ongoing proliferation efforts that it failed to formulate a clear strategy for dealing with the almost inevitable charges that it would conceal the facts. It was similarly unprepared for challenges in the UN over the lifting of sanctions.[29]

The mix of biologists, chemists, nuclear experts, arms control experts, computer and document experts, and special forces troops put together by the United States to search for Iraq's weapons of mass destruction and delivery systems was tailored around the case that Saddam had deployed WMD and had given his commanders authority to use them under certain circumstances.[30] It did not really have the scale, expertise, or language skills to deal with other types of Iraqi proliferation activity—such as covert research and development efforts, tracking down complex patterns of illegal imports, locating and interviewing scientists, searching out concealed and dispersed facilities, and analyzing possible destruction sites.

The United States made little preparation for conducting a timely disarmament and inspection effort with a credible audit trail. It relied on U.S. teams operating without international support and observers. It did not aggressively seek to include the UN. The inclusion of UNMOVIC and the IAEA would certainly have created political problems, but the United States does not seem to have been sensitive to the need to create teams that would have a high degree of international credibility.[31]

The Initial Search Effort

During the war, the U.S. military tasked various elements of Special Forces and other units to search for weapons of mass destruction as U.S. forces advanced into Iraq. The overall level of equipment and training was limited, however, and many units overreacted to suspected sites and failed to properly characterize the weapons, equipment, facilities, and substances they found.[32] Task Force 20, the U.S. Army Special Forces team that had a key mission in this search, was deployed in March, evidently before the actual fighting began. However, the team in Task Force 20 was relatively small and had the much broader mission of looking for key figures in the Iraqi leadership. Similar problems in resources and mission focus affected many of the other special purpose teams involved.[33]

The main initial U.S. effort was conducted by a 600-person group called the 75th Exploitation Task Force. It was supported by the 513th Military Intelligence Brigade and a smaller effort sent in by the Defense Threat Reduction Agency. These specialists spent most of their time at first going through known facilities slowly and by the numbers. They focused on the facilities most likely to have been vacated months earlier because they were known to be targets both for UNMOVIC and U.S. military action. But they failed to ensure that the United States secured key declared facilities like the nuclear facilities subject to IAEA inspection. [34]

There are conflicting reports about the pace of the initial search effort. One source reports that as of early May, the United States "had secured only 44 of the 85 top potential weapons sites in the Baghdad area and 153 of the 372 considered most important to rebuilding Iraq's government and economy."[35] Another states that the U.S. inspections teams had visited 19 top weapons sites, with two left for investigation, and that they had surveyed another 45 out of 68 top "non-WMD sites"—sites without known links to weapons of mass destruction, but suspect as potential sites.[36] In still another report, the 75th Exploitation Task Force was reported to have visited some 300 facilities by the end of May.[37] The true scale of the targeting and search problem may best be indicated by the fact that Stephen A. Cambone, the under secretary of defense for intelligence, announced on May 30 that only 70 of roughly 600 potential weapons facilities on an "integrated master site list" prepared by U.S. intelligence agencies before the war had been examined.[38]

Expanding the Effort and Creating the Iraq Survey Group

As time went on, the growing political and military problems created by the lack of an effective wartime and early postwar search effort forced the United States to greatly expand its search team and give it far more capability. In late May, the United States announced it would supplement the 75th Exploitation Task Force with a much larger Iraq Survey Group (ISG) that included elements from the U.S., British, and Australian intelligence communities. The search effort expanded to the point where the ISG was manned by between 1,300 and 1,400 people from the U.S. government and from the United Kingdom and Australia.

The way the United States initially approached the postwar effort to survey Iraq's weapons of mass destruction, and the reasons for creating the ISG, are described as follows in a Department of Defense briefing on May 7, 2003:[39]

> The command, USCENTCOM, has a command inside of Iraq known as the Coalition Land Component Commander—Coalition Forces Land Component Commander or CFLCC...And each day, within that organization in what they have as their operation center, which is known as the C3, they sit down and work through their priorities. That priority list itself has been pulled together as a consequence of information that we had going into the conflict of sites that we thought important. As you know, there are some thousand sites that we identified; those sites included not just weapons of mass destruction sites, but also prisoner of war—prisoner camps—prisons, rather, prisoner of war locations, terrorist camps and facilities, as well as regime and leadership targets. So there are some thousand of them, roughly, of which about half are related to weapons of mass destruction..
>
> ...As it stands now, we have been to about 70 sites that we were looking to cover. Now, what's interesting about that is that those are the 70 sites that were on the list when we started. Since then, we have been to about another 40 which have come to light as a consequence of this process that I have been describing to you here. And the way this works is with respect to a WMD site in particular, once it's been identified, there is a survey team, which may have been there already, having come up with the troops as they came through the countryside, or sent out in advance. And they will go to the site, they will do a survey and determine whether or not it's important for more advanced

units to come in and take a look at what's there. So, it's a site survey team. And so their job is done.

Next would come in a mobile exploitation team, an MET, as they're being called, which would do a much more thorough assessment of the site and also inspect any additional sites that USCENTCOM might have recommended.

And then, to the extent you need disablement of a facility or a capability in the site, there are disablement teams that are sent out to disarm, or render safe or destroy those—any delivery systems, weapons, agents or facilities that might be found.

Now, the organization that currently is assigned this mission is...known as the 75th Group. It is assigned this discovery and exploitation mission. It, in turn, is supported by a military intelligence brigade, the 513th. These units have been, by the by, in theater for a very long period of time.

The expertise within the 75th Group extends across some 600 people, and they are distributed across interrogators, interviewers, people who do the document exploitations, the material exploitation and the analysts; that is, the people who each day sort of come together, take the information that's come on board and try then to make recommendations about what might be done next. The expertise within the group is made up of people from the Central Intelligence Agency, the Defense Intelligence Agency, from the individual services, from DTRA, the Defense Threat Reduction Agency, the FBI, and then there are coalition partners who, themselves, are part of this ongoing effort.

That group, the 75th, will soon, toward the end of this month, begin to have an augmentation take place, and that will be done under the auspices of what we're calling the Iraq Survey Group. That group will be headed by a two-star general, a major general, Keith Dayton, who, as it turns out, is a member of Admiral Jacoby's staff. He will take the lead for the discovery and the exploitation that we have been talking about. And in particular, its mission is to discover, take custody of, exploit and disseminate information on individuals, records, materials, facilities, networks and operations as appropriate relative to individuals associated with the regime, weapons of mass destruction, terrorists and terrorist ties and their organizations, information having to do with the Iraqi Intelligence, Security and Overseas Services, and those accused of war crimes and crimes against humanity, and POWs. So it's a very large undertaking of which the weapons of mass destruction effort is a part in an important part of that effort, but only a part.

The organization will pretty much double or triple in size. There'll be some 1,300 experts who will be associated with this organization, plus another support element of maybe another 800. So you're talking about 2,000 people, more or less, who will begin arriving with the lead elements of the command starting toward the end of this month and the expertise, again, from the organizations I described a moment ago and will include, as well, people from Treasury, some of whom are already in theater, by the way, as well as U.S. citizens who had been in the past UNSCOM inspectors, some other contractors, and again, our coalition partners.

Now, that effort is going to be supported by a fusion cell that is being constructed here in Washington, again under the executive agency of the Defense Intelligence Agency. It is made up of experts from around the United States government. And they receive information from the 75th Group now, and they will receive it from the ISG as it stands up. And their job is going to be to do that kind of in-depth analysis that's necessary in order to make this a successful effort over time.

...When one comes across a site where we think that we need to be taking samples, for example, there are roughly four sets of samples taken, one for processing in-theater, two are sent here to the United States, and another one is sent to a non-U.S. laboratory for independent analysis and the verification of the results of those tests. And there is a very strict chain of custody process that is put in place to assure that those samples are not tampered with either in the theater, in transit, when they're in the laboratories, or when the results come back to us here. That's all supplemented, then, as I said a moment ago, by interviewing the personnel who we think are involved. I made mention to you that the subordinate scientists as well as the lead scientists are being interviewed. The regime figures are interviewed. We go through the documents and so forth. And then, if we find we've got to dispose of materials, we do so in a way that is safe for all concerned.

The ISG's main center of activity remained in Iraq, with a headquarters in Baghdad and additional facilities in Qatar. Its collection operation included a joint interrogation debriefing center, a joint matériel exploitation center, chemical and biological intelligence support teams, and an ISG operation center. Its main analytic effort was co-located with the CENTCOM forward headquarters in Qatar, along with its combined media processing center. The ISG had liaison elements with CJTF-7 in Kuwait and with other U.S. government agencies inside Iraq and an intelligence fusion center in Washington, D.C. All of its elements were linked electronically.[40]

Conversion to a Forensic Search Effort

Somewhat ironically, the coalition's search for Iraqi weapons of mass destruction was forced to take on much of the character of the previous UNMOVIC effort. It had to shift from a search for war-fighting capability to a much more forensic effort to search through Iraqi records and facilities, a task greatly complicated by its inability to safeguard many key facilities against looting. Douglas Feith, the under secretary of defense for policy, and Lt. General Norman Schwartz, director of operations of the Joint Staff, testified to the House International Relations Committee in May that the Bush administration now estimated that the process of determining Iraq's true level of proliferation could take years, and that no new chemical and biological weapons had yet been found.[41] Moreover, the United States was forced to allow the International Atomic Energy Agency to resume its inspection efforts.[42]

It is still unclear what this search effort will find. In late June, U.S. officials were talking about the need to go through tons of documents. They noted that the United States had taken custody of only 69 of some 255 top Iraqi officials who might know something about Iraq's WMD effort, and only 7 of some 3,152 lower-ranking officials. They also stated that the United States had conducted meaningful inspections of 157 of 578 suspect sites.[43]

As of July 2003, the U.S. search effort still had not shown that any suspect site was a valid military target. It also had not found valid evidence that Iraq had any significant capability to use weapons of mass destruction before the war. In addition, it had not found that Iraq had any major imminent capability to produce such weapons. The only meaningful discoveries were buried plans and parts for a centrifuge design dating back to 1991 and what appeared to be two trailers designed to produce biological weapons.[44]

It seems certain, given the results of the UNSCOM and UNMOVIC effort, that the United States will find some evidence of an ongoing WMD program. But it is far from clear what kind of Iraqi program and effort will emerge. The centrifuge discovery did nothing to shed significant light on recent Iraqi efforts.[45] The trailers may well be a more significant discovery, and the CIA has made a powerful case to this effect. But even experts within the U.S. intelligence community—particularly within the State Department—dispute whether the trailers were really being used for biological weapons purposes.[46] This again illustrates the inherent uncertainty surrounding estimates of proliferation and foreign WMD capabilities.

LESSONS FOR THE FUTURE

The end result so far of the entire intelligence and search effort relating to Iraqi weapons of mass destruction has been to strengthen those who argued against the war and who have since sought to discredit or block a coalition-led nation-building effort. It also threatens to become a specter that will haunt any future U.S. and allied efforts to deal with the threat of proliferation, particularly in winning domestic and international political support for military or preemptive action.

The solution to some extent is to admit the scale of problems that exist in the collection and analytic effort and then make major efforts to reduce them. It is also to lay the groundwork for any future action in a crisis by systematically educating decisionmakers, the media, and the public about the inevitable level of uncertainty in such assessments. This can be done through a series of classified and unclassified intelligence products that are as detailed and objective as possible. Credibility and understanding have to be created over a period of years, not in a crisis. Moreover, the United States and Britain need to understand that the Iraq War has left a heritage of distrust that must be overcome.

It is not enough to have a preemptive strategy. The key argument for preemptive attack must be that it is in fact preemptive and that the potential threat is real enough to justify a major war. Legalistic arguments over whether threats must be imminent may have only secondary value in the real world. The need to unambiguously resolve the kind of uncertainties that surrounded the Iraqi effort in weapons of mass destruction in both the Gulf War and Iraq War is a critical national priority, however. So is the need to examine far more intrusive methods of data gathering, such as unattended ground sensors. If the choice is between infractions of national sovereignty, on the one hand, and war or unacceptable risks on the other, aggressive intelligence gathering and infractions of national sovereignty are by far the better course.

There are two important corollaries of this lesson. The first is that until this aspect of intelligence can be greatly improved and made far more accurate and reliable, the United States, Britain, and other nations must place primary reliance on both operational and national defense and response capabilities. Missile defense is only one of these capabilities and currently may have limited cost-effectiveness. The fact that the United States could never characterize Iraqi links to terrorism or Iraq's ability to make covert use of weapons like smallpox is a warning that defense and response must look at the full range of threats and possible asymmetric attacks.

The second corollary is that the problems involved go far beyond any failures on the part of the United States. More than a decade of the most intrusive international inspection of a country in history also failed to characterize its efforts in weapons of mass destruction and delivery systems, and failed to disarm it. It is easy to focus on the fact that the United States and Britain may have exaggerated the threat and miss the point.

The United Nations accomplished a great deal, and the work of the IAEA, UNSCOM, and UNMOVIC merits the world's gratitude and respect. What could be done was done. Nevertheless, an intensive international arms control effort by UNSCOM, the IAEA, and UNMOVIC—using better means of inspection and arms control to deal with Iraq than now cover any other nation in the world—was still inadequate. This is a grim warning that major improvements are needed in the scope, intrusiveness, technology, and intelligence support provided for international arms control efforts if they are to be effective, and if they are ever to be an effective substitute for preemptive or other military action.

Notes

[1] Many of the comments made in this section are based on interviews with U.S., British, and Australian officials, officers, and experts after the war, and the author's prior experience in analyzing proliferation. Many useful press reports have emerged since the war. In addition to those referenced later in this chapter, they include Warren P. Strobel and John Walcott, "CIA Lacks Info to Counter Claims about Iraqi Weapons," *Miami Herald,* June 3, 2003; James Risen, "Iraq Arms Report Now the Subject of a CIA Review," *New York Times,* June 4, 2003; Maggie Farley, "Blix's Final Words to Security Council Are Words of Caution," *Los Angeles Times,* June 6, 2003; Tony Capaccio, "Pentagon 2002 Study Reported No Reliable Data on Iraq Weapons," Bloomberg.com, June 6, 2003; Bruce Auster, Mark Mazetti, and Edward Pound, "Truth and Consequences," *U.S. News & World Report,* June 9, 2003; Evan Thomas, Richard Wolffe, and Michael Isikoff, "Where Are Iraq's WMDs?" *Newsweek,* June 9, 2003; Michael Duffy, "Weapons of Mass Disappearance," *Time,* June 9, 2003; James Risen, "Word That US Doubted Iraq Would Use Gas," *New York Times,* June 18, 2003.

[2] All of the following points are quoted, with minor editing and reformatting, from the British ("Iraq's Weapons of Mass Destruction—The assessment of the British Government," September 24, 2002, www.pmo.gov.uk/output/page271.asp) and U.S. (CIA, "Iraq's Weapons of Mass Destruction Programs, "October 4, 2002, www. governmentguide.com/govsite.adp?bread=*Main&url=http%3A//www. governmentguide.com/ams/clickThruRedirect.adp%3F55076483% 2C16920155%2Chttp%3A//www.cia.gov) white papers. Additional British charges against Iraq for concealing evidence of its weapons of mass destruction can be found in a second white paper: "Iraq: Its Infrastructure of Concealment, Deception and Intimidation," October 7, 2002, www.number-10.gov.uk/output/Page1470.asp.

[3] For an interesting discussion of the problems in assessing dual-use facilities in Iraq, see Walter Pincus, "Weapons Linked to Dual Use Facilities in Iraq," *Washington Post,* June 2, 2003.

[4] For some additional data on this aspect of these assessments made of Iraq, see Bill Gertz, "Iraqi Group Aid CIA Intelligence," *Washington Times,* June 12, 2003; John Diamond, "Broad Purges Wiped Out Most Iraqis Helping CIA," *USA Today,* June 17,

2003; and John Diamond, "Weak Spy Network Hurt Hunt for Arms," *USA Today*, June 17, 2003.

[5] Earlier unclassified CIA reports on problems like the ballistic missile threat often projected alternative levels of current and future capability. The qualifications and possible futures are far less well defined in more recent reports. For example, see CIA, Unclassified Summary of a National Intelligence Estimate, Foreign Missile Developments and the Ballistic Missile Threat through 2015," National Intelligence Council, December 2001, www.cia.gov/nic/pubs/other_products/Unclassified ballisticmissilefinal.htm.

[6] There is no way to determine just how much the Special Plans Office team set up within the Office of the Secretary of Defense to analyze the threat in Iraq was designed to produce a given conclusion or politicized intelligence. The department has denied this and stated that the team created within its policy office was not working on Iraq per se, but on global terrorist interconnections. It also stated that the Special Plans Office was never tied to the Intelligence Collection Program—a program to debrief Iraqi defectors—and relied on CIA inputs for its analysis. It states that it simply conducted a review and presented its findings in August 2002, and that its members returned to other duties. See Jim Garamone, "Policy Chief Seeks to Clear Intelligence Record," American Forces Information Service, June 3, 2003; and briefing on policy and intelligence matters, Douglas J. Feith, under secretary of defense for policy, and William J. Luti, deputy under secretary of defense for special plans and Near East and South Asian affairs, June 4, 2003, www.defenselink.mil/transcripts/2003/tr20030604-0248.html.

Some intelligence experts dispute this view, however, and claim the team's effort was used to put press on the intelligence community. Such "B-teams" also have a mixed history. They did help identify an intelligence community tendency to underestimate Soviet strategic nuclear efforts during the Cold War. The threat analysis of missile threats posed to the United States by the "Rumsfeld Commission," however, was a heavily one-sided assessment designed to justify national missile defense. Also see Greg Miller, "Pentagon Defends Role of Intelligence Unit on Iraq," *Los Angeles Times*, June 5, 2003; and David S. Cloud, "The Case for War Relied on Selective Intelligence," *Wall Street Journal*, June 5, 2003.

[7] Some press sources cite what they claim is a deliberate effort to ignore a September 2002 DIA report on Iraqi chemical weapons capabilities called "Iraq-Key WMD Facilities-An Operational Support Study." See James Risen, "Word that US Doubted Iraq Would Use Gas," *New York Times*, June 18, 2003 and Tony Capaccio, "Pentagon 2002 Study Reported No Reliable Data on Iraq Weapons," *USA Today*, June 6, 2003.

In fact, the unclassified excerpts from the DIA report show that DIA was not stating that Iraq did not have chemical weapons, but rather that it had "no reliable information on whether Iraq is producing and stockpiling chemical weapons, or where Iraq has—or will—establish its chemical weapons facilities." The report went on to say that "although we lack any direct information, Iraq probably possesses CW agent in chemical munitions, possibly including artillery rockets, artillery shells, aerial bombs, and ballistic missile warheads. Baghdad also probably possesses bulk chemical stockpiles, primarily containing precursors, but that also could consist of some mustard agent of stabilized VX."

If anything, the report is a classic example of what happens when intelligence reports do state uncertainty and of how the user misreads or misuses the result.

[8] See Felicity Barringer, "UN Inspectors Say Baghdad Never Resolved Arms Issues," *New York Times*, June 3, 2003; Maggie Farley, "Blix's Final Words to Security Council on Iraq Are of Caution," *Los Angeles Times*, June 6, 2003; Bob Drogin, "UN Nuclear Experts Back in Iraq," *Los Angeles Times*, June 6, 2003; "UN Nuclear Team Heads for Iraq," BBC News, June 4, 2003, 0943 GMT.

[9] "The Executive Chairman provides the Security Council with an update required by the Security Council 60 days after the resumption of inspections in Iraq," www.un.org/Depts/unmovic/. Taken from transcript provided by ABC News.

[10] www.iaea.org/worldatom/Documents/. Transcript provided by ABC News.

[11] "The Executive Chairman provides the Security Council with an update on UNMOVICs work, www.un.org/Depts/unmovic/. Taken from transcript provided by ABC News.

[12] "Twelfth Quarterly Report," Note by the Secretary General, February 28, 2003, S/2003/232, www.un.org/Depts/unmovic/.

[13] Hans Blix, Executive Chairman of UNMOVIC, "Notes for briefing of the Security Council on the thirteenth quarterly report of UNMOVIC," June 5, 2003, www.un.org/Depts/unmovic/.

[14] Rolf Ekeus, "Iraq's Real Weapons Threat," *Washington Post*, June 29, 2003, sec. B, p. 7. For the full text of the report, see the thirteenth report of the Executive Chairman of the UN Monitoring, Verification, and Inspection Commission, S/2003/580, May 30, 2003.

[15] Dana Milbank and Walter Pincus, "Bush Aides Disclose Warnings from the CIA," *Washington Post*, July 23, 2003.

[16] In addition to the previous sources, see James Risen, "CIA Studying Prewar Reports on Iraqi Threat," *New York Times*, May 22, 2003, p. 1; Walter Pincus, "Officials Defend Iraq Intelligence," *Washington Post*, June 9, 2003; Walter Strobel and John Walcott, "CIA Lacked Info to Counter Claims about Iraq Weapons," *Miami Herald*, June 3, 2003; David S. Cloud, "Case for War Relied on Selective Intelligence," *Wall Street Journal*, June 5, 2003; James Risen, "Iraq Arms Report Now the Subject of a CIA Review," *New York Times*, June 4, 2003; Dan Plesch and Richard Norton Taylor, "Straw, Powell Had Serious Doubts over Their Iraqi Weapons Claims," *The Guardian*, May 31, 2003; Julian Borger, "The Spires Who Pushed for War," *The Guardian*, July 17, 2003; Glenn Frankel, "Blair Accused of Exaggerating Claims about Iraqi Weapons," *Washington Post*, May 30, 2003; John Diamond, "Uranium Reports Doubted Early On," *USA Today*, June 13, 2003; Walter Pincus, "CIA Says It Cabled Key Data to White House," *Washington Post*, June 13, 2003; Walter Pincus,

"Bush Recantation of Iraq Claim Stirs Calls for Probes," *Washington Post*, July 9, 2003; Dana Milbank and Mike Allen, "Bush Skirts Queries on Iraq Nuclear Allegation," *Washington Post*, July 10, 2003; Walter Pincus, "Tenet Says He Didn't Know about Claim," *Washington Post*, July 17, 2003.

[17] In addition to the previous sources, see Walter Pincus and Dana Priest, "Analysts Cite Pressure on Iraq Judgments," *Washington Post*, June 5, 2003.

[18] In addition to the previous sources, see Bill Gertz, "Iraqi Group Aided CIA Intelligence," *Washington Times*, June 12, 2003; Warren Hoge, "Iraq Report Mishandled, Blair Aide Concedes in Letter," *New York Times*, June 9, 2003; Mark Huban and Mark Turner, "Evidence about Iraqi Uranium Not Fake," *London Financial Times*, June 6, 2003, p. 3; Andrew Sparrow and Benedict Brogan, "Blair: I Have Weapons Proof," *London Daily Telegraph*, June 2, 2003.

[19] Glern Frankel, "Allies Didn't Share All Intelligence on Iraq," *Washington Post*, July 17, 2003; Mike Allen and Jim Vandhei, "Uranium Flap Dims Brief Visit by Blair," *Washington Post*, July 17, 2003.

[20] "Serving Officer was 45-Minute claim Source," Times On Line, June 15, 2003.

[21] Statement by Senator Carl Levin regarding Iraq Intelligence, Office of Senator Carl Levin, July 15, 2003, Tara_Andringa@levin.senate.gov.

[22] For the full details, see House of Commons Foreign Affairs Committee, "The Decision to Go to War in Iraq," Ninth Report of Session 2003-03, House of Commons, London, July 3, 2003.

[23] Ibid.

[24] Ibid.

[25] Ibid.

[26] John Hendren, "Weapons Reports Called Lacking," *Los Angeles Times*, June 26, 2003.

[27] Lt. Gen. James Conway, commander, 1st Marine Expeditionary Force, "Live Briefing from Iraq, May 30, 2003, www.defenselink.mil/transcripts/2003/tr20030530-0229.ht.

[28] Commanding General, 1st Marine Division, "Operation Iraqi Freedom (OIF): Lessons Learned," MEF FRAGO 279-03, May 29, 2003.

[29] For example, see Seymour M. Hersh, "Annals of National Security: Selective Intelligence," *New Yorker*, May 12, 2003.

[30] Barton Gellman, "Frustrated, U.S. Arms Team to Leave Iraq: Task Force Unable To Find Any Weapons," *Washington Post*, May 11, 2003, sec. A, p. 1.

[31] Bob Drogin, "New Hunt for Iraqi Arms Resembles Old," *Los Angeles Times*, June 18, 2003.

[32] William J. Broad, "U.S. Civilian Experts Say Bureaucracy and Infighting Jeopardize Search for Weapons," *New York Times*, April 16, 2003; Dan Morse, "U.S. Troops Go House to House in Search of Chemical Weapons, "*Wall Street Journal*, April 16,

2003; Judith Miller, "U.S. Inspectors Find No Forbidden Weapons at Iraqi Arms Plants," *New York Times*, April 16, 2003.

[33] Barton Gellman, "Covert Unit Hunted for Iraqi Arms," *Washington Post*, June 13, 2003.

[34] John J. Fialka, "U.S. Readies a Different Army to Search for Weapons in Iraq," *Wall Street Journal*, April 17, 2003.

[35] Barton Gellman, "Frustrated, U.S. Arms Team to Leave Iraq: Task Force Unable To Find Any Weapons," *Washington Post*, May 11, 2003, sec. A, p. 1.

[36] See Hersh, "Annals of National Security: Selective Intelligence"; and Gellman, "Frustrated, U.S. Arms Team to Leave Iraq.."

[37] "Briefing on the Iraq Survey Group," Stephen A. Cambone, under secretary of defense for intelligence, and Army Maj. Gen. Keith W. Dayton, director for operations, Defense Intelligence Agency, May 30, www.defenselink.mil/transcripts/2003/tr20030530-0231.html.

[38] Hersh, "Annals of National Security: Selective Intelligence." The best reporting on the issue at this writing, however, can be found in Gellman, "Frustrated, U.S. Arms Team to Leave Iraq: Task Force Unable to Find Any Weapons."

[39] Department of Defense Briefing, Stephen A. Cambone, USD (Intelligence) presenter, May 7, 2003, www.defenselink.mil/transcripts/2003/tr20030507-0158.html.

[40] "Briefing on the Iraq Survey Group," Stephen A. Cambone, under secretary of defense for intelligence, and Army Maj. Gen. Keith W. Dayton, director for operations, Defense Intelligence Agency, May 30, www.defenselink.mil/transcripts/2003/tr20030530-0231.html.

[41] Bill Nichols, "Weapons Search Could Take Years," *USA Today*, May 16, 2003, p. 1; Judith Miller, "Radioactive Material Found at Test Site Near Baghdad," *New York Times*, May 12, 3003; Barton Gellman, "Seven Nuclear Sites Looted," *Washington Post*, May 10, 2003, p. 1.

[42] Bob Drogin, "UN Nuclear Experts Back in Iraq," *Los Angeles Times*, June 6, 2003; "UN Nuclear Team Heads for Iraq," BBC News, June 4, 2003, 0943 GMT; Bob Drogin, "New Hunt for Iraqi Arms Resembles Old," *Los Angeles Times*, June 18, 2003. The U.S. Department of Defense spokesman explained the role of the IAEA by stating: "The purpose of the inspection is to inventory and assess the condition of the material that is under IAEA safeguards at the Baghdad yellow-cake storage facility. The material at this facility includes approximately 500 metric tons of safeguarded uranium and several non-fissile radioisotope sources that are not under IAEA safeguards. The uranium is mostly in the form of yellow cake, an isotopically natural form that is an impure oxide. There is a small quantity of low-enriched and depleted uranium. Typically, the IAEA would conduct an NPT safeguards inspection at this location annually. The last inspection was conducted in December of 2002. Given the changed circumstances, the United States has determined it would be helpful to have the IAEA reinventory this location. I would like to underscore, though, that this is a cooperative

effort. The coalition will be providing necessary transportation, security and other minimal logistics to the team, which will consist of seven IAEA experts. The safeguards activity will be led by the IAEA under the protection and auspices of coalition forces. To ensure safety and protection, coalition forces will accompany the IAEA at all times. Coalition nuclear experts will also participate in the inspection and the inventory. Upon completion of the inventory, the IAEA will repackage the material as necessary, reseal all safeguarded rooms, buildings and containers as appropriate, and the coalition will, as appropriate, assist in this effort. I want to note that this access to the IAEA is not an IAEA inspection pursuant to the U.N. Security Council resolutions and does not set any precedent for future IAEA involvement in Iraq in any disarmament or UNSCR-related activity. And lastly, we expect that the IAEA will share their findings with us as we work cooperatively on this effort. "

A U.S. Department of Defense spokesman explained the looting problem as follows: "Tuwaitha, as has been stated earlier, is about a 23,000-acre facility that's about 20 kilometers to the southeast of Baghdad. And Site Charlie, where radiological materials, principally yellow cake were stored, consists of three buildings, and they're surrounded by a fence and a wall of concrete barriers about 12 feet tall on three sides. According to reports from civilians in the area, on or about the 10th of March, Iraqi army forces who were guarding the site reportedly left their weapons—some of their weapons with the local civilians—and abandoned the site. We also believe, from talking to the local civilians, that on or about 20 March, the 20th of March, the civilians guarding the site abandoned it also. And, of course, we were conducting our attack across the Kuwaiti border on the 21st.

"On the 7th of April, U.S. Marines from our land component first arrived at Tuwaitha Site Charlie and assumed the security, and remained there until the 20th of April, when they turned over control of the facility to U.S. Army soldiers from another unit. And Tuwaitha Site Charlie has been secured and under the positive control of U.S. forces since the 7th of April. When the U.S. forces first arrived, they found the Tuwaitha site facility, Tuwaitha Charlie facility, in disarray. The front gate was open and unsecured, and the fence line and barrier wall on the back side of the facility had been breached. And the troops reported that there were no seals on the exterior doors of the buildings. But since taking control of Tuwaitha Site Charlie, no thieves or looters have been allowed inside the facility. We have taken several positive steps to try to mitigate any risks from Tuwaitha Charlie to either the soldiers or the population in the surrounding area or to the environment. And I'll list of a couple of those.

"Between the 8th and 10th of April, a team conducted an initial survey outside the buildings at Tuwaitha Charlie, and they determined that additional exploitation was required beyond their capability. And so the exploitation task force, the folks responsible for that operation, decided to keep the security at the site and to deny access to anyone except properly trained personnel. On the 18th of April, some Iraqi scientists from the Iraqi Atomic Energy Commission, who had worked at the facility, were allowed in to check the site and to mitigate any radiological hazards within their capability. And they moved some sources into a building from the concrete outside.

"On the 12th of May, our Threat Reduction Agency personnel arrived in Iraq and began planning for its operation at Tuwaitha Charlie. And between the 15th and 20th of May, our task force disablement and elimination team conducted its technical assessment and an inventory of what was there. And from what we know at this time, the quantity of materials we have found at the site exceeds the quantity of materials that we had assessed would be present at the site. On the 18th of May, a direct support team teamed up with the Coalition Provisional Authority personnel and some additional people from IAEC, the Iraqi Atomic Energy Commission, and they decided to conduct a buy-back operation because the troops were starting to hear stories that some of the barrels—there were barrels in the local community that resembled those that were at the site. The team went to two villages and offered to pay $3 a piece for any items that may have come from the facility, and they pointed out what these items might look like. The team recovered over 100 barrels of various sizes and shapes and condition, as well as five radioactive sources and some other items. But virtually none of the people admitted to having taken the items from the facility. They said they had bought them. And indeed, barrels like these are ubiquitous around Iraq. And although there are some similar containers available in markets—and the same type barrels are sometimes found in people's homes. The team checked the items for radioactivity and also checked the people to reassure them. None of the people registered any radiation above normal background levels. And these barrels of various sizes and shapes and colors—none of them registered more than background level or slightly above normal background radiation. They then transported the items to Tuwaitha Charlie and secured them. And so, there's no way to tell at this point if they came from Tuwaitha, but they were taken back there just in case, for safety. The technical assessment also determined that outside the fence line at Tuwaitha Charlie, there was negligible risk to the soldiers guarding the site and to the population within a wide area out to a kilometer from the fence line. But the site had apparently been looted before U.S. soldiers arrived. Uranium materials and some other stored materials had been dumped on the floor in places, and in one building, there were a number of radiological sources scattered around the floor. Radiological readings measured only background levels out at the fence line, and readings at the buildings and inside were somewhere between two and 10 times background readings.

"We've been conducting weekly meetings with the Iraqi Atomic Energy Commission, with our coalition forces experts and with the Coalition Provisional Authority experts to continue the way ahead in a joint manner. We've developed a plan and objectives for improvement of the site. This week, the Center for Health Promotion and Preventive Medicine, commonly called CHPPM, arrives from the United States. And they'll conduct a risk assessment on the soldiers and Marines who were there and those who are still there. And the purpose of that is to reassure those soldiers and Marines, but also to determine what, if any, risks they might have occurred—incurred, rather, from being at—near the site. Together with the Iraqi Atomic Energy Commission and the Iraqi Ministry of Health, CHPPM will also help to conduct a wider search and a health risk assessment of the surrounding civilian area, out to about five kilometers. Iraqi scientists and physicians began that work this week by conducting an initial assessment and a census of those people out there. We also formed a joint team with the Iraqi experts and repaired and sealed the buildings as a further measure of safety, so that even if the weather changed to something severe that we hadn't expected, the buildings would still be secure. We've also recruited a 100-man Iraqi guard force. And we're in the process of training them so that once they meet standards, they'll eventually take over the security. And of course, IAEA arrives in Baghdad this weekend to begin its work. And that's about all I have for opening comments." (Senior Defense Department official, "Background briefing on the upcoming IAEA nuclear safeguards inspection and the Tuwaitha Nuclear Facility in Iraq," June 5, 2003, www.defenselink.mil/transcripts/2003/tr20030605-0250.html.)

[43] Judy Keen, "U.S.: Weapon Search has Barely Begun," *USA Today*, June 20, 2003.

[44] See William J. Broad, "US, In Assessment, Terms Trailers Germ Laboratories," *New York Times*, May 29, 2003.

The CIA summarized the importance of this discovery as follows in "Iraqi Mobile Biological Warfare Agent Production Plants," a report dated May 28, 2003 (www.cia.gov/cia/reports/iraqi_mobile_plants/index.html):

"Coalition forces have uncovered the strongest evidence to date that Iraq was hiding a biological warfare program.

- Kurdish forces in late April 2003 took into custody a specialized tractor-trailer near Mosul and subsequently turned it over to U.S. military control.

- The U.S. military discovered a second mobile facility equipped to produce BW agent in early May at the al-Kindi Research, Testing, Development, and Engineering facility in Mosul. Although this second trailer appears to have been looted, the remaining equipment, including the fermentor, is in a configuration similar to the first plant.

- U.S. forces in late April also discovered a mobile laboratory truck in Baghdad. The truck is a toxicology laboratory from the 1980s that could be used to support BW or legitimate research.

"The design, equipment, and layout of the trailer found in late April is strikingly similar to descriptions provided by a source who was a chemical engineer that managed one of the mobile plants. Secretary of State Powell's description of the mobile plants in his speech in February 2003 to the United Nations (see below) was based primarily on reporting from this source.

"Secretary Powell's speech to the UN in February 2003 detailed Iraq's mobile BW program, and was primarily based on information from a source who was a chemical engineer that managed one of the mobile plants:

- Iraq's mobile BW program began in the mid-1990s—this is reportedly when the units were being designed.

- Iraq manufactured mobile trailers and railcars to produce biological agents, which were designed to evade UN weapons inspectors. Agent production reportedly occurred Thursday night through Friday when the UN did not conduct inspections in observance of the Muslim holy day.

■ An accident occurred in 1998 during a production run, which killed 12 technicians—an indication that Iraq was producing a BW agent at that time.

"Analysis of the trailers reveals that they probably are second- or possibly third-generation designs of the plants described by the source. The newer version includes system improvements, such as cooling units, apparently engineered to solve production problems described by the source that were encountered with the older design. The manufacturer's plates on the fermentors list production dates of 2002 and 2003—suggesting Iraq continued to produce these units as late as this year.

"The source reported to us that Iraq in 1995 planned to construct seven sets of mobile production plants—six on semitrailers and one on railroad cars—to conceal BW agent production while appearing to cooperate with UN inspectors. Some of this information was corroborated by another source.

■ One of the semitrailer plants reportedly produced BW agents as early as July 1997.

■ The design for a more concealable and efficient two-trailer system was reportedly completed in May 1998 to compensate for difficulties in operating the original, three-trailer plant.

■ Iraq employed extensive denial and deception in this program, including disguising from its own workers the production process, equipment, and BW agents produced in the trailers.

"Examination of the trailers reveals that all of the equipment is permanently installed and interconnected, creating an ingeniously simple, self-contained bioprocessing system. Although the equipment on the trailer found in April 2003 was partially damaged by looters, it includes a fermentor capable of producing biological agents and support equipment such as water supply tanks, an air compressor, a water chiller, and a system for collecting exhaust gases.

"The trailers probably are part of a two- or possibly three-trailer unit. Both trailers we have found probably are designed to produce BW agent in unconcentrated liquid slurry. The missing trailer or trailers from one complete unit would be equipped for growth media preparation and postharvest processing and, we would expect, have equipment such as mixing tanks, centrifuges, and spray dryers.

"These other units that we have not yet found would be needed to prepare and sterilize the media and to concentrate and possibly dry the agent, before the agent is ready for introduction into a delivery system, such as bulk-filled munitions. Before the Gulf war, Iraq bulk filled missile and rocket warheads, aerial bombs, artillery shells, and spray tanks.

"The majority of our information on Iraq's mobile program was obtained from a chemical engineer that managed one of the plants. Three other sources, however, corroborated information related to the mobile BW project. The second source was a civil engineer who reported on the existence of at least one truck-transportable facility in December 2000 at the Karbala ammunition depot. The third source reported in 2002 that Iraq had manufactured mobile systems for the production of single-cell protein on trailers and railcars but admitted that they could be used for BW agent production. The fourth source, a defector from the Iraq Intelligence Service, reported that Baghdad manufactured mobile facilities that we assess could be used for the research of BW agents, vice production.

"Our analysis of the mobile production plant found in April indicates the layout and equipment are consistent with information provided by the chemical engineer, who has direct knowledge of Iraq's mobile BW program. The source recognized pictures of this trailer, among photographs of unrelated equipment, as a mobile BW production plant similar to the one that he managed, even pointing out specific pieces of equipment that were installed on his unit.

"Common elements between the source's description and the trailers include a control panel, fermentor, water tank, holding tank, and two sets of gas cylinders. One set of gas cylinders was reported to provide clean gases—oxygen and nitrogen—for production, and the other set captured exhaust gases, concealing signatures of BW agent production.

"The discovered trailers also incorporate air-stirred fermentors, which the source reported were part of the second-generation plant design. Externally, the trailers have a ribbed superstructure to support a canvas covering that matches the source's description. Data plates on the fermentors indicate that they were manufactured at the same plant the source said manufactured equipment for the first generation of mobile plants. The plant also was involved in the production of equipment used in Iraq's pre-Gulf war BW program.

"Employees of the facility that produced the mobile production plants' fermentor revealed that seven fermentors were produced in 1997, one in 2002 and one in 2003. The seven fermentors appear to corroborate the source's reporting that Iraq in the mid-1990s planned to produce seven mobile production plants. The two fermentors produced in 2002 and 2003 reportedly were sent to the al-Kindi Research, Testing, Development, and Engineering facility in Mosul—the site where the second trailer was found—and probably are the fermentors found on the trailers in U.S. custody.

"There are a few inconsistencies between the source's reporting and the trailers, which probably reflect design improvements. The original plants were reported to be mounted on flatbed trailers reinforced by nickel-plate flooring and equipped with hydraulic support legs. The discovered plants are mounted on heavy equipment transporters intended to carry army tanks, obviating the need for reinforced floors and hydraulic legs. The trailers have a cooling unit not included in the original plant design, probably to solve overheating problems during the summer months as described by the source. The original design had 18 pumps, but the source mentioned an effort to reduce the number to four in the new design. The trailer discovered in late April has three pumps.

"Coalition experts on fermentation and systems engineering examined the trailer found in late April and have been unable to identify any legitimate industrial use—such as water purification, mobile medical laboratory, vaccine or pharmaceutical production—that would justify the effort and expense of a mobile production capability. We have investigated what other industrial processes may require such equipment—a fermentor, refrigeration, and a gas capture system—and agree with the experts that BW agent production is the only consistent, logical purpose for these vehicles.

"The capability of the system to capture and compress exhaust gases produced during fermentation is not required for legitimate biological processes and strongly indicates attempts to conceal production activity. The presence of caustic in the fermentor combined with the recent painting of the plant may indicate an attempt to decontaminate and conceal the plant's purpose. Finally, the data plate on the fermentor indicates that this system was manufactured in 2002 and yet it was not declared to the United Nations, as required by Security Council Resolutions.

"Some coalition analysts assess that the trailer found in late April could be used for bioproduction but believe it may be a newer prototype because the layout is not entirely identical to what the source described.

"A *New York Times* article on 13 May 2003 reported that an agricultural expert suggests the trailers might have been intended to produce biopesticides near agricultural areas in order to avoid degradation problems. The same article also reported that a former weapons inspector suggests that the trailers may be chemical-processing units intended to refurbish Iraq's antiaircraft missiles.

"Biopesticide production requires the same equipment and technology used for BW agent production; however, the off-gas collection system and the size of the equipment are unnecessary for biopesticide production. There is no need to produce biopesticides near the point of use because biopesticides do not degrade as quickly as most BW agents and would be more economically produced at a large fixed facility. In addition, the color of the trailer found in mid-April is indicative of military rather than civilian use.

"Our missile experts have no explanation for how such a trailer could function to refurbish antiaircraft missiles and judge that such a use is unlikely based on the scale, configuration, and assessed function of the equipment. The experts cited in the editorial are not on the scene and probably do not have complete access to information about the trailers.

"Senior Iraqi officials of the al-Kindi Research, Testing, Development, and Engineering facility in Mosul were shown pictures of the mobile production trailers, and they claimed that the trailers were used to chemically produce hydrogen for artillery weather balloons. Hydrogen production would be a plausible cover story for the mobile production units.

"The Iraqis have used sophisticated denial and deception methods that include the use of cover stories that are designed to work. Some of the features of the trailer—a gas collection system and the presence of caustic—are consistent with both biopro-duction and hydrogen production.

"The plant's design possibly could be used to produce hydrogen using a chemical reaction, but it would be inefficient. The capacity of this trailer is larger than typical units for hydrogen production for weather balloons. Compact, transportable hydrogen generation systems are commercially available, safe, and reliable.

"We continue to examine the trailer found in mid-April and are using advanced sample analysis techniques to determine whether BW agent is present, although we do not expect samples to show the presence of BW agent. We suspect that the Iraqis thoroughly decontaminated the vehicle to remove evidence of BW agent production. Despite the lack of confirmatory samples, we nevertheless are confident that this trailer is a mobile BW production plant because of the source's description, equipment, and design.

- The initial set of samples, now in the United States, was taken from sludge from inside the fermentor, liquid that was in the system and wipes from the equipment. A sample set also was provided to a coalition partner for detailed laboratory analysis.

- As we expected, preliminary sample analysis results are negative for five standard BW agents, including Bacillus anthracis, and for growth media for those agents. In addition, the preliminary results indicate the presence of sodium azide and urea, which do not support Iraqi claims that the trailer was for hydrogen production.

- Additional sample analysis is being conducted to identify growth media, agent degradation products, and decontamination chemicals that could be specific for BW agents, as well as to identify a chemical associated with hydrogen production.

"Although individuals often interchangeably use the terms production plant and laboratory, they have distinct meanings. The mobile production plants are designed for batch production of biological material and not for laboratory analysis of samples. A truck-mounted mobile laboratory would be equipped for analysis and small-scale laboratory activities. U.S. forces discovered one such laboratory in late April.

"The mobile laboratory—installed in a box-bodied truck—is equipped with standard, dual-use laboratory equipment, including autoclaves, an incubator, centrifuges, and laboratory test tubes and glassware. These laboratories could be used to support a mobile BW production plant but serve legitimate functions that are applicable to public heath and environmental monitoring, such as water-quality sampling."

One Iraqi defector has made claims of a much more serious ongoing biological weapons effort, but these have not been validated. See Bob Drogin, "Iraq Had Secret Labs, Officer Says," *Los Angeles Times*, June 8, 2003.

The CIA issued the following statement on the discovery of the centrifuge on June 26, 2003 (www.cia.gov/cia/wmd/iraqi_centrifuge_equipment.htm):

"The head of Iraq's pre-1991 centrifuge uranium enrichment program, Dr. Mahdi Shukur Ubaydi, approached U.S. officials in Baghdad and turned over a volume of centrifuge documents and components he had hidden in his garden from inspectors since 1991. Dr. Ubaydi said he was interviewed by IAEA inspectors—most recently in 2002—but did not reveal any of this.

"Dr. Ubaydi told us that these items, blue prints and key centrifuge pieces, represented a complete template for what would be needed to rebuild a centrifuge uranium enrichment program. He also claimed this concealment was part of a secret, high-level plan to reconstitute the nuclear weapons program once sanctions ended.

"This case illustrates the extreme challenge we face in Iraq as we search for evidence of WMD programs that were designed to elude detection by international inspectors.

"We are working with Dr. Ubaydi to evaluate the equipment and documents he provided us.

"We are hopeful that Dr. Ubaydi's example will encourage other Iraqis with knowledge of Saddam's WMD programs to come forward."

[45] Joby Warrick, "Iraqi Scientist Turns over Nuclear Plans, Parts," *Washington Post*, June 26, 2003, p. 14.

[46] Douglas Jehl, "Agency Disputes View of Trailers as Labs," *New York Times*, June 26, 2003.

CHAPTER THIRTEEN

OTHER LESSONS

There are a number of other lessons that have emerged from the war.

THE ROLE OF WOMEN IN COMBAT

Women made up roughly 15 percent of U.S. military forces during the Iraq War, ranging from a high of 19 percent in the air force to 6 percent in the marines. The number of women in high-risk jobs increased strikingly compared with those in the Gulf War, although women are still barred from ground combat positions. Perhaps the most striking aspect of this change is that there are no meaningful reports of gender problems in combat or high-risk positions. Although scarcely unexpected, this experience is a further refutation of the arguments that women cannot perform such duties or will disrupt operations in wartime.

MILITARY MEDICAL FACILITIES AND CAPABILITIES

The Iraq War reflected continuing progress in military medicine, which has steadily reduced the level of fatalities relative to wounds and injuries. It also reflected the critical importance of new on-the-scene bandages and treatments focused on the most serious wounds and reducing the need for aerial medical evacuation. Some 110 medical evacuation sorties were flown between G-Day and April 11 involving some 1,300 patients but only 50 urgent patients.

The U.S. forces took other innovative steps. They stationed surgeons nearer the battlefield to provide rapid treatment in the critical first 60 minutes of combat. They provided a wide range of new equipment such as ultrasound to look inside the body, Doppler machines to measure blood flow, and new equipment to stabilize arm injuries. They deployed new blood-clotting bandages and better body armor with ceramic plates.[1]

One critical change growing out of the problem of "Gulf War Syndrome" from the previous Gulf War was the use of force-wide medical surveys for each soldier sent to the theater, followed by in-theater surveys and exit surveys, with annual blood sampling. In addition to smallpox and anthrax shots to guard against biological attacks, medical treatment also shifted from a focus on general global needs to a far more detailed survey of the specific risks in the theater. Even so, questions have emerged about the range of sampling, the speed of testing samples, and the need for something approaching near-real-time analysis.[2]

More generally, field reports indicate that there are still major problems in tracking and managing the flow of medical treatment at the division level and below and that problems in tactical communications inevitably affect medical services. Scattered reports also raise questions about the efficacy of the new bandages issued during the war.

SAFETY—BECOMING MORE CRITICAL

As has been discussed in chapter 7, it is easy to focus on more high-profile issues like fratricide, but safety is clearly a critical issue. Military operations have always been "accident prone," but the ratio of accidents to steadily diminishing combat casualties is making safety consciousness and discipline a new priority. Some 36 of the 123 U.S. deaths from G-Day to April 15 were classified as accidents. The figures for British forces were 16 accidental deaths out of a total of 31 deaths. Of the total of 52 accidental deaths for U.S. and British forces, 28 occurred in helicopter accidents and some 12 in vehicle accidents. The accidental discharge of firearms accounted for a significant number of the others.

These figures help explain why Lt. General William Wallace, commander of the U.S. Army forces in Iraq, was forced to issue a warning to all of the U.S. Army forces deployed in the Iraq War on April 15 regarding safety: "We cannot, cannot, cannot allow our soldiers to relax their guard." At the same time, such a warning scarcely solved the problem. A total of 138 U.S. deaths occurred during the war (March 19–April 30); of those, 89 were the result of hostile action, one was the result of illness, 28 were the result of accidents other than in helicopters, and 15 were the result of accidents in helicopters. Two occurred because a U.S. noncommissioned officer shot several other soldiers in his unit (the "Camp PA" incident), and three were the result of known cases of friendly fire.

If one looks at the "postwar" pattern in accidents, there were 61 U.S. deaths between May 1 and June 27. Of that total, 19 were the result of hostile action, 4 came from nonhostile action, 31 were the result of accidents other than in helicopters, 7 were the result of accidents in helicopters, and none were the result of known cases of friendly fire.[3] As of July 17, 2003, the number of deaths since May 1 had risen to 85, with 32 killed by hostile fire and 53 by other causes, almost all accidents. The total killed since March 19 had risen to 229, with 161 deaths due to hostile causes and 68 due to nonhostile causes, again largely due to accidents. These figures do not include wounded or nonfatal injuries due to accidents. As of July 17, 258 U.S. soldiers had been seriously injured in accidents. This total was more than 30 percent of the total of 830 that had been wounded—either in action or in accidents— between March 19 and July 17.[4]

These totals clearly illustrate the importance of "safety" in modern war. They also help to explain why the Department of Defense launched a campaign in late May 2003 on a worldwide basis to try to reduce the number of aviation accidents by 50 percent over the next two years, and why theater commanders in Iraq made similar efforts to improve safety in June 2003.[5] The good news is that a decline in combat losses allows the U.S. military to focus far more on safety than in the past. The bad news is that casualties from accidents remain a serious issue.

Notes

[1] For a good summary, see Larry Copeland, "Faster Treatment, Better Gear, Save Lives on the Battlefield," *USA Today*, April 18, 2003.

[2] Jon Ward, "More Data Sought on Soldier's Health," *Washington Times*, May 1, 2003, p. 7; Russ Byman, "Watching for Gulf War Syndrome II," *Philadelphia Inquirer*, June 3, 2003.

[3] Estimates differ as to the causes. According to the *Wall Street Journal*, the United States lost 92 dead between the fall of Baghdad on April 19 and June 25, versus 102 during the peak fighting between March 19 and April 19, and 52 Americans had been killed since President Bush had announced the formal end of combat action on May 1. Alexei Barrionuevo and Michael M. Phillips, "Mounting Troop Deaths in Iraq Raise Questions of US Control," *Wall Street Journal*, June 25, 2003.

[4] Brian Hartman, ABC News, July 17, 2003, from data provided by the U.S. Department of Defense.

[5] "DoD Launching Campaign to Reduce accidents by Half," *Aerospace Daily*, May 21, 2003.

CHAPTER FOURTEEN

LESSONS FROM IRAQI PROBLEMS AND SHORTCOMINGS

Many of the lessons regarding Iraqi failures have already been discussed in chapter 3 and, in talking about the advantages U.S. and British forces had, in chapters 6 and 7. In many ways, Iraq's military faults and shortcomings were virtually the reverse image of U.S. and British military capabilities.[1]

Iraq may also have made the mistake of fundamentally underestimating the nature of U.S. military capabilities. Secretary of Defense Donald Rumsfeld suggested this in the Department of Defense briefing on April 15:

> …this is speculation, but I would speculate that they very likely expected Gulf War II, a long air war that would give them time to do whatever they thought they wanted to do, leave or take cover and what have you, followed at some distance by a ground war, and probably a massive ground war, probably including the 4th Infantry Division, which was still up in the Mediterranean.
>
> And it's entirely possible when people are interviewed after this is all over that we'll find that they did not expect a ground war to start before an air war and they did not expect a ground war to start without the 4th Infantry Division while it was still up in the Mediterranean. I also suspect that they didn't expect the first air attack that took place the day before the ground war began on the Dora Farms. But one can't know these things; you can't climb into their minds and know what they were thinking.
>
> But we do know that because of the way General Franks conducted the conflict, a lot of bad things didn't happen. The oil wells were not set afire like they were last time. We don't have massive internally displaced people. We don't have a million refugees flooding into neighboring countries.
>
> We didn't have high collateral damage because we didn't have a long air war. We had precision weapons instead of dumb bombs. The ground war went so much faster, that the opportunity for people to reorganize and to reconstitute forces in areas where they could provide a more aggressive defense didn't exist; they were passed very rapidly. So there were a lot of things that — there wasn't time to use ballistic missiles in the western part of the country to

attack neighboring countries as happened last time. There's just a whole list of things that didn't go wrong, that could have been terrible and didn't happen, because of the way that General Franks and his team conducted that. They did a superb job.

Others argue that Iraq did have a relatively good idea of how the United States would fight, but simply lacked the tools to respond effectively.

It may be years before the Iraqi view of the war is fully understood, if ever. Only the top Iraqi leadership probably knows the calculations involved. Still, however, there are some potential lessons about the Iraqi approach to the war that are worth mentioning.

IRAQ REALLY WAS A TYRANNY

There is almost no evidence of broad popular support for Saddam Hussein, although the Iraqis scarcely showed an overwhelming welcome to U.S. and British forces. The Popular Army did not emerge as a meaningful force. Virtually all of the resistance in the south came from loyalist cadres and forces Saddam had used to reestablish control over the south after the uprisings in 1991. The same factors meant that Saddam could not develop a popular defense of Baghdad, and his loyal cadres could only fight in scattered areas and without cohesion and coordination.

The regular—heavily conscript—army showed far less commitment to the regime than the Republican Guard did. In spite of Saddam Hussein's attempt to buy its loyalty, many officers saw the regime as corrupt and as favoring the Republican Guard and security forces at the expense of the nation and the regular army.[2]

IRAQ HAD RIVAL POLITICIZED, BUREAUCRATIC, AND COMPARTMENTALIZED FORCES

At the start of the war, Iraq was still the most effective military power in the Gulf, despite the Gulf War and the loss of some 40 percent of its army and air force order of battle. Iraq still had armed forces with around 389,000 full-time actives. Its army had some 350,000 actives, including some 100,000 called-up reservists, before it began a serious buildup in reaction to U.S. and British deployments, and an inventory of some 2,200 to 2,600 main battle tanks, 3,700 other armored vehicles, and 2,400 major artillery weapons.

The Iraqi Air Force had 20,000 men and more than 300 combat aircraft with potential operational status. It had a 17,000-man air defense command with more than 850 surface-to-air missile launchers and some 3,000 anti-aircraft guns. Iraq's small, 2,000-man navy was equipped with nine small combat ships and an unknown number of mines and Silkworm land-based anti-ship missiles

But Iraq's overlapping structure of forces and security elements were often better at watching one another and at securing the regime than at fighting. There was little coordination except at the local level, and command and control could not direct cohesive action. Iraq also suffered from the fact that it had rebuilt its post–Gulf War forces more around internal security missions, regime stability, and static defense than around the lessons of that war.

Large parts of the Iraqi force structure were designed to cover the Iranian border, secure the Kurdish security zone, and fight a low-level battle against the Shi'ites in the south. Others were designed to protect the regime against other elements of the armed forces. The result was a garrison force optimized around the wrong missions that was not trained to fight as a cohesive force, whose command and control structure was focused around the command of disparate force elements in border defense and internal security missions, and that had limited capability for actual war fighting. This, in turn, exacerbated the divisions between the different elements of the ground forces and security forces, effectively leaving coordination to Saddam, his sons, and the elite around him rather than creating a C4I structure capable of developing any kind of comprehensive operational picture, coordinating maneuver on a national level, and reacting within the tight time limits forced on Iraq by the speed and intensity of the U.S. drive deep into Iraq.

The Iraqi air force and ground-base air defense forces, in turn, came to emphasize survival against low-level U.S. and UK air operations in the northern and southern no-fly zones between 1991 and 2003, although they did try occasionally to challenge or trap the U.S. and British aircraft enforcing the no-fly zones.

The Iraqi air force did virtually nothing to improve its capability to conduct joint operations with any element of Iraq's ground forces during the period between the end of the Gulf War in 1991 and the beginning of the Iraq War in 2003. It did equally little to improve its tactics and operations to deal with large-scale air operations. Rather than prepare for war during the months before the war, it executed plans and exercises it had been developing since 1991 to strip the wings from its combat aircraft and disperse them in fields, towns, and shelters. For reasons that are not yet fully apparent, this plan was executed in February 2003, effectively taking the Iraqi Air Force out of the fight.

The regime seems to have compounded these problems by largely ignoring the air force in its command and communications activity once the war began. Moreover, coordination among the military services was so poor that the Iraqi Air Force did not receive the additional weapons it requested to defend its air bases, and many air force units were left with little more than assault rifles for defense.[3]

As is described in chapters 3 and 4, Iraq's Air Defense Command was a numerically strong force with a command structure based on sectoral operating centers. Its actual war-fighting capability, however, had been seriously degraded by extensive U.S. and British strikes to "enforce the no-fly zone." These U.S. and British strikes had been intensified in both the northern and southern no-fly zones in November 2001 in reaction to increased Iraqi efforts to shoot down a U.S. or British aircraft. They were further intensified in the summer of 2002 as part of Operation "Southern Focus, " which was designed to suppress Iraqi air defense capability in the event of a U.S. and British invasion. The intensity of these strikes is indicated by the fact that the allies struck 349 Air Defense Command targets in southern Iraq, and fired 606 munitions, between June 2001 and March 19, 2003.[4]

During this time, Iraq not only lost many of its radars and surface-to-air missile fire units, but also a significant amount of its command and control system. These losses included part of its buried fiber optical communications capability, including the key repeater stations that provided point targets that affected much of the operation of the entire system. It should have been clear to the Iraqi high command months—if not years—before March 19, 2003, that it was critical to develop more effective deployments and uses for the forces of the Air Defense Command. Air Defense Command units fired on allied aircraft at least 651 times during the period immediately before and during Operation Southern Focus, and never successfully destroyed a single aircraft.[5]

Nevertheless, Iraq did little or nothing to develop a coordinated defensive strategy between its air force and the Air Defense Command. It failed to develop a cohesive strategy for relocating the sensors and fire units of the Air Defense Command, although it did attempt such activity on a largely uncoordinated basis once the war began. It did not take steps to make effective use of the mobile forces of the Air Defense Command to provide cover for Iraqi land maneuver units like the Republican Guards. Moreover, once the war began, the Iraqi Special Republican Guards and security forces interfered with ground-based air defense operations in the Baghdad area and further complicated the problems the Iraqi Air Defense Command had in the face of coalition air dominance and constant attacks on its command centers, radars, and fire units.

WASTING THE BEST FORCES WASTES ALL THE FORCES

A full history of the destruction of the Republican Guard may take years to research and document. As described in chapter 3, however, the Iraqi regime sent the Republican Guard forces out into exposed maneuvers and combat, and some estimates indicate that all but two dozen or so of the Guards' operational tanks were destroyed or abandoned by the end of the war. It seems far more likely that many were actually abandoned, and such counts must be kept in careful perspective because there were serious problems in the coalition's battle damage assessment efforts throughout the war.

At the same time, the U.S. Air Force has confirmed that the Iraqi Republican Guard and other ground forces became the major focus of the coalition air attacks and its use of precision weapons. Although the numbers the United States and Britain issue do not always agree from briefing to briefing, Lt. General T. Michael Moseley, the commander of coalition air operations during the war, stated that some 1,800 aircraft delivered some 20,000 strikes, and that 15,800 of these were directed against Iraqi ground forces versus 1,800 against the Iraqi government, 1,400 against Iraqi Air Force and Air Defense Command targets, and 800 against suspected sites, forces, and installations that might have weapons of mass destruction or surface-to-surface missiles. This meant that 80 percent of the coalition air strikes hit at Iraqi ground forces.[6]

Losing the Republican Guards in Open Warfare

It is not surprising, therefore, that this treatment of the Republican Guard forces compounded the impact of all of the political and other problems in the Iraqi command structure, the divisions between its military services, and its problems in mounting a cohesive defense of Baghdad. A journalistic after-action survey by *Time* magazine of the Guards performance on seven battlefields in the war—Hindiyah, Hillah, Al Kut, Yusufiyah, Mahmudiyah, Suwayrah, and Dawrah—found that the Guard units quickly realized that they simply could not survive in the face of U.S. sensors, targeting capabilities, and precision strikes. As a result, most of them stopped sleeping with their vehicles and abandoned them quickly after initial losses. Many units also had mass desertions after their initial clashes with U.S. land forces or after they began to take serious equipment losses because of coalition air attacks. The end result was that casualties were probably surprisingly limited, as the forces ceased to be operational when they came under air attack and often could not recover from the resulting desertions.[7]

Iraq effectively wasted most of the Baghdad, Medina, Nebuchadnezzar, and Hammurabi divisions of its Republican Guard by sending them into exposed positions some 100 miles south of the capital. There they could be located by UAVs and aircraft like the E-8C and hit from the air. Some reports indicate that more than half of the air munitions dropped by U.S. forces were directed against the Guard units.

Once the Republican Guards came under this intensive level of attack, their armored forces had nowhere to go and could do nothing but clash with U.S. Army and Marine forces, whose sensors, helicopters, tanks, artillery, and anti-tank guided weapons could generally destroy the remaining elements before they could close on U.S. forces.

Making Urban Warfare in Baghdad Difficult to Impossible

Evidence is gradually emerging from various postwar interviews that Saddam Hussein's regime tried to create extensive physical defenses around Baghdad, but never tried to create a cohesive defensive structure in which the various elements of Iraqi ground forces and the Air Defense Command had clear assignments and roles. The leaders of the regime never created a command and control system that could unite their air and ground forces in the face of the lack of any effective prewar C4I system that cut across these elements and the different security services.

This left the defense of Baghdad to be improvised around the Republican Guards as the only force that was truly loyal to the regime and willing to fight. In practice, however, the Guard units were shattered and demoralized before U.S. forces reached Baghdad. This meant there was no cohesive or leading element to ensure that the regular forces, Special Republican Guards, and most popular forces would fight to defend the greater Baghdad area.

The regime lacked the command and control capability, and possibly the communications capability, to conduct any kind of cohesive retreat and concentration of forces around Baghdad. Although the historical record is far from clear, the way in which the regime had effectively wasted its Republican Guard forces seems to have convinced most of the Special Republican Guards and different security services that there was little point in continuing the fight.

Those elements that did initially remain loyal largely collapsed when the U.S. Army and U.S. Marine Corps began their "Thunder Runs" and launched armored raids into central Baghdad. According to some interviews, the sudden appearance of U.S. forces at the international airport, after regime claims that this was not happening, added to the demoralization. So did the knowledge that the city was cut off from further Republican Guard reinforcements from the south, that other reinforcements could no longer come from the north, and that escape out of Baghdad was becoming steadily more difficult should the regime collapse.

THE PROBLEM OF SANCTIONS AND EQUIPMENT MODERNIZATION

The UN embargoed all arms shipments to Iraq after August 1990. Iraq was extremely dependent on arms imports in spite of grandiose efforts to create its own arms industry. Not only did it need the latest technology to compensate for poor military organization and training; it used imports to flood forward supplies and replacement equipment to make up for its lack of effective combat recovery and repair and a modern and efficient logistics system.

Sanctions and the impact of the Gulf War had a major impact on Iraqi war-fighting capabilities. Iraq was not able to fund and/or import any major new conventional warfare technology to react to the lessons of the war or to produce any major equipment—with the possible exception of limited numbers of Magic "dogfight" air-to-air missiles and erratic smuggling of radars, night vision devices, munitions, and spare parts through Syria.

Iraq's inability to recapitalize and modernize its forces meant that much of its large order of battle was obsolescent or obsolete, that its combat readiness was uncertain, and that much of its equipment was difficult to sustain in combat. It also limited the ability of its forces to conduct long-range movements or maneuvers and then sustain coherent operations.

Iraq did maintain much of the clandestine arms-purchasing network it had set up during the Iran-Iraq War. It had prior experience in buying from some 500 companies in 43 countries and set up approximately 150 small purchasing companies or agents. Intelligence experts felt that Iraq also had an extensive network of intelligence agents and middlemen involved in arms purchases.

Iraq probably obtained some air defense equipment from countries like Ukraine and China, and it may have been able to smuggle in some spare parts through Turkey and Jordan as well as Syria. Deliveries through Syria became significant after mid-2001 and included parts and weapons assemblies for MiG and Shukoi aircraft, armor, and land-based air defenses.

Nevertheless, Iraq was not able to restructure its overall force structure to compensate for its prior dependence on an average of $3 billion a year in arms deliveries. It did not visibly deploy any major new weapon system after 1991. Nor did it show that it could recapitalize any aspect of its force structure. About two-thirds of its remaining inventory of armor and its aircraft became obsolete by Western standards.

In addition to lack of funds and spare parts, Iraq lacked the production capabilities to help sustain the quality of its consolidated forces. It had domestic military production facilities, but they were limited to the production of guns and ammunition and had never succeeded in mass-producing more advanced weapons. Many of its modernization efforts showed some technical skill, but others were little more than unintentional technical practical jokes.

In contrast, Saudi Arabia alone had taken delivery of more than $66 billion worth of new arms since 1991. Kuwait had received $7.6 billion, Iran $4.3 billion, Bahrain $700 million, Oman $1.4 billion, Qatar $1.7 billion, and the UAE $7.9 billion. Equally important, the United States had made major upgrades to virtually every aspect of its fighter avionics, attack munitions, cruise missile capabilities, and intelligence, reconnaissance, and targeting capabilities.

IRAQI WARTIME PREPARATIONS EMPHASIZED THE WRONG IDEOLOGY AND TYPE OF PSYCHOLOGICAL OPERATIONS

Iraq circulated literature to its field commanders and troops that emphasized defensive warfare. It did not prepare them for air and missile attacks, and it called for Jihad and Islamic martyrdom rather than effective tactics and combat. It prepared Iraqi units for U.S. and British use of chemical warfare against them, and trained them to disperse rather than make the kind of rapid conventional response that might have delayed the coalition's advance

Instructions to units like the 51st Division near Basra emphasized reliance on faith and sacrifice, tactics like climbing palm trees for reconnaissance purposes, using alternative methods of communication, living on farms and digging wells, and other impractical activities totally unrelated to modern warfare.

Rather than being trained properly for asymmetric warfare, troops were often given pointless ideological nonsense. Martyrdom and suicide attacks do present problems for conventional forces, and some extremist elements will support and carry out such operations. But large-scale military forces are more likely to take every opportunity to desert or avoid fighting. Ideological extremism motivates a small number of ideological extremists, not popular forces and modern armies.

IRAQI COMMAND AND CONTROL: A BLIND FORCE AS WELL AS ONE WITHOUT A BRAIN

It is unclear just how much of the Iraqi collapse was the result of attacks on its C4I assets, the ability of allied air power to paralyze its operations, and the slow-moving nature of Iraq's land forces. Iraq had no satellites, minimal UAV assets, no survivable reconnaissance assets, poor artillery radar capability, and no other airborne intelligence assets. It conducted minimal active reconnaissance. If its C4I problems deprived it of a functioning brain, its lack of modern IS&R assets effectively left it blind in most aspects of combat beyond visual range.

It is clear, however, that Iraq was thrown off balance by the speed of U.S. maneuver as well as by the flanking movement through the western edge of the Euphrates and, then, the drive along the eastern edge of the Tigris.

Once the United States approached Baghdad, Iraqi forces could neither maneuver quickly enough to establish a cohesive, in-depth defense nor cope with U.S. penetrations. The Iraqi decisionmaking cycle fell steadily behind the realities on the ground. By the time the United States entered Baghdad, Iraq had lost force cohesion and committed its best forces—the Republican Guards—in a piecemeal way in meeting engagements that virtually ensured their destruction.

IRAQI IRREGULAR WARFARE TACTICS: UNEXPECTED BUT MORE AN IRRITANT THAN EFFECTIVE

Iraq seems to have badly exaggerated the potential importance of using irregular forces and trying to draw U.S. and British forces into the cities in the south. In practice, these tactics produced clashes and occasional successes. But the United States quickly adjusted its own tactics to bypass most cities, secure key bridges and routes, and give the pacification of cities secondary importance.

The regime was often creative, but it failed at fundamentals like blowing up bridges and oilfields and at creating large, popular army forces that could present a serious threat to the U.S. flanks. Rather than frightening or paralyzing U.S. and British forces, the regime largely succeeded in making them angry and delaying humanitarian efforts.

Irregular Tactics Have Limited Success Unless They Have Popular Support

As has been mentioned, the regime fundamentally misjudged the popular support it could obtain from its people. It cached massive levels of arms in facilities for an "Al Quds" or Popular Army it was never able to call up, arm, and deploy. This may in part have been a function of time and disorganization at the top. But it seems clear that many, if not most, of the Popular Army simply did not support the regime and did not want to fight.

Problems in Urban Warfare

Iraq deployed some of its most loyal irregular forces, like Saddam's Fedayeen, in the south. These units had some successes in ambushes, but could not survive open combat with U.S. or British forces and lacked mobility other than light civilian vehicles. This made them relatively easy to bypass or force out into open combat. One ironic sub-lesson of the war is that the bypasses and roads that went around many cities in Iraq greatly reduced their importance as potential defenses and barriers, and that one way to win an urban war is to avoid one.

It seems equally clear that the divisions and political tensions between various elements of the Iraqi armed forces severely limited the regime's ability to use irregular forces in the defense of Baghdad. There is no real evidence that the regime ever had a master plan to pull together its irregular forces, the Special Republican Guards, the Republican Guards, the regular army, and the security services into a cohesive defense.

Baghdad's physical defenses, the rings of trenches around the city, and use of burning oil-filled trenches, concealed a reality where every Iraqi force element pursued its own goals, power, and survival rather than the actual defense of the city. The more the United States advanced, the more survival became the key goal, and the more the various Special Republican Guard, Republican Guard, and security service elements that might have led the irregular forces lost the will to fight and deserted.

IRAQ FAILED TO USE ITS WEAPONS OF MASS DESTRUCTION *IF IT HAD THEM*

As has been discussed in chapter 12, there is no way to know how many weapons of mass destruction Iraq had or what its plans might have been. The war caught Iraq at the moment it was trying to prevent a conflict by complying with the IAEA and UNMOVIC, and it may have destroyed many of its WMD holdings or dispersed them too far to recover.[8]

Allied air power may have paralyzed any efforts to recover dispersed or hidden weapons, and it certainly destroyed many potential delivery systems. U.S., UK, and Australian Special Forces were much better organized and equipped for the mission of suppressing missile attacks than they had been in the first Gulf War in 1991, and were much better supported with intelligence. The impact of eight years of UNSCOM and IAEA activity may also have done much to force Iraq to destroy its holdings,

There is also the possibility that Iraq had felt sufficiently secure from an invasion during the years from 1991 on that it destroyed its weapons and shifted to a strategy of research and development and reliance on dual-use facilities to produce more weapons in the future. If so, it never had the chance to produce and deploy them before and during the Iraq War.

As is discussed in chapter 17, however, there are so many uncertainties regarding Iraq's actual holdings of weapons of mass destruction that there has never been an assurance that Iraq could not use such weapons, and the Iraq War does not provide any lesson that other proliferating nations will not use them in the future.

OTHER FAILURES

Failure to Use Missiles Effectively

Missiles, like bombs, are not terror-producing weapons unless they can be used in sufficient numbers or with sufficient lethality to cause major killing or destruction. Iraq was never credited with having more than 12 to 25 surviving Scuds, and its Al Samoud II and Ababil missiles and rockets lacked the range, accuracy, and lethality to be much of a threat. Missile defenses and attacks on delivery systems further degraded a largely symbolic capability.

Failure to Use Water Barriers

For whatever reason, Iraq moved too slowly to make use of water barriers. It blew only a few bridges and often only partially, and it failed to defend against bridging and crossings as effectively as it should have.

Force Protection

Iraq left many of its soldiers without meaningful protection gear and body armor, it wasted committed personnel in suicide attacks, and it could not evacuate personnel effectively. Attacks against unprotected civilians are one thing; attacks against alert and well-protected soldiers are another. Committing forces without proper personal protection does not produce martyrs, simply needless casualties.

Notes

[1] The reader should understand that much of this text is based on the author's experience in dealing with members of the Iraqi armed forces since his first visits to

Iraq in the early 1970s, and on interviews with Iraqi exiles and Australian, British, and U.S. experts on Iraq after the war. Such interviews are necessarily uncertain compared to detailed historical analysis that combines systematic interviews with an analysis of captured records and a detailed analysis of the behavior of each element of the Iraqi forces during the course of the fighting.

[2] For good postwar interviews of Iraqi officers, see Molly Moore, "A Foe that Collapsed from Within," *Washington Post*, July 20, 2003, sec. A, p. 1. This article reflects the same range of Iraqi views found by a number of U.S. experts interviewing Iraqi officers after the war.

[3] Ibid.

[4] Michael Gordon, "US Attacked Iraqi Air Defenses Starting in 2002," *New York Times*, July 20, 2003; Bradley Graham, "US Moved Early for Air Supremacy," *Washington Post*, July 20, 2003.

[5] Ibid.

[6] Ibid.

[7] As the previous chapter showed, these conclusions track well with the other data available on this aspect of the war. See Terry McCarthy, "Whatever Happened to the Republican Guard," *Time*, May 12, 2003, p. 38; and Moore, "A Foe that Collapsed from Within."

[8] For an interesting report on this possibility, see Judith Miller, "Illicit Arms Kept Till Event of War, An Iraqi Scientist Is Said to Assert," *New York Times*, April 21, 2003. There is as yet, however, no evidence to confirm this interpretation.

CHAPTER FIFTEEN

_____

LESSONS REGARDING THE
VALUE OF ALLIES AND BUILD-UP TIME

The Iraq War provides important lessons about regional friends and allies. In spite of all the tensions between the United States and the Arab world over terrorism and the Second Intifada, the United States obtained sustained open support from Kuwait, Oman, Qatar, and the United Arab Emirates and quiet support from Jordan and Saudi Arabia. This illustrated both the general value of regional friends and alliances and the dangers of assuming that force transformation is a substitute for foreign bases and the support of foreign states.

Both Britain and Australia took considerable political risks in supporting the United States, and the prime ministers of both countries did so in the face of considerable parliamentary opposition and uncertain public opinion. Both have paid a political price since the war for the exaggerated statements made about the risk posed by Iraqi weapons of mass destruction. One lesson of the Iraq War is that there are generic "allies" and there are real allies. It is often easy to talk about NATO or large blocs of allies, but only a few allies are actually willing to take risks in both political and war-fighting terms. It is the real allies that count.

ALLIES AND INTEROPERABILITY

The fact the United States now has no military peer, and faces interoperability problems in integrating its forces with those of most allies, does not mean that it does not need NATO or allied countries. It is inconceivable, for example, that the United States could fight North Korea without South Korea's taking on most of the military burden and without Japan's support in terms of basing. Designing transformational forces to be interoperable may have its costs, but the value of allies like Britain and Australia has long been clear, as is the value of new allies like Poland.

As has been touched on in previous chapters, this means that the United States must design its forces for as much interoperability as possible and must train with its allies. Just as modern joint warfare requires the United States to blend its military efforts with those of its civilian agencies, true jointness means interoperability. This is a point raised many times in the British Ministry of Defense report on the lessons of the war, particularly in its conclusions regarding coalition warfare:[1]

> Working in a coalition brings political, diplomatic and military advantages, including the aggregation of capabilities, flexible war-fighting options and the sharing of intelligence and risk. Indeed, the operation showed the importance of constructing a force package that allowed a greater range of operational options than the enemy. The importance of the UK's contribution to the coalition lay in the military capability we provided to the front line both in the core coalition disciplines and in unique specialist areas.
>
> At the operational and tactical levels, the planning and conduct of the operation was facilitated by the close professional relationship that has grown up between the UK and US, not only as leading members of NATO, but also through numerous bilateral institutional and personal contacts at every level. Equally important were the benefits of training and operating together over many years, especially in the Gulf, Afghanistan and the No-Fly Zones over Iraq.
>
> Given US technological and military dominance, we should continue to track, align with and integrate US developments in areas where our force balance and resources allow, particularly in terms of the organization of enhanced HQs, communications and information systems, and Combat Identification (ID). We should also ensure that our command structures can engage and influence key US decision-makers with appropriate weight and at the right levels. Based on recent experience, the UK must plan to work in "coalitions of the willing" for future operations as well as within established structures. This may result in the requirement to work with unfamiliar partners, with the attendant challenges associated with force packaging, training, and standardization of procedures and equipment.
>
> ...This was overwhelmingly a US shaped and led operation. The UK contribution was taken into the US plan where it could best complement and enhance US capabilities, both political and military. Most of what UK forces achieved took place under the umbrella of US dominance of every warfare environment. The coalition had naval and space dominance from the start, moved from air and information superiority to dominance and thereby quickly overcame Iraqi opposition on the ground. Coalition forces had technical superiority in virtually every area of combat and could operate through most conditions of visibility and weather and at night. In sum, the coalition dominated the political, diplomatic, military and economic levers....

...The UK force contribution had to be generated within very tight time-lines, using mechanisms and pragmatic solutions that in some cases by-passed established readiness profiles and resourcing assumptions. Given the unpredictable nature of future operations, this may be inevitable, and we need to review how we prepare for operations in such complex politico-military environments.

The overwhelming success of rapid, decisive operations in Iraq reflects the deployment of fast moving light forces, highly mobile armored capabilities and Close Air Support, which made use of near real-time situational awareness by day and by night. The US ability to combine land and air operations and support them from the sea and from friendly bases at very high tempo enabled the mix and impact of joint assets to be adjusted to operational need or events across the whole theatre of operations. This is likely to shape US doctrinal development and impact on potential partners. The implications of maintaining congruence with an accelerating US technological and doctrinal dominance need to be assessed and taken into account in future policy and planning assumptions.

The risk of the United States becoming isolated from the war-fighting capabilities of even its closest allies is also illustrated by the statement of Admiral Sir Michael Boyce, chief of the defense staff at Britain's Ministry of Defense, after the Iraq War. Admiral Boyce took the opportunity of his retirement to state a few lessons from the Iraq War that act as yet another warning about the growing gap between U.S. and allied capabilities. He said that Britain's armed forces were overstretched and should not pursue another war for 18 months: "If you asked us to go into a large-scale operation in 2004, we couldn't do it without serious pain. We must allow ourselves time to draw breath....If it was to be something of the scale that we have done this time, it would have to be something that the government is convinced is pretty important because I would tell them it would take a while to recuperate."[2]

In Admiral Boyce's estimation, Britain's armed forces could not handle another "discretionary conflict, a conflict waged by choice" if it were launched in 2004. Admiral Boyce also questioned the need to spend £18 billion on 232 Euro fighters when bombers had proved much more important than fighters in the conflict. He did say, however, that British plans for two new "super aircraft carriers" had been proved necessary by the diplomatic difficulties of flying planes over sensitive countries in the run-up to the invasion of Iraq. The fact that transformational changes are at least as difficult for allies as for the United States is not a casual lesson. Cooperation and interoperability are critical unless the U.S. military wishes to become very lonely.

THE VALUE OF REGIONAL ALLIES

Another lesson is the value of regional allies. Access to allied territory in the Gulf allowed the United States and Britain to deal with the key logistic problems in their buildup by slowly delivering virtually all of their supplies and major land combat equipment by sea over a period extending from June 2002 to February 2003. The two major coalition partners had access to the critical bases in the Gulf that they needed for operations. Their allies in the Gulf then made substantial adjustments to accommodate a democratic Turkey's refusal to allow the United States to create a northern front or use facilities in that country.

In spite of tensions over the aftermath of the terrorist attacks on the United States on September 11, 2001, Saudi Arabia allowed overflights by U.S. aircraft and missiles; it allowed the expanded use of its airbases for "no-fly-zone" missions that helped weaken Iraq's air defenses both before and during the war; it provided fuel at minimal cost for AWACS and E-8C missions on Saudi soil; it allowed the use of the Combined Air Operations Center (CAOC) to manage coalition air operations; and it made facilities at Ar'ar available for Special Forces search and rescue missions. Above all, it ensured the flow of oil exports in ways that helped compensate for the loss of Iraqi and Venezuelan exports.[3] Although U.S. combat forces will leave Saudi Arabia following the Iraq War, it is important that the U.S. advisory teams will remain in the Kingdom, that the Kingdom is still taking delivery on tens of billions of dollars worth of U.S. military exports, and that U.S. and Saudi joint exercises continue. Saudi Arabia may be of great value to the United States and Britain in the future.[4]

Other Arab allies also helped. Egypt allowed free transit through the Suez Canal and Egyptian airspace. Jordan permitted U.S. overflights and allowed U.S. Patriot units and missile warning systems to operate on its soil. It quietly allowed the USAF and U.S. Special Forces to operate from bases in eastern Jordan. At least 24 F-16s equipped with LITENING II targeting pods and armed with weapons like the GBU-27 laser-guided bomb operated from Jordanian soil and flew roughly 700 sorties, while U.S. Special Forces operated from Jordan to search for Scud launch boxes in western Iraq.[5]

The United States had assistance from still another ally. Israel permitted overflights, did not increase the tempo of its operations in the Second Intifada, and relied on defense in the initial phases of the war.

In short, no discussion of the lessons of the Iraq War should ignore the continuing value of alliances and foreign bases and the need for coalition partners. Equally, it should not ignore the value of decades of military relations and engagement with friendly Arab states, and the willingness of those states to support the United States even when they sometimes opposed the war or when their support presented serious problems in terms of domestic political opinion. It is all too easy for the United States to be blinded by the beauty of its weapons and ignore these lessons. Regardless of force transformation and any new way of war, U.S. strength remains dependent on coalitions even when these are coalitions of the partly willing.

THE VALUE OF REBUILDING ALLIANCES

It is also clear that the defeat of Iraq does not justify any negligence in rebuilding the relations that underpin the U.S. alliance with Europe. As important, there is no room for negligence in efforts to strengthen relations with Russia or strengthen U.S. ties to the Arab world. War-fighting allies are the most important allies in a crisis. It is all too clear, however, that even the most impressive U.S. military victories still leave political alliances as important as ever and that nations that do not support the United States in war can be very important in conflict termination, peace-making, and nation building.

As the next chapters show, it is all too easy to talk about transforming Iraq and the Middle East and far more difficult to achieve even moderate success. The success of U.S. arms has not been matched by the success of U.S. diplomacy. Nation building is not only not a science, it is not yet an art form.

It is absurd to talk about "fourth world wars" with states that have generally been friendly. It is equally absurd to talk about regime change in the Middle East without explaining exactly how this change is to be accomplished, why it will meet the needs of the peoples involved, and why it will produce better and more stable results than encouraging self-reform that addresses demographic, economic, and cultural issues and is not simply a demand for instant democracy. Trading Arab friends and allies for radical religious regimes or "one man, one vote, one time" elections is not a strategy likely to serve any nation's interest.

Once again, military victory in Iraq is not a reason for American "triumphalism." If anything, it should be a prelude—to readjusting the U.S. military presence in the Gulf and Middle East to reflect the downfall of a dangerous tyrant and reduction in the Iraqi military threat to other countries; to concentrating on nation building in Iraq; to strengthening and rebuilding ties to Arab allies; and to using diplomacy and the momentum of victory to discourage proliferation and the threat of terrorism. It is also a time to try to use U.S. prestige and power to offer Israel real and lasting security by advancing a peace process that can seek to end the Second Intifada and do so on terms that give Israel security and the Palestinians dignity. The United States cannot do this alone, but nothing can succeed without such a U.S. effort.

Notes

[1] British Ministry of Defense, "Operations in Iraq: First Reflections" (London: Her Majesty's Stationery Office, July 2003), pp. 7, 19.

[2] Bill Jacobs, "Defense Chief Warns against Another War," *Edinburgh Evening News*, April 29, 2003, www.edinburghnews.com/index.cfm?id=488602003.

[3] See Michael Dobbs, "US-Saudi Alliance Appears Strong," *Washington Post*, April 27, 2003, sec. A, pp. 20–21; Usha Lee McFarling, "The Eyes and Ears of War," *Los Angeles Times*, April 24, 2003, p. 1.

[4] Vernon Loeb, "US Military Will Leave Saudi Arabia This Year," *Washington Post*, April 30, 2003, p. 1; Eric Schmitt, "US to Withdraw All Combat Units from Saudi Arabia," *New York Times*, April 30, 2003. p. 1.

[5] David A. Fulghum and Robert Wall, "Baghdad Confidential," *Aviation Week*, April 28, 2003, p. 32.

CHAPTER SIXTEEN

MILITARY LESSONS RELATING TO CONFLICT TERMINATION, PEACEMAKING, AND NATION BUILDING

There is nothing new about the lesson that it is harder to implement grand strategy than to be successful in implementing strategy and tactics. It is one of the iron laws of military history that armies are far better equipped to win the war than to win the peace, and that strategic objectives in warfighting are far easier to achieve than the grand strategic objectives necessary to shape a peace that has lasting value.

It is also unfair to exaggerate the scale of the problems that emerged during conflict termination, peacemaking, and the transition to nation building. The war itself did considerably less damage than many feared:

- There was little initial resistance to U.S. and British forces, and Saddam's regime failed to mobilize any significant portion of the Iraqi people to resist the coalition advance.

- An expected humanitarian crisis did not emerge. Problems rapidly developed in security, in terms of looting, in medical services, and in the material aspects of life—ranging from the availability of utilities like water and power to continuity in trade and employment. In broad terms, however, there were no major life-threatening problems with food or basic services.

- Although they failed to halt looting, the United States and Britain largely succeeded in preventing Saddam's supporters from destroying Iraq's oil production and export facilities or crippling the economy.

- For all of the postwar chaos and tensions in Iraq, the "Battle of Baghdad" was quick and involved minimal collateral damage, and most Iraqi cities emerged intact.

- No major crises or clashes emerged in the north between Kurds and Arabs, and Turkey did not intervene.

- Iran did not intervene, and the Iranian-sponsored outside opposition did not take military action.

- Although attacks on coalition forces and sabotage began almost immediately, the level of such action was very low for a nation of some 25 million people that had been ruled by Saddam and the Ba'ath Party for nearly 30 years, whose economy had begun to collapse as early as 1982 as a result of the cost of the Iran-Iraq War, and where power had always been given to a small Sunni elite at the expense of a Shi'ite majority and a large Kurdish minority.

Many of the problems that occurred during conflict termination and early in the nation-building phase were beyond the coalition's control. They were the result of some 30 years of mismanagement by an Iraqi tyranny that stifled initiative and prevented market forces from working. Iraq's economy, crippled from 1982 onward by the costs of the Iran-Iraq War, never recovered from the costs of the Gulf War and from Iraq's refusal to put an end to sanctions by meeting the terms of UN Security Council resolutions.

The fact remains, however, that many of the problems the United States encountered were caused by the failure of it and its allies to provide adequate security, prevent looting, and take immediate action to ensure continuity of government. The coalition's success in joint warfare was not matched by its success in conflict termination, peacemaking, and transitioning to nation building. This was partly a matter of force ratios: The same strategy designed to deliver a carefully focused attack on the regime did not provide enough manpower to simultaneously occupy and secure the areas that the coalition liberated.

THE IMPACT OF LIMITED MILITARY RESOURCES

Virtually all wars involve a chaotic transition from war to peace. The U.S. and British governments had ample warning from their intelligence services, diplomats, and area experts that this might be the case in Iraq. Yet, neither the governments nor their military forces were properly prepared to secure the areas they liberated and deal with the wide range of local, regional, ethnic and religious divisions they encountered. Key objectives were not secured against looting, the flow of aid was slow, and there was little preparation to deal with long-standing historical tensions.

Once again, there are mitigating factors. The problems during and immediately after the fighting were partly a result of the sheer speed of the regime's collapse at the end of the war and Iraqi tactics that made it impossible to enter cities without diverting forces to secondary missions. Not having a second front from Turkey and anything like the force totals originally planned also created problems.

The statements of senior U.S. military officers also emphasize the need for rapid military action and giving priority to the battle against Iraqi military forces. General Myers, the chairman of the Joint Chiefs, described the problem as follows in the Department of Defense daily briefing on April 15, 2003:

> [S]ome have suggested, "Well, gee, you should have delayed combat operations to protect against looting, or you should have had more forces, should have waited till more forces arrived." To that I would say this: The best way to ensure fewer casualties on [the] coalition side and fewer civilian casualties is to have combat operations proceed as quickly as possible and not prolong them. And so it gets back to…a matter of priorities. And we're dealing with some of those issues that you just brought up…the first thing you have to deal with is loss of life, and that's what we dealt with. And if you remember, when some of that looting was going on, people were being killed, people were being wounded.

Lt. Gen. David D. McKiernan, the commander of the Coalition Forces Land Component Command, described the military reasons as follows:[1]

> [W]e had to fight our way into Baghdad. Now, that fight was characterized by decisive armor and infantry actions into Baghdad before he could set an urban defense of Baghdad. And the speed of our campaign allowed us really to seize the initiative and to exploit success, but even with that, we had to fight our way into Baghdad. So I can tell you from being here that those lead formations, both Marine and Army that maneuvered into Baghdad first of all, were killing bad guys, and secondly, were protecting Iraqi people. And so if some of the facilities became subject to looting over that period of time by Iraqis, I will tell you that our priority was to fight the enemy and to protect Iraqi people.
>
> …I am satisfied that the forces are here (now) and are continuing to flow here that will allow me to execute what are my phase four missions, and that is to provide a degree, a certain degree of stability and security in Iraq as we transition back to Iraqis in control of their own country. I would caveat that, though, by reminding everyone that there aren't enough soldiers or Marines to guard every street corner and every facility in Iraq, so there's some risk-taking in some areas. And we try to focus our forces where our intelligence and mission sets drive us to focus those forces. But I am satisfied that I have had enough forces on the ground to execute the campaign very decisively to this point. And we have the additional forces we need for phase four flowing in now.

Lt. General William Wallace defended 5th Corps problems in dealing with looting and civil unrest in much the same way:[2]

> We train for war fighting, but peacekeeping is something that we do. If you look across our formation, I would bet that 30 percent or more of our soldiers have had some real-world peacekeeping experience in the Balkans. So we have a lot of experience in how to deal with civil affairs, with civilian populations, with establishing institutions to get civilian populations involved in their own destiny. There is just a lot of experience in our forces with this civil-military dynamic, largely as a result of our operations in Bosnia and Kosovo.
>
> ...One day our troops are kicking down doors, and the next they're passing out Band-Aids. And in some cases, they're kicking down doors without really knowing if they are going to have to pull a trigger or pass out a Band-Aid on the other side. And it's really a remarkable tribute to the mental acuity of our soldiers that they are able to do that.

The coalition might have been better prepared if, as had originally been planned, it had been able to internationalize some aspects of conflict termination and nation building by gaining the support of a second UN Security Council resolution. Similarly, preparations might have been better if it had been able to draw upon the support of a wide range of other nations immediately after the end of the war. This is questionable, however. It is easy to task the UN and "international community," but they have no resources other than those contributed by individual states. Moreover, only a limited number of countries have forces trained and equipped for actual "peacemaking" under conditions that involve actual combat.

Most foreign forces are not capable of dealing with local military and security threats in actual combat and would have had little value. They would have presented a host of interoperability problems, from language differences to a lack of self-protection skills. Moreover, other nations have a very finite supply of either "peacemakers" or "peacekeepers." Most of these resources were already deployed in other contingencies and crises. International forces also would have had to rely on the United States for lift and sustainment at a time when the United States had limited capacity and Iraq did not have functioning ports and airports.

AVOIDABLE PROBLEMS

The fact remains that many of the problems and limitations in military resources the coalition faced during and after the war, and certainly its lack of a coordinated military-civilian effort, were the result of U.S. failures before the war to plan properly for conflict termination and to then provide the proper resources.

In retrospect, the United States—the leader of the coalition and the only power with the necessary resources to act—failed to effectively terminate the conflict for three principal sets of reasons: problems in international coordination; failures in U.S. policymaking and leadership; and failures at the field and tactical levels.

Problems in International Coordination

- It may have been impossible to shape an international consensus on how to deal with the problems involved, but the United States and UK did not seem to have a clear plan to seek such a consensus within the UN, or a clear back-up plan if that effort failed.

- The coalition drew on many Arab allies for bases and support in war fighting but failed to get the level of regional support for peacemaking and nation building it needed after the fighting.

Failures in U.S. Policymaking and Leadership

- The Bush administration had received advice from a number of sources that U.S. experience in Panama, Haiti, Bosnia, and Kosovo had showed that it was critical to introduce a trained constabulary or military police force into urban areas immediately after the fall of local and national authority to prevent looting, civil unrest, and acts of revenge. U.S. military forces do not have training for these missions, however, and the countries that do did not participate in the coalition. As a result, there were no personnel on the ground with the dedicated mission of maintaining order and with the training and skills to do so.

- The coalition conducted a psychological warfare campaign, but failed to conduct a meaningful campaign to tell the Iraqi people how it planned to allow them to shape the peace and what the coalition would do to make that possible. Iraqis had no clear idea of what to expect when the coalition arrived, and many saw its goals and motives as part of a conspiracy to take over the country and its resources.

- At least some senior U.S. political leaders ignored warnings from intelligence, military, and regional experts that the coalition forces would not be greeted as liberators, and that the coalition should expect to deal with a mixture of anti-Western/anti-colonial sentiment and deep ethnic and religious tensions and divisions. Deputy Secretary of

Defense Paul Wolfowitz admitted in July 2003 that the U.S. Defense Department officials leading the planning estimate had (1) underestimated the risk that the Ba'ath Party and other irredentist hard-liners would present a continuing security threat after Saddam Hussein fell from power; (2) counted on large numbers of Iraq military police to quickly join the United States and its allies in the nation-building effort; and (3) overestimated Iraqi popular support for the war. Other sources indicate that U.S. intelligence sources warned repeatedly from April 2002 on that Hussein loyalists would attempt to sabotage the reconstruction effort and that these warnings were ignored by the Office of the Secretary of Defense, the Office of the Vice President, and the White House.[3]

- The National Security Council failed to perform its mission. It acted largely in an advisory role and did not force effective interagency coordination. Several former staff members of the NSC and senior officials in the State Department feel that this was a critical failure leading to the lack of any effective planning and execution of a conflict termination and nation building plan during and immediately after the war.

- The United States failed to develop a coordinated interagency approach to planning and executing peacemaking and nation building before and during the war. A State Department–led effort called the Future of Iraq Project began in April 2002 and produced many of the needed elements of a plan. Much of the results of the State Department's planning efforts for nation building were lost or made ineffective, however, because of the deep divisions between the State Department and Department of Defense over how to plan for peacemaking and nation building. When President Bush issued National Security Directive 24 (NSD-24) on January 20, 2003, he put the Office of the Secretary of Defense in charge of the nation-building effort, evidently because the problem of establishing security was given primacy. The result, however, was that the State Department and other interagency conflict termination and nation-building efforts were dropped, ignored, or given low priority.

- The Office of the Secretary of Defense staffed its nation-building effort as a largely closed group composed of members who had strong ideological beliefs but limited practical experience and serious area expertise. Senior defense officials like Secretary Donald Rumsfeld, Deputy Secretary of Defense Paul Wolfowitz, and Undersecretary Douglas J. Feith believed that the coalition would have strong popular support from the Iraqis, that other agencies were exaggerating the risks, that the task of nation building could be quickly transferred to the equivalent of a government in exile, and that the United States and its allies would be able to withdraw quickly. As a result, the nation-building effort focused on humanitarian problems that failed to materialize, and the coalition partners were unprepared to deal with the political, economic, and security problems that did.

- Although the full details are not clear, at least some senior members of the team in the Office of the Secretary of Defense dealing with nation building believed that the Iraqi National Congress, led by Ahmed Chalabi, should form a government in exile and take over much of the nation-building effort once war began. The idea was rejected because of State Department and other warnings that Chalabi, who had left Iraq in 1958, had little credibility in leading a government in exile. The Office of the Secretary of Defense, however, continued to treat Chalabi as a potential leader and did not prepare for the inevitable internal struggles for power in Iraq once Saddam Hussein's regime fell. In April, while the war was under way, the Department of Defense had Chalabi and 700 of his followers flown to Iraq.

- The result was that the United States saw its mission in terms of defeating Iraqi military forces in main battles, rather than ending all armed opposition. It may have understood that the enemy had to be fully defeated, the remnants of the regime had to be purged, and order had to be established to allow effective nation building to be established. The U.S. military did not, however, properly size and train its forces for these missions. It did not properly train forward and combat units for dealing with activities like looting and the problems in distinguishing between hostile and nonviolent civilians and irregular forces and enemies. In many ways, troops were trained to fight asymmetric warfare up to the point of dealing with the consequences of victory.

- The mistakes of senior U.S. civilian policymakers were compounded by a U.S. military approach to the doctrine and planning for asymmetric warfare that in practice reflected the strong desire of U.S. military commanders to avoid deep involvement in the complex political issues of nation building and to avoid prolonged military commitment to missions other than direct war fighting.

Failures at the Field and Tactical Levels

- The direction of the nation-building effort initially lacked the kind of driving leadership needed for success, and few involved had real area expertise or experience with peacemaking and nation building. This led to an embarrassing change in the midst of conflict termination and the start of nation building from the Office of Reconstruction and Humanitarian Assistance (ORHA), directed by Lt. Gen. Jay M. Garner, to the Coalition Provisional Authority (CPA) directed by Ambassador L. Paul Bremer III.

- The United States failed to create an effective structure for managing the peacemaking and nation-building effort in the field; to clearly subordinate the military to General Garner and Ambassador Bremer on a timely and effective basis; and to task the military accordingly. The problem of establishing an actual interim authority was addressed by creating a semi-civilian body that was unprepared to enter and operate a still-hostile country at the earliest possible period.

- The National Security Council failed to organize effective interagency cooperation in Washington. It did not have a full-time coordinator or representative in the field to oversee the conflict termination and nation-building efforts and ensure suitable coordination between Washington, ORHA, and the U.S. military.

- The lack of civil-military coordination greatly complicated the practical problems in actually providing aid and keeping promises. It also interacted with a lack of practical U.S. military planning for continued violence and "guerrilla warfare" during a prolonged period of conflict termination. The military gave priority to security and only limited support to nation building. The nation builders had no real security capability or safe transportation of their own.

- From the start, a major gap existed among the State Department personnel serving in the field, the civilian team sent to Kuwait and then Iraq under General Garner, and the U.S. military in the Gulf and the field. State Department personnel were largely excluded. General Garner and his team refused an invitation from the land forces commander, Lt. General David McKiernan, to collocate with the U.S. military forces that would advance into Baghdad, and instead stayed in the Hilton Hotel in Kuwait, out of touch with conditions in the field and waiting for a humanitarian crisis that never came.

- Until mid-July 2003, the nation-building team had little meaningful guidance from the Office of the Secretary of Defense or the National Security Council and was not coordinating effectively with the State Department. It was not organized or equipped to move forward with U.S. combat forces and act immediately in rear areas; it took far too long to move to Iraq; and it then chose a location isolated from the U.S. military forces that were its only practical source of logistic support and security.

- When the team under General Garner finally did relocate to Iraq, it made a classic U.S. mistake in choosing its headquarters. It located in a highly visible site in downtown Baghdad, in the Al Rashid Hotel, and in the former palaces of Saddam Hussein. Although the real-world conditions were scarcely luxurious, the image this created and sustained was one of luxury and an occupying proconsul with a filled swimming pool at a time when many Iraqis had no water. The situation was made worse by the fact that this physically isolated the nation-building team from the U.S. military and created unnecessary security and transportation problems.

- This was done despite the fact that past efforts that had created a "downtown palace" had caused tension in many friendly countries like South Korea. In Iraq it reinforced the gap between the nation-building team and the military at a time when the military was giving priority to security, and it helped ensure that the military gave less support to nation building. It also cut the nation builders off from the military communication and support infrastructure and added to the team's security and transportation problems.

- The "downtown palace" approach also forced the U.S. military to create a major security or "no-go zone" in the middle of Baghdad, draining troops and creating problems for the Iraqis who had to drive around an "occupier" in the center of their own city.

- Quite aside from these problems in leadership and focus, the nation-building team often had to rely on experts in U.S. activities relating to nation building who had little meaningful expertise in working in developing countries. Its experts on the Middle East often had little or no prior experience in working in Iraq and/or little experience in the activities involved in conflict termination and nation building.

- These problems were compounded by the failure to ensure that members of the team were committed to full-time, long-service support of the effort. Far too many team members were short-termers or part-timers.

- Looting and criminal activity were not seen as major problems during the war or in preparing for conflict termination despite several thousand years of warning that this could be the case. It was clear that Iraq's prewar economy was driven by nepotism and influence and that much of Iraq's population had reason to feel justified in acting against the regime and strong reasons to do so.

- Humanitarian efforts and expertise were sometimes confused with the very different missions of nation building and conflict termination. Critical weeks were wasted making the transition from planning for a nonexistent humanitarian crisis to dealing with the very real and immediate problems in peacemaking and nation building. Key issues like jobs and economic security were addressed much later than should have been the case.

- Military commanders do not seem to have fully understood the importance of the peacemaking and nation-building missions. They often did not provide the proper support or did so with extensive delays and little real commitment.

- The "jointness" that helped the United States win the war was almost totally lacking during the conflict termination and peacemaking stage. No U.S. commander seemed to have responsibility. Even within the army, major differences emerged in how given units performed their tasks. (The 3rd Infantry Division favored reacting to incidents; the 4th Division aggressively patrolled.) There was no cohesion to the military effort.

- Even where military resources were clearly available, too little emphasis was placed on immediately securing key urban areas and centers of government.

- The two U.S. Army divisions, the U.S. Marine forces, and the British forces all took different and inconsistent approaches to enforcing security. These problems were compounded in the case of the U.S. Army by a lack of consistency in supporting the nation-building effort in the field as well as in the treatment of Iraqis in carrying out the security mission. In many cases, the emphasis on force protection ignored the political impact on the Iraqi population and the fact that it might prove more provocative than helpful in enforcing security.

- In urban areas, the initial security efforts were generally reactive rather than part of a cohesive effort to provide security for the entire area. This left constant gaps in coverage and allowed looting, firefights, and ambushes to occur before an effort was made to act.

- U.S. forces lacked enough people with the necessary language and area skills, and the limited numbers of such experts that were available were dedicated to war-fighting tasks.

- The effort to create an effective Iraqi police force and to provide local security using Iraqis, rather than relying on occupying troops, came too late and had too few resources and too little support at the outset. The analysis of the Iraq police force before the war was misleading and led U.S. planners to assume it had far more capability than it did. Once the truth became apparent, U.S. planners were slow to react; they did not rush to put together an advisory team with the necessary mix of police and area expertise or to provide the necessary resources.

- The United States and its allies failed to assess the motives and competence of the outside Iraqi opposition. Members of the Iraqi opposition had their own goals and ambitions and often proved to be unreliable. Some U.S. policymakers planned to rely on the secular, pro-U.S. opposition to act as a de facto government in exile when it lacked the unity, competence, and popular support in Iraq to do so.

- At least initially, the United States tried to select leaders and representatives from within Iraq on the basis of its views of what Iraq should be, rather than letting such leaders emerge from within key Iraqi ethnic and sectarian groups.

- The "de-Ba'athifcation" effort was handled in too rigid a way for a country that had been under the same dictatorship for nearly three decades. Senior officials and officers were excluded from the nation-building effort simply because of rank and Ba'ath membership, rather than screening on a person-by-person basis. The end result was to compound the power vacuum created by the systematic murder and purging of secular opposition from 1979 onward.

- Many aspects of the U.S. operation initially were overcentralized in Baghdad and in General Garner's and Ambassador Bremer's offices. Teams were needed to work with the local governments of each of Iraq's governates and in its major cities. The United States was particularly slow to see the need to establish a large number of liaison offices to deal with the divided Shi'ite majority in the south and the Kurds in the north, even though the offices that were established quickly demonstrated their value.

- The United States and its allies lacked an accurate picture of the problems in Iraq's infrastructure and an understanding of the problems a dictatorial command economy would face once the regime fell, despite considerable warnings from area experts and some intelligence experts. The Iraqis as a whole were unprepared to take the initiative in any major ministry or area of economic activity without guidance and direction. A long history of nepotism and of seizing any opportunity to gain wealth or power also created large numbers of Iraqis who were far more ready to loot than participate in nation building.

- As with security and the prevention of looting, neither the U.S. nation builders nor the U.S. military were ready for the attacks on nation builders and advisory teams or for acts of sabotage. They had to be reactive when they should have focused on prevention and deterrence.

- The problems in the U.S. effort greatly complicated the problems for NGOs, international organizations, and other countries in the nation-building effort. Humanitarian and nongovernmental organizations do not operate in hostile military environments, but require high levels of protection to perform humanitarian missions with short-term goals that ignore the need to fully secure areas and create the political basis for nation building. In contrast, military organization have not yet adapted to the need to provide suitable protection for humanitarian organizations and NGOs. Both sides need to change their present procedures.

These failures did much to create a climate of continuing violence after May 1 and to create the threat of low-intensity and asymmetric warfare. To an important degree, they contributed to the killing or wounding of every U.S. soldier, British soldier, and Iraqi civilian that became a casualty in the months following the "end" of the war.

A FAILURE OF U.S. LEADERSHIP AND ORGANIZATION

The full history behind the previous list of problems has yet to surface. It is clear, however, that two problems on this list have a special importance in terms of lessons learned. One is the failure at the highest policy levels to give conflict termination the proper priority. The second is the failure by the U.S. military to properly recognize the importance of making conflict termination and the transition to nation building a critical part of its doctrine and planning for asymmetric warfare.

At the policy level, the failure to understand the scale of the problems in conflict termination and nation building was compounded by major organizational problems within the U.S. government. These problems included deep divisions between the Office of the Secretary of Defense, the State Department, and other agencies. The State Department had attempted to coordinate systematic planning for nation building during the course of 2002. This effort took the form of interagency consulting bodies that never had clear authority or unified cabinet-level policy support. These bodies also were largely civilian and not capable of handling the security problems that arise in liberated areas during combat as well as the problems in securing a nation after the most intense phases of combat ended.

The Office of the Secretary of Defense was formally given the lead for conflict termination and the early phases of nation building in January 2003. President Bush seems to have made this decision because U.S. military forces were the only instrument that could perform the security mission during and immediately after combat. In assuming this mission, however, the Office of the Secretary of Defense ignored most of the previous interagency process or left it hanging in limbo, and it took a heavily ideological approach that assumed the coalition would have far more popular support in Iraq, particularly in the south, than it actually did.[4]

The Office of the Secretary of Defense assumed that Saddam Hussein's regime would fall in ways that left much of the Iraqi government and economy functioning—an assessment that ignored both the acute limits to the process of government under Saddam and the equally acute limits to the efficiency of the Iraqi economy and the ability of Iraqi officials to act without direct orders from above. The department also ignored case after case in which earlier collapses of authoritarian regimes ended in looting and sectarian or ethnic divisions and violence.

Put differently, the Office of the Secretary of Defense had large numbers of policymakers who earlier had viewed the Clinton administration's focus on nation building as a waste of U.S. resources. They shared a strong ideological belief that the war would free popular support for democracy that would transform Iraq and the Middle East, and they had little or no practical experience with either Iraq as a nation or the problems in nation building. They concentrated instead on war fighting and assumed that conflict termination would be a more limited priority.

They also did so in the face of advice to the contrary from many area experts within the U.S. government, U.S. officials with experience in peacemaking and nation building, experts within the intelligence community, and the wide assortment of outside experts that had been brought in to advise the interagency planning groups. There certainly was no consensus among these as to how the security and nation-building problems should be dealt with. There was, however, a consensus that the problems would probably be far more serious and immediate than the Office of the Secretary of Defense was planning for.

These organizational failures were compounded by the failure of the National Security Council to act as a forceful body that could make the interagency process work. This was partly a matter of personalities and partly a lack of clear lines of responsibility and administrative capability within the NSC. But it also reflected a deliberate decision by the president to treat the NSC more as an advisory body than as an active manager.

There may be good intellectual and theoretical arguments for having the NSC stay in an advisory capacity and for relying on a government based on lines of responsibility that pass through cabinet-level officials. The problem is that such an approach simply does not work in practice when demanding interagency coordination must take place and action must be taken. The stronger the cabinet members are, the stronger the role of the NSC must be. The tensions and competition between the leadership of Vice President Cheney, Secretary Powell, and Secretary Rumsfeld have led to stronger interagency rivalries under President George W. Bush than at any time in recent memory.

The need for "jointness" does not apply simply to the U.S. military; it must apply to the entire U.S. government. It seems far easier for civilians to press the military for "jointness" than to recognize the need for it in their own operations. A weak and ineffectively led NSC is not capable of dealing with problems like conflict termination.

THE INABILITY OF THE U.S. MILITARY TO PROPERLY CONCEPTUALIZE AND UNDERSTAND GRAND STRATEGY

The failure of the U.S. military to prepare and implement effective plans for conflict termination also merits additional attention. Western military forces are not political forces, and professional war fighters like the U.S. and British military tend to see peacemaking and nation building as a diversion from their main mission. It seems fair to argue that conflict termination and the role of force in ensuring stable peacetime outcomes have always been weaknesses in modern military thinking. Tactics and strategy, and military victory, have always taken priority over grand strategy and winning the peace.

The U.S. military culture has failed to look beyond war fighting in defining the role and responsibility of the U.S. military. The subordination of the military to civilian control in the United States leads to a natural reluctance by the military to become involved in planning for "political" activities like conflict termination, peacemaking, and nation building or to challenge civilian policymakers in these areas. Soldiers naturally focus on war rather than conflict termination.

U.S. military staff colleges have begun to explore these issues, but force transformation and the tactics and strategy of dealing with new threats like terrorism, proliferation, and asymmetric warfare have had priority. As a result, U.S. military thinking tends to focus on winning the war rather than winning the peace, although defeat of the enemy in battle is pointless unless it results in a successful grand strategic outcome.

Resource limitations reinforce the military's traditional focus. Global deployments encourage military planners to try to avoid committing high-technology soldiers to largely low-technology missions. There is a natural desire to avoid tying troops down in open-ended security, peace-making, and nation-building efforts. Moreover, dedicated forces for such missions need area expertise and language skills as well as specialized training and equipment for activities such as security and paramilitary police functions, humanitarian assistance, and nation building. The creation of such forces comes at the direct expense of war-fighting capabilities. Quite naturally, U.S. military planners and commanders see such activities as a diversion from their main mission, as a further stress on an overdeployed force structure, and as missions that should be performed by less capable allied forces.

What military planners and commanders want, however, is not necessarily what they should get or be ordered to do. Even in World War II, the failure to plan for conflict termination helped create many of the problems that led to the Cold War, and successful nation building in Germany and Japan occurred more because these were already strong, cohesive nations than because of "nation building" efforts per se.

The challenges involved have also grown far more urgent since the end of the Cold War. Most of the wars of the twenty-first century are likely to be fought in developing countries and nations that lack an effective political structure and government and have serious ethnic and sectarian divisions. In many cases, the United States and its allies will be fighting nations or terrorist/extremist movements with hostile ideologies, different cultural values, and societies operating on the margin of poverty with limited practical ability to function as modern economies. Basic functions of the state, such as the effective rule of law, will be missing or so flawed that they must be rebuilt from the ground up. The defeated country may be generally hostile to many aspects of Western and secular culture, and it may have no meaningful political parties or political processes. Iraq is scarcely likely to be the last conflict in which the United States and its allies must fight without cohesive international support. Even when the United States has that support, there are no large pools of trained peacemakers to draw upon. Many nations that claim to structure their forces for peacekeeping missions cannot project or support them for sustained missions, and many are unwilling to use them in situations where they must actually fight to create and maintain a peace. Nongovernmental organizations (NGOs) are organized primarily for humanitarian missions in a peaceful, or at least permissive, environment and can provide only limited support. NGOs will always be a critical source of help, but they will never be a substitute for military operations.

The result is that the U.S. military needs to fully accept that conflict termination, peacemaking, and nation building are as much a part of their mission as war fighting. These must have the same priority as combat if terrorists and unstable countries are not to mutate, change tactics, and reemerge in a different form. No strategy for asymmetric warfare can be adequate that does not address these tasks as being as critical as the defeat of most enemy forces in battle.

The U.S. military did not learn this lesson from the first Gulf War, the Balkans, and Afghanistan. In the case of Afghanistan, it was not really ready to act on even the most basic lessons of conflict termination, such as the critical need to secure the country during the period between the fall of a regime and the moment self-appointed leaders try to seize local power. The scale of these problems has been much more serious in Iraq, and it should not take another conflict to realize that the need to see conflict termination and the transition to nation building as a critical military mission is one of the most important single lessons of modern warfare.

THERE IS NO "NEW WAY OF WAR" WITHOUT SUCCESSFUL CONFLICT TERMINATION, PEACEMAKING, AND NATION BUILDING

The United States and its allies must also make this lesson a basic part of force transformation. This is a dangerous time to talk about a new way of war without talking about a new way of peace. In the twenty-first century, planning and training for conflict termination, peacemaking, and nation building have to be given the same priority as planning for peace. Like it or not, most limited wars will only be won by success in these efforts—and the morality and ethics of the use of force can only be justified in these terms.

As a result, jointness must be restructured on a civil-military and interagency basis to provide more capability in these missions if U.S., British, and other Western power-projection forces are to get the domestic, allied, and other foreign support they need to act. Stable war-fighting outcomes can be achieved only if the country defeated or fought over becomes stable after the war. Put differently, even the best military victory cannot, by itself, win the peace.

This requires that both political decisionmakers and military planners and commanders accept the lesson and make the same commitment to winning the peace they make to military victory. The only justification for war is the pragmatic result. Defeating today's enemy without creating the conditions for future stability is a near-certain recipe for future conflict. As a result, peacekeeping and nation building are even more essential aspects of grand strategic planning for political leaders than they are for the military.

Such planning requires the proper organization of civil as well as military activity, the creation of staffs with the skills necessary to carry out the mission, and, above all, the understanding that there has to be a political commitment to take the necessary time and spend the necessary resources. Military leaders can be forgiven for concentrating on winning wars; political leaders cannot be forgiven for failing to win the peace.

Any effort to act on this lesson of the Iraq War must also recognize that peacemaking and nation building are still experimental activities. No one yet has a clear history of success in these undertakings. There are no rules and procedures that guarantee what will or will not work, and most case studies fail to apply clearly to the next case. Priorities often become apparent only once activity begins. It is also virtually impossible for an effort that is intended to create a more democratic government in a nondemocratic state to avoid some tension and violence between suppressed factions and groups.

INTELLIGENCE ON CONFLICT TERMINATION AND NATION BUILDING

There is another critical set of problems that must be addressed. Intelligence did provide analyses and warnings of many of the problems to come.[5] It seems clear that intelligence warned of many of the security problems U.S. forces encountered on entering Iraq and in the immediate aftermath of their advance toward Baghdad. Intelligence also warned that there was a serious risk of pro-Ba'ath and pro-Saddam sabotage, terrorism, and low-level conflict after the regime fell. Some members of the U.S. Army staff indicate that these warnings were serious enough that they recommended that significant security forces be provided to bring order to the areas occupied as the United States advanced.[6]

Intelligence does not, however, seem to have produced an accurate overall assessment of key problems in conflict termination and nation building, and it certainly did not effectively communicate such an assessment to senior policymakers. These problems are discussed in the following chapter and include such issues as the true nature of the Iraqi opposition, the attitudes of the Iraqi people, and the impact of the divisions within Iraq as a nation. All have proved to be of critical importance during conflict termination and the initial phases of nation building.

Adequate intelligence cannot focus simply on "enemies." It must also assess the strengths and weaknesses of potential "friends," and it must do so objectively and without policy-level interference. The United States in particular seems to have failed to accurately assess information from exiles and defectors, many of whom lied or exaggerated their own importance. At least some elements of the U.S. government exaggerated the value and capabilities of outside Iraqi opposition movements like the Iraqi National Congress. In at least some cases, they also failed to objectively assess information from defectors, using information more because it supported policy than because the source had real credibility.

These problems in intelligence did not apply simply to the outside opposition. They applied to the assessment of key parts of the Iraqi population like the Shi'ite south, where the United States and Britain seem to have expected far more support than was forthcoming. It is unclear that a full risk analysis was performed of the probable impact of the U.S. and British advance, and it is unclear that the intelligence effort had a good picture of the power structure within the Shi'ite south and the divisions within it. It seems virtually certain that intelligence underestimated the problems caused by the lack of any secular political structure within the Shi'ites, the importance of Shi'ite religious leaders and their search for political influence and power, and the relative strength of Iranian-backed Shi'ite resistance movements versus other opposition movements.

Similar problems occurred in assessing the nature of the mixed areas near Baghdad and the Sunni areas in central Iraq. The intelligence effort was not capable of distinguishing which towns and areas were likely to be sources of continuing Ba'athist resistance and support. The intelligence community exaggerated the risk of a cohesive Ba'ath resistance in Baghdad, the Sunni triangle, and Tikrit during the war, and was not prepared to deal with the rise of a much more scattered and marginal resistance in these same areas by Ba'ath and Saddam Hussein loyalists after the war.

It is less clear that intelligence failed to assess the problems likely to occur within the Kurdish areas of Iraq, the deep divisions between the Talibani and Barzani factions, and the potential divisions between Kurd, Arab, and Turkoman. Nevertheless, the United States and its allies still seem to have been unprepared for these problems.

Many of the problems in analytic and collection capability were almost certainly in part the failure of U.S. policymakers, who failed to provide proper tasking—and who may sometimes have discouraged such analysis. At the same time, the CIA at least was very slow to address the issues involved and began to do so only in late 2002, months after an interagency effort and State Department task force had highlighted the importance of such work. Once the work did begin, it was weakly staffed, demonstrated a serious lack of analytic depth and area expertise, and had a high degree of theoretical content.

Again, these intelligence failures during the Iraq War reflect a broader policy-level failure to come to grips with the problem of conflict termination and nation building before, during, and at the end of modern wars. U.S. strategy seems to have correctly identified the fact that threats are becoming more and more asymmetric and have a steadily greater ideological and regional content. U.S. practice has failed to come to grips with the fact that military forces can defeat the main elements of such threats—whether they are military forces as in the case of Iraq or guerrilla and terrorist forces as in the case of Al Qaeda and the Taliban—but that only a successful nation building effort can prevent such threats from mutating or new threats from emerging. In any case, a major change is needed in the mindset, focus, and analytic/collection capabilities of the intelligence community to deal with conflict termination and nation building.

LESSONS RELATING TO POLITICAL, DIPLOMATIC, AND PSYCHOLOGICAL WARFARE

Finally, the United States and Britain need to learn painful lessons about the political, diplomatic, and psychological dimensions of the war. Their tactical efforts in psychological warfare seem to have had significant successes. One key lesson of the war, however, is that the United States and Britain failed to conduct a successful political, diplomatic, and psychological campaign at the strategic and grand strategic level.

Limited Success in Psychological Warfare

The United States and Britain had considerable success in those aspects of psychological warfare, such as dropping leaflets, that helped cause inaction among the Iraqi military and helped expedite surrenders. The psyops effort involved some 58 EC-130E Commando Solo sorties, 306 broadcast hours of radio, and 304 hours of television. Compass Call flew another 125 EC-130H sorties, and many made an effort to jam Iraqi communications. The psyops team prepared some 108 radio messages and 81 different leaflets. The coalition flew 158 leaflet missions and ultimately dropped nearly 32 million leaflets over both civilian and military areas. Interestingly, the missions included 32 A-10 and 68 F-16CJ HARM sorties—a strong indication that leaflet drops were timed to go to Iraqi combat troops at the most critical moment. The evidence to date indicates that these missions helped considerably to persuade Iraqi forces either not to fight or to defect, desert, or surrender.

The coalition failed to silence Iraqi radio and TV, however, even though at least 10 major media targets were included among its total of 116 C4I targets. The daily televised briefings of Iraq's minister of information took on the character of a popular farce in the West, but they had considerable impact in Iraq and the Arab world. The continuing presence of the media in Iraq also allowed Iraq to exploit both Arab and Western media and to have a major voice in the world up to the day the regime abandoned its effort to defend Baghdad.

More generally, the psychological warfare effort failed to lay the groundwork for conflict termination and nation building. This was partly the result of the intelligence failure to accurately assess Iraqi attitudes and public opinion; the coalition clearly misread the level of popular support it had among Iraqis at the time it attacked. The United States, in particular, missed the cumulative impact of (1) its failure to support the opposition uprising in Iraq in 1991; (2) its failure to conduct a meaningful public diplomacy campaign to explain that it was not responsible for the suffering of the Iraqi people under UN sanctions; (3) Iraqi and Arab hostility to the United States because of its support of Israel and the Arab portrayal of the Second Intifada; and (4) the coalition's failure to convincingly rebut various regional conspiracy theories, such as an assumption that its goals were "neoimperialist" or that it was fighting to seize Iraqi oil.

As a result, far too little effort was made before, during, and immediately after the Iraq War to persuade key factions within Iraq—and the Iraqi people as a whole—that the coalition was not seeking to oust Saddam Hussein for its own benefit and that it was not fighting the war to take control of Iraqi oil, or use Iraq as a military base, or serve Israel's interests. The tactical psychological and political warfare effort failed to address conspiracy theories in a country and region where such theories usually have far more impact than vague promises about liberation and democracy, and whose history gives it little reason to trust the West.

Perhaps because the United States and Britain put too much faith in the reassurances of the outside opposition, the psychological and political warfare campaign made little effort to reassure Iraq's Shi'ites and failed to understand the importance of dealing with their religious leaders—the only meaningful opposition to the regime inside Iraq after Saddam's political purges of 1979. Similar problems occurred with the Kurds and the need to avoid Kurdish versus Arab and Turkoman confrontations in the north. The United States also made attempts to bribe and subvert Iraqi Sunni officials and commanders, but failed to provide any clear picture of their fate after the liberation.

One of the most inexplicable failures was the lack of a coherent effort to use radio and television to reach the Iraqi people before, during, and after the war. This failure was particularly striking after the war. Even in July 2003, the United States and Britain still did not have an effective radio broadcast effort to reach the Iraqi people. The programming that was provided had very limited news content, and the timing of the news broadcasts ignored the fact that many Iraqis spent most of the afternoon in their homes and left them in the evening when the news was broadcast.

More generally, the United States and Britain failed before, during, and after the war to set clear goals for their nation-building effort and make them a key element in psychological and political warfare. They failed to assure both the Iraqi people as a whole and key elements within Iraq that the coalition had workable plans for nation building—plans that would meet immediate and urgent needs and also produce the kind of "Iraq for the Iraqis" that would give people a strong incentive to cooperate with the coalition. No psychological and political warfare effort is competent that focuses only on defeating the enemy and fails to deal with conflict termination and nation building. The failure to carry out effective programs in this area was a serious defect in the U.S. and British efforts.

Long-standing Failures in Public Diplomacy

The coalition failed in the strategic aspects of psychological and political warfare for a number of reasons. Part of the problem lay in the fact that the Clinton administration never developed a meaningful or effective public diplomacy for dealing with Iraq and the Iraqi people. Instead, it relied largely on the impact of the victory in the Gulf War and the Arab-Israeli peace process. It did not attempt to explain the reasons for the United Nations' sanctions against Iraq and the nature of the UN oil-for-food program, or to deal with aggressive Iraqi efforts to persuade the Iraqi people and many others that the United States and the United Kingdom were responsible for their suffering. It also failed to conduct any meaningful public diplomacy in the Gulf and Arab world to explain and justify its military presence.

The Clinton administration also never rebutted the exaggerated charges that the United States had strongly encouraged public uprisings in Iraq in 1990–1991, when a limited U.S. campaign focused largely on persuading the Iraqi military to overthrow Saddam Hussein. The administration allowed the myth to be disseminated that it was somehow responsible for Saddam Hussein's ability to put down the uprisings because the cease-fire agreement did not prevent Iraqi use of combat helicopters. It failed to explain why the United States had not actively sought to overthrow Saddam Hussein immediately after the Gulf War, and it allowed the Iraqi National Congress to claim that it could somehow have threatened Saddam Hussein militarily if only it had had more active U.S. backing.

The Clinton administration attempted to make a case against Iraqi proliferation without seeming to understand that much of the region, although it feared Saddam Hussein, saw proliferation as a legitimate reaction to Israel's possession of nuclear weapons and the conventional strength of the United States.

Problems Stemming from the Bush Administration

The Bush administration inherited these failures and the backlash from the breakdown of the Arab-Israeli peace process. It does not seem to have understood, however, just how angry Arab public opinion had become over the Second Intifada and U.S. ties to Israel, as a result of the way these subjects were portrayed by much of the Arab media, hostile Arab governments, and Arab and Islamic extremist movements.

The Bush administration also dealt with the aftermath of the September 11 attack on the United States by allowing a climate to develop in which much of the Arab world perceived it as anti-Arab and anti-Islamic. That this was untrue simply magnified the U.S. failure in failing to conduct the kind of broader political and psychological warfare that is vital to winning the war on terrorism and to lay the political groundwork for war against Iraq. This was compounded by the administration's failure to explain its support for democracy in terms that did not appear to threaten its Arab allies or, sometimes, appear to be an attack on—if not contemptuous of—Arab societies.

As has been touched on earlier, both the United States and Britain left their efforts to explain the threat posed by Iraqi weapons of mass destruction until the last moment, when their propaganda-like statements and briefings seemed to be more a rationale for war than a legitimate warning. They made only belated cases for regime change and then failed to clearly define their goals for Iraqi nation building in ways that defused the host of fears, Arab resentments, and conspiracy theories that were the almost inevitable byproduct of the decision to go to war. The United States also badly miscalculated the support it could gain in the UN, as well as its problems with its traditional allies in Europe and with key bilateral partners, such as Turkey.

Finally, and most critically, the United States assumed that it had largely already won the hearts and minds of the Iraqi people and that it did not need a massive political and psychological warfare effort to win their hearts and minds during conflict termination and the transition to nation building.

The Strategic and Grand Strategic Aspects of Psychological and Political Warfare

The key lesson for the future should be that the strategic and grand strategic dimensions of psychological and political warfare are at least as important as the tactical dimensions of such warfare, and that effective operations must focus on conflict termination and nation building long before any actual fighting begins.

THE OVERALL IMPORTANCE OF CONFLICT TERMINATION AS A CRITICAL PART OF WAR FIGHTING

The United States was unprepared for effective conflict termination in the Gulf War, and it sought to avoid the security and nation-building missions in the Afghan conflict. Going back further, it had encountered serious problems in dealing with conflict termination and the aftermath of war in the Spanish American War, World War I, World War II, Korea, and Vietnam. Virtually all of history's major military victors, in fact, have failed to capitalize on their victories in grand strategic terms in at least some important respects.

Conflict termination has generally been treated as a secondary priority, and the end of war has often been assumed to lead to a smooth transition to peace or been dealt with in terms of vague plans and ideological hopes. The United States and its allies are now paying for this failure to look beyond immediate victory on the battlefield. Much more could have been done before, during, and immediately after the war *if* the coalition, and especially the United States, had not seen conflict termination, peacemaking, and nation building as secondary missions, and *if* a number of senior U.S. policymakers had not assumed the best case in terms of Iraqi postwar reactions to the coalition attack. The United States was the only

516 THE IRAQ WAR: STRATEGY, TACTICS, AND MILITARY LESSONS

country in the world that could have provided the necessary resources to ensure a successful transition from conflict to nation building, and it failed to do so.

This should be the last war in which there is a policy-level, military, and intelligence failure to come to grips with conflict termination and the transition to nation building. The United States and its allies should address the issues involved before, during, and after the conflict. They should be prepared to commit the proper resources, and they should see political and psychological warfare in grand strategic terms. A war is over only when violence is ended, military forces are no longer needed to provide security, and nation building can safely take place without military protection. It does not end with the defeat of the main forces of the enemy on the battlefield.

Notes

[1] Department of Defense briefing on April 23, 2003, www.defenselink.mil/transcripts/2003/tr20030423-0122.html.

[2] Interview with James Kitfield, "Attack Always," in *National Journal*, April 25, 2003.

[3] Peter Slevin and Dana Priest, "Wolfowitz Concedes Errors on Iraq," *Washington Post*, July 24, 2003.

[4] Ibid.

[5] The reader should be aware that this analysis is based on unclassified interviews and discussion and not on a review of any of the classified documents involved.

[6] Interviews.

CHAPTER SEVENTEEN

GRAND STRATEGY:
THE CIVILIAN ASPECTS OF NATION BUILDING AND THE CHALLENGE OF WINNING THE PEACE

There are two sets of lessons the United States and its allies need to learn about nation building as a result of the Iraq War. The first set deals with the problems growing out of early failures in conflict termination and nation building, and the problems of asymmetric warfare discussed in chapter 7. The second set comes out of the longer-term problems in nation building in Iraq that in many ways repeat the lessons of previous conflicts.

Like conflict termination, nation building has proved critical to transforming a strategic victory into a grand strategic victory. It again illustrates the need to combine military and civilian planning and policy direction in order to integrate the war plan with a clear plan for both conflict termination and nation building. At the same time, Iraq has already shown the difficulties in making the transition from conflict termination to nation building, and these short-term challenges are only the prelude to the mid- and long-term challenges to come.

SHORT-TERM CHALLENGES AND THE RISK OF GUERRILLA WAR

Some three months after the fall of Baghdad, it was still unclear whether the United States and Britain were really in the conflict termination phase and moving toward nation building or whether they were moving toward low-intensity conflict. On July 18, 2003, the number of U.S. deaths in the Iraq War reached 148, surpassing the 147 casualties in the Gulf War. Although many of the casualties after May 1 had come from accidents, 34 had died from combat and a significant number of the more than 80 deaths from accidents had been the result of security measures like high-speed convoys.

In mid-July 2003, General John Abizaid, the new commander of US-CENTCOM, described the "postwar" level of violence in Iraq as a guerrilla war. In doing so, he recognized a pattern of escalating violence:[1]

> [we are] picking up a lot of information that indicated that there were significant terrorist groups and activities that we were having to be concerned about, as well; most of this all happening in what we call the Sunni Triangle, that area vaguely described by Tikrit, Ramadi and Baghdad, but often stretching up into Mosul.
>
> ...we're fighting Ba'athist remnants throughout the country. I believe there's mid-level Ba'athist, Iraqi intelligence service people, Special Security Organization people, Special Republican Guard people that have organized at the regional level in cellular structure and are conducting what I would describe as a classical guerrilla-type campaign against us. It's low-intensity conflict, in our doctrinal terms, but it's war, however you describe it.
>
> ...I would think it's very important for everybody to know that we take casualties and we cause casualties to be inflicted upon the enemy because we are at war. And it's very important to know that as many of the casualties inflicted upon us have come at the initiation of military action offensively by the United States as by our troops being attacked by the enemy.
>
> We're seeing a cellular organization of six to eight people, armed with RPGs, machine guns, et cetera, attacking us at sometimes times and place of their choosing. And other times we attack them at times and places of our choosing. They are receiving financial help from probably regional-level leaders. And I think describing it as guerrilla tactics being employed against us is... a proper thing to describe in strictly military terms.
>
> ...But there are some foreign fighters, some of which may have been stay-behinds. Remember in the early stages of capturing Baghdad, there were an awful lot of foreign fighters, and it's possible that we missed some of them, they stayed there and they've reformed and reorganized. So foreign fighters are present on the battlefield, but I would state without any...any hesitation that the mid-level Ba'athist threat is the primary threat that we've got to deal with right now.
>
> ...there is some level of regional command and control going on. And when I say regional, probably you look over at the Al Ramadi area, there's probably something going on over there, if you look up in the Tikrit-Baiji area, there's something up there, Mosul. That they are all connected? Not yet. Could they become connected? Sure, they could become connected.

General Abizaid went on to say, however, that there was as yet no central direction of the attacks on the United States, and that such attacks could be defeated:

[W]ar is a struggle of wills. You look at the Arab press; they say, "We drove the Americans out of Beirut, we drove them out of Somalia; you know, we'll drive them out of Baghdad." And that's just not true. They're not driving us out of anywhere.

…The most important thing in all of this is causing the level of violence to go down so that governance can move forward. And governance has moved forward in a pretty interesting way. And I think that—you have to understand that there will be an increase in violence as we achieve political success, because the people that have a stake in ensuring the defeat of the coalition realize that time is getting short as the Iraqi face becomes more and more prevalent on the future of Iraq. And that's precisely what's going on now.

If you look at the local level throughout Iraq, in the South and in the North in particular, local government is moving ahead in a pretty spectacular way.

In the areas where we're having difficulties with the remnants of the regime, it's less secure, and people that cooperate with us are at risk. We have to create an environment where those people do not feel at risk. That means we have to take our military activity to the enemy, and we have to defeat these cells.

In addition, [you] have to understand it's not a matter of boots per square meter. Everybody wants to think that, but that's just not so. If I could do one thing as a commander right now, I would focus my intelligence like a laser on where the problem is, which is mid-level Ba'athist leaders. And we're trying to do that. And I think, as we do that, we'll find that we have more success.

…the level of resistance…is getting more organized, and it is learning. It is adapting. It is adapting to our tactics, techniques and procedures, and we've got to adapt to their tactics, techniques and procedures.

…At the tactical level, they're better coordinated now. They're less amateurish, and their ability to use improvised explosive devices and combine the use of these explosive devices with some sort of tactical activity—say, for example, attacking the quick-reaction forces—is more sophisticated. It's not necessarily a problem that we are not—that we can't handle. We can handle the tactical problems that are presented.

NATION BUILDING VERSUS GUERRILLA WARFARE: BEST, WORST, AND PROBABLE CASES

It is important to note that this fighting was still limited and localized, and did not mean that the United States and Britain could not succeed in conflict termination and nation building. As General Abizaid had pointed out, the hostile threat still came largely from small Ba'ath cells and cadres loyal to Saddam in central Iraq. According to Ambassador Bremer, some 85 percent of the attacks came from the relatively small area including the Baghdad area and the "Sunni triangle" shaped by Tikrit in the north, Ar Ramadi in the west, and Baq'uba in the east.

The attackers were able to strike and hide largely because the Sunnis in the areas where they operated still feared the return of the old regime, and because much of the population resented the U.S. and British occupation for its initial failures in providing security and aid. It was not clear that there was popular support for such attacks; indeed, some polls showed just the opposite. The attacks were also taking place at a time when the U.S. and British nation-building effort was only beginning to gather momentum, and the United States and Britain still had ample opportunity to succeed. Moreover, on July 21, the United States was able to kill Saddam's sons, Uday and Qusay, demonstrating that it could find and capture or kill even the most senior Ba'athist. By that time, it had also captured or killed 37 of the 52 top leaders in the "deck of cards" it had used to list the most threatening members of Saddam's regime, and it had some 600 to 800 other Ba'athist and former regime leaders in custody.[2]

At the same time, the rise of localized violence in Iraq did create the risk of more serious forms of guerrilla warfare and again illustrated the need for a well-managed military and strategic linkage between warfighting and nation building. Instead of a true end to the conflict, there were three major scenarios for the success or failure of nation building.

The best-case scenario was that the U.S.-led nation-building and security endeavors got enough direction, coordination, and resources to steadily gather momentum in spite of early mistakes and Ba'athist and other attempts to sabotage the nation building. Effective Iraqi police forces would supplement the coalition security effort. The United States and its allies would begin to work with the Iraqis to set clearly defined goals for nation building that won the hearts and minds of the Iraqi people. Efforts to draft a new constitution would gather popular support and succeed. Some form of pluralist federalism would be created to deal with Iraq's ethnic and sectarian divisions. The nation-building program would find a way to resume oil exports and obtain enough outside investment to support economic reform and development in ways that the Iraqi people did not see as an attempt to seize their patrimony.

The most probable scenario was mixed success in nation building. This would be success of a kind that put Iraq on a better political and economic path, but did so in a climate of lingering low-level security threats and continuing ethnic and sectarian tensions. Such success would have many limits but would be far better for the Iraqis than the rule of Saddam Hussein. It would still give the United States and other nation builders a victory and allow them to leave. It would scarcely be the "shining city on a hill" that would transform the entire Middle East that some neoconservatives had predicted, but it would certainly be Iraq.

The worst-case scenario was very different and illustrated the kind of linkage between military action and nation building that occurred in Afghanistan. This was the scenario of a steadily escalating guerrilla war that would slowly gather popular support, and of a broadening of the fighting to include the Kurdish-Arab areas in the north and the Shi'ite areas that dominated southern and much of central Iraq. It was a case where the United States and the UK would come to fight the equivalent of a third Gulf War and where violence and sabotage would paralyze nation building.

This worst case could occur, however, only as the result of a combination of failures in nation building that the United States, Britain, and their allies had ample opportunity to avoid:

- **The nation-building effort continued to blunder.** Progress was too slow and too many promises were not kept. Local security continued to falter, the growth in Iraqi jobs and economic activity was too slow, and many well-intended reforms either did not work or paid off too late to develop any real Iraqi support or gratitude among the populace.

- **The problems in nation building increasingly led the United States and its allies to act as occupiers rather than liberators.** Rather than Iraq for the Iraqis on Iraqi terms—with clear goals in terms of milestones, political and economic action, and a transition to Iraqi rule—the United States muddled through in ways that increasingly appeared to involve a presence of 5 to 10 years, rather than one of 12 to 24 months. Rather than goals that could attract real Iraqi support, and win hearts and minds, the United States appeared to be embarked on an effort to rebuild Iraq in its own image.

- **The United States and its allies continued to select the leaders they wanted, rather than the leaders the Iraqis wanted.** Rather than screening the Ba'ath and Iraqi military, large blocs of Iraq's best people were rejected because they went along with Saddam's dictatorship to survive. Not only was there a major power vacuum, but an increasing incentive to oppose the U.S.-led nation-building effort.

- **The U.S. security effort to halt the largely Sunni violence in central Iraq had only partial success—even if Saddam and his sons were caught.** It had its tactical successes, but alienated a large number of

Sunnis in the process, who felt increasingly disenfranchised as the Shi'ites and Kurds gained a fair share of wealth and power for the first time.

- **The U.S. and British nation builders and military forces increasingly huddled behind their own security barriers, creating a growing distance from ordinary Iraqis.** This created more and more physical barriers to the movement of the population and larger "no go" zones. The United States continued in its efforts to seal off much of central Baghdad and in its symbolic occupation of Saddam's palaces. At the same time, the failure to properly integrate the military and civil sides of the U.S. nation-building effort that began before the war in Kuwait continued to present coordination problems in Iraq.

- **The remnants of the Ba'ath and the cult of Saddam became a major force in the Sunni part of the population,** and low-level violence and sabotage combined with a poorly managed nation-building effort to create centers of organized opposition to the United States and Britain that could not be eliminated and which undercut much of the nation-building effort. Even those Sunnis who did not want Saddam back, came to want the United States and Britain out.

- **The United States sought to ignore the lack of any meaningful secular opposition leaders in the Shi'ite south, and to avoid having religious Shi'ites come to power.** This increasingly alienated Iraq's Shi'ites, who earlier had tolerated—not supported—the U.S. and British military advance. The end result played into the hands of Iraqi Shi'ite religious hard-liners and Iran. The same pattern of resistance and violence emerged in the south that already exists in central Iraq. It not only opposed the U.S.-led nation-building effort, but political secularism in Iraq and any reassertion of Sunni/Ba'ath/ purely secular authority. The result was growing sectarian divisions that further complicated the nation-building effort.

- **The Kurds continued to support the United States and Britain, but this did not mean Kurdish unity.** Barzani and Talibani moved back towards a power struggle as the cash flow from oil for food and smuggling dropped. Moreover, ethnic cleansing and Kurdish power struggles with the Arabs and Turkomans complicated the problems the United States has with the Arabs and relations with Turkey. The United States was blamed by Sunnis and Turkomans for the assertion of Kurdish power.

- **U.S. efforts to try to create a federal structure that could bridge over** the ethnic and sectarian differences between Sunni, Shi'ite, and Kurd came too late to prevent civil tension and violence, and no Iraqi faction was convinced that such efforts would give them a fair share of real power. Fear of prolonged occupation, and the feeling among most Iraqis that those who went along with the U.S. effort did do so as appeasers and for their own benefit, further undercut the nation-building effort and added to the level of anti-nation-building/anti-U.S. and UK violence.

- **The United States tried to handle all of these problems as inexpensively as possible in a country that had no meaningful exports other than oil and dates before the war, and earned only $ 12.5 billion in oil exports in 2002.** It continued to talk about oil wealth in a country that has already lost some six months of oil export revenues by July 2003, and whose export capacity had dropped from over two million barrels a day in 2000 to around 800,000—and where every effort to revitalize oil exports met with sabotage. The U.S.-led nation building effort never got the money it needs to succeed, and the United States and Britain tried to mortgage future oil revenues to pay for current nation-building activities.

- **Rather than conduct an open and transparent effort to rehabilitate Iraq's petroleum industry, with Iraqi technocratic and political advice, the United States acted on its own priorities and perceptions.** Ordinary Iraqis came to feel their oil was being stolen. Oil revenues were not used as the "glue" to unite Iraq's divided factions in some form of federalism. Ideas like "securitizing" Iraq's oil revenues to make direct payments to Iraqi citizens deprived the new Iraqi government of financial power and leverage. Iraqis with no experience in dealing with such funds became the natural prey of Iraqis who knew how to manipulate money and such payments.

- **The United States failed to confront its allies with the need to forgive Iraqi reparations and debt**—claims potentially amounting to more than $200 billion—leaving Iraq angry and without a financial future. It continued to leave the contingency contracts Saddam signed with Russia, France, and other oil firms as valid—although these contracts were clearly political efforts to win support to end UN sanctions.

- **Other aspects of the nation-building effort lacked transparency, such as nation-building contracts, assistance to Iraqi businesses, and the search for foreign investment.** The United States and British improvised solutions in Western market terms, failing to realize that the end result is to operate in a climate of hostile Iraqi conspiracy theories that believe the United States and Britain are in Iraq to seize its oil revenues, benefit from contracts, and finance an occupation. The United States and its allies did the right thing in economic and technocratic terms, but every such action ended in increasing Iraqi distrust and hostility because it lacked transparency and a quick transition to Iraqi planning and control.

- **A token 40,000-man Iraqi Army was seen as leaving Iraq defenseless and as dependent on U.S. and British occupiers.** This left Iraq without any clear plan to create a meaningful capability for self-defense against Iran and Turkey and to deal with Iranian proliferation. There also was not a clear plan for sharing control over military power equitably among Iraq's ethnic and sectarian factions. This made the new force seem like a puppet army. Even those officers who seemed to support the United States and Britain secretly became increasingly nationalistic and hostile.

- **Each step ended in making the United States and its allies more dependent on friendly Iraqi "leaders" with limited real influence and credibility** and on Iraqis willing to go along with the "occupying" powers for their own benefit. The result was to create a climate that was increasingly oriented toward security rather than nation building. U.S. and allied forces spent more and more time in "fortress" casernes and headquarters and in patrolling for self-defense purposes.

In military terms, the key lesson from all three of these scenarios is the same. Iraq is a case example—and there will be many future cases—of the fact that victory in asymmetric and regional conflicts is directly tied to a major commitment to nation building. Victory is not defined by having a successful exit strategy; it is defined by winning the end game.

LESSONS FOR NEAR-TERM ACTION

There is no way to predict how well the United States will do in the near term. It seems unlikely that enough elements of the worst-case scenario will occur to create a large-scale guerrilla war. The United States and Britain have come to recognize the seriousness of many of the risks they face in the months since May 1, and they are seeking to correct their past mistakes. At the same time, this scenario shows how much each step in avoiding a serious guerrilla conflict is tied to short-term success in nation building and to correcting mistakes made during the early stages of conflict termination.

A CSIS team visited Iraq during late June and early July 2003 to examine these issues. Its findings and recommendations further illustrate these lessons:[3]

Rebuilding Iraq is an enormous task. Iraq is a large country with historic divisions, exacerbated by a brutal and corrupt regime. The country's 24 million people and its infrastructure and service delivery mechanisms have suffered decades of severe degradation and under-investment. Elements of the old regime engage in a campaign of sabotage and ongoing resistance, greatly magnifying the "natural" challenges of rebuilding Iraq. Given the daunting array of needs and challenges, and the national security imperative for the United States to succeed in this endeavor, the United States needs to be prepared to stay the course in Iraq for several years.

The next 12 months will be decisive; the next three months are crucial to turning around the security situation, which is volatile in key parts of the country. All players are watching closely to see how resolutely the coalition will handle this challenge. The Iraqi population has exceedingly high expectations, and the window for cooperation may close rapidly if they do not see progress on delivering security, basic services, opportunities for broad political involvement, and economic opportunity.

The "hearts and minds" of key segments of the Sunni and Shi'a communities are in play and can be won, but only if the Coalition Provisional Authority (CPA) and new Iraqi authorities deliver in short order. To do so, the CPA will have to dramatically and expeditiously augment its operational capacity throughout the country, so that civilian-led rebuilding can proceed while there are still significant numbers of coalition forces in Iraq to provide maximum leverage over those who seek to thwart the process.

To succeed, the United States and its allies will need to pursue a strategy over the next twelve months that: recognizes the unique challenges in different parts of the country; consolidates gains in those areas where things are going well; and wins hearts and minds even as it decisively confronts spoilers.

Seven major areas need immediate attention.

1. **The coalition must establish public safety in all parts of the country.** In addition to ongoing efforts, this will involve reviewing force composition and structure, as well as composite force levels (U.S., coalition, and Iraqi) so as to be able to address the need for increased street-level presence in key conflictive areas; quickly hiring private security to help stand up and supervise a rapid expansion of the Iraqi Facility Protection Service, thereby freeing thousands of U.S. troops from this duty; ratcheting up efforts to recruit sufficient levels of international civilian police through all available channels; and, launching a major initiative to reintegrate "self-demobilized" Iraqi soldiers *and* local militias.

2. **Iraqi ownership of the rebuilding process must be expanded at national, provincial, and local levels.** At the national level ensuring success of the newly formed Iraqi Governing Council is crucial. This will require avoiding overloading it with too many controversial issues too soon. The natural desire to draw anger away from the coalition by putting an Iraqi face on the most difficult decisions must be balanced with a realistic assessment of what the council can successfully manage. At the provincial and local levels, coalition forces and the CPA have made great progress in establishing political councils throughout the country, but they need direction and the ability to respond to local needs and demands. To achieve this, local and provincial political councils need to have access to resources and be linked to the national Iraqi Governing Council and the constitutional process.

3. **Idle hands must be put to work and basic economic and social services provided** immediately to avoid exacerbating political and security problems. A model economy will not be created overnight out of Iraq's failed statist economic structures. Short-term public works projects are needed on a large scale to soak up sizable amounts of the available labor pool. Simultaneously, the CPA must get a large number of formerly state-owned enterprises up and running. Even if many of them are not competitive and may need to be privatized and downsized eventually, now is the time to get as many people back to work as possible. A massive microcredit program in all provinces would help to spur wide-ranging economic activity, and help to empower key agents of change such as women. The CPA must also do whatever is necessary to immediately refurbish basic services, especially electricity, water, and sanitation.

4. **Decentralization is essential.** The job facing occupation and Iraqi authorities is too big to be handled exclusively by the central occupying authority and national Iraqi Governing Council. Implementation is lagging far behind needs and expectations in key areas, at least to some extent because of severely constrained CPA human resources at the provincial and local levels. This situation must be addressed immediately by decentralizing key functions of the CPA to the provincial level, thereby enhancing operational speed and effectiveness and allowing maximum empowerment of Iraqis. The CPA must rapidly recruit and field a much greater number of civilian experts to guide key governance, economic, social, justice, and also some security components of the occupation.

5. **The coalition must facilitate a profound change in the Iraqi national frame of mind—from centralized authority to significant freedoms, from suspicion to trust, from skepticism to hope.** This will require an intense and effective communications and marketing campaign, not the status quo. The CPA needs to win the confidence and support of the Iraqi people.

Communication—between the CPA and the Iraqi people, and within the CPA itself—is insufficient so far. Drastic changes must be made to immediately improve the daily flow of practical information to the Iraqi people, principally through enhanced radio and TV programming. Iraqis need to hear about difficulties and successes from authoritative sources. Secondly, the CPA needs to gather information from Iraqis much more effectively—through a more robust civilian ground presence, "walk-in" centers for Iraqis staffed by Iraqis, and hiring a large number of Iraqi "animators" to carry and receive messages. Thirdly, information flow must be improved within the CPA itself through an integrated operations center that would extend across both the civilian and military sides of the CPA, and by enhancing cell-phone coverage and a system-wide email system that could ease the timely dissemination of information to all CPA personnel.

6. **The United States needs to quickly mobilize a new reconstruction coalition that is** significantly broader than the coalition that successfully waged the war. The scope of the challenges, the financial requirements, and rising anti-Americanism in parts of the country make necessary a new coalition that involves various international actors (including from countries and organizations that took no part in the original war coalition). The Council for International Cooperation at the CPA is a welcome innovation, but it must be dramatically expanded and supercharged if a new and inclusive coalition is to be built.

7. **Money must be significantly more forthcoming and more flexible.** Iraq will require significant outside support over the short to medium term. In addition to broadening the financial coalition to include a wider range of international actors, this means the president and Congress will need to budget and fully fund reconstruction costs through 2004. The CPA must be given rapid and flexible funding. "Business as usual" is not an option for operations in Iraq, nor can it be for their funding. The enormity of the task ahead cannot be underestimated. It requires that the entire effort be immediately turbo-charged—by making it more agile and flexible, and providing it with greater funding and personnel.

THE MEDIUM-TERM AND LONGER-TERM CHALLENGES IN NATION BUILDING

If the United States and its allies are to have true success, they must also deal with the broader challenges of nation building. This requires a medium- and long-term effort, and one that must deal with the fact that there are deep divisions within Iraq, within the nations surrounding it, and within the world over how Iraq should change and evolve.

The list of factors that will determine success in these aspects of the nation-building effort is long and complex:

- the speed with which security, jobs, and conditions of ordinary life can be restored and improved;
- the quality of U.S. and British peacemaking and nation-building efforts, and their management and funding of the process;
- the effectiveness of peacekeeping and intervention in bringing Iraqi factions together, and/or the level of internal conflicts, if any;
- the role and effectiveness of other states, the UN, and NGOs;
- the scale of humanitarian and economic aid;
- the ability to create a stable form of Iraqi federalism and pluralism that can integrate ethnic and sectarian factions into an effective and stable government;
- the ability to limit interference by neighbors into Iraqi affairs, and to minimize regional competition for influence in Iraq;
- the effectiveness of efforts to reform the criminal and commercial justice systems and protect human rights;
- the ability to restructure the Iraqi economy from a command to a modern market economy;
- the level of de-Saddamization of the state system, including the national oil company;
- the legal status of Iraq as new or inheritor state, and its ability to deal with foreign debt, reparations, and existing contingency and ongoing international contracts;
- how well the Iraqi oil industry is reshaped, repaired, and renovated;
- the role of Iraq in OPEC and the world oil market;
- Arab and Islamic perceptions of war, conflict termination, and the nation-building effort—pro or con; and
- the ability to rebuild Iraqi military forces and integrate Iraq into a stable security structure in the region.

The United States and Britain cannot succeed in meeting all of the challenges involved in transforming Iraq into a modern nation during the time they have anything like their present control over Iraq. Creating stable new patterns of Iraqi political, social, economic, and energy development to deal with these fracture lines will take at least 5 to 10 years, and it seems doubtful that outside powers like the United States and Britain can have an controlling impact on Iraq's decisions for more than a year or so.

The key to grand strategic success, and to winning the peace, will, however, be determined by whether the United States and Britain can succeed in putting the Iraqis on a path where they can transform their country into some form of stable federal republic and one that is on the road to economic development.

FRACTURE LINES IN THE POSTWAR INFRASTRUCTURE

Transforming Iraq into a modern nation will not be easy. All nations face difficulties in their development, and Iraq faces unusually serious internal political and economic problems after 30 years of dictatorship and two decades of war. These problems became all too apparent from the initial surveys U.S. officials made of Iraq's infrastructure, the impact of these problems on the Iraqi people, and Iraq's vulnerability to sabotage:[4]

> [T]he real problem here is decades of neglect to this infrastructure, lack of investment in operations and maintenance, and also the looting and sabotage that's occurred since the end of fighting. We've made incredible progress in the last 12 weeks since the war ended. We are engaged in a very wide range of reconstruction and rehabilitation projects all over the country. In the last six weeks, we've committed almost a billion dollars in several thousand projects, from high-impact, relatively low-cost things that brigade commanders are doing out in the field to large infrastructure investments that will have a huge impact on the future.
>
> When I say "we," I'm talking about the collective efforts of the coalition military, the U.S. Agency for International Development and their British counterpart, DFID. We're talking about the private sector, nongovernmental organizations.
>
> ...Electricity is probably the most important thing we're doing right now, because without it, nothing else works in the country. It's an antiquated system. It's basically 1960s technology. It's an amalgamation of systems that, due to a number of circumstances, the Iraqis have not had a consistent investment approach, and they have a wide variety of manufacturers and types of systems that make up the electrical system. Hence, it is very complicated and difficult to maintain.
>
> The capacity of this system is about 7,800 megawatts. And the real important figure here is the fact that due to its age and condition, they can only generate about 4,500 megawatts. The national demand right now is about 6,000 megawatts, and so you can see that right away, there will be shortages of electricity. And this always has been for the Iraqi people. It's something they're used to. So that just means that we have to do a program of load shedding, which essentially is rolling blackouts, so that people have their power cut off at different times during the day. It's very difficult to control because

the control systems they did have in place were largely looted and destroyed following the war. The distribution system that moves power around the country is also very unstable and not very reliable, so it's difficult for us to give any predictability to the Iraqi people about when their power will be on or when it will be off.

...The fuel system is also in fairly poor condition. They rely heavily on the oil industry and direct feeds from refineries to power the generators. And with the shutdown of the oil system and also the lack of maintenance in that system, getting fuel to the generators has been a real challenge to us.

...On 12 April when we arrived in the city of Baghdad, it was a complete blackout. And through a very, very complex process, working with the Iraqis, we were able to bring up the electrical system. We now have 39,000 electrical workers back on the job. We have today about 3,200 megawatts of power being generated, and by the end of the month [July] we'll have about 4,000, which is about where they were pre-war. We should continue to see rises in power as we make additional investments and repairs in the system. We've also reconnected the national grid, which has been very important in moving power around the country.

...So we will not be where they tell us they were last year. But it should not be a crisis situation, because much of the nation's power demands have been diminished. For example, the military is no longer drawing the huge amounts of power that they did before the war. So I think what we'll see here by the end of July is the status quo ante bellum with the exception of the people of Baghdad, who will begin to feel the pinch, because power is being shared throughout the country more so now than it was before.

...Where water and foods are concerned, again, the electrical system is the real key there to power pumps and move the commodities through the system. Here in Baghdad, before the war we were getting about ... 2,000 million liters per day of drinking water, right now we're about 1,400, and we should be back to 2,000 in the next three months or so.

In the southern part of the country, about 60 percent of the people in the urban population have access to drinking water, and about 30 percent of the rural population. Those are about the numbers they had pre-war. But we are going to continue to improve on those, and we think we'll get it up to about 80 percent by the end of October. No one is really going without water. We are supplementing with tankers, wells, and river water to purify, and feed the people.

...Sewage is a big problem, especially here in Baghdad. None of the sewage here in the city is being treated, because of damage to the sewage treatment plants following the war. It's going to be several months before we are able to get up any level of sewage treatment. This certainly has some down-river consequences, which we're very sensitive to, but so far we haven't had any

Map 4
Population Density in Iraq

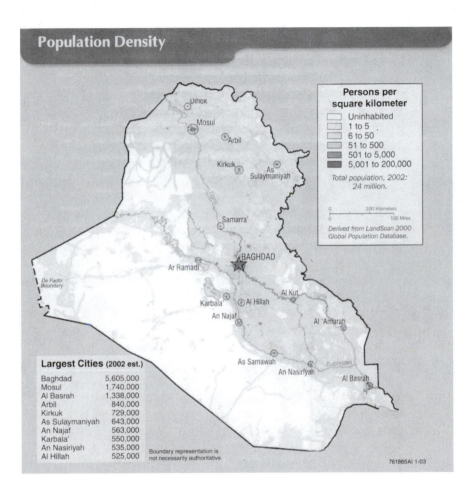

Population Density

Persons per square kilometer

- Uninhabited
- 1 to 5
- 6 to 50
- 51 to 500
- 501 to 5,000
- 5,001 to 200,000

Total population, 2002: 24 million.

Derived from LandScan 2000 Global Population Database.

Largest Cities (2002 est.)

Baghdad	5,605,000
Mosul	1,740,000
Al Basrah	1,338,000
Arbil	840,000
Kirkuk	729,000
As Sulaymaniyah	643,000
An Najaf	563,000
Karbala'	550,000
An Nasiriyah	535,000
Al Hillah	525,000

Boundary representation is not necessarily authoritative.

761865AI 1-03

Source: U.S. Government, CIA.

Map 5
Land Use in Iraq

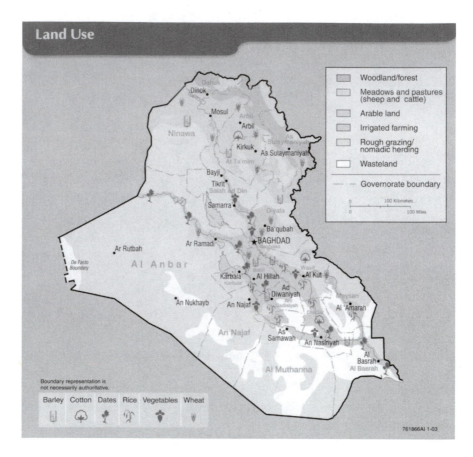

Source: U.S. Government, CIA.

significant outbreaks of disease as a result of that. Our big challenge is just to continue to move the sewage through the system.

...Roads and bridges. The highway network here in Iraq was in fairly good shape before the war. It did suffer some neglect, and that's been, really, the focus of our effort...to maintain some of those damaged sections of road. Thirty highway bridges were knocked down during the war, by both us and the Iraqis. Ten of those are very high priority, and we're building on five of them right now. The other five are being covered by temporary military bridging. So no real significant issues on roads and bridges at the moment.

The rail line is an important transportation network for the Iraqis. They moved all commodities from their port of Umm Qasr all the way up to Mosul in the north. That line is now open. There is one section of the road that is being worked on, about a 70-kilometer stretch south of Nasiriyah, so we're investing about $20 million in doing that.

The ports, both air and sea ports, obviously, are very important as we get the country back on its feet. The port of Umm Qasr is open and, in fact, has a higher capacity than it's had in many years. We're dredging the port, removing wrecks, and we've got it pretty much down to 12.5 meters. So we can get deep-draft vessels in here to bring in relief supplies and begin to stimulate the economy. We're also quite busy removing wrecks that are in the waterway there.

Air traffic should be reinitiated here in about two weeks. It will be the first time we've had commercial air traffic here coming into Baghdad in 12 years, so it's a big event for the people. It will then be followed very closely by the airport at Basra opening, and then eventually up at Mosul in the north.

In irrigation, agriculture is very important to the people here. And again, that system has suffered from years of neglect. And we have a specifically focused program to put people back to work in the irrigation sector. So we're going to have about 100,000 people at work over the next couple of months clearing about 5,500 kilometers of irrigation system.

We've surveyed the major dams throughout the country. We found some structural problems, which we're addressing with the Army Corps of Engineers and with USAID. We've restarted a number of irrigation projects that were put on hold for various reasons.

We're also doing a significant amount of environmental work and investigation, particularly down in the Mesopotamian marshes, in the Shi'a area. This is a very social and—socially and politically charged issue. Saddam drained the marshes down there...as a way of punishing the Shi'as and essentially changed a...many thousand-year-old culture in the process. He has also, in the process, caused us problems with fresh water down in the Basra area. So we're looking into how we can restore those marshlands.

The communications network…really took some beating during the war. We are currently replacing four switches in Baghdad. We're putting in an international gateway, and we're putting in a fiber-optics backbone, which would connect about 75 percent of the users in the nation here with access to telephones.

Government buildings have been a huge problem for us, especially here in Baghdad, but throughout the nation, with hospitals, schools, police stations, fire stations and so forth. So we've (got) a very, very large effort, about $150 million so far, in putting those facilities back on line.

One of the most important ones…are the schools, and we're going to fix about 1,350 schools in 12 different cities over the next few months. So when they open schools in the fall, the children will have a much better learning environment. And in the process, we'll put about 1,500 people to work on those jobs.

The oil infrastructure…without oil, this country does not run. Again, we are gratified with the small amount of damage done to the oil fields. They had a wonderful military campaign that was able to capture the system intact, in spite of some of the Iraqis' attempts to destroy it. But the oil infrastructure also suffers from looting and vandalism following the war.

…We're pleased to announce that we had the first oil out of Turkey on the 20th of June and out of Mina al-Bakr terminal here in Iraq on the 28th of June. So the system is now up and functioning…. And by the fall, we should break the…million-barrel mark and begin to really stimulate the economy here.

…we're actually producing about 800,000 barrels of oil today. Iraq uses about 20 percent of that for internal consumption through the refineries. We are not at the moment exporting any of that oil. We sold about 7.5 million barrels to Turkey at the end of June, and we emptied the storage banks at Mina al-Bakr here just recently. So we're now in the process of recharging the storage tanks. In terms of the ultimate capacity, we think that we can get up to over 2 million barrels per day -2.2, 2.5, something like that -in about a year's time. And that is about the normal export level that the Iraqis have been accustomed to.

Let me close by just saying a few words about security. I know there's been a lot of reporting about this lately. There have been attacks, and this is not surprising or unexpected. As conditions improve, the opposition is going to get more and more desperate in their attempt to destabilize the country and to discredit the coalition and our efforts here to put the nation back on its feet.

We have in recent weeks put a lot more effort into security of infrastructure, particularly the linear lines of communications for power and oil, and I think we're beginning to see the benefits of that.

...When we talk about sabotage, at the moment we're talking about the sabotage of public utilities. We're talking about hundreds and hundreds of miles of power cables, hundreds and hundreds of miles of pipelines and all the associated facilities. And there just aren't enough tanks in the world to put one tank on every electricity pylon. So when we look at security for that system, what we're looking at is a holistic approach. We're looking at the incredible efforts being made by the U.S. military and other coalition forces. But we're also looking at local Iraqi security forces, the new Iraqi police force, in due course we're looking at the new Iraqi security force as well, but also we're looking at the ordinary Iraqi people, because the only way you can protect a system of that size in any country in the world, but obviously here, is by the whole network of everything from starting at the top with security forces to getting right down to the bottom to having people who will give you a tip-off and say, "Look, I've heard that somebody may be thinking of attacking that facility," or, "I've heard this rumor or that rumor."

...another aspect of security is to reduce the vulnerability of the systems through these investments we're making. As I said, it's a very fragile system, does not have a lot of redundancies, so when it does get attacked, it can have catastrophic impact. So the work we're doing in making these investments will make the infrastructure less vulnerable to attack. And we're also putting into place a response mechanism with the Iraqi work crews to be able to respond quickly and get things back on line when we do have interruptions of utilities.

...It's been awfully difficult for us to really understand exactly what level of service the Iraqis had prior to the war. There's never been enough electricity to go around, and Saddam definitely used the provision of utilities as a political tool to reward those he wanted to reward and punish those he wanted to punish. So it's been awfully difficult for us to really get at exactly what the average Iraqi had. We know, for example, that here in Baghdad they typically enjoyed 23 to 24 hours of power. But there are other places in the country that got two. And as we have brought the system back on line, we've tried to get more equitable in the distribution of that power. So what you're seeing here is the people of Baghdad are receiving less than they did before, but...about 80 percent of the population is receiving more.

...As far as the information campaign is concerned, the simple answer is that we use any means that we find, because the infrastructure for the media here is much less complete than one would wish. It was, of course, completely and utterly state-controlled by Saddam Hussein. A lot of elements of that have quite likely now vanished. And it's taking time for things like new television stations, new radio transmitters to come up, and for newspapers. And people here are very poor at the moment. So not all of them can afford to buy newspapers. So with every information campaign that we do, my guiding principle is we do absolutely everything: we do flyers, we do posters, we do word of mouth, we do television, we do radio, we do anything we can, because at this stage of the game you can't be confident that any one media outlet is going to hit the audience that you're looking for.

POLITICAL FRACTURE LINES

Internal Political Fracture Lines

These immediate problems in infrastructure are compounded by the challenges in developing political stability in Iraq. A war can defeat a regime, but it cannot create a new culture or set of values, or suddenly create a modern and stable political system and economy. Iraq may be a sophisticated state with some 25 million people, but, after a 30-year old dictatorial regime, it is also a nation with no viable political parties.

Iraq has many political fracture lines, summarized in table 17.1 (page 540). These include major religious and ethnic fault lines that date back to the Ottoman Empire. It is 60 percent to 65 percent Shi'ite but has been ruled by a Sunni elite that was not based on broad representation even of the Sunni community. Iraq is largely urban but has had a ruling elite more clan- and tribally oriented around village society. It is largely Arab (75+ percent) but has a large Kurdish minority, a significant Turkoman minority, and other minorities, including Assyrian Christians. Its minorities have deep internal fault lines, but all have faced significant Arab persecution.

As table 17.1 shows, there are divisions within divisions. Saddam encouraged a steady growth of tribal and clan divisions between 1992 and 2003 as part of his divide-and-rule tactics. The Kurds have long been divided between a "Barzanistan"—that was more than willing to make alliances with Saddam, the Turkomans, and the Turks—and a "Talibanistan" that made occasional alliances with Iran. The shell of a modern Kurdish democracy developed after 1992, but the economy and stability of the Kurdish enclave depended on aid, smuggling, and oil-for-food income— not economic development. At least some Kurds also took the side of Saddam. The Turkomans came to regard both Kurd and Arab as potential oppressors, and Saddam used the Assyrian Christians to displace Kurds in the north in ways that may come back to haunt them.

The ruling Sunni minority feuded and divided by town, clan, and family. The Shi'ite majority divided between secularists, modern religious Shiites, traditional religious Shi'ites, and those who supported the regime. The development of the south received far less attention than the development of Sunni areas, except for Basra. A low-level civil war by Shi'ite opponents of the regime targeted fellow Shi'ites as well as the regime, and

Map 6
Ethnoreligious Groups and Major Tribes in Iraq

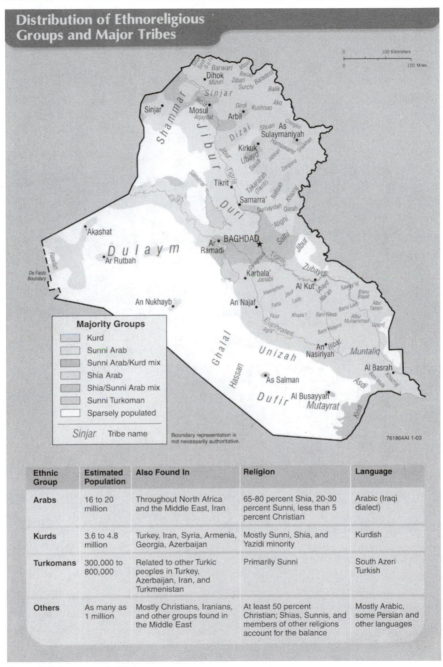

Distribution of Ethnoreligious Groups and Major Tribes

Majority Groups
- Kurd
- Sunni Arab
- Sunni Arab/Kurd mix
- Shia Arab
- Shia/Sunni Arab mix
- Sunni Turkoman
- Sparsely populated

Sinjar Tribe name

Boundary representation is not necessarily authoritative.

761864AI 1-03

Ethnic Group	Estimated Population	Also Found In	Religion	Language
Arabs	16 to 20 million	Throughout North Africa and the Middle East, Iran	65-80 percent Shia, 20-30 percent Sunni, less than 5 percent Christian	Arabic (Iraqi dialect)
Kurds	3.6 to 4.8 million	Turkey, Iran, Syria, Armenia, Georgia, Azerbaijan	Mostly Sunni, Shia, and Yazidi minority	Kurdish
Turkomans	300,000 to 800,000	Related to other Turkic peoples in Turkey, Azerbaijan, Iran, and Turkmenistan	Primarily Sunni	South Azeri Turkish
Others	As many as 1 million	Mostly Christians, Iranians, and other groups found in the Middle East	At least 50 percent Christian; Shias, Sunnis, and members of other religions account for the balance	Mostly Arabic, some Persian and other languages

Source: U.S. Government, CIA.

Map 7
Kurdish Areas in Iraq

Source: U.S. Government, CIA.

long-standing feuds over the control of Shi'ite religious shrines and revenues continued to affect Najaf, Karbala, and other cities. As the initial outbreaks of violence showed after the war, there are also tensions between the religiously oriented segment of Shi'ites led by the Iranian-backed Mohammed Baker Al-Hakim and the more moderate and pro-Western Shiites led by the Khoei family and the INC.

External Political Fracture Lines

As chapter 18 discusses, Iraq's internal fracture lines have impacts outside Iraq, as well as within it. Rather than act to stabilize or "reform" the region, they pose potential threats of regional tensions and conflicts. While it is unclear how the resulting tensions will affect Iraq's stability and nation building, there is a significant risk of outside interference in several areas.

Iran has been deeply involved in Iraqi Shi'ite religious politics ever since the Iranian revolution in 1979, and it is deeply concerned about the role that Iraqi Shi'ites will play in a new Iraqi government. Several of the emerging Shi'ite religious leaders in Iraq have been in exile in Iran, and while some have cooperated with the CPA, others have threatened to create their own militias and to seek to win political power by force. Iran may well seek to create a Shi'ite dominated Iraq to ensure that it has at least some of the features of an Islamic state, to remove a long-standing risk to its borders, and to help secure itself from U.S. pressure or intervention.

Turkey has strong economic interests in Iraq in terms of trade and oil pipeline fees. Its major concern, however, is that Iraq's Kurds do not acquire a state or sufficient autonomy to serve as the base for new efforts to create some form of "Kurdistan" that would encourage separatism and new forms of violence from Turkey's Kurds. Turkey intervened militarily in northern Iraq during the Iran-Iraq War, and on a far more serious scale after the Gulf War, to strike at violent Turkish Kurdish extremists that were using Iraq as a sanctuary. It sent small special forces teams into northern Iraq during and after the Iraq War, although they were forced to leave by U.S. troops. Turkey will almost certainly keep up its pressure on Iraq's Kurds and the emerging Iraqi central government to prevent Kurdish separatism, serve its economic interests, and protect the Iraqi Turkomans—which Turkey sees as a minority it can use as a proxy to put pressure on the Iraqi Kurds.

Saudi Arabia, Syria, and the other Sunni Arab states will seek to limit the growth of the power and influence of Iraq's Shi'ites, and to protect the role of the Sunni Arab minority. The southern Gulf states will be particularly

Table 17.1
The Detailed Fracture Lines within Iraq

Insiders versus Outsiders

- Outsiders vs. Insiders: Iraqi National Congress (INC), Iraqi National Accord (INA), Hakim—The enemy of our enemy is not our friend.

- National "interests" include conflicting political lifestyles; competing economies based on the same resource—oil—or lack thereof; sectarian and tribal enmities; and level of comfort with a prolonged U.S. military presence in the region.

- Of Iraq's 25 million people, up to 3 million have been in exile, primarily in Jordan, Europe, and the United States. Many of them represent the cream of Iraqi society— its scholars, writers, scientists, intellectuals, technicians, and craftsmen.

- Three wars and the long years of sanctions have decimated the ranks of Iraq's middle class—the talented, educated doctors, lawyers, professional bureaucrats, and civil servants—who ran the government civil service, schools, offices, and hospitals.

- Many who remained in Iraq belonged to the Ba'ath Party, but most probably joined for the perquisites a Party credential guaranteed—education, careers, and the promise of a secure future, albeit one in a dangerous political environment. Some, however, were either true Ba'athists or loyal to Saddam Hussein.

- Elements of the Iraqi opposition in exile, such as those led by the Iraqi National Congress and Ahmad Chalabi, may promise a broad coalition crossing ethnic, political, and sectarian elements, but they have no practical experience in governance and are often unpopular inside Iraq.

- The Iranian-backed Supreme Council for the Islamic Revolution in Iraq (SCIRI) led by Ayatollah Muhammad Baqr al-Hakim was the most effective outside force in creating a military challenge to Saddam Hussein and has considerable support among Iraq's Shi'ites.

- Other outside opposition groups like the Iraqi National Accord (INA), led by a former general and a Baa'th Party refugee, and other once-prominent military and political defectors will compete for power.

- More marginal outside factors include Iraq Sharif Ali, representing the Constitutional Monarchists.

- The Kurds inside Iraq are divided into two major factions, the Barzani-led Kurdish Democratic Party and the Talabani-led Patriotic Union of Kurdistan.

- There are divisions between and within the Turkoman, Assyrian, and Chaldean Christian communities inside Iraq and between them and the Kurds and other factions.

- Coalitions have an unlucky history in Iraq. None have survived long enough to govern, the last being the July 17, 1968, coalition that the militant Ba'athists and Saddam Hussein replaced two weeks later.

Political Heritage and Governance Problems

- Iraq has no democratic tradition. It did not have one under the British, under the king, or under the authoritarian military- and party-dominated regimes that have ruled Iraq since 1920.

- Iraq's political society has been ruthlessly purged since 1979. There are no surviving modern and effective political parties, and there is a serious risk that most factions and political parties will act to serve the interests of their leaders and/or followers and not the interests of the nation.

Table 17.1
(continued)

- There is no effective rule of law or functional legal system based on proper legal procedures, human rights, or commercial codes.

- There is no stable pattern of separation of the executive, legislative, and judiciary, and the military and security services have sometimes acted as independent branches of government. Presidential and parliamentary systems create the risk of electing another strong man or one man, one vote, one time.

- Iraq will have to build new political institutions that are democratic, pluralistic, transparent, and diverse. At the same time, Iraq's Kurds talk about federalism, and many outside Iraq believe the country can be easily divided among its ethnic and religious communities.

- Iraq cannot be easily divided into ethnic and religious areas for the purposes of governance. Sunni, Shi'ite, Turkoman, and Kurdish areas overlap in terms of key urban areas, oil reserves, and control of water.

- Iraq's Sunni Arabs face serious problems in dealing with democratization, pluralism, and federalism. They constitute only 17 percent of the population and have ruled Iraq since Ottoman times. The Shi'ites, however, make up 60 to 65 percent of the population. The Kurds make up 15 to 20 percent, and the Turkomans, Assyrians, and Chaldeans total 5 percent.

Restructuring a Shattered Military

- If a new Iraqi military is to reflect the shape of the new government, it must be turned into a more diverse institution, bringing the right proportion of Shi'ites, Kurds, and Turkomans into all echelons of the military.

- Some Kurds were among the senior ranks but very few.

- Shia recruits made up nearly 80 percent of the regular army but few made it into the Republican Guard or the ranks of senior officers.

- Under Saddam, the Iraqi Regular Army was stripped of its status, prestige, and weapons and subordinated in the 1980s to the Republican Guard, whose members were recruited from especially loyal Sunni Arab tribes, including the al-Ubayd, al-Jabbur, al-Shammar, and al-Ani.

- Iraq must deal with major military debts to Russia, France, China, and other states. It also must find some way to fund major imports to rebuild and modernize its forces.

- Some form of paramilitary and security forces must be created to provide local security and to help control internal and ethnic divisions that are led and largely staffed by the worst of Saddam's loyalists.

Tribal Chiefs and Leaders

- Saddam exploited the traditional tribal chiefs and leaders, especially outside the large cities and in the more isolated south and west. He restored tribal rights to administer local justice and impose taxes so long as chiefs and leaders did not contravene national law and maintained law and order. Tribal elements manned local police and security posts, while the national police and security organizations manned border posts.

- The constant suppression of Shi'ite secular leaders and well-recognized clerics created a power vacuum in the south that favored Shi'ite religious factions, including the Iranian-backed SCIRI.

Source: Compilation by author.

concerned about any alliance between Iraq's Shi'ites and Iran that could create a new power bloc in the north once the United States and Britain leave. Like Iran, Syria has every incentive to try to limit U.S. and British influence in Iraq and to seek their earliest possible departure from the country.

DEMOGRAPHIC FRACTURE LINES

The challenges in shaping a postwar Iraq go beyond politics. Despite decades of war and sanctions, Iraq has serious demographic problems that create additional fracture lines. Iraq's population rose from 5.2 million in 1950 to 6.8 million in 1960, 9.4 million in 1970, 13.0 million in 1980, 17.3 million in 1990, and 22.9 million in 2000. UN and U.S. Census Bureau estimates indicate it will rise to 30 million in 2010, 37.1 million in 2020, 43.1 million in 2030, 48.4 million in 2040, and 53.6 million in 2050.

The sheer momentum of this population increase is creating major problems in terms of scarce water and arable land resources and a decline in real per capita oil income. Per capita oil revenue was a little over $700 in 2002 versus more than $6,000 in 1980, and had dropped far more in constant dollars. To put this in perspective, Saudi Arabia with somewhat similar population growth saw its per capita income drop from around $23,820 in 1980 to $2,563 in 2001.

Iraq has a very young population. Roughly 48 percent of the population is 14 years of age or younger. In 2000, the younger job-age population between the ages of 15 and 30 totaled some 2.5 million, or 28 percent of the population, while the total "bow wave" population aged 14 years or younger totaled 9.6 million. This part of the population has never lived under any rule other than Saddam Hussein's, has seen its education collapse since the later 1980s, and has little experience with modern jobs and commerce.

ECONOMIC FRACTURE LINES

Iraq has great mid- and long-term economic potential, but its postwar government will inherit a command economy crippled by decades of grandiose mismanagement, war, and UN sanctions. There has been a steady decline in relative wealth since 1982, not 1991; and 70 percent of the cut in Iraq's GDP per capita occurred before the Gulf War. The Iraqi economy has not really functioned as a market economy. It has been ruled by an elite that treated it more as a base for a profiteering kleptocracy than for national development. Iraq's criminal justice system was corrupted by

Saddam Hussein's regime, but its civil law also failed to develop and implement a modern and effective commercial code.

Economic Strains and Weaknesses

Iraq has long imported more than half its food because of a failure to institute effective agricultural reform and invest in and modernize the agricultural sector. Its banking and commercial sectors are outdated and government-dominated. Aside from a state-controlled construction industry, it has no efficient heavy or light industry and its service sector needs major reform.

Iraq's economy has been dependent on the UN's Oil-for-Food Program and on the country's "black" market sector in order to operate. Some estimate that Iraq will still have a 50 percent to 70 percent dependence on food imports once the economy recovers. Iraq must pay for a major modernization and expansion of medical and educational services, stabilize its currency, and remove the artifacts of a command economy that has been centered around a dictatorship for three decades. It has some solid economic institutions but no real market system in terms of modern market-driven distribution, banking, insurance, or a uniform commercial code.

Although the current war may have done only limited damage to Iraq's infrastructure, the infrastructure has suffered from underfunding since the first years of the Iran-Iraq War and from a lack of recovery and investment since the Gulf War. According to one estimate, Iraq had 9,800 megawatts of generating capacity before the 1991 Gulf War; Desert Storm left it with only 380. Saddam Hussein restored about 4,800 megawatts, but the country would need as much as 14,000 megawatts to match its 1990 capacity, adjusted for population growth.

Debt, Reparations, and Contingency Contracts

There are many estimates of Iraq's debt and reparations burden. An analysis by Frederick Barton and Bathsheba Crocker of CSIS (table 17.2) shows a total of $127 billion in debt (including $47 billion in interest), $320 billion in reparations claims ($148 billion settled), and some $57 billion in pending contracts the regime signed with nations like Russia and the Netherlands.

These burdens could cripple any hope of recovery even more than the Treaty of Versailles and World War I reparations claims crippled the economy and political stability of Weimar Germany. To put them in perspective, U.S. intelligence estimates that in 2002 the entire GDP of Iraq was only $28.6 billion at purchasing power parity rates, and only $15.5 billion

Table 17.2
Iraq's Financial Burden

Total debt: $127 billion

- Interest: $47 billion
- Gulf states: $30 billion
- Kuwait: $17 billion
- Russia: $12 billion
- Bulgaria: $1 billion
- Turkey: $800 million
- Poland: $500 million
- Jordan: $295 million
- Morocco: $32 million
- Hungary: $17 million
- France, Egypt, Others: ?

Pending contracts: $57.2 billion

- Russia: $52 billion (90 percent)
- Netherlands: $3.6 billion (6 percent)
- Egypt: $740 million
- China: $80 million

Reparations (less claims from Iran-Iraq War): $320 billion claimed

- $148 billion settled
- $172 billion unsettled
- Status of interest on payments unsettled

Source: Frederick Barton and Sheba Crocker, *A Wiser Peace: An Action Strategy for a Post-Conflict Iraq* (Washington, D.C.: CSIS, January 2003; updated May 2003).

at market exchange rates. Iraq's total merchandise exports were only $13 billion for 2002, of which $12.3 billion were oil export revenues—including the estimated value of some $3 billion worth of smuggled oil.

ENERGY AND OIL EXPORT FRACTURE LINES

The glue that will hold Iraq together, or the wealth that will divide it, is the revenue from petroleum and petroleum-related exports. Oil underpins Iraq's exports, market economy, and government revenues. Iraqi oil revenues are critical to the country's development, as is the proper sharing of such revenues to any hope of its political stability. Iraq's oil wealth is acutely limited in comparison to the past. The U.S. Department of Energy's Energy Information Administration (EIA) estimates that Iraq's oil revenues peaked at $57.8 billion in 2000 dollars in 1980. They were only $15 billion in 2001, and $12.3 billion in 2002. They would have been only $15.7 billion in 2003 with no war and no discount for smuggling.

At the same time, Iraq's oil reserves give it immense future potential. The EIA estimates that Iraq contains 112 billion barrels of proven oil reserves, the second-largest proven oil reserve in the world (behind Saudi Arabia). Iraq's true resource potential may be far greater than this, however, as the country is largely (90 percent or so) unexplored due to years of war and sanctions. Deep oil-bearing formations located mainly in the vast western desert region could yield large additional oil resources (possibly another 100 billion barrels).

The National Iraqi Oil Company (NIOC) has a large number of competent technocrats and managers, and had only a light top layer of thugs and killers under Saddam Hussein. Iraq has not had adequate development funding, planning, and management since 1982, however—the year during the Iran-Iraq War when Syria closed its pipeline to Iraq and Iraq ran out of money. UN surveys by Saybolt are only preliminary but indicate that Iraq's fields suffer from waterflooding and overpumping in most areas, and that before the war only 24 of 73 fields were working and 12 percent to 40 percent of the oil wells were at risk.

Iraqi Oil Development Needs

Iraq needs major funding to rehabilitate and modernize its oil fields, as well as to pay for any wartime damage. At best, its present economic production capacity is 2.8 million bbl/d (barrels per day) and possibly only 2.5 million bbl/d. This amounts to about 3 percent of world markets and makes it roughly equivalent to Nigeria.

There is no way to predict the short- and mid-term future of Iraqi oil development. Experts simply have too little knowledge about Iraq's problems and about investment priorities, costs, and opportunities. An Iraqi study in 1996 claimed it would cost $35 billion to increase production capacity to 3.5 million bbl/d. Other sources estimate it would take $7 billion and a minimum of three years to increase capacity to that level, and $20 billion plus to raise capacity to 6 million bbl/d by 2010.

In December 2002, the Council of Foreign Relations and the Baker Institute released a report that concluded the following:

- Iraq's oil sector infrastructure was being held together by "Band-Aids" and was experiencing a production decline rate of 100,000 bbl/d per year.

- Increasing Iraqi oil production would require "massive repairs and reconstruction...costing several billions of dollars and taking months if not years."

- The costs of repairing existing oil export installations would be around $5 billion, while restoring Iraqi oil production to pre-1990 levels would cost an additional $5 billion, plus $3 billion per year in annual operating costs.

- Outside funds and large-scale investment by international oil companies would be needed; existing oil contracts would need to be clarified and resolved in order to rebuild Iraq's oil industry, with any "prolonged legal conflicts over contracts" possibly "delay[ing] the development of important fields in Iraq."

- Any "sudden or prolonged shutdown" of Iraq's oil industry could result in long-term reservoir damage.

- Iraq's oil facilities could easily be damaged during any domestic unrest or military operations.

Given these problems, it is unrealistic to expect massive rises in oil export earnings in the near future. According to the *Middle East Economic Survey*, Iraq's oil sector suffers from years of poor oil reservoir management; corrosion problems at various oil facilities; deterioration of water injection facilities; lack of spare parts, materials, equipment, etc.; and damage to oil storage and pumping facilities requiring major investment. MEES does estimate, however, that Iraq could reach a production capacity of 4.2 million bbl/d within three years at a cost of $3.5 billion, and a production capacity of 4.5–6.0 million bbl/d within seven years.

Contingency Contracts Signed under Saddam

The challenge of rebuilding and expanding Iraq's petroleum industry and dividing up its resources and revenues is compounded by another problem. The EIA reports that Saddam Hussein's regime signed several multibillion dollar deals with foreign oil companies, mainly from China, France, and Russia. Deutsche Bank estimates the contracts are worth a total of $38 billion for new field development—with a potential production capacity of 4.7 million bbl/d.

In 1992, Iraq announced plans to increase its oil production capacity to more than 6.3 million bbl/d following the lifting of UN sanctions. This plan, which was to be accomplished in three phases over a five-year period, assumed the availability of billions of dollars of foreign investment. Much of the production was to come from developing giant fields in the south (Halfaya, Majnoon, Bin Umar, West Qurnah), plus the Mishrif reservoir (Luhais, North and South Rumaylah, Zubair, etc.), East Baghdad, and others.

The EIA estimates that Russia signed a $3.7 billion, 23-year deal with Saddam's regime to rehabilitate Iraqi oilfields, particularly the 11-billion-barrel to 15-billion-barrel West Qurna field (located west of Basra near the Rumaylah field). In October 2001, a joint Russian-Belarus oil company, Slavneft, signed a $52 million service contract with Iraq to develop the 2-billion-barrel Suba-Luhais field in southern Iraq. Full development of the Suba-Luhais field could result in production of 100,000 bbl/d (35° API) at a cost of $300 million over a period of three years.

These contracts may not have been signed under duress, but they certainly were intended to buy political support for Saddam in freeing Iraq from sanctions. The economic competitiveness of the French and Russia contracts is unclear, and Iraq may have a strong interest in renegotiating them.

The Ethnic Fracture Lines of Oil Development and Control

The divisions between Kurds, Sunnis, and Shi'ites could greatly complicate the future development of Iraq's present fields, much less its proven and unproven reserves. Although some of the current fields are in Sunni areas and major new potential reserves exist in the Sunni west, Iraq's proven oil reserves are not distributed evenly throughout the country. In fact, before Iraq's invasion of Kuwait in 1990, about two-thirds of Iraq's production was coming out of the southern fields of Rumaylah, Zubair, and Nahr Umr in Shi'ite areas. Other potentially huge fields such as Majnoon and West Qurna are also located in the southern part of the country.

The EIA data on these fields show that recently Iraq's main exports of crude oil have come from the country's two largest active fields: Rumaylah and Kirkuk. Iraq clearly needs investment to rehabilitate and modernize these fields, as well as develop others, but the cost and time required can only be guessed at.

Iraq also needs money to develop its gas resources to allow it to meet domestic energy demand while freeing oil for export and to restore and expand its downstream operations. Iraq's refining capacity in January 2003 was about 417,000 bbl/d, compared to a pre-Gulf War nameplate capacity of 700,000 bbl/d. Iraq has 10 refineries and topping units. The largest are the 150,000-bbl/d Baiji North, 140,000-bbl/d (or higher) Basra, and 100,000-bbl/d Daura plants.

Iraq needs to create a modern downstream sector. The country currently lacks light-end products and relies on low-quality gasoline. The

EIA reports that Baiji in northern Iraq as well as the refineries at Basra, Daura, and Nasiryah were severely damaged during the Gulf War. Rising pollution levels because of a lack of water treatment facilities are also problems for Iraq's refining sector. Iraq's prewar/post-sanction plans called for attracting foreign investment to perform refinery upgrades (Iraq identified dozens of such projects) and for a new $1 billion, 290,000-bbl/d "central" refinery near Babylon.

The Fracture Lines of Oil and Gas Exports

The movement of Iraqi oil creates additional ethnic and international fracture lines. Iraq's most efficient and profitable shipping route is through the oil terminals in the Gulf to Asia, but then no country other than Iraq benefits. The Kirkuk-Ceyhan pipeline goes through the Kurdish area but favors Turkey. The Kirkuk-Banias pipeline favors Syria. Iraq's oil shipments to Jordan have been a politically motivated subsidy. Smuggling oil by truck into Turkey and by barge through Iranian waters was one result of UN sanctions. Each nation can be expected to put some form of political pressure on Iraq to ship oil in ways that serve their own interests.

The war itself does not seem to have damaged Iraq's export facilities, but postwar looting and sabotage have done such damage. In addition, Iraq's oil facilities and export capabilities still reflect damage from the Gulf War and have suffered years of underinvestment since the beginning of the Iran-Iraq War and the early 1980s. The EIA reports that the 600-mile, 40-inch Kirkuk-Ceyhan pipeline is Iraq's largest operable crude export pipeline. It has a design capacity of 1.1 million bbl/d, but reportedly can handle only around 900,000 bbl/d. A second, parallel, 46-inch line has an optimal capacity of 500,000 bbl/d and was designed to carry Basra Regular exports, but at last report was inoperable. The two parallel lines have a combined design capacity of 1.5–1.6 million bbl/d.

Iraq has three tanker terminals in the Gulf—at Mina al-Bakr, Khor al-Amaya, and Khor az-Zubair (which mainly handles dry goods and minimal oil volumes).These are Iraq's only means of exporting without paying a premium for shipping from a foreign pipeline. Mina al-Bakr is Iraq's largest oil terminal, with four 400,000-bbl/d capacity berths capable of handling very large crude carriers (VLCCs). Gulf War damage to this terminal has been largely repaired and the terminal can handle up to 1.2–1.3 million bbl/d. A full return to Mina al-Bakr's nameplate capacity apparently would require extensive infrastructure repairs. Mina al-Bakr is also constrained by a shortage of storage and oil processing facilities, most of which were destroyed in the Gulf War.

Map 8
Iraq's Oil Infrastructure

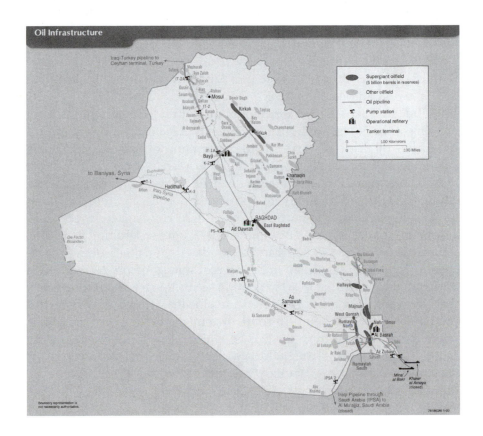

Source: U.S. Government, CIA.

The EIA reports that Iraq's Khor al-Amaya terminal was heavily damaged during the Iran-Iraq War (and completely destroyed during Operation Desert Storm in 1991) and has been out of commission since then. As of March 2001, reports indicated that Iraq had largely completed repairing two berths at Khor al-Amaya. Once repairs are completed, Iraq projects that the terminal's capacity will rise to 1.2 million bbl/d.

Iraq's pipelines through Kuwait and Saudi Arabia have been shut since the Gulf War, and its only other line goes through Syria. On August 20, 1998, Iraq and Syria signed a memorandum of understanding for the reopening of the 50-year-old, rusting, Banias oil pipeline from Iraq's northern Kirkuk oil fields to Syria's Mediterranean port of Banias (and Tripoli, Lebanon). The pipeline had been shut for 17 years.

Iraq does have an internal pipeline network that cuts across its internal ethnic and religious divisions. To optimize export capabilities (i.e., to allow oil shipments to the north or south), Iraq constructed a reversible, 1.4-million-bbl/d "Strategic Pipeline" in 1975, but the resulting flow of oil reached only about 120,000 barrels per day. Iraq's other options have been providing subsidized oil to Jordan and smuggling products through Turkey and Iran, neither of which option seems to have much future now that the regime has gone. The reversible pipeline consists of two parallel 700,000-bbl/d lines. The north-south system allows for northern Kirkuk crude to be exported from the Persian Gulf and for southern Rumaylah crudes to be shipped through Turkey. The pipeline was disabled during the Gulf War after the K-3 pumping station at Haditha as well as four additional southern pumping stations were destroyed.

Gas exports are also an issue. The EIA reports that Iraq has a major natural gas pipeline with the capacity to supply around 240 MMcf/d (million cubic feet per day) to Baghdad from the West Qurna field. The 48-inch line was commissioned in November 1988; phases II and III of the project, meant to supply Turkey, were never completed due to war and sanctions.

Iraq's Northern Area Gas Project, which came online in 1983, was damaged during the Gulf War and the Kurdish rebellion of March 1991. The system supplied liquefied petroleum gas (LPG) to Baghdad and other Iraqi cities, as well as dry gas and sulfur to power stations and industrial plants. Iraq also has a Southern Area Gas Project that was completed in 1985 and came online in 1990. Natural gas also used to be pumped from Rumaylah into northern Kuwait via a 40-inch, 105-mile pipeline. The gas was used to supply Kuwaiti power stations and LPG plants, but was halted following Iraq's invasion of Kuwait in August 1990.

TRANSPARENCY AND CONSPIRACY THEORIES

The challenges can be met in a wide variety of ways. A key problem the United States and outside powers face, however, is that no single issue is more likely to arouse Iraqi distrust and conspiracy theories, and any successful nation-building effort must do much more than find a economically and technically valid set of solutions. Iraqis must believe that the solutions are honest and in Iraq's interests, and, wherever possible, formulated by Iraqis.

Rebuilding and expanding Iraq's energy sector is also the only path to creating a source of money that can fund an Iraqi federal government, and act as the financial glue that ties the country together. At the same time, no resource is more attractive to try to dominate or steal, and Iraq's heritage as a functional kleptocracy—with no real history of foreign investment or popular experience with the market system and stock markets—makes any market-driven solution or form of privatization extremely suspect. Power struggles, corruption, and efforts to seize any privatized part of the energy sector are inevitable.

The United States virtually had to award emergency contracts to U.S. firms in the period immediately after the war to get production under way again and to deal with the impact of years of underfunding, and the looting following the war. It is not clear, however, that the United States is prepared for the political reality at hand—that transparent management of every detail of this aspect of nation building is critical; that the United States must now do everything possible to prove that neither it nor Britain will benefit from the postwar development of the energy sector; and that the political aspects of nation building are inevitably tied to how energy money and resources are to be allocated.[5]

THE NEW FRACTURE LINES CAUSED BY DISARMAMENT AND THE NEED TO REBUILD IRAQI MILITARY FORCES

Another set of fracture lines emerges out of the need to both disarm Iraq of its weapons of mass destruction and to rebuild its conventional forces to give it new capabilities for self-defense. The fact that the United States and Britain did not find large "smoking guns" in the form of Iraqi forces capable of using chemical and biological weapons, and/or a major nuclear weapons development effort, has led many to believe that Iraq was not a serious proliferators despite eight years of discoveries by UNSCOM and the IAEA and new discoveries by UNMOVIC.

It seems likely that the United States and Britain will gradually find evidence that Iraq continued to research and develop weapons of mass destruction at the time the Iraq War began, and that it probably dispersed and concealed some weapons or assets to hide them from UNMOVIC. It is also possible, however, that Iraq had adopted a different strategy: continuing covert research; destroying its overt holdings of weapons; buying dual-use facilities and equipment it could later devote to WMD production; and, finally, trying to both break out of UN sanctions and defer a U.S. and British attack. If so, one lesson of the aftermath of the war is that the failure of the United States and Britain to internationalize the WMD disarmament effort from the start may lead many countries and experts to question the validity of whatever the Americans and British find, and lead others to question whether Iraq was ever a serious threat.

The practical lessons of intelligence and targeting have been discussed earlier. Iraq will face further fracture lines because it has lost many of its conventional forces and will see most of its remaining missile and WMD assets destroyed. It will still exist in a heavily armed neighborhood, however, where powers like Israel, Iran, Pakistan, and Syria have their own weapons of mass destruction. Regardless of any U.S. and British disarmament efforts, Iraq will also retain a large amount of human capital in terms of expert knowledge about how to build and use weapons of mass destruction, and any economic development program will give it new dual-use facilities that presumably will not be under UN inspection.

The full nature of the problems to come in rebuilding Iraq's conventional forces remains unclear. Intense land and air combat and the use of some 18,000 precision weapons have almost certainly left Iraq with limited defense capability. When these effects are combined with the near destruction of the Republican Guard, the massive air and surface-base air defense losses, and massive desertions in the regular forces, the net result would seem to be that Iraq has lost the vast majority of its conventional war-fighting capabilities.

The burden of rearming Iraq will also add to all of the economic and energy barriers discussed earlier. It seems extremely unlikely that Iraq will ever return to the militarism it had before the Gulf War. Iraq was spending some 20 percent of its GNP and 30 percent of its government revenues on military forces in the late 1970s before the Iran-Iraq War. During the most intense periods of that war, the percentages rose to some 45 percent of GNP and 50 percent of government revenues.[6]

Iraqi arms imports averaged more than 35 percent of all imports in the late 1970s and roughly 60 percent of all imports in the 1980s.[7] According to U.S. estimates, Iraq spent some $29.7 billion on arms imports during 1984–1988: $15.4 billion on arms imports from the former Soviet Union; $3.1 billion from France; $2.8 billion from China; $30 million from the UK; $675 million from West Germany; $675 million from Czechoslovakia; $750 million from Poland; $370 million from Italy; $650 million from Bulgaria; and $5.2 billion from other countries—largely North Korea and Vietnam.[8]

If one looks at the period between 1983 and 1990, the "run-up" to the Gulf War, and considers only arms purchases in excess of $50 million, another source indicates that Iraq imported some $39.6 billion worth of major arms—$19.5 billion from the Soviet Union; $6.4 billion from major West European nations; $6.4 billion from other European nations; $4.0 billion from China; and $3.2 billion from all other nations. (The United States sold less than $50 million worth.) Even though Iraq decisively won the Iran-Iraq War by August of 1988, it still placed orders for $9.97 billion worth of new arms between 1987 and 1990, virtually all with the Soviet Union and Europe.[9]

Nevertheless, after the UN imposed an embargo in the summer of 1990, Iraq had only several hundred million dollars worth of smuggled arms imports, and it lost many during the Iraq War. In contrast, Saudi Arabia alone imported some $65.8 billion worth of arms during 1994–2001, and Iran imported $3.0 billion. The smaller southern Gulf states imported $19.1 billion.[10] Given the fact that Iran is a major proliferator, the challenges of rebuilding an Iraqi security structure, war-fighting capability, and deterrent are anything but easy.

As a result, the problems in rebuilding Iraqi military forces will be affected not only by the political and economic fracture lines discussed earlier; they will be affected by the following challenges to both Iraq and the U.S. and British effort to turn their military victory into a more stable structure of security within Iraq and the region.

- How can Iraq's conventional military capabilities be rebuilt? What force levels, arms modernization, and costs are involved?

- How does one disarm a nation like Iraq that has practical experience in making and using weapons of mass destruction? How does one "disarm" Iraq's intellectual capital and deny it the future capability to make use of what will be steadily growing dual-use facilities?

- How can the "new" Iraqi state deal with the mid- and long-term impact of Israeli, Syrian, Iranian, Pakistani, and Indian proliferation?

- How can Iraq's military and paramilitary forces be restructured to provide security and prevent factional forces or warlords?

- How can these forces be restructured to support a transition to a true Iraqi rule of law, the enforcement of human rights, and national police activity?

- Finally, the issue arises as to whether the United States and UK will guarantee Iraq suitable security in a region where key neighbors like Iran and Syria are major proliferators and an exposed Iraq could be vulnerable to pressure and attack.

At least two lessons can be drawn from this experience. First, it is impossible to disarm a state of weapons of mass destruction as long as it retains the intellectual capital to build and use such weapons and as long as its economy provides large-scale dual-use facilities that can be used to produce such weapons. The second lesson is that the security aspects of nation building require the victors in modern wars to determine how to rearm their opponent—a challenge that will prove anything but easy.

The United States may well have made a serious mistake in mid-May 2003 when it dismissed the entire regular structure of the Iraqi armed forces with a month's pay. Iraqi officers had already demanded a role in shaping Iraq's future. The dismissal treated them as an extension of Saddam and the Ba'ath's rule, however, rather than as patriots who had fought for their country. It also added several hundred thousand young men to the labor pool when there were virtually no jobs, and it effectively told all officers of the rank of colonel and above that they had no future in a post-Saddam environment. At the same time, it implied to all Iraqis that the new Iraq Army might be so weak that Iraq would remain little more than a client of the United States and Britain in the face of the threat from Iran and possible future intervention by Turkey.[11]

The United States stated later that it would pay the dismissed soldiers a stipend. But it also indicated that it would try to create a new Iraqi Army from the ground up and that this would be largely an internal security force of some 40,000 men.[12] Like many other aspects of the initial U.S. nation-building effort, the end result was a plan that made no coherent effort to build on existing capabilities—and instead excluded many potentially competent personnel at the possible cost of making them opponents or enemies—and that took no account of Iraqi nationalism. A plan for a military force so small that it would obviously be unable to deal with Iran, a Turkish incursion, or any other regional threat is scarcely one that will reassure Iraqis. It also, by default, leaves Iraq obviously dependent on the occupying powers for its security. Small beginnings are one thing; lasting strategic dependence is another.

LESSONS FOR PEACEMAKING AND NATION BUILDING

All of these issues and problems reinforce the lesson that modern war-fighting must be ready to make the transition from war to peacemaking and nation building as combat actually proceeds and as each area is liberated. Another lesson is the need to prepare the country involved, its people, the nations around it, and the world for the concept of peacemaking and nation building that will be employed. This may not always win popular support. But it will greatly reduce many of the fears and conspiracy theories that arise in the absence of any clear plan and public statements. In this sense, no psychological operation is complete that only focuses on winning the war; "psyops" must give equal weight to preparation for peacemaking and winning the peace.

This lesson must be acted upon in a world that has moved well beyond the point where it will tolerate the delays and problems in dealing with humanitarian needs, reconstruction, and nation building that occurred in Germany and Japan after World War II. The United States and the West cannot afford to ignore the fact that an era of asymmetric warfare will also be an era of political warfare in which true victory means not only successful conflict termination but defeating enemy ideologies and political groups by creating stable successor governments and societies. Cutting one head off the Hydra may be militarily impressive, but it has little grand strategic purpose. All it does is to force the enemy to mutate or create new enemies for the future.

A dependence on "coalitions of the willing" also means that the United States must recognize that its future ability to form coalitions requires those who actively participate in a conflict to believe in the justice and adequacy of the peace. The same changes in the morality of war that force powers like the United States to fight in ways that minimize civilian casualties and collateral damage also force them to commit themselves to shaping the peace in ways that win the approval of the peoples of the nations they defeat, the nations around them, their coalition partners, and the world. There is no significant operational difference in grand strategic terms between altruism and pragmatism.

Here it is well worth noting the comments of Carl Bildt, one of the few voices with great practical experience in nation building, about the broader lessons of nation building for Iraq and for any war to come. Looking at the situation in Iraq immediately after the fall of Baghdad, Bildt outlined seven major lessons based on his experience in the Balkans. All now seem valid in Iraq, and they seem likely to be equally valid in any future conflicts:[13]

Lesson 1: It is imperative to establish a secure environment very fast. In Bosnia, we failed in the critical transfer of territories in Sarajevo. In Kosovo, the mandate for the troops was clearer, but we still failed to protect minorities. In both cases, we still suffer from the consequences of these initial failures. In Afghanistan there are grave question marks over the consequences of limiting the international security presence to Kabul. As long as the gun remains the fastest way to power and property, there simply will not be room for democratic politics and entrepreneurship. With national police in disarray and international police always taking time to recruit, there is no alternative to using soldiers and armies to keep order.

Lesson 2: The central challenge is not reconstruction, but state-building. Reconstruction of the physical scars of war is certainly important, and it can be costly and take time. But building a political infrastructure that unites competing forces and ensures some sort of order, and an infrastructure of economic governance that promotes jobs and growth, is far more complex. Priorities must be right.

Lesson 3: To build a state, you need to know what state to build. Normally this requires some sort of a peace agreement or constitution. When this is not the case, as in Kosovo, any initial success risks being short-lived. In the Balkans, we have seen the immense challenge of doing so in a multiethnic environment. We must recognize that Iraq has some issues in common with other former parts of the Ottoman Empire, such as Kosovo and the Kurdish region.

Iraq's potential for disintegration is obvious, as are the consequences if this were to happen. Thus there has to be an early and fast agreement on a constitutional structure that will unite Arabs, Kurds, Turkmen, and Assyrians of different beliefs in a state structure acceptable to them all.

Lesson 4: While humanitarian problems are always in the forefront in the initial phase, it is dangerous to let them predominate over the long-term issues. There must be an early focus on economic questions such as currency, customs, taxation systems, commercial law, banking, debt restructuring, and accessing international capital markets.

The sanctions that were provoked by Saddam Hussein have destroyed much of Iraq's economy. Because Iraq has experienced a population explosion, oil income per capita is unlikely to be substantially more than a tenth of what it was in the early 1980s. Job creation and bringing back a vibrant middle class are the keys to long-term stability.

Lesson 5: There has to be a benevolent regional environment. In the Balkans, regime change in Zagreb and Belgrade was key to improving prospects in Bosnia and Kosovo; in Afghanistan, the open or tacit cooperation of Pakistan and Iran is critical. If neighbors try to destabilize, they will sooner or later succeed.

Iraq is now a fragile zone in one of the most volatile areas of the world. Just about everyone recognizes that if the liberation of Iraq from tyranny is not followed by the liberation of Palestine from occupation (giving true security to Israel, too), the presence of U.S. and other NATO forces in Iraq will be an extremely challenging operation.

Lesson 6: Nation building takes a longer time, and requires more resources, than most initially believe. As the first High Representative in Bosnia, I was told that everything should be concluded within a year. When the folly of this was recognized, a new deadline of two years was given. But five years after that has expired, the fourth High Representative is hardly less busy than the first. Bosnia and Kosovo might be easy cases compared with Afghanistan and Iraq. Peace-building requires an abundance of patience.

Lesson 7: The greater the international support, the easier the process. If there is international disagreement over the state-building process, this sooner or later risks translating into conflicts in the country in question. Some sort of UN framework normally helps, although it is not a guarantee. Building peace is a far more fragile, complex, costly, and drawn-out process than fighting a war. So a peace coalition normally needs to be much broader than a war coalition.

There is no current way to determine how much the United States and Britain can do now to act upon these lessons or to predict how much they can accomplish in helping Iraq while they still have a dominant impact on the country's development. The divisions and fracture lines within Iraq run so deep that achieving a stable path toward unity, pluralism, and economic development will take years—if not a decade.

Events may prove that the United States and Britain do not succeed in nation building. Yet, events may well prove that U.S. and British efforts do succeed because Iraqis themselves come to want them to succeed. If so, the Iraqi people will continue to seek these goals years after U.S. and British forces have left. Everything will ultimately depend on the level and quality of international effort over time, and above all, on whether the nation-building effort can heal enough of Iraq's fracture lines to produce a lasting change in Iraqi goals and perceptions.

Notes

[1] DOD news briefing. Participating were Lawrence Di Rita, acting assistant secretary of defense for public affairs, and Gen. John Abizaid, commander, U.S. Central Command, July 16, 2003. Department of Defense transcript, www.defenselink.mil/transcripts/2003/tr20030716-0401.html.

[2] Interview, senior U.S. government official; Tomas E. Ricks, "Hussein's Two Sons Killed in Firefight with US Troops," *Washington Post*, July 23, 2003.

[3] John Hamre, Frederick Barton, Bathsheba Crocker, Johanna Mendelson-Forman, and Robert Orr, "Iraq's Post-Conflict Reconstruction: A Field Review and Recommendations—Report of the Iraq Reconstruction Assessment Mission, June 27–July 7, 2003" (Washington, D.C.: CSIS, July 17, 2003).

[4] Quotes taken from transcript of press briefing by Army Maj. Gen. Carl Strock, deputy director of operations for the Coalition Provisional Authority, and Andrew Bearpark, director of regional services for the Coalition Provisional Authority, Monday, July 7, 2003, Coalition Provisional Authority Live Video-teleconference briefing from Baghdad, Iraq.

[5] Colum Lynch, "Potential Iraq Donors Seek Great Accountability from US on Oil Plans," *Washington Post*, June 26, 2003, p. 16; L. Paul Bremer, "Operation Iraqi Prosperity," *Wall Street Journal*, June 20, 2003; Michael Slackman, "Ruled by Rumors in Iraq," *Los Angeles Times*, June 5, 2003.

[6] U.S. Department of State, *World Military Expenditures and Arms Transfers, 1989* (Washington, D.C.: GPO, 1990), p. 51.

[7] Ibid., p. 93.

[8] Ibid.

[9] Richard F. Grimmett, *Conventional Arms Transfers to the Third World, 1983–1990* (Washington, D.C., Congressional Research Service 91-578F, August 2, 1991), pp. 54 and 67.

[10] _____, *Conventional Arms Transfers to Developing Nations, 1994–2001* (Washington, D.C.: Congressional Research Service RL31529, August 6, 2002), p. 58.

[11] Ceasar C. Soriano, "Iraqi Troops Now Request Postwar Roles," *USA Today*, May 16, 2003, p. 16.

[12] Riad Kahwaji and Barabara Opall-Rome, "Rebuilding Iraq's Military," *Defense News*, June 2, 2003.

[13] This list, with minor edits, is taken from Carl Bildt, "Hard-earned Lessons on Nation Building: Seven Ways to Rebuild Iraq," *International Herald Tribune*, May 7, 2003, p. 6.

CHAPTER EIGHTEEN

GRAND STRATEGY:
THE OUTCOME OF THE IRAQ WAR
AND THE NEW OLD MIDDLE EAST

The broader lessons of grand strategy are even more speculative than the future of nation building in Iraq. It seems increasingly likely, however, that the Iraq War will provide yet another iteration of the lesson that small wars have fewer transformational effects on the regions where they are fought than many of their protagonists thought in choosing to fight such wars. In fact, this is often true of much larger wars as well. The war to make the world safe for democracy did not; and the war to end all wars began more wars than it ended.

In the case of the Iraq War, some neoconservatives and liberals felt before and immediately after the war that it would produce fundamental changes in the Middle East region that would put an end to old regimes and many of the region's tensions and conflicts. In contrast, some Arabists reversed the cloak of Samuel Huntington and warned of "clashes of civilization" and outbreaks of terrorism. Like most developments in history, the ultimate reality is likely to be different. The impact of the war on the region is likely to be more limited and more mixed. In fact, the "new" postwar Middle East may look surprisingly like the old.

AN EXAMPLE OF WHAT?

One key problem is the one raised in the previous chapter. Nation building takes time. It may be years before Iraq is an example of anything other than U.S. military strength, and it is very unclear what Iraq will become:

- At a minimum, Iraq will be a work in progress for several years. It will be a work that outside powers will seek to influence in political and economic terms, with pressures from the United Nations to internationalize the nation-building effort, pressure from the United States to maintain control while internationalizing the border, and French, Russian, and other pressures to serve their respective commercial interests and weaken U.S. influence. Turkey, Iran, Syria, and the southern Gulf states will compete for influence and control over Iraq almost regardless of what government emerges.

- If Iraq becomes hostile to the U.S.-led nation-building effort, or if there is a serious guerrilla war, the initial U.S. military victory may be seen as a defeat and the nation building as a failed occupation. The worst case would be a U.S. and British departure in the face of Iraqi popular hostility and/or guerrilla war. The second worst case, however, would be to stay at the cost of doing so by force, in at least part of the country, and without winning a popular mandate.

- If Iraq becomes a weak, client democracy, the new regime will do nothing more than appear to validate all of the regional conspiracy theories that see the United States as an aggressive power with neo-imperialist goals and the desire to take over Iraq's oil resources.

- If Iraq emerges as weak and divided, with feuding or warring Kurdish, Sunni, and Shi'ite factions, this will create a dangerous power vacuum. At a minimum, it will lead Turkey, Iran, Syria, and the southern Gulf states to intensify their competition for influence and control.

- If Iraq should tilt toward Iran and/or Syria, or toward any form of theocratic state, this would create a new pattern of instability in the Middle East.

- If Iraq becomes a strong and united state willing to act as a "have power" and concentrate on internal development, it will still have to rebuild its military forces and rearm. Even if Iraq is peaceful and democratic, rebuilding its military will lead to tensions with some of its neighbors.

- No matter what Iraq becomes politically, much depends on the level of success in economic development, energy development, and creating security and a rule of law for ordinary Iraqis. Democracy and political stability are certainly important, but Iraq's impact as an example will depend at least as much on the physical and economic well-being of its people.

- The problem of proliferation has become an issue in itself. The political controversies regarding U.S. and British claims about Iraqi activity, and the failure to make early discoveries of weapons of mass destruction, have undercut the credibility of the reasons for going to war and the entire effort to halt and counter proliferation. Iraq will be an even weaker example of dealing with the problems of proliferation if other regional powers like Iran continue to proliferate with little meaningful outside interference.

It is far too early to know which future Iraq will pursue or how soon the choice of this future will be apparent. It also is far too early to know how the Iraqi people will view the U.S. and British role in shaping that future. It now seems that most are grateful for Saddam's fall, but not for the war or for American political and economic influence over the peace process. The images of the Second Intifada, the problems of trying to establish a balance among Iraq's factions, and the natural desire for instant economic benefits are all problems in Iraqi perceptions of the United States and Britain. So are the many Iraqi conspiracy theories about the United States' role in shaping Iraq's oil industry and contracts.

Even if the United States succeeds in putting Iraq on the road to successful nation building, success does not necessarily mean popularity and gratitude. Foreign intervention of this kind has rarely, if ever, met with broad approval, and Iraq remains a very different culture, society, and ethnic/religious mix. In any case, Iraq cannot be an example of anything to the region other than the military defeat of a tyrant until it is (1) clearly Iraq for the Iraqis and (2) clearly successful. It is hard to see how this can take less than a few years.

ISRAEL AND THE SECOND INTIFADA

There is no reason to assume that the "new" Iraq will be a major military threat to Israel or willing to subsidize Palestinian suicide bombers. At the same time, there is no reason to assume that Iraq will emerge as pro-Israel unless it comes under intense pressure from the United States or there is a settlement to the Israeli-Palestinian conflict. Iraqis have seen all of the same images of the Second Intifada in the Arab media as other Arabs, and those images will not become more favorable because Saddam has fallen. If anything, those same images are likely to reinforce any resentment of the United States.

Many in the Arab world see the end of the Iraq War as the time for more American action to resolve the Arab-Israeli conflict and to advance the "road map" of a peace plan developed by the United Nations, European Union, Britain, and the United States. The United States has already begun such an effort. It is clear that the Bush administration's wartime agreement with Prime Minister Blair has led the United States to make another major attempt at advancing a peace plan. It is also clear that American officials have become more sensitive to Arab concerns in the region and the need to defuse the Second Intifada, both to maintain U.S. alliances in the Arab world and to reduce Arab hostility toward the United States.

Making progress will be extremely difficult, however—with or without true Palestinian reform. Israel sees deep flaws in the "road map," and Palestinian "acceptance" of it is probably more a matter of tactical maneuver than any real support. The United States also will not sacrifice Israel's interests, and it is unclear whether the United States will take enough action to really alter Israeli-Palestinian tensions or the broader tensions between Israel and the Arab world. There is a good chance that the Second Intifada will continue, and even intensify, regardless of such U.S. efforts and the outcome of the Iraq War.

IRAN

Iran has interests in both Iraq and the region different from those of the United States. On the one hand, Iran has seen a key threat disappear. On the other hand, Iran has seen America triumphant on its borders and heard U.S. rhetoric that is at least indirectly threatening. Although former Iranian president Ali Akbar Hashemi Rafsanjani, among others, talked about finding some way to legitimize a political dialogue with the United States after the war, the internal tensions in Iran have prevented any progress, as has the reluctance of the Bush administration to deal with the Iranian government. There has been no informal U.S.-Iranian dialogue of the kind that led to informal cooperation in Afghanistan; the United States has relied more on threats. The end result may deter Iran from some adventures, but it could provoke it into others. It could also exacerbate the many fault lines within Iranian politics.

Iran will not stand aside from Iraq. Iran has a long-standing interest in Iraqi Shi'ite religious politics and in the role and power of Shi'ites in Iraqi society and politics. This interest encompasses religion (key shrines and seminars are in Iraq), ideology (Iran favors a more theological Shi'ite power structure), security (avoiding another war and limiting the impact of a U.S. presence on its border and in the Gulf), political power (a weak Iraq is a strong Iran in terms of Gulf power politics,), energy (oil production and quotas), and the economy (Iran has reparations claims left over from the Iran-Iraq War and would like to clear the Shatt Al Arab.)

The Iranian "game" in Iraq is almost certain to be to play pro-Iranian Shi'ites off against other factions, seeking to create a friendly and Shi'ite-dominated Iraq. Certainly, Iran has done little to encourage SCIRI and other pro-Iranian Shi'ites to cooperate with the U.S. nation-building effort in Iraq, and it is unlikely to do so unless it sees a clear tactical value in doing so. Iran will be careful because of its own military weakness, its need to maintain friendly relations with the southern Gulf states, and its desire to keep up its efforts at developing missiles and nuclear weapons without provoking the United States into any form of military action. The result, however, is likely to be a more disruptive Iranian role in Iraq than in Afghanistan and a constant pressure to internationalize the nation-building effort and to push U.S. forces out of Iraq and the Gulf.

It is far from clear that there is any major political faction in Iraq that can both take power and then be willing to meet U.S. goals by halting proliferation or eliminating Iran's support to anti-Israeli movements. The result could be a "kinder and gentler" proliferator and opponent of Israel. The political dynamics of Iran have not been kind to its "moderates" in recent years, however, and its hard-liners continue to control the military, security services, judiciary, and much of the media. The pro-Khatami faction may now be more willing to compromise and seek dialogue. The pro-Khomeini and hard-line factions, however, are more likely to feel threatened and to take a hard line internally while trying to play the nation-building game in Iraq against the United States, and exploit Arab resentment against the United States to reduce its presence in the Gulf.

These problems are further complicated by postwar discoveries that Iran has far more nuclear facilities than previously estimated, and that at least two of those facilities seem to be part of a nuclear weapons program. Similarly, Iran's ongoing missile program has also demonstrated a growing Iranian capability to deliver weapons of mass destruction. This has inevitably increased tensions with the United States, Israel, and Iran's neighbors.

In balance, the aftermath of the Iraq War may do more to harden the hard-liners than to push Iran toward a more pro-Western position. In any case, the course of nation building in Iraq will be seen as both a potential win for the United States and as a potential threat to Iran's vital interests. At the least, some degree of competition with the United States seems inevitable.

SYRIA

The radically differing ideological views of the Bush administration and Syria make for troubled relations at best. Syria has lost a major trading partner and counterbalance to Israel. Although little love was lost between the two Ba'ath regimes, a rapprochement in recent years had led to better relations and more trade. Iraq's proliferation and strong conventional forces also acted as a threat to Israel, and a new Iraqi regime with far fewer military forces is far less reassuring.

Syria clearly sees the U.S. victory in Iraq as "anti-Arab," removing a potential ally against Israel and placing American forces next to Syria for the first time. Syrian pan-Arab rhetoric and conspiracy theories reinforce a very real fear of U.S. "neocolonialism" and a follow-on threat to the Syrian regime. Syria also sees the U.S. effort in nation building in Iraq as a threat to Ba'ath ideals and goals—regardless of the fact that they have had limited realization in Syria.

It is not surprising, therefore, that Syria initially played a game in Iraq of a spoiler, seeking to rebuild some form of Ba'athist role and Syrian influence and harassing the United States while pressing for the internationalization of the nation-building process. The United States seems to have intimidated Syria into being more supportive in terms of counterterrorism and suppressing the efforts of Iraqi Ba'athists and other hostile elements that attack the U.S.-led nation-building effort. Such actions may well last only so long as Syria is more afraid than ambitious, however, and postwar clashes between U.S. and Syrian forces in the areas near the Syrian-Iraqi border have scarcely smoothed relations.

The future of the Syrian-Iranian alliance that helped support the Hezbollah in Lebanon is another issue. It is still uncertain whether it will extend to cooperation in trying to influence the outcome of nation building in Iraq or whether Arab versus Persian becomes the more important fault line.

TURKEY

It is too soon to determine how much residual tension will exist between Turkey and the United States because of Turkey's refusal to base U.S. forces. What is clear is that Turkish democracy now has a strong Islamic element and that the Turkish economy faces what could be a half-decade of crisis. Turkey has already attempted to infiltrate its forces into northern Iraq in an effort to limit the power of Iraq's Kurds.

Like all of Iraq's neighbors, Turkey has a strong national interest in shaping nation building in Iraq to serve its own goals and objectives, rather than view it as an example. Turkey fears Kurdish autonomy and a lack of security along the border of its own Kurdish area. It is politically committed to supporting Iraq's Turkoman minority.

Turkey needs oil pipeline revenues from Iraq and sees Iraq as a major trading partner—one where its exports, including agriculture and manufactures, can be far more competitive than in the European Union. As a result, Turkey does not want to see Kurdish control of Mosul or Kirkuk or see the Kurds taking on a major role in the control of Iraq's northern oilfields. Iraq's Kurds, in turn, still have some ambitions for creating an independent Kurdistan that would include Turkey's Kurds. They fear and resent the Turks, who sent in troops five times between 1991 and 2003 to hunt down Turkish Kurdish guerrillas hiding in Iraq, and Turkey has since attempted to infiltrate special forces and other troops into northern Iraq.

The Iraq War is not going to help stabilize Turkey. The Kurdish and Turkoman problems in Iraq will be a constant source of tension, and serious questions will arise over Turkey's future role in Iraq's economy. Oil shipments, for example, could shift toward more exports through the Gulf. Iraq's Kurds may prefer other trading partners and seek to influence Iraq toward trade policies that favor other countries.

The result is unlikely to become a major crisis unless the Kurds show very little judgment and discretion. Still, the Iraq War will scarcely make things easier for Turkey, at least in the near term.

SAUDI ARABIA AND THE SOUTHERN GULF STATES

As is the case in most other parts of the Arab world, much of the popular reaction to the war in Saudi Arabia and the southern Gulf depends on how successfully and how quickly the United States can help create a stable Iraq for the Iraqis. Much of the population in the southern Gulf has initially seen the coalition victory as having been motivated by a U.S. and British search for control of Gulf oil, military dominance in the Gulf, and/ or helping Israel to secure its position in the region. Southern Gulf regimes may be less concerned about the more extreme version of such fears, but they quietly share deep concern about the United States' ability to create a unified and stable Iraq.

More broadly, it is difficult to see why a Saudi Arabia so concerned with its own internal political, cultural, and economic issues is going to see Iraq as a useful example of anything. The cultures and societies of the two states are simply too different. While Iraq has been a tyranny resisting change, Saudi Arabia has been a nation where the more progressive princes, technocrats, and businessmen have sought to modernize a deeply conservative people and Ulema. If anything, there is the risk that any U.S. and British failures in nation building in Iraq will provide more ammunition to those conservative and extremist Islamists in Saudi Arabia (and the rest of the region) who oppose secular reform and see the United States as a hostile, neo-imperialist power.

The governments of Saudi Arabia and the southern Gulf states will be relieved at the fall of Saddam Hussein, but neither these regimes nor most of their citizens welcome an increase in the power and role of Shi'ites and Kurds in Iraq. Saudi Arabia and the Gulf Arab states fear the breakup of Iraq's territorial integrity, a loss of Sunni control, and a shift in the balance of power in the Gulf. All Arab states fear any weakening of Arab control of Iraq and any breakup that would give Iraq's Kurds independence. The southern Gulf states are afraid that Shi'ite separatism or control of Iraq would create a major new pro-Iranian power center in the Gulf, potentially destabilizing the balance of power in the region. They are already concerned that the loss of so much of its military forces and equipment has gravely weakened Iraq's ability to deter Iran.

The Kuwaiti reaction has been more favorable in terms of seeing Saddam go. But Kuwait now lacks a unifying threat. In addition, the two leading members of the royal family are ill to the point of incapacity, the National Assembly is bogged down in service politics, and the power of Islamists, who are scarcely pro-American, is growing.

The other southern Gulf states will continue to focus on their own political dynamics, with a Shi'ite problem in Bahrain and succession issues in Oman. These countries that are so dependent on foreign labor and oil wealth will show limited interest in the Iraqi "example"—even if there is an "example" worth following.

In general, the initial impact of the outcome of the Iraq War has been to demonstrate to the southern Gulf regimes that the United States is a preeminent military power that they must continue to deal with. At a popular level, however, its impact has been to add to the concerns and tensions between the United States and southern Gulf states that have grown out of the Second Intifada, the U.S. reaction to 9/11, and the U.S. military presence in the region. The postwar reduction of the U.S. presence in Saudi Arabia may ease some of these tensions, but will scarcely eliminate them. Saudi concern about U.S. efforts at regime change has increased, and many Saudi officials feel the United States is unwilling to recognize their efforts at economic reform and the problems the regime faces with an ultraconservative population.

JORDAN

The Iraq War has removed a potential military and political threat to Jordan's regime, but it has increased Jordan's other problems, at least in the short term. Jordan fears the loss of trade and low-cost oil: Jordan has long benefited from Iraqi oil subsidies and from the fact that Iraq imported goods through the port of Aqaba because of UN sanctions and Iran's closing of the Shatt al Arab. The future of such subsidies and trade is now unclear.

The popular reaction to the war and to the initial nation-building effort has not been favorable. Some Jordanians recognized that Saddam was a tyrant in his own country, but most saw him as a supporter of the Palestinians and the Second Intifada. They now see King Abdullah's support of the United States as at least a partial betrayal, and their expectations are likely to be focused more on postwar U.S. efforts to create an Arab-Israeli peace than on Iraqi nation building. The Iraq War will not make things in Jordan radically worse, but—at least in the short term—it is unlikely to make them even marginally better.

EGYPT

The Egyptian government is likely to perceive the Iraq War with a sense of relief that it is over and did not make the fracture lines between the United States and the Arab world even worse. Egypt also is deeply concerned, however, about the potential emergence of an Iraq that is less Sunni Arab. Popular reactions are far more critical, and many Egyptians view their government as having betrayed the Arab cause by giving the United States basing aid and transit rights through the Suez Canal.

The result so far has been to increase the resentments growing out of the Second Intifada and the U.S. treatment of the Arab and Muslim world since 9/11. The Egyptian "street" is filled with conspiracy theories about U.S. and British motives in Iraq, the Gulf, and the Arab world. While some Egyptians do see the fall of a tyrant as desirable, even they view nation building in Iraq in terms of unrealistic demands for instant success, instant internationalization, and instant U.S. departure.

In broad terms, however, Iraq is a sideshow to the internal politics of Egypt. These politics are driven by increasing tension over the government of an aging "pharaoh," the lack of a clear successor to President Hosni Mubarak, a lack of valid political alternatives, and the problems of the Egyptian economy. The successful suppression of Islamist challenges to the Egyptian government has been suppression, not defeat or movement toward a more stable form of pluralism, and successful Iraqi nation building will not change this situation. It is also doubtful that Egypt's noisy media and secular politicians will shape the post-Mubarak era. It is more likely to be a struggle between Egypt's army and Islamists.

In any case, years of troubled nation building in Iraq are not going to reshape the perceptions and attitudes of an equally troubled Egypt.

NORTH AFRICA

Iraq is too far away to have much impact on the Maghreb states, except to serve as one more example of Western interference in Arab affairs—at least in the short term. The image of the Iraq War is likely to blur with the image of U.S. support for Israel and the hostility much of the U.S. media has shown to Islam and the Arab world since 9/11. But it is unclear that the impact will be particularly strong or negative.

A truly successful Iraq in political and economic terms might have a long-term influence on the Arab states in North Africa. The internal problems of Morocco, Algeria, Libya, and Tunisia are so great, however, and so driven by internal factors, that Iraq is not likely to have a major impact even if it does become a striking success story.

ISLAMIC EXTREMISM AND TERRORISM

Arabists have argued that the Iraq War will polarize and anger the Arab world, creating new groups of Islamic and other extremists and a new wave of terrorist attacks. Neoconservatives have argued that defeating Iraq will serve as a deterrent and, at worst, will be the first phase in a series of military operations to defeat terrorist states.

In practice, it is difficult to see why either view should be correct. The war may well stimulate some sources of terrorism and deter others, achieving a rough balance. It is difficult to imagine that those Arabs and Islamic extremists who already resent the United States will resent it that much more because of a conflict removing a secular dictator.

As for deterrence, the message of the war to extremists and terrorists may well be that although conventional forces cannot do serious damage to the United States, irregular forces can. In any case, it is far from clear how the message of military victory will deter suicide bombers and violent extremists any more than the U.S. victory in Afghanistan did, and Iraq's role as a supporter of terrorism was so tenuous that it is unclear why removing Saddam's regime will make that much of a difference.

Once again, it is the quality of nation building in Iraq, and the mid- and long-term message this sends, that is likely to be more important than the military outcome.

THE U.S. ROLE AND PRESENCE IN THE REGION

The Iraq War is not likely to make the presence of U.S. forces in the region radically more—or less—popular than it was at the start of the war. Fear may lead some states to want the United States to reduce its presence because of the risk that it will push for regime change. On the other hand, fear may make others less willing to differ from the United States and fail to support its power projection efforts. The United States as yet has no way of estimating how many forces it needs to keep in Iraq in the short term, or what America's security needs will be relative to Iran in the longer run.

In any case, many of the tensions shaping the U.S. presence in the Gulf are more the long-term legacies of the U.S. military presence in Saudi Arabia, and the tensions that grew up between Saudi Arabia and the United States following 9/11, than new tensions tied to Iraq. The U.S. decision to remove its combat forces from Saudi Arabia should ease these tensions, but, as has been discussed, it will scarcely eliminate them.

The U.S. presence in Bahrain, Qatar, and Oman has never led to serious popular pressure for their removal. It also has generally been more tied to these countries' perception of the threat posed by Iran than the threat posed by Iraq, although Kuwait's fundamentalists may be more willing to oppose U.S. and Kuwaiti military ties now that the threat from Iraq has diminished.

The situation affecting the U.S. presence in the region may be more destabilizing in terms of Egypt and Jordan. The Iraq War has made the quiet support their governments gave to the United States more visible, and they already face serious problems because of the Second Intifada, the state of their economies, and other internal issues. Much will depend on progress in the Arab-Israeli peace process and on the quality of the nation-building effort in Iraq.

ENERGY IMPORTS AND ENERGY SECURITY

One of the ironies of the Iraq War is that while it was a war about the stability of a region with some 60 percent of the world's oil reserves, and a war about the security of oil exports, there is little prospect that it will offer the United States or the UK any particular advantages beyond a more stable global oil market. The liberation of Iraq may ease the squeeze on world oil prices once Iraqi oil exports resume. Once the United States and Britain leave Iraq, however, no oil deals made by them can survive unless the Iraqis feel that those deals clearly benefit their own country. In fact, there is no area where both the United States and Britain must do more to show Iraq and the world that all transactions and actions are in the interest of the Iraqi people.

"Oil imperialism" has little practical value to a modern economic power. The flag a multinational oil company uses is no indication of economic benefit to its "host" country; and the tax and revenue streams from foreign operations have a limited impact on national revenues—if any. The international political costs of backing an oil company in a non-market-driven foreign operation almost inevitably outweigh the tenuous economic advantages. Any control over the end-destination of the oil produced is negligible and subject to International Energy Agency (IEA) sharing agreements in an energy emergency. Creating a strong national Iraqi oil industry that can attract global investment and operate on market terms offers far more advantages than a return to the nineteenth century and a failed colonialism.

In any case, large-scale expansion of Iraq's oil exports is likely to come only after the United States and the UK have gone from Iraq, and the supply and price impact of such an increase in Iraqi exports has long been anticipated in forecasts by OPEC (Organization of Petroleum Exporting Countries), the IEA, and the Department of Energy. These projections call for Iraqi oil production to increase to 3.1 million bbl/d by 2005, 3.9 million bbl/d in 2010, 4.5 million bbl/d in 2015, and 4.8 to 5.5 million bbl/d in 2020 if the world is to meet expanding demand with moderate prices. Iraq may or may not meet or exceed these goals; but it will do it long after U.S. and British influence has faded, and it will do so on its own terms. In practice, Iraq is far more likely to be driven by the world economy, its internal needs, the availability of sustained investment, and the energy politics of its neighbors and OPEC.

THE UNDERLYING FACTORS THAT SHAPE THE NEW OLD MIDDLE EAST

The greatest factor limiting the grand strategic impact of the Iraq War on the region is that the outcome will not affect the larger forces pressing on the Middle East. The outcome of the Iraq War will be a factor, but only one factor among many affecting the future of the Gulf and the Middle East. The outcome of the war has removed a major tyrant, but it has not fundamentally changed the Middle East or even disturbed most fracture lines. In any case, it will be several years before the victory in Iraq, and the nation building that follows, can be a key example of anything. Even when the outcome of nation building in Iraq is clear to the other peoples and nations in the region, it seems doubtful that it will have a definitive impact on any of the other 22 countries in the region, each of which has its own problems, goals, and imperatives.

The broader forces that shape the Middle East are too powerful for any one conflict or example to reshape the region. These factors include massive population growth and the failure of effective economic development and reform in virtually every country in the region. They include the precipitous decline of agriculture, water shortages, urban migration, hyper-urbanization, and the destruction of traditional social structures and the forced restructuring of extended families because of social and economic change.

Iraq's future politics are important, but it is equally important to understand the scale of the other forces at work. The World Bank's report *Global Economic Prospects 2003* shows a sharp decline in economic growth as measured by GDP in constant prices in the Middle East from 6.5 percent during 1971–1980 to 2.5 percent during 1981–1990. While growth rose to 3.2 percent during 1991–2000, it barely kept pace with population growth. In fact, growth in per capita income in constant prices dropped from 3.6 percent during 1971–1980 to –0.6 percent during 1981–1990, and was only 1 percent from 1991 to 2000—reflecting static income over nearly 20 years in a region with extremely poor equity of income distribution.

While interregional comparisons may be somewhat unfair, the economic growth in East Asia and the Pacific over the same time periods was 6.6 percent during 1971–1980, 7.3 percent during 1981–1990, and 7.7 percent during 1991–2000. The growth in real per capita income for that region was 3.0 percent during 1971–1980, 4.8 percent during 1981–1990, and 5.4 percent during 1991–2000.

Demographics are a major problem. The total population of the Middle East and North Africa has grown from 78.6 million in 1950 to 101.2 million in 1960, 133.0 million in 1970, 177.9 million in 1980, 244.8 million in 1990, and 307.1 million in 2000. Conservative projections put it at 376.2 million in 2010, 449.3 million in 2020, 522.3 million in 2030, 592.1 million in 2040, and 656.3 million in 2050.

This growth will further exhaust scarce natural water supplies and increase permanent dependence on food imports. Meanwhile, the young working-age population—those aged 15 to 30—is projected to rise from 20.5 million in 1950 and 87.8 million in 2000 to 145.2 million in 2050. The age group 14 years and younger now totals more than 40 percent of the population in the region, creating an immense bow wave of future strain on the social, educational, political, and economic systems.

The resulting social turbulence is compounded by overstretched and outdated educational systems and the failure of the labor market to create productive jobs, or any jobs at all, for many of the young men entering the labor force. Emigration is another source of social turbulence, while religious and cultural barriers to the effective employment of women compound problems in productivity and competitiveness with other developed regions.

All of these forces affect any regime where political structures remain fragile and largely authoritarian regardless of the formal structure of government. Traditional monarchies often interfere less in matters of human rights and normal social conduct than supposed democracies do. In broad terms, however, no state in the region has managed to create a secular political culture that provides effective pluralism.

The Middle East is also a region where competing secular ideologies have failed: Pan-Arabism, socialism, capitalism, Marxism, statism, and paternalism have all proved unable to provide adequate development and to meet social needs. The fact that so many in the region have turned back to more traditional social structures and religion is scarcely surprising, but it is unclear that this offers any meaningful solution to the problems involved.

Given these regional divisions and pressures, the grand strategic lesson of the Iraq War seems to be that both the results of the war and the outcome of the nation-building process must be viewed as a one-country solution to a twenty-plus country problem. The war in Iraq is an important move in the three-dimensional chess game that will shape the region over the next ten years, but only a move.

ABOUT THE AUTHOR

ANTHONY H. CORDESMAN holds the Arleigh A. Burke Chair in Strategy at CSIS. He is also a military analyst for ABC News and a frequent commentator on National Public Radio and the BBC. His television commentary has been featured prominently during the Iraq War, the Gulf War, Desert Fox, the conflict in Kosovo, and the fighting in Afghanistan. The author of numerous books on U.S. security policy, energy policy, and Middle East policy, he has served in senior positions for the Office of the Secretary of Defense, NATO, and the U.S. Senate.